EDUCATION 84/85

Fred Schultz, *Editor*
The University of Akron

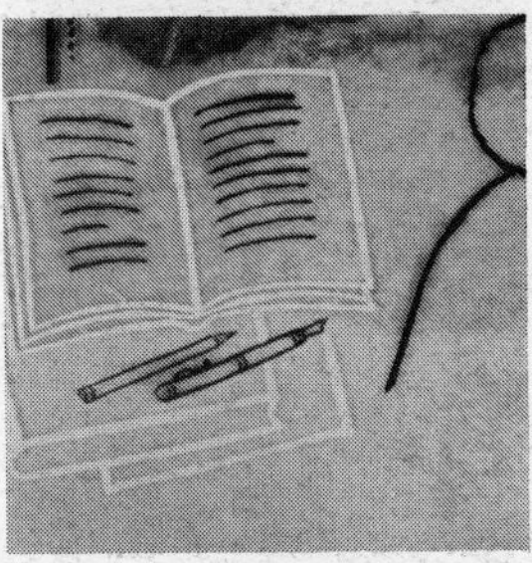

Cover Credit: Tom Goddard, artist.

ANNUAL EDITIONS

The Dushkin Publishing Group, Inc. Sluice Dock, Guilford, Ct. 06437

Volumes in the Annual Editions Series

- Abnormal Psychology
- ● Africa
- ● Aging
- ● American Government
- ● American History, Pre-Civil War
- ● American History, Post-Civil War
- ● Anthropology
- ● Biology
- ● Business
- ● China
- ● Comparative Politics
- ● Criminal Justice
- Death and Dying
- ● Deviance
- ● Early Childhood Education
- ● Economics
- ● Educating Exceptional Children
- ● Education
- ● Educational Psychology
- Energy
- ● Environment
- Ethnic Studies
- Foreign Policy
- Geography
- ● Health
- ● Human Development
- ● Human Sexuality
- ● Latin America
- ● Macroeconomics
- ● Management
- ● Marketing
- ● Marriage and Family
- ● Microeconomics
- ● Personal Growth and Behavior
- Philosophy
- Political Science
- ● Psychology
- Religion
- ● Social Problems
- ● Social Psychology
- ● Sociology
- ● State and Local Government
- Twentieth Century American History
- ● Urban Society
- ● Western Civilization, Pre-Reformation
- ● Western Civilization, Post-Reformation
- World History
- ● World Politics

● Indicates currently available

Eleventh Edition

Manufactured by George Banta Company, Menasha, Wisconsin 54952

Library of Congress Cataloging in Publication Data
Main entry under title: Annual editions: Education.
1. Education—Addresses, essays, lectures. I. Title: Education.
LB41.A673 370'.5 84-78580
ISBN 0-87967-528-4

ADVISORY BOARD

Members of the Advisory Board are instrumental in the final selection of articles for each year's edition of *Annual Editions.* Their review of articles for content, level, and appropriateness provides critical direction to the editor and staff. We think you'll find their careful consideration well reflected in this volume.

AND STAFF

CONTENTS

1

Perceptions of Education in America

2

Continuity and Change in American Education

3 The Struggle for Excellence: Striving for Higher Achievement

Morality and Values in Education

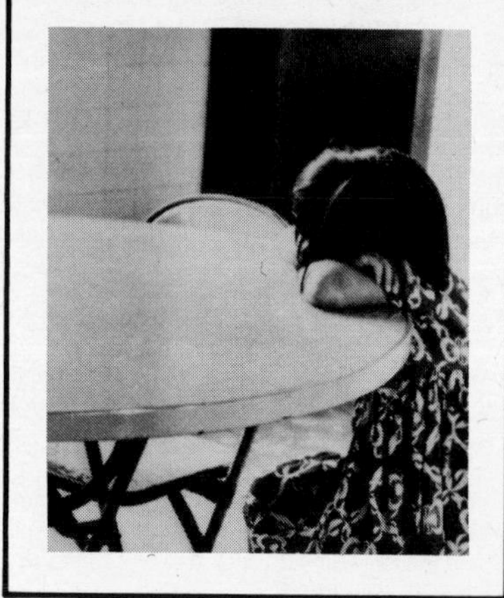

Discipline Problems in the Schools

6

Equality of Opportunity and American Education

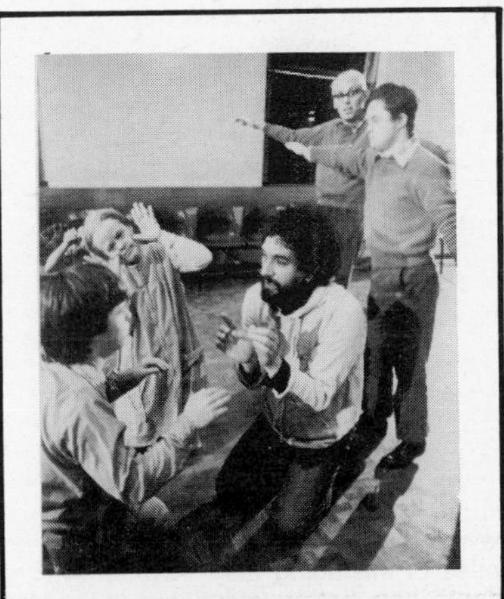

7

Serving Special Needs and Individualizing Instruction

8

The Profession of Teaching Today

A Look to the Future

TOPIC GUIDE

This topic guide can be used to correlate each of the articles in *Annual Editions: Education 84/85* to one or more of the topics normally covered by education books. Each article corresponds to a given topic area according to whether it deals with the subject in a primary or secondary fashion. These correlations are intended for use as a general study guide and do not necessarily define the total coverage of any given article.

TOPIC AREA	TREATED AS A PRIMARY ISSUE IN:	TREATED AS A SECONDARY ISSUE IN:
Academic Freedom	47. Scapegoating the Teachers 48. The Art of Teaching	2. When Rituals Are Not Empty
Affirmative Action	37. The State of Education for Black Americans 38. The Education of Black America	34. Human Rights 35. Beyond Racial Balance Remedies
Alternatives in Education	11. Video Games Go to School 15. The New Pioneers of the Home Schooling Movement	
Back to Basics	4. Elementary and Secondary Education Policy 16. The Debate About Standards 17. A Nation at Risk 18. A Nation at Risk: How's That Again? 19. The Bold Quest for Quality 20. A Time for Re-examination	5. How to Save the Public Schools 6. End of the Permissive Society? 22. Are Soviet Schools as Good as They Look?
Collective Bargaining	53. Reflections on the Profession	
Compensatory Education	9. Restructuring the Schools 13. Bilingual/Bicultural Education 16. The Debate About Standards 19. The Bold Quest for Quality	3. The Educational Pendulum 14. Multiethnic Education 21. The Decline of American Education
Compulsory Schooling	15. The New Pioneers of the Home Schooling Movement	1. Hard Times, Hard Choices
Computers and Teaching	10. Keys to Computer Literacy 11. Video Games Go to School 12. Computers and a New World Order	
Continuity and Change	1. Hard Times, Hard Choices 8. What's Still Right with Education 9. Restructuring the Schools 10. Keys to Computer Literacy 11. Video Games Go to School 12. Computers and a New World Order 13. Bilingual/Bicultural Education 14. Multiethnic Education 15. The New Pioneers of the Home Schooling Movement 20. A Time for Re-examination	3. The Educational Pendulum 6. End of the Permissive Society? 19. The Bold Quest for Quality
Creativity	2. When Rituals Are Not Empty 9. Restructuring the Schools	40. A Holistic View of Mainstreaming 48. The Art of Teaching 54. Curriculum in the Year 2000
Desegregation	34. Human Rights 35. Beyond Racial Balance Remedies 36. Achieving Quality Integrated Education 37. The State of Education for Black Americans	38. The Education of Black America
Discipline	29. Disciplinary Strategies 30. Defusing Discipline Problems 31. The Discipline Problem in Our Schools 32. There's Only One True Technique for Good Discipline 33. The Myths of Discipline	6. End of the Permissive Society?
Educational Innovations	9. Restructuring the Schools 10. Keys to Computer Literacy 11. Video Games Go to School 12. Computers and a New World Order	8. What's Still Right with Education 13. Bilingual/Bicultural Education 14. Multiethnic Education
Equal Opportunity	13. Bilingual/Bicultural Education 14. Multiethnic Education 34. Human Rights 35. Beyond Racial Balance Remedies 36. Achieving Quality Integrated Education 37. The State of Education for Black Americans 38. The Education of Black America 39. Expectations and Realities 41. Mainstreaming	3. The Educational Pendulum 21. The Decline of American Education 22. Are Soviet Schools as Good as They Look?
Excellence	2. When Rituals Are Not Empty 16. The Debate About Standards 17. A Nation at Risk 18. A Nation at Risk: How's That Again? 19. The Bold Quest for Quality 20. A Time for Re-examination	6. End of the Permissive Society? 9. Restructuring the Schools 21. Decline of American Education 22. Are Soviet Schools as Good as They Look?

TOPIC AREA	TREATED AS A PRIMARY ISSUE IN:	TREATED AS A SECONDARY ISSUE IN:
Exceptional Children	39. Expectations and Realities 40. A Holistic View of Mainstreaming 41. Mainstreaming 42. Comparison of Soviet and American Approaches to Special Education 44. Overplacement 45. The Teacher's Role in Facilitating a Child's Adjustment to Divorce 46. Helping Children Cope with Death	13. Bilingual/Bicultural Education 14. Multiethnic Education
Future and Education	54. Curriculum in the Year 2000 55. Instructional Computing in 2001 56. The Coming Enrollment Crisis	1. Hard Times, Hard Choices 13. Bilingual/Bicultural Education 24. Schools and Democratic Values 43. Our Investment in Public Education
History of Education	1. Hard Times, Hard Choices 3. The Educational Pendulum 4. Elementary and Secondary Education Policy 13. Bilingual/Bicultural Education 21. The Decline of American Education 26. Values and Morality in Early Twentieth Century Elementary Schools 47. Scapegoating the Teachers	6. End of the Permissive Society? 8. What's Still Right with Education 35. Beyond Racial Balance Remedies
Human Rights	34. Human Rights 35. Beyond Racial Balance Remedies 36. Achieving Quality Integrated Education 37. The State of Education for Black Americans 38. The Education of Black America	13. Bilingual/Bicultural Education 14. Multiethnic Education
Law and the Schools	13. Bilingual/Bicultural Education 35. Beyond Racial Balance Remedies 39. Expectations and Realities 49. Tenure	15. The New Pioneers of the Home Schooling Movement 36. Achieving Quality Integrated Education 37. The State of Education for Black Americans 38. The Education of Black America
Mainstreaming	39. Expectations and Realities 40. A Holistic View of Mainstreaming 41. Mainstreaming	
Merit Pay	51. Merit Pay: The Great Debate	
Morality and Values in Education	23. The Conflict in Moral Education 24. Schools and Democratic Values 25. The Role of Self-Discipline 26. Values and Morality in Early Twentieth Century Elementary Schools	6. End of the Permissive Society? 9. Restructuring the Schools 21. The Decline in American Education

TOPIC AREA	TREATED AS A PRIMARY ISSUE IN:	TREATED AS A SECONDARY ISSUE IN:
Morality and Values in Education (cont'd)	27. No Empty Heads, No Hollow Chests 28. How to Encourage Moral Development	
Multicultural Education	13. Bilingual/Bicultural Education 14. Multiethnic Education 34. Human Rights 35. Beyond Racial Balance Remedies 36. Achieving Quality Integrated Education 37. The State of Education for Black Americans 38. The Education of Black America	3. The Educational Pendulum 22. Are Soviet Schools as Good as They Look
Public Opinion of Schools	6. End of the Permissive Society? 7. The Fifteenth Annual Gallup Poll 19. The Bold Quest for Quality	21. The Decline of American Education 23. The Conflict in Moral Education 34. Human Rights
Quality of Education	16. The Debate About Standards 17. A Nation at Risk 18. A Nation at Risk: How's That Again? 19. The Bold Quest for Quality 20. A Time for Re-examination 21. The Decline of American Education 22. Are Soviet Schools as Good as They Look	24. Schools and Democratic Values 25. The Role of Self-Discipline 27. No Empty Heads, No Hollow Chest
Soviet Education	22. Are Soviet Schools as Good as They Look? 42. A Comparison of Soviet and American Approaches to Special Education	
Teacher-Administrator Relations	49. Tenure 50. To Improve Schools 53. Reflections on the Profession	51. Merit Pay: The Great Debate 52. Teacher Burnout
Teacher Burnout	52. Teacher Burnout	
Tenure	49. Tenure	
Urban Education	35. Beyond Racial Balance Remedies 36. Achieving Quality Integrated Education 37. The State of Education for Black Americans	34. Human Rights
Teaching as a Career	2. When Rituals Are Not Empty 47. Scapegoating the Teachers 48. The Art of Teaching 49. Tenure 50. To Improve Schools 51. Merit Pay: The Great Debate	8. What's Still Right with Education 9. Restructuring the Schools 56. The Coming Enrollment Crisis

PREFACE

Annual Editions: Education 84/85 reflects major shifts in thought concerning the state of education in the United States. The past year has been one of significant movement for quality. Several national commission reports on the state of the nation's schools, and commentary concerning the national mission that lies ahead are coming to the fore. We have embarked on a new period of critical analysis of the American experience in education. Such an intense period of critical revision of the qualitative standards of schooling in the United States has not been evident since the mid-1960s. In addition, we may be experiencing the early stages of significant, if not academically revolutionary, changes in the content and manner of conducting instruction.

The critical historical assessments of the American educational experience in the 1960s and 1970s, and the moderate revisionist critiques and syntheses of that experience have led us to a more mature and balanced perspective through which to examine our educational past and present. The continuing reinterpretation of the American educational past and present has given us a broader and more accurate perspective on which to base judgements of theory and practice in the field of education.

Hard economic times and the continuing pressures for greater emphasis in improving the quality of educational achievement in the nation have had a significant effect in the shaping of current thought about American education. What can the schools do? How much should they do? The contents of this volume reflect these current themes.

This eleventh edition of *Annual Editions: Education 84/85* is designed to be a very readable and usable volume in teacher education, as well as an informative source for general readers. It is the only volume published in the field of education that is revised annually. All of the sections are constructed to raise important questions regarding American educational development. The volume represents an integration of many new essays with valuable ones from last year's edition. The essays are selected from both general "trade" and professional publications. This anthology is revised annually. You can have some input into the next edition by filling out and returning the article rating form on the last page of this volume.

Fred Schultz
Editor

UN DAY

Perceptions of Education in America

1

The present issues concerning education in the United States reflect public demands for the optimum development of our possibilities as a people. Some advocates of quality education are striving for national excellence and others are seeking to renew basic ideals. Social, political, and economic realities of the mid-1980s have different effects on certain sectors of the American population, and in turn affect how they view the state of education today and the direction in which it should move.

The essays included in this section concentrate on some of the changes in the roles of schools in a period of change and reassessment. The lead article develops themes relating current educational problems to their historical origins and supports more coherent reassessments in planning our educational future. The new articles concern major issues such as the primary purposes of education, the role of the school on social and economic life in recent years, and public opinion toward the public schools. An important issue in the coming years will be just what the priorities should be in American educational development.

We are entering a period of major transition in public attitudes toward education. We cannot be certain where the final shifts in public and governmental opinion regarding education will lead us, but we can be certain that assessments of the mission and quality of public and nonpublic education will continue.

Looking Ahead: Challenge Questions

What are the primary purposes of American education? How best can we achieve them in these times?

What issues in American education are new? What old issues are still being raised?

To what extent, if any, do educators influence public attitudes about schooling?

What goals do you think our national educational system could achieve?

Is the United States a "permissive" society? What changes in national educational priorities seem to be reflected in the struggle to reassess the quality of American educational institutions?

What's wrong with American education? What is still right with it?

How does the opinion of the American public affect national educational development?

Hard Times, Hard Choices:
The Case for Coherence In Public School Leadership

David Tyack and Elisabeth Hansot

DAVID TYACK is Vida Jacks Professor of Education and History at Stanford University, Stanford, Calif. ELISABETH HANSOT is an associate professor of political science at the University of Nevada-Reno. *The authors wish to acknowledge the support of the National Institute of Education through the Institute for Research on Finance and Governance at Stanford.*

At the turn of the 20th century the British educator Michael Sadler observed that "the American school is radiant with a belief in its mission, and it works among people who believe in the reality of its influence, in the necessity of its labors, and in the grandeur of its task."[1] Today no one talks that way about public education; it would sound corny and unconvincing. But such a faith — and the coherence of program, governance, and purpose it helped to produce — has been a powerful force in the history of education in the U.S. A public philosophy of education as Thomas Jefferson or Horace Mann or John Dewey would have understood the term has deteriorated in recent years, a casualty of the same fragmentation that has splintered politics and instruction in public schooling.

Fragmentation

Today both a sense of the past and hopes for the future are in disarray in public education. Few would now affirm that the teacher is "the prophet of the true God and the sharer in the true kingdom of God" or would recall that John Dewey wrote those words in *My Pedagogic Creed*.[2] Today the media focus on pathologies: violence in classrooms, falling test scores, warring interest groups, tax revolts, and discord within the education profession itself. Public education, traditionally an expanding enterprise based on a consensual ideology, has begun to constrict and become litigious. Older histories portraying the emergence of the common school as the result of providential design or the progressive evolution of a unified profession have given way to revisionist accounts that stress the gaps between aspirations and achievements. People are uncertain about the forms and direction that leadership in education should take — or even whether leadership is possible.

Coherence is not the strong suit of contemporary public education. Public school leaders in recent years have absorbed most demands for change by accretion, scarcely altering the central core of instruction. As a result, U.S. education has been both faddish in its particulars and resistant to change in its basic mode of operation. Reformers of the 1960s, cheerfully ignoring history, promised quick pedagogical fixes to old and intractable problems. Much of the current skepticism about schools and the desire to reemphasize the three R's result from disenchantment with curricular fragmentation. In governance the changes in recent years have created an incoherent patchwork. And as a multitude of special interest groups have pushed their divergent goals, the larger purposes that once gave resonance and integration to the complex enterprise of public education have atrophied.[3]

One could easily predict a dismal future for the public schools. Retrenchment could set in motion the haphazard process of incrementalism, only in reverse: Educators could initiate an equally haphazard decrementalism by peeling away parts of the system with little sense of common purpose. The economics of scarcity could stimulate factionalism and bitter competition among the various interest groups in education. As loyalty to the common goal of public schooling erodes, parents who have the opportunity could choose exit from rather than improvement of public schools, leaving the public system to become a place of last resort.[4]

This gloomy future is neither desirable nor inevitable. It should be possible to consolidate the real gains achieved for neglected groups in the last generation while creating greater coherence in education where it counts the most — in the actual classrooms where children learn. Americans can create a greater sense of common purpose in public education without losing the energy and variety generated by pluralistic politics. But to do so will require leaders adept at building pro-school coalitions, willing to abandon narrow professional perspectives and ideologies, and skillful in creating coordinated programs in individual schools. To ask for such leadership is not to demand implausible heroes; there have been — and are now — many who have demonstrated such talents. But hard times will force hard choices, and those choices will require a vision of the whole that can make sense of the parts. Let us use adversity to our advantage: The need to decide what is essential — and to enlist colleagues and community in that debate — can help to remedy the incoherence produced by easy money and rapid growth.

Faced with the uncertainties of the present, school leaders often wish that they could peer into the future to help guide their policy making. Past efforts at prognostication, however, do not increase one's faith in futurist predictions. Americans have often anticipated futures that never came to pass. Advocates of technological panaceas, for example, have confidently argued that their particular solution — chalkboard, radio, films, television, programmed instruction, or computers — would solve the problems of public schooling. Their enthusiasm for the new made them scornful of what had gone before; too many avid reformers rejected the past.

We start from a different point of departure: history. Through a study of the past people may gain a sense of the trajectory of events and may use that knowledge of where they have been to gain some perspective on where they might go. One reason why futurism may miss the mark is that to make causality flow from the present into the future deprives events of the particular density and momentum they acquire in historical time. The Harvard

From *Phi Delta Kappan*, April 1982. Excerpted from MANAGERS OF VIRTUE, political scientist James Q. Wilson argues that successful policy analyses — the kind that can help in making hard choices — have this historical dimension: "They involve statements about what has happened in the past, not speculations about what may happen in the future. They are evaluations of policies that have already been implemented."[5]

We turn, then, to a brief recapitulation of two dominant modes of coherent leadership in the past, move to challenges in the last generation, and then propose a case for new forms of coherence today.

Evangelists and Experts

In our forthcoming book, *Managers of Virtue*, we suggest three different kinds of school buildings as symbols of stages of development of U.S. public education. The first is the fast-disappearing one-room school that once represented the mainstream of public education. Small, resembling a church with its bell tower, mixing all ages in a family-like manner, simple in aspiration and curriculum, this school was coherently related to the community that built it. The second symbol is the large urban high school built about 1915. It looks rather like a factory with some classical ornamentation. Inside, it is complexly and sternly organized, with an elaborate inner office for the principal and all the emblems of bureaucracy in the outer office, classrooms for instruction in dozens of subjects, cubicles for counseling, workshops and kitchens, and a gym and playing fields. Like the factory, it is separate from family and community, hierarchical in organization, planned, purposive, consequential. The third is the sprawling, one-story suburban complex that might as easily be a shopping center as a high school. Soft-edged, divided into segments, united mostly by a common parking lot and heating system, it offers nearly endless choices. It is blurred in purpose, adapting to individual tastes but not articulating common values. It is the quintessential educational expression of a postindustrial consumerist society.[6]

The one-room school, the remarkably uniform product of the decentralized social movement of the mid-19th century called the common school crusade, symbolizes one kind of coherent leadership. Reformers of the mid-19th century sought to mobilize people at the local and state levels to construct a system that was public in control and support and to send their children to that common school. Leaders worked within a nation that was overwhelmingly rural. State departments of education were small and weak, and the federal government exerted little influence over public schools. Schooling was largely unbureaucratized and unprofessionalized. For the most part, these common school crusaders did not devote their entire careers to education but saw it as one among several occupations and causes that demanded their attention. They believed that schooling was crucial to the development of the United States as a capitalist nation and were themselves usually members of local elites, but the economy they knew was mostly small-scale and decentralized. Largely Protestant in religion and Anglo-Saxon in ethnic background, they shared a common millennial notion of the role of public education in shaping a Christian society and a republican civic culture. It was this common ideology, common set of economic interests, and similar ethnic and religious backgrounds that gave coherence to their leadership. Their shared earnestness and civic activism have caused us to call them an "aristocracy of character."

Although early leaders turned to state governments in carrying out their educational plans, they relied heavily on the consciousness-raising and institution-building activities of voluntary associations. They exchanged ideas in regional and national networks, but the chief action took place at the local level. A useful way to understand their leadership is to see it as mobilizing a vast institution-building social movement similar to the religious movement that spread small Protestant churches — similar in purpose and architecture to the one-room school — across a far-flung rural nation. They were evangelists of education.

By contrast, the administrative progressives who dominated educational leadership in the early 20th century — and whose characteristic achievement was the urban high school — saw themselves as social engineers and scientific managers. Their source of coherence and authority was not so much shared ethical ideas as it was the expertise of science and the power of hierarchical position. Their goal was to bring about a smoothly meshing corporate society. Largely sons of small-town pietist families, they shared similar cultural values with the crusaders of Horace Mann's generation; unlike them, they saw themselves as scientists and as career professionals in education. In some respects their optimism about the potential of schooling was as utopian as that of their predecessors, but their version of a millennial society was far more secular. Their task was not to create but to redesign the public school system, not to arouse public participation in school governance but to constrain it by substituting "administration" for "politics," not to campaign for a common curriculum in education so much as to differentiate instruction according to the needs of a complex urban-industrial society. They sought — and gained — an awesome power: the ability to define what was normal or desirable. Translating numbers into norms, they shaped their preferred policies into a standard template of reform that they applied in state after state, district after district, in their school surveys and legislative proposals. Through training programs and "old boy networks" they developed a cohesive group of leaders with similar values and strategic positions of leverage.

The earlier religious-political legacy was not abandoned, however. The 19th-century social movement for the common school continued to give education leaders much of their moral capital, a lasting fund of metaphors, an overarching sense of purpose to animate work that was often mundane. Until the last generation the rhetoric of moral charisma and millennial hope complemented the dream of professionalism and the language of social efficiency. In many 20th-century leaders of public education the evangelist merged with the scientist.

Challenge to Business as Usual

In the last generation much of this composite ideal of educational leadership has come under attack for being a "closed system" of governance by education experts and for imposing white Anglo-Saxon Protestant values on what is in fact a highly pluralistic society. As protest has proliferated, traditional leaders have been assaulted by dispossessed groups and delegitimized by competing elites; social scientists, for example, have questioned, one after another, the key articles of the American faith in schooling and have undermined educators' claims to expertise. Beginning with blacks and their white allies in the civil rights campaign, successive groups — feminists, Hispanics, the handicapped, Native Americans, and many others — have mounted powerful social movements to win practical and symbolic gains, demanding equal dignity as well as equal opportunity. Within the education profession, the older professional consensus has eroded and internecine battles have erupted. Many factions have found the law a ready instrument for challenge and reform, both for groups and for individuals, and thus public schooling has become litigious. Federal and state governments have created a kaleidoscope of new programmatic reforms, each with its own regulations and accounting system.[7]

One result of these changes — many of them long overdue attempts to achieve social justice for excluded groups — has been fragmentation and discord in the governance of education. Leaders have lost the power to command securely either as aristocrats of character or as experts. Indeed, amid the litigiousness, the competing claims of interest groups, the infighting within a once united education profession, the confusing and sometimes conflicting requirements of the new paperwork empire of categorical programs, people have sometimes wondered if *anyone* was in charge, if *anyone* spoke with authority and wisdom about public education. Amid the claims of single-issue reformers, it has been hard to find a common ground, a belief system that could make the parts of public education coherent. The older notion of public education as a common good seems to some as antiquated as the one-room school.[8]

Both the common school crusaders and the administrative progressives believed in public education as an instrument of progress. In retrospect, the belief systems that undergirded their optimism may appear to be myths, but myths are not the same as lies. Organizational myths are a way of making vivid a sense of what institutions can be; by elaborating a heroic past, they direct people toward an equally potent future. Embedded in myths are images of potentiality.[9]

Are a new coherence and a community of commitment possible? We believe so, but it will be no easy task to recreate — on new terms — coherence in governance and program in a fragmented society and school system. It will be even more difficult to negotiate a new social contract between the people and their public schools, for there has been a subtle but powerful erosion of the traditional American faith in public education. The public school system is probably the closest Americans have come to creating an established church. Challenges during the last generation have amounted to a new reformation, undermining the authority of established leaders, demystifying beliefs, and splintering coalitions and allegiances.

Coherence in governance has always been difficult to achieve, and never more so than now. The starting point of wisdom is to recognize that, in a federated system such as ours, local/state/federal relations are, and should be, always in some tension. In the last generation we have experienced sharp swings of the pendulum, both rhetorically and actually, between centralization and decentralization. Liberals and activists in protest movements, aware of how local control fostered inequities among districts and how local school boards could and did discriminate against groups that had little power, have typically wanted federal and state governments and the courts to intervene in the interest of social justice. Categorical programs were one instance of centralized intervention in favor of underserved groups. State legislators have passed minimum competency legislation and accountability laws to force local educators to toe the line. Court decisions and collective bargaining have also increased centralization. By contrast, minority groups have pressed in some places for "community control" of schools, and federal laws have mandated school/community councils. Conservatives wanting "the government off our backs" have glorified local control and advocated block grants rather than centrally administered categorical programs. The result of all of these counterpressures has been governmental and administrative arrangements so complex that Rube Goldberg himself would have been baffled.[10]

One way out of the maze is to ask which kinds of decisions are best made at which levels of the system. What should be centralized and what decentralized? For all the bad press it is now receiving, centralization has been necessary to achieve certain kinds of equity and justice. Fiscal equity, for example, can rarely be achieved purely at the local level. Only state and federal legislatures can mitigate the great disparity in wealth between school districts. Outside subsidies have been, and will continue to be, important in equalizing education for underserved groups such as the handicapped, the poor, and those who need assistance in learning English. In addition, basic constitutional rights cannot be left to the discretion of local boards and education officials, who all too often have violated basic civil rights with respect to race, gender, due process, and freedom of expression. The courts and civil rights laws will still be necessary forms of centralization. Americans cannot achieve a democratic form of coherence in governance by ignoring the just demands of low-power groups or by denying constitutional rights.[11]

Decisions about what and how to teach bridge the boundaries of governance and program. Our view is that centralization of decisions about instruction has had ambiguous results. Instructional reforms imposed on teachers from without and from the top down — the so-called "teacher-proof" curricula — rarely work. Reform in instruction requires the support and understanding of the people who carry it out. No one knows more about how to reach children effectively than the educators who encounter them daily. Teaching is the core function of schools, and no one has yet devised, nor is anyone likely to, so foolproof a technology of instruction as to justify centralized dictation of curriculum and methods. This is not to say that some form of minimum competency requirements prescribed at the state level is noxious; it may even help in focusing attention on important skills and knowledge. But considerable autonomy should remain with local educators to achieve results in the ways they know best. This suggests that most basic decisions about instruction are best made at the level of individual districts or even individual schools.[12]

For achieving such coherence in program at the local level we suggest two approaches. One is learning what makes effective schools work well. Another is making some hard choices about what is nourishing educational fare and what is junk food. Retrenchment may force such decisions.

In recent years, researchers such as Michael Rutter, Ronald Edmonds, and John Goodlad have gone beyond asking why programs fail. They have asked why some schools, even in tough neighborhoods, succeed. From such studies it has become apparent that what counts most in the academic and social learning of children is a coherent experience of learning in their individual schools and classrooms. Principals, students, teachers, and parents must share a sense of being a community of instructors and learners working toward definite goals, with clear but cooperative leadership and high expectations. Such schools have an ethos that Philip Selznick has called an institutional "success myth." Such a "socially integrating" sense of purpose allows people to complete a sentence that begins: "What we are proud of around here is. . . ."[13]

The plethora of changes in schools in recent years and expanded funding have allowed the curriculum to grow by accretion in a largely unplanned way, like a coral reef in warm water. One result has been a great increase, especially in secondary education, in electives and in activities that only marginally belong in schools. The wide popularity of the back-to-basics movement reflects popular unrest with the lack of focus of much of the curriculum. We do not favor a narrow construction of "basics" — excluding art and music, for example — but we do believe that coherence in program requires careful reappraisal of what schools can do best and elimination of nonessentials that occupy too much time in the classroom.[14]

Our final argument — about coherence of purpose — relates closely to the other two issues of governance and program. The old unifying philosophy of public education is in severe disarray. The vital idea of the common school as a common good has atrophied, while hyperpluralism and possessive individualism seem to be the order of the day. Now, many people of various political persuasions regard schooling as simply a consumer good, which prompts them to welcome plans for vouchers or tuition tax credits that would permit them to send their children to private schools. The traditional notion that public schools are a collective responsibility of all society has lost its force, its rationale obscured by the narrowing of the professional ideology that was the legacy of the administrative progressives and by the splintering of interest groups in recent years.

Common ideals have counted in history, and community of commitment is sorely needed today. There is perhaps no more important task facing education leaders now than the reformulation of the purposes of public education in a tough-minded and coherent way that fits our own time.

Debate over the direction of public education offers Americans perhaps their best forum for shaping a common future. It deals with a compelling question: How shall the next generation be educated? This issue is not of interest to parents alone; it concerns everyone, for ultimately the education of all affects the welfare of all. In that sense education is both an individual good and a collective good.

Educational leaders who want to be catalysts in such a reformulation of purpose and commitment need many talents. They need to be skilled at hearing different criticisms and aspirations and at interpreting diverse people to one another. People who want to influence education are potential allies, for voice can lead to commitment. But educational leaders are not only negotiators and interpreters among individuals and groups. They are also professionals with rich experience, trustees of *all* the children, those whose adult representatives successfully voice concerns and those who have no spokespeople. As leaders, they need to seek the welfare of the entire community and to see the education system whole.

When one concentrates only on the failings of the public school system — and they are many — it is easy to forget what a sturdy achievement public education has been and how well it compares with other social services both here and abroad. America has lagged well behind other industrial democracies in the public services it has provided to the old, in day care for little children, in housing, and in public health care. The public school represents the *only* commitment by which this society has guaranteed to look after the needs and interests of all of its citizens, at least while they are young. Now this collective sense of responsibility is threatened — and at a time when public trusteeship may be more important than it has been for decades.

We now face the appalling fact that an increasing number of children may grow up in impoverished circumstances in the wealthiest nation on earth. It has been estimated, for example, that one-half of U.S. children alive in 1976 will at some time live in a one-parent family, and typically that means in a low-income family. Immigrants have flooded into the U.S. in the last decade in numbers rivaling immigration in the early 20th century. Big-city schools are increasingly populated with minority children living at or near the poverty line. Teenage unemployment is near Depression levels. Can this really be time to cut back on school lunches, job training, or special classes for non-English-speaking children?[15]

Many people — ourselves included — have criticized the gap between the aspirations and the performance of public schools. No reformulation of the purposes of public education should become simply a public relations campaign that neglects unfinished business. But it is useful to compare schooling not only with its own high ideals but also with the performance of other social agencies. And in that light, there is much room for pride. What other major social institution displays *less* bias with respect to race, sex, or class than do public schools? What other institution does *more* to promote equal dignity among groups or equal opportunity for all? What other public institution is *more* responsive to public influence than are the public schools? And where else can citizens find a better forum for debating the shape of a common future?

---

1. Michael Sadler, "Impressions of American Education," *Educational Review*, vol. 25, 1903, p. 219.
2. John Dewey, *My Pedagogic Creed* (1897; reprint ed., Washington, D.C.: Progressive Education Association, 1929), p. 17.
3. David Tyack, Michael Kirst, and Elisabeth Hansot, "Educational Reform: Retrospect and Prospect," *Teachers College Record*, vol. 81, 1980, pp. 253-69.
4. On decline in organizations, see Albert O. Hirschman, *Exit, Voice, and Loyalty* (Cambridge, Mass.: Harvard University Press, 1970).
5. James Q. Wilson, " 'Policy Intellectuals' and Public Policy," *The Public Interest*, vol. 64, 1981, p. 41.
6. A full exposition and documentation for the argument in this section is found in David Tyack and Elisabeth Hansot, *Managers of Virtue: Public School Leadership in America, 1820-1980* (New York: Basic Books, 1982).
7. Edith K. Mosher, Anne H. Hastings, and Jennings L. Wagoner, Jr., *Pursuing Equal Educational Opportunity: School Politics and the New Activists* (New York: ERIC Clearinghouse on Urban Education, 1979).
8. Gene I. Maeroff, "Harried School Leaders See Their Role Waning," *New York Times*, 5 March 1974, p. 1.
9. David K. Cohen and Bella H. Rosenberg, "Functions and Fantasies: Understanding Schools in Capitalist America," *History of Education Quarterly*, vol. 17, 1977, pp. 125-32.
10. Michael W. Kirst, "Organizations in Shock and Overload: California's Public Schools, 1970-1980," *Educational Evaluation and Policy Analysis*, vol. 2, 1979, pp. 27-30; John W. Meyer, "The Impact of the Centralization of Educational Funding and Control of State and Local Organizational Governance" (Stanford, Calif.: Institute for Research on Educational Finance and Governance, Stanford University, 1980); and William L. Boyd, "The Public, the Professionals, and Educational Policy Making: Who Governs?," *Teachers College Record*, vol. 77, 1976, pp. 539-77.
11. On race, for example, see J. Harvie Wilkerson III, *From Brown to Bakke: The Supreme Court and School Integration, 1954-1978* (New York: Oxford University Press, 1979).
12. Arthur Wise, *Legislated Learning: The Bureaucratization of the American Classroom* (Berkeley: University of California Press, 1979).
13. Michael Rutter et al., *Fifteen Thousand Hours: Secondary Schools and Their Effects on Children* (Cambridge, Mass.: Harvard University Press, 1979); Ronald Edmonds, "Some Schools Work and More Can," *Social Policy*, March/April 1979, pp. 28-32; John Goodlad, "Can Our Schools Get Better?," *Phi Delta Kappan*, January 1979, pp. 342-47; and Philip Selznick, *Leadership in Administration: A Sociological Perspective* (New York: Harper & Row, 1957), p. 151.
14. On the proliferation of high school courses, see Philip Jackson, "Comprehending a Well-Run Comprehensive: A Report on a Visit to a Large Suburban High School," *Daedalus*, vol. 110, 1981, pp. 82-85; and Michael Kirst, "Loss of Support for Public Secondary Schools: Some Causes and Solutions," *Daedalus*, vol. 110, 1981, pp. 45-68.
15. On the effects of cutbacks in funding, see Daniel L. Duke and Adrienne M. Meckel, "The Slow Death of a Public High School," *Phi Delta Kappan*, June 1980, pp. 674-77.

When Rituals Are Not Empty

Harry S. Broudy

Harry S. Broudy is Emeritus Professor of Philosophy of Education, University of Illinois at Urbana-Champaign. Educated in the public schools of Milford, Massachusetts, he attended the Massachusetts Institute of Technology, Boston University, and Harvard University where he was awarded the PhD in Philosophy. After teaching at the North Adams and Farmington state colleges, Dr. Broudy joined the University of Illinois faculty in 1957. He retired in 1974 and is now Coordinator, Committee for Interdisciplinary Studies, Urbana-Champaign campus. He is a former Fulbright Professor and a member of Phi Beta Kappa and various academic and professional organizations.

I am honored by this invitation to take part in the ritual of your College's Fiftieth Anniversary observance. And it is a ritual, with incantations, costumes, and music, all according to a formula, a formula perhaps less fixed than that of weddings, funerals, and college commencements—but a formula nevertheless. Until the appropriate words and gestures are instantiated, the significance of the event is incomplete. Ritual transforms an event into a celebration.

Rituals and ceremony have had a bad press in a scientifically rational and technologically omnipotent world. Science clears away mystery and technology creates its own magic at will, and so the locution an "empty ritual" becomes a motto. And yet one hesitates to stage a college commencement without a ritual, and although banquet speakers are routinely regarded as boring, it would be a brave banquet that did not have one. If ritual and ceremony are really empty and do not affect the substance of the events they celebrate, why do we persist in enacting them and feel uncomfortable when they are omitted?

One answer is that ceremony and ritual fix the significance of an event by giving it a clear and emphatic form. Another is that whatever society regards as significant it shapes by ritual and ceremony so that it becomes part of the communal memory. This ceremony today is designed to remind ourselves of the significance of the occasion not only for us but also for this College, all colleges, and society itself.

The establishment of a College of Education at this University fifty years ago marked the entry of a calling into the learned professions. It brought into being the structure of another learned guild, but underneath the physical and ritual founding of the College lay a compact with society—an ancient and solemn compact, so ancient and so tacit that on this anniversary it behooves us to remind ourselves of it.

As we do try to remind ourselves of this auspicious event, we cannot avoid asking just how auspicious was it? In 1931 the world was not a happy place. In the United States the Depression was still deepening. In Europe and Asia the clouds that were to produce the torrents of the Second World War were already gathering. It seemed as if the physical, political, and spiritual resources of humankind were inadequate to meet the impending crisis. Yet at that very time the faith in education was on the rise. Not only were the schools not blamed for the Depression and the political storms, but, on the contrary, the requirements for the preparation of classroom teachers were being raised from two years at normal schools to three and four years in collegiate institutions. The establishment of this College was a declaration that there was enough scholarly activity in education to warrant systematic study of its theory and practice. In other words, teaching, pedagogy, and its ancillary functions were making a bid for professional status.

It is rueful as it is remarkable to compare attitudes of the public toward education and the schools today. At a

"When Rituals Are Not Empty," Harry S. Broudy, *Educational Perspectives*, Spring 1982. Reprinted by permission.

time when consumer spending is at an unprecedented height; when technology is leaping forward almost out of the bounds of our understanding; when prospects for life and health in the United States have never been better, the public is sour on schooling, sour on teachers, sour on the faith that the schools can produce an enlightened citizenry for a democratic society. Is this saddening change perhaps a sign that the compact with the social order implicit in the profession of education has been breached in some way?

The learned professions use their special skill and knowledge to serve as intercessionaries for those who cannot cope by themselves in critical life predicaments. Physicians intercede in crises of health, lawyers in encounters with the law, clergymen in crises of salvation. Educators, one would like to think, are our intercessionaries when we are threatened with ignorance, albeit the fear of ignorance if not so fearful as that of pain, prisons, and damnation. Professionals, therefore, always have been considered a quasi-priestly class garbed in black robes or white coats devoted to the welfare of their clients even if—and this is a crucial condition—the client cannot pay enough for the rescue operation.

No business firm, craftsman, or laborer is expected to provide goods or services *gratis*; the professional—especially the learned professional—is! Clients are—and yet are not—customers.

For this reason the payment of fees to doctors, lawyers, clergymen, and yes, even teachers is not simply a business transaction. Health, life, freedom, justice, and knowledge have no fixed price. The rich can pay a lot; the poor cannot, even when both are equally grateful for the intercession of the professional. Gratitude, when expressed in money, becomes a gratuity. To say that professionals work for tips is an odd notion indeed for professionals do send bills, often for high fees, school teachers and college professors occasionally strike, yet they are reluctant to come out and say, "We do it for the money." The public is even more reluctant to believe that they do, myriads of facts to the contrary notwithstanding.

This lingering reluctance to regard their service as a market commodity is witness to the importance of a profession's credibility. Because we cannot, as laypersons, judge their expertise by our own knowledge, we have to take it and their integrity, on faith. We rely on professionals' fidelity to their calling, to their code of ethics, to their moral commitment to their clients and their guild. We cannot as laymen check the safety of foods, or the dangers and benefits of drugs and surgery, or the justice of laws, or the efficacy of the teacher. In a complicated world, made no less so by every technological advance, the growth of science demands a growth of faith in scientists. We have to believe that scientists do not fudge the evidence; that our physicians and lawyers and clergymen and educators, not to speak of our statesmen, know what they are doing, and doing it in the public interest. We have to *believe* that the media are telling us all we need to know.

When that faith is shaken, we become fearful, frustrated, and angry. How do we react to this fear and frustration? We may shrink into our cocoons, bolt the doors, stay off the dark streets, and listen to those who advise us to buy gold. Cults, nostrums, astrologers, and gambling casinos flourish; *we* vacillate between saving it all against the day of doom or spending it all out of fear that that day is near.

Or we lash out at what we think is the cause of our frustration. We join single-interest groups and threaten our legislators. Neighbors are attacked—verbally, physically, or both. The pleasure of hate and revenge is supposed to offset the fears of danger, and the danger of fear.

What is the alternative to mindless withdrawal and mindless aggression? Education says that enlightenment through reliable knowledge is the only real alternative. However, if we can no longer master or test that knowledge ourselves, then we have to place our faith in the guilds of scholars who have dedicated themselves to the discovery, development, and dissemination of knowledge.

So while this anniversary observance is a ritual, it is not an empty one. It deserves the special costumes, the decorations, music, and the heightened emotions of the participants, because these are our ways of marking and renewing the commitment of and to the guild of scholars. This is our pledge of allegiance to the compact we are making with society; staking out our claim to its respect and faith, and promising our loyalty to the best that the human mind has thought and said and wrought.

The guilds of scholarship are the custodians of a long, critical tradition; they may not always be right but society expects them always to be upright in building and guarding that tradition. The State in building and supporting schools, colleges, and universities recognizes the import of that tradition for the public good. It expects returns in the form of applications to industry, business, agriculture, medicine, and, one must suppose, to all forms of the public good. Nevertheless, there is an even deeper faith expressed by the continued existence of this College; it is, that for knowledge to be good for man and society it must first be sought for itself. This is the cornerstone of academic credibility.

That credibility is endangered when academics get too close to the marketplace. And in recent years they have been tempted to do so by grants, consultation, opportunities in industry and government. A taste for power and money is easily acquired. Even more tempting and threatening is the tendency to measure academic values in monetary terms. The distinguished professor commands a higher salary than the less distinguished. The professor who can take a position in business commands a higher salary than one who is condemned to the classroom. Prestigious institutions are rarely indigent. But academic quality is not the same as money quality, or price, or value. Each mode of human value is unique: a $150,000 tennis star is not equal or the same as a $150,000 award for personal injury or a $150,000 painting or a $150,000 research grant. Using a single money scale for all human values—as the media seems to be doing—destroys their individual, intrinsic quality and leads to depersonalization and, in time, to dehumanization.

Scholarship and teaching is not a likely road for those who seek a fortune. If it does not give intrinsic satisfaction, its other rewards may be disappointing. And this brings us back to our compact with society. It gives us freedom to teach, to speak, to inquire. It gives into our care its most precious resource: its hostage to the future.

Indeed one of the most precious freedoms is the freedom to *play with ideas* and to play idea games with our students. The power of the mind to expand in imagination is the engine of creativity in every art and science. This is a dangerous freedom, as all important freedoms are likely to be, and that is why the scholarly tradition is needed to criticize and assess the hypotheses and theories issuing from the minds of the guild members.

To study and learn to use the rules of the basic disciplinary guilds with relevant facility is a fair definition of the disciplined mind; the educated mind is a disciplined mind. Within each discipline, research and controversy can be carried on rationally even when there is no agreement; outside of it there is only opinion held with more or less passion.

It is no small matter, therefore, for the College of Education—on this occasion—to recall to its students, graduates, faculties, and the community the year of its birth. It is an occasion for pride and the renewal of its pledge to serve society as a guild of the learned, many of whose members have also become good and wise.

The Educational Pendulum

DIANE RAVITCH

Diane Ravitch is the author of The Troubled Crusade: American Education, 1945-1980 *(Basic Books) and is an associate professor at Teachers College, Columbia University.*

The schools of America are in crisis—again. In spring, four major commissions declared that the inadequacies of the schools threatened the future of the nation, and this fall several new reports are expected to add to the indictment. Now that the ills of American education are once more a significant public issue, it is a good time to reflect on how we reached this point.

At any given time during most of the past half-century, schools have been the object of well-intended crusades to change or save them. These periodic waves of reform, from one extreme to the other, have led many observers to wonder whether the worst problem of American education is its faddishness. In the 1940s and early 1950s, a "good school" used progressive methods based on student interests and activity projects. After the Soviets put Sputnik into orbit in 1957, a "good school" was defined as one with high academic standards and special programs for gifted students, especially in subjects such as science, foreign languages, and mathematics. By the late 1960s, the once-high standards started to fall, and the "good school" was one where student participation and choice were emphasized. Since the mid-1970s, the educational pendulum has swung back toward "basics," "standards," and a coherent curriculum, and away from the free-wheeling experimentation of the '60s and '70s.

Why so much faddism? Why the constant shift from spontaneity and student interests in one decade to rigor and standards in the next? More than anything else, our educational faddism stems from the deeply ingrained conviction among many Americans that the best way to reform society is to reform the schools. Awareness of a social problem typically leads to the creation of a new school program: To curb the rate of traffic fatalities, a driver-education curriculum is devised; a rise in the divorce rate is followed by new courses on family life; demands for racial integration are met with school busing. Since the needs of society change depending on the social, political, and economic climate, the educational pendulum is pushed first in one direction, then in another.

Through the years, efforts to make the schools relevant to the needs of society have provoked intense struggles over the curriculum between groups with differing views. One source of this tension has been generated within the education profession itself. As the profession emerged and became self-conscious in the early 20th century, it developed a "new class" of policymakers and theorists who were not primarily classroom teachers. As the profession sought to define itself and find its social role, its leaders sought ways in which the profession could make a significant contribution to solving social problems. Unlike the classroom teacher, who had little time or reason to wonder whether the study of history or literature would change society, the growing number of professionals in schools of education, city education departments, state education departments, and professional associations interminably debated how to change the schools in order to serve society better.

While their agreement is widespread that schools exert an important influence on the next generation, a sharp divergence characterizes the question of how schools should meet this responsibility. Historically, the debate on this issue within the education establishment has raged between the progressive educators and the traditionalists. The progressives argue that professional educators must determine how to fit the individual to the society and design their course offerings accordingly; traditionalists, on the other hand, contend that the only way to reform society is by making individuals more intelligent. The zigs and zags in educational development during the past 50 years directly mirror this debate.

The traditionalist idea—that the central purpose of education is to increase students' intellectual powers—dominated American schools until the 1930s. At that time, however, the beliefs of educational philosopher John

> *"The objectives of education are preparation for citizenship; for home and family life; for vocational life; for physical health; for effective personality; for effective use of leisure time; and for development of information, interests, and skills . . . It cannot be expected that the great mass of the populace will spend its leisure time with the classics, the arts, or higher mathematics. Leisure education must then be attuned to the primitive instincts for physical and practical activity, the more familiar pursuits of the masses—the home and its furnishings, nature, sports, games, the radio, and social activities."*
>
> Harl R. Douglass
>
> Secondary Education for Youth in Modern America, 1937

CULVER PICTURES

Growing up to be a good citizen, however, sometimes meant learning how to be a practical consumer.

Dewey and his followers made substantial inroads in schools of education, professional associations, and public-school systems. Because of the Depression, which destroyed the job market for adolescents, many young people who would normally have gone to work stayed in high school. The swelling of the high-school enrollment by non-college-bound students made many educators dissatisfied with the traditional academic curriculum. The progressive philosophy—which argued that in school there should be a society that would define what the larger society should be—encouraged broadening the curriculum for this new brand of student. Under the influence of progressivism, many schools introduced vocational and personal-service courses while reducing academic offerings.

After World War II, this kind of progressivism came to be known as "life-adjustment education" and became a major force in American education. Principals boasted that their programs adjusted students to the demands of real life, freeing them from dry academic studies. The new curriculums centered around vocation, leisure activities, health, personal concerns, and community problems. The schools in Des Moines, Iowa, for example, offered a course called "Developing an Effective Personality," while junior-high-school students in Tulsa learned what shade of nail polish to wear and how to improve their appearance. Some schools had no curriculum at all, while others pointed with pride to new courses in which projects or activities such as running a barbershop or decorating the girls' washroom replaced traditional studies.

Since the public never fully understood why these innovations were introduced, some communities became embroiled in heated political controversies. In Minneapolis, for example, a progressive superintendent merged English and social studies into a new required course called "Common

> *"To what desirable patterns of group behavior does [education] contribute? With any child, the secret for success is being fitted . . . It is vain and wasteful to take a girl who would make a fine homemaker and try to fit her into the patterns of training which make a lawyer, or to take a boy who would be successful in business and try to fit his training to that which produces doctors."*
>
> Paul R. Mort and William S. Vincent
> A Look at Our Schools: A Book for The Thinking Citizen, 1946

Learnings" in which pupils studied their own personal and social problems. A parent group, led by university professors including poet and novelist Robert Penn Warren, persuaded the local school board to permit their children to choose traditional academic subjects instead of "Common Learnings."

By the early 1950s, "life-adjustment education" had been introduced in many school districts across the nation, and it became the target of ridicule by scores of critics, most of whom were concerned laymen, such as Mortimer Smith, who later went on to found the Council for Basic Education, and university professors such as Arthur Bestor, who wrote the controversial book, *Educational Wastelands*. Critics charged not only that life-adjustment education was conformist and anti-intellectual, but that it was undemocratic because it provided academic studies only to college-bound students. Among the most outspoken critics was Robert Hutchins, chancellor of the University of Chicago, who complained that schools were failing to equip youngsters with intellectual power, feeding them instead a poor diet of vocational training and miscellaneous dead facts. By trying to meet all the needs of students, Hutchins charged, the schools were disintegrating their program since students have so many needs. "Perhaps the greatest idea that America has given the world," Hutchins wrote, "is the idea of education for all. The world is entitled to know whether this idea means that everybody can be educated, or only that everybody must go to school."

Although progressive educators defended their programs and charged that the critics were reactionaries, out of touch with the modern world, the launch of Sputnik finished the debate, at least for the moment. Almost overnight, the nation became obsessed with the failure of the schools. School boards hastily installed new programs in mathematics, science, and foreign languages. Admiral Hyman Rickover insisted that the schools had damaged the nation's security by neglecting those with talent. And the federal government, which had refused to approve any general federal aid to education for nearly a century, appropriated nearly $1 billion in the National Defense Education Act, which spurred the teaching of the hard sciences and foreign languages.

The post-Sputnik effect was almost immediate. For the first time in the century, enrollments in foreign-language classes rose. With federal funds, more teachers of science, mathematics, and foreign languages were trained, and schools had money to modernize their laboratories. Through the encouragement of the National Science Foundation, courses in the physical sciences, mathematics, and social science were substantially rewritten by leading scholars to reflect recent advances in knowledge.

By the time the new curriculums were ready for use in the classroom in the mid-1960s, however, the furor over Sputnik had abated. The calls for academic excellence had faded away, drowned out by the rising tide of social conflict in the cities and the disorders on college campuses.

The contemporary climate of social unrest, racial tension, and anti-war protest produced a new wave of critics and reformers, who—in keeping with the American tradition of saving society by changing the schools—pointed the finger of blame at the schools for all that had gone wrong. According to the typical analysis, society was in deep trouble because the schools were too authoritarian in their insistence on standards of academic performance, dress, and behavior and, in addition, were responsible for perpetuating institutional racism.

The federal government responded to the mood of crisis by enacting a major school-aid program whose primary beneficiaries were poor children. Critics contended that this would not alter the fundamental structure of education or society. What was needed, they said, was more freedom and spontaneity, which would surely produce higher motivation and therefore better learning. In the universities, students demanded courses that were relevant to political and social issues of the day.

During the late 1960s and early 1970s, schools again swung towards progressivism. Many elementary schools adopted "open education," which varied from place to place but often meant that the walls between classes were knocked down, and that students could exercise considerable choice about what to do each day. At the high-school level, graduation requirements were lowered, enrollments fell in such "hard" subjects as science, mathematics, and foreign languages, and alternative schools were established for students with special interests. Traditional subjects gave way to independent study, student-designed courses, and topical electives.

The subject areas affected most in the new era of student freedom were English and social studies. Typically, these courses gave way to a plethora of electives. In many schools, English was replaced by courses on the mass media, pop culture, and popular fiction. Writing, once a part of every student's daily regime, became a special course. Social studies, or history, was often splintered into mini-courses on black history, women's history, or "rap" sessions about values.

By the mid-1970s, academic indicators began to reveal a steady, nationwide downturn. For example, the number and proportion of students who received high scores on the SAT dropped dramatically. Not only college entrance examination scores but other tests taken by students in junior and senior high school showed a marked drop. In 1977, a blue-ribbon panel appointed by the College Board identified such in-school phenomena as grade inflation, absenteeism, frivolous courses, the absence of homework, and a striking diminution in reading and writing assignments as reasons for falling test scores. Other studies

> *"Parents are slow in realizing how unimportant the learning side of school is. Children, like adults, learn what they want to learn. All prize-giving and marks and exams sidetrack proper personality development. . . . All that any child needs is the three Rs; the rest should be tools and clay and sports and theater and paint and freedom."*
>
> A.S. Neill
>
> Summerhill: A Radical Approach to Child Rearing, 1960

> *"There is no inherently indispensable body of knowledge that every single child should know. . . . What children carry in their heads as 'chair' or 'aunt' or 'black' will never be absolutely identical. . . . In open education the teacher is mainly assistant to, not director of, the child's activity."*
>
> Charles Rathbone
> Open Education: The Informal Classroom, 1971

consistently found that during the 1970s high-school students took more nonacademic courses and fewer of the advanced courses necessary for college preparation.

As evidence accumulated that the schools were slipping as academic institutions, public confidence plummeted. Parents called for a "back-to-basics" curriculum, demanding the restoration of academic standards and discipline. In every year but one since 1969, the Gallup Poll has reported that the public's greatest educational concern has been the lack of discipline in the schools.

As usual, the schools followed society's shifting mood. One of the first things to go was the "new math," a prominent post-Sputnik curriculum reform, which most students and many teachers and parents found incomprehensible. Many schools that had torn their walls down for open education now replaced them. While alternative schools survived, their numbers shrank and their purpose became more clearly defined. By 1978, nearly 40 states adopted minimum competency tests to ascertain whether students had learned enough to be promoted or to graduate.

The latest swing of the educational pendulum has now taken us back, at least rhetorically, to the post-Sputnik era, when educators, policymakers, and parents feared that America's schools were producing (as one book was titled) "second-rate brains." The fear expressed in the most recent batch of commission reports is that the United States, through the failings of its schools, is losing the international competition for jobs and markets. When Sputnik was first launched by the Soviets, critics worried that the United States was falling behind in the race for space, technological prowess, and military superiority. Today, they worry less about falling behind in the space race, but just as much about the lags in our technological innovation and our place in the world economy.

While it is likely that American education will continue to be responsive to social change, certain facts will moderate future swings of the pendulum. For one thing, the use of polls in sounding school issues will restrain faddism to some extent, because the public has consistently expressed fairly traditional ideas about curriculum and student behavior. For another, the continuing spread of interdependence in the global economy will make it difficult for American schools to neglect the basic subjects.

What has been the effect of this history of educational fads? It is impossible to say how society has been changed as a result. For one thing, no single educational innovation has ever been universally adopted; even when a fad was at its height, many teachers and schools simply ignored the fashion. For another, there is no simple barometer with which to measure social change or with which to tie together causes and effects. What is clearly discernible, however, is the effect of these trends in the schools. When high school graduation requirements fell, enrollment in courses such as science, mathematics, and foreign languages dropped; in some high schools, foreign languages were eliminated, as were advanced courses in numerous hard disciplines.

If the past is any guide, we can expect that the current interest in excellence will last as long as there is a general perception that society's welfare depends on our ability to compete successfully in the international marketplace of goods and ideas. If we experience an internal crisis of confidence comparable to the Depression or to the late 1960s, then we may expect a return to the kind of educational progressivism that stresses self and community rather than competition and achievement.

Whatever the state of politics and society, America's schools need an anchor, an informed constituency of citizens and professional educators who will continue to press for the kind of liberal education that all children should have. Even back in the 1930s, when progressives and traditionalists first began to battle, they all agreed on the importance of literacy. The appeal of educational progressivism to parents lies in its promise to improve children's learning by increasing intrinsic motivation. Traditionalists have insisted that some kinds of extrinsic motivation, some external discipline such as grades and course requirements, are necessary. In either case, it is clear that parents and the public want children to become literate in school.

That is why, today, educators speak not just of reading and writing but of scientific literacy, cultural literacy, and historical literacy. Fads may come and go, but American schools now appear to be aiming at this broadened definition of literacy.

> *"Excellence in education means several related things. At the level of the individual learner, it means performing on the boundary of individual ability in ways that test and push back personal limits, in school and in the workplace. Excellence characterizes a school or college that sets high expectations and goals for all learners, then tries in every possible way to help students reach them. Excellence characterizes a society that has adopted these policies, for it will then be prepared through the education and skill of its people to respond to the challenges of a rapidly changing world."*
>
> A Nation at Risk
> The National Commission on Excellence in Education, 1983

The Twentieth Century Fund Task Force Report on Federal Elementary And Secondary Education Policy

Patricia Albjerg Graham

PATRICIA ALBJERG GRAHAM, who was a member of the Twentieth Century Fund Task Force, is Charles Warren Professor of the History of Education and dean of the Harvard Graduate School of Education, Cambridge, Mass. She presented an earlier version of this report before the U.S. House of Representatives Budget Committee on 22 June 1983.

THE REPORT of the Twentieth Century Fund Task Force on Federal Elementary and Secondary Education Policy joins a growing chorus of concerned critics in asserting that U.S. schools are in dire straits. Despite a number of specific examples to the contrary, an emerging national consensus suggests that U.S. schools do not come close to living up to expectations.

The diversity of these expectations contributes to the difficulty; we Americans have consistently reaffirmed our faith in schooling by increasing both the number and the variety of tasks that we expect the schools to perform. More than ever before, we expect – even require – the schools to be all things to all people. We expect them to serve not only as agents of education, but as vehicles of social, political, and even legal changes as well. We expect no other societal institution to serve so many masters. We may find it disappointing, but we should not be surprised that the schools have failed to meet these expectations.

The Twentieth Century Fund Task Force believes that elementary and secondary schools, pressed to play so many roles, are in danger of losing sight of their fundamental purpose: providing "the basic skills of reading, writing, and calculating; technical capability in computers; training in science and foreign languages; and knowledge of civics." Although the Task Force heartily supports the diversity of educational practice that results from a historical commitment to state and local control of U.S. schooling, its members believe in the value for the nation of a common curricular "spine" that includes both the basic skills associated with mastery of the primary and elementary curriculum and the complex skills taught in the high school. Schools must provide students with the competence to exist in, to sustain, and to further develop a complex economic and technological society. Schools must nurture in individuals those qualities of mind and character that are necessary to maintain an ethnically diverse democracy. Schools must imbue students with the desire to acquire knowledge, so that both they and their society may grow and prosper. Few schools accomplish these tasks adequately; all schools need to do them well.

Thus the Task Force believes that educational improvement is a preeminent national need. U.S. society in general and individual Americans in particular would benefit from an enhancement of elementary and secondary education. The Task Force further believes that, since a prime national need for educational improvement exists, the federal government must contribute to such improvement without interfering with state or local responsibility and accountability for the public schools.

The Federal Role

Throughout our history, we Americans have recognized the distinction between a national problem and a federal responsibility for its solution. We have considered certain issues of great national importance, such as defense or diplomacy, solely as federal matters. In other instances, such as our national concern for the prosperity of commerce and agriculture, we initially thought the matters best handled privately; only later did public efforts trigger federal support and regulation.

We Americans have always viewed education as a significant national need that requires governmental support. Ever since the Revolutionary War, we have believed that a democratic society such as ours requires an educated citizenry. But since the late 18th century we have viewed this particular national need as a matter to be handled by state and local governments. This is not surprising, given the hesitance of early national leaders to offend the political sensibilities of those who sought strong roles for state governments. Furthermore, the evolution of a public system of education, with primary administrative and fiscal responsibility located at the state and local levels, has generally served the nation well.

The Twentieth Century Fund Task Force does not challenge that tradition. The advantages that accrue from a local/state system of public education are great: educational flexibility, the building of local and regional community support for education, the avoidance of pitfalls associated with a highly centralized bureaucratic administrative structure, and the recognition of this nation's cultural diversity. Yet, as U.S. society has become more complicated, higher levels of educational achievement have become essential for all citizens. The U.S. can no longer afford to have substantial portions of its population handicapped by limited literacy skills. Current estimates of illiteracy in the U.S. range from about 1% of the population (those individuals who lack even the barest rudiments of reading and writing) to nearly 20% (those individuals who lack the "functional literacy" required for coping effectively in this complex society). Thus the U.S. today requires both higher levels of literacy skills for participation in the society and universal — not partial, as in the past — acquisition of these higher-order skills.

The current public perception of elementary and secondary education in the U.S. — a perception that the Task Force shares — is that the performance of students, especially those in the secondary schools, does not meet this new and higher standard. The problem is national in scope and acute in intensity. Therefore, the Task Force believes that the federal government should supplement local and state efforts in some specific areas of education. The Task Force believes that efforts by the federal government to accomplish the vital and awesome task of improving elementary and secondary education can be grouped under three broad headings: 1) quality, 2) equality, and 3) quality control.

Quality

Concerns for quality pervade the degree and kind of national leadership given to elementary and secondary education, as well as the basic issues of who teaches and what is taught.

National Leadership

Although there is a historical tradition of federal concern for education, much of that concern has been indirect. If in recent years the judicial branch has taken the most active (to the point of interventionist) role in educational affairs, this has been, at least in part, a result of the failure to act that has characterized the executive and legislative branches. As a general recommendation, the Task Force calls on the executive and legislative branches of the federal government to reiterate and emphasize that better schools and better education for young Americans are pressing national needs.

Teachers

The Task Force acknowledges the depressed state of the teaching profession. For a wide variety of reasons, many of our best educators have left teaching for more financially rewarding work. Few of our ablest college graduates are choosing careers in teaching. The Task Force believes that the status of teaching must be reinforced, incentives for entering the profession must be provided, educators must be encouraged to improve their pedagogical skills, and excellent teachers must be rewarded and encouraged to remain in the classroom.

The Task Force recommends that the federal government fund a national Master Teachers Program to recognize and reward excellence in the classroom. Awards would:

- go to teachers in every state (with one or more recipients from every congressional district),
- be monetary grants above the top levels of existing salary schedules, and
- be granted for five-year periods (the first year to be spent in professional development, the last four in further teaching and in sharing skills with other teachers).

What Is Taught

The Task Force believes that issues of quality in education may be most directly addressed in two specific content areas: 1) language training and 2) science and mathematics education.

A comprehensive approach to the study of languages. The Task Force believes that, although Americans are increasingly conscious of the fact that they live in a pluralistic society, those citizens who are unable to speak or write in the national language will be at a perpetual disadvantage. Similarly, if the U.S. is to sustain its role as an international leader, there is an increasing need for U.S. citizens to develop fluency in a second language. Accordingly, the Task Force recommends:

- that the federal government clearly identify the development of literacy in English as the most important objective of elementary and secondary education in the U.S. and that the government promote and support proficiency in English for all public school children, especially for those who have only a limited command of the language or none at all;
- that federal funds now allocated to bilingual education be used to teach non-English-speaking children how to speak, read, and write English (although the Task Force does not recommend a pedagogy by which such English fluency is to be achieved); and
- that every U.S. public school student have the opportunity to acquire proficiency in a second language and that, to begin to remedy the great deficiency in foreign language teachers, the federal government sponsor a matching grant program, to be administered by the states, for the training of foreign language teachers.

Mathematics and science education. Although training in mathematics and science is a crucial national need, the number of teachers qualified to prepare U.S. children in these areas is rapidly diminishing. To assure an adequate level of training and an adequate force to accomplish such training, the Task Force recommends:

- that the federal government emphasize programs to develop basic scientific literacy among all citizens and to provide advanced training in science and mathematics for secondary school students; and
- that the federal government sponsor an incentive program to augment the supply of teachers in science and mathematics, as well as in foreign languages, through loans to students who are preparing to teach in these areas, with 10% of each loan forgiven for every year (up to five) of actual classroom teaching.

Equality

The Task Force applauds federal efforts, both past and current, to insure that the needs of special categories of students — the poor, the handicapped, the non-English-speaking — are met, despite the inability of state or local governments to do so. Such federal efforts act as a goad for those districts unwilling to act and as a support for those districts that — although willing — cannot afford to implement these often costly programs. Consequently, the Task Force recommends:

- that the federal government continue its efforts to provide categorical or special education programs for the poor and the handicapped; and
- that those categorical programs required by the federal government be paid for from the federal treasury.

The Task Force also wishes to draw federal attention to the fiscal problems of school districts that are required by federal mandate to provide equal educational opportunities to large numbers of illegal aliens, a task well beyond the financial capabilities of such districts. Using as a model the federal "impact aid" originally awarded to districts overwhelmed by a sudden influx of children of military personnel, the Task Force recommends:

- that federal "impact aid" be reformulated to assist school districts overburdened by substantial numbers of immigrant children; and

- that federal assistance – through specifically targeted, flexible federal grants – be given to depressed localities with large concentrations of immigrant and/or impoverished groups, as well as to districts making strong efforts to improve their educational performance.

In line with this concern for districts in which economic issues complicate the task of education, the Task Force has turned its attention to those locales with large numbers of students whom the public schools serve poorly, if at all. Students who repeatedly fail city or state competency examinations or who fail in other ways to achieve at levels commensurate with their abilities should not be abandoned to "social promotion" or to repeated retention. The Task Force believes that the substantial sums now being spent on remediation for these students have not borne fruit. Accordingly, the Task Force recommends:

- that special federal fellowships be established for these students, to be awarded to school districts to encourage the creation of small, individualized programs staffed by certified teachers and run as miniature academies.

Quality Control

Since the establishment of the Office (now Department) of Education in 1867, the federal government has been involved in gathering data on American education. These federal efforts broadened after World War II to include support for basic research in education. The findings from federally supported data collection and basic research have helped to identify areas of progress or emerging difficulties within education; sometimes these findings have also pointed toward possible solutions or focused national attention on the schools. In recommending continued federal support for the collection and investigation of data on education and learning, the Task Force has not ignored the potential of such support for abuse or misdirection. Those individuals and institutions receiving federal support must be held accountable for it; moreover, federally supported educational programs need consistent and careful evaluation. With these caveats in mind, the Task Force advocates federal support for:

- the continued collection of factual information about various aspects of the educational system itself;
- the collection of information about the academic performances of students, teachers, and schools across the U.S.;
- the continuation of fundamental research into the learning process; and
- the evaluation of federally sponsored educational programs.

All of these activities will inform and guide our attempts to improve U.S. public schools. Meanwhile, careful monitoring of these activities will insure that the federal support has been neither misdirected nor misplaced.

Conclusion

The mother wit and character of its people are this nation's most valuable resources. Many institutions in the society – families, communities, religious organizations – have some responsibility for nurturing these resources, but one institution has the preeminent responsibility for fostering their development. That institution is the school. No government can afford to ignore its most precious resources, particularly when ample evidence suggests that those resources are not being developed adequately. Such is now the situation of the federal government with regard to the elementary and secondary schools. To protect and promote the wit and the character of Americans, the Twentieth Century Fund Task Force has argued that the federal government must increase its efforts related to education. The fact that federal support for U.S. schooling should supplement, not supplant, state and local financing makes the need for federal support no less pressing. Only the federal government can assert and emphasize the national interest in having schools of high quality and in insuring that all children have access to such schools. The intellect and character of all Americans need support, and the federal government must take responsibility for helping to meet this preeminent national need.

How to Save the Public Schools

PHIL KEISLING

Phil Keisling is an editor of *The Washington Monthly.*

In 1960 six-year-old Ruby Bridges braved the taunts of white racists to become the first black to enroll in New Orleans's then-segregated public school system. Two decades later, Bridges took her three children out of that same school system and placed them in a parochial school. "I don't like to put down public schools," she said to a reporter about her son, "but he wasn't really learning the way he should have."

As Bridges painfully learned, integrating the public schools is only half the battle—and probably the easier half. A more insidious evil than segregation is a public school system that's bad and getting worse. The signs of decline—from the nineteen-year stretch of plummeting SAT scores (broken only this year by a minuscule rise) to the three hundred thousand "functional illiterates" who graduate from American high schools each year—are already familiar. Less often considered are the millions of children, many already victimized by racial prejudice and poverty, who will be consigned to lives of failure because their high school diplomas are the educational equivalent of worthless notes from the Weimar Republic.

So Bridges and a growing number of other parents are defecting to private schools, motivated not so much by strong religious convictions or a desire to ensure their children's high social status as by a conviction that the public schools have betrayed them. Some of their children are landing in plummy institutions such as Andover and Phillips Exeter; at this gilded end of the private school spectrum, competition has grown so fierce that kindergartens in Washington, D.C., charging $4,000 a year are now turning away four times as many applicants as they accept. Other children—to the delight of the new right and the outcries of liberals—are turning to fundamentalist Christian schools and white academies.

Nevertheless, the typical private school in America remains the one Bridges chose: a parochial school operated by the Catholic Church. Two-thirds of the nation's five million private school students attend such schools and, contrary to popular misconceptions, they are relatively inexpensive (tuition seldom exceeds $1,000 a year); involve little overt religious instruction (explained partly by the fact that 75 percent of all parochial school teachers are lay instructors); and have relatively unrestrictive admission and retention policies (according to one recent study, 60 percent of these schools don't expel a single student during the school year.) In many inner cities—Chicago, Detroit, Washington, D.C., and New Orleans, to name just a few—the majority of parochial school students are black.

Private schools have co-existed with public ones throughout American history, but until recently they've escaped the scrutiny of the professional sociologist. University of Chicago professor James Coleman, along with associates Thomas Hoffer and Sally Kilgore, has now put an end to that neglect with this path-breaking study. Coleman surveyed 58,000 students in 893 public and 122 private high schools, gathering information that ranged from each school's financial resources to the attitudes of its students. Achievement tests were then given to students in the 10th and 12th grades. After performing the various mysteries of the sociologists' craft—ordinary least squares regression analyses, standard deviations, independent variable weightings—Coleman came to a disturbing conclusion. Students in a typical private school—a parochial school with larger classes, lower paid teachers, and substantially fewer

resources—achieve more than those in the average public school.

WHEN COLEMAN first announced his results a year ago (this book reprints his study in more detail and includes a rebuttal to some of the major criticisms), many in the educational establishment reacted as if he'd just endorsed public hangings for juvenile delinquents. Fellow sociologists assaulted Coleman for his methodological "sloppiness" and criticized the specific techniques he used to filter out the effects on achievement of family income and race. The criticisms went beyond the normally staid bounds of academic discourse. Professor Arthur S. Goldberger of the University of Wisconsin, for example, claimed the report "reeked of incompetence and irresponsibility." Political liberals were no less upset, particularly when Coleman endorsed tuition tax credits. This last criticism—that Coleman was inappropriately enlisting social science on behalf of a controversial political issue—was somewhat ironic, since many of the same critics had used a previous Coleman study, *Equality of Educational Opportunity* (1966), to justify large-scale busing to promote integration.

It doesn't take a sociologist to detect methodological shortcomings in Coleman's book. For example, Coleman doesn't fully account for the effect on a child's achievement of having parents who care enough about education to begin with that they're willing to pay private school tuition. Likewise, the achievement tests Coleman used partly measure the effects of elementary education, not high school.

Such flaws aren't surprising; after all, the only unimpeachable scientific comparison would require sending a child through a public high school, deprogramming him of everything he learned there, reversing the aging process, and after all that sending him back through a private school. But of far more interest to the general reader is the almost banal simplicity of Coleman's major conclusions. Whoever once dubbed sociology the "quantification of the intuitive and the glorification of the obvious" might have had this study in mind. Despite an occasional surprise—for example, if income and religion are equal, blacks are more likely to send their children to parochial schools than whites—his findings seem obvious. Private schools are more rigorous; their students, for example, are 50 percent more likely to have over an hour's worth of homework every night than students in public schools. Private schools impose stricter disciplinary rules and maintain more order in their classrooms. Most important, private schools put a much greater emphasis on academic subjects. Seventy percent of their students are enrolled in an academic program compared to only 34 percent for public school. Fourteen percent of private school students take a third-year language, compared to just 6 percent in the public schools. For chemistry the comparable figures are 53 percent and 37 percent; for geometry, 84 percent and 53 percent.

In other words, private schools demand more of their students—and they get more. But Coleman doesn't suggest that private schools are automatically better than public ones; in fact, according to his comparison of "high performance" public and private schools, there is little difference between the two in student achievement. Rather, Coleman's important finding is this: the characteristics that result in higher achievement are much more likely to be found in a private school than in a public one.

IT'S A SIMPLE, even obvious, conclusion; what's most interesting are the great number of people who choose to distort or ignore it entirely. Their reaction reveals the paucity of thinking these days about public education, particularly on the left. Among most Democrats, the educational agenda has only two major items: opposition to tuition tax credits and support for increased educational spending. It's a distinctly unimaginative agenda—which perhaps explains why, among those leading Democrats urging the party to formulate new ideas in response to the new right, education is barely on the radar screen. Paul Tsongas's *The Road from Here* doesn't list education among the "eight realities" Democrats need to reconsider. Mark Green's *Winning Back America* and Tom Hayden's manifesto, *The American Future*, are similarly silent.

Tuition tax credits aren't a good idea; they're more an admission of defeat than a sensible way to improve public education. But just as tuition tax credits won't revitalize our public schools, neither will the traditional liberal panacea of simply dipping deeper into the public purse. Is there good reason to believe that higher salaries for public school teachers will automatically make a substantial difference in student achievement when private school teachers work longer hours, have to manage larger classes, and make about $5,000 less per year? Unfortunately, there is no good reason, and those desiring proof need look no further than the experience of the last two decades. During that period expenditures for public elementary and secondary education increased nearly sixfold to almost $120 billion, more than keeping abreast of inflation. Meanwhile, the quality of our schools has plummeted.

ONE CAN POINT accusing fingers at the influence of TV, apathetic parents, and even junk food, but the lion's share of the blame must fall on that segment of the educational system with the most direct influence on children: the nation's 2.2 million teachers. Never particularly high, the quality of the nation's teaching corps today is embarrassingly low, and sinking further. The profession is attracting the nation's least academically gifted and creative students. Just one measure: in 1979-1980 those college students planning to major in general education scored an average of 339 on the verbal portion of the SAT—80 points below the already dismal national average. Those who justifiably might point out the imperfect link between SAT scores and teaching ability should also consider the experience of the Lemon Grove School District in Southern California. There a literacy test scaled to eighth-grade levels was given prospective teachers, all possessed of paper degrees and certificates. Thirty-five percent flunked one or more parts.

The education methodology courses required for a teacher's certificate—usually so stultifyingly dull that most college students avoid them—are partly to blame. As J. Myron Atkin, an education professor at Stanford, has observed, "It is doubtful if as many as two dozen of the 1,300 institutions that prepare teachers are maintaining programs that a bright youngster would find demanding." Another cause is more heartening, but no less reassuring. A quarter-century ago widespread sexism gave intelligent, motivated women access to few professions other than teaching; today, those same women are pursuing careers in law, medicine, and business. Unfortunately, what is long-overdue equity for women is also our children's loss. Indeed, the aversion to the classroom of talented men and women alike provides but a sad commentary on contemporary values. Something is seriously amiss when a society gives more financial reward to those who hunch over a convoluted legal brief, in search of some new obstructionist tactic to use in an obscure contract dispute, than to those who teach a child to appreciate the eloquence of the written word or the elegance of mathematics.

THE NATION'S two major teachers' unions—the American Federation of Teachers and the National Education Association—don't dispute the low quality of teachers so much as enlist this unhappy situation in arguing for higher teachers' salaries. Their argument is simple: when it comes to public schools, Americans are getting what they pay for. And if they want better schools, they'll simply have to pay substantially more for better teachers.

Welcome to the great circular argument of public education. In the abstract, higher teacher salaries are both fair and sensible. Yet in the real world, what would be the result if teachers' salaries were doubled overnight? Very little, except that the incompetent and mediocre teachers now in the classroom would get a lot more money—and would probably be that much less inclined to quit.

That latter point is important because replacing bad teachers with good ones, after all, is the whole raison d'être of raising salaries. But retirement or resignation now are about the only ways to get rid of incompetent teachers; administrators, school board members, and even candid teachers will admit that firing a tenured teacher—and most fall into that category after just three years' experience—is virtually impossible. In the name of the great liberal shibboleth of "due process," such a warren of legal obstacles has been erected that only in the most egregious cases do school districts even bother to initiate dismissal proceedings. In the last six years, for example, Philadelphia has dismissed only 24 of its 13,000 teachers; a typical dismissal takes two years, and involves expensive legal fees.

Short of changing various rules governing tenure and due process, both the AFT and the NEA contend that better teachers can be incorporated into the ranks over a period of years. (To help ensure the quality of these new teachers, the AFT favors some competency testing; the NEA steadfastly opposes any measurement attempts.) But putting aside the question of whether the nation's children should be forced to wait several decades for these better teachers so no one has to be fired, this gradual approach has a graver flaw: it won't work.

Again, it's important to focus on the educational world as it is. The American Federation of Teachers predicts 55,000 existing teachers will be laid off this school year—which hardly leaves much room for those bright, new hirees. (Incidentally, union contracts usually dictate that lay-offs be on the basis of seniority, not competence—yet another way bad teachers are protected while our schools deteriorate). Nor is there much reason to expect such lay-offs will abate, notwithstanding the unions' warnings that a slight rise in student enrollments toward the end of this decade will help spawn a new teacher shortage. Student enrollments peaked twelve years ago, yet in 1981 there were more elementary and secondary teachers than at any other time in the nation's history. The explanation lies in the "shrinking classroom": in 1962 there were 25.6 students per teacher while today there are just 18.9. If the nation were to return to the 1962 ratio, it could lay off almost 500,000 more teachers. That would be unwise, to be sure, but further decreases are hardly unreasonable, especially when one considers that the traditional argument for smaller classes has been improved quality of education. But in light of recent history, that's hardly a compelling argument—which perhaps explains why both the AFT and the NEA are increasingly trying to make classroom size a negotiable item in collective bargaining agreements.

Higher salaries for some teachers may prove necessary to improve our public schools; indeed, the dire shortage of math and science teachers now plaguing most districts can be resolved in the near term only by paying more for these specialities. (Again, the NEA and to a lesser extent the AFT oppose such salary differentials, insisting that salaries for all teachers, even those in oversubscribed fields such as English and social studies, rise together.) But absent other changes in our public schools, spending more money will only produce more dashed expectations.

This is where the Coleman report holds its most important lesson. Rather than glorifying private education, the report suggests that public schools would be wise to emulate the best aspects of private schools—aspects which have little to do with money. One of the most obvious places to begin is with academic requirements. Fewer than half of our public high schools now require more than one year of math and science for graduation; little wonder a recent National Science Foundation report warned that ours is a nation fast approaching "scientific illiteracy." As reflected in the dearth of third-year language students, foreign language requirements are virtually unknown in American schools. Our schools' neglect of both science and foreign languages stands in glaring contrast to the schools of Western Europe and Japan, countries whose economies, not so incidentally, are more robust than our own.

Certainly not all private schools offer adequate academic programs. Some—particularly fundamentalist Christian schools—lose more from narrow-mindedness than they gain in rigor. Even so, as Coleman discovered, parochial schools have proved far less susceptible to the academic relativism in which a course entitled "TV—The Medium is the Message" is put on a par with one teaching the basics of grammar and expository writing.

Another characteristic that Coleman linked to higher achievement is the private school's insistence on a more orderly learning environment. Not only did parochial schools have stricter disciplinary standards, but their students were more likely to feel they were treated "fairly" than their public school counterparts. Perhaps more important, whereas one in ten public school students rated their teachers' interest in them as "excellent," for parochial schools, where the classes were even larger, the figure was one in four. Of course, one cannot expect public schools to duplicate the spiritual mystique of parochial schools, where the implied presence of a higher moral authority suffuses the classrooms. But public schools can and should pay far more attention to fostering a coherent set of shared values and establishing more clear-cut lines of authority—if for no other reason than students themselves seem to prefer it.

As for specific disciplinary measures, the Coleman report suggests that public schools need to reevaluate some dearly held notions. In theory, any child can be transformed into an attentive student with a little understanding and patience. In practice, that noble sentiment is one of the most destructive illusions of modern education. It takes only a few disruptive students to poison the learning atmosphere for everyone. Many of these students should be removed from regular classrooms so that teachers can focus their energies on students who've shown a willingness to learn. This at first may sound harsh and uncompassionate, but it's far less cruel than denying a much greater number of students a decent education. In our insistence on giving as many children as possible the traditional token of success—the high school diploma—we've inadvertently ensured that far too many of them will fail later in life.

PERHAPS the most important lesson of private schools—and one Coleman unfortunately didn't examine—involves teachers. Almost no private schools require teaching certificates; instead, the emphasis is on whether instructors know their subjects and can teach them well. Pay in private schools is substantially lower than in public ones, but outstanding performance is usually rewarded with merit pay. Teachers who prove to be incompetent can be easily fired or simply not re-hired when their contracts come up for renewal.

Compare this with public schools. Only people with proper credentials can teach, even though many without them know their subject far better than those who hold them. Once in the classroom, most of these teachers are paid without regard to ability or the need for their services, but according to seniority and the possession of additional academic degrees. While a beginning math teacher might get $12,000 a year (assuming the school district can find one), an English teacher with 15 years' experience and a master's degree can command twice as much or more—even though he performs far worse than his younger, lesser-paid colleagues. The result is a system that protects incompetent teachers, demoralizes excellent ones, and makes mediocrity the best most of our children can hope for.

The major defenders of this system—the AFT and the NEA—once offered their members badly needed protection from the caprices of administrators and the penury of school boards. But the unions have succeeded all too well, having grown sufficiently powerful to undermine the quality of public education in the name of protecting their members. When a bad teacher is kept in the classroom while a far better candidate waits in the wings for a job opening, the children are the real losers.

SOLVING THIS PROBLEM doesn't require abolishing the unions so much as forcing them to stop having it both ways. On the one hand, the unions demand that their members be treated as "professionals," with commensurate salary and status; on the other, that they should effectively be immune from judgments of quality. As is the case with academic requirements, the relativism behind the credo that "all teachers are equal" allows schools to avoid difficult decisions about the merit of individuals—but in the process undermines excellence. A similar attitude has been all too prevalent on automobile assembly lines, where quality control is ultimately someone else's responsibility. The defective automobile that results can always be recalled; unfortunately, the same is not true for children with defective educations.

Instituting stricter curricular and disciplinary standards will be relatively easy; what will truly test the sincerity of liberals who claim they want to reverse the decline of public education is their treatment of teacher's unions. They are among the nation's most powerful lobbies; the NEA alone provided over 10 percent of the delegates and alternates to the 1980 Democratic National Convention. Their power is even greater on the state level, where they often lead the PACs in spending for legislative races. The bulk of their largesse is lavished on Democrats.

Unfortunately, most liberals aren't showing the stomach for this necessary battle with their traditional allies, preferring instead to tell themselves that the problems with our nation's schools can be solved with a bit more money here, a few more specialized programs there. But such incrementalism is a prescription for the continued deterioration of our public schools, and as they fail the nation loses more than just the well-educated citizenry it needs to compete successfully in an increasingly competitive international economy. The failure of our schools also threatens democracy itself. As more people abandon the public schools to those too poor to escape them, ours becomes a society increasingly stratified, not so much by race as by social class.

Is such a bleak outcome inevitable? Not at all. In fact, for all its criticism of the public schools, Coleman's study is strangely heartening, far more so than his 1966 study mentioned earlier. Fifteen years ago, Coleman concluded that the most important determinant of a child's achievement was his socioeconomic background and that of his peers; little could alter the educational outcome except perhaps trying to mix rich white children with poor black ones—hence the resulting passion for busing.

This latest report suggests an opposite and far more optimistic conclusion: schools *do* make a difference. Though Coleman found that the achievement gap between white and minority students widened between the 10th and 12th grade in public schools, he found it actually narrowed in private ones. Strange as it may sound, that should be comforting news *especially* to liberals, for it suggests that schools really can overcome the debilitating effects of poverty and race.

This is why it's so distressing that, so far, the lessons of the Coleman report have been embraced mainly by conservatives. Indeed, one of the most dismaying failures of American liberalism has been its allowing the right to assume the initiative in calling attention to the deterioration of our public schools. The public understandably has grown impatient with those who make excuses for poor schools or seek refuge in unrealistic—and discredited—solutions such as large, new infusions of public money. Conservative nostrums such as tuition tax credits aren't much better and are probably worse; unfortunately, for many parents concerned about their children's education, they're the only game in town.

Good public schools needn't become an endangered species. But if their ostensible friends continue to ignore danger signs such as the Coleman report, it won't take a sociologist to perform a post-mortem. Parents like Ruby Bridges could just as easily explain what went wrong.

High School Achievement: Public, Catholic, and Private Schools Compared by James S. Coleman, Thomas Hoffer, and Sally Kilgore (Basic Books, 277 pp., $20.75)

End of the Permissive Society?

Americans in rising numbers are joining in a fight to halt the permissiveness that has spawned a host of social and moral conflicts over the past two decades.

Violent-crime rates, drug and alcohol abuse, laxity in school standards—these and many other ills that have spread since the early 1960s are prompting concerned citizens to forsake the benign inaction of that era and enlist in a sometimes controversial drive to strengthen authority—

- Many states this spring, heeding citizens' demands, have enacted laws aimed at cracking down hard on drunk drivers—who accounted for more than half of last year's 50,000 highway deaths—and others are mapping similar action.
- Under public pressure, state after state is moving to curb rising crime with more mandatory sentencing, tougher handling of parole and longer confinement for repeat offenders.
- Public schools in more than two thirds of the states have imposed a minimum-competency requirement for promotion or graduation—only one of several measures being pushed to meet public concern about long-declining academic standards.
- Parents with out-of-control teenagers are joining by the thousands a self-help program using firmness and discipline to restore a more normal family environment.

At the same time, a self-styled "citizens' war on drugs" is making an impact in almost every state, with new laws aimed at everything from smuggling to shops dealing in drug equipment. Several cities are forcing out downtown pornography peddlers through local rezoning restrictions. Public pressure against sex and violence on television is mounting, spurred by a White House survey of network fare that warned of adverse effects on children.

The demand for a stronger hand in dealing with such national woes parallels closely the conservative political swing that brought Ronald Reagan to the Presidency. Yet, as one Midwestern political scientist views the backlash against permissiveness: "There is more involved than a conservative desire to turn the clock back. A good many Americans, whatever their political leanings, feel it is high time to come to grips with many problems that in years past were met with little more than guilt-obsessed hand wringing."

Certain trends that surfaced in the era of "doing your own thing" are proving particularly resistant to change.

The sexual freedom proclaimed in the 1960s—reaching even into junior high schools—is undergoing new strains, yet shows little sign of retreating. In fact, a Reagan administration plan that would require federally funded birth-control organizations to notify parents when teenagers obtain contraceptives has drawn a flood of protest mail—including statements of opposition from 34 state governments.

Even where the battle against permissiveness has made measurable changes, setbacks have come. The censoring of schoolbooks, now particularly strong in the South, recently suffered a widely publicized reverse in Virginia. Heeding a storm of opposition, the Fairfax County school system in mid-April rejected a recommendation that *The Adventures of Huckleberry Finn* be dropped as "racist."

Still, the trend to push back what many Americans see as the excesses and abuses of "letting it all hang out" for two decades is surging ahead in more and more parts of national life. To find out what's going on in the spreading grass-roots rebellion, *U.S.News & World Report* correspondents took soundings across the country.

Crackdown on Alcohol and Drugs

Says the National Safety Council's Charles Vance: "Public pressure to tighten drunken-driver laws has reached an all-time high. Ordinary people are up in arms at the sharp rise in road fatalities involving consumption of liquor. They are demanding—and getting—greater penalties in one statehouse after another."

The pressure is showing results. In recent weeks, 11 states have passed tough laws aimed at intoxicated motorists, and 26 others are considering similar measures—or even stiffer ones. Both Virginia and Florida have just enacted mandatory 48-hour jail sentences for first offenders. Under most of the new laws, repeat offenders will be facing longer jail sentences, bigger fines and license suspensions.

Irate citizens are following through in other ways. One citizens' group, Mothers Against Drunk Drivers (MADD), drums up votes for candidates for public office—including judgeships—who pledge stronger action against drunken drivers. In a number of states, MADD has played a key role in obtaining mandatory sentences for such offenders.

Hand in hand with campaigns to rid the roads of drinkers are ones to raise legal drinking ages. In 16 states, citizens' groups have gained legislative support to hike the age minimum from 18 to as high as 21. These lobbyists cite a survey by the Insurance Institute for Highway Safety that shows a 28 percent decrease in traffic deaths in states that have done so.

Widening antidrug war. Nowhere have citizens' groups sprung into action more effectively than in the war against marijuana and other drugs. Within the last two years, the antidrug campaign has grown from a few community organizations formed by outraged parents to a well financed and nationally organized political force.

Early results have been impressive. Laws making it a crime to sell drug paraphernalia—such as water pipes and tweezer-like "roach clips" for holding the dwindling butt of a marijuana cigarette—have been enacted in at least 25 states. Stiffer penalties and enforcement procedures against illegal drug traffic have been passed in six states. In others, new actions range from crackdowns on sales of caffeine tablets in drugstores to the use of military helicopters and Navy vessels against drug trafficking.

Says Lee Dogoloff, executive director of the American Council on Marijuana: "No longer are there the hopelessness and frustration about pot and other drugs that inhibited so many Americans before. The prevailing mood now is that the battle can be won."

Local drug-control officials differ on tactics. Some contend that curbing the sale of paraphernalia is as difficult as trying to stamp out prostitution and pornography. "It just drives dealers underground," warns one official, "much as liquor dealers became bootleggers during Prohibition." Yet, until authorities started going after drug equipment, says Bob Kramer, program coordinator in Anne Arundel County, Md., "we seemed to be giving out conflicting signals—that drugs were bad but paraphernalia legal. Now the message is clear."

Texas has taken a lead by pressing one of the most closely coordinated and comprehensive state antidrug campaigns. It has long served as the country's main port of entry for drugs, with an estimated illegal traffic of 3 billion dollars yearly across its 500-mile border with Mexico and the 400-mile Gulf Coast. But now Texas law-enforcement agencies are armed with such Draconian new measures as a maximum sentence of life imprisonment for dealing in marijuana—which one defense attorney called "quite a change from a decade ago when people were talking about legalizing pot."

Those involved in the antidrug war can point to some signs of progress among teenagers. Jerald Bachman of the University of Michigan's Institute for Social Research, which has been plotting trends in adolescent drug use since 1975, reports that marijuana consumption has waned "appreciably" since 1979 and that the use of certain other drugs has lessened or leveled out. Why? Bachman's finding: "The kids say they are more concerned now both about the health consequences and the fear of disapproval. In other words, they are realizing there's no such thing as a free high."

"Stampede" Toward Crime Control

Crime has become a prime target of the movement to restore order and discipline to national life. Many experts note a shift of massive proportions toward more-stringent laws, longer sentences and more actual time served by convicts.

Judge Seymour Gelber of Florida's 11th Circuit Court, who is a member of the American Bar Association's Task Force on Crime, sizes up the trend this way: "There isn't just a move away from permissiveness; a stampede is occurring. It is evident in the rush to build prisons and jails, in the demand for mandatory sentences, in cutting parole, in doing away with community-based rehabilitation programs."

Says former U.S. Attorney Charles Ruff, now in private practice in Washington: "People are saying that earlier experiments with parole and community-based rehabilitation did not work. This is leading to efforts at the other end of the spectrum."

California voters approved on June 8 a sweeping anticrime measure that requires higher penalties for repeat offenders, restitution by criminals to their victims and curbs on both the insanity defense and "plea bargaining" by suspects. State after state is adopting mandatory sentencing—under which a judge is required to impose a specific penalty for a given crime—to assure longer confinement. Forty-six states now have lengthened their prison sentences for repeat offenders, and many others include maximum penalties up to a life term if a criminal is convicted of more offenses.

Even when mandatory sentencing does not apply, both appointed and elected judges are handing down stiffer sentences. A number of states now automatically shift teenagers arrested for serious crimes away from juvenile courts, where traditionally the treatment is more lenient, to adult criminal courts—a new Vermont law allowing this as early as age 10. Parole has been abolished in four states, while nine now impose "determinate" sentences that cannot be shortened by parole boards.

The combination of mounting crime rates and stiffer sentencing has led to an 88 percent increase in the number of state and federal prisoners since 1972. The total number now stands at 369,009, with a record 12.1 percent jump last year generating a new round of prison construction in several states.

At the same time, public support for the death sentence appears to be returning after a long decline. Recent public-opinion polls show an overwhelming majority of Americans favor capital punishment. Thirty-seven states now provide for execution as the supreme penalty.

Yet there's a significant gap between what the laws allow with death penalties and what actually takes place. Although some 1,000 prisoners are in death cells today, only four have been executed in the last 10 years—compared with 72 a year in the 1950s. The rest have benefited from drawn-out appeal proceedings or lingering official qualms.

The trend to more punitiveness as an answer to crime is drawing criticism from some judges, lawyers, criminologists and civil-rights groups. The American Civil Liberties Union and the National Moratorium on Prison Construction argue against imprisoning more criminals for longer periods. They maintain that rehabilitation, fines and community service for criminals would not only ease the growing burden on the taxpayer and salvage many offenders, but be more consonant with the goals of a democratic society. One critic, John Ackerman, a Houston defense attorney and former dean of the National College of Criminal Defense, says: "We have been putting people into prison for 200 years, and that hasn't lessened the problem. How many more years before we realize that?"

Opinion analysts doubt that such criticism will do much to temper the present public mood. In a recent telephone survey by Research & Forecasts, Inc., of New York, 4 out of 10 Americans expressed fear they would become victims of such violent crimes as murder, rape, robbery or assault.

Focus on Youth and Schools

The growth of a program called Toughlove, for families that have out-of-control teenagers, is one of the outstanding phenomena of the recent turnaround. With strong support from Ann Landers, the nationally syndicated advice columnist, this nonprofit self-help movement has grown to 400 chapters in the U.S. and Canada and has a mailing list of more than 50,000.

The logotype of Toughlove, a fist within a heart, emphasizes its prime goal: To restore parental authority through firmness and discipline. Parents are encouraged to set specific penalties, such as forbidding use of the family car, limiting phone calls, refusing to intervene when a child gets into trouble, or sending a repeatedly troublesome one to live elsewhere.

"You're the boss," says a Toughlove manual. "The sooner your youngster understands this, the better." Successful users of the program say it rids them of parental guilt feelings and helps other family members to lead a more normal life.

The program has come in for criticism from some psychiatrists and professional therapists as "a quickie, short-term solution to complex teenage problems" and "lacking in sensitivity and compassion." But many specialists approve. Dr. Barry Schwartz, past president of the Philadelphia Society for Adolescent Psychiatry, finds particular value in it for drug abusers. "For those kinds of problems, you need something dramatic," Schwartz said in a recent interview. "I like Toughlove—not for starters, but when more traditional methods have failed."

As another means of reducing juvenile misbehavior, a number of communities are moving to revive the ancient practice of curfews. One model for these is Detroit, which four years ago imposed a curfew that requires anyone under 18 to be off the streets between 10 p.m. and 6 a.m., with an extension until 11 for 16 and 17-year-olds on Friday and Saturday nights. If out later, young people must carry a note or some other proof of "legitimate reason." For citizens of Detroit, the nightly restriction has the double advantage of protecting young people from the risks of crime and serving as a less expensive means of law enforcement. The city recently laid off 1,000 police officers.

Some parents and civil-rights groups have voiced opposition to curfews. In Keene, N.H., parents testified in a recent unsuccessful suit against a reimposed curfew—aimed at vandalism and car theft—that it usurped their choice to grant or limit freedoms in the raising of their children. But the majority in Keene appeared to support one resident's view that the important thing is to try "to make parents more responsible for their kids."

Tightening up on students. Public schools, under attack for years for allegedly winking at rising student misbehavior, are increasingly responding to the push for greater discipline. In New York City, under a program launched at 10 school sites, police and school officials go on "sweeps" to nail youngsters skipping classes. In the first year, 17,300 truants were picked up, including 1,300 repeaters.

"Behavior contracts" are showing up as a means of maintaining tighter control. At Alhambra High School in Martinez, Calif., students and their parents are required to sign a four-page contract setting out exactly what is and what is not considered acceptable conduct. Punishments for various infractions also are detailed, topped by a special "Saturday school" with compulsory classes for weekday offenders.

Schools in Burbank, Calif., last fall adopted a dress code prescribing acceptable attire from kindergarten through high school. This has drawn inquiries from 60 other school districts in the United States. Banned in Burbank classrooms: Lightweight jogging shorts with slits up the sides, swimsuit-type tops and bare midriffs.

A "spare the rod and spoil the child" philosophy is making a comeback in some places. Last year the Los Angeles school district, the nation's second largest, decided to restore spanking, which had been abolished in 1975. According to the National Center for the Study of Corporal Punishment and Alternatives in the Schools, at Temple University, there are more than 1 million cases of corporal punishment a year.

Over all, school surveys show a measurable improvement in the level of serious misbehavior in recent years. A big reason, says J. William Rioux of the National Committee for Citizens in Education, is the growing involvement of parents in school matters. "For years in the past," says Rioux, "the public generally accepted and even contributed to a letdown in the schools, many figuring that professional educators know best. The new generation of parents seems

High School '82: "You Know You Have to Work Hard"

ROCKVILLE, Md.

Rockville High School is a very different place these days from what it was 10 years ago when permissiveness held sway in classrooms, schoolyards and students' homes. Discipline, student attitudes and behavior, academic standards—all have changed.

Today, order prevails. Skipping classes used to be common, with no real policy governing attendance. Now, says Rockville's principal, Joseph Good, "if a student has five unexcused absences from a class, he or she loses credit in the subject."

Rules on marijuana and other drugs have stiffened as well. If a student is found with any drugs on school property, officials immediately call the police, then the student's parents—and the student is suspended for five days. A repeat violation can mean expulsion for a year.

Good says that the students have, for the most part, taken remarkably well to these and other measures to curb misbehavior. "Kids have cleaned themselves up," he notes. "They are taking care of their hair and wearing decent clothes. They're pretty respectable."

Many students welcome the change. Says Mike Pugliese, a junior: "When you're 15 or 16 years old, you're old enough to understand what you're supposed to do. You're responsible for your actions and you should understand the consequences."

Some in the new student generation even have a good word to say for police officers. "I have great respect for the police and the job they do," says freshman Gary Goldstein. "I also like learning about new laws on drunk driving and drugs."

The more responsible attitudes and behavior at Rockville High extend to studies. "Before," says Good, "you rarely saw kids get on the bus with a book. We had lowered our standards. They never had any homework. Now, you rarely see a student get on the bus without a book."

Contributing to the new student mood, the principal believes, are the drying up of jobs in the ailing economy and tighter college-admission policies. Goldstein, the freshman, remarks, "Even in the ninth grade you hear how much tougher it is to get into college. You know you have to work hard."

Still, students feel it is important not to become too conformist. Jacqueline Kelly, a Rockville senior, says: "I want the opportunity, the freedom to make my own decisions. I'm following a lot of the same ideals as my parents—work hard, do well and generally live your life for what you want to get out of it. But I don't want to be stifled. If I felt like I lived in a police state, I would be very uncomfortable."

By LUCIA SOLORZANO

determined to build more rigor into children's training."

One of the most significant consequences of that mood is a concerted effort to restore academic standards, which are considered to have fallen off alarmingly in public schools over the past two decades. Declining scores on achievement tests, simpler textbooks, teaching letdowns and easy "human development" courses—all are now coming in for fresh attention with a view to sweeping changes.

A measure of the progress in the upgrading drive: Thirty-nine states have adopted minimum-competency tests at various levels of the educational process. These are meant to assure that a student has mastered the work at one grade level before passing on to the next—replacing the automatic "social" promotions that produced many poorly trained students in the 1960s and 1970s.

Teachers themselves are having to pass muster by taking competency examinations. In an effort to upgrade the caliber of instruction, 19 states have established such tests. Some require all new teachers to take them—just as graduate lawyers must pass a state bar exam—while other states start the competency exams in an education student's sophomore year in college to determine who may become teachers.

Much of the pressure for better education has come from employers in various fields who complain about the level of preparation of recent graduates. Heeding such comments, Massachusetts Institute of Technology just recently required that its engineering students take special new courses in writing to earn a degree. Other colleges are restoring mathematics, science or language requirements that they had dropped in the era of permissiveness.

Many colleges—including an estimated two thirds of the state universities—are tightening admission standards to put new pressure on high schools. In response, authorities at that level are beginning to cut back on such popular courses as music, art, home economics and driver training. This has drawn criticism from educators who regard certain of the courses "an essential enrichment experience." William Spady, director of the National Center for Improvement of Learning, cautions: "Some of that cutting back may be healthy, but in some places it can be indiscriminate."

Whatever the case, the "back to basics" approach is making a strong recovery. Scott Thomson, executive director of the National Association of Secondary School Principals, reports that most school districts have increased graduation requirements over the last four years by adding one or two more challenging courses, usually in English, mathematics or science.

Outlook: Fears and Hopes

What is the outlook for the counterattack on the permissiveness that has pervaded America for two decades? How far will the changes go, and to what effect on the country?

Most social scientists stop short of making broad predictions, pending clearer patterns in key fields. But some already express a concern that the pendulum could swing so far as to impinge on basic rights and liberties.

Says Dr. Perry Ottenberg, chairman of the American Psychiatric Association's committee on emerging issues: "The trend runs the risk of going overboard if it brings on too many restrictive new rules, regulations and expectations. To carry authority that far diminishes the freedom of choice necessary to an open society."

Another expert who is uneasy about the trend, Richard Gerstein, chairman of the American Bar Association's Task Force on Crime, declares: "People are far more concerned today about criminal conviction than they are about civil liberties." He finds it unsettling that the U.S. now has the longest prison sentences of any democratic country in the world.

Still, even many criminologists, educators and social scientists who hold such reservations view current crackdowns on various excesses in U.S. life as positive steps that could contribute to the building of a better society.

There is much agreement with David Riesman, Harvard sociologist and author of the classic study of American society, *The Lonely Crowd*, who regards the trend to re-establish authority and reinforce conventional values as one with far-reaching possibilities. "It is almost inevitable," says Riesman, "to see some corrective action after the many and dramatic changes of the recent past. We could be in for another period of profound transformation."

By DAVID B. RICHARDSON with JEANNYE THORNTON, TED GEST, STANLEY N. WELLBORN and the magazine's domestic bureaus

THE 15TH ANNUAL GALLUP POLL OF THE PUBLIC'S ATTITUDES TOWARD THE PUBLIC SCHOOLS

George H. Gallup

Purpose of the Study

THIS SURVEY, which measures the attitudes of Americans toward their public schools, is the 15th annual survey in this series. Funding for this survey was provided by Phi Delta Kappa, Inc. Each year the poll attempts to deal with issues of greatest concern both to educators and to the public. New as well as trend questions are included in this and every survey.

To be sure that the survey would embrace the most important issues in the field of education, Phi Delta Kappa organized a meeting of various leaders in the field of education to discuss their ideas, evaluate proposed questions, and suggest new questions for the survey.

We wish to thank all those who contributed their ideas to this survey.

Research Procedure

The Sample. The sample used in this survey embraced a total of 1,540 adults (18 years of age and older). It is described as a modified probability sample of the United States. Personal, in-home interviewing was conducted in all areas of the U.S. and in all types of communities. A description of the sample can be found at the end of this report.

Time of Interviewing. The fieldwork for this study was carried out during the period of 13-22 May 1983.

The Report. In the tables that follow, the heading "Nonpublic School Parents" includes parents of students who attend parochial schools and parents of students who attend private or independent schools.

Due allowance must be made for statistical variation, especially in the case of findings for small groups in which relatively few respondents were interviewed, e.g., nonpublic school parents.

The findings of this report apply only to the U.S. as a whole and not to individual communities. Local surveys, using the same questions, can be conducted to determine how local areas compare with the national norm.

Impact of the Report of the President's Commission on Excellence in Education

This year's survey was conducted shortly after the report of the National Commission on Excellence in Education was released. Thus it was possible to obtain some indication of the initial reaction of the public to the report.

The survey results reflect only the first reactions of the public, however. The debate over the Commission's findings is sure to continue and may become part of the campaign rhetoric in the 1984 Presidential race.

At the time this survey was conducted, the Commission report was only two weeks old. At that time only 28% of those interviewed in the national sample had heard or read about the report. Of those, 79% could cite some of the facts and conclusions of the report. In short, at the time of the survey, the report had reached an audience of approximately one person in five in the U.S. adult population.

Examination of the survey results indicates that the Commission report had not substantially changed the

Figure 1. Major Problems Confronting The Public Schools, 1981, 1982, and 1983

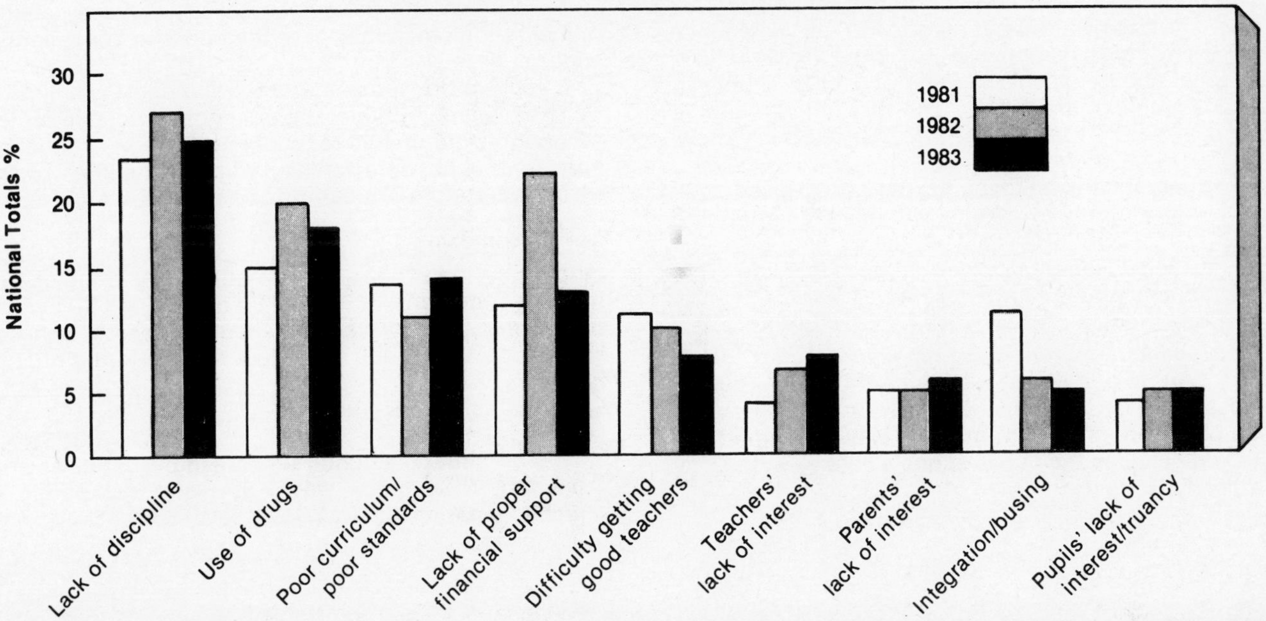

Illustration by Charmaine Dapena

views of the public about public education. One reason, perhaps, is that the public already agreed with many of the Commission's main conclusions.

The survey results that follow will point out how the views of those familiar with the report differ from the views of other groups in those instances in which the Commission report deals with issues covered in this survey.

Major Problems Confronting the Public Schools in 1983

When respondents in this year's survey were asked to name the biggest problems facing their local public schools, the answers were quite similar to those recorded in earlier surveys. The top four problems cited continue to be "discipline," "use of drugs," "poor curriculum/poor standards," and "lack of proper financial support." Parents who have children now attending public schools cite the same four problems and in the same order as the public at large.

Although discipline continues to be regarded as the number one problem, the frequency with which other problems or concerns have been recorded has changed. For example, "integration/busing" and "lack of proper facilities" were named frequently in earlier surveys; they are now far down the list of major concerns.

Because discipline is so frequently cited as a major problem in the public schools, this year's survey has sought to shed further light on underlying causes that may contribute to the perceived lack of discipline. These will be described later in this report.

Here is the question:

What do you think are the biggest problems with which the *public* schools in this community must deal?

	National Totals %	No Children In School %	Public School Parents %	Nonpublic School Parents %
Lack of discipline	25	23	29	31
Use of drugs	18	17	20	16
Poor curriculum/poor standards	14	14	14	19
Lack of proper financial support	13	12	17	8
Difficulty getting good teachers	8	8	9	7
Teachers' lack of interest	8	9	6	9
Parents' lack of interest	6	6	9	5
Integration/busing	5	6	8	4
Pupils' lack of interest/truancy	5	6	4	1
Moral standards	4	4	4	6
Drinking/alcoholism	3	3	4	5
Large schools/overcrowding	3	2	5	6
Lack of respect for teachers/other students	3	3	2	6
Mismanagement of funds	2	2	1	1
Problems with administration	1	2	1	-
Crime/vandalism	1	1	1	-
Teachers' strikes	1	1	1	6
Communication problems	1	1	2	1
Lack of proper facilities	1	1	1	3
Parental involvement with school activities	1	1	1	1
Lack of needed teachers	1	1	2	1
Fighting	1	1	*	1
Non-English-speaking students	1	1	1	-
Government interference	1	1	*	1
There are no problems	1	1	3	1
Miscellaneous	2	2	3	3
Don't know/no answer	16	19	7	15

(Figures add to more than 100% because of multiple answers.)
*Less than one-half of 1%.

1983 Rating of the Public Schools

The public's rating of the local public schools in 1983 follows the downward trend reported in the years since 1974, when this question was instituted. In 1974, 48% gave local public schools a rating of A or B. This year, the comparable figure is 31%. (The 1974 ratings were: A, 18%; B, 30%; C, 21%; D, 6%; FAIL, 5%; and Don't know, 20%.)

More significant, perhaps, is the rating given their local public schools by parents with children attending public schools. In 1974, 64% of the parents gave the schools their children attended an A or B rating. This year, the comparable figure is 42%.

The question:

Students are often given the grades A, B, C, D, and FAIL to denote the quality of their work. Suppose the *public* schools themselves, in this community, were graded in the same way. What grade would you give the public schools here — A, B, C, D, or FAIL?

Ratings Given The Local Public Schools	National Totals								
	1983 %	1982 %	1981 %	1980 %	1979 %	1978 %	1977 %	1976 %	1975 %
A rating	6	8	9	10	8	9	11	13	13
B rating	25	29	27	25	26	27	26	29	30
C rating	32	33	34	29	30	30	28	28	28
D rating	13	14	13	12	11	11	11	10	9
FAIL	7	5	7	6	7	8	5	6	7
Don't know	17	11	10	18	18	15	19	14	13

Rating of the Local Public Schools

By Adults with:	A %	B %	C %	D %	FAIL %	Don't Know %
Children in public schools	11	31	36	10	7	5
Children in nonpublic schools	5	22	24	23	9	17
No children in school	5	23	31	13	6	22

Rating of Public Schools Nationally

Respondents in the survey gave their local schools higher ratings than they gave the public schools nationwide.

It appears that the report of the National Commission on Excellence in Education had some influence on the ratings of the public schools nationally. Those respondents who were familiar with the findings of the report were more critical of U.S. schools than was the public at large.*

Only 12% of the group familiar with the Commission report gave the public schools nationally a rating of A or B; at the same time, 30% gave them a rating of D or Fail. By contrast, 19% of the general public gave the schools a rating of A or B, and 22% gave them a rating of D or Fail.

The question:

How about the public schools in the nation as a whole? What grade would you give the public schools nationally — A, B, C, D, or FAIL?

	A %	B %	C %	D %	FAIL %	Don't Know %
Public schools in this community	6	25	32	13	7	17
Public schools in the nation	2	17	38	16	6	21

*One must also consider the possibility that those individuals who are already strongly critical of the schools would be more likely than others to pay attention to media reports that say that "the educational foundations of our society are presently being eroded by a rising tide of mediocrity. . . ."

Figure 2. Rating of Public Schools Nationally

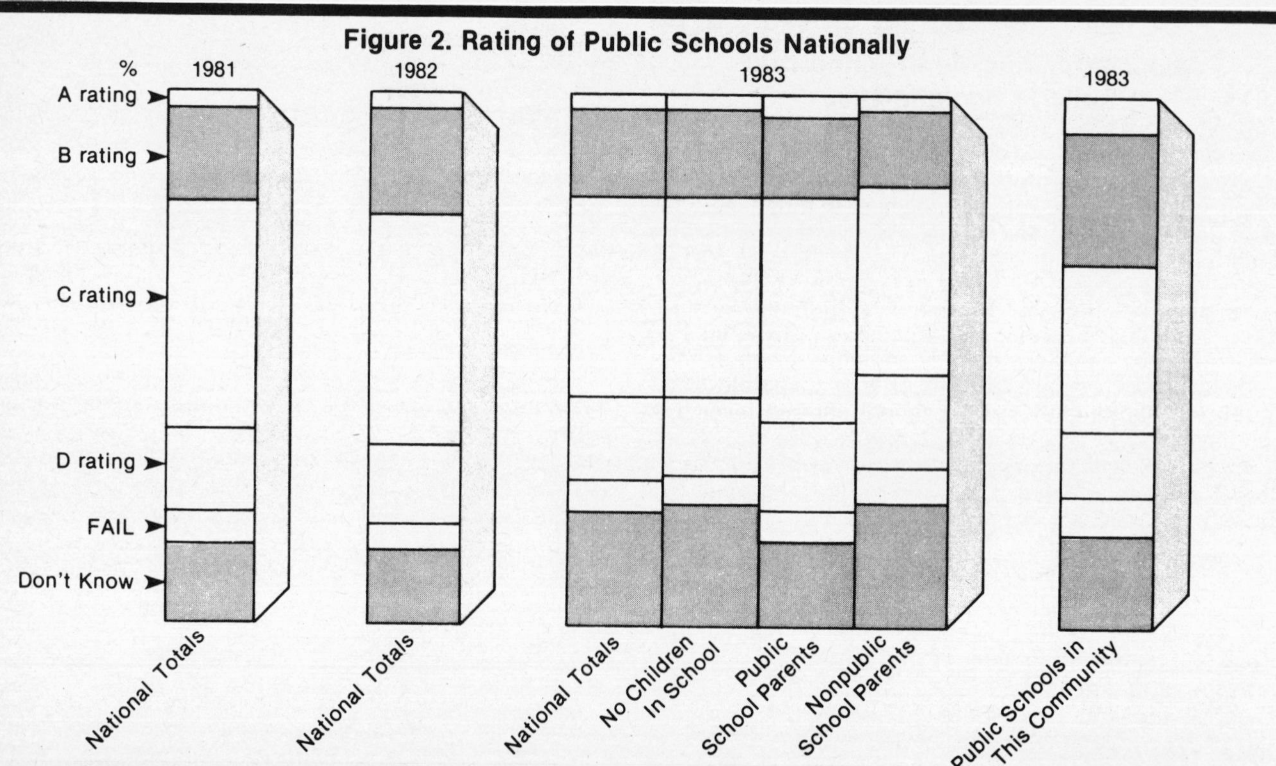

Illustration by Charmaine Dapena

Why Is There a Discipline Problem?

The problem of discipline continues to loom large in the public's mind. Thus, this year we attempted to find out who or what is chiefly to blame for the lack of discipline that the public says is a major problem in the local public schools. A card listing 11 reasons for a lack of discipline was handed to each respondent included in the survey.

The question:

Many people say that discipline is one of the major problems of the public schools today. Would you please look over this list and tell me which reasons you think are most important to explain why there is a discipline problem?

Those identified with the public schools can take comfort from the fact that the chief blame is laid on the home, with disrespect for law and order throughout society ranking second in frequency of mention.

The percentage of votes given each of the 11 statements are as follows, listed according to frequency of mention:

1. Lack of discipline in the home (72%)
2. Lack of respect for law and authority throughout society (54%)
3. Students who are constant troublemakers often can't be removed from school (42%)
4. Some teachers are not properly trained to deal with discipline problems (42%)
5. The courts have made school administrators so cautious that they don't deal severely with student misbehavior (41%)
6. Viewing television programs that emphasize crime and violence (39%)
7. Punishment is too lenient (39%)
8. Decline in the teaching of good manners (37%)
9. Teachers themselves do not command respect (36%)
10. Failure on the part of teachers to make classroom work more interesting (31%)
11. One-parent families (26%)

The Voucher System

The idea of the voucher system — a plan whereby the federal government allots a certain amount of money for the education of each child, regardless of whether the child attends a public, parochial, or independent school — is favored today by a clear majority of the public (51% to 38%). Significantly, public school parents favor the voucher system by a margin of 48% to 41%.

The current support for the voucher system represents a substantial shift in the public's attitude. Between 1970 (when the question was first asked) and 1981, the idea elicited a mixed reception. In 1970 a slightly higher percentage opposed the idea than favored it. This was also true in 1971. In the 1981 survey those in favor held a slight majority over those opposed.

The question:

In some nations, the government allots a certain amount of money for each child for his or her education. The parents can then send the child to any public, parochial, or private school they choose. This is called the "voucher system." Would you like to see such an idea adopted in this country?

	National Totals %	No Children In School %	Public School Parents %	Nonpublic School Parents %
Favor voucher system	51	51	48	64
Oppose voucher system	38	37	41	30
No opinion	11	12	11	6

NATIONAL TOTALS	Favor %	Oppose %	No Opinion %
1970 survey	43	46	11
1971 survey	38	44	18
1981 survey	43	41	16
1983 survey	51	38	11

Promotion Based on Examinations

Promotion from grade to grade based on examinations and not "social" promotion is favored by a substantial majority of the survey respondents. This view is shared by parents of schoolchildren and by those who have no children in school — and by almost the same percentages.

The question:

In your opinion, should children be promoted from grade to grade only if they can pass examinations?

	National Totals %	No Children In School %	Public School Parents %	Nonpublic School Parents %
Yes	75	75	73	71
No	20	19	23	27
Don't know	5	6	4	2

NATIONAL TOTALS	1983 %	1978 %
Yes	75	68
No	20	27
Don't know	5	5

National Test Scores Used for Comparison Purposes

The results of the question about the use of national tests as a way of judging the local schools reveals the public's faith in tests and, at the same time, the public's desire to have another measure of the quality of education in their own local schools.

One important provision should be added, however. Earlier survey reports have pointed out that comparisons should take full account of the composition of the school population. Comparisons are only valid if the local school population reflects the national population. Schools that draw students from poor neighborhoods where parents have had little education and where language barriers exist obviously cannot be expected to achieve the same levels of test scores as schools in high-income communities.

The question:

Would you like to see the students in the local schools be given national tests, so that their educational achievement could be compared with students in other communities?

	National Totals %	No Children In School %	Public School Parents %	Nonpublic School Parents %
Yes	75	72	80	79
No	17	17	16	18
Don't know	8	11	4	3

NATIONAL TOTALS	1983 %	1971 %	1970 %
Yes	75	70	75
No	17	21	16
Don't know	8	9	9

Too Much or Too Little Schoolwork for Students?

Are students in elementary schools or high schools made to work too hard? Widespread agreement exists on this issue among parents of schoolchildren and those without children in the public schools.

Two-thirds of all respondents, in both the case of elementary school children and of high school students, agree that the workload given students is too light. An earlier survey of students found that students themselves say that they are not given enough homework.

A significant change has been recorded since the 1975 survey when the same questions were asked of the public. At that time 49% said that students in elementary school were not required to work hard enough. In this year's survey the percentage has increased to 61%. In 1975, 54% said that high school students were not required to work hard enough; now that percentage is 65%.

The 1983 survey includes another question related to this issue. When respondents were asked if they thought that what is now covered in the first two years of college could be covered before graduation from high school, a total of 65% predicted that this would happen by the year 2000.

The question:

In general, do you think *elementary* school children in the public schools here are made to work too hard in school and on homework, or not hard enough?

	National Totals %	No Children In School %	Public School Parents %	Nonpublic School Parents %
Too hard	4	3	6	4
Not hard enough	61	62	60	70
About right amount	19	15	27	16
Don't know	16	20	7	10

NATIONAL TOTALS	1983 %	1975 %
Too hard	4	5
Not hard enough	61	49
About right amount	19	28
Don't know	16	18

The question:

What about students in the public high school here — in general, are they required to work too hard or not hard enough?

	National Totals %	No Children In School %	Public School Parents %	Nonpublic School Parents %
Too hard	3	3	4	-
Not hard enough	65	66	63	69
About right amount	12	11	14	9
Don't know	20	20	19	22

NATIONAL TOTALS	1983 %	1975 %
Too hard	3	3
Not hard enough	65	54
About right amount	12	22
Don't know	20	21

Increasing the Length of the School Year

Although more individuals oppose than approve increasing the length of the school year in their communities by one month, more respondents favor a 10-month school year in this year's survey than in last year's. Moreover, those who were familiar with the report of the National Commission on Excellence in Education are strongly in favor of such a change. More of those parents with children in nonpublic schools approve than disapprove of extending the school year. Individuals who have no children attending school show the least enthusiasm for increasing the school year from the present 180 days.

The question:

In some nations, students attend school as many as 240 days a year as compared to about 180 days in the U.S. How do you feel about extending the public school year in this community by 30 days, making the school year about 210 days or 10 months long? Do you favor or oppose this idea?

	National Totals %	No Children In School %	Public School Parents %	Nonpublic School Parents %
Favor	40	39	43	50
Oppose	49	47	52	44
Don't know	11	14	5	6

NATIONAL TOTALS	1983 %	1982 %
Favor	40	37
Oppose	49	53
Don't know	11	10

Subjects the Public Would Require in High School

A majority of the American public would require high school courses in mathematics and English, regardless of whether students plan to continue their education in college or to get jobs following graduation. For those students who plan to go on to college, the public would require courses in history/U.S. government, science, business, and foreign language. For those who plan to end their education with high school, the public would require vocational training, business, history/U.S. government, and science.

Those respondents who would require a foreign language were asked, Which foreign language(s)? The preferred language, by a large margin, is Spanish, followed by French and German, in that order. A surprising number of parents with children in school (12%) would require that the Russian language be taught.

The question:

Would you look over this card which lists high school subjects. If you were the one to decide, what subjects would you require every public high school student who *plans to go on to college* to take?

	1983 %	1981 %
Mathematics	92	94
English	88	91
History/U.S. government	78	83
Science	76	76
Business	55	60
Foreign language	50	54
Health education	43	47
Physical education	41	44
Vocational training	32	34
Art	19	28
Music	18	26

(Figures add to more than 100% because of multiple responses.)

The question:

What about those public high school students who do *not plan to go to college* when they graduate? Which courses would you require them to take?

	1983 %	1981 %
Mathematics	87	91
English	83	89
Vocational training	74	64
Business	65	75
History/U.S. government	63	71
Science	53	58
Health education	42	46
Physical education	40	43
Foreign language	19	21
Art	16	20
Music	16	20

(Figures add to more than 100% because of multiple responses.)

The question (asked of those who would require foreign language for high school graduates):

What foreign language or languages should be required?

	National Totals %	No Children In School %	Public School Parents %	Nonpublic School Parents %
Spanish	56	58	54	44
French	34	35	32	34
German	16	16	14	20
Latin	8	6	11	12
Russian	8	7	12	7
Japanese	6	6	5	7
Other	4	4	5	10
Don't know	24	23	21	30

(Figures add to more than 100% because of multiple responses.)

Instruction in Special Areas

In addition to traditional school subjects, the public would like the schools to give special instruction in many other fields, presumably because other institutions, including the home, have not been notably successful in dealing with these areas of instruction. This is especially true in the case of education about the abuse of drugs and alcohol.

More than seven in 10 adults would require driver education. A majority would also require instruction in the use of computers, as well as training in parenting.

This year's survey included several additional subject areas; all of these except the dangers of nuclear war were approved by a slight majority.

The question:

In addition to regular courses, high schools offer instruction in other areas. As I read off these areas, one at a time, would you tell me whether you feel this instruction should be required or should not be required for all high school students?

	Should Be Required %	Should Not Be Required %	No Opinion %
Drug abuse	81	14	5
Alcohol abuse	76	18	6
Driver education	72	23	5
Computer training	72	21	7
Parenting/parent training	58	32	10
Dangers of nuclear waste*	56	33	11
Race relations*	56	33	11
Communism/socialism*	51	38	11
Dangers of nuclear war*	46	42	12

*These topics were not included in the 1981 survey.

Availability of Computers in the Schools

Computers are now available to students in a surprisingly large number of U.S. schools. Nearly half of the parents of children attending the public schools and the nonpublic schools say that these schools now have computers that their children can use. And eight in 10 of the parents with children in schools that do not have computers say they would like to have computers available for their children.

Schools in the East and in the Midwest are much more likely to have computers that are available to students than are schools in the West and South.

The question:

Does the school your child attends have a computer that students can use?

	Public School Parents %	Nonpublic School Parents %
Yes	45	47
No	32	33
Don't know	23	20

The following question was asked of those whose children do not have access to a computer in school:

Would you like the school your child attends to install a computer that students could use?

	Public School Parents %	Nonpublic School Parents %
Yes	81	56
No	10	30
Don't know	9	14

Importance of a College Education

It will come as good news to college administrators that in the last five years the public has changed markedly in its view about the importance of a college education. Since a question about the importance of a college education was first asked (1978), the percentage of individuals who say that a college education is "very important" has increased from 36% to 58%. Those with children now attending school are even more convinced of the importance of a college education.

The question:

How important is a college education today — very important, fairly important, or not too important?

	National Totals %	No Children In School %	Public School Parents %	Nonpublic School Parents %
Very important	58	57	60	60
Fairly important	31	31	32	30
Not too important	8	8	7	6
Don't know	3	4	1	4

NATIONAL TOTALS	1983 %	1978 %
Very important	58	36
Fairly important	31	46
Not too important	8	16
Don't know	3	2

Teaching as a Career

In five surveys, beginning in 1969, respondents have been asked if they would like a child of theirs to take up teaching as a career. This year, substantially more respondents were undecided than in earlier years when the same question was asked. The percentage giving a definite yes answer this year is slightly lower than in 1981 and substantially lower than in 1969, when 75% of all respondents said that they would like a child of theirs to take up teaching in the public schools as a career. The comparable figure today is 45%.

To help explain this marked change, respondents were asked why they would, or would not, like a child of theirs to become a public school teacher. The answers to this question from those who said no, listed in order of frequency of mention, are: 1) low pay; 2) discipline problems; 3) unrewarding, thankless work; and 4) low prestige of teaching as a profession. Those who said that they would like a child of theirs to enter the teaching profession said that teaching: 1) is a worthwhile profession, 2) contributes to society, 3) is a challenging job, and 4) can make a real difference in a child's life.

The question:

Would you like to have a child of yours take up teaching in the public schools as a career?

	National Totals %	No Children In School %	Public School Parents %	Nonpublic School Parents %
Yes	45	42	51	40
No	33	33	33	39
Don't know	22	25	16	21

	1983 %	1981 %	1980 %	1972 %	1969 %
Yes	45	46	48	67	75
No	33	43	40	22	15
Don't know	22	11	12	11	10

Personal Qualities Most Desired in Teachers

When respondents were asked in an "open" question about the personal qualities they would look for if they could choose their child's teacher, their responses indicate that they would seek a model of perfection — someone who is understanding, patient, friendly, intelligent, and who has a sense of humor and high moral character. Farther down the list the public would seek out a person who has the ability to motivate and inspire children and possesses enthusiasm for the subject being taught.

The question:

Suppose you could choose your child's teachers. Assuming they had all had about the same experiences and training, what *personal* qualities would you look for?

The qualities respondents named most often, in order of mention:

1. Ability to communicate, to understand, to relate
2. Patience
3. Ability to discipline, to be firm and fair
4. High moral character
5. Friendliness, good personality, sense of humor
6. Dedication to teaching profession, enthusiasm
7. Ability to inspire, motivate students
8. Intelligence
9. Caring about students

Teachers' Salaries

About one person in four of those questioned in this year's survey registers no opinion about whether teachers' salaries are "too high," "too low," or "just about right." Of those who do have an opinion, many more say that salaries are too low than too high.

When the "no opinion" group is eliminated and percentages are based on those with opinions, a sharp increase in the number saying that salaries are "too low" has been registered in the last two years.

The question:

Do you think salaries for teachers in this community are too high, too low, or just about right?

	National Totals %	No Children In School %	Public School Parents %	Nonpublic School Parents %
Too high	8	8	9	5
Too low	35	33	37	42
About right	31	30	35	32
No opinion	26	29	19	21

NATIONAL TOTALS	1983 %	1981 %	1969 %
Too high	8	10	2
Too low	35	29	33
About right	31	41	43
No opinion	26	20	22

NATIONAL TOTALS (with "no opinion" group eliminated)	1983 %	1981 %	1969 %
Too high	11	13	3
Too low	47	36	42
About right	42	51	55

Figure 3. Teachers' Salaries

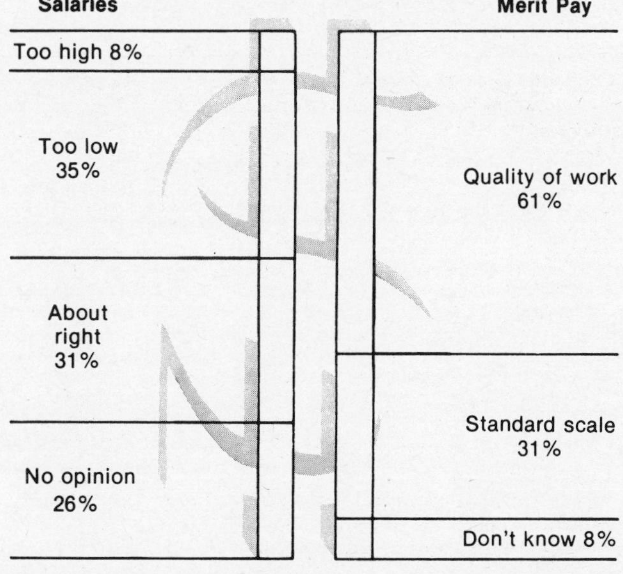

Illustration by Charmaine Dapena

Merit Pay for Teachers

The public votes nearly two-to-one in favor of merit pay for teachers. The percentage favoring merit pay has increased slightly since 1970, when the same question was asked of a similar cross section of U.S. adults. In 1970, 58% of the public favored merit pay and 36% favored a standard scale. Today, the comparable percentages are 61% and 31%.

Parents of schoolchildren favor merit pay by almost the same margin as the general public. Those who were familiar with the report of the President's Commission are more strongly in favor of merit pay, voting 71% to 25% in favor of it.

The question:

Should each teacher be paid on the basis of the quality of his or her work, or should all teachers be paid on a standard-scale basis?

	National Totals %	No Children In School %	Public School Parents %	Nonpublic School Parents %
Quality of work	61	61	61	64
Standard scale	31	30	34	30
Don't know	8	9	5	6

NATIONAL TOTALS	1983 %	1970 %
Quality of work	61	58
Standard scale	31	36
Don't know	8	6

Willingness to Pay More Taxes To Raise Educational Standards

The report of the President's Commission may have a positive effect in helping communities increase tax revenues for their local public schools — provided that such increases are aimed at raising educational standards.

In an earlier question, included in this same survey, respondents were asked if they would vote to raise taxes if their schools claimed that they needed much more money. The vote on this question was 39% yes and 53% no. Although this represents an appreciable increase in the yes vote over 1981, it is far less than the 58% who say that they would be willing to pay more taxes to raise the standard of education throughout the nation.

Two points need to be borne in mind. First, the public would obviously like to have the federal government contribute more to help finance the public schools. And second, respondents see a need for raising the educational standard throughout the nation.

The question:

Would you be willing to pay more taxes to help raise the standard of education in the United States?

	National Totals %	No Children In School %	Public School Parents %	Nonpublic School Parents %
Yes	58	54	70	57
No	33	35	24	38
Don't know	9	11	6	5

Looking Ahead to the Year 2000: Changes That the Public Foresees In the Educational System

Many suggestions for improving the educational system were presented to respondents to determine what chance they think these suggestions have of being carried out between now and the year 2000.

Those respondents who were familiar with the report of the President's Commission differ little in their views from those who now have children attending the public and nonpublic schools.

The question:

As you look ahead to the year 2000 (that's 17 years from now), what do you think the schools will be doing then to educate students?

	National Totals %	No Children In School %	Public School Parents %	Nonpublic School Parents %
Do you think that all students will have access to a computer and be trained in its use?				
Yes	86	84	92	90
No	6	6	5	7
Don't know	8	10	3	3

1. PERCEPTIONS

	National Totals %	No Children In School %	Public School Parents %	Nonpublic School Parents %
Do you think that more importance will be given to vocational training in high school?				
Yes	76	76	77	69
No	11	11	13	19
Don't know	13	13	10	12
Do you think that more attention will be given to teaching students how to think?				
Yes	70	68	73	72
No	16	16	17	15
Don't know	14	16	10	13
Do you think that what is now covered in the first two years of college will be covered before graduation from high school?				
Yes	65	62	71	67
No	19	20	19	23
Don't know	16	18	10	10
Do you think that more attention will be given to individual instruction?				
Yes	53	53	51	59
No	32	31	37	28
Don't know	15	16	12	13
Do you think children will start school at an earlier age — such as 3 or 4 years old?				
Yes	51	49	52	55
No	37	37	38	37
Don't know	12	14	10	8
Do you think that taxpayers will be willing to vote more favorably on bond issues and give more financial support to the schools?				
Yes	45	44	47	49
No	36	35	37	38
Don't know	19	21	16	13
Do you think that the school program will cover 12 months of the year — with less time for holidays?				
Yes	33	30	38	40
No	53	53	54	53
Don't know	14	17	8	7

COMPOSITION OF THE SAMPLE

Analysis of Respondents

Adults	%
No children in schools	68
Public school parents	27*
Nonpublic school parents	6*

*Total for both starred categories exceeds 32% because some parents have children attending more than one kind of school.

Occupation	%
Farm	3
Undesignated	8

Political affiliation	%
Republican	24
Democrat	41
Independent	30
Other	5

Sex	%
Men	48
Women	52

Race	%
White	86
Nonwhite	14

Religion	%
Protestant	54
Catholic	30
Jewish	3
Other	13

Age	%
18 - 29 years	27
30 - 49 years	36
50 and over	37

Occupation	%
Business/professional	26
Clerical/sales	6
Manual labor	38
Non-labor force	19

Income	%
$40,000 and over	11
$30,000 - $39,999	10
$20,000 - $29,999	19
$10,000 - $19,999	30
$9,999 and under	24
Undesignated	6

Region	%
East	28
Midwest	27
South	27
West	18

Community size	%
1 million and over	20
500,000 - 999,999	13
50,000 - 499,999	26
2,500 - 49,999	14
Under 2,500	27

Education	%
College	30
High school	56
Grade school	14

DESIGN OF THE SAMPLE

The sampling procedure for this survey is designed to produce an approximation of the adult civilian population, age 18 and older, living in the U.S., except for those persons in institutions such as prisons or hospitals.

The design of the sample is that of a replicated probability sample, down to the block level in the case of urban areas and to segments of townships in the case of rural areas. Approximately 300 sampling locations are used in the survey.

The sample design included stratification by these four size-of-community strata, using 1970 census data: 1) cities of population one million and over, 2) 250,000 - 999,999, 3) 50,000 - 249,999, and 4) all other populations. Each of these strata was further stratified into seven geographic regions: New England, Middle Atlantic, East Central, West Central, South, Mountain, and Pacific. Within each city-size/regional stratum, the population was arrayed in geographic order and zoned into equal-sized groups of sampling units. Pairs of localities were selected in each zone, with probability of selection of each locality proportional to its population size in the 1970 census, producing two replicated samples of localities.

Within localities so selected for which the requisite population data are reported, subdivisions were drawn with the probability of selection proportional to size of population. In all other localities, small definable geographic areas were selected with equal probability.

Within each subdivision so selected for which block statistics are available, a sample of blocks or block clusters was drawn with probability of selection proportional to the number of dwelling units. In all other subdivisions or areas, blocks or segments were drawn at random or with equal probability.

In each cluster of blocks and each segment so selected, randomly selected starting points were designated on the interviewers' maps of the areas. Starting at these points, interviewers were required to follow a given direction in the selection of households until their assignments were complete.

Interviewing was conducted at times when adults, in general, were most likely to be at home, which means on weekends, or, if on weekdays, after 4 p.m. for women and after 6 p.m. for men.

Allowance for persons not at home was made by a "times-at-home" weighting procedure rather than by "callbacks."* This procedure is a standard method for reducing the sample bias that would otherwise result from underrepresentation in the sample of persons who are difficult to find at home.

The prestratification by regions is routinely supplemented by fitting each obtained sample to the latest available Census Bureau estimates of the regional distribution of the population. Also, minor adjustments of the sample are made by educational attainment by men and women separately, based on the annual estimates of the Census Bureau (derived from their Current Population Survey) and by age.

*A. Politz and W. Simmons, "An Attempt to Get the 'Not at Home' into the Sample Without Callbacks," *Journal of the American Statistical Association*, March 1949, pp. 9-31.

WHAT'S STILL RIGHT WITH EDUCATION

Harold L. Hodgkinson

HAROLD HODGKINSON was director of the National Institute of Education in the Ford Administration. He has just left the presidency of the National Training Laboratories to become a Senior Fellow at the Institute for Educational Leadership, Washington, D.C.

In November 1979 the *Kappan* published my article, "What's Right with Education." That article provided numerous examples of the successes of public schooling; response to it has been favorable and intense. Now, three years later, my intent is to discuss newly available evidence on the achievement of the public schools.

One impressive development since my earlier article is the new concern for and competence in providing the media with accurate, effective information on actual school performance at the local, state, and national levels. In Atlanta, for example, Superintendent Alonzo Crim has started a campaign to promote enthusiastic support from citizens by publicizing the educational achievements of Atlanta schools. Such states as Minnesota, Oregon, and New York have produced excellent, readable documents reflecting educational challenges and achievements. At the national level, most educational associations are placing more accurate information into the hands of their members and are also assisting members in informing the public. The public information officer is becoming a key staff member at both the local and state levels. Educators today seem far more aware of the importance of informing the public about school achievements. Such achievements are not new, but our ability to communicate them has improved notably.

End of the Psychic Recession

Periodically, Americans seem to sink into a deep depression, during which the average citizen loses faith in the worth of the U.S. and proclaims that its institutions are not responsive to the needs of the citizens. The decade of the 1970s was such a period. Now this psychic recession is beginning to reverse itself. As one indication of this reversal, birthrates in the U.S. are rising, and increased birthrates tend to reflect a general optimism, a greater national concern about the importance of investing in human resources (the public schools being the prime target of such investment), and an increased awareness that such investment pays off — not only in dollars and productivity but in improved quality of life.

There are other indications of an end to our psychic recession. The Gallup Organization reports an increasing percentage of the American people who now consider the public schools to be excellent, above average, or average. The 1982 survey, for instance, showed that 8% of the American public think the schools are excellent, 29% think they are above average, and 33% think they are average. Only 14% think the public schools are below average, and 5% think that the schools are failing. The National Opinion Surveys on public confidence in various societal endeavors now show that education is listed third among institutions in which people have a great deal of confidence — immediately behind medicine and science. In 1982, 33% of the American people indicated that they had "a lot of confidence" in their systems of education. And in a September 1982 poll Gallup reported the following:

1. What would *best* guarantee a strong America in the future?

Strong educational system (#1 for *all* groups)	84%
Strong industrial system	66%
Strong military	47%

2. If more federal money *were* available, where would you spend it?

Public schools	21%
Health care	19%
Welfare	16%
Military	14%

3. How should school districts respond to budget crunches?

Cut teachers' salaries	17%
Don't cut teachers' salaries	76%

In his book, *New Rules*, Daniel

1. PERCEPTIONS

Yankelovich argues that the essential task of the Eighties is to help adults develop a dual value system that emphasizes both institutional loyalty and a commitment to self-development. When this begins to happen, people's attitudes should generally become more positive, as they are able to link their new concern for personal health and emotional and intellectual growth with their service-oriented desires to be loyal to the institutions in their society. As Americans turn this corner in their private lives, it is likely that they will become more loyal to the society that made this transformation possible.

One of the most bewildering aspects of the past decade was the rapid transformation of the U.S. economy and workforce from an industrial/manufacturing base to an information/service base. The wrenching consequences of this transition have been as great as those suffered when we moved from an agricultural economic base to a manufacturing one. Today, less than 20% of U.S. workers manufacture products, while more than 65% provide information or services. Although this transition is far from complete, we have at least recognized it and are beginning to learn how to cope with it. Figure 1 presents several examples of our changing economy.

Our values are also changing, but the health of the U.S. as measured by comparative studies of values appears to be quite good. One such study of 18 nations, performed by the Center for Applied Research in the Apostolate (CARA) in 1982, arrives at the following general conclusions. Compared to western Europeans and the Japanese, for example, Americans are: 1) most willing to fight for their country, 2) most proud of their national identity, 3) most likely to take pride in their work, and 4) most deeply religious. Table 1 presents a breakdown by country on two of these questions.

A more useful measure of our national well-being can be found in our phenomenal ability to encourage new business;

Figure 1. Performance of Key Industries (by Revenues, 1980)

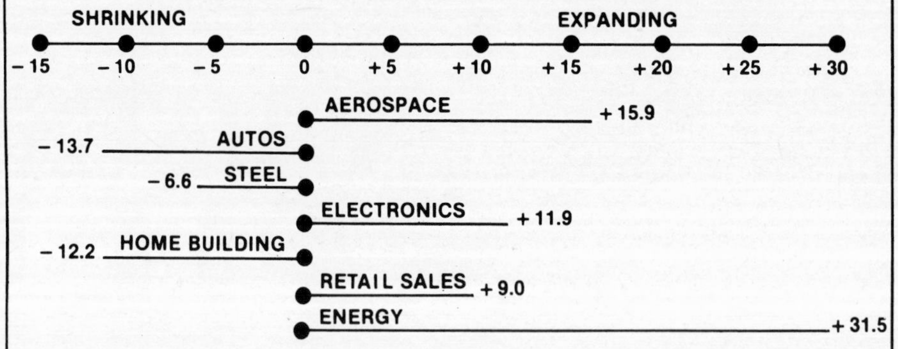

SHRINKING — EXPANDING

−15 −10 −5 0 +5 +10 +15 +20 +25 +30

AEROSPACE	+15.9
AUTOS	−13.7
STEEL	−6.6
ELECTRONICS	+11.9
HOME BUILDING	−12.2
RETAIL SALES	+9.0
ENERGY	+31.5

Sources: *Annual Review* (Washington, D.C.: U.S. Department of Labor, 1981); and *Research Bulletin: The U.S. Regional Outlook* (New York: Conference Board, 1981).

Table 1. Comparative Values

Proud to be a citizen.	
U.S.	80%
Ireland	60%
Great Britain	55%
Japan	30%
West Germany	21%
Proud of my work.	
U.S.	84%
Japan	37%
West Germany	15%
France	13%

Source: CARA News Release, Washington, D.C., 25 May 1982.

nearly 40% of the U.S. gross national product is produced by new companies employing fewer than 25 people. Here is where new jobs and innovations will be created, and there is little evidence that we are slowing down in this area (Figure 2).

The American genius for creating innovative technologies is about as active as ever: We now export six times as many technical innovations (in patent form) as we import. Although most innovations produce more jobs than they eliminate, the new jobs tend to require higher levels of education (intellectual skills) than did the older jobs (see Tables 2 and 3).

Table 2. Ten Most Rapidly Growing Jobs, 1978-90

Jobs	Growth Rate %
Data-processing machine mechanics	147
Paralegal personnel	132
Computer systems analysts	107
Computer operators	88
Office machine services	80
Computer programmers	74
Aero-astronautical engineers	70
Food preparation personnel (fast foods)	69
Employment interviewers	67
Tax preparers	65

Source: Max Carey, "Occupational Employment Growth Through 1990," *Monthly Labor Review*, August 1981, p. 48.

Finally, although the U.S. is still gripped by recession, some demographic changes are clear. Unemployment is bound to lessen as the number of youths seeking access to the labor force continues to decline. The number of blacks in the labor force will increase to about 15 million by 1989, with men and women represented about equally. The number of employed Americans will rise by more than 16 million workers to about 113 million by the end of the Eighties. We have in prospect a decade of rising living standards for most Americans, with modest but orderly economic growth, speeding up in the second half of the decade.

All of these trends bode well for the public schools. Despite the concern about the new importance of private and independent schools, these institutions still are educating only 10% of U.S. children, while 90% attend public schools. Moreover, recent increases in the birthrate — particularly in sunbelt states — are creating an increased interest in education at local and state levels, as well as teacher shortages in some sunbelt states.

Educators can be encouraged by the fact that, in the 1980s, our knowledge about how schools work is beginning to jell — and to be put to use. No profession can be any better than its base of knowledge. Other professions have accumulated their knowledge bases over the last 50 to 100 years. Agriculture and medicine, for example, have enjoyed 100 years of steady federal support to develop the existing knowledge base in those fields. Educational research, however, has received only 20 years of consistent federal funding. Let us ask, though, how our knowledge base has developed in this brief span of 20 years. For one thing, a series of correlational studies has established the factors that tend to be present when learning occurs. These factors do not cause learning, but they are associated with it in a systematic way. They include:

- social class;
- race (less powerful than class);
- sex (women superior in verbal areas, men superior in quantitative areas);
- urban, rural, or suburban residence (related to class);

• region (the Southwest, for example, is improving rapidly on tests of achievement);

• birth order (oldest children tend to achieve at higher levels);

• family size (small family equals greater learning);

• prenatal and infant nutrition;

• amount of activity shared with parents;

• television (increases scores of children aged 3-8 but decreases teenagers' scores); and

• age (very small decline in ability to learn after age 30).

We have also gathered some important data about learning rates (within a normal population of schoolchildren, the learning rate varies by a factor of four) and differential abilities (in a third-grade class, some students operate on a first-grade level in some areas, while others operate on a sixth-grade level in the same areas).

Our search for the "best" reading program is somewhat analogous to the search for the cure for cancer. Just as medicine has found no "cure" but *has* discovered significant information about carcinogens and their effects on the human body, so educators have discovered that there is no one best method of instruction in reading (assuming that phonics is a factor in all reading programs, which seems to be the case). The difference between successful and unsuccessful reading programs is related to these environmental factors:

• local school involvement in the decision-making process;

• the principal's leadership and support from community and superiors;

• a "critical mass" of teachers who share attitudes and values; and

• the use of local ideas originated in each individual school.

The total school environment figures prominently in such major studies of school effectiveness as the British research report, *Fifteen Thousand Hours*, as well as in a number of similar studies in the U.S. These studies seem to agree that educational improvement occurs at the building level and that the most important single factor in school improvement is the leadership of the individual school principal. In addition, schools must provide for parent involvement, and some easily communicated definition of quality of student performance must be available.

Table 3. Job Skills for 1990

1. Evaluation and analysis
2. Critical thinking
3. Problem solving (including math)
4. Organization and reference
5. Synthesis
6. Application to new areas
7. Creativity
8. Decision making with incomplete information
9. Communication skills in many modes

Source: *Information Society*, Denver, 1982.

Earlier research (e.g., the work of James Coleman and Christopher Jencks) examined the entire range of schools and students and concluded that schools make little difference. Within these samples, however, were many examples of highly successful schools in highly unlikely locations. Today, researchers are working to discover the traits of good schools and then trying to duplicate those traits elsewhere. Clearly, these efforts are beginning to pay off; in many schools today, we see new emphasis on strong leadership from the principal, high expectations for all students, an orderly atmosphere, an emphasis on reading skills, and frequent diagnostic evaluation of student progress.

In addition, federally funded labs and centers have — particularly in recent years — provided important new information about teaching and learning and have produced new instructional materials that have significantly increased student performance, particularly in the areas of math and reading skills. Naturally, our knowledge base in education is not nearly complete. In a relatively short time, however, with minimal funding, we have made a significant beginning at developing useful knowledge about how schools and individual children can do better.

Access vs. Quality

The access/quality dichotomy is a specious and dangerous one. Arguments in its favor usually take the following form. As access to public education increased in the 1970s, the quality of education declined. If educators seek to increase further the quality of education in the coming decade, they risk limiting access to our educational system. But there is no reason to think that quality and access cannot work together. Even if handicapped children, for example, do not score as well as children without handicaps, access to education has unquestionably increased the quality of education available to handicapped children. Removing such students from the mainstream of education might raise the mean scores of the remaining students — but at an unacceptably high cost.

In the last two decades especially, a key task of U.S. public schools has been to increase access for all youths, regardless of race, sex, or social class. Access to higher education has been a means of enhancing the quality of human life, and we now have data to support that commonsensical connection. Since 1947, the "yield" of those going on to higher education has increased significantly (see Figure 3). In 1954, 28% of those youngsters who had been fifth-graders seven years earlier entered college. By 1977 that percentage had risen to 43%. Fifty-five percent of that earlier group of fifth-graders graduated from high school; 74% of the group from the Seventies did so. This represents a major achievement for the U.S. and a major improvement in quality of life for its citizens.

Let us consider the matter of access in another way: In 1950 approximately 55% of white students graduated from high school, whereas 30% of black students graduated. Today, 85% of white students and 75% of black students are graduating from high school. Moreover, various economists have estimated that between one-quarter and one-half of the increase in the U.S. gross national product over the last two decades can be attributed to the increased educational level of the workforce.

In addition, more U.S. youngsters are enrolled as full-time students than youths in most other western nations. About 75% of U.S. youths aged 15 to 19 are full-time students. In France that figure is 51%; in Germany, 51%; in Great Britain, 44%; and in Italy, 40%.

Even though a far higher percentage of U.S. youths are enrolled in schools than is true of youths in any other country except Japan, the average comparative levels of performance in science, mathematics, and reading show a strong performance by U.S. students. In literature, for example, U.S. students scored highest among the countries tested. In reading comprehension, U.S. students outscored those from the Netherlands and the United Kingdom, while Italian youngsters did slightly better

Figure 2. New Business Starts in U.S., 1970-81

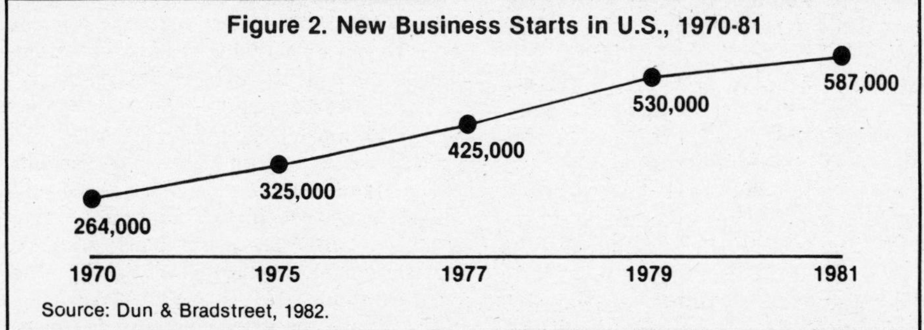

Source: Dun & Bradstreet, 1982.

Figure 3. A Comparison of Educational Outcomes, 1954 and 1977

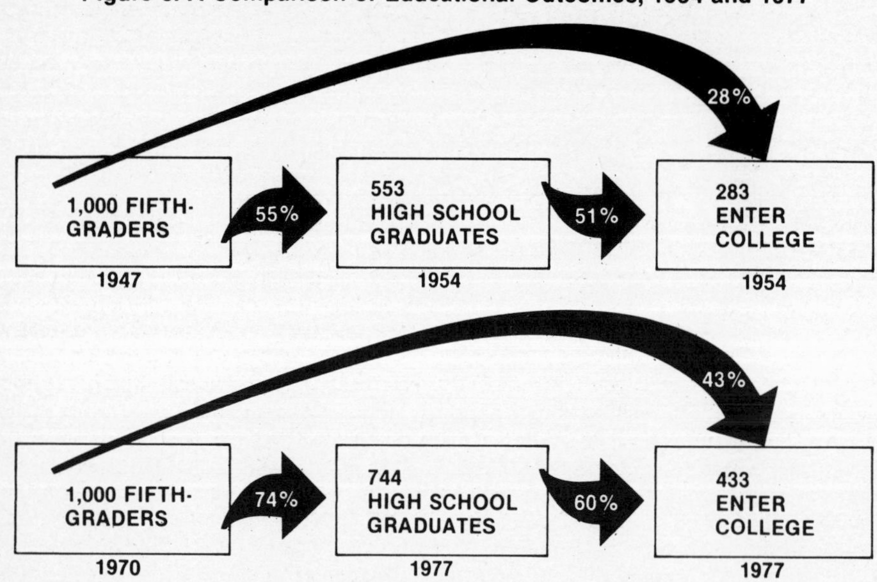

Source: House Education Committee Hearings, June 1980.

than American youngsters. In science, American students scored as well as or better than students from Italy, the Netherlands, Sweden, and the United Kingdom.

One of the few reliable studies of reading achievement across a wide time span indicates that in 1944 Indiana students did not read as well as students in the sixth and 10th grades did in 1976. Given the fact that access to education has increased greatly and the fact that we are now educating 75% of our youths, it appears we are educating them to a higher standard than we managed to do with only 30% to 40% of their counterparts in 1944.

It is also important to note that, even though our major mission has been to provide access to public education for the largest possible number of youths, the top 5% of the U.S. school population is as skillful as the top 5% from any nation in the world — however small a percentage of its youngsters it educates. The 22nd International Mathematics Olympiad, held in 1981, included competing teams from 27 nations. The eight-member U.S. team placed first. Even though our public school system is non-elitist in nature, we do as well for our very brightest young people as any other nation in the world.

SAT Scores

Critics of the public schools have used testing and test scores to show a decline in the general quality of the schools. Others maintain that tests do not measure achievement accurately. The argument has centered on aptitude testing. For example, scores on the Scholastic Aptitude Test (SAT) have declined somewhat in recent years, but that decline seems to have stopped. However, the profile for both verbal and mathematical SAT scores differs markedly from that of scores on the American College Testing Program (ACT) exams, which presumably measure the same aptitudes. The Preliminary Scholastic Aptitude Test (PSAT), given to high school sophomores, has shown *no* decline in scores, even though it purports to measure the same qualities as are measured by the SAT. Similarly, the Graduate Record Examination (GRE), taken by graduates of U.S. colleges, has shown no significant decline. This is also true of the Medical College Admission Test (MCAT) and the Law School Admission Test (LSAT). If the public schools were doing such a terrible job, declines in graduate school admission test scores should certainly follow. No such decline is generally evident.

With this in mind, the announcement that SAT scores have risen slightly needs to be taken with several grains of salt. The SAT was never intended to serve as *the* national barometer of school success and is obviously faulty when used in this way. Some numbers beat no numbers, however, and, unless the National Assessment of Educational Progress (NAEP) receives more national attention than has been the case, the public will probably continue to pay more attention to SAT scores than their predictive performance merits. This year, scores are being published with norms for each state — a practice that will undoubtedly give further impetus to competitive attitudes among the states, stemming from scanty information and mistaken interpretations. (The percentage of high school graduates who have taken the SAT varied from 2% in South Dakota and 3% in Iowa, Mississippi, and North Dakota to 69% in Connecticut and 51% in Georgia. This does *not* mean that public schools are better or worse in Connecticut and Georgia than they are in Iowa or Mississippi.)

I believe that the education profession has allowed the public to develop a stereotyped and erroneous notion of the meaning of SAT scores. It is time that we returned these tests to their proper use: one of several measures designed to help college admissions officers do a better job of selecting freshmen. The decision of the College Board to publish state SAT score distributions may help to sell copies of the test, but it has no other educational objective. The tests do not indicate the quality of education at the state level.

We could better devote ourselves to the testing of specific school achievements, particularly reading. Since 1980, student reading scores have shown significant increases in Atlanta, Boston, Chicago, Houston, Minneapolis, New Orleans, Newark, Philadelphia, and many other large cities. New York City, for instance, has markedly reduced the number of third-graders scoring below the minimum competency level in reading. There is no doubt that U.S. schools are teaching young people to read better than they have in the past, particularly in the early years of schooling. In addition, a number of standardized tests show that today's elementary school children do better than did their counterparts tested in 1960.

Another area in which U.S. schools excel is in educating young people with special needs. Handicapped youngsters in America have more education geared to their special needs than handicapped youngsters in any other nation. It may be true that handicapped youths as a group score lower than nonhandicapped youths, but there is no doubt that our handicapped young people achieve a higher level of education than the handicapped young people of any other country. Rather than becoming expensive, passive wards of the state, most are able to engage in productive work and become useful citizens.

In our quest to offer equal opportunities to handicapped students, we may not have offered a wide enough range of programs for the gifted. This problem seems to be handled very well in some communities and not well at all in others. Unlike programs for the handicapped, programs for the gifted and talented will have to be developed at the local and state levels, without federal largesse.

Additional NAEP data indicate that the reading performance of 9-year-olds rose significantly (while black 9-year-old students have made even more impressive gains). Thirteen-year-old black students are also achieving significant gains on the NAEP exams.

Overall, the gaps in school performance have narrowed. Students in the Southeast, who used to lag considerably behind the rest of the U.S., have improved significantly. Blacks have moved toward the national average. And rural students have made significant gains in reading and reference skills.

One additional point involves the number of students who are prepared to take Advanced Placement tests for college. In 1970 only 58,000 students took Advanced Placement tests; in 1981 about 134,000 high school students took Advanced Placement tests. These are tests of knowledge, not aptitude.

During the 1960s and 1970s, some astonishing things happened in U.S. public schools. As a nation, we have assimilated 12 million immigrants during the Seventies alone. This is the largest wave of immigration of any decade in U.S. history. The public schools have been the key mechanism for assimilating these immigrants into U.S. society.

U.S. public schools are also a system in which academic achievement at the upper end of the range is as good as the best of any other nation. Eighty percent to 85% of our young people graduate from high school, and 65% to 70% go on to attend college. Of those who do attend college, 50% graduate. Enrollment in U.S. colleges and universities rose from six million in 1966 to about 12 million in 1981. In England, only 20% of youths graduate from high school, and in Italy the figure is 16%. The life chances of young Americans are significantly increased because of this educational advantage.

Head Start

Next I must mention one of our areas of greatest improvement. Compared with those of other countries, U.S. provisions for day care and educational programs for preschoolers have lagged far behind. We now know, however, that one such program, Head Start, has proved to be a striking success. The Head Start program began in the Sixties as an attempt to give disadvantaged 3- and 4-year-olds an advantage in school through a carefully designed program of enrichment. The first Head Start group is now of high school age, and comparing them with a control group indicates very significant differences. As sophomores, the Head Start students scored one grade level higher on reading and mathematics than did similar non-Head Start students in the control group. Only 19% of the Head Start group were in special classes for slow learners, compared with 39% of the control group. The number of chronic offenders in the Head Start group was half the number in the control group. The Head Start students were also more likely to complete high school, to work after school, and to enter the world of work or college after high school graduation. They were also much less likely to end up on welfare. The $6,000 per child that is invested in programs of this sort can save $15,000 per child in later remedial and special services.

New Alliances

American industry is showing renewed interest in and support for the public schools. For the most part, this support stems from enlightened self-interest; the better the educational programs in a community, the higher the quality of workers who can be attracted to that community.

More than 200 Adopt-a-School programs now exist. The city of Philadelphia has four high schools for students who intend to enter business, engineering, and related fields. These schools work closely with local firms. Many companies are providing school systems with various kinds of equipment (from furniture to computers), which can then be used as tax deductions. Non-cash contributions are increasing; some companies will give executives released time to share their skills, do printing in their own print shops for school systems, or provide trained specialists for energy audits, financial procedures, and a variety of other services.

The linking of public schools with networks of business and community organizations will be a key factor in this period of scarce fiscal resources. Schools can increase their resources without actually raising dollars, through participating in cooperative networks. Foundations have also discovered that their grants to schools have greater leverage if the money is supplemented by a variety of these resource-raising methods. For example, the Piton Foundation found that, in its community development project in Denver, every dollar it put into the project raised seven additional dollars in facilities, human talent, and services. This "leveraging" principle is an important one for the 1980s, as we attempt to stretch limited resources.

Looking to the Future

Several demographic trends will be important in the Eighties. First is the "two nations" trend — the result of the population shift to the sunbelt. In addition, the birthrate per thousand females of child-bearing age has shown striking changes. Severe teacher shortages are already appearing in many sunbelt states, and the economy seems unprepared to provide additional funds for larger numbers of youngsters of elementary school age. The increasing number of women in the workforce will create a huge demand for day care, particularly in the sunbelt.

These trends will force us to view education as though there were two United States — one primarily in the North and East, the other primarily in the South and West. Their educational needs and strategies will be vastly different. Moreover, differential fertility data tell us that a larger percentage of U.S. public school children will be coming from minority group backgrounds than in the past; from 30% to 35% of the public school population will be minority by the year 1990. In some states, that percentage will approach half of all youths. Additional problems may arise in attempting to educate children of single-parent families. Policy decisions are increasingly likely to come from the state and regional levels and less from the federal government. Certainly the next decade will be a time of change and challenge, given the increasing numbers of relatively poorly prepared students, coming often from single-parent families, more frequently members of racial minorities, and increasingly from sunbelt and not from frostbelt states.

But, those challenges notwithstanding, we should anticipate excellent performance in U.S. public elementary schools. The secondary schools will have to undergo some drastic changes, particularly in preparing people for a remarkably changed workforce. High performance in the "basics" will not be enough for the workplace of the late 1980s. The workforce will depend more heavily on information and analysis and less on the physical production of goods. The increased need in the workplace for higher-order skills will require major changes in the American public high school. However, we should have great confidence in our ability to meet this challenge, knowing that elementary school performance is now reliable and successful.

The U.S. public education system is a remarkably successful institution. It is designed for every student, and yet its very best students are as good as those of any nation in the world. It provides a high return on dollars invested. The future of America depends on investment in human resources. American public schools are obviously the best place to find the highest return on that investment.

IBM

Continuity and Change in American Education

Every year brings several recommendations for the improvement of schooling in America. This year is no exception. Although many of the same suggestions for helping the nation's schools achieve success are made year after year, they are seldom acted upon. The form and practice of education in the United States is under severe criticism, however, and alternative modes of learning are being considered.

The articles in this section deal with alternative approaches to different dimensions of educational practice that are being implemented in some schools today. Enormous advances in electronic technology have brought about the microcomputer. Microcomputer software has provided a new approach to individualized instruction in the schools, thereby making it possible for children to learn in different ways.

Other significant and often controversial curricular developments that have evolved over the past decade and are now being operationalized in the nation's schools include bilingual and multicultural education. However, approaches such as these have been subject to severe criticism by many of the more traditional educators and conservative political forces in the nation. The new immigrant populations are coming, for the most part, from Latin America, the Caribbean cultures, and Asia. Critics of special programs for the children of new immigrant families argue that such extensive special programming didn't exist for the children of earlier generations of minority students. The critics also say that such programming is divisive. Advocates of multiethnic education argue that present day minority populations face a more advanced, technologically oriented society. The fact that the schools of the nation did not always respond constructively to cultural differences in the past is no reason why they ought not to respond to such differences now.

Though the best and noblest of our traditional educational values are still in place, the search for alternative approaches to the development of educational goals and to educational programming will continue.

Looking Ahead: Challenge Questions

What changes in the way schooling is conducted might foster improvement in the quality of schooling?

What do you know about educational microcomputer software? How can it best be used? How can we learn about it?

What is bilingual education? Do you think it is necessary? Why was it ordered by the federal courts?

What is the controversy surrounding multicultural education? In your opinion, does it have divisive or unifying connotations?

What social conditions in the United States brought multicultural educational programming into the nation's schools?

Should parents be free to educate their children at home? What are the advantages and disadvantages to having children educated informally in the home and community?

RESTRUCTURING THE SCHOOLS: A SET OF SOLUTIONS

AMITAI ETZIONI

Amitai Etzioni is a professor at George Washington University in Washington, D.C. This article is excerpted from An Immodest Agenda: Rebuilding America Before the Twenty-first Century *by Amitai Etzioni.*

In the first article of this two-article series, Etzioni focused on the current status and criticisms of American schools. His conclusions: Although many, maybe as many as half, of the schools have failed in their mission to educate, it's not true of all schools, and it's not for the reasons usually given. These schools, he says, have failed not in teaching reading, writing and arithmetic, but in providing the psychic foundation children need to learn those skills in school and later to function effectively in the adult world of work, community and citizenship. What's more, this failure is not a result of too much structure in the schools, as open classroom advocates and proponents of an ego-centered mentality would have us believe, but of the wrong* kind. *Schools need structure to instill in children—and future adults—self-discipline as well as self-organization, for these attributes are at the core of the mutuality and civility that are needed to bring about a healthy society.*

In Part II, Etzioni outlines the kinds of measures that must be taken in restructuring the schools, beginning with studying those schools that have proved successful in developing positive personality traits in students.

*See first article of series on page 211.

In considering a reconstruction of American schools, one approach is to look at those schools that provide creditable to excellent education, for such schools inform us whether or not the factors we consider essential for education are present. There are several studies of such schools, although much work is yet to be done.

One informal account comes from an observer who visited successful elementary schools (at least half of the sixth graders were reading at or above grade level) in poor neighborhoods (at least 60 percent of the kids were eligible for free lunches). These schools, he found, showed unmistakable marks of structure: clear goals, high expectations and monitoring of students' progress.

A quite different set of observations came out of a grand tour of 750 "alternative schools." Despite the popular notion that alternative schools never require a student to do anything he doesn't want to do, the two educators who visited these schools (both alternative school advocates) reported that "*no* public alternative school that has survived more than two years gave students such a veto. Successful public alternative schools . . . soon learned that they needed rules about behavior, attendance, graduation requirements, respecting rights of others, and so on." At the same time, the observers noted, "students had opportunities to help make, review and revise many rules." However, in schools that survived two years or more, these opportunities did not include a right of students to ignore rules.

A finding of the National Assessment of Educational Progress may be relevant to this discussion. It points out that as reading scores have improved somewhat, the ability of high school and junior high school students to draw inferences and to apply knowledge to problem solving has declined. There are no compelling data to explain this decline. Among the possible causes nominated by the research team are excessive TV viewing and a focus on "basics" at the cost of more advanced skills. My hypothesis is that this development also shows lack of intellectual self-discipline. Interpretation and application, much more than basic reading skills, require following certain rules (e.g., check out all main options, avoid premature closure) and a measure of patience (i.e., control of impulse). The data suggest to me that these attributes declined. This is not to deny the possible role of other factors; for example, under most circumstances extensive television watching develops neither self-discipline nor the ability to think.

Two Major Studies Point to the Need for Structure

The large-scale comparative study of public and private schools conducted by James S. Coleman and his associates presents a more in-depth analysis of the attributes of effective schools. What this study of 1,016 public, parochial and other private schools shows is that effective schools, both private and public, have two features in common: Their structure enables them, first, to impose discipline, and second, to uphold academic standards. Schools with these attributes graduated students with significantly higher knowledge and skills than those without them.

From *Learning*, March 1983. Excerpted from AN IMMODEST AGENDA: REBUILDING AMERICA BEFORE THE TWENTY-FIRST CENTURY, by Amitai Etzioni, ©1983 Gertrude Falk.

The single most important difference between more effective and less effective schools was the disciplinary structure. While Coleman relied on such measures as enforcement of a dress code and strictness in dealing with those who cut classes, are absent or attack teachers, he also drew on student-based measurements. These indicated that in the more effective schools, discipline was not merely imposed but by and large was accepted as legitimate—that is, the majority of students perceived discipline not as a set of dictates but as worthy of their commitment; they found the discipline "fair."

The fact that Coleman's analysis comes out favoring nonpublic schools is only because private schools are more commonly able to maintain these structural prerequisites of learning. However, when they are available in public schools, they work there too. Also, at first reading it may seem that Coleman's findings combine the psychic agenda with the cognitive one, since they stress both discipline and academic standards. However, the second most important factor determining high performance, after disciplinary structure, is also more a structural item than a cognitive one. This is the proper authority relationship between teacher and student, the ability to compel task-relevant behavior and to have the class, peers and parents support it, or at least not negate it.

Another large-scale study relevant to the question of what makes schools effective was one conducted in Britain, from 1970 to 1974, of 12 secondary schools, all in London's inner city. Holding constant the social background of pupils, the study found substantial differences among the schools in students' learning and behavior.

The single most important factor in these differences was the schools' character as a social institution—their structure and the processes that administrators and teachers used. In the schools that provided clear incentives and rewards, that had a strong academic emphasis and gave priority to student learning, that expected students to carry out clearly defined responsibilities, students not only did better in school and attended more regularly, they also were less involved in delinquent behavior outside of school. And schools with clear and well-established standards of behavior and discipline did better than those where teachers had to struggle alone to establish these standards.

The more successful schools in this study provide a good illustration of the difference between creating the structural conditions for evolving self-organization and self-discipline, and merely imposing discipline from the outside. The better schools created a climate of respect for students as responsible individuals and held high expectations of both their behavior and their academic work. Students accepted specific supervisory tasks in corridors, classrooms and assemblies, for example. Teachers provided many occasions for students to work independently, in effect saying to them, "We trust you to use your time for productive, self-guided work." At the same time, the results of work students did on their own was checked, and some students did indeed need help to develop study habits for independent work. The point, though, is that expecting students to take responsibility and work independently encourages self-regulation rather than reliance on constant close supervision.

Another important finding of the London study is that appreciation and praise—that is, positive sanctions rather than negative ones—were highly effective, although teachers did not use these tools often. Indeed, what "discipline" brings to mind most immediately is restraining and setting limits, not encouraging or promoting any particular behavior. My own studies show most clearly that involvement based on positive feelings is psychologically much more productive than the same degree of compliance attained by fear, pressure or negative sanctions. Educators must use both sets of motivational tools; to give up either would undercut their capacity to discharge their duties. However, the more they can use the positive ones, the more likely the result will be students' self-organization rather than compliance limited to the time and scope of actively present disciplinary agents.

Of course, other factors affect the quality of schooling. A community uninterested in or hostile to learning, one lacking in successful role models (or rich in the wrong ones, such as "making it" by circumventing school and being a numbers runner or drug peddler), one ravaged by unemployment, crowded housing, garbage and rats, will undermine learning. Teachers who are underpaid and who do not feel respected will not be paragons of education. Extensive exposure to TV seems to be a negative factor. And there are some pupils—of all classes and races—who do have low IQs or severe learning disabilities. However, so far as the effective working of schools is concerned—holding constant, so to speak, their environment and the cognitive abilities of the pupils—school structure is in my view the prime factor. Cognitive deficiencies are secondary and often reflect in part the other factors. True, the circle closes: Once cognitive deficiencies accumulate, they tend to pose personality problems, as evident in learning disabled pupils who become disruptive. But the main vector points the other way: Studies of effective schools suggest that even children with cognitive problems learn when they can mobilize and commit self.

Reconstruction: School as an Experience

The first step toward reconstruction of the schools from the inside will require a higher level of awareness and analysis of the school as a *set of experiences*, as a structure. When you look at a school, don't see teachers, pupils, classrooms, curriculum. See, instead, young people being rewarded for work well done, finding that self-organization and achievement are a source of social gratification, as long as students abide by the rules (e.g., compete fairly) and are sensitive to others (e.g., do not deride slower learners).

Some educators refer to the merits of "learning by experience" rather than by lecture, evoking the work of Dewey or Montessori, for example. This is quite a different matter from the kinds of experiences I'm talking about. They refer, by and large, to teaching methods that enhance cognitive learning. A child is said to learn more about Egyptian pyramids, for example, by building a small one out of toy bricks than by a teacher talk. The educational experiences I refer to are as a rule imparted by life in school, and they affect most immediately personality and character development, not task-oriented learning.

The significant effect of such experiences in school *has* been widely recognized in one area. Sports have often been held up as the arena in which character is formed. The British evolved the dictum that the playing field is where you learn that how you play—cooperating with your own team and, above all, being fair to the other—is more important than whether you win. In other words, a commitment to shared rules outweighs personal—or group—gains.

It is symptomatic of the American condition that in forming character, sports in schools are often not geared to this element of civility, but to Richard Nixon's favorite quote from football coach Vince Lombardi: "Winning is not the most important thing; it's the only thing." A common lesson is, hence, that violating rules, often with impunity, is the shortest way to personal and group gains.

My point is not that sports with this emphasis form people who are willing to vote for politicians on the take, or who embark on unbounded quests for personal and corporate gain. My point is that *all* school activities are like sports in two pivotal ways: First, the experiences generated—not by what teachers say, but by the way they conduct themselves, deal with students, with each other, with assignments, and so on—affect pupils' characters. Second, like sports, these experiences are often counterproductive in many, maybe as many as half, of America's schools.

In about 15 to 20 percent of the schools, especially public schools or schools in large cities, the dominant issue is custodial maintenance (i.e., coping with violent or disruptive students). In many other schools, especially suburban or private schools, a variety of ego-centered psychological approaches hinder education. Since most educators, parents and citizens seem to think about schools in terms of academic achievements, content of teaching and teaching styles—or to think about personality-shaping experiences as a matter reserved for extracurricular activities, not the whole school—the first step to correction must occur through a change in awareness of how schools affect personality development, the direction on their current effect, and how it might be redirected.

Other Steps Toward Reconstruction

At the same time schools heighten their awareness of character development, factors external to the schools will have to be tackled. The schools have been overloaded with assignments, from making up for the preschool education millions of families do not complete to scores of educational goals promoted by various interest groups, from sex education to religious teaching, from foreign languages to "non-competency-based" promotion. The question is not the merit of these assignments; when each is viewed in isolation, many are quite valuable. But taken altogether, they clearly overwhelm the schools' ability to carry out all of them, or even a fair share.

Correctives might come from several directions. Certainly the schools' load could be eased if families did more of their educational duty before their youngsters reached school. In addition, it would be helpful for families to work more closely with schools, and for the schools to make greater efforts to involve parents in their work rather than shut them out or manipulate them in PTAs and other such groups.

Another corrective would be for the general public to raise its level of involvement somewhat, to countervail single-issue and other interest groups. More broadly based public pressure would make it easier for the schools to avoid the costly and ultimately counterproductive programs to which they have been pushed, for example, by extreme advocates of bilingual education, who want almost everything taught in a child's native language, and not merely for a transition period.

As a result of greater mobilization of the public, interest groups would have to moderate their demands on schools, if only because they would be made to recognize that unless the schools are allowed to attend more actively to their first business, nobody's goal will be served. They might also be more inclined to work *with* the schools to find mutually satisfactory ways of meeting legitimate needs. Thus, the American Civil Liberties Union, to protect students' civil rights, has insisted that schools meticulously observe due process in suspending students. The result has been procedures that are so cumbersome and time-consuming that in practice very disruptive students often stay in school. The urgent need is to work out ways to make it easier to remove from public schools truly disruptive students, without opening the door to violation of their civil rights.

Some deregulation and reduction of the role of state and federal agencies would also help. In the matter of suspending students, for example, procedures prescribed by state and federal agencies push schools in the same direction as the safeguards urged by the ACLU—toward protecting the rights of a disruptive student at the expense of the need of all students for an educational environment. Reducing state and federal intervention would also serve to reduce the mountain of paperwork that now takes time and energy away from the schools' primary task.

In addition, there are several major shifts in public policy that would help to restructure the schools. These include a substantial "downward" shift in educational resources; more opportunity for combining work and study for students aged 16 to 18; and the implementation of a year of national service. It is my purpose here not to explore these reforms in detail, but merely to outline them for consideration.

• **A Downward Shift of Educational Resources.** If one looks at American schooling as a whole, one sees that it is top-heavy. A very high proportion of the young population stays much longer in the educational sector, especially in colleges, than in other societies. For instance, as many as 50 percent of Americans in the relevant age range attend college, compared to about 10 percent in countries such as West Germany or France. (This is not to suggest that the United States should have as few of its young in college as these countries, but just as 10 percent may be much too restrictive, 50 percent may be too expansive.)

One reason for this overeducation is that many colleges, especially junior and community colleges, are having to do the work the high schools failed to do—so-called remedial education. As concern for the scarcity of resources has increased in recent years, the time is ripe to try to complete more of the educational task at earlier age levels, where it is more cost-effective. A downward shift of resources could be achieved by adding no new public resources to colleges, and instead adding resources to primary and high schools.

Two other considerations lead to the conclusion that resources should be shifted downward. One has to do with prevention versus correction. It is much more efficient to teach a subject effectively the first time around than to allow pupils to waste high school, acquire poor study habits and grow in alienation, then try to correct for all these later. More important, since we stress the role of personality in these matters, personality is shaped early and is particularly difficult to reshape once it is misformed. Some data suggest that little progress on this front occurs after the sixth grade, roughly age 12.

• **Greater Work-Study Opportunities.** A more radical reform would start schooling at age 4 and continue it until age 16, to be followed by two years of mixed work and study. Schools could either recognize certain kinds of work as providing educational experiences equivalent to classroom time (e.g., work as an apprentice instead of in the schools's carpentry shop) or provide internships in voluntary or government agencies on a part-time basis.

The work-study years should be aimed at easing the transition from the school to the work world, and at adapting the last years of schooling to a large variety of needs, e.g., allowing some pupils a more vocational and less academic mix. This would work best if the work were meaningful and properly supervised, i.e., more educational.

• **A Year of National Service.** A year spent serving the country, interrupting the "lockstep" march from grade to grade, right into and through college, has been widely recommended. While the suggested programs vary in detail, many favor a year of voluntary service, with options including the armed forces, Peace Corps, VISTA and Conservation Corps. Some would have it occur in the senior year of high school; I prefer for it to follow high school, replacing the first year of college for those who wish to continue, or providing a year between school and work for those not college-bound.

The merits of a year of national service are multiple. To begin with, high unemployment among teenagers and young adults is generating a demoralizing experience for the many individuals involved. A year of national service could provide a positive, constructive experience with which to start one's post-school life, enhancing the individual's self-respect, sense of worth and outlook on the future.

In terms of future employment, a year of national service could furnish young people with an opportunity to try their hands at a skill they might later want to develop. For those planning to go on to college, service after high school would provide a break between "work" in two institutions, and time out to consider their goals in an environment that is largely noncompetitive.

National service would provide a strong antidote to the ego-centered mentality as youth become involved in vital services for shared needs. And finally, the program could serve as the "great sociological mixer" America needs if a stronger national consensus on fundamental values is to evolve. A year of national service, especially if it were designed to enable people from different geographical and sociological backgrounds to work and live together, could be an effective way for boys and girls, whites and nonwhites, people from parochial and public schools, North and South, big city and country, to get to know one another on an equal footing while working together at a common task.

Focus on Recovery

To state the obvious, that the first duty of schools is education, turns out not to be self-evident. First, there is a strong tendency to equate education with teaching, transmitting skills and knowledge, which it is not; at least that is not the school's only major task. Second, there is a lack of understanding of how important character formation, education's core subject, is *in itself* for the purpose for which teaching is usually sought—as a source of basic skills for work, for mutuality, for membership in a civil community.

The single most important intra-school factor that affects education is not the curriculum or the teaching style, at least not as these terms are normally used, but the experiences the school generates. In many schools, perhaps as many as half, these experiences are not supportive of sound character formation, mutuality and civility. While many factors combine to account for this weakened condition of many American schools, the ego-centered mentality is probably the easiest to reverse; it is almost certainly a good place to start the reconstruction of the schools, by providing legitimation for a structure under which self-organization will be more likely to evolve. Reconstruction must also draw upon other factors, many external to the schools, ranging from greater parental support for the schools' primary educational mission to a reduction in the number of other missions, which currently dissipate their resources and blur their focus.

Keys To Computer Literacy

Dr. Gene Geisert

Dr. Gene Geisert is Associate Professor in the Division of Administrative & Instructional Leadership at St. John's University, Jamaica, NY.

FOR LEVELS K THROUGH 12

You can feel it coming! The school board has been pressing the superintendent to recommend a plan for computer use in instruction. Local parent organizations are talking about buying computers and donating them to your school. Children are asking excitedly, "When will we be able to use computers?" The teaching staff is also becoming excited but for a different reason. Nothing in their training or experience has prepared them for this new technology. You are beginning to wonder how to control the computer before it controls you!

What can be done to assist teachers and district administrators to plan for the use of technology? How can the classroom teacher effectively integrate the microcomputer into the instructional process? To answer these questions, it is important that planners of computer-related in-service programs recognize the multiple uses of the computer.

At the Region 10 Workshop in Dallas (February, 1983) Sandra Pratscher, Director of Computer Education for the Texas State Department of Education said in a talk entitled "Training Teachers To Use The Powerful Tool"—"We now have a tool for instruction that is not only something we can teach with and use for many purposes, but also something we need to teach. Computers in school are bound to affect the way we teach almost every conceivable subject."

For the past two years, I have been conducting a series of workshops designed to enable school district administrators, teachers, and curriculum teams to develop plans for the use of computer technology in instruction.

The suggested training model that follows has proven to be effective in helping educators become more confident, capable and flexible professionals to cope with the new technology. The overall program goal of this workshop is to provide assistance to teachers and administrators in the development of plans for the use of computers in the instructional process.

The workshop objectives are designed to help teachers obtain an understanding of the uses, capabilities and limitations of computers—not programming.

Each training session focuses on a single objective. The approach and rationale for each objective in this basic literacy program follow—

Objective 1: Identify Long Term Trends for the Use of Instructional Technology

Approach: Identify the state of the art in the microcomputer revolution and its impact on instruction. Study research findings and listen to what the experts are saying about instructional use of computers. Investigate relationships between society and computers.

Rationale: Teachers must be given honest information about the computer's promise for the future. They should not be led to believe that the computer is a panacea for curing all the ills of education. On the other hand, teachers must be aware of the outer limits of potential computer technology holds for the improvement of instruction. With greater understanding, educators willl not only use the new technology more effectively, but will begin to influence future developments.

Objective 2: Identify Current Practices of Model School Districts Using Instructional Technology

Approach: Provide information describing model programs. Present model plans. Identify how districts have approached the integration of technology into the curriculum. Identify current practices in the use of technology in "lighthouse" districts.

Rationale: Teachers need to see a variety of ways in which computers are already being used in instructional activities. In this session, the focus is on the computer's relationship to instruction rather than on the computer as an object of study. It enables teachers to become knowledgeable about innovative and creative uses of the computer as developed by other teachers.

Objective 3: Provide Basic Hands-On Workshop Experiences

Approach: This section of the workshop should include the development of teacher competencies in the use of beginning commands; the capabilities, uses and limitations of computers; computer terms; and practice on simple problems written in BASIC. The morning is spent in group instruction; the afternoon, in hands-on practice with each teacher having access to a computer.

Rationale: Classroom teachers should attain a working knowledge of computer use and develop some background in computer literacy. Since many students already know how to communicate with the system, it naturally follows that teachers should be on an equal footing with their students. Much of the mystique surrounding computers may be dissipated, and as a result, an increase in teacher willingness to use the computer as a classroom aide may result.

Reprinted with permission of the publisher Allen Raymond, Inc., Darien, CT 06820. From the October 1983 issue of *Early Years.*

Objective 4: Establish Goals for the District Concerning the Use of Computers in Instruction

Approach: Using a small group approach, do an instructional needs assessment covering where a district *is*, and then where it wants to be. Establish a priority listing of district goals for instruction. Identify which of the instructional goals can best be met using the new technology. Use a system-analysis approach in which needs are identified and matched with computer resources.

Rationale: Although the computer has a wide range of uses and great potential as an instruction tool, lack of planning frequently results in ineffective use. Schools are purchasing computers without the slightest consideration being given to how the new technology is to be used in existing instructional programs. To paraphrase Alice in Lewis Carroll's *Through the Looking Glass*, "If you don't know where you want to go or don't care, then it doesn't make any difference what you do." However, if you know what it is that you wish to accomplish, knowing how to accomplish it becomes very important.

Objective 5: Identify and Demonstrate Each of the Standard Types of Instructional Software Programs. Learn How to Evaluate Quality Software and Integrate It Into Classroom Activities

Approach: Teachers are shown examples of effective and ineffective instructional software. Evaluation forms are reviewed in order to help teachers discover what to look for when considering software purchases. Sources of specific software packages that will meet a variety of instructional needs are provided. (Ed. note: See *EY's* article "By Chance Or Choice" on selecting microcomputer software elsewhere in this computer portfolio.)

Rationale: Much of the early instructional software programs available for classroom use was unusable. Widespread use of microcomputers has led to a sizable demand for better instructional software. Commercial enterprise has responded to this demand with an influx of new products. Marketing firms range from reputable to "fly-by-night," and the quality of programs from exceptional to inappropriate. Teachers must become involved with the evaluation of computer software and learn to apply rigorous standards which promote quality education regardless of media.

Objective 6: Identify and Demonstrate Each of the Major Microcomputers Used in School Settings, Along With the Preferred Hardware Which Should be Considered When buying a Computer

Approach: Profile the major microcomputers that educators are using for applications ranging from computer literacy, to computer assisted instruction, to administrative functions. Where practical, include a "Computer Fair" which provides participants the opportunity for testing and comparing the major brands.

Rationale: At last count, there were over 250 different brands of microcomputers vying for market recognition. With so many different models to choose from, the question regarding the right one becomes difficult to answer. Part of the solution to this dilemma is to know what you want the computer to do. What goals do you wish to achieve? Do you want to use the computer for management purposes (attendance, grades, etc.)? Or is your aim to familiarize the children with the machine so they can become computer literate? Or perhaps you want the computer solely for drill and practice? What software is available that will help you meet your goals? Once the answers to these questions have been identified, the challenge of finding the right hardware is considerably eased. Having comparative equipment and specifications at hand reduces the risk of buying inappropriate hardware.

Objective 7: Develop a Strategic Plan for Using the New Technology in the Classroom

Approach: Participants are provided with a "blank" strategic planning guide which will enable them to:

1) Select one or more priority goals for the use of microcomputers in instruction
2) Determine what stage they're at
3) Determine where they should be
4) Determine the steps to get there
5) Determine the resources needed

Using small group techniques, enable participants to develop a strategic plan for micro-based instruction which meets the needs of their district.

Rationale: The greatest misuse of the microcomputer revolution occurred when educators rushed to buy computers in order to keep up the district image. Many school board members and superintendents "jumped on the band wagon" and as a result bought computers that ended up as expensive paperweights. Systematic planning for the use of computers as an instructional tool is key to any hope for success. Since teachers will be the ones using the new technology, it is imperative that they be fully involved in planning for that use.

The major reason this type of workshop is so successful is it's emphasis on teaching computer *use*—not programming. Experience has shown that when teachers feel comfortable using the computer, understanding its potential strengths and weaknesses, know what tasks they want the computer to accomplish for them, and how to select the right software to accomplish the task, technophobia (fear of technology) is diminished.

Teacher participation is a key factor in any successful implementation of comuters into instruction. Without teacher support little change will take place in the classrooms. Thoughtful administrators must begin to "bridge the teacher-training gap" and provide workshops. Why not make it a priority at your school!

Suggested Readings For Workshop Participants

Informational Technology and Its Impact on American Education, Congress of the United States, Office of Technology Assessment, Washington, D.C. 20510.

Computer Classroom. Emphasis is on using sound educational techniques in the classroom. One year $16.00. Published by Intentional Educations, Inc., 51 Spring Street, Watertown, MA. 02172.

Computing Teacher, The. Designed for educators interested in the instructional uses of computers and calculators. Nine issues. Published by the Oregon Council for Computer Education, Computing Center, Eastern Oregon State College, LaGrande, Oregon 77850.

Electronic Learning. A well written and entertaining magazine that provides information about developments in electronic learning, especially computers. Eight issues $19.00. Published by Scholastic Magazine, 902 Sylvan Avenue, Englewood Cliffs, New Jersey 07632.

Educational Computer. A bi-monthly publication for teachers on using computers, especially microcomputers, in the classroom. $12.00 P.O. Box 535, Cupertino, California 95015.

Educational Technology. Published by Educational Technology Publications, 140 Sylvan Avenue, Englewood Cliffs, New Jersey 07632.

Timely TIES Topics. On Instructional Services, Total Information Educational Systems, Minnesota School District, Data Processing Joint Board, 1025 West County Road B2, St. Paul, Minnesota 55133.

Author's note: The American Association for Supervision and Curriculum Development is now offering several comprehensive programs in planning for the use of micro technology, one of which stresses administrative applications in education. Contact: Cerylle Fritts, Staff Development Contract Manager, Association for Supervision and Curriculum Development, 225 N. Washington Street, Alexandria, Virginia 22314, (703) 549-0110.

Video Games Go to School

HOWARD RHEINGOLD

Howard Rheingold is coauthor with Howard Levine of Talking Tech, A Conversational Guide to Science and Technology *(Morrow/Quill, 1983) and with Rita Aero of the upcoming* New Technology Coloring Book *(Bantam, 1983).*

Corinne Grimm, of Mountain View, California, like many other 13-year-olds, often parks herself in front of a video screen, wraps her fingers around a control device, and transports her consciousness to a cathode cosmos of glowing phosphors and electronic sound effects. Yes, she has that suspicious look of concentration on her face, and yes, she handles a joystick with the telltale skill of a video addict. Yet if you were to look over her shoulder, you would discover that Cori is not zapping intergalactic invaders. She is building a logic machine.

The game she is playing, designed for children as young as 7, is called Rocky's Boots, and it is a particularly good example of a new, fast-growing hybrid of educational philosophy and software marketing. At its best, the infant educational software industry seems to be manifesting a whole new way of thinking about learning that uses the capabilities of computers to exploit children's natural capacity to learn.

A few researchers who have studied the potential of computers as learning tools tend to believe that the new approach is more than just another flashy medium for presenting the same old ideas. Unlike the technologically hyped "computer-assisted education" that came into vogue in the 1950s and '60s, they say, the "learning environments" and "discovery tools" of new educational software herald a profound transformation of the way children will be educated.

Cori, whose mother designs such software, is unquestionably a talented computer kid. Cori has been designing software graphics since she was 9. But she is hardly an isolated case, as the microcomputer becomes a fixture in public and private schools. In 1982, there were some 150,000 personal computers in American public schools, according to an estimate of the National Center for Education Statistics, a figure likely to double in the next few years. Many educators worry that the computers' full potential will be dissipated for lack of analysis and leadership within the education community. "The implications of computers for learning are vast," writes George W. Bonham in a recent issue of *The Chronicle of Higher Education*, "but the dazzling possibilities may also lead to a stampede that could come dangerously close to education's earlier failed flirtations with television- and computer-aided instruction." Bonham, the executive director of the Council on Learning, is alarmed at "the volume of the babble . . . that characterizes much of the instructional adaptations of information technology." Other educators, however, regard the microcomputer as the most revolutionary education tool since the advent of chalk.

Thus far, the enthusiasm for the new uses of classroom computers is based largely on observations of students working under an artificially high level of instructor assistance. "There is clearly a need for disinterested research on what really happens in a normal classroom," says Karen Sheingold, director of the Center for Children and Technology at the Bank Street College of Education in New York City.

The theory on which computer-learning advocates base their claims comes from an unexpected synthesis of several lines of thought which have evolved in the fields of education, psychology, and computer science. The products of this theory—fashioned from the skills of artists, musicians, writers, and educators—are, in effect, bringing the seminal thinking of John Dewey and Jean Piaget into the age of the silicon chip.

Dewey, whose work encouraged generations of progressive educators, stressed that important learning occurs during aimless play. Psychologist Piaget also saw play as a spontaneous form of research. According to him, children are natural epistemologists, continually formulating hypotheses about how the world works and revising them when they are proved false. During years of observation of how children think, Piaget developed a distinction between declarative knowledge—the name of the capital of Norway, for instance, or the elements in the periodic table—and procedural knowledge, which guides skills such as reading, speaking, or bike riding.

The computer's forays into the classroom can be similarly distinguished. The teaching machines of computer-assisted instruction transfered declarative knowledge with assembly-line efficiency but did nothing to upset the stale notion that learning is little more than the acquisition of facts. Software programs of today, on the other hand, teach process: not new skills per se but how to learn new skills, even how to think. Indeed, modern Piagetians believe that computers allow children to conduct their research about the world on a scale never before possible in a sandbox or a playground.

To know the basic learning processes is to be in command of "powerful ideas," says Seymour Papert, a colleague of Piaget for five years and a professor of mathematics and education at Massachusetts Institute of Technology. LOGO, designed by Papert and colleagues at MIT in 1970, was the first programming language that children could really use. It is actually an entire computer programming language especially suitable for teaching. It uses a "turtle," a small picture of a turtle on the computer's screen, to serve as "an object to think with," as Papert calls it. The turtle follows the student's computerized instructions to draw geometric shapes, which can become startlingly complex and beautiful.

LOGO is but one of the programs in the new generation of software that harnesses the computer's powerful capacity for simulating the cognitive and physical world. The essence of this new approach to education is not to be found in any particular kind of computer hardware, but in methods of teaching. Although the field is already too diverse to be neatly categorized, the emerging forms of education through computer use can be exemplified by four concepts:

☐ LOGO is the oldest, and perhaps the most powerful, example of an educational philosophy based on computation as an avenue of learning. It creates a computer language designed for children.

☐ "Learning environments," which embed families of concepts to be learned in the structure of computer games, are, like LOGO, designed to be explored and controlled by the students.

☐ "Discovery tools," like programs that produce graphic displays and programs that create other programs, enable students, once they become adept at the embedded problem-solving skills, to alter the learning environment itself.

☐ Peer tutoring and other pedagogical techniques help students to bring computer-related skills into their daily lives and to disseminate these skills to those encountering them for the first time.

Joyce Hakansson, 42, laughs a lot and frequently employs the word "fun" when she talks about educational software. Founder of a new software production company, she is one of the most experienced designers of computer learning games. By January, Texas Instruments and Spinnaker Software will begin distributing the first of her group's products.

Hakansson's involvement with kids and computers goes back to the mid-1970s, when she was involved with the Lawrence Hall of Science's pioneering computer-education project. In 1979, she joined the Children's Television Workshop (creators of "Sesame Street") to create the Computer Gallery, a roomful of educational games for Sesame Place. Her group evolved into the Children's Computer Workshop, and Hakansson eventually returned to Berkeley to form her own company.

"When we began to design our first product, my colleagues—among them musicians, writers, programmer/designers, an educational research expert and a specialist in curriculum development—and I knew we wanted to create nonsexist, nonviolent, and self-learning games. We wanted to go beyond games and to create genuine learning environments," Hakansson says.

To her, a "learning environment" is an engaging, entertaining, interactive computer game in which a learning concept is embedded. Movement through stages of learning is controlled by the child, not by the teacher or the computer.

Hakansson describes a simple example of a way intended to build reading skills. "Imagine a game," she says, "in which a friendly, fun kind of central figure is controlled by the child, who can move the character by means of a joystick or keyboard. As the child moves the character through this environment, she discovers that her task is to collect letters that are embedded in the graphics. This pattern recognition skill is an important step toward reading. More importantly, children find out that learning is empowering and fun. They learn how to gain that power and to experience that fun by learning the language of the environment. That's where the curricular content automatically comes in."

At a certain point in the game, the child will have collected quite a few letters. A voice then asks her how she is going to carry any more letters. Does she have a "b", an "a", and a "g"? If so, she can put up to 10 letters in her "b-a-g." Does she have a "c-a-r-t"? It can hold up to 20 letters. As the character continues along a path, still under control of the child, it reaches a brook. A voice asks if there is a "b-o-a-t" or a "b-r-i-d-g-e" in the bag of letters. The game teaches letter-recognition skills, to be sure, but it does so at a pace and in a manner prescribed by the child, not by a text. Its goal, like that of a great deal of young play, is simply to explore an environment.

Across the Bay from Hakansson's office, on the nothern fringe of Silicon Valley, is Menlo Park, the home of The Learning Company. Founded by educational psychologist Ann Piestrup, former Atari game designer/programmer Warren Robinett, mathematics educator Teri Perl, and designer/programmer Leslie Grimm (Cori's mother), it creates and markets its own kind of knowledge—rich worlds of color, music, and logic.

In 1978 Robinett created a graphic version of a game that originated in Stanford's Artificial Intelligence Laboratory and that became one of Atari's most popular game cartridges. The AI game, a notoriously addictive cybernetic version of Dungeons and Dragons, was known simply as Adventure. A character moves through rooms that contain objects such as swords or snakes; the goal is to avoid dangers and collect treasures by entering keyboard commands like "go north" or "pick up the sword."

Adventure makes use of a basic concept of computer design, Boolean logic. Boolean logic (named for mathematician George Boole) says that a certain operation can be performed only after the digital logic "gate" that leads to that operation is "opened" by performing a previous operation. In Adventure, the game player's commands open gates. Some of the commands lead into blind alleys, so the player must retreat and open the equivalent of a different logic gate in order to proceed.

"In the video version," Robinett recalls, "I made it possible to use a joystick to move a graphic representation of a character. It was a very popular game. But it seemed to me that many other worlds of different objects and fantasies were possible with an adventure format. In the summer of '79, I quit Atari, traveled, and thought about a kind of game in which the player would have to defeat monsters by building a machine out of parts to be found in the fantasy environment. I decided that digital logic gates would make a good model for the building elements, and that logic circuits would make good machines."

In 1980, Robinett met Piestrup and Perl, who were applying for a National Science Foundation grant to teach geometry and logic to gifted second- and third-graders. The result of the trio's collaboration was Logic Tools, a computer game in which youngsters search for treasure in a maze inhabited by 11 voracious ducks, which can be defeated by using "duck detector" and "power thruster" elements in the proper configurations. By September of 1981, it was clear that future federal funding for innovative education was not forthcoming, so The Learning Company was born as a commercial enterprise. Among its earliest projects was Rocky's Boots.

"I came into contact with Piagetian ideas about education long after I started my designs of adventure-type games," Robinett says, "but I think Rocky's Boots is a good example of a way to make abstract concepts concrete enough for young children. Boolean logic has always been considered to be far too abstract to teach to third-graders. Once I started to design the logic gates, I decided to use colors to display the state of the circuits. That meant I could convey an abstraction like logical truth and falsity in concrete terms of orange fire that flowed through pipes."

Conveying abstract information in a visual pattern is the secret to the success of this learning method, for adults as well as children, says Robinett. "I call it the power of graphical interactive simulations. Our games are graphic in that they use the pattern recognition capabilities of the human brain to do a lot of work without burdening conscious awareness. They are interactive because they allow the player to change and experiment with the representation and observe how it responds, thus feeding more information to both conscious and unconscious processes. And they are simulations because the skills they impart can be transfered directly to problems in the real world. And that's where the game can become a tool for educators who want to introduce students to specific idea-domains."

Piestrup's philosophy is similar to Hakansson's. "Joyce was the person who taught me that a computer should never tell children they are wrong," Piestrup says. With a background in educational research and curriculum development, Piestrup was aware that the children who seemed to be attracted to video and computer games were at an age when their thinking skills were maturing in important ways, and she suspected that these colorful, fast-changing displays were somehow related to that natural learning process.

"The idea was to create a world where failure is impossible, success is rewarded with power, and mastery of knowledge leads to greater challenges," Piestrup says. "We wanted to build an environment that is always controlled by the learner, in which the game itself provides a landscape of concepts for students to discover. Risk-taking is encouraged. There is feedback, but it is gentle. Finally, mastery of the game also achieves a curricular goal."

Perl felt that the mental skill of problem-solving was far more important than the "school math" that turned off even the brightest youngsters. Piestrup and Perl were quick to see the educational potential in the fantasy environment Robinett was developing. They began to introduce these learning methods to educators while the early versions of Rocky's Boots were developed, and they critiqued Robinett's creations from an educational perspective. Then they added musicians and graphic artists.

One of the first tools Robinett created was a "graphics editor." By manipulating a cursor with a joystick, the software authors were able to quickly create and modify up to 64 "rooms" or screens through which the learner can move. "At first it was for our own use," says Piestrup. "Teri and I could use the tool to create fantasy characters. Warren would critique them. Then Cori Grimm came along and really warmed to it. So we decided to build 'discovery tools' like the graphics editor into each game. When children master the elements of the game, they can personalize it by learning to make their own graphic characters. We want to enable the computer to be seen as a friendly partner in a mental playground, rather than as a dehumanizing drillmaster."

At the Jordan Middle School in Palo Alto, California, there is no need for special "children's" software. Since 1979, students have been teaching each other how to produce polished reports for their social studies classes, issue party invitations, and generate mailing lists to solicit literary magazine ads with "adult" word processing.

The use of word processing as a teaching tool was pioneered by New York's distinguished Bank Street College. At first, educators looked into the possibility of using word processing as a means of teaching communication skills to students who were intellectually able, but could not coordinate the act of writing because of youth or physical handicap. Programmers were then brought in to create easy-to-operate software. The whole idea worked so well that both educational and commercial versions of their program, called "The Bank Street Writer," are now on the market.

The secret of success in the "Computer Tutor" project of Joan Targ and Jeff Levinsky, using the WordStar word-processing system, is not how the software was designed, but how students are introduced to it. Targ is a teacher, and Levinsky is a computer scientist with Interactive Sciences, a not-for-profit organization that creates programs and organizes summer institutes for teachers and administrators. Targ's regular classroom has a flag with the symbol of a floppy disk flying outside.

"Children learn marbles or jacks without any help from adults, so why not let students teach each other about computers?," Targ says. "It isn't the software that needs to be simplified," adds Levinsky, "but the way it is presented."

"Peer tutoring" pairs students with other students of the same age. In a typical class, a group is initiated into the use of computers by a teacher. From then on, all the teaching is done by students. This procedure has proved particularly successful with people who have been excluded from or were thought to have no interest in computer access—females, minorities, the physically handicapped. "The idea that young women are not interested in computers is a myth," Targ asserts. (See "Second-Class Citizens?," *Psychology Today,* March 1983.) "We just make sure that when a girl comes into this room for the first time, she sees a lot of other girls using computers. The same is true of any group. If you let students see kids like themselves succeeding and having fun, they'll find ways of learning from each other."

The word-processing program not only introduces students to the mechanics of the computer, it also serves as an immeasurable aid in the teaching of clear writing. Traditionally, an essay is laboriously inscribed, not always in the most legible handwriting, read and commented on by the teacher, and returned to the student for rewriting. The labor involved invites compromises on both sides. By contrast, the easy-to-read and easy-to-correct word-processing version requires the student to revise only those words and passages that need amendment. "Now that student and teacher don't have to pay a penalty for rewriting," says Targ, "we can afford to take the time to strive for excellence."

"We have special-education classes," Levinsky adds, "where children who have never written a legible sentence in their lives are soon composing letter-perfect paragraphs and experiencing levels of communication they feared would be denied them forever. That kind of rapid success makes an enormous difference in how people feel about themselves, and about learning."

Cognitive scientists and a growing number of educators now recognize that people learn some tasks because they are enjoyable and because mastery of them conveys a pleasurable sense of control over some aspect of the world, not because it helps them gain any external reward. This concept of "intrinsic motivation" grew out of Piagetian ideas—as well as from more recent research—about the way external reinforcement can actually destroy some students' motivation. For example, psychologist Mark Lepper at Stanford and others have shown that children who liked to play with marking pens began to play with them less after they were promised a reward for doing so. Other researchers found that students learn more effectively when they perceive that the consequences of their actions are under their own control.

Intrinsic motivation is what psychologist Thomas W. Malone attempted to isolate in some of the more popular products of the video-game industry—in the hope that what makes the games fun could be transfered to the creation of educational software. His research method was to expose schoolchildren to various versions of Darts, a learning game, and Breakout, a for-fun-only video game, and then survey the children for their reactions.

Malone found that the most compelling games had seven essential elements: challenge, fantasy, curiosity, control, cooperation, competition, and recognition.

Prophetically, perhaps, Papert had already begun to satisfy some of Malone's criteria for compelling learning experiences with his signal work on LOGO. In 1968, drawing from his association with Piaget, Papert started the LOGO project at MIT. After a decade of research, he wrote the testament of the LOGO movement: *Mindstorms: Children, Computers, and Powerful Ideas* (Basic Books, 1980), and helped design LOGO's software to be a tool for teaching thinking and problem-solving skills to children. One of the most important of these skills is the idea of "bugs." Instead of launching students on an ego-bruising search for the "right" answer, Papert wanted them to solve problems by daring to try new procedures and debugging these procedures until they worked.

Students start a LOGO exercise by pretending to be the turtle and trying to guess what it would do to trace a square, a triangle, or a circle. The student then tells the turtle to go through those steps—e.g., go forward, then turn right three times. If the procedure doesn't work, the next step is to systematically track down the "bug." The fear of being wrong is replaced by the immediate feedback of discovering powerful ideas on one's own.

The purpose of any tool, Papert reminds those of us who are puzzled by the complexity of computer technology, is to help human beings become more human:

"In my vision, the computer acts as a transitional object to mediate relationships that are ultimately between person and person," Papert has written. "I am talking about a revolution in ideas that is no more reducible to technologies than physics and molecular biology are reducible to the technological tools used in the laboratories or poetry to the printing press.

"In my vision, technology has two roles. One is heuristic: The computer presence has catalyzed the emergence of ideas. The other is instrumental: The computer will carry ideas into a world larger than the research centers where they have incubated up to now."

The world of software development is both broader and deeper than the few examples explored here, but each of the four examples exemplifies a trend that is likely to emerge more strongly as the field of educational software matures:

☐ Languages like LOGO will be used to teach not only how to use a computer but also a broad range of problem-solving skills.

☐ Learning environments like those described and created by Hakansson are likely to become important for teaching a broad range of curriculums. For the next few years, at least, most of these environments are likely to be provided by commercial companies. The development of "authoring" software, however, will give teachers who are not expert programmers the tools they will need to custom-design such environments to meet their own particular educational goals.

☐ Discovery tools like the graphics editor of Rocky's Boots will become more prevalent and more powerful. They will give students an increasing amount of control over the way they learn and the software itself. Ultimately, students will use these tools to modify stock learning environments for their own interests.

HOW TO PURCHASE SOFTWARE

☐ Look for the same things you look for in a good game or toy. Will it have play value for a long period of time? Is it constructed so that the child can learn it without extensive adult assistance? Is it colorful and nonviolent? Does the game provide opportunities for the child to take control, rather than acting only at the direction of the software?

☐ Read reviews of the software in computer magazines and write to educational and game software distributors for catalogues.

☐ Write to the manufacturer of your computer for information about compatible education software.

☐ Try the software in retail stores and ask for a demonstration.

☐ The "Consumers Union" of educational software is the Educational Products Information Exchange, P.O. Box 839, Water Mill, New York 11976.

☐ Teachers can learn about peer tutoring and ways to introduce computers into the curriculum by attending the International Institute on Microcomputers in Education at Stanford University, held every summer. For information, write: Interactive Sciences Inc., 1010 Harriet, Palo Alto, California 94301.

—H.R.

☐ The peer-tutoring techniques pioneered by Targ, Levinsky, and others will be important elements in integrating computer-based learning tools into the existing educational system and in bringing computer literacy to groups traditionally denied access to the benefits of technology.

Today's experiments in educational software and research on its psychological effects already are influencing the software industry and educational institutions. Spread through a broad segment of the population, cognitive computing is likely to grow into a powerful new tool for coping with a fearsomely complex 21st century.

Computers and a New World Order

James Dray and Joseph A. Menosky

JAMES DRAY is a researcher with the Communications and Information Technology Division of the congressional Office of Technology Assessment. JOSEPH A. MENOSKY is an associate producer of National Public Radio's current-affairs program "NPR Dateline."

AMID the popular utopian visions of the world's computerized future are some troubling questions about who really will benefit. Must the computer revolution widen the gulf between rich and poor? Will it only perpetuate technological elites?

In reaction to such concerns, the French government has established a research group whose goal is to start a revolution of its own. The World Center for Microelectronics and the Human Resource ("Centre Mondial Informatique et Ressource Humaine") in Paris supports a cadre of scientists who are studying—and suggesting ways to change—the computer's impact on people and societies. The scientists ultimately envision the widespread use of computers by ordinary people in all countries, making them an integral part of human culture. In particular, they hope to transfer microcomputers to Third World countries and the poorer regions of industrial countries. They also hope to design computer languages, software, and hardware simple enough to make the machines truly useful to their recipients.

French President François Mitterrand opened the center early in 1982 with a good deal of fanfare and a budget for the year of $20 million. Since then, the budget has been cut by almost half, the staff has undergone a devastating shakeup, and the program itself has provoked considerable controversy. Now its future is uncertain, and the center remains an intriguing mix of science and politics, savvy and naivete, technical solutions and world-class problems.

Among its founders were Jean-Jacques Servan-Schreiber, the French writer, publisher, and politician who is the center's president; Seymour Papert and Nicholas Negroponte, computer scientists from M.I.T. who took leaves of absence from their academic posts to become the center's directors; and a number of other top computer scientists, educators, and socially active intellectuals. From the beginning, then, the center has been driven by the ideas of a disparate group of people—above all by Papert's vision of the computer as an agent of intellectual freedom, and by Servan-Schreiber's ideal of a new world order based on access to information and high technology.

Over the past decade, Papert has guided the development of a sophisticated computer language, called "Logo," for use as a learning tool. (He wrote about the experience in a book for a popular audience, *Mindstorms*, published in 1980.) His studies of children grappling with Logo convinced him of the radical effect computers could have on the way children learn to reason, and on their subsequent ability to deal with novel situations and complex problems.

Papert thinks that even very young children and uneducated adults can master difficult intellectual concepts if a computer is used to convey the ideas to the learners. For example, he recalls that, as a child, he was fascinated by gears. Later, when he was introduced to algebraic equations in school, he was able to understand them by thinking of an equation as a gear. He writes, "By the time I had made a mental gear model of the relation between x and y, figuring out how many teeth each gear needed, the equation had become a comfortable friend." Papert believes that just as the gear acted for him as a "transitional object," a computer can serve the same function. "Because it can take on a thousand forms and can serve a thousand functions, it can appeal to a thousand tastes," he says.

This potential of computers to alter radically the nature of education and work remains unexploited, Papert argues, because "our society consistently casts computers in a framework that favors the maintenance of the status quo." To counteract this emphasis, he would like to see "alternative computer cultures": minority groups, women, or poets, for example, who would adapt microcomputers to their own interests and needs.

Servan-Schreiber took up some of Papert's themes in his book *The World Challenge*, published in 1981. He claims that countries of the Third World will eventually join together to confront the developed world with a demand for high technology. He argues that former colonial powers have a moral obligation to help developing countries take advantage of the microcomputer's social and economic potential, and that failure to do so will worsen North-South tensions and lead to worldwide political upheavals. But with the assistance of the advanced technological powers, Servan-Schreiber says, Third World countries might someday even "jump above industrial society into the new information society."

The transfer of microcomputer technology that Servan-Schreiber proposed was to be implemented along the lines Papert had suggested for alternative computer cultures, but his full vision goes far beyond. First, individuals who have used the Logo system to learn new ways of thinking would band together in local groups to solve common problems. For

Seymour Papert thinks even young children and uneducated adults can master difficult concepts via computers. He spent a decade developing a computer language called "Logo" for use as a learning tool. Here he's using it with children in Dakar, Senegal.

example, farmers in a small Third World community could use computers to keep better tabs on the availability and distribution of supplies. Moreover, the very act of "exploring" with the computer could engender a flexibility of thought that would, in turn, allow the farmers to find novel ways of combining the efficiency of modern agricultural practices with their traditional cultures.

The next step is for communities to widen their knowledge and power bases by linking up, via satellite, with similar communities across a wide region. For example, farming communities could pool their experience about the success of new agricultural techniques so that each farmer need not start from scratch. Finally, networks of communities could become a new social force, with political and economic systems changing accordingly. Within a developing country, this might mean that historically disenfranchised groups could gain enough power to demand a more equitable distribution of rights and resources. And in Servan-Schreiber's ultimate vision, the entire Third World would become an electronically linked network of countries ready to cooperate or compete with developed nations.

The Politics of Computer Cultures

The center has so far devoted much of its budget to trying computers at two test sites: the West African city of Dakar, Senegal, and Marseilles, France.

In Dakar, a team from the center is working with government-sponsored educators and computer scientists to adapt microcomputers to many aspects of Senegalese life, including industry, agriculture, and medicine. The team has begun by tackling the educational system, and the first project has elementary school children learning to program computers using a French version of Logo. (French is the European language spoken most widely in Senegal.) The system is also being adapted to the local culture, beginning with the translation of Logo programs into Wolof—one of the major Senegalese national languages—which many children speak at home. Once children have mastered the basics of computers, they can use the computer as what Papert calls "an instrument for learning everything," particularly science, mathematics, and language.

Robert Lawler, an educational expert at the center and longtime colleague of Papert's, demonstrated to one of us how a prototype program in Wolof can help children learn language. First, Lawler typed the Wolof word for "sun," just as the children would do when taught to spell it by their teachers. An image of the sun appeared promptly on the screen. Then he instructed the computer, again in Wolof, to put the sun in the sky, and the image on the screen moved up. With a few more commands, the screen soon showed the sun rising over a man as he walked to his house. The computer adds a visible "reality" to keyed words, and Logo permits even young children to add new words and designs to such "microworlds." It is this simplicity, feedback, and adaptability for the individual that Papert and others believe can change minds in fundamental ways—and that make the Logo language suitable for many cultures that would otherwise be out of reach of computer technology.

In Marseilles, researchers from the center are preparing for the delivery of some 500 microcomputers this year to schools, houses, and social-service agencies in a working-class district with high unemployment. In effect, the project will be a large-scale laboratory experiment in creating a "computer culture." The team will study the impact on the community and work with the residents to help them adapt the computers to their own needs. Project staffers hope residents will "seize" the microcomputers, bringing the machines into their lives "as a tool, as a game, as a companion, as a mirror." For example, Papert says unemployed young people, especially high-school dropouts, could make use of their easy access to computers to learn marketable skills. Another possibility is that self-employed artisans will use the computers to boost their productivity. For instance, carpenters might use computers to estimate more accurately the cost of jobs, control inventory, and even design their products.

The rest of the 75 researchers employed by the center are working on an array of other projects. For example, some are improving laser videodisk memory technology that will enable "interactive" computers to respond even faster than when equipped with standard floppy disks. Some are developing new programming languages to make computer systems more flexible and easier for untrained people to use. Some are designing durable and compact microcomputers suited for use in remote areas. And some are developing portable "expert" medical systems to assist rural health workers in diagnosis and treatment of disease.

All these projects are still in their early stages, and most seem to be loosely organized and minimally defined. In fact, many of the center's teething pains seem to arise from its slippery mandate and shifts in its objectives. The center's priorities already seem to have been diverted from the project in Senegal and others planned for Third World countries to social programs that could relieve unemployment in France, and then to research to make the French telecommunications system stronger. "The center is terribly sensitive to the winds of French politics," Lawler says. "There is no buffer between research and the pressing needs of the French nation."

The center's political volatility contributed to Seymour Papert's resignation, in a flurry of publicity, last December. (Since then, Negroponte has announced that, in August, he too will leave.) Papert charged that Servan-Schreiber was using the center to further his political career and aid the French computer industry at the expense of more humanistic goals. For his part, Servan-Schreiber says that Papert is "a very difficult man . . . interested in only one thing—how to train very young children by computer." But, he adds, "It's not a personal thing for me." Observers say the flap between Papert and Servan-Schreiber turned on personal and philosophical conflicts as well as on their noisier disagreements over how the center ought to be administered.

Technological Colonialism?

Problems deeper than these internal matters, however, may prevent the center from ever making significant contributions. An obvious barrier to the transfer of microcomputers to poor and unskilled people is illiteracy; most computer programs depend on written language. One center project has begun to focus on the issue of literacy, and other alternatives are being examined as well. Edward Ayensu of Ghana, who is the president of the Network of African Scientists and one of the center's founding members, claims that it will soon be possible to develop a computer program that understands spoken Wolof. Another suggestion is to design a computer that can recognize physical gestures, allowing for the transmission of a nonwritten, nonverbal "language." But both ideas are pipe dreams, according to Joseph Weizenbaum, a computer scientist at M.I.T. and longstanding critic of the more extravagent claims current in his field. He describes these language programs as "an artificial-intelligence project of absolutely staggering proportions." Weizenbaum argues, "There's no clue to date as to whether these problems are even attackable by any means that we have now."

Critics have also questioned the center's economic, political, and moral premises. For example, American reviewers greeted *The World Challenge* with almost universal disdain, judging Servan-Schreiber's grasp of global economics—and his notion of the Third World leap-frogging its way into the Information Age—to be naive at best. As George W. Ball, the undersecretary of state in the Kennedy and Johnson administrations, wrote in the *New York Times*, "Yes, Virginia, there is noise out there, but what you are hearing is not the [Third World] hammering on the gates of Europe [for technology]; it is only Servan-Schreiber pounding his typewriter."

Servan-Schreiber's ideas in *The World Challenge* were based on the promise of Third World solidarity, as evidenced by the strength of the OPEC cartel. But OPEC is now troubled and divided, and the "challenge" presented to developed nations by the Third World's demands for high technology seems less likely to materialize than he predicted. Indeed, Servan-Schreiber dropped all references to such demands when he testified before a congressional subcommittee in mid-1982. Instead, he predicted that "an army of 50 million jobless will appear on the horizon and signal a situation of despair," unless the developed nations seek creative methods of adapting to computers.

Perhaps the most damaging question raised about Servan-Schreiber and the center concerns the conviction that helping Third World countries acquire computer technologies would be beneficial. To many critics, such a goal is an artifact of colonialism, imposing Western values and definitions of progress on other cultures for less than altruistic reasons. Some have charged that the center was founded because Mitterrand's government saw the Third World as a vast market for the French microcomputer industry—a market largely untouched by American or Japanese firms. "This reminds me of times long ago when white Europeans decided that African women should wear dresses and men pants," Weizenbaum says. "One wonders which came first: the desire to help the Third World or the desire to open up a gigantic new market for cloth."

Those involved in the center's work reject the charge of colonialism, arguing that they wish only to provide a useful tool with which non-Western cultures can meet their needs as they see fit. "Helping people control the most important technology of our time is not colonialism," Lawler says. Servan-Schreiber bristles at those who speak of colonialism. "It is an insult," he says. "It is the Senegalese themselves who have asked for this."

The leaders of Senegal have indeed asked for the center's help, as have the leaders of many other countries. Concluding that the Senegalese *people* also want microcomputers demands a leap of faith, however. And it remains unclear who will enjoy the benefits and who will bear the costs in Third World countries. The technology may be just as easily—perhaps more easily—used by those in power to increase the distance between rich and poor and to monitor dissidents.

Unlike Servan-Schreiber, Papert has always admitted that life in Third World countries could become harder rather than easier with the introduction of computers. "I don't want to present myself as a computer utopian. The computer in Senegal, or anywhere else, could create a little enclave in which there is very rapid development, ultimately at the expense of everything around. It absolutely could happen," Papert says. But for him, this danger is far outweighed by the possibility for good and the need to prepare for the coming microelectronics revolution.

The Mitterrand government still supports the center, which has a budget of about $13 million this year. The center has restructured its social-sciences staff and has signed an agreement with Carnegie-Mellon University in Pittsburgh to exchange staff and expertise. Raj Reddy of Carnegie-Mellon, a longtime ally of the center, will work part-time in Paris directing its scientific efforts. The center has also inspired other countries—Colombia, Canada, and Japan—to consider establishing similar programs.

Those close to the center are convinced that its efforts will pay off. "Adapting computers to the various cultures of the world is an idea whose time has come," Lawler says. "The center began this effort, and if it doesn't succeed in Paris, it will succeed somewhere else. The idea is too powerful not to work." Indeed, Papert has had some amazing successes with children using Logo, but the demonstrations have occurred in controlled environments under the guidance of talented teachers. Whether his results can be replicated in cruder settings is uncertain.

The center's intention to analyze and possibly predict the computer's social impacts in both developed and undeveloped countries is undeniably noble. And the center's proposed "counter-revolution"—to be born out of locally initiated computer cultures—is tantalizing. Perhaps groups of people outside society's mainstream can indeed find radically different, creative uses for computers. There are modest precedents with other technologies.

The "rap music" now popular is an example. Emerging out of the black communities of New York City, rap music involves a rhythmic, verbal bantering accompanied, in its most elaborate form, by records played on two or more turntables. The "rapper" delivers his or her monologue while a disc jockey manually cuts back and forth between turntables, spinning them backward as well as forward and establishing new beats as the rap proceeds.

This is a radical use of an established sound technology—a significant extension of the limited use for which the stereo turntable was designed. Given that the computer is, in Papert's words, "the Proteus of machines," it is interesting to consider what might result if blacks in Harlem appropriated that technology. But whether this sort of appropriation can be the basis for a new world order is open to serious question.

Bilingual/Bicultural Education: Its Legacy And Its Future

Carlos J. Ovando

CARLOS J. OVANDO (University of Southern California Chapter) is director of the Bilingual/Crosscultural Specialization, School of Education, University of Alaska, Anchorage.

Like the intricate baobab tree of Africa, which is a natural haven for myriad fauna, bilingual/bicultural education has become an educational phenomenon that serves many different groups. Beyond this point, however, the simile takes a different turn. For, unlike the baobab tree, with its largely self-regulating web of life, bilingual/bicultural education has many wardens who monitor its status with a great deal of interest. At one extreme are parents who (understandably) want to know what is going on inside the bilingual or English-as-a-second-language (ESL) classroom in terms of curricular content, first- and second-language development, and cultural emphasis. At the other extreme are politicians and journalists who are eager to extract a great deal of mileage from a topic that has consistently, during the past 15 years, touched some of the most sensitive sociopolitical and pedagogical nerves in U.S. society.

Both participants and observers view bilingual/bicultural education in a variety of ways. Some embrace with zeal the revitalization of languages and cultures through the public schools. They see bilingual education as a natural consequence of the sociocultural realities of a pluralistic society. For them, dual language instruction is a logical vehicle for cognitive and language development for those students with limited proficiency in English — and for those students whose first language is English, as well. They believe that bilingual/bicultural education will be personally satisfying to all students and that it will help them to develop the interpersonal skills and attitudes that are essential to a healthy society. Students with limited proficiency in English, these advocates would argue, are entitled to a fair share of the goods and services of the society, and this includes equal access to high-quality educational opportunities through the use of the language spoken in each student's home.

Those individuals at the other extreme argue that the positive effects of bilingual education on academic achievement, dual language development, cultural affirmation, national integration, and psychological well-being have been exaggerated. Such critics often suggest that support for bilingual education springs from faith, not from empirical evidence. They fear that the institutionalization of bilingual education in the public schools will further fracture social cohesion by encouraging youngsters to depend on languages other than English and to adhere to cultural patterns that may be in conflict with the mainstream U.S. culture. Such results, these critics argue, will only hamper upward mobility for students with limited proficiency in English.

Somewhere between these two extremes are those individuals who concede, on ideological and pedagogical grounds, that students with limited proficiency in English are entitled to schooling in their primary language until such time as they can assume the demands of an all-English curriculum — but the sooner, the better. Where this view of bilingual education is dominant, students with limited proficiency in English are generally removed from the bilingual program — somewhat arbitrarily — after one or two years of instruction. Bilingual education is only a means of pushing and pulling the speaker of limited English as quickly as possible into the mainstream American culture (whatever that is).

Finally, some individuals believe in the importance of nurturing ancestral languages and cultures, but they also believe that such endeavors should take place somewhere other than in the public schools. Consider, for example, the Korean community of about 2,000 in Anchorage, Alaska. Sensitive to the fact that its children were forgetting their mother tongue, becoming alienated from their culture, and having trouble communicating with their parents (who speak limited English), the Korean community, with help from the Korean consulate, started a Saturday school to teach these youngsters the Korean culture and language. The Japanese community in Anchorage also operates such a school, as do many other ethnic groups throughout the U.S.

Although it is useful to isolate and examine the myriad voices competing for attention on the topic of bilingual/bicultural education, the debate is much less clear in reality. The formulation of a national policy on language would compel the articulation and examination of language-related issues. Such a policy could function as a sounding board for debates on the homogenization or the pluralization of U.S. society. To what extent, why, how, and by what means should we move in one direction or the other? A national policy on language would resolve the often conflicting language policies that the U.S. has randomly and almost unconsciously followed to date. The National Defense Education Act (NDEA) of 1957 and the Title VII bilingual education legislation of 1968 epitomize this conflict. The NDEA affirmed the significance of foreign languages as integral components of national security; the bilingual education legislation, by contrast, was designed to allow the rich linguistic experiences of the immigrant and indigenous minority communities in the U.S. to atrophy.

To establish the need for a national policy on language, we must look back at the pedagogical and the sociopolitical development of bilingual/bicultural education since the late 1960s. By isolating these two closely interrelated strands of development, we can see that both the pedagogy and the sociopolitics of bilingual education have suffered from a general lack of direction. The usual approach has been one of ad hoc experimentation. This is natural in the early stages of developing a new program, but it also demonstrates more clearly the need for a national policy on language.

Bilingual Pedagogy

Pedagogically, bilingual education was based on the assumption that building instruction on what students with limited proficiency in English already knew would result in more learning than would total instruction in a second language. Those who held this view also assumed that cognitive skills acquired in one language can be transferred to other languages and cultures. The general objective of bilingual education was to open up two-way communication between the world of the limited-English-speaking student and the school in subject-area content, in first- and second-language development, and in cultural awareness. The long-term goal was to improve the academic achievement of students with limited proficiency in English.

The partial institutionalization of bilingual education in U.S. public schools was an admission that defects in the regular curriculum accounted, at least in part, for the poor academic showing of limited-English-speaking students. Through bilingual/bicultural education, educators, parents, and policy makers expected to improve the marginal academic achievement and the equally marginal sociocultural status of these students.

But those educators charged with carrying out this dual mission had no reliable research to guide them. In fact, not until federally sponsored bilingual education was 10 years old, in 1978, did the now-defunct Department of Health, Education, and Welfare direct a Title VII committee to monitor a research agenda in the following areas: 1) assessment of national needs for bilingual education, 2) improvement in the effectiveness of services for students, and 3) improvement in Title VII program management and operations.[1] The data from these research efforts were to be ready for the congressional hearings for reauthorization of Title VII in 1983.

Approaches to language delivery illustrate the experimental nature of bilingual education during the Seventies. Teachers who were bilingual themselves often used the concurrent method — switching back and forth between two languages during lessons — for delivery of content and development of students' language. The concurrent method was a commonly prescribed mode of delivery in early Title VII programs. More recently, this approach has come into disrepute, however. Teachers have found it time-consuming, tedious, and — more important — not conducive to the development of a second language. Rather than actively listening to the second language, students learn to wait passively until the teacher returns to their first language. Similarly, teachers tried and then often discarded many varieties of the alternate and preview/review models for delivering language.

As with modes of language delivery, approaches for developing literacy skills in the bilingual classroom have varied tremendously. Some programs have introduced reading skills exclusively through the first language, while English as a second language is developed separately. Other programs have chosen to immerse children in English exclusively. Still others have experimented with introducing reading and writing simultaneously in students' first and second languages.[2]

Two of the most debated issues in bilingual education have concerned *who* should participate and *for how long*. Educators have used a wide variety of instruments to assess the language skills of learners slated for entry into or exit from bilingual or English-as-a-second-language programs. Some educators have been interested in instruments that would identify only those students most in need of bilingual instruction — and that would deem these youngsters ready for exit from such programs as quickly as possible. Others have looked for instruments that would identify many students with diverse language needs and that would demand higher levels of achievement in the areas of language and literacy before returning these youngsters to regular instructional programs. It was not until 1978 that Title VII made provisions to assess all four language skills — listening, speaking, reading, and writing. Even then, a gap existed between this policy and the availability of instruments to carry out these tasks with sufficient validity and reliability.

The policy regarding which youngsters to include in bilingual/bicultural programs has also been subject to change. The major intent of early bilingual legislation, for example, was to address the needs of limited-English speakers, who were frequently children of poverty. But a 1978 amendment to Title VII encouraged the inclusion of other students, provided that they did not exceed 40% of the total classroom population. Thus it was possible to have in one classroom indigenous minority students whose parents wanted them to reclaim their ancestral languages, English-dominant majority students whose parents saw the benefits of acquiring a second language, highly bilingual children whose parents wanted them to develop in both languages, and students with limited proficiency in English. The instructional implications for each of these groups are quite different. For instance, indigenous minority students whose dominant — or only — language is English may have endured negative experiences associated with their linguistic or cultural identities. To focus in the classroom on a language or culture that a student has rejected may be a delicate endeavor. Furthermore, such children — even though their dominant language is English — may in fact speak a nonstandard version of English. Often, their needs are overshadowed by the glaring language deficits of limited-English-speaking students — and thus not given the attention they deserve.

Such instructional problems stem in part from the shortage of classroom-tested research findings to shape and buttress program designs. Bilingual teachers, many of them novices, have been given a complex charge. They must 1) provide literacy instruction in two languages for a variety of students; 2) understand and apply theories of language acquisition; 3) organize their classrooms for the triple goals of language development, cognitive growth, and intercultural awareness; 4) stay abreast of the latest research findings; and 5) keep up to date on the constantly changing federal, state, and school district regulations. Simultaneously, bilingual teachers must manage their classes, which are characterized by linguistic, cultural, and academic diversity.

What have we learned during the past 15 years that can help us realize more fully the promise of bilingual education? To begin with, linguists have made important progress in understanding first- and second-language acquisition. Their research suggests that the developmental process is similar and predictable for both children and adults. Thus the acquisition of a second language requires time and experiences that are tailored to a learner's developmental stage.

One stage is manifested in the informal language that we all use as we deal with our immediate environments. Because the context is clear, this level of language is characterized by incomplete responses, a limited vocabulary, and many nonverbal cues. An average non-English-speaking student learns to communicate at this level after about two years of instruction.

A second developmental level consists of the language used in school and in many facets of adult life. Here the context is less clear; instead, communication depends on a speaker's (or writer's) ability to manipulate the vocabulary and syntax with precision. Students with limited proficiency in English need at least five to seven years of instruction to master this formal language.[3]

The implications for timing the exit of students from bilingual programs into the regular curriculum are clear. In assessing the language proficiency of such students, we must be certain that they can handle this formal (i.e., context-reduced) language. However, assessments during the Seventies of children with limited proficiency in English often measured only context-embedded communication, not the formal language that students need for sustained academic growth.

During the past 15 years we have also learned that certain methods promote natural acquisition of language, while other methods promote only a mechanical ability to manipulate rules of grammar. Moreover, because learners follow a neurologically programmed sequence of stages in acquiring a second language, we now recognize that our expectations for second-language production should follow that sequence. Likewise, the language to which teachers expose learners during language lessons should reflect those stages. To be comprehensible, teachers should begin with concrete objects, firsthand experiences, and visual contexts. In other words, students with limited proficiency in English are likely to make more progress in one hour of carefully designed, *comprehensible* input than in many hours of simply sitting in a regular classroom listening to what, to them, is "noise." In addition, Stephen Krashen has found that students' attitudes toward the second language are as important as their talents for learning languages; the students' ages, their previous exposures to the second language, and their levels of acculturation are also factors that teachers must take into account.[4]

We have also learned that bilingualism and biculturalism are not detrimental to cognitive development, and that cognitive skills are transferable across cultures and languages. In fact, some evidence suggests that bilingualism may encourage the development of divergent thinking and creativity.[5] This new view of bilingualism challenges the view that researchers held from the Thirties through the Fifties: that bilingualism hindered cognitive and linguistic development because the brain could not deal with multiple linguistic tracks.

The evolution of bilingual education has caused us to recognize the fact that social context affects learning outcomes in bilingual settings. For example, programs that immerse youngsters in a second language are successful only when they do not stigmatize the students' primary languages and home cultures. Thus the attitudes of the host society toward groups that speak another language have an enormous impact on minority students' perceptions of themselves and of the school.

Much pedagogical experimentation and learning took place during the Seventies in the areas of language and cognitive development, but not all the findings were pleasant. The most publicized negative findings were those of the report by the American Institutes of Research (AIR),[6] which suggested that students enrolled in Title VII bilingual programs did not achieve at a higher level than counterparts who were not enrolled in such programs. However, Doris Gunderson points out that:

> Although there is insufficient research documenting the effects of bilingual education, there is no research to substantiate the claim that bilingual education and bilingualism are harmful. Moreover, the available research indicates that bilingual education is either beneficial or neutral in terms of scholastic achievement, giving the student the added advantage of exposure to two languages.[7]

A variety of longitudinal studies have also revealed positive academic gains for students who have been enrolled in bilingual programs for at least four years.[8]

To date, many students who would qualify for bilingual or English-as-a-second-language programs have not received such instruction — and, in general, such students are still not achieving on a par with students whose native language is English. There is still much work to be done. As bilingual educators become better acquainted with theories of language acquisition and the methods they imply, with the relationships that research is disclosing between cognition and language, and with the findings related to the optimal organization of classroom programs and resources, bilingual education will become increasingly effective. But better bilingual education also depends on a supportive sociopolitical environment.

The war of words regarding bilingual/bicultural education has centered on three disputed issues: 1) the use of public funds for special educational programs for students with limited proficiency in English, 2) the function of language as a bonding or polarizing force in society, and 3) the extent to which language — and not other socioeconomic and cultural factors — is responsible for academic failure. Historically, bilingual programs emerged in the U.S. wherever ethnic communities believed that it was in their interest to create such programs. But 1968 marked the beginning of an uneasy relationship between the federal government and such ethnic communities, brought about by the enactment of Title VII of the Elementary and Secondary Education Act. The primary purpose of Title VII was to improve the academic performance of economically deprived children who also had difficulty with English. Congress appropriated the initial funds to teach such students in their home languages, but these students were to transfer into the all-English curriculum as soon as they were able to handle such instruction. Congress did not intend the legislation either to promote minority languages or to pluralize society. Rather, the intention was to use the home languages and firsthand experiences of these students to assimilate them as rapidly as possible into the regular (i.e., English-dominant) school program. Congress supported Title VII on the premise that these low-income youngsters needed all the help they could get to overcome their linguistic, cultural, and environmental handicaps and thus to equalize their opportunities for success in U.S. society.

Title VII recognized the importance of building on what the students already knew. However, this legislation was not intended to maintain the rich linguistic resources that these children represented. Much of the debate about bilingual education during the Seventies focused on this issue. One side favored prolonged attempts by the schools to maintain children's home languages; the other side believed that the period of bilingual instruction should be as short as possible. As the debate on the length of programs grew more heated, participants focused less attention on the quality of bilingual instruction.

From the debate about language maintenance versus rapid transition to English, a second question arose that the public found more worrisome: would bilingual education cause students to develop divided linguistic and cultural loyalties? The federal guidelines for Title VII implied that the schools would encourage a common culture, since they would eventually return bilingual students to regular classes. At the community level, however, ethnic minorities were beginning to see that they could join the societal mainstream politically, educationally, and economically without forgetting their first languages and their cultural traditions.

Should linguistic minority groups have the right to participate fully in American life without being completely assimilated into the mainstream culture? This issue is still not resolved. Court decisions have consistently affirmed the civil rights of all residents without regard to race, language, or national origin.[9] However, many defenders of monolingualism and monoculturalism have argued that, with respect to bilingual education, the courts have limited the rights of local communities to run their schools as they see fit. Therefore, even though the intent of the courts has been to protect the civil rights of all students, many individuals have interpreted these decisions as invidious vehicles for social engineering.

Moreover, bilingual education is intertwined with such sensitive issues as governmental attitudes toward immigrants and indigenous minorities. The U.S. has received in the recent past large numbers of political refugees, economic refugees, and undocumented workers. But consistent policies regarding who can enter the U.S. and on what criteria are nonexistent. Nor do clear policies exist with regard to trade relations with the developing nations or political relations with oppressive regimes. It is hard to examine the pedagogical value of bilingual instruction without becoming entangled in such sensitive political issues as the rights and status of undocumented workers.

Given these tensions and the current trend toward less federal involvement in education, some observers feel that bilingual programs are doomed to extinction. However, the 1982 cutbacks in bilingual education were no more severe than those in other federal programs, and it looks as though Congress will reauthorize funding in 1983. Furthermore, extensive state legislation is now in place to continue the funding of bilingual education. It would be pedagogically unsound and sociopolitically imprudent to return to the sink-or-swim methods of the past. Bilingual education is a reality that even Nathan Glazer, one of its most ardent critics, admits is here to stay.[10]

This does not mean that bilingual education will have smooth sailing. As we reflect on the experiences of the past 15 years and consider the political, demographic, and economic realities of the future, we must recognize the need to define more clearly the mission of bilingual education. This mission is to meet — rationally and realistically — the linguistic and cognitive needs of students with limited proficiency in English. This mission assumes greater importance when we consider that the non-English-speaking population in the U.S. is expected to increase from 30 million in 1980 to about 39.5 million in the year 2000.[11] There will never be a more appropriate time for the U.S. to develop a clear language policy.

An official language policy toward ethnolinguistic minorities would create a better balance between the learning needs of students with limited proficiency in English and the national interest. Such a policy would stress the universal language needs of all learners; it would also consider both the importance of breaking down the social barriers between ethnic groups and the potential for cognitive development of intracultural and cross-cultural affirmation. Likewise, such a policy would recognize the role of language in the promotion of academic excellence, and it would encourage the development of multilingualism in the larger society. In this era of global interdependence, such multilingualism would help to advance U.S. trade and political interests. Although it is difficult to quantify, the humanistic rationale for encouraging individuals to maintain or acquire a second language is also important. Through language, human beings discover one another's worlds.

The public is still somewhat uncertain today about the content and the process of bilingual education, about its posture regarding goals for national unity, and about the balance that bilingual education strikes between benefits and costs. But despite these uncertainties, most Americans seem to agree that language development and cross-cultural studies advance national interests. The final report of the President's Commission on Foreign Language and International Studies, *Strength Through Wisdom: A Critique of U.S. Capability*,[12] confirms this positive attitude. Largely as a result of the commission's recommendations, a consortium of 10 organizations involved in language instruction — called the Joint National Committee for Languages — has begun to assess governmental support for a more coherent national policy on language.

Such a language policy must be responsive to the desires and needs of local communities. As it relates to the education of children with limited proficiency in English, however, this policy could aim to accomplish three general goals: 1) the affirmation of children's right to maintain their home languages, 2) the collection and dissemination of research findings on the role of the home language in cognitive development, and 3) the collection and dissemination of research findings that compare the outcomes of carefully designed bilingual education programs with those of undifferentiated instruction in an all-English environment.

The U.S. should nurture the rich linguistic resources that ethnic minorities provide. A national language policy will increase the likelihood of a flexible support system for children whose home language is other than English. Such a policy will also foster the acquisition of second languages among English-speaking students and can be adjusted to meet the needs of local communities.

---

1. Betty J. Mace-Matluck, *Literacy Instruction in Bilingual Settings: A Synthesis of Current Research* (Los Alamitos, Calif.: National Center for Bilingual Research, 1982), pp. 19-20.
2. Eleanor W. Thonis, "Reading Instruction for Language Minority Students," in *Schooling and Language Minority Students: A Theoretical Framework* (Los Angeles: Evaluation, Dissemination, and Assessment Center, California State University, 1981), pp. 162-67.
3. Jim Cummins, "Four Misconceptions About Language Proficiency in Bilingual Education," *NABE Journal*, Spring 1981, pp. 31-44.
4. Stephen D. Krashen, "Bilingual Education and Second Language Acquisition Theory," in *Schooling and Language Minority Students. . .* , pp. 76-77.
5. Elizabeth Peal and Wallace E. Lambert, "The Relation of Bilingualism to Intelligence," *Psychological Monographs: General and Applied*, no. 76, 1962, pp. 1-23.
6. Malcolm Danoff, *Evaluation of the Impact of ESEA Title VII Spanish/English Bilingual Education Program* (Palo Alto, Calif.: American Institutes for Research, 1978), pp. 1-19.
7. Doris V. Gunderson, "Bilingual Education," in Harold E. Mitzel, ed., *Encyclopedia of Educational Research*, Vol. I, 5th ed. (New York: Free Press, 1982), p. 210.
8. See, for example, Wallace E. Lambert and Richard Tucker, *Bilingual Education of Children: The St. Lambert Experiment* (Rowley, Mass.: Newbury House, 1972); William Mackey and Von Nieda Beebe, *Bilingual Schools for a Bicultural Community: Miami's Adaptation to the Cuban Refugees* (Rowley, Mass.: Newbury House, 1977); and Bernard Spolsky, "Bilingual Education in the United States," in James E. Alatis, ed., *Georgetown University Round Table on Languages and Linguistics: International Dimensions of Bilingual Education* (Washington, D.C.: Georgetown University Press, 1978).
9. See, for example, *Aspira of New York* v. *Board of Education of the City of New York*, 423 F. Supp. 647 (S.D.N.Y. 1967); *Lau* v. *Nichols*, 414 U.S. 563, 566 (1974); and *Castañeda* v. *Pickard*, 648 F. 2d 989 (5th Cir., 1981).
10. Nathan Glazer, "Pluralism and Ethnicity," in Martin Ridge, ed., *The New Bilingualism: An American Dilemma* (Los Angeles: University of Southern California Press, 1982), p. 58.
11. *The Prospects for Bilingual Education in the Nation: Fifth Annual Report of the National Advisory Council for Bilingual Education, 1980-81*, p. xii.
12. President's Commission on Foreign Language and International Studies, *Strength Through Wisdom: A Critique of U.S. Capability* (Washington, D.C.: U.S. Government Printing Office, 1979).

Multiethnic Education: Historical Developments And Future Prospects

Geneva Gay

GENEVA GAY (Lafayette Indiana Chapter) is an associate professor of education at Purdue University, West Lafayette, Ind., and an editorial consultant to the Phi Delta Kappan.

What began in the late 1960s with the political demands of racial minority groups — that their heritages and experiences be reflected accurately in school curricula — has now extended to other ethnic groups and to all aspects of the education enterprise. As the idea of ethnic education continues to mature, other expansions are evident, too.

Today, the arguments in favor of multiethnic education have become more pedagogical than political, and its espoused objectives, goals, and functions have broadened in scope. Whereas multiethnic education was at one time regarded as strictly compensatory, today its aim is to help improve the overall quality of general education. The mission of multiethnic education is no longer seen simply as the transmission to minority students only of cultural information about ethnic minority groups. It has moved from the correction of errors of omission and commission in portrayals of ethnic experiences to the promotion of ethnic pluralism as a social value at all grade levels. Thus multiethnic education today requires more than mere tinkering with the curriculum.

Although the years since its inception have been productive, the progress of multiethnic education has been uneven — especially in moving from theory to practice. Most theoreticians and scholars of multiethnic education have come to view it as comprehensive and multidimensional, but many school-based practitioners continue to view it in rather narrow, simplistic, and rudimentary ways. Decision makers at one level of schooling establish policies that encourage multiethnic education, while their colleagues at another level institute rules and regulations that discourage it. Mandates for minimum competency testing often include objectives that are directly related to a familiarity with various ethnic groups, but most colleges of education are still reluctant to require multiethnic education in the preparation of teachers. Some educational planners and practitioners have been quick to endorse the notion of infusing multiethnic education into the entire curriculum without first having a sufficient understanding of its characteristics and components.

As we approach the midpoint of the 1980s, it is appropriate to think about where multiethnic education has come from and to chart future directions. We are indeed at a crossroads. The concept, though still relatively young, is old enough for the novelty to have worn off and for authentic commitment to the idea to surface. Those who remain loyal to multiethnic education do so because they believe deeply in its merits and validity — not because it is the fashionable thing to do.

Multiethnic education is facing difficult times — perhaps even more difficult than it faced in its early, formative years. Multiethnic education emerged from the turmoil of the late 1960s, but in the 1980s it will face its trial by combat. To understand why this is so and how some of the challenges to multiethnic education will take shape requires us to reflect on the development of the movement.

The Beginnings

Multiethnic education was not conceived in a vacuum. Like other educational innovations, it originated in a sociopolitical milieu and is to some extent a product of its times. Concerns about the treatment of ethnic groups in school curricula and instructional materials directly reflected concerns about their social, political, and economic plight in the society at large. In the mid-1960s three distinct forces converged to set the scene for the inception of multiethnic education and to shape its philosophical and programmatic contours: new directions in the civil rights movement, the criticisms expressed by textbook analysts, and the reassessment of the psychological premises on which compensatory education programs of the late 1950s and early 1960s had been founded.

The civil rights movement had begun to change its character and tone by the mid-Sixties. Whereas the middle-aged leaders of the movement had previously tried to change laws through passive nonviolence, the movement began to attract a younger following and to advance a more assertive agenda. The arenas of activity moved from courtrooms and the southern states to the northern ghettoes and the campuses of colleges and schools. The ideological and strategic focus of the movement shifted from passivity and perseverance in the face of adversity to aggression, self-determination, cultural consciousness, and political power. Along the way, marching and singing were backed up by burning and rioting. Newly formed student activist organizations, as well as the older established civil rights groups, began to demand restitution for generations of oppression, racism, and cultural imperialism. The shifting ideological focus of the movement was captured in such slogans as "Black is beautiful," "Yellow is mellow," "Black power," and "Power to the people." Moreover, as these slogans suggest, the civil rights movement for Afro-Americans gradually became a movement for recognition of the rights of *all* minority groups, including Mexican-Americans, Native Americans, Asian-Americans, and Puerto Ricans. Poets, writers, musicians, and revisionist scholars joined politicians and philosophers in speaking for the movement.

It is not surprising, then, that, when campuses became centers of civil rights activities in the late Sixties, their instructional programs became targets of criticism. After all, these sources of oppression and racism were what the young activists knew most intimately. Whereas other activists could speak passionately and from personal knowledge about racist practices in employment and housing, many of the students could not. But they did know from personal experience what it was like to spend 12 or more years in school without ever seeing their ethnic peoples and experiences portrayed except in stereotypic, derogatory ways. These educational practices became the targets of their protests.

From within the ranks of the education community itself some new developments complemented the students' activism and reinforced their demands. Two particularly significant ones were the emergence of new philosophies about the learning potential of minority youths and the continuing analyses of instructional materials. Many educators and social scientists who had endorsed the deprivation theory that undergirded compensatory education in the 1950s began to rethink their premises. Some completely abandoned the idea that the poor academic achievement of racial minority youths was caused by some lack in their backgrounds or some dysfunction in their families. Others argued vehemently that the academic failure of minority youths was due more to the conflicting expectations of school and home and to the school's devaluation of minority group cultures than to any inherent failing in the cultures of racial minorities. William Ryan argues the point eloquently in *Blaming the Victim*. Ryan writes:

> We are dealing, it would seem, not so much with culturally deprived children as with culturally depriving schools. And the task to be accomplished is not to revise, and amend, and repair deficient children but to alter and transform the atmosphere and operations of the schools to which we commit these children. Only by changing the nature of the educational experience can we change its product. To continue to define the difficulty as inherent in the raw materials — the children — is plainly to blame the victim and to acquiesce in the continuation of educational inequity in America.[1]

Another noteworthy defense of the abilities that ethnic minority youths brought to classrooms was *The Study of Nonstandard English*, by William Labov. He concluded:

> [T]he principal problem in reading failure for speakers of nonstandard English dialects is not dialect or grammatical differences but rather a cultural conflict between the vernacular culture and the schoolroom. . . . Some of this conflict proceeds from the pluralistic ignorance which prevails in the classroom: the teacher does not know that the student's dialect is different from his own, and the students do not know just how the teacher's system differs from theirs.[2]

Textbook analysts provided additional support to minority demands for an accurate depiction of their heritages and experiences in the school curriculum. Textbook critics had been actively pursuing the question of how racial minorities were treated in instructional materials since the 1980s. Edward Johnson observed that the earliest criticisms — that white textbook authors committed sins of omission and commission against Afro-Americans, that books seemed to be written exclusively for white children, and that they either ignored the creditable deeds of Afro-Americans or taught that Afro-Americans were innately inferior — remained as pertinent as ever 70 years later.[3]

The textbook analyses that appeared from the 1930s through the 1960s reported similar results for Afro-Americans, Hispanics, Native Americans, and Asians. In fact, textbooks continued to report ethnic distortions, stereotypes, omissions, and misinformation as recently as the mid-1970s. In 1970 Juanita Roderick reported that, although the most blatant derogatory stereotypes of Afro-Americans had been eliminated, textbooks still tended to "type" Afro-Americans negatively by habitually showing them in occupational uniform, by not naming them, and by not giving them speaking roles in stories.[4] In 1971 a state task force in California found that the books it reviewed were ignorant of the bilingual/bicultural realities of minority children, provided inadequate portrayals of minorities, and were written chiefly from a white middle-class point of view.[5] Jeannette Henry's analysis of 300 books led her to conclude that "not one could be approved as a dependable source of knowledge about the history and culture of the Indian people in America. Most . . . were . . . derogatory. . . , [and] contained misinformation, distortions, and omissions of important history."[6]

Since 1968 the state department of education in Michigan has sponsored biennial studies of instructional materials, especially in social studies, to determine how accurately they portray America's pluralistic society. A study released in 1980 of four elementary social studies programs concluded:

> The programs deal with minority groups in some context and make an effort to present with accuracy and honesty the pluralistic character of the American society, historically and in contemporary context. The degree of effectiveness differs with each of the programs reviewed. Minority groups are discussed with sympathy and respect. The characteristics which are universally shared and differences from one culture to another are presented in a positive style, although generally only through Western eyes and with ethnocentric attitudes.[7]

The student activists, abetted by the efforts of textbook analysts and by the new thinking about cultural differences, provided the stimulus for the first multiethnic education programs. They employed many of the strategies pioneered by the first civil rights activists. They, too, marched, boycotted, sat-in, locked-out, and issued lists of demands. Instead of demanding direct social change, however, they demanded that educational institutions stop their racist, oppressive practices of ignoring and distorting the cultural heritages and contributions to society of ethnic minorities.

As a result of these charges, claims, and demands, a bevy of minority studies programs were launched. Some were as simple as supplementary lessons or units on heroic deeds and "ethnic firsts," on the virtues of ethnic cuisine, and on the festivities of ethnic celebrations. Others were as complex as a series of courses that constituted a program of ethnic studies. Most were poorly conceived and hastily designed; they overlooked some necessary and basic principles of pedagogy, learning, and curriculum design. The first ethnic studies courses aimed to correct distortions of existing programs about ethnic experiences. They concentrated on racial minorities and had their greatest impact on the humanities, the social sciences, and the language arts. They were "crisis programs" in that they arose in response to a need to placate pressure groups rather than from pedagogical foresight.

The goals and priorities of these early programs were justifiable because of the ideological premises on which they were founded. As early as 1964 Milton Gordon had proclaimed the vitality and perseverance of ethnicity in shaping human behavior and attitudes.[8] He argued that networks of organizations and interpersonal relationships develop within an ethnic group, which encourages an individual to look first to the group for the fulfillment of fundamental needs throughout life. The persistence and significance of the ethnic factor in the lives of individuals (and by extension the social character of American society) make it imperative that ethnic pluralism be included in the education of young people — if schools hope to realize their goals of maximizing human potential, improving the quality of life for students, and advancing such values as freedom, justice, and dignity.

Prime Times

The first seven or eight years of the movement — roughly the middle of the 1970s — were "prime times" for multiethnic education. This was an era of growth and expansion, both quantitative and qualitative. The educational and sociopolitical climates were receptive to innovation and change; a wave of exploration and experimentation swept the nation and the schools. Traditional American values were reassessed. The youth counterculture, the anti-war movement generated by Vietnam, and experimentation with alternative lifestyles flourished. Such critics of education as Charles Silberman, Paul Goodman, Jonathan Kozol, John Holt, and Nat Hentoff were publishing exposés of the crises and chaos that seemed to be pandemic in urban schools. Ethnic groups celebrated their heritages, experiences, and cultures in movies, books, plays, films, concerts, classrooms, and pulpits. This era, tagged the "me generation," committed its intellectual, personal, and ideological resources to achieving self-understanding and human liberation and to improving the overall quality of life.

Everyone got into the ethnic act. White ethnics (Poles, Slavs, Germans, Greeks, Italians, etc.) began to rediscover their heritages and joined racial minorities in demanding that their cultures and experiences be included under the umbrella of multiethnic education. An avalanche of revisionist materials — including pedagogies, psychologies, ethnographies, histories, and sociologies — appeared. A wide variety of ethnic books, films and filmstrips, recordings, audio-visual packets, course outlines, and study guides were readily available.

At the same time, legal precedents and changing practices established the legitimacy of multiethnic education. The *Lau* decision and the Bilingual Education Act legitimated bilingualism. The Ethnic Heritage Act made federal funds available to support research, curriculum design, and dissemination projects that dealt with cultural studies of ethnic groups, particularly those of European ancestry. State legislatures and departments of education adopted goal statements and endorsed minimum competency testing plans that included competence in areas directly related to ethnic pluralism. School districts and professional associations sponsored conferences, workshops, seminars, and publications to help educators learn about ethnic groups, their cultures, heritages, lifestyles, and experiences. Commercial publishers established policies to govern the production of instructional materials, so that the ethnic and cultural diversity of America would be clearly reflected. The National Council for Accreditation of Teacher Education included multiethnic education among its new set of requirements for the certification of teacher education programs.

Advocates of multiethnic education enjoined policy makers, diagnosticians, evaluators, administrators, and teacher educators, as well as classroom teachers and curriculum developers, to implement ethnic pluralism in schools. High-quality programs involved systemic and systematic reform; they were designed to influence all aspects of schooling for all students, at all grade levels, kindergarten through graduate school. Rather than merely adding on separate and supplementary techniques, the new models of educational change were integrative and inclusive.

The goals of multiethnic education expanded, too. Conceptual mastery replaced factual information as the primary objective. Clarifying attitudes and values became standard procedure, and promoting ethnic pluralism as necessary to the health and vitality of society gained prominence. Thus, as the idea grew to conceptual maturity, multicultural education came to mean both content and process, curriculum and pedagogy, ideology and policy. Three essential ideological orientations emerged: teaching ethnically different students differently, using insights into ethnic pluralism to improve all educational decision making, and teaching content about ethnic groups to all students.

Yet even during these "good times," multiethnic education had its problems. Many skeptics expressed fears that emphasizing differences among ethnic groups would balkanize American society. Others felt (and some of them said) that multiethnic education was a self-indulgent fad, an excuse for people not to exert the efforts necessary to succeed according to the standards set by society and its institutions. The revival of ethnic interest among whites was labeled a backlash intended to weaken the cause of racial minorities. Others saw this "new ethnicity" as the romanticized delusions of aimless white middle-class young adults who were trying to authenticate something that was long since lost. Many of the efforts to implement multiethnic programs lacked sufficient conceptual understanding, clearly defined goals, long-range planning, adequate diagnoses of needs, and the necessary pool of professionally prepared and committed personnel. Hence, the theory was advancing, emerging, and evolving with apparent continuity, but multiethnic practice remained largely fragmentary, sporadic, unarticulated, and unsystematic.

Future Prospects

Before the 1970s ended, it was clear that multiethnic education would face perilous prospects in the near future. The challenge for the 1980s will be to survive. Multiethnic education must be vital enough to weather the skepticism and retrenchment of a chilly educational climate. Many of the new priorities in education — vocationalism, the worship of technology, and an insistence on quantifiable criteria of success — are antithetical to the essential goals of multiethnic education. Multiethnic education is fundamentally an affective, experiential, and qualitative phenomenon that requires, if it is to be effective, a commitment to imagination, innovation, and change.

The survival of multiethnic education is in jeopardy on several fronts. Two of the most potentially devastating challenges are economic and ideological. Even under the best of circumstances, multiethnic education has never been totally accepted, nor has its legitimacy gone unquestioned in the education community. Moreover, fiscal allocations have always been minimal and have usually fallen into the categories of "soft money" and "discretionary funds." The current budgetary cutbacks in education will threaten even the minimal financing that multiethnic education has received. Economic hard times necessitate fiscal reductions and programmatic streamlining. As educational practices go, multiethnic education is still relatively new and has yet to be fully absorbed into the mainstream of U.S. education. Thus, when program reductions occur because of fiscal constraints, multiethnic education tends to be one of the first casualties.

Such reductions are now evident across the board. The number of visible multiethnic programs, courses, units, and lessons now in existence is a mere fraction of those that existed a decade ago. Many centers of ethnic culture at universities now operate on shoestring budgets; others no longer exist at all. The attrition rate of ethnic student organizations (e.g., black student unions) and the declining enrollments in ethnic studies courses are staggering. All of these signs point to a lean time ahead for multiethnic education. Advocates of multiethnic education must find creative and unorthodox ways to achieve their objectives in the absence of adequate financial resources.

Changing ideologies and shifting values are as threatening to the future of multiethnic education as are economic constraints. The current societal and educational emphases on basics, conservatism, fundamentalism, and the cost-effectiveness of human services are not conducive to educational ideas that run counter to the status quo. Given its history of struggle for legitimacy and acceptance (even in the 1970s when American society and education were more open to innovation), we can expect the 1980s to be unreceptive to multiethnic education.

Therefore, it seems unwise for proponents of ethnic pluralism to squander their energies in advocating multiethnic education as an entity separated from other aspects of education. A more pedagogically plausible and politically expedient strategy is to demonstrate, conceptually and programmatically, that multiethnic education can improve the overall quality of general education. One way to do this is to show how multiethnic education can be infused into all other aspects of education without compromising the integrity of either. This demonstration must convey the message that it is virtually impossible to teach or learn any subject, lead a school or a district, diagnose and assess students' potential and actual performances, and create school and classroom climates conducive to learning without simultaneously teaching, learning, and responding to ethnic pluralism. More attention must be paid to modeling ways to make educational programs ethnically diverse and to providing empirical evidence of the effectiveness of multiethnic education. These efforts represent a major change in strategy for supporters of multiethnic education, much of whose energy has, up to now, been devoted to conceptual clarification.

Another potential threat to multiethnic education comes from within. Although any educational idea must grow and change if it is to stand the test of time, such growth must remain within reasonable boundaries and retain a certain degree of continuity. If many new dimensions are added to an idea too rapidly, the original idea may be distorted beyond recognition. This may be beginning to happen to multiethnic education.

The original aim of multiethnic education was to include information about the lifestyles and the heritages of American ethnic groups in school programs. But this notion has expanded considerably since the late 1960s. Now, discussions of multiethnic or multicultural education frequently include the diversities, dilemmas, and experiences of women, the handicapped, the aged, and the poor. Donna Gollnick and Philip Chinn exemplify this eclectic view of multiethnic/multicultural education. They write:

> Our approach to multicultural education is based on a broad definition of culture. By using *culture* as the basis of understanding multicultural education . . . we focus on the complex nature of pluralism in this country. An individual's cultural identity is based not only on ethnicity but also on such factors as socioeconomic level, religion, and sex. . . .[9]

These issues are legitimate areas of study, and they are clearly intertwined with ethnicity. But including them under the conceptual rubric of multiethnic or multicultural education may tend to divert attention away from ethnicity.

The fact that the initial dimensions of multiethnic education have matured conceptually is also a source of strength. These broader dimensions can make the concept more acceptable to a variety of constituents in a variety of educational circumstances. However, this very growth may cause multiethnic education to become a synonym for "pluralism" in its broadest sense. Should this happen, there may be so many "pluralities" vying for attention in educational programs and policies that ethnic pluralism will be lost in the shuffle. Add to this the tendency of educators to extol any idea that is in vogue or politically expedient to the virtual exclusion of all others, and the threat that these tendencies pose to the authentic survival and further development of multiethnic education is clear. Multiethnic education is definitely not in vogue now, although the need for it is as great in 1983 as it was a decade ago. Supporters must find ways to protect the integrity of multiethnic education. One way to do so is to reaffirm its original intentions and to insist on reasonable demarcations of its conceptual boundaries.

The future of multiethnic education is in some ways more uncertain and challenging than it was when this discipline emerged. One kind of political expediency gave it birth; another, coupled with economic and ideological constraints, threatens its existence. Whereas much of the history of multiethnic education to date has been devoted to its justification and conceptual clarification, its future will require long-range pragmatic planning, practical models for implementing ideas, and demonstrations of its effectiveness (both in terms of student performance and of fiscal expenditures). The major challenges for the future of multiethnic education are to translate theory into practice, to institutionalize the concept, and to provide hard evidence of its efficacy.

---

1. William Ryan, *Blaming the Victim* (New York: Pantheon, 1971), p. 60.
2. William Labov, *The Study of Nonstandard English* (Urbana, Ill.: National Council of Teachers of English, 1970), p. 43.
3. Edward A. Johnson, *A School History of the Negro Race in America from 1619 to 1890* (Chicago: W.B. Conkey, 1891).
4. Juanita Roderick, "Minority Groups in Textbooks," *Improving College and University Teaching*, Spring 1970, pp. 129-32.
5. California State Board of Education, "Task Force to Re-evaluate Social Studies Textbooks, Grades Five Through Eight," mimeographed, December 1971.
6. Jeannette Henry, *Textbooks and the American Indian* (San Francisco: Indian Historian Press, 1970), p. 11.
7. *1978-79 Michigan Social Studies Textbook Study*, Vol. I (Lansing: Michigan State Department of Education, 1980), p. 103.
8. Milton M. Gordon, *Assimilation in American Life: The Role of Race, Religion, and National Origins* (New York: Oxford University Press, 1964).
9. Donna M. Gollnick and Philip C. Chinn, *Multicultural Education in a Pluralistic Society* (St. Louis: C.V. Mosley, 1983), p. viii.

The New Pioneers Of the Home-Schooling Movement

Diane Divoky

DIANE DIVOKY covers California education for the Sacramento Bee.

"Parents have a right to educate their children at home, and this right bears constitutional protection."

That credo comes not from a radical educator or libertarian theorist, but from the Rockland (Massachusetts) School Committee, which last August approved a home-schooling policy that gives school officials the right and responsibility to approve home education programs but provides parents with significant control over the *way* their children will be educated at home. For example, the Rockland policy states that, in line with recent state court rulings, the school committee will not pry into parents' reasons for wanting to educate their children at home. Furthermore, the committee will not worry about "the lack of a curriculum identical to that of the public schools" or the lack of group experiences for home-schooled children.

The Rockland policy, developed by parents and school officials, gives those who wish to educate their children at home clear guidelines under which to apply for program approval. Parents are also afforded the right to a hearing to explain and answer questions about their plan; at this hearing, they may be represented by counsel and call witnesses.

"We believe that people can be educated in places other than schools," explains John Rogers, superintendent of the Rockland schools. "I don't think we have a monopoly on education. Who's to say where children can get a proper education?" The Rockland school district is one of a handful that are known to be friendly to home schoolers; as a result, people who want to school their children at home "are moving into town, knowing they won't be hassled," Rogers says. He adds that the district is willing to provide books and programs for home-schooled children; in fact, he plans to start placing such youngsters on the district rolls, in order to collect state funds for them.

The tiny San Juan Ridge Union School District in Nevada City, California, has had home-schooled youngsters on its rolls for several years. When administrator Marilyn DeVore realized that about a dozen children who lived within the district were being schooled at home, she decided to work with their parents rather than to fight them. Under the arrangement she devised, the students are tested by the district, and DeVore herself supervises the courses of study that the parents propose and teach. "The board approves each individual course of study," she says. So far, the children learning at home are performing very well on district tests.

A subversive activity until a very few years ago, home schooling is quickly becoming a national movement with its own gurus, publications, and support networks. Not many school systems are as cooperative with parents who educate their children at home as Rockland or San Juan Ridge. But few superintendents are unaware of the movement and of parents' reasons for choosing this option, according to Kathleen O'Malley, an attorney with a Harrisburg, Pennsylvania, law firm that handles a sizable number of home-schooling cases. "In some cases, the superintendent will still say, 'If I let you do this, everyone will want to do it,' " O'Malley notes, "but usually superintendents can be educated about the legal rationale for home schooling and are willing to negotiate some sort of compromise."

"The New Pioneers of the Home-Schooling Movement," Diane Divoky, *Phi Delta Kappan*, February 1983. Reprinted by permission.

The home schoolers themselves — estimates put the number at about 10,000 nationally — are coming out of the closet. Ten years ago, such parents would have insisted that their children stay inside the house during school hours, for fear that neighbors would report them to the truant officer. Today, home schoolers are more likely to appear on TV talk shows and to grant interviews to reporters about this educational option. For example, Joyce Kinmont of Brigham City, Utah, who schools her seven children at home, publishes books, makes tapes, and speaks frequently before groups about the advantages of home schooling.

In Grants Pass, Oregon, Jane Joyce writes favorably about home schooling for an area newspaper; she charges that the public schools quash creativity and foster dullness. "Why is education compulsory, if it's so good?" she asks. Joyce, who has been willing to submit her home learning program to the local district for approval and to have her children tested, is no longer certain that she wishes to continue accommodating the system to that degree. She contends that it is her right to educate her children in any way she chooses, and she chafes at the idea that "my papers must be in order and approved so that I can do this." Joyce urges other home schoolers in her area to deal more confidently with school officials. "You can't be Little Miss Muffet," she exhorts. "You don't have to be mealy-mouthed and embarrassed about what you're doing."

Meanwhile, home schoolers in Indiana are going on the legal offensive for the first time. A sudden flurry of prosecutions of home schoolers has arisen in that state, despite a fairly liberal state policy. Parents are responding by joining a suit filed in federal court in February 1982 by a South Bend area family, the Mazanecs, against the North Judson-San Pierre School Corporation. The suit charges that the school district — under cover of the compulsory education laws — has violated the civil rights of the Mazanec family by harassment. The plaintiffs are asking $310,000 in damages for the emotional stress they claim to have suffered because of school officials' actions.

"It's a model case," says Ed Nagel, director of the National Association for the Legal Support of Alternative Schools in Santa Fe, New Mexico, an organization that supports home schoolers. "We're signaling the system that it can't use public money to intimidate parents, to make them live in fear. We're saying to school officials that, if you go after parents, they'll turn around and sue you. It's time the bureaucrats begin to assume responsibility for their vindictive prosecution of parents under vague, ambiguous laws."

Nagel adds that, although parents have a high win rate — somewhere between 90% and 95% — when districts take them to court, "individual wins aren't enough, because in every case parents have to be on the defensive, and it's an expensive and time-consuming business. We're trying to turn that around." He describes home schooling as "a rapidly growing movement that school administrators cannot thwart."

John Holt, best known for his books on education reform and perhaps the preeminent spokesman for home schooling, agrees with Nagel. "These parents are tough, determined, and slippery, with a real pioneer spirit," says Holt, whose bimonthly newsletter, *Growing Without Schooling*, provides support, legal information, ideas, and resources to some 3,600 subscribers.*

"The beauty of the anarchistic structure of the home-schooling movement," according to Holt, "is that it spans quite comfortably a wide range of views," including those of every ideological and political stripe. Both Holt and Nagel come out of the liberal school reform movement; by contrast, Raymond Moore, an educational researcher from Michigan who writes in favor of home schooling and provides expert court testimony for parents, is a conservative — a Seventh-Day Adventist who believes that children should learn religious and moral principles from their parents before being exposed to the secular culture of the schools.

Parents choose home schooling for a number of reasons. For some, the decision springs from personal experiences as teachers or parents who have worked to reform the schools from within. Linda Ashton of Lawton, Oklahoma, says that her years as a third-grade teacher taught her "how much time had to be wasted by virtue of having 30 students" in the classroom. "It was either hurry-up or busywork," Ashton recalls. "I knew that I couldn't give the children the kind of attention they needed. One-on-one makes so much more sense."

An Esparto, California, mother who didn't become involved in home schooling until her youngest child was 12 explains: "Over the years I became more and more disillusioned with the schools. I've raised seven children. I've worked as an aide in the classroom and served on all the committees. I asked questions about accountability and why the schools couldn't teach composition. I watched youngsters pick up more bad habits in school than their parents could counteract. And finally I got wise and realized that the school is not our friend, that those people really don't care about us and our children."

Other home schoolers are simply working for self-sufficiency in a society that they perceive as too technological and too institutionalized. For them, home schooling is an extension of a lifestyle that often includes living on the land and growing their own food. And life in a rural environment — where children necessarily spend more time with their families than with peers — seems unusually compatible with home schooling.

For example, in rural Plumas County, California, the Gorbet children begin the day with three hours of studying under their mother's tutelage; in the afternoon they do outdoor chores around the family ranch and care for their own horses. Accomplished riders, they often win prizes at local and regional horse shows. Similarly, Pat Mattison of Middlebury, Vermont, explains that her home-schooled children are responsible for feeding and watering the family's farm animals. "These are not token chores — but real work that is necessary in order for us to have the life we choose," she points out.

Probably a majority of home schoolers are religious fundamentalists, unhappy with the failure of the public schools to teach religious and spiritual tenets and with what they sometimes describe as the "secular humanism" that these schools allegedly espouse. Gina Gorbet says that the primary reason for schooling her eight children at home is so that "they will absorb the traditional Catholic philosophy," which, she explained, stresses modesty in dress and speech, separation of the sexes, and the importance of proselytizing. Ruth and Peter Nobel of Dorr, Michigan, who gained national publicity in 1980 when a court ruled that they had a constitutional right to educate their children at home, are devout Calvinist Christians who rejected the public schools because of "the immorality, the dress, the attitudes, the speech" that they found there.

Florence Wolf of Brooks, California, who teaches her two children and a nephew at home, complains that in the public schools "there is no right or wrong; values are variable." She also believes that children can pick up dangerous ideas in sex education classes. "As Christians, we're concerned with children's self-worth, their ability — with God's help — to say no when that is required," explains Brit Fillmore of Gridley, California, an Adventist who is schooling her children at home. "Children can be swayed so easily by peer pressure."

In spite of the diverse reasons that draw parents to home schooling, they share a profound belief that the public schools are not providing a healthy environment for their children. They also share a need to have some control over their children's learning and development. And they are all willing to be different, to take a socially unorthodox route to rearing the kind of children they want.

2. CONTINUITY AND CHANGE

On a political level, home schooling is an act both revolutionary and reactionary: revolutionary because it flies in the face of the established social order, reactionary because it means turning one's back on the larger society and on the time-honored assumption that parents and society share in the rearing of the young. On a more practical level, home schooling is a remarkably gutsy effort. Parents must be willing, first of all, to negotiate with, stare down, or hide from school authorities — and to live as outsiders in their own communities. They must also develop enough confidence to be able to ward off doubts about whether they are doing right by their children.

Most difficult of all is the nonstop, year-in, year-out job itself. Even in the rare cases where two parents share the work, it is psychologically and physically demanding. Most often, however, the mother alone becomes the unpaid teacher in uncharted territory. "Home schooling requires enormous personal confidence, enterprise, and tenacity," notes a home schooler in Sacramento, California. "It is not a step taken lightly — or done as a protest or an ego trip." She points out that, if nothing else, most parents are grateful to use the schools as a baby-sitting service. "Because I am both educating and caring for my children, I have no time for myself, no break," she says.

For the majority of families with young children, home schooling is logistically impossible, no matter how attractive the idea seems. The current economy does not allow most parents to remain at home, even when career advancement is not at issue.

Holt likes to think that it is possible to school children at home, even when both parents work. He suggests that children over age 8 "don't need to be baby-sat," that like-minded families can rotate home-schooling responsibilities, that working parents with younger children can send them to homes where older home-schooled children can supervise them, and that older people in the community can be recruited to do the job. These are all interesting ideas — but probably not practical, except in special circumstances.

Nagel suggests that, to avoid the mom-stays-at-home-and-does-it-all routine, an older son or daughter might serve as tutor or a college student might be offered room and board in exchange for tutoring. A number of families might share a tutor, he says, as long as parents keep the arrangement small enough so that it doesn't grow into a school, with all the same problems that the families are trying to avoid.

The hardest part of the job for many home schoolers appears to be getting started, given their preconceived notions about how children learn. Kinmont warns interested parents that they probably won't do a very good job the first year, as they work to overcome their ingrained sense of what school is all about. She advises parents to give themselves at least a year to try out home schooling before abandoning the idea. Angel Eberlein of Brooks, California, says that, when she began schooling her two children at home, she hired a teacher to check on their progress periodically; as she grew more confident, she no longer needed that backup, however. "Common sense and dedication are the main ingredients needed to teach one's own children," according to Eberlein. "When I started out, I didn't have any of the confidence I have now," Gorbet concurs. "But slowly I learned my strengths and where I was weak, where I needed to call for some help."

Many parents said that the shakiness of the first few months was replaced by confidence, as they saw their children thriving. A number, whose children had attended public schools before beginning home schooling, also noted that the youngsters had needed some time to shed bad habits and to regain a sense of self-direction.

"We had a specific curriculum for the first three or four months when we started this," says Francis Turano of Somerset, Massachusetts, whose daughters — now 12 and 14 — have been schooled at home since 1978. "But then we found we didn't need it, so now we just use it as a reference or guide. At first, when we took them out of public school, they seemed to have lost the ability to think and learn on their own — their zest and curiosity. They had lost the natural instinct to learn. Then, after a period of time, it was like: 'Look out, here we come.' They're studying more now, on their own, because they want to. My wife (who was a public school teacher for seven years) and I just oversee their studying now. We assist them, but they're pretty much on their own."

The goal, many veteran home schoolers suggest, is to be able to get out of the way of children's learning, to simply provide an environment that allows youngsters to be self-directed. "We leave Krista pretty much on her own," says Karen Elder of Princeton, New Jersey, of her 7-year-old, who is schooled at home. "We have a lot of books, some textbooks (which are the least used, because they are the least interesting), lots of paper, various machines (typewriter, calculator, TV, tape recorder, stereo, electronic games, and a borrowed minicomputer), sports equipment, small animals, and ourselves and our work."

Holt recommends a free-flow curriculum for home-schooled children, which exposes them to as many community resources as possible. "Let the interests and the inclinations of the children determine what happens, and give children access to as much of the parents' lives and the world around them as possible," he advises, adding that three to five hours of formal instruction per week is "perfectly sufficient."

However, the popularity of such highly structured correspondence courses as the Calvert Home Instruction Courses and the Christian Liberty Academy program suggests that many parents need a crutch for their home schooling. These programs provide for a structured morning or afternoon of study each day. They also give parents some feedback about their children's progress by evaluating their work, scoring their tests, and reporting back with grades.

Many programs — and many experienced home schoolers — urge parents to spend their time working side by side with their children, integrating skill development with such tasks as cooking, shopping, planning menus, gardening, and doing carpentry and repairs. Home schoolers who wish their children to have time to socialize with their peers are also advised to sign them up for such out-of-school activities as Scouts, sports teams, church groups, hobby clubs, and community classes.

In spite of the growth of the home-schooling movement, there is still little consistency among the school districts in a given state — much less from state to state — regarding the acceptability of home schooling. "Often, it's up to the individual superintendent's interpretation of state law, his particular bias," says attorney Kathleen O'Malley. "In Pennsylvania, for example, the state department of education has never decided whether correspondence courses fulfill the compulsory education law. So you have superintendents who are suspicious of home schoolers, and others who will wink at home schooling."

Turano, a police officer, notes that his home state, Massachusetts, "has districts that are both the toughest and the most lenient" with home schoolers. "Each system here has its own idea of how much it can invade the privacy of families," he says.

In general, California is benign in dealing with home schoolers — requiring only that they file an affidavit each fall that registers them as private schools. However, the largest school district, Los Angeles, interprets the law strictly and does not allow home schoolers to register as private schools, even if the parents hold proper credentials for teaching the grades in which their children are enrolled. "We consider any home-teaching situation a tutoring situation; we require that the teacher have the proper credentials — and, in any case, the teacher cannot be the parent," says Kathleen Smith, a district official. To enforce that policy, any school with fewer than six or seven students is investigated, and parents who persist in home teaching are turned over to the city attorney.

At about the same time that the highest court in West Virginia tightened the home-schooling policy in that state, denying that parents have a religious right to teach their children at home without the approval of the local school board, the Arizona legislature passed a law allowing parents to teach their children at home without the permission of the local school board — a major victory for home schoolers in that state.

Amid the patchwork of court decisions and regulations, parents use a number of ploys to avoid legal controversy. Some enroll their children in private schools that are willing to serve as fronts for home-schooling families. Such "shelter schools" often provide materials and lesson guides or testing services for parents; some actually allow home-schooled children to attend one day or so each week. Other parents do what is legally required in a particular district or state to meet compulsory education laws: hire a certified teacher as a tutor, become certified teachers themselves, or write curricula for their children and submit them to the district for approval.

Michelle Carnevale of Grass Valley, California, who is educating her daughter at home, thinks that most problems with school officials can be avoided if children are kept out of school from the beginning, so that their absence is never noticed. Other parents simply tell a district that they are moving elsewhere when they begin home schooling. Even these tactics may not be discreet enough, particularly in urban areas. Raymond Moore maintains that three-fourths of the children who are pursued by school districts come to the attention of school officials because neighbors report them.

Given the diminishing financial resources of the schools, engaging the parents of each home-schooled child in a protracted legal battle seems a ludicrous and ultimately self-defeating task for school districts. By contrast, a cooperative arrangement between a district and home schoolers — one that allows parents to use district resources, while the district continues to receive state funds for each child — may satisfy the needs of both parties. "It's such a sensible arrangement," says Holt. "There's nothing in the laws that says that attendance has to mean that bodies are in certain classrooms all day, that districts should be prevented from collecting aid if students are schooled at home."

"The legal decisions are going against the system anyway," echoes Nagel. "So if districts want to hold on to their average daily attendance, why don't they make materials and resources available to these parents in exchange for enrollment? How much more sense it makes to set up an educational center for the use of home schoolers and others, instead of spending that money fighting them. The superintendents can't stop the movement anyway, so why not work with it?"

The Struggle for Excellence: Striving for Higher Achievement

We are presently witnessing a new search for excellence in education. The struggle is an old one, but the latest form it has taken has been sparked by a recent presidential commission report. Several reports have also been issued by private foundations calling for renewed emphasis on the quality of achievement in the field of education. The teachers of teachers, the elementary and secondary school teachers of the nation, and the whole question of the quality of schooling in the United States have again been the subjects of severe criticism. The President's National Commission on Excellence in Education has made far reaching recommendations for the improvement of the quality of learning in American schools. The various private foundation reports suggest a basic refocusing of our national priorities.

The articles in this section focus on the debate which has been generated by these reports and by increasing concern on the part of many citizens over the quality of schooling in America. All across the nation, thousands of local school districts have been implementing new forms of educational programming and new methods and criteria for the evaluation of the learning achievement of students. Teachers are under increasing pressure to improve the quality of instruction. Local boards of education are involved in critical re-examination of the quality of school programs at the local level.

In a period of hard economic times for local and state public school systems, they are being asked to strive for excellence above all else. This struggle will test the courage, commitment, and resourcefulness of the nation's educational system. The struggle for quality in the field of education may become a major national issue in the mid- and late 1980s.

Looking Ahead: Challenge Questions

What economic, political, and ideological forces seem to have sparked this new drive for excellence in American education?

What are your reactions to the recommended changes proposed to improve the quality of schooling in America?

Where do we seem to be headed as a nation in the struggle for excellence?

What can we do to improve the quality of the conditions for teaching and learning in the United States?

What caused the educational climate in the United States that has led to greater demands for excellence in the field of education?

What counter forces may inhibit or prevent the success of our efforts to achieve excellence in the conduct of schooling?

What would you list as the defining criteria of excellence?

Are American schools better or worse than schools in other nations? Explain. Why is it difficult to compare different nations' educational systems?

Where do we go from here? What can we do to improve the quality of schooling?

The Debate About Standards

Where Do We Go From Here?

Diane Ravitch

Diane Ravitch is associate professor of history and education at Teachers College, Columbia University, New York City, and author of The Great School Wars: New York City, 1805-1973 *and* The Revisionist Revised: A Critique of the Radical Attack on the Schools.

EDUCATORS HAVE argued the issue of standards during most of the twentieth century. Traditionally, the discussion of standards focused on the secondary schools, particularly on the nature of the curriculum, on requirements, and on the use of grades and promotion policy. Recently, as concern about the number of nonreaders in secondary schools has grown, districts across the country have begun to apply standards like promotional "gates" and have introduced minimum competency tests in the elementary grades. For the moment, at least, standards are "in," and it is important to understand why this has happened and the context in which the debate takes place.

In theory, everyone is in favor of good education, but people differ about what is good and even what is education. The historic debate about standards in secondary schools well illustrates the competing ideas that have brought us to the current situation. A good starting point for understanding the present is the 1893 report of the Committee of Ten, which prescribed what the ideal high school curriculum should be. According to the Committee, which included several university presidents and the U.S. Commissioner of Education, all high school students were to receive a liberal education—composed of subjects like history, English, mathematics, foreign language, and science—whether they intended to go on to college or not. In the years following this report, course enrollments in these subjects were high.

In 1918, however, the report of the Committee of Ten was superceded by a document called "The Cardinal Principles of Secondary Education," which asserted that the chief objectives of high school were functional goals like health, vocation, worthy use of leisure time, character, citizenship, worthy home membership, and—almost incidentally—"command of fundamental processes." The "Cardinal Principles" was undoubtedly the single most influential document ever issued by a group of educators. (In contrast to the university-oriented Committee of Ten, the authors of the "Cardinal Principles" were mostly school superintendents and professors of education.) Over the next three decades, under steady pressure from various arms of the National Education Association to accept the "Cardinal Principles" as the goals of secondary schooling, states and school districts reduced graduation requirements and sought to deemphasize subject matter. As educators interpreted their mission to be one of keeping all children in school for as long as possible, the practice of "social promotion" became commonplace. Anything that might have diluted the "holding power" of the school, such as failing marks or difficult course requirements, was to be avoided. It became an accepted principle among educational theorists that only those who intended to go to college should take such courses as chemistry, algebra, physics, and foreign language. As the number of "life-adjustment" courses grew—that is, courses devoted to family relations and to students' personal social problems—educators all too rarely questioned the value of the schooling that they were providing to ever-increasing numbers of students.

Revulsion against these trends led to a great debate about standards in the early and middle 1950s. Critics like Arthur Bestor, Robert Hutchins, and Mortimer Smith accused the schools of debasing educational standards and distorting the purpose of schooling to narrow, utilitarian ends. Defenders of the movement

This article first appeared in the Fall 1981 issue of the *AMERICAN EDUCATOR*, the quarterly journal of the American Federation of Teachers.

away from academic studies responded by saying that the critics advocated a return to narrow, aristocratic schools, which would exclude or fail to interest the great mass of students. On one side were the critics who claimed that a truly democratic education would offer the same intellectual stimulation to all children, not just to the college bound; on the other were those who argued that a truly democratic education offered each child the education best suited to his needs, interests, and abilities. Echoes of this heated debate have been heard in recent years, as one side characteristically identifies its views with "quality," while the other takes "relevance" and "meeting the needs of children" as its banner.

THE LATEST round of controversy over standards has come about as a result of a growing perception that there have been substantial declines in educational achievement, which reflect real deterioration in the ability of Americans to read and write thoughtfully. These are consequences, it is believed, of the trend in schools and colleges to promote students without regard to competence and to set low demands in terms of student effort. Undoubtedly, the most important spur to this perception has been the steady drop in college admission scores, notably on the Educational Testing Service's Scholastic Aptitude Test (SAT). Median verbal scores, which reached a peak of 478 in 1963, fell to a new low of 424 in 1980; in the same period, mathematical scores fell from 502 to 466. Girls' scores on both tests fell more sharply than those of boys. At first, the score drops were attributed to the expansion in the mid-1960s of the pool of test-takers to include more minorities, females, and low-income students, but even after the pool itself became relatively stable in 1970, scores continued to fall. What has been even more striking than the fall of the average for all test-takers has been the shrinkage in the number of high-scoring students. The number of seniors who scored over 650 (in a range from 200 to 800) fell from 53,800 (5.3 percent) in 1972 to 29,000 in 1980 (2.9 percent). The diminution of the number of top-scoring students cannot be attributed to the overall composition of the test-takers.

If the SAT scores were the only test scores that had fallen, then one might well wonder whether the test was somehow defective, as some have charged. But those who have analyzed other major standardized tests have observed the same pattern: rising achievement levels until the mid-1960s, then a steady decline, which grew more pronounced as students reached higher grades and which was most noticeable in verbal areas. Annegret Harnischfeger and David E. Wiley, in their examination of the score declines, noted that there was a striking parallel with enrollment declines in traditional subjects. They observed that fewer students were taking regular English, American history, mathematics, and science courses. Increasing numbers of students, it seemed, were taking nonacademic courses, off-beat options, or work-study programs.

The blue-ribbon panel appointed by the College Board to analyze the score decline found it impossible to isolate a single cause and noted the possible influence of such things as the decline of the family; the Vietnam War; television; drugs; sex-role stereotyping; and even the fallout from atomic bomb testing. Yet, although the panel was evidently reluctant to attach primary responsibility for declining academic performance to school policies, it nonetheless noted that "there have unquestionably been changes over the past ten to fifteen years in the standards to which students at all levels of education are held. Absenteeism, formerly considered intolerable, is now condoned. An 'A' or 'B' means a good deal less than it used to. Promotion from one grade to another has become almost automatic. Homework has apparently been cut about in half." The report observed ruefully that "less thoughtful and critical reading is now being demanded and done" and that "careful writing has apparently about gone out of style."

Now, there is a logical principle known as "Occam's Razor," which means that one doesn't look for a complicated answer when a simple answer is sufficient. Why, one might reasonably ask, is it necessary to seek grand sociological and political explanations of declining academic performance when obvious reasons are at hand? If, as the panel suggests, standards of performance have fallen, if critical reading and careful writing are endangered species, if grade inflation is widespread, and if homework is out of style, are these not sufficient explanations for declining verbal skills?

The belief that particular school policies contribute directly to diminished academic performance, as well as to a climate that undercuts the schools' seriousness of purpose, has provoked the most recent criticisms of the schools and has led to demands for higher standards of performance. Although many teachers will admit privately that the climate of schooling has deteriorated since the mid-1960s and that many able but demoralized colleagues retired early, nonetheless, most teachers understandably resent yet another round of recriminations directed at the schools, yet another season of scapegoating by critics whose forerunners saddled the schools with many of the reforms, theories, and gimmicks that have contributed to the present situation.

It would be a mistake, however, to view the present calls for change as an attack on teachers; instead, they should be understood as an attack on the conditions that undermine teaching. There is a growing and significant body of research that establishes beyond doubt that at the heart of good education is the well-prepared, purposeful teacher. What is particularly worth noting is that recent research, such as Michael Rutter's *Fifteen Thousand Hours: Secondary Schools and Their Effects on Children,* N.L. Gage's *The Scientific Basis of the Art of Teaching*, and James Coleman's *Public and Private Schools*, effectively rebuts the destructive notion that "schools don't make a difference," which was certainly the most demoralizing doctrine of the past fifteen years. This conclusion flowed from the findings of the famous *Equal Educational Opportunity Survey* (known as the Coleman

Report) of 1966; *EEOS* held that "schools are remarkably similar in the effect they have on the achievement of their pupils when the socioeconomic background of the students is taken into account" and that variations in the facilities and curricula of schools "account for relatively little variation in pupil achievement." This was taken to mean that, when compared to the influence of family background, there was little that schools could do to affect student achievement. Subsequent writings, such as Christopher Jencks's widely discussed *Inequality: A Reassessment of the Effect of Family and Schooling in America* and the publications of the heavily subsidized Carnegie Council on Children, reiterated the now-familiar themes that schools were ineffectual instruments of social policy and that schools could make little or no contribution to social progress. Small wonder in the face of such disparaging claims that men and women with a desire to make a difference, to play some useful role in their professional lives, were discouraged from entering teaching or from staying in the profession.

The gist of the new research, which is becoming increasingly convergent, is that schools *do* make a substantial difference in children's lives and that there are important differences between schools, even when children of similar backgrounds attend them. *Fifteen Thousand Hours*, a report by a British research team led by Michael Rutter, found that high schools differed significantly in terms of pupil behavior (in school and out of school), attendance rates, and achievement scores, even when students' family background was matched. Rutter found that each school had an "ethos," or climate, with its own norms, values, and expectations. In good schools, the staff shared high expectations for student behavior and academic performance and understood that teachers served as role models. Rutter observed that the best results were obtained when the teacher was well prepared and was a good manager of classroom time.

In *The Scientific Basis of the Art of Teaching*, N.L. Gage summarized the research on teaching in the early grades to see whether there was any relationship between teaching style and what pupils learn. In study after study, the children showed the greatest educational growth in terms of higher cognitive achievement, lower levels of anxiety, and even enhanced creativity in classes that were traditional and structured rather than in classes that were "open," innovative, and informal. As Jerome Bruner wrote in the introduction to one of the comparative studies of teaching style, "The more formal the teaching, the more time the pupils spend working on the subject matter at hand. And in general...the more time pupils spend working on a subject, the more they improve at it...." What Gage found is what many other researchers have confirmed: the importance of time-on-task, which is to say that there is a relationship between the amount of time spent learning and what is learned. It may sound like a rediscovery of the wheel, but given the history of the past fifteen years in education, the wheel—which, in this case, would be the importance of direct instruction by a skilled teacher—needs to be rediscovered.

Coleman's study, *Public and Private Schools*, has attracted attention largely because of its conclusion that private high schools are on the whole better than public high schools. Yet, what is most significant about the study is that it represents a dramatic refutation of the earlier Coleman Report that found little variation between schools after pupils' family background was taken into account. In the 1981 Coleman Report, the overriding fact is that school policies have a significant effect on student achievement and student behavior. Good secondary schools, Coleman shows, have high academic expectations, high enrollments in academic courses, and a disciplinary climate that is respected by students as fair and effective. Coleman holds that private high schools are on the whole more effective because they "create higher rates of engagement in academic activities...school attendance is better, students do more homework, and students generally take more rigorous subjects." In public high schools, only 34 percent of students are in an academic curriculum, compared to 70 percent of those in private high schools. Students in public high schools do less homework yet get higher grades than do their counterparts in private schools or their public school predecessors of 1972. Only 25 percent of public school sophomores spend more than an hour each school night on homework, compared to close to 50 percent of private school sophomores. The findings on enrollments in advanced courses show that in every area, whether science, mathematics, or foreign languages, public school students are enrolling at substantially lower rates than their counterparts in the private sector.

The new Coleman Report reveals some of the consequences of those policies adopted by school boards and administrators that have disintegrated the common curriculum, lowered course requirements, and reduced academic standards. It also criticizes the intrusion of courts and governmental agencies into the ability of public schools to discipline disruptive students. In any discussion of the revival of standards, Coleman's findings offer documentation of the view that students perform best when the school expects them to work hard and to take seriously their responsibilities as students.

FOR MANY people, these studies will offer little more than confirmation of common sense about educational practice. Children learn best when teachers are productive and purposeful and when instructional time is well prepared and well used; students achieve most when the expectations of the school are consistent and high; schools function best when they create a climate based on shared values, norms, and expectations with regard to student performance, both academic and personal.

The key word in all of this is "expectations." Pupils respond to teachers' expectations, and constant reinforcement of high expectations can contribute to good behavior and to increased academic effort. Another word for expectations is standards. By our standards, we tell others what we expect them to accomplish, we define what we consider to be excellent, good, fair, or unacceptable. Some current practices, which have become widespread in recent years, communicate low expectations and low standards. These include:

- grade inflation, which means that students get high marks for mediocre work and that those who might work harder if expectations were higher are robbed of incentive;
- the decline of enrollments in courses in foreign language, science, and mathematics, which follows, in most cases, the abandonment of requirements by the school district or the state and which tells students that the school does not expect them to work at challenging tasks, either because they presumably lack the ability or because their occupational futures are too constricted to need knowledge of basic disciplines;
- the proliferation of insubstantial courses that students may take in place of demanding courses, which tells students that the school makes no distinction between, for example, an inspired course in chemistry and a fluffy course in astrology;
- the reduction in the amount of homework, which, besides extending the amount of time-on-task, also, in Rutter's words, is "of symbolic importance in emphasizing the school's concern for academic progress and its expectation that pupils have the ability and self-discipline needed to work without direct supervision"; and
- the apparent decline within the context of courses like English, history, and social studies of systematic writing instruction of the sort that involves thinking through a topic, preparing multiple drafts, receiving written and oral comments from the teacher, and revising papers after the teacher returns them.

If we are serious about renewing the promise of American schools, we will have to begin to think seriously again about the nature of the curriculum, about the consequences of abandoning requirements, and about how to prepare children and young people to live in a world in which they will need to know a great deal about language, history, politics, economics, science, mathematics, music, art, and technology. We will have to be sensitive to all of their needs but set priorities among them in terms of what schools know how to accomplish. We will have to convey to them through our attitudes that their education will be their most important resource in the years to come and that we care enough about them not to give them a cheapened, fraudulent version of the real thing. We will have to exemplify through our behavior the expectation that there is a difference between good work and poor work and that each of us, teachers and students alike, can strive to improve our past efforts. The basic premise of education is the belief in the possibility of learning and improvement. Without a clear sense of what is to be learned, good teaching cannot go forward. Without a clear sense of standards, improvement cannot take place.

When educators believe that schools do not make a difference, then it really doesn't matter what courses students take or how much effort they expend. But when it is acknowledged that the schools are institutions in which young people learn to use their intelligence and develop their abilities to the fullest, then it becomes clear once again that schools must carefully, thoughtfully, and purposefully plan both the content and the process of education.

A Nation at Risk: The Report of the National Commission On Excellence in Education

Milton Goldberg and James Harvey

MILTON GOLDBERG, former acting director of the National Institute of Education, is executive director of the National Commission on Excellence in Education. JAMES HARVEY is a senior research associate with the Commission.

TWO HUNDRED leaders of U.S. education, industry, and government gathered in the White House on April 26 to watch the ceremonial presentation to President Reagan of the report of the National Commission on Excellence in Education. Nearly five months later, the tumultuous reception of the report by the press and the public has yet to subside.

Such magazines as *Time, Newsweek*, and *U.S. News & World Report* have provided detailed coverage of the report, which has also been the focus of extensive discussions on several network television programs, among them "The McNeil-Lehrer Report," "Good Morning America," and "Nightline." Prompted by this publicity, the public demand for the Commission's report has been astonishing. The Government Printing Office, besieged by requests for the report, is now into the fourth printing; at least 200,000 copies of the text have been printed separately by various education publications, and an estimated three million readers have had access to shortened versions of the report in such newspapers as the *Portland Oregonian*, the *Washington Post*, and the *New York Times*.

The public's response suggests that Secretary of Education Terrel Bell, who created the Commission in 1981, is correct in hailing the report as a possible "turning point" in an era when U.S. schools face "the challenge of the postindustrial age." Bell also vowed not to allow the report "to be remembered as the warning our Nation failed to heed."

If the public response to the report has been remarkable, so are the activities already under way in response to it. The Pennsylvania State Board of Education recently announced its intention to adopt new high school graduation requirements that will triple the amount of science and mathematics required for graduation and that will add computer science as a diploma requirement. Within weeks of the release of the report, the school board in Ypsilanti, Michigan, announced its intention to lengthen the school day for elementary students and to increase high school graduation requirements. The Tulsa, Oklahoma, superintendent published an extensive "Open Letter to the People of Tulsa," outlining the standing of schools in that city with respect to the National Commission's recommendations.

Not since the heady days following the launching of Sputnik I has U.S. education been accorded so much attention. Although the Commission released its report almost five months ago, major U.S. newspapers and network television programs continue to focus on the problems of education. President Reagan has already discussed the report at several regional forums, with other such forums scheduled for early fall. Individual members of the Commission and of the Commission staff continue to be deluged with requests to address meetings and convocations across the nation. Meanwhile, other prestigious individuals and panels have added their voices to the rising chorus of concern about the quality of U.S. schools; these include the Twentieth Century Fund, the College Board, and the Task Force on Education and Economic Growth (chaired by Gov. James Hunt of North Carolina).

The unprecedented attention now being paid to education is evidence of public concern. But this attention also provides – as the president of the American Federation of Teachers, Albert Shanker, pointed out to his constituents in early July – "unprecedented opportunities" for education in the coming months.

The Imperative for Reform

What has generated all this fuss? The answer is: a deceptively short report to the nation, in which a panel of distinguished Americans warns that the "educational foundations of our society are presently being eroded by a rising tide of mediocrity that threatens our very future as a Nation and a people." Titled *A Nation at Risk: The Imperative for Educational Reform*, this report has sparked a national debate on education that could prove to be seminal to the development of an ethic of excellence in education and in American life.

Commission Aims and Process

That debate was quite consciously sought by members of the Commission, under the leadership of David Gardner, then president of the University of Utah, who has recently assumed the presidency of the University of California. It was Gardner's idea that the report be in the form of an open letter that would, in the words of Commission member Gerald Holton, serve as a "clarion call" to the American public. The call was intended to remind Americans of the importance of education as the foundation of U.S. leadership in change and technical invention and as the source of U.S. prosperity, security, and civility.

The National Commission conducted its work and collected its information in an extraordinarily open manner, which also helped to encourage public response to *A Nation at Risk*. Practically everywhere one turned in the last two years, there was evidence of the Commission at work. Six public hearings and three symposia were held across the U.S., so that administrators, teachers, parents, and others could discuss their perceptions of the problems and accomplishments of American education. Forty papers were commissioned from a variety of experts and presented to the full Commission.

In virtually every city in which the Commission held a meeting or a hearing, the Commission members also visited local schools and corporate training facilities. It has been estimated that, during the 18 months between the first Commission meeting and the release of *A Nation at Risk*, Commission members were involved in a public event somewhere in the U.S. every three weeks. All of this highly visible activity created a national audience for the Commission's work; indeed, we knew several months before the report was issued that the response to it was likely to be unprecedented in education.

The Commission also examined the methods that other distinguished national panels had used to generate public and governmental reactions to their findings. The commissioners learned that the effective reports concentrated on essential messages, described them in clear and unmistakable prose, and drew the public's attention to the national consequences of continuing on with business as usual.

Essential Messages

The first essential message from the National Commission on Excellence in Education is found in the title of the report: the nation is at risk. It is at risk because competitors throughout the world are overtaking our once unchallenged lead in commerce, industry, science, and technological innovation. As the Commission observed, the problem has many causes and dimensions; education is only one of them. But education is the primary factor undergirding our "prosperity, security, and civility."

The Commission is not the first national body to draw attention to the central importance of education to our national well-being. Indeed, in 1980 the President's Commission for a National Agenda for the Eighties reported that "the continued failure of the schools to perform their traditional role adequately . . . may have disastrous consequences for this Nation."

Just as assuredly, the Commission is not the last national body to draw attention to the central importance of education. One week after the release of *A Nation at Risk*, the Twentieth Century Fund Task Force called U.S. schools "the Nation's most important institution for the shaping of future citizens" and warned that "threatened disaster can be averted only if there is a national commitment to excellence in our public schools."

But the Commission may be the first national body to insist — as the essential first premise, not simply as an afterthought — that inattention to the schools puts the very well-being of the Nation at risk.

The second essential message from the Commission is that mediocrity, not excellence, is the norm in American education. *A Nation at Risk* paid tribute to "heroic" examples of educational excellence, but it made clear the fact that, on balance, "a rising tide of mediocrity" threatens to overwhelm the educational foundations of American society. And the consequences of that tide are staggering.

- On 19 international assessments of student achievement, U.S. students never ranked first or second; in fact, when compared only with students from other industrialized nations, U.S. students ranked in last place seven times.
- Some 23 million American adults are functionally illiterate.
- About 13% of U.S. teenagers (and up to 40% of minority adolescents) are functionally illiterate.
- From 1963 to 1980 a virtually unbroken decline took place in average scores on the Scholastic Aptitude Test (SAT).
- Similarly, a dramatic decline took place in the number of students who demonstrate superior achievement on the SAT.
- Between 1975 and 1980 the number of remedial mathematics courses offered in four-year public colleges increased by 72%.
- Only about one-fourth of the recent recruits to the Armed Services were able to read at the ninth-grade level, the minimum necessary to follow safety instructions.

The third essential message from the Commission is that we don't have to put up with this situation. We *can* do better, we *should* do better, and we *must* do better.

That message is found most clearly in a section of the report titled "America Can Do It." This section cites the remarkable successes of the American educational system in responding to past challenges as justification for the Commission's optimism that we can meet the current challenges. The past successes of U.S. education have included:

- the research and training provided by land-grant colleges and universities in the 19th century, which helped us develop our natural resources and the rich agricultural bounty of the American farm;
- the educated workforce that U.S. schools provided from the late 1800s through the mid-20th century, which sealed the success of the Industrial Revolution and provided the margin of victory in two world wars; and
- the schools' role to this very day in transforming vast waves of immigrants into productive citizens.

The message that "America Can Do It" also appears in the letter from Gardner that accompanied the formal submission of the Commission report to Bell. Said Gardner: "The Commission deeply believes that the problems we have discerned in American education can be both understood and corrected if the people of our country, together with those who have public responsibility in the matter, care enough and are courageous enough to do what is required."

The message can be found as well in the first paragraph of the report, which notes that Americans can take "justifiable pride in what our schools and colleges have historically accomplished and contributed to the United States and the well-being of its people." But the Commission's optimism is perhaps most apparent in the recommendations it sets forth in *A Nation at Risk*. These recommendations provide more than a prescription for improving American schooling; they also provide a framework within which parents and educators across the U.S. can consider their own unique situations and then determine for themselves how best to proceed. The elements of this framework — the amount of time devoted to learning, the content to which students are exposed, the expectations we hold for ourselves and our children, the teaching, and the leadership – constitute, in the final analysis, the tools that local districts can use to improve the processes of education.

Recommendations

The Commission made five broad recommendations, each with several implementing recommendations.

Content

The recommendations regarding content were grounded in the Commission's conclusion that secondary school curricula have been homogenized, diluted, and diffused to such an extent that they no longer have a central purpose. According to *A Nation at Risk*, today's U.S. high schools offer "a cafeteria-style curriculum in which the appetizers and the desserts can easily be mistaken for the main courses."

The Commission recommended that all students seeking a high school diploma be required to lay a foundation in "five new basics" by taking four years of English, three years of mathematics, three years of science, three years of social studies, and one-half year of computer science. Several implementing recommendations suggested the kinds of skills that high school graduates should possess in each of these areas. The implementing recommendations also stressed the desirability of proficiency in a foreign language and stated that the teaching of foreign languages should begin in the elementary grades. In addition, the Commission recommended that the schools offer rigorous coursework in the fine and performing arts and in vocational education; that the elementary curriculum be improved and upgraded; and that such groups as the American Chemical Society and the Modern Language Association continue their efforts to revise, update, improve, and make available new and more diverse curricular materials.

Standards and Expectations

The Commission concluded that we expect far too little of our students and that we get, by and large, exactly what we expect. Evidence of our low expectations is widespread. For example:

- the schools are requiring less and less homework of students;
- two-thirds of the states require only one year of mathematics and one year of science for a high school diploma;
- one-fifth of the four-year public colleges and universities offer open admissions to all graduates of high schools in the state, regardless of the courses they have taken or the grades they have earned; and
- many U.S. colleges and universities reported lowering their admissions requirements during the 1970s.

The Commission recommended that high schools, colleges, and universities adopt more rigorous and measurable standards and higher expectations, both for academic performance and for student conduct, and that four-year colleges and universities raise their requirements for admission. The implementing recommendations focused on improving the reliability of high school grades as indicators of academic achievement, on raising college and university admissions requirements (including the scores required on standardized achievement tests in the five basics), on establishing a nationwide – but not federal – program of achievement testing for students who are passing from one level of schooling to another, on upgrading textbooks, and on the need for new instructional materials that reflect the most current applications of technology.

Time

The members of the National Commission were struck by the fact that many other industrialized nations have much longer school days and far longer school years than does the United States. Because the level of mastery of curriculum content is directly related to the amount of time that students devote to learning, the Commission made a number of recommendations designed to use available time more effectively and to prompt consideration of extending the amount of time available for learning.

The Commission recommended that significantly more time be devoted to learning the "five new basics." This will require more effective use of the existing school day, a longer school day, or a lengthened school year. The implementing recommendations included more homework, the provision of instruction in study and work skills, consideration of a seven-hour school day and of a 200- to 220-day school year, the reduction of disruption, the improvement of classroom management, and stronger policies on school attendance.

Teaching

The Commission concluded that too few academically able students are attracted to teaching; that teacher preparation programs need substantial improvement; that the professional working life of teachers is, on the whole, unacceptable; and that a serious shortage of teachers exists in key fields. The recommendation on teaching has seven parts, quoted here in full:

1. Persons preparing to teach should be required to meet high educational standards, to demonstrate an aptitude for teaching, and to demonstrate competence in an academic discipline. Colleges and universities offering teacher preparation programs should be judged by how well their graduates meet these criteria.
2. Salaries for the teaching profession should be increased and should be professionally competitive, market-sensitive, and performance-based. Salary, promotion, tenure, and retention decisions should be tied to an effective evaluation system that includes peer review so that superior teachers can be rewarded, average ones encouraged, and poor ones either improved or terminated.
3. School boards should adopt an 11-month contract for teachers. This would ensure time for curriculum and professional development, programs for students with special needs, and a more adequate level of teacher compensation.
4. School boards, administrators, and teachers should cooperate to develop career ladders for teachers that distinguish among the beginning instructor, the experienced teacher, and the master teacher.
5. Substantial nonschool personnel resources should be employed to help solve the immediate problem of the shortage of mathematics and science teachers. Qualified individuals, including recent graduates with mathematics and science degrees, graduate students, and industrial and retired scientists, could, with appropriate preparation, immediately begin teaching in these fields. A number of our leading science centers have the capacity to begin educating and retraining teachers immediately. Other areas of critical teacher need, such as English, must also be addressed.
6. Incentives, such as grants and loans, should be made available to attract outstanding students to the teaching profession, particularly in those areas of critical shortage.
7. Master teachers should be involved in designing teacher preparation programs and in supervising teachers during their probationary years.

Leadership and Fiscal Support

Finally, the Commission recommended that citizens across the U.S. hold educators and elected officials responsible for providing the leadership necessary to achieve these reforms – and that citizens provide the fiscal support and stability required to bring about the reforms. The implementing recommendations in this area concentrated on the leadership roles of principals and superintendents; on the roles of local, state, and federal governments; and on the need for educators, parents, and public officials to assist in implementing the reforms proposed by the Commission. This section of *A Nation at Risk* concluded with these words: "Excellence costs. But in the long run mediocrity costs far more."

Other Issues

Although the overall response to the Commission's report is gratifying, several of us associated with the report have been disappointed at the scant attention paid to several major themes.

Learning Society

For example, the press has frequently misinterpreted *A Nation at Risk* as an attack on education and educators. Far from it. The report stands instead as an eloquent reaffirmation of education as a key element undergirding our society. Indeed, in light of new developments in computers, miniaturization, robotics, lasers, and other technologies, the report calls for the development of a learning society. The Commission states that:

> At the heart of such a society is the commitment to a set of values and to a system of education that affords all members the opportunity to stretch their minds to full capacity, from early childhood through adulthood, learning more as the world itself changes. . . . In our view, formal schooling in youth is the essential foundation for learning throughout one's life. But without lifelong learning, one's skills will become rapidly dated.

Excellence

In similar fashion, little comment has been forthcoming about the Commission's careful definition of "excellence" in education, particularly the Commission's view of excellent individual performance. For the individual, the Commission defined excellence as performing on the boundary of individual ability in ways that test and stretch personal limits, both in school and in the workplace.

Implicit in this definition is the notion that each of us can attain individual excellence – although the boundaries that each of us tests and extends will clearly differ. This concept of excellence prompted the Commission to state that "our goal must be to develop the talents of all to their fullest." It also led the Commission to insist that the pursuit of excellence and the pursuit of equity are not incompatible educational goals and that we cannot permit one to yield to the other "either in principle or in practice."

Public Commitment

There has also been little attention given to the Commission's stand that, of all the tools at hand for improving education, "the public's support . . . is the most powerful." On the contrary, when informed of the report's findings and its recommendations, many educators and legislators have asked how these suggested reforms can possibly be funded. In the eyes of many of the commissioners, this response puts the cart before the horse. As one of them said, "If education demonstrates that it is willing to put its house in order, then the public will respond with increased support." As justification for this belief, the Commission cites results of national polls that indicate the public's steadfast regard for education as a major foundation of the nation's strength, the public's conviction that education is important to individual success, and the public's support for rigorous curricular offerings.

But it was toward another facet of the public's support for education that the Commission turned in seeking constructive reform:

> The best term to characterize [this facet] may simply be the honorable word "patriotism." Citizens know intuitively what some of the best economists have shown in their research: that education is one of the chief engines of a society's material well-being. They know, too, that education is the common bond of a pluralistic society and helps tie us to other cultures around the globe. Citizens also know in their bones that the safety of the United States depends principally on the wit, skill, and spirit of a self-confident people, today and tomorrow. . . .
>
> And perhaps more important, citizens know and believe that the meaning of America to the rest of the world must be something better than it seems to many today. Americans like to think of this Nation as the preeminent country for generating the great ideas and material benefits for all mankind. The citizen is dismayed at a steady 15-year decline in industrial productivity, as one great American industry after another falls to world competition. The citizen wants the country to act on the belief, expressed in our hearings and by a large majority in the Gallup Poll, that education should be at the top of the Nation's agenda.

Parents and Students

Finally, although our correspondence provides ample evidence that educators understand the importance of the Commission's message to parents and students, the message has received too little attention. Because the roles of parents and students in the improvement of educational quality are even more important than the responsibilities of teachers, administrators, or legislators, the Commission took the unusual step of addressing these groups directly in its report.

A Nation at Risk bluntly reminds parents of their responsibility to launch their children into the world with the soundest possible education, coupled with respect for first-rate work. It also reminds them of their right to demand the best that our schools and colleges can provide and of their obligation to serve as living examples of the kind of excellence the U.S. requires.

Students receive equally forthright advice: "You forfeit your chance for life at its fullest when you withhold your best effort in learning. When you give only the minimum to learning, you receive only the minimum in return. . . . [I]n the end it is *your* work that determines how much and how well you learn."

From Risk to Confidence

Americans have not only lived with change in the past but also welcomed and encouraged it. Faced with the dangers of an uncharted continent, they spanned and mastered it; awed by the vastness of space, they investigated and explored it; perplexed by the mystery of the atom, they plumbed and solved it. Now a new challenge beckons: how to use our enormous educational system to turn to advantage the current risk to our values, our standard of living, and our international security.

The evidence that we can do so successfully is all around us. It can be found in the past successes of American education, from the development of the one-room schoolhouse to the development of our great research universities. It can be found in the attention paid to the Commission's report by the President and the secretary of education, as well as in the high visibility of education as a major issue on the national agenda. It can be found in the spirited debate we are witnessing on the issue of merit pay for teachers, for this issue touches on many of the elements we must address in seeking excellence – merit, reward for performance, evaluation, and the role and status of teaching.

The evidence can be found in the letters that the National Commission has received from students. Predictably, some students have complained about increased homework or a longer school day. One letter writer suggested that President Reagan contact his junior high school and cancel the book reports that teachers had assigned for the summer vacation. Other letters have been less amusing.

3. THE STRUGGLE FOR EXCELLENCE

One seventh-grader wrote a six-page letter of despair. Teaching study skills during study hall would be fine, she wrote, "if there was anything to study, and if anybody did any studying. There isn't and they don't." She said she would opt instead for six demanding hours of history, math, composition, foreign languages, geography, literature, and science. "Then my school days would be worth getting up for. To lengthen our existing days would be merely to extend the monotony, boredom, frustration, and agony. . . ."

The evidence that we are up to the challenge is perhaps most apparent in the many schools, districts, and states that have already responded to the Commission's report or have appointed task forces and commissions of their own to chart their next steps. But it is also apparent in corporate and foundation boardrooms, in legislative cloakrooms, in meetings of the Cabinet, and in meetings of learned societies, where discussions of the report, of its implications for the nation, and of what the discussants should do about it are the order of the day.

All of this is as it should be, for it was precisely this kind of discussion, debate, and excitement about education that the Commission set out to provoke. If the level of interest remains high and leads to the kind of positive responses anticipated by the Commission, then we may eventually look back on the release of *A Nation at Risk* as a turning point in American education.

Clearly, the Commission's report has touched that chord in the American consciousness which governs the hopes, aspirations, and apprehensions of Americans about the future well-being of their children, their schools, and their society. The task for all of us now is to take this renewed commitment and dedicate it to the creation of a learning society. That responsibility does not belong solely to any one group. As *A Nation at Risk* concludes:

> It is . . . the America of all of us that is at risk; it is to each of us that this imperative is addressed. It is by our willingness to take up the challenge, and our resolve to see it through, that America's place in the world will be either secured or forfeited. Americans have succeeded before, and so we shall again.

A Nation at Risk: How's that again?

Remember how we promised (*Embrace excellence; tinkerers be damned,* July) we wouldn't mislead you about the report of the National Commission on Excellence in Education? Not so others in high places. Seems misrepresentations of that august body's findings have been insinuating themselves into the record, and now the commissioners themselves (or at least some of them) are trying to tell us what they *really* meant to say.

The problem started almost before the ink was dry on *A Nation at Risk.* On April 28—just two days after the report was unveiled to a fanfare of slightly off-key White House trumpets—the *Washington Post* reported "confusion" over the commission's recommendations. As news buffs no doubt will recall, President Reagan used the occasion of the report's release as a convenient soapbox for reiterating his support of tuition tax credits, education vouchers, and school prayer—issues never mentioned in the report itself.

As if that weren't enough, the President went on to call the report "consistent with our task of redefining the federal role in education"—a task his Administration has openly avowed to be more a matter of reduction than of redefinition. Commission member Gerald Holton, a Harvard physics professor, found Mr. Reagan's interpretation of the report startling, to say the least. "Contrary to Reagan," Holton told the *Post,* "we made a clarion call for the federal government to identify the national need and finance what's necessary. . . . If the states cannot afford it, and it's a national emergency, then the money must come from the only source that has it—the federal government."

Since that April day, President Reagan has wasted no opportunity to make political hay of the commission's report. But what were the commissioners really asking for—a New Federalism for education, or a continued, even strengthened, federal role? Late this summer, Representative Carl Perkins (D-Ky.), chairman of the House subcommittee on elementary, secondary, and vocational education (and no friend to the President's education policies), decided the time had come to set the record straight. His tactic: to survey the 18 commission appointees for their "individual views" on such questions as these: (1) Does the report conclude that additional federal funds should be provided for education? (2) What about state and local funds? (3) Are tuition tax credits, education vouchers, and school prayer "discussed, suggested, or endorsed" in the report?

Now, anyone who has had even a remedial course in reading comprehension can take a stab at answering those questions simply by scanning the pages of *A Nation at Risk.* But what Representative Perkins was looking for—and what he says he got—was a horse's-mouth refutation of the President's reading of the commission's handiwork.

Take federal support for public education, for example. Eight out of the ten commissioners who responded to Perkins's survey agreed the report assumed more, not less, of it. The key word here is *assumed.* Yale president and commission member A. Bartlett Giamatti explains: "The report clearly envisions a partnership among local, state, and federal entities in order to meet the needs of the 40 million-plus students in our public schools. Yes, I believe the report foresees federal money joining state and local money. No, I do not believe this is a 'conclusion' of the report; I believe it is an assumption. Clearly, the commission was not of one mind about federal aid."

The commission, it seems, had agreed to come up with a unanimous report, one that would not in any way be qualified or diminished by dissenting opinions. "But one price to be paid for [that unanimity]," Gerald Holton observed, "was that some issues were not spelled out in detail—and above all the question of 'additional federal funds,' a prospect which was ideologically . . . unacceptable from the beginning to at least two or three of the 18 appointees." Holton went on to say that he, and "probably the majority" of the commission members, would favor increased federal aid to public schools.

Among the respondents to Perkins's survey, only commissioners Annette Kirk (of Kirk Associates, a communications consulting firm in Michigan) and New Rochelle high school teacher Jay Sommer were opposed on this point.

As for tuition tax credits, education vouchers, and school prayer—reform notions on which the current Administration has pinned some hope for educational excellence—nine out of ten respondents agreed these proposals were not treated by the commission in its deliberations nor included in its report. The lone holdout was Annette Kirk, who said, "While such proposals are not endorsed as such in the report, it would be possible to extract from the document support for them."

But remember: Only ten of the 18 commission members responded to the survey, and at press time, Perkins's office told the JOURNAL that replies from the remaining members still had not been received. If you've kept careful count you'll realize, then, that on the crucial issue of education funding, only 8 of 18 commissioners *actually* say Mr. Reagan has read them wrong—a not-so-resounding 44 percent, in other words. (On tuition tax credits and the like, the percentage edges up to 50.)

We're not gifted in telepathy, so we don't presume to speak for the silent commissioners. Still, we note (as Representative Perkins undoubtedly has) the presumably unanimous paragraphs in *A Nation at Risk* in which the commission spells out the federal government's role in public education: "The federal government has *the primary responsibility* [the commission's emphasis] to identify the national interest in education. It should also help fund and support efforts to protect and promote that interest."

That language provides plenty of latitude, and although we might not agree with Representative Perkins's claim that his survey adds up to "an emphatic No" to funding cuts, we quietly applaud his statement to the House that cutbacks in federal funding for education "are hardly responsible when the need for educational improvement is imperative."

The Bold Quest For Quality

The nation's public schools are shaping up

The 19 students in a junior English class are discussing a George Eliot novel, which they have read in the three days between orientation day and the start of school. Five students are debating with the teacher about the time frame of the novel, as well as the use of first-person narrative. Near by, a class of sophomores listens intently as the teacher fires off volleys of French. Not a word of English is spoken. The same spirit of curiosity and dedication seems to flow through other rooms at Lincoln Park High School in Chicago, where students from the ghetto mingle with those from glass palaces on the lakefront. Says French Teacher Maureen Breen: "Something is very definitely happening in the air once these kids walk through those doors. We can all feel it."

Kansas City threw a huge pep rally last month, complete with a 25-member song-and-dance troupe. Yet there were no football players proudly strutting through tissue-paper arches. The head cheerleader was president of the Chamber of Commerce. The team being hailed: the city's public school teachers.

Johnson Elementary School in Benton Harbor, Mich., is a one-story building that sits a few hundred yards east of Interstate 94, the heavily traveled highway between Chicago and Detroit. The impoverished school district does not have a sign to put on the building. But in the small lobby, which doubles as the school's library, there is an award from the Michigan Department of Education congratulating the school's fourth-graders for scoring 20% higher than their predecessors on a state assessment test. Beside the plaque, in bold construction-paper letters, is the school's motto: "We demand excellence."

As 44.3 million students settle down to another school year, a growing number are finding—and responding to—a new demand for excellence in the classroom. More required courses and tougher graduation requirements. No-frills curriculums featuring basic skills. Old-fashioned homework and computer literacy. Rigor without the customary mortis.

Once again, Americans have decided that good public schools are essential for the public good. Parents, educators, business people and politicians everywhere are forming grass-roots coalitions to raise standards and improve the quality of instruction from kindergarten to senior year. Their vigor is bringing a new vitality to education, the institution that has been called America's secular religion. Says Terrel Bell, U.S. Secretary of Education: "There is currently in progress the greatest, most far-reaching and, I believe, the most promising reform and renewal of education we have seen since the turn of the century."

Report cards on the nation's public schools have been dismal for a decade: teachers cannot teach; students cannot, or will not, learn. The short-comings of the schools have been documented by lower Scholastic Aptitude Test scores, a national high school dropout rate of some 25%, the shrinking elite of students taking calculus and physics, the proliferation of remedial courses in colleges and in businesses to repair the damage. One study in the '70s found that 30% of 18-year-olds (47% of black youths) were functionally illiterate, unable to read or follow a set of simple directions.

Over the past year a flurry of reports have chronicled a nation with declining basic skills, foundering will and a diminishing ability to compete with a hi-tech rival like Japan. In May, the National Commission on Excellence in Education (NCEE) stirred the most concern when it reported that the U.S. was "at risk" from "a rising tide of mediocrity." Its judgment: standards are too low, the school day is too short, teachers are paid too little and education is too far down the list of national priorities. The report's ringing indictment: "If an unfriendly foreign power had attempted to impose on America the mediocre educational performance that exists today, we might well have viewed it as an act of war."

What the NCEE failed to report, however, is that the tide of mediocrity has already begun to ebb. There are plenty of weaknesses still, but excellence has once again become part of the agenda in hundreds of school districts across the country. Statistics only sketch out the dimensions of the turnaround. Over the past three years, 53% of the 16,000 school districts nationwide have increased the number of credits they require in such core subjects as English, science and math; 38% more will upgrade their standards by 1985. During this same period, 69% of school systems have launched efforts to increase daily attendance. No fewer than 20 states have passed tougher certification laws, with the goal of making sure that a teacher has mastered basic skills before ever entering a classroom.

What is remarkable is that all this activity comes at a time when student enrollment is shrinking and funding is scarce. In hard-pressed Michigan, for instance, where the recession lingers (last month's unemployment: 13.4%), some schools almost had to close in the 1982-83 school year for lack of funds; during the same year 90% of all school tax renewal proposals were approved, a good showing under the circumstances. Poll after poll has disclosed that the public would pay higher taxes for better schools. David Gardner, chairman of the NCEE, now admits, "I hadn't realized how deep and wide the concern was. This is a classic example of why this country works."

The Carnegie Foundation for the Advancement of Teaching last month released a thoughtful study that rejects the notion that public education has failed. After spending a total of 30 months compiling observations of high schools across the nation, the report's author concluded that the best American high schools, which educate 10% to 15% of all students, are the world's finest. Says Ernest Boyer, president of the Carnegie Foundation and former U.S. Commissioner of Education under Jimmy Carter: "School is in a very real sense a mirror of its community. Time and time again, we saw that community support or community conditions were shaping the school. So, in a very real sense, the report card on the school is a report card on the nation."

No wonder that education is becoming a hot presidential campaign issue. Ronald Reagan was the first to sense the opportunity, demanding tougher standards and extra, or "merit," pay for outstanding teachers. But Reagan sees little role for the Federal Government or federal dollars in the quest for excellence. Indeed, the Administration got Congress to cut back 10% on public school funding over the past three years, and only recently stopped vowing to dismantle the Department of Education.

Caught off guard by Reagan, the potential Democratic candidates are trying to devise reform plans that will score points with voters. Walter Mondale has called for an $11 billion annual infusion of federal money for, among other things, a national $4.5 billion fund for excellence that would grant sums to schools to help them improve instruction. Senator Ernest Hollings wants $14 billion, in part to give certain qualified public school teachers $5,000 raises. Senator John Glenn's $4 billion plan would include loans to math and science majors that would be forgiven for students who go on to teach those subjects.

While the presidential candidates talk of their plans, the real leadership is coming from the state level: from Governors, from local superintendents, from business people. In a spirit of enlightened self-interest, state officials equate better schools with healthier economies. Some 45 states have put together task forces to consider school reform. In Mississippi, traditionally one of the educationally benighted states, Governor William Winter got the legislature to pass a $69 million bill last December to improve teacher pay and to implement compulsory attendance for the first time since the 1950s. Florida Governor Bob Graham's $228 million school-reform package, passed in June, will toughen student requirements, provide summer institutes for classroom teachers, buy computers for classes, and provide money to attract math and science teachers. Governor James Hunt of North Carolina, who led the Task Force on Education for Economic Growth and who has done part-time teaching during his gubernatorial tenure, has spearheaded everything from an elementary school reading program to the North Carolina School of Science and Mathematics, a public boarding school for the state's most gifted students.

In a sense, the prophets of doom and the harbingers of progress are both right about the public schools. The American education system is so complex and diverse that signs of hope mingle with tokens of disaster even within the same schools. Says Theodore Sizer, former headmaster of Phillips Academy in Andover, Mass., and head of a new study on high schools: "You find marvelous things going on and not so marvelous things going on." Any report card on the public schools would have to consider at least four major areas: curriculum and standards, teaching, funding and community support. In all of them, there is cause for rejoicing as well as alarm.

The Curriculum: Shows Progress

There is no question that expectations for curriculum and standards dropped over the past 20 years. In many schools, the art of diagramming sentences went the way of *Wuthering Heights,* and survey literature courses were transformed into cotton-candy electives like "Expressions of Love." Nationally, average scores on the verbal portion of SATs dropped more than 50 points from 1963 to 1980. A California survey found that many math and science texts now in use are ten to 20 years old. One book still used as a reference in a second-grade classroom near Cape Canaveral even tips off students: "Soon we may land on the moon. Watch for it."

Lowered expectations affect students at all levels. Says Northwestern University Sociologist Christopher Jencks: "What we are seeing is not so much a decline in basic skills as a decline in advanced skills." During the past few years, 13 states, from California to Florida, have sent a strong message to high schools by demanding more requirements of freshmen entering state universities; some have demanded higher grades as well. Says University of Chicago Education Professor Philip Jackson: "Any kid who can follow the intricacies of an N.F.L. football game can follow the turns of plot in a Jane Austen novel or a Dickens tale."

School districts have devised a variety of imaginative and promising strategies to challenge the unchallenged and to brighten the best. New York State is considering a proposal that would require foreign language proficiency by ninth grade. Tennessee has approved a program that will award "honors diplomas" to students who voluntarily complete an accelerated course of study with strong emphasis on English, math, science, arts and foreign languages. Louisiana has opened a residential state school in Natchitoches for students gifted in math, science and the arts, modeled on North Carolina's boarding school. In Iowa, where only 1,500 students took calculus last year (but 17,500 elected driver's education), the state is instituting an incentive program. Students who take upper-level math and science courses will be eligible for a special, one-time tuition grant of $500 to attend any college in the state. Furthermore, the Iowa legislature has approved bounties to school districts: $25 for each student who enrolls in physics, chemistry or advanced math courses, and $50 for each first-year foreign language student.

While the suburban schools got lots of credit for innovation and honors programs two decades ago, urban schools now appear to be on the cutting edge of reform. One reason, says Carnegie's Boyer, may be that many parents in ghetto areas fight fiercely for better schools for their children. The Council of the Great City Schools, a coalition of 30 of the nation's largest urban school systems, reports that 27 of these predominantly minority systems have had increases in elementary school reading and mathematics test scores during the past five years.

To be sure, some of the progress came about because there was nowhere to go but up. But much of the improvement in inner-city schools is due to the energy and dedication of strong leaders who are imposing standards of discipline as well as excellence. Their strategy: make the students believe they can succeed.

When Alonzo Crim, 55, took over as superintendent of Atlanta's schools in 1973, the first year that a court-ordered desegregation program went into effect, only 30% of students were reading at the national norm. Says Crim: "We had to focus on reading. Handling the language arts is perhaps the most fundamental building block to the whole educational program. If you can't read, write, speak and listen, you won't do anything else well." In June, Crim announced that the average student in kindergarten through tenth grade was reading at the national level; math achievement was slightly above the norm. The dropout rate last year was 4% (down from 12% in 1973), and the average daily attendance was 94% (up from 86%). Says Crim proudly: "Our kids voted with their feet. They stayed in school."

Before Robert Alioto, 49, arrived in San Francisco in 1975 from Yonkers, N.Y., the school district was considered unmanageable. The superintendent's office did not even know how many teachers were at work. Alioto's first success was putting the district's finances in order.

Then he began cutting down on the bureaucracy: of the 100 or so administrative jobs in 1975, only 42 are left. In 1978 he closed 30 schools because enrollment had dropped, a move that earned him many enemies in the community. Nor did he win friends among teachers by laying off 1,197 of them in 1979. Says Alioto: "Too many people in education are mealy-mouthed wimps. I think you can sleep better if you fight for what you believe in."

The performance of San Francisco pupils on achievement tests has improved so rapidly (reading scores of third-graders at one school rose nearly ten percentage points in one year) that the state education department conducted a secret check in 1978 to make sure everything was on the up and up; it was. As a result, about 1,000 private school students return to the public schools each year. In 1982 Mayor Dianne Feinstein showed her confidence in Alioto by giving $4 million of the city's surplus funds to the schools.

Anthony Alvarado, 41, was appointed chancellor of New York City schools last spring after working educational magic as superintendent of East Harlem's District Four, an area where rubble spills out of abandoned buildings and youths loiter in empty lots. When Alvarado, son of Puerto Rican immigrants, was assigned to District Four in 1973, it ranked dead last among the city's 32 districts on reading test scores: only 18.5% of students read at grade level or above. Last year the district ranked 15th in the city, and 48.5% of its students were up to par in reading. Alvarado's success was due in part to his ability to attract bright and dedicated teachers and his willingness to take risks with new programs. Says Alvarado: "My view has always been that you increase expectations and you support students at the same time."

Some of the schools trying the hardest are those with the worst problems. About 30% of the students at Edison High School in Miami's riot-scarred Liberty City are Creole-speaking Haitians; another 14% are students, predominantly Hispanic, who are learning English as a second language. Principal Craig Sturgeon believes that discipline is essential for learning. "We make our expectations and the punishment clear," he says. "When people are late, they are taken to the cafeteria to work on their basic skills. The second time it happens, we contact the parents, and the third time, they are forced to do work around the school." The percentage of Edison's students who passed language assessment tests went up from 54% in 1981 to 83% in 1983. This fall the school is starting a special program in solving word, math and logic problems.

In Boston, Superintendent Robert Spillane is improving one of the nation's most racially torn school systems. An apt symbol is South Boston High School, where whites clashed with blacks in the mid-'70s. Today Southie is a well-balanced school with a population of 856 students that is 43% black, 34% white, 11% Asian and 12% Hispanic. In 1976 Headmaster Jerome Winegar began an in-school suspension program: students who get into trouble are assigned special help under a supervising teacher instead of being tossed out. Since the program's inception, three-day suspensions have dropped from 1,660 to 83 last year.

Southie is also the only district school that requires all ninth-graders to study a foreign language. In addition to a mandatory English course, ninth- and tenth-graders must take a reading and writing workshop that continues in the eleventh and twelfth grades if the student does not do well. Daily attendance rates have risen 14% in the past year. Says Winegar: "You don't change a school with programs. You change a school with philosophy. We want to help young people battle their way into the mainstream."

In Benton Harbor, Mich., the adult unemployment rate is 32%, more than half of the city's 14,000 residents are on some form of welfare, and 77% of the 8,900 public school students are either black or Hispanic. Most of the town's central business district is boarded up. Benton Harbor's students had scored 40% below the statewide average for the past five years. Two years ago, with solid support in the community, Superintendent James Hawkins began a program that requires every student to master basic minimal skills before being promoted to the next grade.

Hawkins is willing to hold back even kindergarteners unless they can meet certain standards: they should be able to follow simple verbal directions, know at least ten letters of the alphabet, write numbers up to ten as well as their first name, and recite a four-line nursery rhyme. Results of the reforms: scores on the California Achievement Test have gone up 13% for first-graders and 24% for second-graders, but 15% of first- and second-graders have been kept back. Hawkins is unapologetic. Says he: "Retention is not necessarily destructive to self-image. If you really want to see trauma, go to a high school and see a twelfth-grader reading at fourth-grade level. That's trauma."

Another approach to higher standards favored by Alvarado and other reformers is the establishment within a district of a so-called magnet school, featuring specialized programs in the sciences, arts or humanities along with a core curriculum. Its purpose: to achieve integration by creating an inner-city school with an irresistible claim to academic excellence. Waller High School in Chicago, once a mere holding pen, was transformed by District Superintendent Margaret Harrigan into Lincoln Park High. It has a school of science with a college-level course in biochemistry, a school of languages that offers French, German, Italian and Spanish, and a school of arts that offers everything from the Stanislavsky acting method to Baroque music.

About 95% of the students at Waller were black; enrollment at Lincoln Park is 56% black. This year 200 applied for the 30 places in Lincoln Park's International Baccalaureate program, an academically demanding two-year curriculum, and students who scored in the 97th percentile on the entrance exam were turned away. Says Stephen Ballis, an insurance executive and neighborhood parent: "This used to be a half-filled building, isolated from the community. Now it's overcrowded. Excellence and expectations of excellence are contagious."

Teaching: Needs Improvement

The most ambitious plans for longer school days, more demanding courses and higher standards are meaningless without teachers who can make school worth attending. The cold truth is that the kind of inspired teachers who can transform an English class at Lincoln Park High or a kindergarten in Benton Harbor are in woefully short supply. Warns John Goodlad, former dean of the U.C.L.A. graduate school of education and author of *A Place Called School: Prospects for the Future:* "The proposed curricular changes, if not accompanied by substantial improvements in pedagogy, could increase the high school dropout rate."

More than 60% of Houston public school teachers taking a competency exam last spring failed. The example is not surprising. Nationwide, education majors tend to come from the lowest strata of students: last year they scored 32 points below the national average on the verbal portion of the SAT test and 48 points lower on the mathematics section. Says James Guthrie, former chairman of the department of education at the University of California at Berkeley: "In the past, the quality of American education was maintained by women and minorities. Now these people can do other things."

The lack of talented and trained teachers is especially critical for math and science. Only 50% of such teachers are qualified in their subjects; most have been recycled from other areas. The undergraduates who excel at math or physics are smart enough to know that they can make considerably more money in industry than in teaching. From 1971 to 1980, the number of math teachers dropped 78% nationwide. Massachusetts universities produced only two graduates last June certified to teach chemistry on the high school level and only two who could teach physics. Berkeley, the proud flagship of the California system, did not graduate a single one.

Some 33 states have passed, or are considering, incentive programs to attract students and qualified teachers to science labs and math classrooms. In Kentucky, 95 students last year received up to $2,500 toward their college costs; if they spend one year as math or science teachers in a Kentucky public school, one year of their loan will be canceled. At least half a dozen states are reconsidering their certification procedures to emphasize knowledge of subject matter over teaching methodology. Such changes could open the teaching field, largely dominated by education majors, to graduates with liberal arts degrees.

Still, teachers' hours remain long (at least for the conscientious), working conditions are often poor, and the pay is terrible. While the average teacher's salary is just over $20,000, that figure reflects the pay of a corps of veterans. The average salary for beginning teachers with a B.A. is $12,769, about $4,200 less than a fledgling accountant can make. Even worse, after 15 years the accountant will probably be making between $40,000 and $50,000, while the teacher will be earning less than $25,000. A Carnegie Foundation report last month concluded that teachers' salaries declined 12.2% between 1972 and 1982, when inflation was factored in, while total personal income increased by 17.8% in real dollars during the same period. Reason enough for sporadic strikes. Chicago teachers, for instance, may go out this week.

To improve the situation, Reagan and Mondale, among others, have recommended some form of merit pay for good teachers. However, teachers' unions—the American Federation of Teachers (580,000 members) and the National Education Association (1.7 million members)—have traditionally opposed merit pay, out of suspicion that bonuses would be given out unfairly and would cut into general pay raises for entire faculties.

As interest in merit pay has increased, both the A.F.T. and, more reluctantly, the N.E.A. have agreed at least to consider the proposal, provided that some mechanism can be worked out to make sure the selection process is fair. A study conducted this summer by the *American School Board Journal* found that nearly two out of three teachers support the concept of merit pay. Seven states now have some form of it in one or more local school systems, nine more are considering specific legislation, and 29 are studying the idea. But the jury is still out on the potential impact. In Los Angeles, 200 of the city's 25,000 teachers last year were awarded $1,008 extra for superior performances and extra work; the program is generally well received by the teaching staff. It has also worked for more than 30 years in the Ladue School District of suburban St. Louis, and more than 20 years in Dalton, Ga. Darien, Conn., however, halted its three-year experiment in merit pay because the paperwork involved had become a bureaucratic nightmare.

The Dallas school system has just started a trial year with what may be the nation's first computerized merit-pay plan. Says the district's Director of Employee Relations Robby Collins: "Once you have human beings evaluating other human beings, the systems produce jealousies, morale problems. The beauty of our system is that it's done totally by computer." Each school will receive projections on how students should score on national achievement tests, based on the past three years' performances. In schools that outperform the computer projections, every teacher will pocket an extra $1,500.

An extra 1,500 bucks will not revitalize a profession, though. More important than better pay, say disgruntled teachers, is the need to improve the prestige and power of the job, to restore its practitioners' self-respect. Says A.F.T. President Albert Shanker: "We give people poor salaries, then we lock them in a room with a bunch of kids and instead of letting them teach a subject they know—Shakespeare or math—we have them doing everything else, teaching 'Living,' 'Loving,' 'Life Adjustment.' " Maintains San Francisco School District Administrator Carlos Cornejo: "We don't give teachers the recognition they need. We have them teaching in leaky rooms and supervising the boys' john in between classes. We're going to have trouble until we make teaching a profession again."

There is one reform that could go a long way toward revitalizing the profession of teaching. It would provide something that does not now exist in most school systems: a career ladder that offers opportunities for advancement. Tennessee Governor Lamar Alexander's "master teacher" plan, which has yet to pass the state legislature, would provide more money ($115 million a year) and four career steps: apprentice, professional teacher, senior teacher and master teacher. Movement through the four stages would give teachers more pay for more responsibility. Those at the top could earn as much as 60% more than the base salary. The A.F.T.'s Shanker, for one, endorses the idea.

Charlotte-Mecklenburg, N.C., boasts another intriguing teacher-development program. With the help of his faculty, Superintendent Jay Robinson is now working out a career plan that would identify 26 qualities an instructor should exhibit. Teachers would receive extensive training through a center that already houses a library of curriculum materials and sets up workshops to sharpen skills. Favorable evaluations would lead to pay bonuses as teachers advanced up a three-step career ladder to tenured status. Says Robinson: "Merit-pay plans attempt to identify excellence and reward it. Our plan's emphasis is on creating great teachers through training them and then putting them on a career salary schedule."

Higher education is beginning to take some responsibility for the improvement of public school teaching. One such program is the Yale–New Haven Teachers Institute. Each semester eight senior Yale professors conduct seminars with 80 city teachers on such topics as Greek and Roman mythology and the elements of architecture. In addition, the teacher "fellows" become part of the Yale community, with privileges ranging from parking to library use. Says junior high Math Teacher Sheryl DeCaprio: "It sort of makes you feel professional again."

Colleges and universities are also trying to send more talent the way of the public schools. Faith Dunne, head of Dartmouth's education department, has helped put together a 15-member Consortium for Excellence in Teacher Education, made up of 15 top private colleges that will use exchange programs to pool resources and attract able students. Says Dunne: "I think we could have better teachers if we got to the point where influential professors would stop discouraging their students from going into elementary and secondary school education."

Dunne has found one unexplained source of opposition: the parents of some students she has encouraged to become teachers. Asks Dunne angrily: "Why is it that people will go from suburb to suburb refusing to buy a house until they figure out where the best schools are, and at the same time forbid their children to become teachers?"

Harvard's Graduate School of Education started an elite program this fall to help professionals switch to teaching in mid-career. One of the seven "students" in the pilot program is Jim Selman, 59. With his children through college and his mortgage paid off, Selman is quitting his $50,000-a-year job as an electrical engineer at Mitre Corp. Mitre is paying Selman's $8,320 tuition. When he finishes the program, which includes 14 weeks of student teaching, Selman will be accredited to teach science and math in Massachusetts schools, and he is looking forward to being "able to effect a permanent change in a student's intellect or attitude."

Funding: More Required

Behind all the plans for reform is a fundamental but unanswered question: Who will pay? Traditionally, America's public schools were financed primarily by local property taxes. A surge of court decisions in the 1970s found that such funding had fostered great inequalities between wealthy and poor local districts. School funding became more of a state matter. Today, on average, states provide 50% of the money for community public schools and local taxes 42%, while the Federal Government contributes only about 8%. As Dade County Assistant Superintendent Paul Bell has observed: "We have had a major shift of control from the local level to the state board of education, with the legislature acting as a superboard."

State legislatures, hit hard by the recent recession, have tried to hold down taxes and, with them, school funding. But a few states have been able to buck the trend and raise taxes to fund education reforms. When the Florida legislature turned down his costly reform program this spring, Governor Graham countered with proposals for taxes on liquor and corporate profits earned abroad. By late June, when legislators reconvened for a special session, Graham showed that he could raise an extra $100 million to lengthen the school day, increase teacher pay by 5% to 7% and purchase new science equipment.

One of the nation's most ardent advocates of reform, California's new Superintendent of Public Instruction William Honig, has conquered the land of Proposition 13. Last November Honig, a former elementary school teacher, beat the incumbent and popular superintendent by hitting again and again on the need for homework, discipline, high standards. California had ranked among the top three states in the nation on school spending per pupil until the mid-1960s. It dropped to 17th place in 1969, and after Proposition 13, to 31st place in 1981-82. And a marked decline in California education performance accompanied the decline in funding.

Soon after his election, Honig asked Sacramento legislators to toughen high school graduation requirements, raise beginning salaries for teachers to $18,000, make loans for teacher training, and fund master teacher programs. Cost: $800 million. Governor George Deukmejian, who had won office on a promise of fiscal austerity, balked. But a public opinion poll indicated that Californians by a 2-to-1 majority would support increased taxes to improve public schools.

Honig immediately started a campaign that rivaled his bid for office. In one day in July, he held press conferences in three different cities. Then he talked to the California Round Table, a group of 88 chief executive officers already concerned about educational reform. The Governor began to get letters. "Dear George," wrote J.R. Fluor, head of a multibillion-dollar engineering and construction firm, "I am urging you to reconsider the position you took during your campaign—a position which we all admired at the time—and relent just a bit so that sufficient revenues can be raised to ensure the reform and then the financial support so necessary to improve the quality of education here in California." Deukmejian relented, and the bill passed this summer.

Across the country, the business community is acknowledging a responsibility and stepping in to help. Corporations are "adopting" schools, providing everything from laboratory equipment to volunteer instructors. In Chicago, 176 firms have established links with 600 schools; in Los Angeles, the figures are 189 and 225. Seven of Atlanta's largest banks, as well as the local Federal Reserve branch, have collaborated in establishing the city's newest magnet school, Harper High. The banks provide not only money but their own employees for financial courses and internships for interested students. Such programs have a variety of benefits. Memphis Schools Superintendent W.W. Herenton believes that business involvement in his area has been partly responsible for the return of 1,400 white students from private schools in the past two years.

Another new source of funding is a variation on the old parent bake sale. Citizens are banding together into public school foundations to raise extra money. In California, at least 60 such organizations sponsor phonathons and benefit events to finance important extras, including theater arts, special math programs, remedial reading classes and even computers. In Washington, D.C., the Parent Group Fund taps local and congressional donors to fund field trips and special tutoring for public school children. Early this year, the Ford Foundation set up the Pittsburgh-based Public Education Fund, which will help start up some 40 local education foundations across the nation in the next five years.

Community Support: Growing

The great fear of educators like Carnegie's Boyer is that the current enthusiasm for school reform will not endure in the face of rising costs and slow progress. It has happened before. After the Soviets launched Sputnik in 1957, the nation underwent a similar convulsion of reforming zeal as schools geared up to beat the Russians. The ardor cooled after the success of U.S. space explorations made it seem that America was first once more.

Just as the Sputnik reforms were waning, the nation was also subjected to a decade of social turbulence. The civil rights movement raised issues of equal opportunity, and the Viet Nam War shook faith in American institutions. The public schools were directly affected: by busing, by a decline in discipline, by the drive for equity. Says Christopher Jencks: "In the late '60s and early '70s, there was a collapse of consensus about what was worth teaching and what was worth learning." In addition, with many of the functions formerly assigned to home, community or church also breaking down, schools suddenly had to advise students on love, divorce and drugs. The Federal Government further complicated the schools' role by demanding that those who could not speak English be instructed in their native languages, that the disadvantaged be given free lunch at school, and that the handicapped be accommodated in all classrooms.

Some of the duties taken on by the schools were positive, notably much of the new egalitarianism. Diane Ravitch of Columbia University, who chronicles the postwar history of school-reform movements in a new book, *The Troubled Crusade,* says, "The challenge is to turn [that egalitarianism] into a commitment to educate all children and to educate them very well. We must watch in our passion for excellence that it doesn't bear only on the elite, that it means we are going to have a school system that works for everyone and not just 'the winners.' "

There are forces today, however, that may impede public school reform in the near future. The U.S. is an aging nation with fewer children and a population that may be less eager to increase taxes in support of schools. Warns Carnegie's Boyer: "In many ways, we're addressing not just a school problem, but a youth problem. We have a generation of young people who feel essentially unattached, who are genuinely adrift." The alienation between the young and the old, he adds, could intensify over how tax moneys should be used. Furthermore, with a declining white birth rate, minorities could make up one-third of public school enrollments by 1990 (they are already 27% today). If, as a result, public schools are perceived as institutions for the underprivileged, middle-class support may diminish even more.

The driving force behind much of the current revolution is the desire for economic revival. What will happen ten years from now if the results are spotty? Theodore Sizer worries about present motivations: "The rhetoric of toughness is so predominant today. There isn't the idealism and compassion that has been behind significant school reform in the past."

In short, Americans still need a larger vision of their schools' educational mission. Says Ravitch: "We went through a period of ethnic revivalism and separatism, and it may be that we are now ready to go beyond that to think about our common needs as people and as Americans, our needs as a community."

Virginia Beach, Va. (pop. 262,000), has already tried to work out its goals for the future and how to gain them. The school board in this tidewater city near Norfolk has spent two years and $250,000 to develop a 21st century reform plan that recommends 138 changes in the present school system. Phase 1 began a month ago when classes resumed, and included such currently celebrated reforms as longer days and stronger basics. But Virginia Beach will go much further. Students will be encouraged to take harder courses by a new grading system that will assign added weight to an A in an upper-level course. Phase 2, to begin this year, will call for innovative teacher training and in some cases retraining, so that as competence improves, a teacher's higher expectations will inspire student performance. Visiting scholars will be invited to address both students and teachers. Says School Superintendent Ed Brickell: "It was time to stop operating piecemeal, patching here, adding on there; it was time to redesign our entire system."

Although the Virginia Beach plan could cost taxpayers as much as $14 million during the next few years, the community is behind Brickell. When the city manager cut $5 million from the school budget two years ago, 30,000 citizens signed petitions opposing the cut; hundreds came to a public hearing to praise the school system and attack the city manager.

"Revolutions happen not suddenly but after a long accumulation of grievances and awareness of defects," says Philosopher Mortimer Adler, who is optimistic that the reforms will continue. "This is the first time that the central matter is being discussed: teaching and learning. Not civil rights or free lunches or girls *vs.* boys."

If state legislatures, public forums and PTA meetings are any indicators, Americans seem to be reaffirming a strong commitment to education. A Gallup poll shows that 84% of Americans believe that a superior educational system is "very important" to the nation, while only 47% believe that a strong military force is as important. "There is now considerable resolve to see reform through to the end," says Chester Finn, a professor of education and public policy at Vanderbilt University. Yet he warns, "These changes will take some years, and when they happen they will be characteristically American, which is to day, uneven and sporadic."

After watching the past year's crescendo of public concern, Ruth Love, superintendent of Chicago's rallying system, says, "Whenever we get in trouble as a nation, we always turn to education, and those of us in education must seize this opportunity—it won't be here always." California's Honig agrees that educators must make the most of this golden moment. But he notes, "There is no one secret answer to turn our schools around. It takes the commitment of thousands and thousands of people, people who are committed to kids and education and good human values." Those people appear to be rallying.

—By Ellie McGrath.
Reported by Dorothy Ferenbaugh/New York, J. Madeleine Nash/Chicago and Dick Thompson/San Francisco

A TIME FOR RE-EXAMINATION AND RENEWAL COMMITMENT

David Pierpont Gardner

Mr. Gardner is chairman of the National Commission on Excellence in Education.

The American educational system has long enjoyed a deserved reputation for both its egalitarian nature and the excellence of its program and product. From the days of Thomas Jefferson's call for an educated citizenry, to Horacc Mann's crusade for the common schools, to John Dewey's eloquent advocacy for the public schools, and to our nation's more recent effort dramatically to expand access to our schools and colleges, our country's educational effort stands as an enviable, albeit imperfect, record of solid achievement.

The egalitarian dimension in American life and character, as noted by the young French aristocrat Alexis de Tocqueville and other observers, has been and will continue to be a pervasive and important characteristic of our evolving educational system. An equally important dimension of American life and its educational system has been the seeking of authentic distinction or excellence with an ever-expanding number of students.

Our schools serve a much larger segment of the school-age population than do the schools of most other countries. Nevertheless, we have produced as able individuals as a percentage of the school-going pool as has any nation, irrespective of the pool's size. For example, Dr. Torsten Husén of the Institute of International Education at the University of Stockholm, Sweden, recently testified before the National Commission on Excellence in Education and reported that the top nine percent of American students perform just as well on standardized achievement tests as the top nine percent in other industrialized countries. Similarly, our colleges and universities, which admit a far larger proportion of 18-year-olds than other countries, produce exceptionally able students and direct graduate and research programs that are the best in the world.

Excellence as an Issue

Why then is excellence in education an issue of intense current interest today?

First, public confidence in education, as measured by opinion polls, shows significant declines which go well beyond normal cyclical patterns. For example, a recent analysis of Gallup Poll findings over the past 12 years reveals that in 1974 approximately two-thirds of parents with public school children felt that their local schools were superior or above average. In 1979, the percentage responding so favorably dropped below 50 percent.

The sources of such dissatisfaction tend to be increasingly associated with issues of educational quality. A recent Washington *Post*/ABC News Poll indicates that about four parents in ten of high school or near high school age students criticize schools for offering "pass through" education, for having unmotivated teachers, and for grade inflation. A similar level of support was accorded the statement: "Too many students are allowed to graduate from high school without learning very much."

Second, the well-publicized declines in test scores of college-bound students, as measured both on ACT and SAT examinations, reinforce perceptions of weakening quality in our schools. Similarly, declines in the proportion of students taking mathematics, science, and other more academically challenging courses or "solids" suggest to many observers that students are being inadequately prepared for the demands that will be made of them in an increasingly complex and technological world, not to speak of what our colleges and universities will be expecting of them as they pursue their studies beyond high school.

Third, the number and kind of remedial offerings now embodied in the lower-division programs of our colleges and universities have grown enormously in recent years. These programs are diluting higher education's resources, deflecting their mission, and weakening the conventional pressures that more exacting college and university standards have historically exerted on secondary school curriculums.

Thus, public and professional concern over the quality dimension of our educational system has become widespread in recent years and is growing. The formation of the National Commission on Excellence in Education by Secretary Bell is but one example of this concern. Similar efforts in several states have been undertaken. Legislators, governors, foundations, scientific and scholarly societies, teacher associations and societies, educators, and parents are discussing the subject with increasing frequency. Television news programs, magazine articles, and

Reprinted, with permission, from *American Education* Magazine, August/September 1982. U.S. Department of Education.

newspaper reports just this past year further reflect the high level of interest in the status and quality of education in America. And there are nearly 25 major national research studies on the American high school currently under way.

Role of the Commission

The National Commission on Excellence in Education is, of course, an initiative of the federal government. The federal interest and record in promoting excellence in education is long-standing and ranges from development of science curriculums to peer review and funding of basic research, to support of centers of excellence, and to enrichment programs for teachers. Quality education and educational access have historically been regarded as in the national interest, although the role of the federal government in expressing that interest has ebbed and flowed with the times, politics, and economic conditions.

Education, of course, is now and has historically been a state and local function. Any lasting changes in our schools, colleges, and universities will be a function of decisions made by local school boards, parents, teachers, professors, principals, superintendents, state school boards, legislative committees, governors, boards of trustees, boards of regents, scholarly and scientific societies, and the general public.

To presume that the federal government or a federal commission can effect comprehensive and sustainable changes in our nation's educational system is to misunderstand the workings of both our system of government and the purposes of this Commission, just as to believe that the federal government and the Commission can have no impact is similarly to misunderstand their respective roles and potential.

The National Commission on Excellence in Education, by its very existence as well as by its *modus operandi,* can be an effective force for focusing attention on the issue of excellence, for bringing to the fore problems which bear upon it, for teasing out data and testimony of a kind that is known or new and casting it in a fresh perspective, and for offering its recommendations to those whose opinions count at all levels in our country.

The Commission is composed of 18 persons whose experience with the educational system, its purposes, processes, financing, politics, and governance is wide-ranging and personal. It includes teachers, principals, superintendents and school board members at the local and state levels, professors, a Nobel laureate, university presidents, a business leader, and a governor, among others. The Commission, taken as a whole, has a breadth and depth of experience and contacts uncharacteristic of many national commissions.

Secretary Bell regarded the composition of the Commission as critical to its success, both for purposes of preparing a useful and insightful report with the help and assistance of interested parties, societies, associations, and constituent organizations and of having a capacity to reach out and to influence the educational system at district, state, and national levels as well, once the report has been submitted. The Commission's staff, directed by Dr. Milton Goldberg, was chosen with equal care.

Charge and Agenda

The Commission's charter, as detailed by Secretary Bell, charges the Commission with the following responsibilities:

- Assessing the quality of teaching and learning in our nation's schools and colleges;
- Comparing the American educational system with the systems of other advanced countries;
- Studying the reciprocal relationship between college admission requirements and high school curriculum/high school student achievement;
- Assessing the degree to which major social and educational changes in the last quarter century have affected educational achievement;
- Defining problems which must be faced and overcome if we are to pursue successfully and promote excellence in education;
- Holding hearings and receiving testimony on how to foster high levels of quality in the nation's educational system.

In contrast to most of the national studies currently underway on the American high school, the Commission intends to generate relatively little in new research findings. Rather, it intends to gather, evaluate, and synthesize existing research findings and field experience. This information, together with invited and volunteered testimony and commissioned papers, will enable the Commission to construct its findings, arrive at its conclusions, and formulate its recommendations. Scientific and scholarly societies throughout the country, the national educational laboratories, individual scholars, teachers, school board members, and others have already been of material help and, without exception, willing, indeed eager, to be of assistance. The Commission's final report is to be submitted to the Secretary and the nation in March of 1983.

Completing the tasks outlined above in such a short time will require a major effort on the part of Commission members and staff, as well as the involvement of the educational community, broadly defined.

Public Hearings

The Commission is in the midst of a series of six public hearings scheduled across the United States over a period of several months. These hearings constitute the cornerstone for the Commission's work, since they provide Commission members with access to both factual information and informed opinions about current education problems and how to overcome them, as those facts and opinions bear upon issues of educational quality and excellence.

The first of these hearings was held at Stanford University in Palo Alto, California, during the second week in March. The topic of the hearing was science, mathematics, and technology education. The hearing was chaired by Commission member Glenn T. Seaborg, holder of a Nobel Prize in Chemistry and presently a University Professor of Chemistry at the University of California, Berkeley.

In mid-April, a hearing on the topic of language and literacy was held in the board auditorium of the Houston Independent School District in Texas. The hearing was chaired by Commission member Jay Sommer, 1981–1982 National Teacher of the Year and currently a foreign language instructor at New Rochelle High School in New York State.

A third public hearing was conducted at Georgia State University in Atlanta in May. Teaching and teacher education comprised the scope of this hearing, chaired by Commission member Annette Y. Kirk, parent, civic leader, and former high school teacher.

The Commission's remaining three scheduled public hearings this year will cover college admission standards (Chicago, June 23), education and work (Denver, September 16), and education for the gifted and talented (Boston, October 15).

Each hearing follows a similar format. In the morning, Commission members hear invited testimony from national experts on the topic under consideration. Following the presentation of testimony, the invited experts discuss issues and respond to questions from Commission members. Following lunch, local and regional experts present testimony about their experiences and perspectives on the topic. The last portion of each hearing day is open to members of the public wishing to express their viewpoints individually or collectively. These presentations are expected to address the day's topic and, thus far, such opinions have been well prepared, succinctly presented, and very helpful to the Commission.

In addition to the personal testimony the Commission receives on the day of each hearing, individuals and organizations across the country are invited to submit two to five pages of written testimony on each hearing topic. All testimony pertaining to a particular hearing will be placed on the official record, if received no later than one month following the hearing date.

Aside from the hearings, two full Commission meetings have been scheduled in the upcoming months. These have been scheduled in addition to four earlier ones, the most recent of which was given over to a discussion of the nature of schooling and transitions between levels. The agenda of each of these remaining meetings has not yet been fully determined. However, a substantial part of the full Commission meetings is devoted to examining specific issues raised in the charter. In addition, several panels and symposiums have been scheduled in various topics, such as student performance expectations.

Importance of Excellence

I wish to stress two points in connection with the work of the Commission and the notion of excellence.

The first is that the Commission is genuinely open to informed and responsible advice from interested groups and individuals. These opinions are invited and will be welcomed, read, and considered. The Commission is wholly uninstructed, except for its charter, and is in no respect whatsoever bound to the opinions and views of Secretary Bell, the White House, Congress or any part of government, or to any other interested public or private party or organization.

The Commission, therefore, actively solicits advice from individuals and groups, particularly from those who observe educational successes and failures on a daily basis. Please send us any information which you believe might help us understand the problems inhibiting excellence in our schools and the solutions that might allow us to improve the quality of schooling. Examples of exemplary programs and successes are, obviously, of equal interest. We also are attempting to seek out examples of schools that are unexpectedly succeeding as well as those that are inexplicably failing. We believe there is much to be learned from these examples, whether they are encouraging or not.

The second point is that, while diversity of background and experience characterizes membership of the Commission, we are unanimous in our concern for, and commitment to, excellence in education. While our views of what constitutes excellence will not always coincide, there is unanimity in our belief that excellence and quality will be the overriding educational issue of this decade. This statement is not intended in any way to slight the egalitarian dimension of American education. This nation has attempted, and rightly so, to pursue both equal educational opportunity and excellence in education. I feel confident that Commission members, along with educational, business, and political leaders, remain committed to pursuit of that ideal.

A Concluding Note

There is a tendency on the part of some to view a recommitment to excellence in education as elitist and as hostile to the need for expanded educational opportunity. My own view, and I cannot speak here for anyone else, is that the egalitarian dimension, as expressed for example in the educational philosophy of John Dewey, is compatible with, and reinforcing of, the quality dimension in education. For Dewey, the aim of education is to allow individuals to live their lives to the fullest, to enable them to expand their horizons, to provide for both individual and societal growth. This philosophy is at base egalitarian and democratic in that everyone, irrespective of race or background, is considered capable of, and is afforded an opportunity for, personal growth and an educational experience worthy of each person's potential.

This view is in no respect inconsistent with excellence if one is willing, as I am, to accept the notion of excellence as John Gardner so many years ago and with such understanding and insight put it:

> A conception (of excellence) which embraces many kinds of excellence at many levels is the only one which fully accords with the richly varied potentialities of mankind. . . . Our society cannot achieve greatness unless individuals at many levels of ability accept the need for high standards of performance and strive to achieve those standards within the limits possible to them. . . . The tone and fiber of our society depend upon a pervasive and almost universal striving for good performance. And we are not going to get that kind of striving . . . unless we can instruct the whole society in a conception of excellence that leaves room for everybody who is willing to strive. . . .*

The time is ripe for schools, colleges, and universities to work more closely and cooperatively than they are inherently wont to do, to answer the public's cry for educational programs that will truly prepare young people to function in our society with success and happiness, and to draw from them what they are capable of giving, students of limited academic promise as well as those possessing such promise in greater measure. We should be clear in our own minds about the kinds of schools and institutions we have—what they can do well and what they should not be asked to do because they would do it either poorly or because in doing it, they dilute schooling's central purpose. By assessing the strengths and weaknesses of American education and identifying ways in which levels of excellence can be raised, the Commission hopes to set forth viable and enduring strategies for rebuilding confidence in the educational system.

The French novelist Marcel Proust once observed, "The real voyage of discovery consists not in seeking new lands but in seeking with new eyes." A fresh perspective and re-examination will, we earnestly hope, recommit our nation to the belief that the improvement of education in our country will expand individual choice, tap unrealized promise and potential, enliven sensibilities and understanding both at home and abroad, inform our civic discourse, enrich our lives, invigorate our economy, improve our security, assure our future as a free people, and restore confidence in and support of our schools, colleges, and universities.

For comments or information, write to: National Commission on Excellence in Education, 1200 19th Street, N.W., Washington, DC 20208.

---

*John W. Gardner, *Excellence* (New York: Harper & Row, 1961), pp. 131–132.

The Decline of American Education in the '60s and '70s

Andrew Oldenquist

Dr. Oldenquist is a professor of philosophy and member of the Mershon Center senior faculty at Ohio State University.

Despite limited successes, public schooling since about 1963 has presented a pattern of overall decline. That (or thereabouts) was the magic year, when scores started going down and all sorts of bad indicators—crime, suicide, illegitimate births—started going sharply up; in terms of such data the boring, eventless, Eisenhower '50s were the best we've ever had. The raw data that have been most damning for education are Scholastic Aptitude Test scores, which declined nearly every year since 1963. Iowa Tests, administered to primary school children and not only to the college-bound, show a marked, though not quite so drastic, decline during the same period. By these measures of verbal and analytical ability, for 18 years virtually every high school graduating class has been dumber than the preceding year's class. Universities now spend millions for remedial courses, and at my own university most freshman humanities texts used 15 years ago cannot be used today because the students cannot read them: The vocabulary is too rich, the sentences too complex, the ideas too difficult.

During the mid-'70s the magnitude of the failure began to penetrate the American consciousness and many who could afford it fled the public schools. Between 1970 and 1978, while public school enrollment declined, private school enrollment increased by 60 percent;[1] it increased in communities that do not bus for racial balance. Black enrollment in Catholic schools rose sharply in the big cities;[2] nationwide, nonwhites in private high schools increased from 3.3 percent in 1960 to nearly 8 percent in 1979.[3]

What went wrong?

The speculations of journalists and government commissions about why children can't read (and more recently, why they assault their teachers) have been incomplete and occasionally silly: Too much TV, old fashioned curricula, the decline of the family, Vietnam, the elimination of school prayer, and government interference have all been indicted. The cures have been simplistic, sometimes harmful, and very American—new buildings, ever more money, new experimental curricula, better racial balance. The only thing we are certain of is that public education did not improve.

Speculations about what went wrong largely neglected changes in our conception of the nature and purpose of education. So the cause that was left out was not a gadget like television or an event such as the Vietnam War, it was an *idea*. It was really a set of ideas which came primarily from professors in the colleges and departments of education and from a number of social scientists. They taught a radical individualism that alienated people from all of their social affiliations excepting the most local, an individualism-gone-mad that sometimes borrowed the slogans of the Left but in reality had practically nothing in common with socialism or collectivism. They preached the equal rights of individuals to respect, to reward, even to truth itself; they taught the supremacy of self-interest over the common good, of the emotions over knowledge and intellect, of children's autonomy over society's need for their socialization; and a thorough relativism according to which the very idea of one person's performance, ability, or even conduct being better than another's was considered demeaning, stigmatizing, and elitist. What is important, of course, is the effect these ideas had on young teachers and, particularly, on the inner-city schools where the federal funds could be spent.

The public schools' problems have multiple causes and it would be mistaken as well as mean to blame everything that happened on the education professors. However, ideas do guide policies, and the history of the ideas ascendant during the '60s and '70s reveals philosophical goals and assumptions which, through the usual kind of time lag, affect us for years after the ideas themselves have had their day. That is one good reason for beating a dead horse; I also hope to convince doubters that the horse

Reprinted, with permission, from *American Education* Magazine, May 1983. U.S. Department of Education, and the author.

is indeed dead and to contribute to an understanding of its fatal illness.

Ethics and avocados

Simple logic tells us that if Tom says something is so, and Mary says it isn't so, at least one of them is wrong. Either that, or they are arguing about whether avocados taste good and there is no right and wrong of the matter. But the idea of calling someone "wrong" offended the sensibilities of the period, focused as they were on such ideas as "middle class values" and "ghetto values," and many were led to treat ethics like avocados.

The elitism implied by standards in science, ethics, or everyday affairs— the simple idea that some things are better than others and some people better than other people at doing something—is not the same as the "elitism" of fixed social classes or of experts looking down their noses at everyone else. But in the turmoil of the '60s and '70s educators couldn't see the difference between standards and arbitrary privilege. After all, privilege typically hides behind the maintenance of standards and there were millions of blacks, women, disadvantaged, and handicapped who had long been excluded by such rationalizations. By about 1970 logic had become the professors' enemy; reasoning was "playing head games." The Law of Non-contradiction outraged them: it was elitist, indeed, downright un-American, because it ruled out the possibility of everyone's being right.

For educational policy it followed that academic standards had to be subjectified, made a matter of self expression, sincerity, and good will. Otherwise, there would be winners and losers, an elite, and self-esteem would suffer. Testing became an evil, grading of any kind a way of labeling children successes and failures. 1971 gave us the book *Wad-Ja-Get?—The Grading Game in America.* In 1975, a fifth-grade mathematics teacher said to me that while she does give some tests she does not put grades on them, "because I would not want to stigmatize the children."

Grade inflation at all levels

There is a connection between school teachers' reluctance to apply strict standards to their pupils and grade inflation in the colleges and universities. The decline in Scholastic Aptitude Test scores throughout the '60s and '70s is paralleled by an increase in the average grades given by colleges. Typical is the University of California at Berkeley, where the average undergraduate grade point average went from 2.5 in 1960 to 3.0 in 1974.[4] In a study of fifty leading

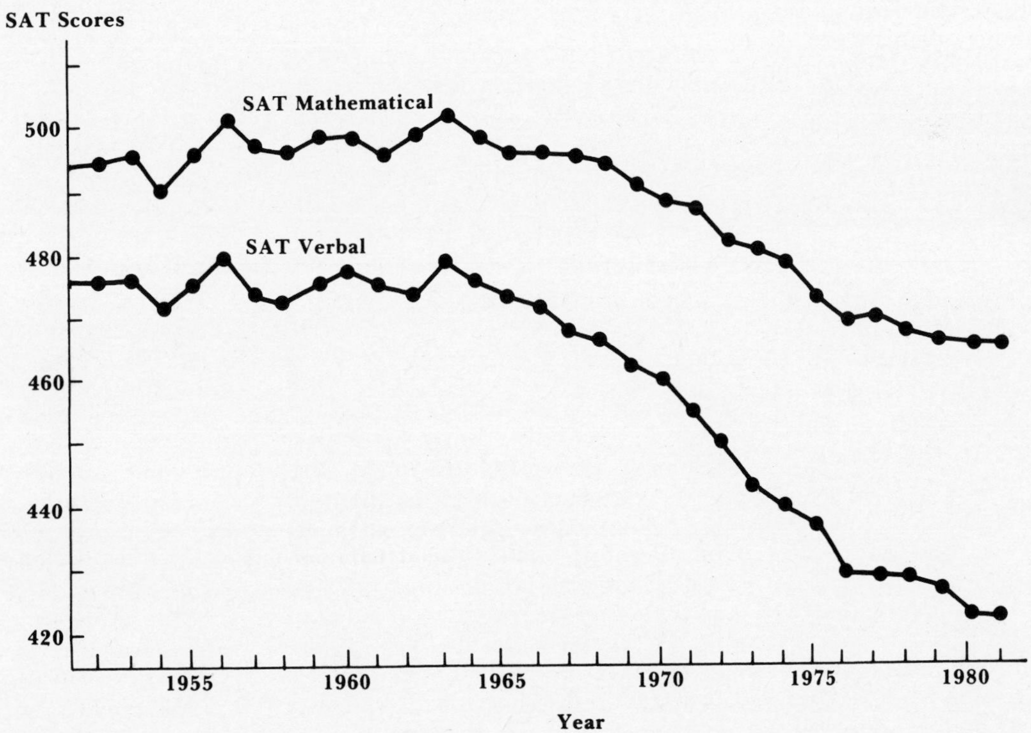

Figure 1. The mean score in mathematics declined from 502 in 1963 to 466 in 1981. The verbal score shows a greater decline. One is tempted to surmise that whatever caused both declines is exacerbated by television in the case of reading skills: TV competes with reading much more than with math; and the widespread acquisition of TV sets in the fifties would start a cohort of seven-year-olds in 1953 on the road to poor reading test scores ten years later.

universities and institutes of technology, Sidney Suslow found that between 1963 and 1974 the average undergraduate grade jumped from C+/B− to B, and the percentage of "A" grades awarded more than doubled, from 16 percent to 34 percent.[5] At some universities, starting in the late '70s, grade inflation has begun to level off.

Nationally, the leaders in grade inflation were the colleges of education, followed by the schools of social work. An evil that affected all departments of a university, in education departments during the late '60s and the '70s grade inflation became a way to sabotage the very concept of grading. The University of Texas at Austin is stricter than many. In 1980 the average undergraduate grade given by its education college was 3.3, nearly an A−, compared with 2.4 in business, 2.5 in engineering, 2.7 in liberal arts. Five years earlier the average education grade was 3.5.[6] Perhaps a more dramatic figure is the percentage of A's given by Texas at Austin. In the spring of 1977 (in undergraduate courses) 45 percent of the grades given by the education college were A's, compared with 27 percent by engineering, 15 percent by business administration, 31 percent by humanities, 24 percent by natural sciences.[7]

When we turn to a large state university in a different part of the country the picture is similar. At Ohio State University in the spring of 1980, the average grade given by the College of Education was 3.45, compared with 2.3 in the College of Mathematical and Physical Sciences, 2.7 in the College of Humanities, and 2.6 in the College of Biological Sciences.[8]

The result was that class after class of future teachers went through school being told that everything they did was excellent, for they received nearly automatic A's in every education course they took, and then, half literate, went forth into the schools and applied the same ideas to the nation's children: Everyone is doing just fine, everyone always passes. The education colleges' grades have been giveaways and bear little relation to acquired knowledge and skills; but the Scholastic Aptitude Test on which the teachers' pupils perform poorly, several years later, is objective and measures knowledge and cognitive skills. Is it whimsical to see a connection between these phenomena? Of course, our effective teachers managed to unlearn this "hidden curriculum" of the education colleges.

How is self-esteem achieved?

Within the education colleges and beginning in the late '60s, self-esteem became the chief good to be achieved by schooling, and its perceived enemies were grading, competition, and standards of any sort that implied that someone might fail to meet them. These included ethical standards with their threats of guilt and shame. The recipe for creating self-esteem emphasized "affective education" (i.e., programs concerned with emotions and feelings), which became a booming industry through the '70s; "cognitive education" (i.e., education) became an embarrassment. The aim, of course, was to humanize schooling and break with the picture that educators painted of martinet schoolmarms convincing tender psyches that they are failures. By the late '70s, what actually went on out there in the trenches, in the classrooms, seemed to depend on which side you were on: The education professors still saw cowed pupils learning dead facts and terrible assaults on self-esteem. Their critics saw the abandonment of basics, class discipline, and homework, and, in the "open classroom" schools in particular, teachers left with little to do with their young pupils beyond trying to keep some order, playing with gerbils, going on field trips to McDonald's, and telling puzzled parents that their child will learn to read "when he is ready." In the large cities, at least, the evidence is that the truth lay more with the critics.

Educators have not to my knowledge produced evidence that classes with strict academic standards and competition for grades have lower self-esteem, even among the bottom half of achievers, than classes in which everyone is told he or she is doing wonderfully and no one ever fails. The informal evidence is the opposite: Self-esteem results from competence and community, not from stroking. Losing sight of this was perhaps the most serious mistake of the "'60s thinkers," but it was a mistake born of compassion. Children feel good about themselves when they feel they are actually learning things, acquiring skills, and participating with others in serious, structured activity. Even when children do not realize this, their future satisfaction with themselves, and society's satisfaction with them, plainly depends on the character and competencies they acquire. But the eye of the period was on differences and on the individual, not on innate human sociality, not on the demands a healthy tribe or society must make for the sake of its common good.

The other side of the rejected coinage of traditional education concerned the nature of "cognitive" education itself. Here the new idea was that real education is learning how to think, to question, and to integrate experiences; it is not just learning "dead facts." Noble as this sounds, what it usually meant in practice is sneering at acquiring facts and substituting sessions devoted to self-expression and "rapping." For it is not as though one had in mind "live" facts to replace dead ones; all factual knowledge is "dead" and its alternative is self-esteem pumping, "hands-on experiences," and self-expression. Learning how to think—how to appraise, to reason, and to research facts—supplements and cannot replace learning lots of facts. Unfortunately the teachers who were supposed to teach children how to think were not themselves taught how to think, nor were *their* teachers (the education professors). No one in this chain was taught the necessary logic and scientific method, for that would require a rigorous sort of training that was contrary to the relativist and self-expressive spirit of the times.

Children respect facts, are proud of new ones they learn; this is also true of most great thinkers and scientists, as well as of ordinary good thinkers, throughout history. It is absurd to be ashamed of teaching or learning lots of facts. But the greatest minds do something creative with their facts that seems to transcend factual knowledge. The professors saw only this culmination and tried a short cut to wisdom and creativity. Perhaps they also forgot that just being able to name the beasts, or trees, or provinces, gives one power and control—the ability to re-identify things and tell about them, together with the taxonomy or social structure that lies behind an organized system of names.

The ideas of the '60s and '70s were uncongenial to the discipline, patience, and sense of wonder characteristic of science, and probably contributed to the present acute shortage of science and mathematics teachers. In 1971 the average college or department of education produced about 22 math teachers and 18 science teachers; in 1980 it was under five math teachers and six science teachers.[9]

The American "Cultural Revolution"

A key to the philosophical basis of educational "'60s think" is not the educators' formula for achieving self-esteem—all that bubble-minded stroking at the expense of learning—but the goal itself. "Self-esteem" is the inward-oriented, ego-centered replacement for the "social adjustment" of earlier decades. To many observers it was disconcerting enough then to see educators emphasizing social adjustment at the expense of mastery of material. But it was at last a *social* goal of teaching children how to live amongst others as social creatures; by the late '60s we had lost even that. Hyper-individualists dropped the "social" and saw the aim of education in terms of "self-image," "feeling good about oneself," and "self-esteem." They no longer sought to train children for life as members of a society; they at best taught them to view society as hostile terrain in which they must cope, at worst to be predators and parasites on society. This move from "social adjustment" to "self-image" as a goal of education is a good example of the individualism-gone-mad of the '60s and '70s. Masquerading behind Leftist rhetoric, it was a very American overreaction to tumultuous racial eruptions, discrimination, and to an unpopular war: We retreated from common, collective values to the individual, from "us" to "me."

There is an interesting parallel with China. Both countries wrecked their educational systems, from ideological excess and at about the same time, during their respective "cultural revolutions." Under the pressure of crisis the dominant ideology of each country hypertrophied, taking an exaggerated form: China aimed at the purest communism, America strove for the most perfect individualism. In America this meant denigrating community, tradition, and ceremony (except at extremely local levels) as bad conformity, as giving up self to serve "them," and substituting a calculated selfishness.

The effects on minority students

The educational ideas of the period had their greatest impact on minority students, because they appeared most in need of the professional educators' help, because they could not so easily escape to private schools, and because the big federal grant money was earmarked for them. That youngsters from black slums need help is statistically demonstrable in a number of ways; one way is to look at college performance figures. The attrition rates at state universities that enroll large numbers of ill-prepared students are frustrating to taxpayers, students, professors, and parents. The record is especially dismal for blacks. Consider the class of 1979 at Ohio State University. Of all students, black and white, who entered in the autumn of 1975, only 25 percent graduated after four years. The graduation rate for blacks after four years was 8.5 percent, and for black males, 4.9 percent, which is less than one in twenty. When we give students five years to graduate, the overall graduation rate is about 40 percent (obviously higher for whites alone) and under 21 percent for blacks.[10]

While Ohio State is worse off than most because it is an open admissions university, the graduation rates at state institutions across the country are lower for blacks than for whites. At some universities, while the overall graduation rate is still very low, the race difference is very small—for example, at the University of Texas at Austin. Consider again the class of 1979: 37.5 percent of the whites who entered in autumn 1975 graduated after four years, compared with 34.3 for blacks and 27.5 for Hispanics. The dismissal rate at Texas, at the end of four years, was 8.4 percent for whites and 21.9 percent for blacks (15.6 percent for Hispanics).[11]

The assumption of the education professors was that when a lower economic class black student enters college his main problems are psychological and societal—perhaps a defeatist attitude coupled with an uncaring and still partly racist academic environment—rather than more devastating shortcomings that have nothing especially to do with race: great ignorance of facts and of how to reason, very poor work and study habits, or poorly formed character. We are understandably loath to admit we are bringing up large numbers of children to be truly stupid, permanently so after a certain age, and worse, bringing up some to have characters so poor they are incapable of living lives useful to themselves or society. Consequently, the tendency has been to locate the problems of even the worst-off slum children exclusively in what is external, or superficial, or temporary—to describe the children in any way that does not imply that after age eight or nine, or even age 15, their inmost minds and characters are ruined.

A large part of the problem in the schools today is that teachers and administrators are less willing to force blacks than they are whites to do homework, perform up to standards, and behave civilly. We should also remember that poor blacks have been the primary guinea pigs for the educational experiments of the '60s and '70s, with the result that they and other poor children have been taught silly things, if anything, and deprived of crucial kinds of self-discipline by educators who were trying to help them. For example, my black freshmen, more often than my white ones, neglect an assigned paper topic and "express themselves" on some vaguely related idea; that, apparently, is what they were permitted to do in high school. The capacity to accurately explain a passage is poorer in my black than in my white students: another aspect of education that apparently had become obsolete in inner city schools. White college students make mistakes in papers or exams and ask (though not as often as 15 years ago) about the right way to do it. My black students, with the exception of those obviously from educated, middle class backgrounds, seldom ask about the actual text or theory they were to explain; they don't seem to think it related to how their paper was graded. I don't mean they assume they were given poor grades because they were black, but rather, they appear simply unused to being penalized for failing to master specified material.

What we demand of school children in slums should be the same as what we demand in private and suburban schools: hard work, prompt and accurate performance, and a trained capacity to postpone gratifications. A school in a wealthy, educated neighborhood might unavoidably have a larger college preparatory program than a school in a very poor neighborhood; but there can be no excuse for any difference in the effort that is demanded or in the habits we try to create. God knows, a school cannot do these things by itself: We now know that simply coming from a single-parent family, white or black, poor or wealthy, is correlated with poor school performance and with other problems, and that half of all black children are from single-parent families.

Educators practiced social triage

But the public education establishment hasn't even been firing in the right direction. Its general approach to school children in black slums has been timid and undemanding. More ominously, for a number of reasons it has rejected the indoctrination in character traits and work habits that *any* American needs in order to be a well functioning, useful, and reasonably satisfied member of society. The thrust of "'60s think" was that hard work and a work ethic, promptness and accuracy, and civility, cannot reasonably be imposed on children in black slums, that the "value systems" of children in black slums require different kinds of traits.

What this came to in practice was a system of social triage for a large minority of American children. Like military triage teams who set aside the wounded who look like hopeless cases, the educators who practice social triage fail to insist on the same levels of performance, self-discipline, and hard work that they demand of "more advantaged" children. It is "Catch 22": One of the most important ways the more advantaged children are more advantaged is that these things are demanded of them. Slum children are trained how to live in their slum, with a character, education and speech appropriate for the slum, and nowhere else. This is a policy that is racist in effect if not intention. On matters of race, "'60s think" was such an intellectual mess that many felt obligated to conclude that black slums were nice; indeed, they thought, simultaneously, that (a) black slums are dreadful and socially and spiritually harmful to the people who live in them, (b) since all values are relative, the black slum lifestyle is just as good as any other, and (c) we ought to be ashamed of our white, middle-class lifestyle.

The poor performance of slum children, particularly black slum children, in school and college today has very little to do with money or facilities; it has much to do with *ideas*—philosophical ideas about human nature, the work ethic, responsibility, the good society, and the methods and purposes of education. Spending billions of additional dollars on buildings, gadgets, and special programs will not do a thing to improve the performance of inner-city black kids in school and in business if the philosophy of education remains the same. What is needed, within the limits of what schools can provide, is very simple: Tough, demanding teachers and school officials, with authority to put pressure on parents, and who will kick kids' behinds, metaphorically speaking, until they do their homework, do lots of it, do it accurately, do it on time, do it in correct English, and take criticism with civility. But *nobody,* black or white, will learn how to study, gain self-discipline, and acquire competencies, under the philosophy of education of the '60s and '70s.

The Terror of the revolution

It was the glory of that period that it produced our first public, national commitment to racial equality and sensitized us, as did no preceding decades, to the rights of women, the handicapped, and others. But every social revolution has its Terror, in this case a fixation on rights and the self that extended to rejecting the most basic socialization and civilizing of the young. The self was everything, all the filaments between individuals and their society were cut, and a sense of belonging was lost.

Hyper-individualism leads to alienation and societal fragmentation that are in no one's interest. The issue of Black English is an example. Black English is an argot spoken by many low economic class urban blacks, but not by black people brought up in middle or upper class families except as an affectation. It is isolating because those who speak only Black English cannot be well understood by outsiders, nor can they adequately communicate in the larger worlds of business, science, and government. It is, for just that reason, an inferior means of communication for an American, unless his aim (or his teachers' aim) is that he spend his life in black slums. The relevant question for educators is, why pay any attention to Black English? I don't mean, why even think of it, for knowing that at home a pupil speaks Vietnamese, Russian, Spanish, or an American slum vernacular may be worth knowing when we detect problems in his or her speech and reading. But why should teachers fail to correct it in class, and why should they pay fulsome compliments to it or use books written in it? In doing such things we make it easier for Cubans, Soviet Jews, and Vietnamese to fully join the ranks of Americans than for blacks who have been here three hundred years.

It is ultimately a question of moral and cultural self-confidence: Insistence on mastering the national language is as much a sign of the non-demoralized society as is insistence on a common core of social morality. Each requires the indoctrination of the young; the acquisition of each is a principal badge of societal membership, its absence a badge of alienation. By lack of moral and cultural self-confidence I mean that the "language relativists" and "ethics relativists" have, fundamentally, given up. They are ashamed to be proud of anything and are saying, in effect, that either our society is no longer worth joining or it lacks the spiritual force to incorporate these people.

Perhaps another way to illustrate the philosophy of the period is to mention a few '70s examinations for the Ph.D. in education. In one, a candidate was asked what she would do, as a teacher, if a pupil told her to shut up. She would, we were told, try to find out "whose problem it was"; it was, she said, most likely her problem, and she would let the pupil know she realizes adults impose their wills on kids too much. She would, in effect, apologize to the pupil for his telling her to shut up. In another exam, a candidate for the Ph.D. defended the thesis that teachers must always connect their teaching with students' pre-existing interests. No one present seemed interested in whether doing this, as a general practice, could interfere with students learning how to postpone gratifications.

Results of relativistic philosophy

We have gone through a period of a decade and a half during which teachers and pupils have been taught that "values" and ethics are relative; that feeling good about oneself is the main goal of education; that a work ethic and even standard English are just white, middle class values, the imposition of which on blacks, Hispanics, and the poor is a kind of cultural imperialism; that children will learn to read "when they are ready"; that grading, criticizing, or punishing pupils is wrong because it may stigmatize them and damage self-esteem; that self-expression and learning to question and criticize are more important than learning "dead facts"; that children have rights to decide what they will learn and what is "relevant" to their lives; that doing work on time and accurately is uptight and middle class; that nothing is better than anything else, just different. Well, they have learned what we have taught them. Where the above educational philosophy is perfectly implemented we have its perfect products: Students who can barely read, who "turn off" when an explanation gets difficult, who know nothing of science, their history, or their culture, and who are suckers for astrology, witchcraft, and similar nonsense; who believe everyone is always selfish and that morality is hypocrisy; and who view their society as their enemy, are unable to persevere at onerous tasks, cannot accept authority or follow instructions, and insist on constant entertainment.

These suggested causes of recent failings of public education concern what is in our power to change: It is not "late capitalism," Laws of History, or worn-out DNA that is makng our children stupid and bad citizens, but educational philosophy and policy regarding how young humans must be trained in order to be competent, civil, productive, and relatively satisfied members of their societies.

NOTES

1. "Private-School Boom," *U.S. News and World Report* (August 13, 1979).
2. Fred Reed, "The Color of Education," *Harpers* (January 1981).
3. Bureau of the Census, *Statistical Abstracts of the United States, 1981* (Washington: U.S. Department of Commerce, 1981).
4. Sidney Suslow, "Grade Inflation: End of a Trend?", *Change* (March, 1977).
5. *Ibid.*
6. William F. Lasner, "Memorandum on Grade Trends," (The University of Texas at Austin: Office of Institutional Studies, 1981).
7. "Report of the Faculty Senate Committee on Grade Inflation," (The University of Texas at Austin, 1978).
8. "Annual Report of the Registrar," (Columbus, Ohio: The Ohio State University, 1980).
9. Worthy Ward, "Classroom Crisis in Science and Math," *Chemical and Engineering News,* July 19, 1982, pp. 9–16.
10. Survey by the office of Michael Young, The Ohio State University, released 1981.
11. "Memorandum on Student Flow by Ethnic Group," (The University of Texas at Austin: Office of Institutional Studies, 1980).

Are Soviet Schools As Good as They Look?

Russian students seem to outclass American graduates. But there are doubts over how much they actually learn.

MOSCOW

The Soviet Union would be a hands-down winner over the U.S. in a test of which nation turns out high-school graduates with a wider exposure to mathematics, science and foreign languages.

The question, however, is what use do Soviet high-school students make of the technical knowledge they acquire?

Unlike some American youths who leave school without learning to read, Soviet students all are literate. Their handwriting is legible. They use pen and ink to solve arithmetic problems—with few errors. They follow instructions.

Soviet teenagers sometimes use calculators, but few have access to computers. In a country where the centuries-old abacus is used more often than the cash register, conservative Russians believe a calculator spoils a youth's ability to work mentally with numbers.

The fact that the 3.9 million Soviet youths who finish high school each year are steeped in science and technology worries Izaak Wirszup, a University of Chicago mathematician and expert on Soviet education. He contends that "Soviet education mobilization poses a formidable challenge to the national security of the United States, one that is far more threatening than any in the past and one that will be much more difficult to meet."

Yet Russian officials—and parents—are concerned about the quality of work done by students, a majority of whom receive mediocre marks in final examinations. Official statistics show that only 17.7 percent of the graduates receive 4s and 5s, equivalent to B's and A's in America.

Going to school in Russia is no snap.

Students attend classes 6 days a week, 9 months a year, for 10 years, not 12 as in the United States. About 35 percent of classroom work is in science, 40 percent in the humanities and the rest in vocational training and sports.

Heavy on math. Starting in the first grade, or "class," as grades are known in Russia, students take five years of arithmetic, then are introduced to algebra and plane geometry, followed by calculus in the ninth and 10th classes. The national curriculum also calls for 1 year each of mechanical drawing and astronomy, 4 years of chemistry, 5 years of physics and 6 years of biology.

Boys and girls take close-order military drill during the final two years of school and are taught how to assemble rifles and use gas masks.

Outsiders find it difficult to assess the impact on Soviet society of this intensive concentration on science. But some experts say the fact that mathematicians emigrating to the West have no trouble finding teaching jobs proves that the Russian system works.

It is in the teaching of humanities that Westerners spot weaknesses.

The handful of American and British educators invited to Russia each year to teach English are impressed by class discipline and the seriousness with which pupils approach their work. But they note that students fail to think questions through on their own.

Says one American: "In a Russian literature class I visited, the teacher remembered my comment that students weren't forced to think for themselves. So he asked questions which would require them to use their minds.

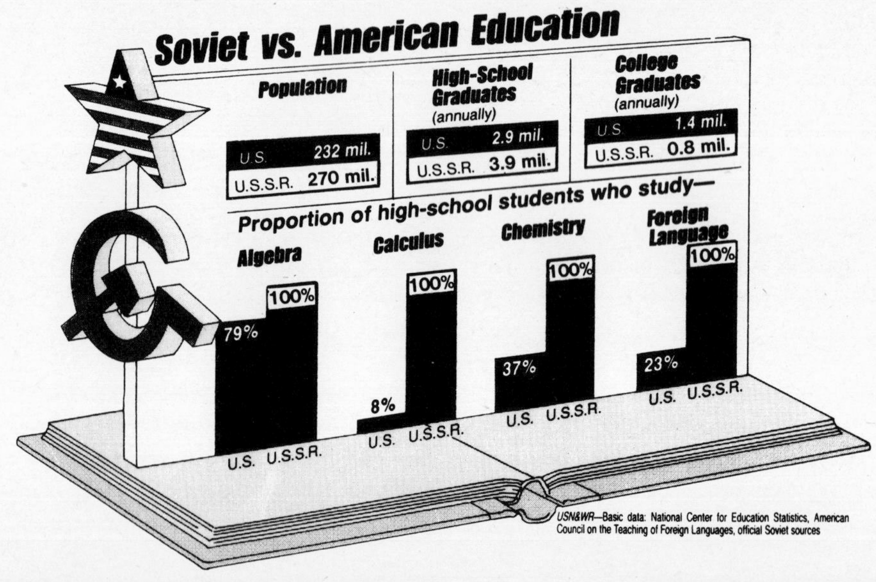

"The students couldn't answer the questions—which proved my point."

Many Soviet parents share the American teacher's skepticism about the quality of the system. Among their complaints: Teaching standards are falling. Some subjects are irrelevant. The six-day school week is too heavy a burden for children, as well as for teachers, who often work 60 to 80 hours a week.

Parents also fault the system for inflexibility on college admissions. Only about 10 percent of all high-school graduates are permitted to enroll full time in universities. However, statistics show that more than 40 million adults are enrolled in part-time, advanced-education programs.

The major reason cited for the ceiling on university admissions is the pressure to send high-school graduates with technical knowledge and skills directly into industry and the military to relieve manpower shortages.

This policy creates intense competition for university slots and favors candidates whose parents can afford to hire tutors to prepare their children for entrance exams. Says an engineer who credits his degree to luck in finding a good tutor:

"Some of these tutoring outfits are like factories. A teacher gets one group going in a room of his apartment, then moves on to a second room where he already has another group at work."

As in the U.S., quality of instruction varies from area to area. But the low level of pay—the ruble equivalent of $135 to $207 a month, or half what a skilled worker earns—makes teaching a relatively unattractive profession.

Another point: One half of the Soviet school-age population resides in the countryside, where living conditions are difficult and cultural and recreational facilities are few. Highly qualified teachers try to avoid rural assignments. The result is that even the top graduates of rural schools often score poorly on the college-entrance tests.

A distinguished professor at Moscow State University is scornful of today's instructors. "When I was in school before World War II," he says, "my teachers were experienced and demanding. They had been educated before the [Soviet] Revolution. Now, youths are taught by graduates of teacher-training colleges, people who don't have a thorough grasp of what they are supposed to be teaching."

A critical problem in the U.S.S.R. is the high student-to-teacher ratio, currently about 35 and 40 to 1. Thus, teacher-student relations tend to be formal and distant. There is little time for individual instruction.

A few dozen of Moscow's 1,200 secondary schools specialize in physics, mathematics and foreign languages. Emphasis is on discipline, Communist Party ideology and patriotism.

Take Moscow School No. 36, which specializes in teaching English. The neatly painted corridors are decorated with signs: "Learn to live and work in the Communist way." "Lenin lived. Lenin lives. Lenin will live." And in English: "Read, think, follow out."

For eight years, School No. 36 taught English and American literature entirely in English, without explanations in Russian. This tough approach has been revised, according to Director Nikolai Sonin, "because it was too difficult for the children. Parents complained."

This is what visitors hear when boys, dressed in blue gabardine uniforms, and girls, in brown dresses and black pinafores, demonstrate their skills.

Teacher: "Why was John Reed [American author of *Ten Days That Shook the World*] buried in the Kremlin wall?"

One youth: "Because he propagandized the October Revolution."

Another boy: "Because he fought for our Great October Revolution."

Their answers conformed to a law requiring schools to spread "the Marxist world view" among students.

Historical omissions. The role propaganda plays in Russian schools was disclosed by an in-depth study of Soviet and U.S. high-school textbooks made by scholars from the two nations in the early days of détente. The Americans were critical of Soviet textbooks that omitted important aspects of their own country's history.

Omission rather than falsehood is the usual technique in presenting history. The 1980 textbook used nationwide by students in class 9, for instance, provides no details of Stalin's reign of terror and fails to touch on the Moscow purge trials of the late 1930s.

The 10th-class textbook devotes one paragraph to Nikita Khrushchev, the top Soviet leader from 1953 to 1964. The Cuban missile crisis of 1962, set off by Khrushchev, is not mentioned.

Comparing the Soviet and American educational systems is much like equating oranges and apples. Views differ.

Some U.S. educators fret that intensive concentration on science and mathematics rapidly is moving Russia ahead of the U.S. in developing new technology. But in Moscow, worry centers on what is seen as U.S. superiority in turning scientific research into applied technology.

Director Sonin of Moscow School No. 36 notes that "scientific knowledge doubles every 10 years." Therefore, a major Soviet problem is how to impart that knowledge to students in just 10 years of schooling.

Why not add one or two years more? "The state doesn't want kids to delay their entry into life," he explains—life for most being either the military or the labor force.

Another judgment, this one by a Soviet parent: "Our schools have this in common with the military: They teach conformity and discipline. They try to mold children into obedient citizens. What they don't do is teach children to think for themselves."

By NICHOLAS DANILOFF

Morality and Values in Education

4

The definition of "morality" depends on the criteria persons use to evaluate the choices one makes in a variety of life situations. Since 1966 (and probably before that), there has been continuing interest in different possible approaches to helping young people learn about moral decision making. Several interpretations of values clarification, and Lawrence Kohlberg's moral education have been attempted in American public and private schools. These two approaches were conceived differently, and have generated curricular controversies in the schools. But perhaps education should move beyond the position of simply assessing the relative strengths and weaknesses of the two approaches to the fundamental question of what ought to be the relationship between public morals and the teaching about morality in the nation's schools.

Since the years following the American Revolution, many Americans believed that the schools should be involved in teaching certain civic values. Concern for the moral development of persons has been a basic part of the mission of public education in the United States ever since its formation. Issues have centered on what moral standards can or should be taught in the public school systems of a nation committed to the separation of Church and State by Constitutional mandate. This is the source of the recent debate over the establishment of more systematic and more secular approaches to moral education in the public schools. In the United States, the Constitutional requirement for separation of Church and State have, at times, limited what public school educators could perceive as legal or Constitutional forms of moral education. A major controversy exists over what types of moral instruction should prevail in American public schools. The public schools have far fewer degrees of Constitutional freedom in the general area of moral education than do private schools. Factors relating to freedom of expression of one's beliefs, as well as the right to be free from moral indoctrination in tax supported institutions are at work in the dilemma.

What is moral education? We need to take a hard look at what this idea means to each of us. We need to look hard at what specific things private or public schools should or should not do to implement instruction for dealing with choices requiring ethical judgment. There is evidence of widespread public support for some form of moral education in the schools. Before it can be carried out, however, we need to clarify what we mean by the moral education of a person.

Looking Ahead: Challenge Questions

What is moral education?

How does the study of ethics relate to a person's efforts to become a responsible, moral human being?

What is "right" or "wrong"? What is "better" or "worse" with regard to older and contemporary efforts to teach moral values in the schools?

Should schools be involved in helping people learn how to reason about moral questions? What skills are necessary for learning to critically evaluate moral situations? What are the best methods of teaching such skills?

Can teachers take a neutral stand in dealing with valuational concerns or moral issues?

How can teachers avoid indoctrinating their students?

What are the best methods for teaching people how to make decisions?

What ethical principles should prevail in a teacher's conduct in teaching about moral issues?

The Conflict in Moral Education: An Informal Case Study

Martin Eger

Some few years ago, the State of New York released a publication setting forth ten "educational goals" to guide designers of programs and courses. The fifth goal on this list reads as follows:

> Competence in the processes of developing values—particularly the formation of spiritual, ethical, religious, and moral values. . . . [The responsibility of the] school: a. knowledge of the diversity of values, b. skill in making value-based choices. . . .[1]

Three words are remarkable in the above formulation: "competence," "skill," and "process." To elucidate, even in a small way, what these terms may mean within today's cultural setting requires a long story—and we have one; but the words are significant also in a more direct sense.

"Skill" and "competence" are associated with such matters as carpentry, language, and mathematics. They hint at a science or craft, suggesting authority, implicitly relating themselves to proven methods or facts. When social support for moral values seems to be crumbling, new sources of authority are naturally welcomed, especially science.

For the uninitiated, however, there is a serious problem here, because science deals with what *is* or *is possible*, and from this no logical operation can derive what *ought to be*. To claim scientific backing in morals is therefore suspect, and could do more harm than good if the claim proves erroneous or misleading. Apparently, then, we face here a classic dilemma of secular education: That schools omit values from their concern is highly undesirable, and possibly an instance of social negligence, but the appeal to science is fraught with other dangers. Moral judgment does require authority, a ground of legitimation, but where is the *science of value* fit for such a role?

For those who *are* initiated–in the teaching movements that have recently commenced–there is no problem whatsoever. "Sciences" of "value formation" have long been sought and are now available; the "is"/"ought" disjunction is no longer an obstacle. The state's booklet takes this for granted, obviously, and the key to it all is the third word we have noted—"process." If values themselves are not derivable from facts, some theorists believe, the *process* of valuing may well be.

The studies that underlie this view—genetic and humanistic psychologies, associated with such names as Jean Piaget, Lawrence Kohlberg, Carl Rogers, and Abraham Maslow—are widely discussed today. But in addition to psychology, there is another field—increasingly important—that also contributes: the group of "decision sciences" based on computers, initially developed for military and managerial use. What such diverse theories have in common is a concern with the "how" of valuing, with the structure of decisions rather than their outcome. One uses "is" to derive not the "ought" of morals themselves, but another "ought": the manner of thinking about morals, and the way of evaluating that manner.

Those who avail themselves of these achievements see the educational dilemma as essentially bypassed: If we teach value science as political science is taught (without telling the student which party to belong to) then *all* values are within our purview. Logic is not violated, and the student becomes morally responsible in the highest degree, for he gains the "competence" to "develop" his own values, and to justify them in the light of reason. There is little doubt that the apparent advantages of this approach contribute heavily to the proliferation of "values programs" in the schools.

Yet in spite of the new outlook, and in spite of initial public receptivity, there has emerged during the past few years a widespread resistance to the project, including stunned and disillusioned parents, as well as reasoned doubts in scholarly quarters.

The clash points again to the dilemma described, and raises an important question: Is harm already being done? If so, is it related to the "sciences" guiding such policies as adopted by the State of New York? Or are the protests we hear of incidental phenomena, reflecting undue fear, to be expected when anything new is tried?

This is the question we examine here—by probing the connection between one type of values program, in one school district, and the social conflict to which it gave rise. A controversy over *curriculum* that shakes a town is bound to reveal something contemporary about the relation of theory to practice. Recently, such a conflict took place, distinguished by the clear and extensive record it leaves us. Looking at what actually occurred, what was said and done by different sorts of people—teachers, parents, school board members and professors—we immediately find two striking features: on the one hand, a living enactment of what some analysts are trying to tell us; on the other, odd happenings and strange inversions, as thought-provoking as they are unpredictable.

The Case of Spencer-Van Etten

In the hilly region south of Ithaca, New York, only 20 miles from Cornell University, lie the small towns of Spencer and Van Etten. All around are silos, Holstein herds, barns of every style and condition—yet farming is not the only occupation familiar here; far from it. From village homes and those adjoining the cornfields, people drive away each morning or work for Cornell, or for sophisticated industries in Ithaca, or commute south toward the IBM plans along the Susquehanna. Quite a number of families are relative newcomers, having left city and suburb to seek something else still: nature, a less treacherous environment for children, peace, and perhaps a chance for the spiritual side of existence.

For such a purpose the place seems well chosen. But in the Spring of 1979, as the local district prepared for its school board election, an uncommon battle raged through these valleys, and the village of Spencer was a center of intrigue. Neighbors met in each other's homes to make policy; professors were visiting to lecture; reporters from Ithaca, Elmira, and towns unknown were dropping by—even CBS's "60 Minutes" was there, cameras shooting a classroom scene.

The reason for all this was the school system's use of a "technique" known as Values Clarification (V.C.)—to many parents, the antithesis of wholesome moral guidance.[2] The election marked the climax of a protest movement already in its second year, and involving other issues also. But gradually the values program became the main target of criticism; for this, it was felt, was teaching outright what seemed implicit in much of the curriculum.

To picture to some extent the mode of these protests, how logic and bewilderment provoked each other, let us go back still further in time. If months earlier you happened to be nearby and stopped to pick up the local weekly, you might have read an item like this:

> The following are 8th Grade Decision Making questions given to the children of our school.
>
> Q. Which would you prefer to give up if you had to?
> A. Economic freedom? B. Religious freedom? C. Political freedom?
> Q. Are you in love right now?
> Q. Do you think there are times when cheating is justified?
> Q. Do you think people should limit the size of their families to two children?
>
> These are my questions to those questions: Who says one "has to" give up any of these freedoms? . . . Does an 8th grader really know if people should limit their families to two children? . . . What are they talking about? Cheating in school? Cheating in society? I feel these questions are "picking at a child's brain."

Under attack is a course of broad scope called "Decision Making" (D.M.), designed to help youngsters choose not only an occupation, but their lifestyles too. However, before people can make such choices, so it is explained, they must first determine what their true values are; and for this purpose the school had adopted the approach of Sidney Simon and his collaborators. Exercises, questionnaires, and "strategies" brought together by Simon's group in a teachers' handbook are used extensively in this course, as is their basic metatheory of values.[3]

Since parents had not yet discovered professional criticism of this new trend, the complaint quoted deserves notice. Its *style* reveals a level of emotion typical of many letters appearing at that time; but its *content,* just as typical, expresses in terse language several objections to which pages of scholarly prose had been devoted—questionable use of forced choice, violation of privacy, and superficiality.[4]

In Spencer, however, this was only the beginning, a kind of introduction, while really tough arguments turned on the philosophical concept of "choosing freely." And rightly so. For if the values-teaching movement makes any idea crucial it is this: A value must be "chosen" by the individual himself, "free," as much as possible, from authority, "conditioning," and "social pressures." Only in this way does it become one's "own," and therefore something positive rather than oppressive, something to be "prized," "cherished," and to "be proud of."

To many parents this naturally comes as a shock—and, incidentally, to not a few children also. (Some parents became opponents when their children complained.) These people, old and young alike, had thought until now that whether to become an engineer or a farmer was certainly their own choice—truly a "free" and personal decision—but they never believed that whether or not to cheat, for example, was quite in the same category. And this, it seemed, is what the school was saying: "If I teach my child that cheating is wrong" wrote one mother, "and V.C. teaches a child that there are no right answers, no wrong answers but rather to choose freely, it most certainly upsets the house."

Have these parents misunderstood? Have they missed the point in regard to *process?* If so, they are not alone. The charge of ethical relativism is made by scholars as well—in the philosophically grounded disciplines especially. In this case, an average group of parents sees what the academic community sees. The mechanic and farmer agree with the professor of philosophy. "Ethical relativism"—the technical term—had to be defined in Spencer, yet its significance was known long before.

But "relativism" is not taught here, the school retorts in frustration, and "philosophical generalities" are not relevant to what we actually do. The technique is *professional,* and scientifically tested; it raises to consciousness the cause of our ideals. "We understand ourselves as not teaching values," explains the Director of Guidance, "*but* teaching students to identify the values their parents, friends, churches, and society have already imparted to them." This is the local version of the oft-mentioned claim that V.C. "accepts all viewpoints," does not "promote particular values," and should therefore be offensive to no one. Moreover, the advocates insist, to avoid inculcation is not to say all values are equally good. As Simon and his associates put it: "If we urge critical thinking then we value *rationality.* If we promote divergent thinking, then we value *creativity.* . . . If we uphold free choice, then we value autonomy or *freedom.*"

This is the theory. And many parents have shown good will toward it, even in the face of disturbing practice. When the professional speaks, citing surveys and statistics, most people listen respectfully—especially those less versed in the conceptual apparatus of recent trends. But naturally they also listen to their children.

Take for example the afternoon of May 12, 1979. At the Spencer Grange, the seats and benches around the hall are filled. A photographer walks about popping his flashbulb at whoever seems newsworthy, a television camera bobs up and down on someone's shoulder, and in back, near the door, a young woman stands up to speak:

> My little girl came home and told me how she said lying was *wrong*—because Jesus said so—and the teacher told her, "but many people do lie." Well, I don't know . . . maybe I'm wrong, maybe I shouldn't believe what she told me—but I *do* . . . I *beeeelieeeeeve* her!

The mother repeated the key word, drawing it out and raising her voice, and one could not tell whether all its meanings were intentional.

Various people were gathered in this audience—farmers, executives, housewives, engineers, and also teachers from the local school system, their administrators, and members of the Board of Education. They had come to listen to a lecture on Values Clarification and to discuss its problems. The speaker, a philosopher at Cornell, was finished.[5] Now people from the floor were telling their stories, and when the mother of the girl who thought lying was "wrong" sat down, there was a momentary silence in the place. Then a young defender of the new methods answered from the front of the large hall, "Would you like it better if the teacher said nobody lies?"

A man turned to his neighbor with a wry expression. Scholarly debates surrounding the is/ought problem have not reached most parents of the Spencer area, but this they did sense: Not the fact of lying but another kind of "is" was making itself felt at this meeting as it does in the school—the "is" of language, the reality of *style.* What is new and noteworthy is not that "people lie," but what educators now *say* about people who lie—or cheat or steal.

A short distance to the south at Elmira College, an assistant professor hears of the controversy; indeed, it touches his town too. A trainer of teachers in the V.C. technique, he gives a talk to clear up the confusion. Suppose you tell a shoplifter that stealing is wrong—what do you accomplish? "It places the other person on the defensive, and the person making the judgment on a plane above the shoplifter." Some people may clarify their values in accordance with the best methodology, and still decide to shoplift. In that case, explains the educator, "you have to respect that decision if they have reached it intelligently . . . at least in this approach, you are respecting the person as a decision-maker."

Soon afterwards a newspaper version of the professor's views is placed in front of every chair at a meeting of the Board of Education in Spencer-Van Etten. Some parents are puzzled, others shrug; but months earlier, an answer had been given to this now familiar stance:

> If the child "chooses" freely to steal, who do I send the officer to? The school? I tell my children *stealing is wrong.* D.M. states "choose freely"—does that mean D.M. will be responsible for the child they have taught? No, hardly, the parents will be responsible. . . .

And in a formal letter to the Board of Education, the same concern from another viewpoint:

> If the school assumes the responsibility of dealing in areas of personal values, morals . . . does the Board feel it is up to assuming the responsibility to these children that involves seeing them through the hurts and consequences of the decisions about morality? We as parents are suffering with them. . . .

One fear is that the non-judgmental aspect of the program is *formal* only, that indirectly a type of value system is indeed being promoted—not just creativity, justice, and the like. In such a "receptive" atmosphere, parents suspect, the "is" of fashionable attitudes, professionally systematized and synchronized with an assimilated youth-culture, acquires artificially enhanced power; so that thought-structures deemed "advanced" are substituted for the "ought," usurping the normative function of the latter.

Here, for example, is a key general definition used in the controversial course dealing with moral values:

What is a "good decision"? The answer given by the D.M. Teacher's Manual: "the result of a decision is only good or bad in terms of the decision maker's own personal preferences."

And so, from the newspaper, a voice asks about the victims of such personal preference.

> If one chooses to steal, destroy, cheat—the list goes on—what about the victims? . . . *Thou Shalt Not Kill* . . . On the other hand there is values clarification which teaches to "choose freely." I would say that Hitler fit into this category. As he chose freely to kill. . . . Bineum Heller, in reaction to the big lie of Hitler and its horrible consequences wrote this:
>
> Perhaps part of the blame falls on me
> Because I kept silent, uttered no cry
> Fear froze my heart and confused my mind
> And I did not resist the lie.
>
> So I have spoken up.

Thus a writer in the *Spencer Needle.*[6] The point must have been made elsewhere too, for in the Adirondack foothills, in a center of V.C. work, a reply for trainers and teachers has already been composed, and appears in a recent book:

> *Could a Person Use the Valuing Process and Become a Hitler?* This question represents a classical test for the morality inherent in the valuing process. . . . *Short Answer:* No. A psychologically disturbed person is severely hampered in his or her ability to make free choices and to rationally examine a wide range of alternatives and consequences. Hitler was clearly paranoid and could not effectively use the choosing process of valuing.

At Cornell, speaking on moral education, a professor recalls those charges of old leveled at "corrupters of youth"—and smiles. The audience, knowingly, returns the smile. The vague resemblances, hurriedly glimpsed, may conjure a distorted image. The quotations above, with their awesome subject, suggests perhaps a truer resemblance—in the emphatic juxtaposition of a "scientific" perspective to the concepts of "good and evil."

The protesting parents did not do particularly well in the school board elections of June 1979—for reasons which will be touched upon. Though they received a respectable portion of the vote, none of their three candidates was elected. (One, however, elected the previous year, remained on the Board.) In September of that year, a new private Christian school opened in North Spencer with a starting class of 23 pupils, and this year there are 50.

It would be misleading to suggest that the values controversy alone was responsible for the fact that children are now being withdrawn from this public school system, though many pupils in the new school are children of the protesters. Scholastic achievement had been a major concern before the values issue arose. Strangely enough, "Decision Making" was in part developed to meet that concern—to combat apathy, and demonstrate how valuable *thinking* could be in making life's crucial choices. And on that basis it was defended.

To disenchanted parents, however, the relation between mental growth and this type of values program is of an entirely different nature. It deepens their despair over the intellectual quicksands into which the schools have now sunk, where each step taken to solve a problem seems to make things worse. They say that in regard to rationality, the effect achieved by methods like V.C. is the opposite of what is claimed; that the desire for knowledge and delight in reasoning, naturally budding at that age, may be channeled into something else: an endless sequence of games, of questions and answers that place the trivial and profound on equal footing, stupefying the student to a point where he is not likely to stop and think—or object—when after innumerable other queries he comes across," . . . enjoy watching movies on T.V.? . . . *enjoy going to church or synagogue?* . . . enjoy going on a picnic?" (Emphasis added.)

The long-term intellectual effects of holistic elements in the curriculum are always hardest to deal with, and in this area parents have the greatest difficulty making themselves understood: "Do you mean that this innocent little question will corrupt your child? You can't be serious." But these parents are serious: "Values Clarification mocks the educational process."

Parent vs. School

For some families, no doubt, V.C. was the last straw, especially in view of the school's response to their considerable and initially hopeful efforts. This response—or rather, the response of the education system at its many levels—when faced with inquiry and criticism, is itself a matter that must receive special attention.

The first reaction was, unfortunately, a denial that any such thing as Values Clarification was included in the curriculum—an inauspicious beginning, immediately rupturing the trust between the school and the community. Unconvinced, some parents began their own education, gradually acquainting themselves with the basic texts of the V.C. movement. It was not long before they could place on the table the handbook by Simon, Howe, and Kirschenbaum, and beside it definitions, voting sheets, and tests that children brought home. From then on, the source of these lessons was never in doubt.

There followed months during which letters of protest and dissent appeared in almost every issue of the local weekly. Not all were restrained, or thoughtful, or distinguished by sensitivity to the teachers' unenviable position—letters to the editor being what they are. It is significant, however, that leaders of the protest group clearly set forth arguments paralleling those in the academic literature—a literature with which they were still unfamiliar. That scholarly criticism of values programs is not as easily found as the many volumes written by proponents was certainly a factor in these events.

The second phase of the school's reaction was to say, in effect: Well, yes, we use this "technique," but what of it? Many school systems do; it is state-evaluated, government funded, and approved by the best educators and universities. Then it is possible to quote Lawrence Kohlberg,[7] use a few psychological terms, mention the formidable name of Harvard, and so on—making it quite clear that behind the local course stands a vast professional world of *science,* prestige and official recognition, in comparison with which the doubting parent is a stumbler, at best. And to insure the final effect, there followed, at a public debate in 1978, this impressive counterthrust:

> Now I want to know who are *your* sources. . . . Where do you *get* these ideas? . . . You made very strong allegations against the school. . . . On what kind of *research* are these statements based, and *where* does this research come from?

Alas, at this point the spokeswoman for the parents' group could cite only the texts of V. C itself—the books speak for themselves, don't they? How could anyone read this and *not* see what we see?

Yet, many did not. What happened instead was totally unexpected by these parents. In the third phase it was they who stood accused:

> We are witnessing an attack by an organized group . . . led by extremists from the far right who would like to see a little more hate than already exists in the world. The philosophy espoused in recent letters is embraced by the John Birch Society, the Heritage Foundation, the Conservative Caucus, the National Conservative Political Action Committee, and other ultra-conservative organizations.

This published outburst from a Spencer citizen became the keynote for much of what followed. The critics were described as anti-intellectual, simplistic, and opposed to independent critical thought. They were charged with "lifting" ideas from outside sources, and their actions were blamed for "dividing" the community. The insights of humanistic psychology and advantages of "process methods" seemed far beyond their understanding. But that was hardly the worst of it: The teachers' spokesman—head of a recently formed "Academic Freedom Committee"—warned of possible "links with the new right coalition in the country, one aim of which is to do away with the public schools."[8]

Actually, the situation was quite different. In over two years of controversy, no evidence of any ties to an extremist organization was uncovered, though at least one Ithaca newspaper went to the trouble of "acting on local tips" and conducting its own investigation. "Are you now or have you ever been a member of the John Birch Society?" was asked by a member of the Board of Education.

In the beginning, lacking political experience, the letter writers did avail themselves of whatever materials seemed to indicate a shared concern—and these, it is true, do not all conform to the highest standards of scholarship. Still, such fragments as appeared in Spencer could not in seriousness be called extreme or "ultra." (Of "outside sources" serving as a true inspiration here, there were C.S. Lewis' *The Abolition of Man* and the Harvard speech of Alexander Solzhenitsyn). Thus the school critics of Spencer-Van Etten acquired a bad name: "We have become the target of much criticism, mockery, segregation . . . not only as a group, but as individuals as well. We are not enjoying this role." And a bad name is not easily shed.

Much later, when the relevant scholarly papers were discovered, when academics came to town and long discussions were held privately and publicly, and when highly respectable professional criticism was offered to the community, the labels still stuck. Repeatedly, the critics had to ask for attention to the substance of criticism, not its alleged sources:

> I am very concerned about being labeled "extreme right wing". . . . If you think what we are saying is wrong, then *talk* to us about those issues, don't call us names. . . .

And even when a scholar experienced with the problem (Professor Baer, of Cornell) came to the aid of the parents' cause—with detailed analyses, and lots of patience—that only discredited the scholar! "An avowed enemy of Sidney Simon," was the teachers' reaction. "Why has an outsider stepped into our local controversy?" asked the president of the Board of Education, "his remarks were . . . an affront to our local people."

Here the issue stands. Those parents who out of religious or moral conviction do not wish to have their child's values "clarified" can with some effort avail themselves of a special procedure: The pupil is separated from his class and placed in study hall. This was the main concession brought about by the protests. Though parents point out the possible psychological harm, the injustice, and the educational waste of such a policy, no further accommodation has been offered. However, as people in this community continue their criticism—drawing in more detailed, credible support—the aura of unquestioned legitimacy surrounding the values program is dispelled. Since the election of June 1980, at least one third of the Board of Education is sympathetic to the case of the protesters.

Six Unsettling Questions

The controversy described obviously touches on issues of greater significance than a particular program used in one community. A critique of the Values Clarification method as such will not be given here. Rather, my aim is to reflect on a few of the more important problems brought to light by the Spencer-Van Etten story; and to pose, in the case of each problem, the basic question involved.

It is perhaps not accidental that the first difficulty encountered in Spencer-Van Etten, that which caused the earliest complaint and much bad feeling, had to do with the question of *truth*—not the problem of what to teach children about truth, but whether the school is telling the truth. Certainly access to fact was hard to obtain for those whom these facts affected most—the families of pupils, the "consumers" of education. A controversial program was part of the required curriculum, but parents were told it was not. When they discovered otherwise, they were assured it played a minor role; when they perceived it was the basis of courses in decision making, the explanation was that no educator could be found to oppose the approach; and when they brought to town scholars who did oppose it—things turned nasty.

We have here a new kind of credibility gap, involving not merely the schools' shortcomings, but their very intentions. And this misinformation or lack of information regarding programs likely to be found objectionable is not unique to the towns we have focused on. It is reported of a district in Anne Arundel County in Maryland that the Board of Education itself "had no idea" of the use of V.C. in their school, and the revelation was "positively electrifying."[9] In a New Jersey course, Transcendental Meditation was apparently practiced with incense, chanting, and invocations to Vishnu, but that did not prevent school officials from blandly denying a religious content. "Inexcusable ignorance . . . bordering on deception," replied parents; a legal suit was needed to eliminate the program.

Did the response in Spencer-Van Etten also border on deception? Many people believe just this. Unfortunately, the V.C. handbooks lend support to that suspicion, since total frankness is not encouraged. What parents see, teachers are told, should be *carefully selected.* Trainers themselves prejudge the source and nature of objections in a way that corresponds exactly to what happened in our story.[10] The patronizing attitudes, so bitterly resented by parents in this case, are less surprising therefore.

National attention is now directed to problems of "truth in lending," "truth in advertising," the Freedom of Information Act, and so on. But "truth in education"—in the same sense—seems to have been taken for granted. Thus, our first question:

1. *Is it acceptable that families of pupils in public schools be denied access to any information regarding curricula, school activities, or teacher training? Or that the standard of veracity for teachers and school officials be lower than that for auto makers, bankers, or the Department of Justice?*

The second point may also be seen in a consumer's perspective: Not only the purpose of a product has to be considered, but unintended results also. Cigarettes, energy use, and certain medicines have taught us that some side-effects are cumulative, long range, and hard to detect. Such experience supports the demand that on every new product or "system" introduced into society there be imposed bounding conditions within which the designers must solve their problem. And to insure not only that positive claims are justified, but that these conditions too are met, *time* is required.

How do matters stand in education in this respect? When Values Clarification was introduced in Spencer-Van Etten in 1974, and the *Handbook of Practical Strategies* was beginning to be used there, this fundamental text of the movement was barely two years old. "Research" on the effectiveness of the approach was "far from conclusive"—by the authors' own admission—and side-effects were not even mentioned. In the following year, evaluators termed these studies "relatively unsophisticated";[11] and the first systematic appraisal of even this doubtful evidence—which did not appear until 1978—essentially refutes the positive claims of the proponents.[12] Thus, when the program was initiated in this school district, detailed professional criticism of Values Clarification had not yet begun. But advocacy by the developers was loud, their materials flooded the libraries, and their activities were gaining favor with the State and the teachers' union.

This situation gave rise to an especially instructive though predictable phenomenon. There was a time—some parents believe—early in the protest, when the protesters were being "listened to" by their community, and indeed by a fair number of the teachers themselves. It was their inability *at the time* to produce unimpeachable professional critiques, supporting at least in part their own objections, that largely determined the ensuing course of sentiment. In the absence of scholarly judgment, the charge of "rightwing sources" dominated the atmosphere. And once public positions were adopted, and commitments made, no amount of credible evidence could alter the outcome, for then a powerful new element had entered the picture—personal prestige.

Whether we take a "consumerist" viewpoint, or that of scholarship and science, the implication is clear: Criticism *follows* innovation; a decent pause between proposal and full-scale use is therefore indispensable. The lack of thorough, many-sided evidence invites leadership by selected expertise and half-baked professionalism, and in such a context the ideal of local control of education through elected boards is hardly meaningful. Our second question, therefore, is:

2. *What checks and balances, if any, exist within the educational system to prevent questionable practices*

from being "sold" to the school before competent evaluation has taken place? What mechanisms are there for communicating to the schools and their communities all aspects of such evaluation at the time they are needed?

Now suppose a new program is in fact developed at the universities and widely implemented—and it does engender opposition. What then have we a right to require of the educational system?

Nothing was more evident, and more embarrassing to the teaching profession, than this fact: After a year of discussion and debate, the protesting parents were in possession of more knowledge, more documentation, and deeper understanding of the subject at issue than were the teachers defending the school's position. The parents, not the school, informed the community of the relevant literature, and brought in scholars to speak. Teachers involved in the controversy seemed caught off-guard, frightened, and badly prepared to handle the intellectual substance of the protest. Perhaps this explains why they never did come to grips with that substance, but concentrated instead on other replies.

"My intention here tonight is to get the facts out, and to demonstrate to you what we have found in our research." So began the teachers' representative in a public forum in Spencer-Van Etten. His posture is flawless. It is indeed the teacher's job to supply facts and dispel prejudice. What followed, however, was breathtaking: "I teach a college course in adolescent psychology and moral development . . . and the only place that I find the statements you people make about Values Clarification is in this right-wing literature." When this statement was made in December 1978, the *Moral Education Forum* had been reporting professional opposition for about three years, and a special issue of *Phi Delta Kappan* featured debates on the same kinds of objections local parents were raising.

The conclusion in Spencer was inescapable: Either school employees knowingly withheld critical opinion from the community, or they honestly did not know of it and could not find it even with effort. In any case, the professional training of these educators is called into question, and the responsibility of the academic world reveals itself as greater than commonly assumed. Criticism of teacher education is nothing new, but the expansion of public schools into the realms of morals, sex, death, the self, and "decisions" in general, raises additional questions.

Can the average teacher with the average training be a "teacher"—or "facilitator"—in such deep waters without comprehensive additional education in ethics, moral history, theory of knowledge, and the like? May we not expect that these modern "teachers of virtue" will themselves have had an education commensurate with the task? It does not inspire confidence to be lectured by an instructor in "moral development" who does not even possess the basic skill of a "library look-up" in his own field.

Unfortunately, most developers of these programs are far more engaged in stocking a veritable supermarket of materials—with films, tapes, games, numberless "strategies" and "moral dilemmas"—than the in-depth education of the teacher. Values Clarification, which recommends itself as "easy to get started," is especially culpable in this respect; to become a practitioner, the novice is assured, "a relatively short training program, as short as a few hours," will suffice! Summing up this side of the problem, then, we ask:

3. *Do the universities—and does society—feel comfortable with a situation in which millions of children in thousands of schools receive systematic moral education from teachers whose study of the subject consists of no more than a one-week workshop and a handbook of strategies?*

Morality and Process

In discussions of whether moral education belongs in public schools at all, two questions always arise. Can you really avoid moral problems? And wouldn't prohibition violate a basic freedom?

Again the drama of Spencer-Van Etten casts the issue in a new light. The controversy there began in earnest not because an individual teacher made an isolated remark or gave a personal opinion, but when parents discovered exercises, questionnaires, and definitions, taken from *handbooks* and systematically applied in classes, and when they realized that this methodology projects a meta-ethic fundamentally different from what C.S. Lewis called the "Tao"—the universal recognition of objective value and "common human law."

Teachers' freedom to express personal views on moral questions, when these questions arise naturally in subject matter or discussion, was *not* contested here. And of course such "dealing" with moral issues cannot be avoided—nor is it. Nor does any serious person suggest it should be. The crucial question seems, rather:

4. *Is the issue of "free speech," when each individual teacher responds on the basis of his own unique background and convictions, the same issue as when a whole school, or district, adopts this or that developer's system of moral education, complete with hardware, software, "trainers," and gurus? In the latter case, may it not actually be a restriction on moral dialogue?*

The opposition in Spencer-Van Etten did indeed believe that a narrowing of moral vision had been imposed. Parents usually find the nature of this narrowing difficult to articulate in a form acceptable to educators, but in this community one school board member rendered the gist of it concisely: "We're not saying our precepts should be taught, but if ours are left out, then leave out all values."

The statement deserves attention. What is meant by "our precepts"? It is not, as sometimes charged, "our religion." The Constitution's stricture in this regard is well known here and not challenged. We arrive therefore at a point where the pervasive effect of *meta*-ethics comes to the fore—the foundation of ethics, its origin, its categories. What is clearly felt by many parents is the exclusion—from the explicit methodology—of a whole realm of moral categories not specific to one religion, but part of that "Tao" encompassed by the heritage of both East and West: the *good*, the *true* (objectively), the *just, soul, faith, courage, moral rebirth,* (or "turning," or "enlightenment") . . . etc. What they see instead is a new set, including such concepts as *self-image, life-style, rich experience, decision-model, risk strategy, maturity, self-actualization,* and *rationality* (in the hypothetico-deductive sense). The only element from the older list often kept is *justice.*

Granted that such a shift in ethical categories accords with trends in psychology and operations research, are there valid grounds for *excluding* from public education the more traditional set? Well . . . there may be. There may, indeed, be—*if* such language is in itself deemed to be religious, and its inclusion unconstitutional. But this raises perhaps the most fundamental question of all:

5. *If the systematic teaching of morals within the bounds of the First Amendment requires systematic exclusion of a whole realm of meta-ethics underlying moral thinking in our society, isn't this in itself a distortion of ethical discourse in the intellectual sense, and injustice in the social sense?*

Yet systematics is the main feature of the values teaching movement today; it meets the requirement that morals too be seen as *skill,* that here also a *science* legitimates. Let us look at the point more closely therefore—this time from a humanist perspective.

The word "humanism" is, of course, what is distinct from "mechanical." The "knowledge factory" and "mega-machine" embody its opposite. It is this anti-mechanistic, anti-rule-following inclination that led reformers to indict so-called traditional education, and to introduce a whole series of reforms to free the schools from needless stifling formalism. And this aim one can easily accept.

But today a curious reversal seems to be occurring. Humanist educators increasingly press to systematize the few realms that have so far escaped this fate. "Traditional" education assumed certain values axiomatically—and for that very reason had no need to explicate them through a system. If a child cheated on a French test, for example, he lost face with his peers and his teachers—and this is how the value was *supported* (not "reinforced," not taught!). Now, however, a pupil is asked whether, according to someone's criteria, that "decision to cheat" is or is not a "critical" one. Again, a child is tempted to "drop a friend who is being made fun of by other kids at school." In a traditional environment, chances are a youngster would *recognize* that act for what it is; but today in Spencer he is *taught*—to identify which of the four "main risk-taking strategies" this decision represents.

Science, by definition, systematizes what it deals with, it formalizes its subject. And the formalization of decision making along the lines of management and computer models, if applied to morals, must obviously reduce that also to a system. It is fair at this juncture to ask, of humanists, especially:

6. *Is it good "strategy," in the long run, to humanize our "knowledge factories" by replacing the axioms and disciplines of one era with the systematics of another? Is rule-following in "how to decide" really less mechanical than rule-following in regard to ends? In short, is an automatic "value-driven decision system" the proper model for a more moral, more humane society?*

A Warning, Ancient and Modern

The final point is not a question at all, but a reminder. The value education movement has justified its mission partly by the rapid social change occurring in our time—the "collapse of the old morality." True, the change is great. It lends urgency to the work of the developers; to do nothing seems dangerously complacent. That is one horn of the dilemma of values education. But in thinking about man, as about nature, there generally has been equal concern with the *invariants*, as science calls them—that which remains constant in the midst of all change. Compare now the dialogues from Tioga County that have occupied us here, with those of another, "simpler" age. In the invariant lies the second horn of the dilemma.

Protagoras, the Sophist, is come to town. And the young Hippocrates is all on fire—for this teacher, famous in all the cities, promises his student not the "drudgery of calculation, and astronomy, and geometry and music," but "prudence in affairs private and public . . . to speak and act for the best." He has a special method, it is told, and all the youth and would-be teachers throng about him like a king's entourage.

But wait a minute, says Socrates—how do we know it's all true?

> When the soul is in question, which you hold to be of far more value than the body, and upon the good or evil of which depends the wellbeing of your all—about this you never consulted either with your father or with your brother or any one of us. . . .
>
> Surely . . . knowledge is the food of the soul; and we must take care, my friend, . . . that the Sophist does not deceive us when he praises what he sells, like the dealers wholesale or retail who sell the food of the body. . . . In like manner, those who carry about the wares of knowledge, and make the round of the cities, and sell or retail them to any customer who is in need of them, praise them all alike; though I should not wonder, O my friend, if many of them were really ignorant of their effect on the soul. . . . If, therefore, you have understanding of what is good and evil, you may safely buy knowledge of Protagoras, or any one; but if not,

then, O my friend, pause. . . . For there is far greater peril in buying knowledge than in buying meat and drink. . . . You cannot buy the wares of knowledge and carry them away in another vessel; when you have paid for them, you must receive them into your soul and go your way, either greatly harmed or greatly benefited. . . .

Plato, *Protagoras*

"You are what you eat," most of us have heard that expression.

There are those who are very concerned about "junk" being served through the school breakfast and lunch programs. They believe as adults we are responsible, and should be choosing nutritious food for school children. . . .

I have heard the phrase, "You are what you think." This also has clear meaning to me. What I think is eventually manifested in my character; the things I say and do. Shouldn't I be equally concerned with the nutritional value of what enters my mind? Shouldn't I be even more concerned as to my children's choice? . . .

Theresa Rimbey
Spencer Needle
August 10, 1978

Notes

[1] *Goals of Elementary, Secondary and Continuing Education in New York State* (The University of the State of New York, 1974).

[2]For a general introduction and critique, see William J. Bennett and Edwin J. Delattre, "Moral Education in the Schools," *The Public Interest,* 50 (Winter, 1978).

[3]Sidney B. Simon, Leland W. Howe, and Howard Kirschenbaum, *Values Clarification: A Handbook of Practical Strategies for Teachers and Students* (Hart, New York, 1972). This is a widely used text.

[4]For example: John S. Stewart, "Clarifying Values Clarification: A Critique," *Phi Delta Kappan,* 56, No. 10, 1975, and other articles in that issue. Alan Lockwood, "A Critical View of Values Clarification," *Teachers College Record,* 77, No. 1, 1975; and "Values Education and the Right to Privacy," *Journal of Moral Education,* 7, No. 1, 1977.

[5]Professor Richard A. Baer, Jr. (Cornell University). See also his "Values Clarification as Indoctrination," *Educational Forum, XLI,* No. 2 (January 1977).

[6]September 14, 1978, p. 7. Most of the local quotations given in this article appeared in the *Spencer Needle* during 1978 and 1979.

[7]Lawrence Kohlberg has criticized Values Clarification for some of the same shortcomings as have the parents of Spencer-Van Etten. But since he has defended the use of V. C. in public schools, his name was used here in support of the controversial course. See "An Exchange of Opinion between Kohlberg and Simon," in *Readings in Values Clarification,* Howard Kirschenbaum and Sidney Simon, eds. (Winston, Minneapolis, 1973).

[8]*Ithaca Journal Magazine,* January 27, 1979, p. 1.

[9]Private communication. See also *Maryland Gazette,* July 30, 1979, p. 1 and *Sunday Sun* (Baltimore), May 27, 1979, p. A-1. In Anne Arundel County, parents apparently won some legal restrictions on the use of V.C.

[10]Howard Kirschenbaum, *Advanced Values Clarification* (University Associates, La Jolla, 1977), Chapters 4 and 13.

[11]Douglas Superka and Patricia L. Johnson, with Christine Ahrens, *Values Education: Approaches and Materials* (Social Science Education Consortium, Inc., Boulder, Colorado, 1975).

[12]Alan Lockwood, "The Effects of Values Clarification and Moral Development Curricula on School-Age Subjects: A Critical Review of Recent Research," *Review of Educational Research, 48,* No. 3 (Summer, 1978).

[13]But "humanism" also connotes an opposition to *theism*: in our culture, Judaism/ Christianity. The confusion of the two meanings of the word greatly exacerbated the conflict in this community, and elsewhere.

SCHOOLS AND DEMOCRATIC VALUES

SANFORD A. LAKOFF

Sanford A. Lakoff is a fellow at the National Humanities Center at Research Triangle Park, North Carolina, and professor of political science at the University of California/San Diego.

THOSE WHO care deeply about democracy have always been concerned about the role of education in preparing the young to assume their responsibilities as citizens. Jeane J. Kirkpatrick, now our representative to the United Nations, addressed this concern thoughtfully, from a modern perspective, in the pages of this magazine two years ago ("The Teaching of Democratic Values," *American Educator,* Spring 1979). In an eloquent essay, she rejected the vogue for "value-neutral" education and pointed out that "democracy makes unusually difficult demands on both rulers and citizens." No other government, she says, "requires so much voluntary participation in power and poses so many limits on its exercise." For just this reason, she concluded, "If democratic government is to survive, schools should teach democratic values."

And so they should—provided there is a clear understanding of the all-important difference between education and indoctrination.

In urging that the schools teach democratic values, Ambassador Kirkpatrick is in good, even venerable, company; the Founding Fathers of this republic shared exactly the same view. They, too, recognized that because it required restraint in the exercise of power, as well as a high degree of citizen participation, a democratic system of government could not be maintained unless loyalty to its ideals could be instilled at an early age.

As usual, it was Thomas Jefferson who put the common conviction most incisively. In drafting a report proposing the establishment of a university in Virginia, he distinguished between the role of the university and that of what he called "primary" education. The university, Jefferson held, should concentrate on developing the talents of those who had shown themselves to be especially gifted and virtuous—the "natural aristocracy" that would provide the country's leadership. Primary education should be universal and should be designed to give each individual not only "the information he needs for the transaction of his own business" but also the moral and civic instruction "to understand his duty to his neighbors and country" and "to know his rights; to exercise with order and justice those he retains; to choose with discretion the fiduciary of those he delegates; and to notice their conduct with diligence, with candor, and judgment."

In prescribing these goals, Jefferson took full account of the need for young people to acquire specific skills and substantive knowledge, but it was not enough, he thought, for schools simply to train people to fend for themselves. Above all else, the aim of schooling in a democracy must be to develop moral and responsible citizens, "to instruct the mass of our citizens in these their rights, interests, and duties as men and citizens."

What beliefs constitute the core values of democracy that schools should aim to inculcate? Ambassador Kirkpatrick admits that no single checklist can be drawn up that can be said to have authoritative standing, but she contends that there must be widespread consensus on certain basic items, amounting to a democratic creed: "A belief in political equality for all citizens; a belief that rulers should be chosen by competitive, periodic elections (and not by force or heredity); a belief that rulers and ruled alike are bound by the ordinary laws of the land and entitled to due process; a belief that all persons have certain rights—including those of life, liberty, and

This article first appeared in the Summer 1981 issue of *AMERICAN EDUCATOR,* the quarterly journal of the American Federation of Teachers.

property—that may not be legitimately abrogated by government."

Here, too, she is on firm ground. Studies of the political theory of American democracy and of the fundamental beliefs held by the overwhelming majority of Americans show that there is a strong consensus over these ultimate values. Americans differ in the emphasis and interpretations they put on the particulars and the means most appropriate for realizing them. There are real and significant differences of opinion between contemporary liberals and conservatives, as there were earlier between Federalists and anti-Federalists, Whigs and Jacksonian Democrats. Nevertheless, compared to the ideological discord that often separates people in other countries into warring camps, controversies among Americans tend to be contained within a more encompassing and unifying commitment to the democratic process.

In fact, the consensus over fundamental values has been so pervasive that it can easily go unrecognized. As the political scientist Robert Dahl explains in a textbook intended for introductory courses in American politics, "Americans are a highly ideological people. It is only that one does not ordinarily notice their ideology because they have, to an astounding extent, all agreed on the same ideology."

GIVEN THIS general agreement on fundamental principles, why should it now be necessary to urge that a deliberate effort be made in the schools to inculcate democratic values? One reason is that a good deal of confusion has grown up in recent years about the nature of these ideals. As Frances Fitzgerald has shown in her recent book *America Revised*, the textbooks used to teach American history have traditionally mirrored (though imperfectly) the general consensus as it changes from decade to decade. Lately, however, they have been tailored to suit a variety of "markets," defined by age, as well as by social class and region. As a result, she points out, with the textbooks of the 1970s in mind, "The messages that children must receive are rather confusing: love everyone in the elementary grades, fight communism in junior high, and face endless intractable problems in high school."

This confusion is compounded by a growing ignorance of the way the political system actually works. As Fitzgerald also points out, a recent survey found that 47 percent of the nation's seventeen-year-olds did not even know that each state is represented by two senators.

Confusion over values and political ignorance go hand in hand. Young people who might otherwise become responsible and active citizens acquire what Thorstein Veblen called a "trained incapacity" for political life because they never really learn what it means to live in a democracy. This, of course, is not just a result of the instruction they receive or do not receive in school. The schools must compete against powerful outside influences, not the least of which is the pervasive output of the media of mass communication. Studies of the political socialization of American school children have turned up dramatic evidence of the growing influence of the mass media. Since the turn of the century, when the media began to acquire its present enormous influence, surveys of children's heroic role models have shown a steady trend toward the replacement of political and patriotic figures by popular idols in the various fields of entertainment and athletics.

Other evidence suggests that in recent years the adults from whom children take their political cues have experienced a loss of confidence in the legitimacy of this country's political institutions. The contributing causes are well known; they include such wrenching social experiences as the controversy over the Vietnam war, the rash of political assassinations, and the Watergate scandal. Now, traditional pride in American ideals is being tested anew by the spread of incivility, drug addiction, crime, and almost casual violence in our major cities and, increasingly, in the suburbs and rural areas.

Ambassador Kirkpatrick lays some of the blame for the deterioration of civic and moral standards on the belief held by too many educators that, for various reasons, it is wrong to impose values in the classroom. She indicts a series of modern ideas, including moral relativism, the notion that objectivity requires moral neutrality, the belief that in a pluralistic society moral values should be left to subcultures, and the objection that to transmit social norms is merely to promote acquiescence to the status quo.

In responding to these attitudes, she points out that some questions, such as genocide and racial discrimination, do not admit relativistic answers. In the daily life of the classroom and playground, moral questions arise that demand to be resolved in accordance with such ethical principles as honesty and fairness. When they teach literature, history, and social studies, teachers inevitably "communicate and inculcate moral principles." Pluralism, she argues, does not require that *all* values be left to subgroups to teach their adherents, but only those, such as religious beliefs, that are not essential to the democratic creed. The rise of totalitarianism in this century, not only in Germany and Eastern Europe but even in "Jonestown," shows all too clearly that democratic values will not be acquired automatically: "The notion of the 'natural' moral man turns out to be no more tenable than the notion that children learn best when left alone to motivate themselves, discipline themselves, teach themselves."

AS COMPELLING as this argument is, especially in comparison with some of the woollier theories of open-ended, "de-schooled," wall-less, and mindless pedagogy that have been advanced in recent years, the conclusions that seem to follow may raise troubling problems unless a clear distinction is drawn between education and indoctrination. If teachers are told nothing more than that they should not be value-neutral and scrupulously objective, what is to inhibit some of them from using their classrooms to subject the young to propaganda on behalf of whatever one-sided version of American democracy they choose to inflict? Some would surely try to promote an uncritical allegiance to some glossily unrealistic, rose-tinted vision of the American Way of Life, as it appears to the most myopic super patriots, while others would use their new license to paint America in more lurid colors—as the home of racism, imperialism, sexism, and assorted other evils.

If the schools are to catechize students in the democratic creed, why not in the religious values of the various communities they serve? What could be said to those who now claim that teachers of biology should not be free to teach Darwin's theory of evolution because it contravenes religious teachings or that they should be allowed to do so only on condition that they give equal attention to "creationism"? Those who take this position are also arguing that education cannot and should not be value-neutral, but the conclusion they draw is that the schools should indoctrinate the young with Christian values, as understood by fundamentalists and evangelicals, even at the expense of scientific education.

There is also good reason to fear that if the schools are made instruments of indoctrination they will become, more than ever, the object of attention not only by self-appointed guardians of public morality but also by the agencies of government. If the Arkansas legislature can mandate the teaching of creationism, what is to prevent any legislature from prescribing the orthodox standard interpretation of American history and government? If a federal investigator can sit in on a class (as one did recently at the Berkeley law school) to investigate the charge that a particular professor was making comments derogatory to women, what is to stop an army of government auditors from being dispatched into every classroom in the country once it becomes the law of the land that schools must indoctrinate students with some prescribed national creed?

Even if the legislatures and courts can be trusted to deny themselves such an exercise of their power (which in view of recent experience, is most unlikely), the idea that society should rely on its teachers to implant approved values is not necessarily any more appealing. There would remain the problem so wonderfully portrayed in Muriel Spark's novel *The Prime of Miss Jean Brodie* and in its memorable film version. As those who know it will recall, the fictional Miss Brodie thought it her mission in life to transform her impressionable charges from mere girls to votaries of the higher morality as understood by the avant-garde. The version of bohemianism then current involved a mixture of aesthetic and political romanticism, including the adoration of Mussolini and his Blackshirts. As a result of her proselytizing, one of her pupils becomes entangled in the Spanish Civil War and comes to a tragic end; another, recognizing that she was being induced into entering a liaison with an older, married art instructor, turns upon Miss Brodie and instigates a review of her conduct that leads to her dismissal. On at least one level of analysis, the moral of this story is that there is a serious distinction between dedicated teaching and the seduction of the innocent.

DOES THIS mean that dedicated teachers must ignore questions of morality and citizenship, that Ambassador Kirkpatrick and Jefferson before her have been wrong in urging that the young be prepared to become loyal and active citizens by an education in the values of democracy? No, far from it. Perhaps an example from my own experience will indicate how the sort of education that is appropriate and necessary can be distinguished from mere indoctrination.

It was my good fortune to be the pupil of an extraordinary teacher in the public high school that I attended. In the classroom, she opened our minds to the work of great writers and essayists. She taught us all how to use our native intelligence to reach out beyond our own limited experience, to see our cultural values with a measure of detachment, and to learn to appreciate, even if we could not accept, the arguments that might be made intelligently from perspectives other than our own. So devoted was she to our education that she also taught a special seminar for the best students in the class (Jefferson's natural aristocracy?) one evening each week. We began by reading the *Iliad* and went on to Plato's *Republic,* more or less in keeping with the "Great Books" approach that was then popular. In retrospect, I wonder whether, had it been up to some committee of public safety, she would have been allowed to introduce us to the *Republic* in view of its scathing attack on Athenian democracy. It was, for me, an especially provocative work not just because it struck a responsive chord in my youthful idealism but was also quite hostile to what seemed to be ideals of my own society. Then and since, I have wrestled with this paradox and reflected on it with my own students. And that, of course, was exactly what my teacher wanted to happen. She wanted to stimulate us to think about our personal values and about what it meant to live in a democracy.

While she was doing such a splendid job of teaching us literature and introducing us to challenging ideas, she also set an example outside class of what it means in practical terms to be a citizen of a democracy, for she was one of the leading spokespersons of the local teachers organization. I remember vividly what happened when the board of education decided to retaliate against the teachers by "exiling" their leaders to grammar schools where they were required to serve as substitute teachers, even though they were not actually needed. My teacher used her first day's free time to sit in the teacher's room and write an essay on the relevance of Machiavelli's *The Prince* to local politics. The piece so delighted the editor of our daily newspaper that he printed it on the front page. Meanwhile, we students circulated a petition demanding that the teachers be reinstated; the board of education, reconsidering its decision, did so. It had been quite a little lesson in the rights and duties of democratic citizenship.

THE LARGER lesson to be drawn from such personal experience as this is that good teaching must begin with the same deeply felt vocation that led Socrates to seek to open the minds of the young to a richer reality than they could possibly appreciate from their own experience. It must proceed with respect for their independence of mind, however immature or premature that independence. It must aim to give them the tools for reading and expression with which they can appease their curiosity and deepen their understanding long after they have completed their schooling. It must introduce them to the most serious moral issues by explaining what is meant by such values as integrity, courage, responsibility, and compassion, and by such democratic beliefs as those guaranteeing individual rights, self-government, and due process of law.

Unlike mere indoctrination, a true education must challenge the young to weigh these values against the alternatives, to test them not only against their own experience of life but also against that of people in other societies and at other times. This sort of education must make it clear how comparatively rare and fragile democracy is and how rampant are dictatorship and terror; it must treat the problems of democracy in our own society but also consider the far worse problems facing those elsewhere who yearn to be free but must struggle against thought control, secret police, and the threat of imprisonment and exile.

Such an education, finally, should aim to help young people recognize that because the highest aim of a democratic society is to promote the liberty of the individual, the fate of that society rests with each of them—with what they make of their talents and with the ways they resolve the ethical and practical choices that will confront them separately and collectively. This is a kind of education that is best conveyed by example, as well as by precept. It is as far from indoctrination as legal tender is from counterfeit—as sound as the other is base, as individual as the other is repetitive, as valuable as the other is worthless. When it comes to the role of the schools in inculcating democratic values, the standard is the same as in all other aspects of academic instruction: education, yes; indoctrination, no!

The Role of Self-Discipline

Amitai Etzioni

AMITAI ETZIONI is University Professor at George Washington University, Washington, D.C. This article is based on Chapter 6 of his latest book, An Immodest Agenda *(New York: McGraw-Hill, 1982).*

Much of the talk about the cognitive deficiencies exhibited by many U.S. pupils tends to focus on teaching methods (e.g., phonics versus sight-reading) and teaching resources (e.g., numbers and qualifications of teachers). Nobody claims that character development is not also important. However, from the pages of the *Kappan* to the staff meetings in my neighborhood public school, character development receives much less attention as a goal of schooling. Most important, character development is not typically seen as directly tied to cognitive achievement. I believe that one character trait, the level of self-discipline, is of central importance (accounts for much of the variance) both for cognitive achievement in school and for the level of performance in society as worker, citizen, and fellow human being. It deserves more attention from both researchers and educators.

To illustrate my thesis, let us look first at a simple incident. A young secretary, recently hired, was asked to use the Yellow Pages of the telephone directory. When she was unable to do so, it became evident that she did not command the alphabet or understand the principles of categorization and subcategorization involved.

Such inability would usually be counted as an example of a cognitive deficiency — an outcome of poor teaching, if not low I.Q. However, if we ask why it is difficult to teach someone a list of 26 items and the principles of a very simple index, we soon realize that something more is amiss than simple lack of teaching time and effort. Nor could this inability be related to I.Q. for most pupils, because learning the alphabet requires little comprehension or intelligence.

What would it take you to memorize, say, a telephone number of 26 digits? A considerable amount of effort, but *not* cognitive effort. Instead, this task would take concentration, control of impulse, self-motivation, and the ability to face and overcome stress (in order to resist distractions and accept the "routine" work involved). This element of psychic organization — the capacity to mobilize and commit psychic energy to a task — is what I hypothesize that those who are not learning well lack most. It is what seems to account for their "inability" to do elementary computation (i.e., to memorize a few rules and adhere to them) or to write a coherent expository paragraph (i.e., to remember the rules of punctuation, syntax, and so on).

In one public opinion survey after another, teachers and parents rank discipline as the number-one problem of the schools. This attention to discipline is highly relevant: It focuses on the school as a structure in which learning is to take place and suggests that — in a classroom where the proper relationships between pupils and their teachers and a proper learning atmosphere cannot be developed and maintained — learning is difficult, if not impossible.

Unfortunately, the focus on discipline is itself partially misdirected. Discipline, as most people understand it, is highly external. Teachers and principals "lay down the law" and will not brook back talk; students "show respect" by rising when their teacher enters the room, not speaking unless spoken to, and so on. But it seems to me that what many pupils — all of them future adults — need more of is *self-discipline*, i.e., the ability to mobilize and commit themselves. This self-discipline is developed in structured situations, not in authoritarian ones.

The line between structure and authoritarianism is easy to illustrate but not to define with great precision. Basically, what students need is not close, continuous external supervision but a school structure — authority figures, rules, and organization of tasks — that will build up their capacity to regulate themselves. This is best achieved, it seems, when what is required of the students is clearly explained and closely linked to educational goals, rather than arbitrarily announced, changed at will, and aimed as much at salving teachers' egos as at educational enhancement. To advance self-discipline requires that assignments be "do-able," appropriately evaluated, and rewarded. When assignments are mechanical (such as excessive memorization) or when rewards are allocated according to irrelevant criteria (such as having influential parents or minority status), requirements become dictates instead of sources of involvement and ways to build commitment.

Externally imposed discipline and a hierarchical structure will tend to produce passive, compliant students, suited at best for repetitive jobs when they graduate. Most jobs, especially in a technological society, require people who are actively involved in their work, who care about the outcomes, and who show a measure of initiative and creativity — all hallmarks of a self-disciplined and committed individual.

Several quite well-known bodies of data seem to lend plausibility to my thesis of the importance of self-discipline. For example, the National Assessment of

From Phi Delta Kappan, November 1982. This article is based on Chapter 6 of AN IMMODEST AGENDA: REBUILDING AMERICA BEFORE THE TWENTY-FIRST CENTURY, by Amitai Etzioni.

Educational Progress (NAEP) has found that, despite an improvement in scores on reading tests, the ability of junior high and high school students to draw inferences and to solve problems has declined.[1] There are no compelling data to explain this decline. Excessive televiewing and a focus on "basic" skills at the expense of more advanced ones are two possible explanations among the 16 that the NAEP advanced. I suggest that this decline in higher-order skills also reflects a lack of intellectual self-discipline, because interpretation and application — much more than basic reading skills — require following certain rules (e.g., check out the primary alternatives, avoid premature conclusions) and a measure of patience. The NAEP data suggest to me that these attributes have declined. Of course, other factors may also play a role. For example, under most circumstances extensive televiewing develops neither self-discipline nor the ability to think.

Another body of data that lends credence to my thesis comes from James S. Coleman's comparative study of public and private schools,[2] which stirred up a major controversy. As far as I can determine, Coleman's data suggest that effective schools, both private and public, have structures that enable them, first, to impose discipline, and second, to uphold academic standards. The single most important difference between effective schools and less effective ones proved to be the disciplinary structure. Coleman took into account such administrative measures as enforcement of a dress code and strictness in dealing with those who cut classes, were truant, or attacked teachers, but he also measured students' attitudes. He found that, in the higher-performing schools, most students accepted rules and regulations as legitimate. They thought that the discipline in their schools was effective and fair, they believed teachers' interest in them was relatively high, they did significantly more homework than students in the other schools (which both affected their achievements and reflected the effectiveness of the disciplinary structure), and — perhaps most revealing — they had high degrees of self-esteem.

Another large-scale study of school effectiveness, *Fifteen Thousand Hours*, was conducted in Great Britain.[3] Researchers found in this study that the single most important factor in pupils' achievement was the school's character as a social institution — its structure and the processes that administrators and teachers had established. In the schools that provided clear incentives and rewards, that gave priority to learning, and that expected students to carry out certain clearly defined responsibilities, the students performed better and attended more regularly than did their peers in other schools; they were also less involved in delinquent behavior outside of school. Moreover, those schools with clear and well-established standards of behavior and discipline helped to promote students who performed better than did those schools in which teachers had to struggle alone to establish such standards.

The more successful schools in this study illustrate the difference between imposing discipline from above and creating the structural conditions that nurture the development of self-discipline. Teachers and administrators in the better schools respected students as responsible individuals and set high academic and behavioral standards for them. The students took over specific tasks in corridors, classrooms, and assemblies, for example. Their teachers provided many opportunities for independent classroom or library work; the implicit message was: "We trust you to use your time for productive, self-guided work." The teachers also carefully checked students' independent work and helped some youngsters to develop the study habits essential for such efforts. The point is that expecting students to take responsibility and to work independently encourages self-regulation instead of reliance on close supervision, which contributes to inadequate internalization of impulse control.

Another important finding of *Fifteen Thousand Hours* was that such positive sanctions as expressions of appreciation and praise are highly effective in motivating students, although teachers in the study did not use these tools often. Indeed, what the word *discipline* brings to mind most immediately is restraining and setting limits, not encouraging or promoting any specific positive behaviors. But my own study of compliance in organizations, a reanalysis of some 1,100 studies of a large variety of organizations, from prisons to schools, also demonstrated clearly that involvement stemming from positive feelings is much more productive than the same degree of compliance attained by fear, pressure, or negative sanctions.[4] Educators must use both sides of the motivational scale; given the paucity of tools available to them, to give up either would undercut their capacity to discharge their duties. However, the more they can use positive motivation, the more likely they are to engender self-discipline among their students rather than superficial compliance, which lasts only as long as they are present to mete out punishment.

Of course, there are other factors that affect teachers' effectiveness. A community uninterested in or hostile toward learning, one lacking in successful role models (or rich in the wrong kinds), or one ravaged by such conditions as unemployment or crowded housing will deter learning. Teachers who are underpaid and who do not feel respected will not be paragons of instructional excellence. Extensive exposure to television seems to affect the academic performance of youngsters adversely. And there are some pupils — regardless of social class or race — who are well below average in intelligence or who display severe learning disabilities. Nonetheless, school structure is, in my view, the primary factor in school effectiveness. Cognitive deficiencies are secondary and often reflect nonschool factors in part. True, once cognitive deficiencies accumulate, they tend to pose personality problems, as evidenced by learning-disabled pupils who become disruptive. But studies of effective schools suggest that even children with cognitive problems will learn, when they can mobilize and commit themselves to the task.

If further research and deliberation were to support the pivotal importance of self-discipline to cognitive achievement, what should the schools do about it? Obviously, children's levels of self-discipline are determined in part by their families, their peers, and their previous experiences. What schools can or cannot do is also determined to a large extent by the communities they serve. However, the schools themselves can take certain steps.

The first step is for teachers and administrators to analyze the school as a structure that provides a *set of experiences*. Don't view the school as simply teachers, pupils, classrooms, curriculum. Look instead for young people who are receiving rewards for work well done — who are finding that self-discipline and the achievements that spring from it are sources of social gratification, as long as they abide by the rules (e.g., compete fairly) and are sensitive to others (e.g., do not deride slower learners). Alternatively, look for teachers assigning work that the students either cannot handle or are not motivated to do, vandalism going unpunished, open selling of drugs, and the rewarding or punishing of students according to criteria other than achievement (such as staying out from underfoot, obeying without question, or simply coming from an affluent or socially preferred background).

Some educators talk about the merits of "learning by experience" rather than by lecture. They refer, by and large, to teaching methods that enhance cognitive learning. A child is likely to learn more about Egyptian pyramids by building a small pyramid out of toy bricks than by a lecture, for example — even if the lecture is backed by visual aids. The educational experiences I endorse are imparted by life in school, and they affect most immediately the personality development, not the task-oriented learning, of students.

With typical disregard for this aspect of schools, David Moore has written in the *Harvard Educational Review* on "Discovering the Pedagogy of Experience." Moore seeks out-of-school, "community settings" that require students to be "engaged in activities in the real world."[5] He goes on to suggest, quite correctly, that these "social encounters" help participants learn "to organize their behavior,"[6] but — like so many other educators — he overlooks the significance of comparable in-school experiences.

The Tavistock Institute of Human Relations in Britain, under the direction of Elliott Jaques, has developed for industrial management a strategy for enhanced self-awareness and change that might well be applied to schools.[7] The Tavistock strategy does not attempt to introduce changes either from the outside (by directives, expert advice, and so on) or by meeting with some of the staff (e.g., the foremen). Instead, self-analysis and change come through dialog that starts with top management and works its way down the corporate hierarchy. This approach greatly increases the probability that the higher levels of management will support, rather than hinder, change and that all levels will be involved and won over. Group therapists or other facilitators may participate — but only to enhance the process, not to dominate it.

In schools, this approach might entail working first with school boards and groups of superintendents, then principals, then teachers, and then Parent/Teacher Associations and students. A good way to start might be to discuss the experiences that schools now generate and to ask what these experiences *ought* to be — what educational outcomes are desired. The next step would be to ask how the desired changes can be achieved. Outside facilitators could help to prevent self-analysis from turning into defensive self-justification or mere gripe sessions.

Specifically, such a dialog should examine every school policy from the standpoint of how it works and how it *ought* to work. Are grades accorded only for academic achievement, or do they also reflect and thus encourage effort? And what are the criteria by which these grades are assigned? Are the pupils aware of these criteria, and do they consider them legitimate? Is grading fair or arbitrary?

Are school incidents — from rowdy behavior on a field trip to acts of vandalism — handled as custodial or disciplinary matters, largely ignored, or used as educational opportunities to build students' self-discipline? Are teachers under great pressure to improve students' scores on standardized tests and to pump knowledge more quickly into their pupils? Or are assignments in the content areas balanced with concern for character development and self-discipline?

As I see it, many families are not able to provide the necessary psychic foundations for character development, and those that do provide such foundations need the schools to reinforce their efforts and achievements. Only if the schools make character building, especially the promotion of self-discipline, a core item of their agendas, will they be able to discharge effectively their other educational and teaching duties.

---

1. National Assessment of Educational Progress, *Three National Assessments of Reading: Changes in Performance, 1970-80* (Denver: Education Commission of the States, 1981). See also Gene I. Maeroff, "Reading Skills: New Problems," *New York Times*, 30 April 1981, p. 19.
2. James S. Coleman, Thomas Hoffer, and Sally Kilgore, *Public and Private Schools*, preliminary draft (Washington, D.C.: Educational Resources Information Center, National Institute of Education, March 1981); and idem, "Public and Private Schools," *Society*, January/February 1982, pp. 4-9.
3. Michael Rutter, Barbara Maughan, Peter Mortimore, and Janet Ouston, with Alan Smith, *Fifteen Thousand Hours* (Cambridge, Mass.: Harvard University Press, 1979).
4. Amitai Etzioni, *A Comparative Analysis of Complex Organizations*, rev. ed. (New York: Free Press, 1975).
5. May 1981, pp. 287-88.
6. Ibid., p. 289.
7. Elliott Jaques, *The Changing Culture of a Factory* (London: Tavistock Publications, 1951).

Values and Morality in Early 20th Century Elementary Schools: A Perspective

JEANNE PIETIG

JEANNE PIETIG is Assistant Professor of Education, University of Virginia, Charlottesville.

As any public school teacher or administrator knows, American taxpayers expect a great deal from public schools. Teaching basic skills is not enough; Americans expect their schools to provide instruction in values as well as the three R's. According to a recent Gallup poll, the public favors instruction in values and ethical behavior as part of the public school curriculum by about four to one. But if American parents agree that public schools should teach values, they do not agree on *how* this should be done. Nor do educators.

Given the renewed interest in moral education, it may be helpful to examine how public school teachers handled this issue in the past. Although American schools engaged in some form of moral instruction from their inception, the opening decades of this century merit special study. During this period, an array of programs was implemented in public schools to develop the ethical character of students. Influential organizations, such as the National Education Association, the Character Education Institution, and the National Council of Better Citizenship, endorsed the movement. National contests were conducted that offered cash prizes to the authors of the best morality codes and the best methods of moral education. Then, as now, teachers wrestled with the following questions: How much time in the school day should be devoted to teaching values? What is the most effective means of developing character in students? Should moral education be taught as a separate subject or should it be integrated into the existing curriculum?

This article examines some of the ways moral education was taught in American public elementary schools during the first three decades of this century. The programs were popularly described as using direct or indirect methods of moral instruction. Examples of both methods are provided to see whether either approach offers today's elementary teachers a sensible way to teach values to children.

Direct Methods

Moral education programs using direct methods most often began with a systematic treatment of a specific virtue or some other desirable character trait. The vast majority of these programs employed slogans, oaths, creeds, codes, and pledges to instill moral responsibility in students.

One example of the direct method was the *Book of Golden Deeds,* developed by Kentucky superintendent M. A. Cassidy in 1903. His plan consisted of a daily 15-minute "Golden Deed" period during which children illustrated the character trait for the day by drawing pictures or writing stories. The best picture or story was then placed in the classroom's Book of Golden Deeds, and awards were given to schools, classrooms, and students for creating outstanding books. This plan is noteworthy because it is a forerunner of our present-day workbooks.

Another example of the direct method was the *Children's Code of Morals for Elementary Schools,* written by William J. Hutchins. The code was composed of 10 "laws," such as the Law of Duty, the Law of Kindness, and the Law of Self-Control. An 11th law, the Law of Truth, was added later:

Good Americans Are True

(1) I will avoid hasty opinions, lest I do injustice and be mistaken as to facts.
(2) I will hunt for proof, and be accurate as to what I see and hear. I will learn to think, that I may discover new truth.
(3) I will stand by the truth, regardless of my likes and dislikes, and scorn the temptation to lie for myself or friends; nor will I keep the truth from those that have a right to it.

Hutchins's Code was the most famous of the morality codes because of the publicity it received as the winning entry in a national contest sponsored by the Character Education Institution in 1916. The author was awarded $5,000 for his efforts.

The *Five Point Plan,* like many other proposals for moral education, made direct use of Hutchins's Code, which was discussed each day so that children could apply its laws to their own lives. Besides leading classroom discussions, teachers rated the moral development of students on Character Charts, planned group projects in good works, and pointed out incidents from school life that illustrated Hutchins's Code. Perhaps the most interesting feature of the Five Point Plan was Uncle Sam's Boys and Girls Club. Students wore badges as members of the club, but the teacher or the class could remove badges from misbehaving students. Upon graduating from eighth grade, worthy students kept their badges and took the following pledge:

I am a citizen of the United States of America.
I pledge myself to Uncle Sam;
To live in loyalty to my Nation, its Constitution, and its laws.
In the spirit of justice, I will do my best to establish peace, goodwill and happiness
And to increase the benefits of civilization to all humanity.

A final example of the direct method was the *Knighthood of Youth Plan,* which was introduced into 12 New York City schools in 1924. Under this plan, children "slew dragons," that is, conquered bad habits; they built castles of good deeds; and they studied ancient and modern knights. After completing required tasks, students were promoted from knights to crusaders.

Later, the program developed a new focus. Classes were organized into clubs with elected officers, and students worked on various committee projects, such as sending letters to sick classmates, reporting on current events, cooperating with Junior Red Cross, and keeping the classroom clean. But the idea of building castles remained: a picture of a castle was placed on the classroom wall, and, as group tasks were finished, new "stones" were added to the structure. Children also were provided with special booklets so they could record knightly adventures undertaken at school or at home. A strength of this program was its concentration on behavior rather than codes, pledges, and discussions of virtues; a weakness was its questionable emphasis on the symbolism of knighthood.

The moral education programs employing direct methods are too numerous to mention, but the examples described here illustrate some of their common features. Educators who favored direct methods maintained that moral education was important enough to merit its own place in the school curriculum.

Indirect Methods

Educators who favored indirect methods were opposed to teaching moral education as a separate subject. Instead of relying on specific lessons in values, teachers were to capitalize on the entire range of school experiences in order to elicit desired behaviors in students. The aim of this method was to show how all the ordinary aspects of school life had character training potential.

Many of the programs employing indirect methods relied on the curriculum as a major means of moral education. Literature, more than any other subject, was used to promote moral growth. One program in Oregon consisted entirely of children's stories selected for their character building qualities. Another project in New York City used biographies of great men and women. Several other cities and states developed similar plans that included careful listings from literature. Classroom teachers also turned to professional books and journals that topically indexed fairy tales, legends, myths, and stories according to their adaptability for moral education.

Another example of the indirect method was the *Iowa Plan,* which was the winning entry in a national contest sponsored by the Character Education Institution in 1921. The authors of the plan, Edwin Starbuck and associates, were awarded $20,000 for submitting the best proposal for moral education in public schools. Like Hutchins's Code, the Iowa Plan was widely publicized and influenced many later plans for moral education.

The best feature of this plan was its comprehensiveness. It examined a broad spectrum of educational resources, such as school organization, curricular materials, instructional methods, and teacher preparation. The bulk of its suggestions, however, were conventional. For example, to teach civic relations, the plan recommended that kindergartners learn songs and stories of patriots, that third graders make a model plantation, and that seventh graders establish a post office. Despite its shortcomings, the Iowa Plan provided a more workable conception of the goals of moral education. Teachers were encouraged to "cultivate *persons who* live gracefully and helpfully, *not virtues that* seem desirable."

Undoubtedly the most famous advocate of the indirect method was John Dewey. Like the authors of the Iowa Plan, Dewey developed a comprehensive proposal for moral education. He maintained that a school was organized on a moral basis if its resources increased each student's social intelligence, social interests, and social power. The resources available to the classroom teacher were three: the curriculum, the instructional methods, and the community life of the school.

In discussing the moral implications of the curriculum, Dewey insisted that any subject that enhanced a student's understanding of social life had ethical import. For Dewey, other conceptions of moral education were too narrow. He disapproved of teachers using literature or any of the arts as a pretext for moral instruction. Not only was the moral outcome questionable, but the studies involved very often had their educational significance destroyed. Dewey similarly examined the instructional methods with a view toward restructuring schools on a moral basis. He wanted students to learn skills of critical inquiry so they might apply them to all areas of human endeavor, ethics included. Finally, in discussing the community life of the school, Dewey urged teachers to provide occasions for cooperation, self-direction, and leadership rather than conformity, passivity, and blind submission to authority.

As with other educators who favored the indirect method, Dewey believed that all aspects of school life had implications for the development of character in students. But Dewey was far more critical of traditional educational practices than were most educators of his day. His proposals for moral education were essentially proposals for school reform.

In Search of the Best Method

What was the most effective means of moral education? Educators who preferred the indirect approach argued that their methods capitalized on naturally occurring settings in school life. Other educators maintained that indirect moral instruction was too haphazard an affair, while direct moral instruction was systematic, thorough, and economical in time and effort. Still others proposed that the ideal form of moral education consisted of a judicious combination of both methods.

Debates about the merits of moral education naturally attracted the attention of psychologists, who conducted several studies to assess the effectiveness of the programs. The most extensive study was the "Character Education Inquiry," a five-year research effort headed by Hugh Hartshorne and Mark May. In one volume of research, *Studies in Deceit,* Hartshorne and May examined cheating, lying, and stealing in children. They found that children who belonged to certain unnamed organizations purporting to teach honesty deceived about as often as children who did not belong. In one organization, length of membership and rank achieved were positively correlated with deceptiveness.

Hartshorne and May concluded that the mere urging of honest behavior by teachers or the discussion of standards and ideals had no necessary relation to the control of conduct: "The extent to which individuals may be affected, either for better or worse, is not known, but there seems to be evidence that such effects as may result are not generally good and are sometimes unwholesome." Again:

> The main attention of educators should be placed not so much on devices for teaching honesty or any other "trait" as on the reconstruction of school practices in such a way as to provide not occasional but consistent and regular opportunities for the successful use by both teachers and pupils of such forms of conduct as make for the common good.

Hartshorne and May's assessment of the effectiveness of direct moral instruction was decidedly unfavorable. Their findings helped accelerate the growing discontent with the direct approach. For even before their research results were published, educators had become largely dissatisfied with direct moral education; the use of slogans, oaths, creeds, codes, and pledges especially fell out of favor. The last phase of the character education movement was thus marked by a decline in confidence in direct methods. By the late 1920s, it was generally agreed that moral education, in the United States, at least, should be indirect.

Conclusion

What can today's educators learn from past attempts to teach values in public schools?

First, moral education should be indirect. Hartshorne and May's study remains a classic work in the field of moral education and their recommendations still merit a careful consideration by educators today. Moral education should not be taught as an isolated subject in the school curriculum since teaching values cannot be limited to a few minutes of instruction each day.

Second, moral education should be comprehensive. It is not enough to integrate moral education into the existing curriculum. Teachers and administrators need to examine the moral implications of all aspects of school life, such as disciplinary procedures, extracurricular activities, instructional methods, and school organization. If this is not done, the hidden curriculum can undermine the educational goals of the overt curriculum.

Third, moral education should be broadly conceived. Many moral education programs failed in the past because they were based on a narrow conception of morality: character was assumed to be a structure of virtues and vices. This trait-inspired approach to morality has long since been discredited. Nevertheless, educators today are still faced with a variety of approaches to moral education that are equally limited in scope.

Moral education, like morality itself, is multifaceted. It involves much more than moral reasoning, much more than clarifying values, and much more than instilling discipline in students. Perhaps John Dewey still offers elementary school teachers the most sensible way for teaching values to students; he emphasized that education is an intrinsically moral enterprise, and he interpreted the ethical responsibility of the school in the broadest and freest spirit.

In summary, there are no shortcuts or guaranteed methods for teaching values in the school just as there are no shortcuts or guaranteed methods for teaching values in the home. Moral education remains one of the most challenging, vital, and necessary tasks facing both parents and educators today.

References

Character Education Methods: The Iowa Plan. Washington DC: Character Education Institution, 1922.

Dewey, John. "Art in Education." In *Encyclopedia of Education.* New York: Macmillan, 1911.

______. *Moral Principles in Education.* Boston: Houghton Mifflin, 1909.

Gallup, George H. "The Thirteenth Annual Gallup Poll of the Public's Attitudes toward the Public Schools." *Phi Delta Kappan* 63 (Sept. 1981) pp. 33–47.

Hartshorne, Hugh. *Character in Human Relations.* New York: Charles Scribner's Sons, 1932.

Hartshorne, Hugh and May, Mark. *Studies in Deceit.* New York: Macmillan, 1928.

McKown, Harry C. *Character Education.* New York: McGraw-Hill, 1935.

Pietig, Jeanne. "Lawrence Kohlberg, John Dewey, and Moral Education." *Social Education* 44 (March 1980) pp. 238–242.

Tuttle, Harold S. *Character Education by State and Church.* New York: Abingdon Press, 1930.

No Empty Heads, No Hollow Chests

Edwin J. Delattre

Edwin J. Delattre is president of St. John's College in Annapolis, Maryland.

EDUCATION SHOULD be committed to the propagation of boys and girls, men and women, whose heads are not empty and whose chests are not hollow—to people, that is, who bring thoughtfully reasoned and passionate conviction to the conduct of their personal and professional affairs.

The first and most fundamental feature of education worthy of the name is that it promotes aspiration in the young, that is, it promotes the desire to become more and better than one is. The encouragement of aspiration depends, above all, on both intellectual and moral propagation.

C.S. Lewis captures this idea with accuracy and eloquence in his book *Abolition of Man* in which he says:

> When a Roman father told his son that it was a sweet and seemly thing to die for his country, he believed what he said. He was communicating to the son an emotion which he himself shared and which he believed to be in accord with the value which his judgment discerned in noble death. He was giving the boy the best he had, giving of his spirit to humanize him as he had given of his body to beget him.

The Roman father, as Lewis sees it, was communicating to his son the truth, as best he was able to grasp it, that courage and fidelity are more worthy of us than selfishness and cowardice. He offered his reasoned convictions about what a worthwhile life amounts to, not for any ulterior purpose, but because of a conception concerning the obligation of each generation to teach those that follow what we have learned about how to live well. Lewis contrasts this idea of teaching with that of teachers who manipulate the young in order to engender service to some ideology or other, when no effort is made to develop their critical faculties or their ability to reflect about what is worthy of us, what deserves our loyalty. He sees, as we all can, much of the latter form of teaching in the world now, and he distinguishes it from the case of the Roman father in this way:

> ...the difference between the old and the new education [is] an important one. Where the old initiated, the new merely "conditions." The old dealt with its pupils as birds deal with young birds when they teach them to fly: the new deals with them more as the poultry-keeper deals with young birds—making them thus or thus for purposes of which the birds know nothing. In a word, the old was a kind of propagation—men transmitting manhood to men: the new is merely propaganda.

Mature adulthood is an achievement. Adults can promote aspiration to it in the young by avoiding the pitfalls of simplistic dogmatism and by taking students seriously in work and at play. The dogmatism that most obviously promotes empty-headedness is the absolutism that teaches that nothing needs to be thought about because everything is already known. This is the absolutism of the totalitarian; for the totalitarian, the tyrant, the demagogue is a coward—afraid to entrust the future to coming generations and to their capacity for insight and understanding. It is this cowardly lack of faith in our own kind and in their potential to take responsibility for the world in their turn that lies at the root of propaganda and of the forms of government that have no use for freedom. Such absolutism is incompatible with the transmission of manhood to men, for at base, it has no respect for men. It disdains giving real instruction in how to learn to think for oneself or even how to learn for oneself.

At the same time, the dogmatism that most obviously promotes hollow chests is that of absolute relativism, the idea that everything is merely subjective, that nothing is genuinely right or wrong, that all matters of value are just matters of personal taste, and that matters of taste are not to be disputed. For this dogma, genocide is like spinach: some people like it, and some people don't, and nothing more can be said. As totalitarianism is cowardly, relativism is naive. As a dogma, it is a plaything of the innocent; nobody who was at the mercy of barbarians, no hostage, no prisoner of war, no person who took life seriously ever concluded that it does not matter how people are treated by others.

These dogmas bear attention because they make propagation impossible. Absolutism cannot seek to transmit manhood to men because it is afraid to do so.

This article first appeared in the Summer 1981 issue of *AMERICAN EDUCATOR*, the quarterly journal of the American Federation of Teachers.

Relativism cannot transmit anything to anyone because it has nothing to transmit, and the irony of this dogma is that it is encouraged because it is supposed to promote understanding of tolerance for people and ideas different from one's own. Yet, if relativism were true, then nothing would be truly right or wrong, good or evil, and, accordingly, tolerance would not be either. If relativism were right, nothing would have any value, including tolerance, and a hollow chest would be the only kind to have.

IN EDUCATION, helping the young to achieve worthy, even noble aspirations means steering a course safely between these dogmas. This is how propagation is made possible. It consists in practice of lessons throughout the curriculum and in extracurricular activities that teach the nature of sound judgment and principled conduct. These, along with the examples set by parents, teachers, peers, public figures, and others, are the mainstays of an education that promotes self-discipline, understanding of the academic disciplines of inquiry and discovery, recognition that personal identity is not a gift but an accomplishment, and appreciation that the ways we live and the ways we act have consequences. These are the lessons that give instruction in the responsible conduct of a life.

For this reason, students deserve to study lessons that enable them to see what empty-headedness, hollow-chestedness, and their opposites are in practice. The examples available within the disciplines we teach are innumerable and spectacular.

The story of *Faithful Ruslan* by Georgi Vladimov, for example, is a wonderful account of courage and loyalty subverted by propaganda. Faithful Ruslan is a guard dog in a Siberian concentration camp who relentlessly does what he has been trained to do, a courageous and loyal dog who has been used to serve the ends of ignoble masters who have no respect for human beings, no respect for civic identity, civil rights, humane conduct, due process, freedom, or the truth. Ruslan is a perfect example of the danger of having a full chest, a capacity for passionate conviction, when one has no critical intelligence by which to determine what deserves loyalty and courageous support. The dog shows the importance of learning to think well and the terrible danger of failing to do so. Ruslan shows that being smart is no adequate deterrent to being ignorant, and he shows how thoroughly people are at the mercy of demagogues and tyrants when they allow their own ignorance about how to gather and assess relevant evidence to persist. He has a full chest, but even though he is smart, he has an empty head, a head incapable of critical judgment.

William Roper, the son-in-law of Thomas More, is like Ruslan in this sense. His empty-headedness is caused by impulsiveness, self-righteousness, and impetuosity, however, rather than by propaganda. In *A Man for All Seasons,* Roper exhibits passionate conviction, and More must repeatedly correct the dreadful errors in his judgment. Consider the following exchange in which Roper seeks to persuade More to arrest Richard Rich, a bad man who ultimately perjures himself for the sake of personal gain but who has, at this point, broken no law:

ROPER: Arrest him.

ALICE: Yes!

MORE: For what?

ALICE: He's dangerous!

ROPER: For libel; he's a spy.

ALICE: He is! Arrest him!

MARGARET: Father, that man's bad.

MORE: There is no law against that.

ROPER: There is! God's law.

MORE: Then God can arrest him.

ROPER: Sophistication upon sophistication!

MORE: No, sheer simplicity. The law, Roper, the law. I know what's legal, not what's right. And I'll stick to what's legal.

ROPER: Then you set man's law above God's!

MORE: No, far below; but let *me* draw your attention to a fact—I'm *not* God. The currents and eddies of right and wrong, which you find such plain sailing, I can't navigate. I'm no voyager. But in the thickets of the law, oh, there I'm a forester. I doubt if there's a man alive who could follow me there, thank God...(he says this last to himself).

ALICE: (exasperated, pointing after Rich) While you talk, he's gone!

MORE: And go he should, if he was the Devil himself, until he broke the law!

ROPER: So now you'd give the Devil benefit of law!

MORE: Yes. What would you do? Cut a great road through the law to get after the Devil?

ROPER: I'd cut down every law in England to do that!

MORE: (roused and excited) Oh? (advances on Roper) And when the last law was down, and the Devil turned round on you—where would you hide, Roper, the laws all being flat?...Yes, I'd give the Devil the benefit of law, for my own safety's sake.

Thomas More, by contrast to Roper, is a study in critical, civilized intelligence and courage, intellectual humility, and moral decisiveness. He is a whole man, one man through and through, as scholar, author, parent, politician, friend, and Christian. He knows the limits of his authority and the extent of his responsibilities and acts accordingly.

The man Roper wants imprisoned, Richard Rich, is a perfect case of a person whose head is empty *and* whose chest is hollow. He cannot believe in anything except his own gain, and because of this, he is prevented from self-knowledge, becomes craven, and is forever susceptible to manipulation by others. He is one of whom nothing transcends self-interest. Consider this exchange between Rich and More in which More understands Rich much better than Rich does. Rich is pleading with More for a political appointment:

RICH: Pardon me, Sir Thomas, but how much do you know about me?

MORE: Whatever you've let me know.

RICH: I've let you know everything!

MORE: Richard, you should go back to Cambridge, you're deteriorating.

RICH: Well, I'm not used!...D'you know how much I have to show for seven months' work?...

MORE: Work?

RICH: Work! Waiting's work when you wait as I wait, hard!...For seven months, that's two hundred days, I have to show: the acquaintance of the Cardinal's outer doorman, the indifference of the Cardinal's inner doorman, and the Cardinal's chamberlain's hand in my chest!...Oh, also one half of a "Good Morning" delivered at fifty paces by the Duke of Norfolk. Doubtless he mistook me for someone.

MORE: He was very affable at dinner.

RICH: Oh, everyone's affable here....(More is pleased) Also, of course, the friendship of Sir Thomas More. Or should I say acquaintance?

MORE: Say friendship.

RICH: Well, there! "A friend of Sir Thomas and still no office? There must be something wrong with him."

MORE: I thought we said friendship....(he considers, then) The Dean of St. Paul's offers you a post; with a house, a servant, and fifty pounds a year.

RICH: What? What post?

MORE: At the new school.

RICH: (bitterly disappointed) A teacher!

MORE: A man should go where he won't be tempted.

Rich does not learn to go where he won't be tempted, to take a position whose temptations he can resist, and, as a result, he ends up taking bribe after bribe until he perjures himself in order to be appointed attorney general for Wales. In taking the oath to testify truthfully, Rich offers himself as credit for the truth of his testimony; when he perjures himself, he forsakes the self he has offered as credit, destroys its value. He becomes, literally, incredible, in the much more important sense than the one that our students see in the television show that has played fast and loose with the meaning of the word.

THE HISTORY of the liberal and fine arts and the sciences is wealthy with such cases, appropriate at virtually all levels of education, at home and in schools and colleges. The materials can be ancient or modern—from the Socrates of the *Apology* to the Will Cain of *High Noon* to the Admiral James Stockdale, who served with such honor as a military officer and prisoner of war and who now writes on such issues as the Garwood case with eloquence and insight. The characters can be as empty-headed and cowardly as Emma's husband, Dr. Charles Bovary, as lucid and courageous as James Madison, as striking in athletics as Bobby Jones, or as pathetic as the Jake LaMotta portrayed in *Raging Bull*. The examples and cases are there for the asking, they are available for every discipline in the curriculum, and they provide the occasion to teach students, for example, how a person learns to think through an issue, as Madison did in arguing for a constitutional republic in the *Federalist* and at the Constitutional Convention in 1787. They are opportunities for students to want to come to know, to aspire to know.

The lesson here for us is straightforward. Being human is not new—it is only new to beginners, and for an individual to learn fully who he is, he must learn who *we* are, what human beings are, and what we have managed to make of ourselves. The examplars of intellectual and moral virtue and vice must be treated as real human beings in the presence of the young.

To learn the sort of thing we can do as teachers and parents, consider the following letter that might be written to children in our time as a way of following the example set by the Roman father described by C.S. Lewis:

Dear Children,
Mommy tells me that in school you have been talking in some of your classes about who your heroes and heroines are and that your classmates are talking about this,too. In my life, I have studied and thought hard about heroes and heroines, and I wanted to write you this letter to tell you something of what I have come to understand.

First, many of your fellow students, and possibly some of your teachers, and certainly many other people you will meet in your lives do not have much of an idea of what a hero is, what sorts of things a person must do to be truly heroic. You will find many people who confuse being heroic with being famous, and so, right away, they will say the name of the first famous person or thing that comes into their minds, like Miss Piggy or R2-D2 or Farrah Fawcett. Now, of course, you don't have to be famous to be a hero, and being famous doesn't make anyone heroic. Some people who are famous are called celebrities; they are people who are famous not for doing anything important but just for being famous. Sometimes they get famous because they are good looking or because they just happened to be somewhere near the center of television or newspaper attention or because someone wanted to sell a product and put them in a commercial, and so on. There is nothing about people who are famous for being famous that makes them of much interest.

But heroes are something else again from celebrities. Heroes are people who do things that are brave. There are lots of ways of being brave, but in general these ways can be given one or more of three descriptions: A person can be physically brave; a person can be morally brave; and a person can be intellectually brave. Of course, a person can be all of these, but when one is, *then* we are talking about the greatest of heroes and heroines).

Now I am going to tell a story about being physically, morally, and intellectually brave that will help you to get the idea.

Once upon a time, there was a fifteen-year-old boy who went to school in New York City. He was a big boy for his age—about six feet tall and 175 pounds. One day in early winter when it was very cold and the water in the rivers in the city was icy cold but not frozen, he and a school friend were walking across a bridge on their way home from school. As they walked and talked, they saw a young woman in the water swimming away from shore. They called to her, concerned about what she was doing and not fully understanding. Maybe, they thought, she was a member of the Polar Bears—a club made up of people who swim in cold water. Or maybe she was trying to drown herself. They quickly decided that she was trying to drown herself, and so one of the boys ran to call the police to bring help while the other, our fifteen-year-old, took off all his clothes but his underwear and plunged into the water to try to rescue the woman. She tried to get away from him and fought against him, but he managed to swim with her back to shore—and so he saved her life. In all, he swam more than seven hundred yards—seven football fields—to save her. Of course, he risked his own life in the rescue, for his muscles might have tightened in the cold, making him unable to swim. The police rushed the three people (for the other boy jumped into the water to help bring the woman ashore) to the hospital in ambulances to get them warm and to see whether they needed further medical care. Now these boys were physically brave, especially the one who risked his life; indeed, his act was heroic.

But there is more to the story than this. The boy was worried as he was swimming that he might be doing the wrong thing—perhaps the woman was so unhappy that he should leave her alone. If she was unhappy enough to try to kill herself, what business, he thought, was it of his? Despite these thoughts, the boy said to himself that he should and would try to save her. Her life mattered, after all, and possibly she would one day be glad. This took moral courage on the boy's part, to act knowing that the consequences of his actions might not be happy ones, and still insisting that one should save a life if one can. And even though the woman might have hated him forever because she really wanted to die, in fact, when he visited her the next day in the hospital, the woman said that she was glad he had saved her and that she was alive.

And now, even though our fifteen-year-old boy has demonstrated two kinds of courage or bravery, there is even more to the story. As you would expect, the newspapers in the city learned about the rescue and printed stories about it. But one of the papers wanted to do more; it wanted to interview the boy and do a big story. It is a newspaper read by many, many people, for it contains lots of stories about things that are sensational—fires, earthquakes, murders, crimes, scandals, astrologers, and so on. When some of the boy's friends heard that he had been asked for an interview, they urged him to do it, because he would be famous. But the boy thought about what kind of paper it was, and he thought about how the paper might write something that would hurt the feelings of the woman he had saved, and so he told his friends that he did not think he should grant the interview. Despite their urging, he concluded that his ideas were better than theirs and refused to be persuaded; he did not give the interview. This took intellectual courage, to insist that he was right (just like it takes intellectual courage to admit we are wrong when we think we are). Thus, our fifteen-year-old boy showed us physical, moral, and intellectual bravery; he behaved like a hero.

Still, heroism is more than this. It doesn't mean just doing particular actions that are brave. It means being the kind of person who does not run away when physical, moral, or intellectual bravery is called for. So, for example, you might have a woman whose husband dies and leaves her to raise several young children by herself. The person who does not run away, who does her best to be a good parent in these difficult circumstances exhibits deep and continuing bravery and so is especially heroic, even though there may be no single events like rescuing a drowning person to catch our attention. It is a quiet, durable heroism that consists of facing up to whatever the world puts before us and refusing to give up. This is the heroism that deserves respect above all, and the place to look for it is in people you know and love, people you respect, people you see in your daily lives. You won't find very much of it in celebrities, although you will find it in some people who are famous.

The question to be asked now is how one becomes heroic. What things should we do to become the kinds of durable people who do not give up? And the answer is not, of course, that we should rush out to find people who are drowning so that we can save them. It is instead to practice not giving up, practice it in all the things we do.

—With love from your daddy

* * *

By means such as these, we can give successive generations of human beings the opportunity to become clear-headed and full-chested.

How To Encourage Moral Development

THOMAS LICKONA

Thomas Lickona is a developmental psychologist who directs Project Change at the State University College at Cortland, N.Y.

"With us an order was an order. . . . Where would we have been if everyone had thought things out?"

"I believed he had the authority to do it."

"The success of this man proved to me that I should subordinate myself to him."

"I was there to follow orders, not to think."

Statements one and three were made by Adolph Eichmann at his trial for crimes he committed in Nazi Germany. Statements two and four were made by defendants in the Watergate trials.

Well before Watergate, social psychologists knew that most people faced with a tough moral decision prefer to pass the buck—they will do what they're told to do. That was the conclusion of Stanley Milgram's well-known experiments at Yale. A sizable majority of subjects, representing all walks of life, were willing to give what they believed to be intensely painful electrical shocks to protesting victims—simply because the experimenter instructed them to do so. Watergate and studies like Milgram's are not, however, the whole story. Unthinking conformity may be one form of moral bankruptcy, but the spreading violence in society seems to indicate that we don't have *enough* conformity to the most basic norms of human decency.

Can schools do anything about these moral problems? Should teachers get involved in the potentially murky waters of moral education? In one Gallup poll, 79 percent of the people interviewed said yes—schools *should* offer instruction in morals and in moral behavior. If you agree with these people, your next question probably will be the crucial one: How do we teach morals?

Understanding Moral Development

Developmentalists like Lawrence Kohlberg of Harvard have argued that the only objective definition of psychological maturity is one based on knowledge of how people actually do develop. Piaget's apparently universal stages of cognitive development provide a definition of maturity in the intellectual realm. Thinking at Piaget's concrete operational level, for example, is more mature than thinking at the preoperational level; thinking at the formal operational level is more mature than thinking at the concrete level, and so on.

So it is, Kohlberg maintains, in the realm of moral development, where similar stages of maturity can be identified. Over the last 20 years, Kohlberg and his colleagues have mapped stages of moral reasoning by presenting children, adolescents and adults with hypothetical moral dilemmas. One dilemma used with children, for example, describes a situation facing ten-year-old Holly: Should she climb a tree to rescue the stranded kitten of a small boy, or should she keep her promise to her worried father not to climb any more trees?

The five stages that Kohlberg's research has identified are described in the chart on the next page. The child at stage 1 believes that the people in power—adult authorities—are the arbiters of morality. The authorities determine what's right and what's wrong. Because the child doesn't yet understand the practical need for moral rules in human relationships, his only motivation to obey rules is his fear of getting caught if he steps out of line. If Holly were at stage 1, for example, she might reason that she shouldn't save the kitten, because if she climbs the tree, she might get in trouble with her father.

With stage 2 comes the first awareness that morality has something to do with human relations and needs. There's an understanding of reciprocity on a tit-for-tat level. One girl in second grade said that Holly should save the kitten because some day Holly might be tied up and the kitten would remember and would come and loosen the ropes for her. Stage 2 reasoning *against* climbing the tree might focus on all that Holly's father has done for her in the past; this might convince Holly that she should pay him back by keeping her promise.

At stage 3, the child grasps the golden rule. Holly should save the kitten—or keep her promise to her father—because it's the "nice" thing to do, not just because of what's in it for her. People are counting on her. With stage 3 comes the ability to put yourself in the other person's shoes and to know simultaneously that they can put themselves in your shoes too. Perhaps Holly's father will understand if she climbs the tree to save the kitten; he'll know that she didn't want to disappoint him but that she felt she just had to help.

At stage 4, concern for others is expanded to a wider scale. One begins to have a concept of society, law, and one's role within a larger social and legal system. You want to do your duty, to set a good example, and to insist that other people do too. Stage 4 is still a morality shaped by external expectations, however. Not until stage 5, the level of principled moral reasoning, can you stand apart from the social framework and say that some things are morally wrong in the system—that some laws or institutions, for example, need changing to protect the rights of individuals. Not until stage 5 can a person understand the moral basis for the Bill of Rights.

At stage 5, universal moral principles define right and wrong. That's what we told the Nazis at the end of World War II: they had an obligation to universal moral laws respecting human rights, and this obligation should have superceded the commands of their superiors. That's what, in effect, we told the Watergate defendants who said they were only carrying out what they believed to be presidential orders.

Over the last two decades, Kohlberg and his associates have conducted substantial research: they have followed for 20 years the moral development of 50 individuals who are now 30 to 36 years old; they have compared moral reasoning in diverse cultures (Taiwan, England, Turkey, Yucatan and the United States); they have experimented with various techniques to stimulate advances to higher developmental stages. Their central findings:

1. The stages of moral reasoning appear to be the same for all persons, regardless of social class or culture.
2. Stages can't be skipped, because one stage builds onto another.
3. Stage change is gradual, because a new stage can't be instilled directly but must be constructed out of many social experiences.
4. Stage and age can't be equated, because some people move much faster through the stage sequence than others; some also get further (only about 25 percent of American adults reach stage 5 of principled morality).
5. Although an individual's stage of moral reasoning is not the only factor affecting his moral conduct, the way a person reasons does influence how he actually behaves in a moral situation. Persons at higher stages, for example, are more likely to help others, more likely to honor a commitment, and less likely to cheat.
6. Experiences that provide opportunities for what Kohlberg calls "role-taking" (assuming the viewpoints of others, putting yourself in another's place) foster progress through the stages. Children who participate a lot in peer relationships, for example, tend to be at more advanced moral stages than are children whose peer interaction is low. Within the family, children whose parents encourage them to express their views and participate in family decisions reason at higher moral stages than children whose parents do not encourage these behaviors.

Kohlberg's Stages of Moral Development

PRINCIPLED LEVEL (Concern for fidelity to self-chosen moral principles)	STAGE **5***	**MOTIVATOR:** Internal commitment to principles of "conscience"; respect for the rights, life and dignity of all persons. **AWARENESS:** Particular moral/social rules are social contracts, arrived at through democratic reconciliation of differing viewpoints and open to change. **ASSUMPTION:** Moral principles have universal validity; law derives from morality, not vice versa.
CONVENTIONAL LEVEL (Concern for meeting external social expectations)	STAGE **4**	**MOTIVATOR:** Sense of duty or obligation to live up to socially defined role and maintain existing social order for good of all. **AWARENESS:** There is a larger social "system" that regulates the behavior of individuals within it. **ASSUMPTION:** Authority or the social order is the source of morality.
	STAGE **3**	**MOTIVATOR:** Desire for social approval by living up to good boy/good girl stereotype; meeting expectations of others. **AWARENESS:** Need to consider intentions and feelings of others; cooperation means ideal reciprocity (golden rule). **ASSUMPTION:** Good behavior equals social conformity.
PRECONVENTIONAL LEVEL (Concern for external, concrete consequences to self)	STAGE **2**	**MOTIVATOR:** Self-interest: what's in it for me? **AWARENESS:** Human relations are governed by concrete reciprocity: let's make a deal; you scratch my back, I'll scratch yours. **ASSUMPTION:** Have to look out for self; obligated only to those who help you; each person has own needs and viewpoint.
	STAGE **1**	**MOTIVATOR:** Fear of getting caught; desire to avoid punishment by authority. **AWARENESS:** There are rules and consequences of breaking them. **ASSUMPTION:** Might makes right; what's regarded by those in power is "good"; what's punished is "bad."

*(Kohlberg recently has redefined his stages so that stage 5 incorporates much of what used to be in a stage 6.)

How Not To Apply the Moral Stages

At first glance, the moral stages might suggest that you should be aware of a child's stage, adapt your behavior to that level, and at the same time provide impetus for the child's advancement up the developmental ladder.

This easy recipe for applying Kohlberg's theories has several problems:

1. It's often hard to diagnose a child's stage of functioning in a specific situation (although diagnostic ability does improve with practice).
2. Keying one's behavior to the child's stage is complicated by the fact that children, like adults, typically operate simultaneously at several different stages.
3. A teacher must come up with an approach to rules and responsibilities that works for the whole class; there can't be two or three different "moral curriculums" in the same classroom.
4. Focusing on the single aspect of a child's dominant stage of moral reasoning results in a kind of tunnel vision that can limit a teacher's perception of the multidimensionality of any child's moral personality. Lois Murphy's extensive naturalistic observations in the 1930s found that preschoolers frequently came to each other's aid—shoving an attacker away from the victim, for example, and showing intense concern for the hurt child. Such sympathetic emotional responses and prosocial actions, like children's early flashes of a sense of fairness, run ahead of their systematic moral reasoning. Teachers who dwell on a child's dominant pattern of moral reasoning may miss these positive moral flashes, which must be noticed and nurtured, because they are the seeds from which a more consistent moral orientation will later grow.

Teachers also can run into difficulties if they assume there's a direct link between age and moral stage. It is true that, in general, the moral reasoning research shows that stages 1 and 2 dominate in the primary school years and persist in some individuals long beyond that. Stage 3 gains ground during the upper elementary grades and often remains the major orientation through the end of high school. Stage 4 begins to emerge in adolescence. Only one in four persons moves on in late adolescence or adulthood to stage 5, the morality of equal rights, justice and democratic process underlying the American Constitution.

Even so general a statement of the research findings, however, can be misleading. For one thing, these norms are based on interviewing subjects on hypothetical moral dilemmas. Piaget points out that children's "theoretical moral thought" on fictional stories may lag behind their "active moral thought" in real-life situations. Thus a child may demonstrate the upper reaches of his moral reasoning—say, stage 3—only if you catch him in his natural environment acting upon a problem that he really cares about. Muddling the picture even more is the fact that a self-interested stake in the outcome of a moral problem may have just the opposite effect, causing a child to reason at a level lower than what he is capable of.

But there *is* a practical value in knowing Kohlberg's moral reasoning stages. They define a natural, nonrelativistic goal for moral education: progress through the developmental stages. Kohlberg's stages also provide rough indicators of what kind of moral understanding you can expect from children during broad developmental periods, and they underscore the idea that becoming moral, like becoming logical, is indeed a developmental process involving step-by-step stage changes and requiring the child's active construction of these stages.

Teachers don't need to worry, then, about tailoring their every behavior to a child's moral stage. It's much more important to provide an overall moral environment that is in harmony with the broad themes of moral growth, such as fairness and a concern for others. This moral environment should provide opportunities for the role-taking that Kohlberg's research suggests is so critical. Consider, for example, this finding: Children who grow up on an Israeli kibbutz—with its intense peer-group interaction, shared decision-making and intermeshing work responsibilities—typically reach stage 4 or 5 in adolescence. By contrast, children reared in situations where there is limited social interchange are often still at stage 1 and 2 even in late adolescence.

Developing Morals Discussions

Moral dilemma discussions were the first method for putting Kohlberg into the classroom. At the elementary level, I've gotten some animated discussions going with commercially prepared dilemmas—Guidance Associate's *First Things: Values* filmstrip series, for example. The most popular of these is "Cheetah (What Do You Do About Rules?)." A schoolteacher in ordinary life, Cheetah is a superhero who must decide whether to keep his solemn oath of secrecy as a member of the Cat-People or reveal his identity to his nine-year-old son, Marcus, who suspects him of being involved in a bank robbery. One third grade class was unanimously in favor of Cheetah's keeping his oath, so I role-played Marcus to dramatize what he would be feeling and to get the kids to think about other ways of looking at the problem. "Cheetah promised never to tell," they said.

"That's an interesting reason," I said. "Tell me, do you think it is ever right to break a promise? Did any of you ever break a promise?"

Most admitted to having done so, and we got into a good discussion of the reasons for breaking promises and for making them in the first place. We moved to other issues, such as whether Cheetah had a responsibility to keep fighting crime, and after 45 minutes the discussion still was going strong.

Sometimes children will say things during a moral dilemma discussion that are textbook examples of Kohlberg's stages, but most of their statements are not so easily pigeonholed, nor do they need to be. What's more important is getting students to think hard about a moral issue, to give reasons for their opinions, and to listen to the reasons others give. The teacher's job is to lead a good discussion: clarify each child's contribution, raise challenging questions, ask for reasons behind opinions, and stretch children's moral awareness to consider the viewpoints of all characters involved in a dilemma.

Phyllis Hophan, a third grade teacher in Lansing, New York, and a participant in Project Change (see resource list at the end of this article), has experimented with several approaches to dilemma discussions and says the following guidelines work best for her:

1. Keep the discussion group small; six is ideal.
2. Encourage children to respond to each other. Ask: "What do you think about what so-and-so said?"
3. List children's opinions and reasons on the chalkboard. Says Hophan: "Under each of the solutions the group mentions, we have many 'becauses' and it's the 'becauses' that we spend our time talking about."

Along with commercially prepared dilemmas, situations from the classroom can provide good stimuli for moral discussions. Teachers often say that they and their students get more involved in trying to solve real moral problems: How should teachers and students deal with a rash of fistfights, pencil jabbings and kickings in the classroom? How can cleanup be organized so all do their fair share? Is it right to revoke everyone's free-time privileges because a few have abused those privileges?

In Phyllis Hophan's classroom there is a chart with an unfinished sentence that anyone may complete: "This was the week when ______." Every Friday the class tackles whatever problems have been logged that week. Examples: "There were three fights on the morning bus." "Someone had money taken." "Another teacher kept the projector too long and we couldn't see our movie." Having these complaints recorded on the chart, Hophan says, gives her and the children a longer time to think about various sides of a problem and its solutions.

Real classroom conflicts are open to many solutions and can offer students the important moral experience of hammering out a fair compromise. Coming to grips with real problems and following through on group decisions help children take a crucial step in their moral growth: *acting* on the basis of their moral reasoning. Follow-through is critical; the solutions that you and your students come up with should be put into practice. As part of the class discussion, students should share the responsibility of determining just how a solution is to be implemented and its success evaluated.

Fostering Cooperative Learning

Moral discussions—whether of fictional dilemmas or of actual problems—can aid greatly in moral development, but they won't do the whole job. The deeper moral curriculum is the day-to-day life in the classroom—the quality of the relationships between the teacher and the children and among children.

Teachers can foster positive moral relationships among children by encouraging cooperative learning. At its best, this kind of learning involves what Piaget calls *co-operation*: doing operations or work-together in a way that forces children to stop centering exclusively on their own viewpoints and to coordinate their ideas and actions with those of their co-workers.

Teacher Hophan's third grade class embarked on a cooperative learning project that spanned four months. Phase one of the project had the children working in pairs trying to figure out how to make dried beans grow without soil. At class meetings, each team shared its conclusions with the rest of the class. If there was general agreement that a reported "finding" was a fact, it was entered in the "Class Bean Book."

The children divided their labors well and showed respect for each other's ability. Said one child to his teammate: "You write in the Bean Book, OK? You write neater than me. I'll empty the water 'cause I don't care if it smells."

In phase two of the project, the class planted beans in soil. At this point, Hophan reports, unexpected competition erupted among the teams. "Partners blamed each other for over- or underwatering. Teams taunted each other and bragged about their plants growing faster or larger. There were even several cases of sabotage; in one instance the class discovered that many containers had been virtually swamped in water and that a book had been placed squarely on top of a lush crop of soybean plants. One team even blamed the death of their lima bean plant on other children's 'talking bad' to it."

The teacher used the class meeting, a regular feature of the classroom since the beginning of the year, to deal openly with the issues of cooperation, competition and jealousy. About half the children said they wanted to work alone, to care for their own plants, rather than having to work with a team member. The teacher agreed to this change.

About a week later, almost all of the children, acting on their own initiative, were back with their partners again. One boy explained that he needed his partner because, "I can't hold this paper [on which he had been recording his plant's growth rate] and mark it too." The members of one reunited team said that when they were apart they forgot to water their plants, but together they could remember.

The third phase of the project took the children on a visit to a greenhouse at Cornell University, which inspired group efforts to build their own greenhouses. As the culminating step in the project, the teacher created an opportunity for the children to engage in an altruistic act that would benefit the whole school: "I asked the principal to speak to the students, telling them that he had heard of their work in growing things and asking their help in beautifying our school by planting flowers. The response was so overwhelming that a parent contacted me that night, wanting to know if I really needed the shovels tomorrow as her son had claimed!"

Not every effort to foster cooperation in the classroom needs to be so ambitious. Ann Caren, who taught a combined second and third grade class in Ithaca, New York, found a class newspaper to be an excellent way to develop cooperative effort and group cohesion. In addition, she recommends stocking the classroom with materials—blocks, Lincoln Logs, Lego, animals, plants, clay, scrap materials, and plenty of paper and pencils—that naturally stimulate children to work together on activities that are meaningful to them. Craft activities are also good; one boy learned how to macramé and for three days straight taught other children how to do it.

The Class Meeting

To create a strong sense of community among children, which is a critical ingredient in a good moral climate, the teachers I've been describing rely heavily on class meetings. A time is set aside—typically 20 minutes at the end of the morning and sometimes again at the end of the afternoon—when children talk about what they enjoyed doing and what they didn't enjoy, discuss how they can make the classroom a better place to learn, share important personal experiences, plan a project, or exchange views about how to solve a problem that has arisen. Every teacher I know who has worked at developing this kind of regular communication among students reports a marked improvement in students' relationships and in the general moral atmosphere of the classroom.

Debbie Wilcox, a substitute teacher, uses a class meeting to begin her first day with a new class. She tells something about herself, asks the children to do the same, and explores with students the question: "What is a substitute teacher?" This discussion makes it possible to establish that a substitute teacher is a "real teacher" (most children do not think so initially) and to talk about problems that could arise during the day. The approach has proved to be very effective in creating rapport and in heading off the "let's-see-what-we-can-get-away-with" games that many classes use to make miserable the lives of substitute teachers.

Teacher Wilcox has also found that it's effective to call an impromptu class meeting during the day to clear the air and nip a problem in the bud, as she did recently when three boys threw spitballs in violation of an explicitly agreed upon rule. No discipline problem, she finds, is too tough to solve if she uses the meeting to compel children to be accountable for their own behavior.

Class meetings don't always work immediate magic, but they are always a step in the right direction—a step toward a fair exchange of perspectives, a willingness on the children's part to take responsibility for their conduct, and a group sense of caring. "This is the time of day," says Anne Roubos, a first grade teacher in Homer, New York, "when I relish the feeling of unity. At our meeting we're all together, becoming more aware of our place within the group. We're individuals, yet part of the whole. We are becoming more aware, little by little, of what respect means, what tolerance means, what sharing means. We have time to reflect, to wonder, to talk about what it feels like when someone laughs at us, or sits at our desk without asking, or crowds in line, or tells on us unfairly."

Developing a climate of moral respect in the classroom may also require directly teaching children how to communicate respectfully with one another. Often they simply don't know how. Peggy Manring, a former second grade teacher in Skaneateles, New York, recounts what she did when the children in her room were using violence to express their feelings: "I brought in a bag of wood scraps from the local toy factory and dumped these on the rug within everyone's reach. I asked the children to make a model of the classroom as they saw it, and I concentrated on their cooperation skills when these became a problem."

Here is an excerpt from the dialogue that took place between this teacher and her students:

David: "That is the dumbest chalkboard, Martha. You put it in a stupid place."

Teacher to David: "You think Martha should put the block in a different place? Would you like to suggest to her where she might put it?"

David: "Yeah, right there. The chalkboard is behind the table!"

Teacher to Martha: "If you accept David's suggestion, you may move your block. If you like it where you put it, you may leave it right there."

Teacher to David: "When you don't use the words 'stupid' and 'dumb,' people like to listen to you. You had an interesting point to make about the chalkboard."

Manring reports: "The next time David wanted to say something, he said, 'Paul, I *suggest* you look where the art table is. It's next to the teacher's desk.' Paul picked up on the 'I suggest'; so did Eddy and Alan. All the children in the class seemed to be stretching to cooperate."

The kind of direct intervention this teacher used can teach children the social skills they need to enter into the positive interactions that foster progress through the moral stages.

Uncovering the Hidden Curriculum

Even more basic than teaching children how to respect each other is setting a good example—practicing what we preach. This may mean a change in the way we use our moral authority with children. Let me give you a personal example: When our son Mark was four, he began issuing commands to his mother and me: "Daddy, read me a story." "Mommy, fix my dinner." Get me this, get me that. After not very much of this, we sat him down for a moral lecture on the virtues of saying "please" and "I would like" and so on. The next day, during the morning hassle of getting him off to nursery school, I barked, "Mark, get in the bathroom and brush your teeth and wash your face!" He took two steps, turned around, and said solemnly, "Daddy, I don't like getting orders either." As a moral educator I could hardly squelch this appeal to reciprocity and fairness, so I negotiated a bargain: I wouldn't give him orders and he wouldn't give us orders.

Piaget says that adults can have an enormous positive influence on a child's moral development if they will place themselves on an equal footing with children and stress mutual obligation with regard to at least some rules. Adults who use their authority in a way that is unilateral and that appears arbitrary to children may retard the child's growth toward understanding that morality is for everybody, big and small.

Kohlberg speaks of the influence of the "hidden curriculum"—all the ways that teachers and other adult authorities transmit, usually unwittingly, moral lessons to children. Most students, for example, must compete for grades with their classmates; helping another person may be defined as cheating. Most kids go to schools in which rules are laid down by authority; children never have a chance to participate in formulating, revising or enforcing moral requirements, and they're expected to obey without question the adult in charge.

I recently came across two stories, each about an incident in which a student called the teacher an obscene name. In one case, a second grade boy called his teacher a "son-of-a-bitchin' whore." The teacher marched the boy down to the principal's office and demanded that the child be expelled, which he was. The lesson that student learned was almost surely: the only reason to respect others is to avoid punishment (stage 1).

In the second incident, reported in Haim Ginott's excellent book *Teacher and Child,* a fifth grade boy was asked by his teacher why he persisted in talking out of turn. "None of your business, you motherfucker!" the boy replied. The teacher answered sternly, "What you have just said makes me so angry that I feel I cannot talk to you." The boy, obviously surprised at not being punished, came up after class and apologized for his behavior.

To punish a child, as Ginott points out, is to arouse resentment and to interfere with education. The essence of discipline is finding effective alternatives to punishment—alternatives that leave the child's dignity intact, show him how he has violated another's rights, and motivate him to change for the better. William Glasser's strategy for dealing with discipline problems [see "A New Look at Discipline," *Learning,* December 1974] by requiring the child to devise a concrete plan for self-improvement is another example of a discipline approach that stimulates a child's moral development and avoids wielding the club of stage 1 authority.

Teachers and parents needn't go overboard, however, worrying if they're retarding a child's moral growth every time they use their authority. Research shows that the parents who have the most morally mature children are those who assert their power with discretion—often by calling a halt to undesirable activity and directing children's attention to considering the moral problem at hand. What counts most is the overall climate an adult creates: Is there a concern for fairness? an opportunity for regular communication and collaboration? a spirit of pulling together and caring about others?

We must make education for moral development as important a part of the curriculum as is education for the intellect, because sharpened intellects alone will not prevent future Watergates and will not instill a respect for the rights of others.

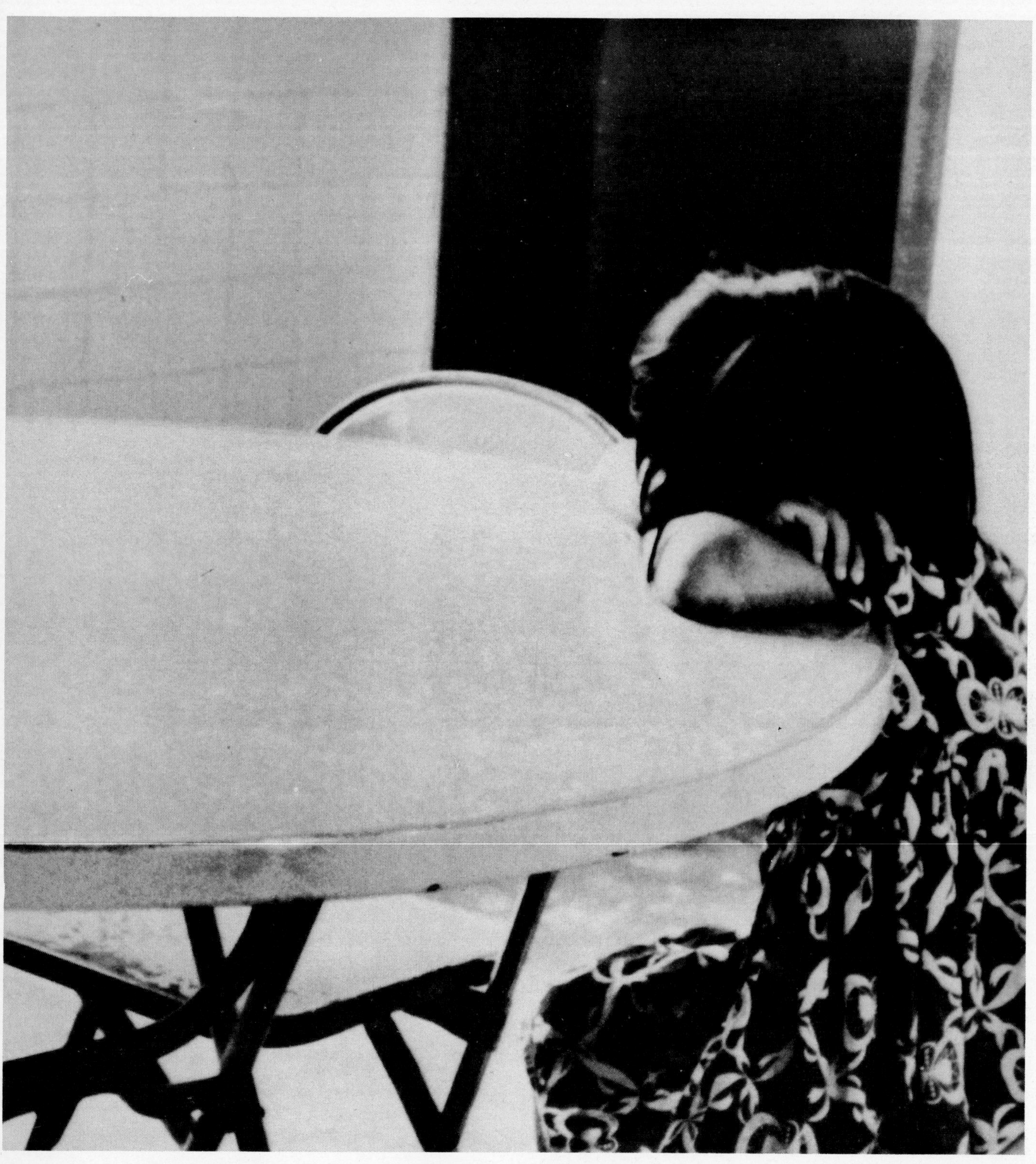

Discipline Problems in the Schools

5

The articles in this section focus on many important dimensions of classroom discipline and contain some guidelines for the control of student behavior in school settings. There are many myths and legends about what constitutes discipline in a school and control in a classroom. The essays in this section deal with both the myths and the empirical data concerning some of the school discipline problems now facing many teachers. Discipline problems and violence in many urban and suburban schools are major issues for the professional organizations representing teachers in the United States. The dimensions and scope of these problems continue to escalate in the expressed concerns of teachers and parents. Disobedience of students, disrespect toward teachers, physical assaults of all types on teachers, and an epidemic of general violence against both students and teachers in some schools are deeply affecting the morale and the professional attitudes of American teachers.

The National Education Association (NEA), the American Federation of Teachers (AFT), members of Congress, and state legislatures are concerned about the level of violence in some American school settings. The costs of maintaining security for the safety of both students and teachers across the nation run into the tens of millions of dollars per year. Threats, violence, extortion, and disrespect are unsavory considerations; yet they are real elements in the total picture of contemporary American education.

It may be helpful to remember that violence can be, and often is, an emotional and psychological, as well as a physical, phenomenon. It is bad enough that many teachers are subject to physical violence. But it is even more intolerable that teachers are so frequently subjected to attacks on their personalities and self-respect as working people. The problem of excessive violence, whether psychologically or physically inflicted, must be solved because such conditions in the schools of one of the most advanced civilizations in the world is reprehensible. If the problem is not solved, professional educators should not be held totally responsible for the possible disastrous consequences of the continuation of such a state of affairs.

Looking Ahead: Challenge Questions

What are some of the best techniques for helping someone learn self-control?

Why is it important for teachers to have a clear understanding of what target behaviors they want their students to exhibit?

What classroom behavior control strategies might be promising alternatives to corporal punishment?

What are the moral issues surrounding the concept of corporal punishment?

Can individualized approaches to classroom behavior control be developed?

What are the minimum levels of support that teachers have the right to expect from their administrative superiors?

What are some of the most common myths about classroom discipline? Why are they myths?

What should be the role of professional organizations such as the NEA and the AFT in helping teachers who experience violence in their work? What specific types of assistance should be available to teachers from such organizations?

Disciplinary Strategies

BARBARA K. TALENT
and SUZANNE G. BUSCH

Dr. Talent is an instructor of Psychology in Pediatrics, Washington University Medical School Department of Pediatrics, and assistant director of the Psychology Laboratory, St. Louis (Missouri) Children's Hospital.

Ms. Busch is the educational consultant, Psychology Laboratory, Washington University Medical School, and Department of Pediatrics, St. Louis Children's Hospital.

Innumerable books, articles, and even whole courses have been devoted to the topic of classroom management. Our experience, however, suggests that there is a great difference between understanding the principles of behavior management on a theoretical level and applying those principles in a real classroom setting.

We, therefore, try to make our suggestions as specific and concrete as possible. Feedback from teachers who have actually used our ideas has helped us do this. We have tried to address the day-to-day issues of classroom teaching and take into account the restrictions with which the average teacher must cope: 30 to 40 children in a classroom, a scarcity of support personnel and resources, limitations on preparation time, and little or no cooperation from parents.

While we believe a teacher plagued by these difficulties can successfully apply our techniques for classroom management, we do not mean to imply that it will be simple. Teachers who use our approaches must be active, creative, flexible, and capable of adapting rules to children's particular needs. Even for such teachers, these approaches will not be a panacea for all behavior problems. Applied consistently and thoughtfully, however, they can be invaluable tools for helping children become more successful in the classroom.

Behavior Patterns

In our experience, most children with behavior problems fall into two main groups (although rarely will any one child fit neatly into one group or the other). In one group are youngsters who are actually fairly compliant; they are willing to work, particularly on a one-to-one basis, and do not openly defy their teachers. On the other hand, they are disorganized, work carelessly, and tend not to finish assigned work. They daydream, seem to have a short attention span, and are easily distracted.

In the second group are the more actively disruptive and openly defiant children. These students are easily frustrated and vent their frustrations in temper outbursts. Adults often say they have a chip on their shoulder. Such children will often refuse to begin an assignment. If they do begin, they give up quickly, often angrily tearing up their papers and throwing them on the floor or scribbling over what they have already done.

After describing ways to get started, we will describe general behavior management techniques that we have found useful for children who behave in either of these ways. Then we will give suggestions aimed more specifically at each type.

Starting the Program

Attempting to change too many behaviors at once almost always guarantees failure. The first step, therefore, in implementing a behavior management plan is choosing the behaviors you most want a child to change. We suggest the following procedure:

1. Make a list of the child's behaviors that you find disruptive. Take a good look at what you have written. A sample list might read—

- Taps pencil against desk
- Never finishes assignments
- Talks out instead of raising hand
- Tips chair back against wall
- Spends a lot of time doodling.

2. Decide which behaviors deserve priority. Which one or two (at most) do you need to deal with immediately? On the sample list, "never finishes assignments" followed by "talks out instead of raising hand" would most likely be the ones you would choose. Although the rest are certainly annoying, you should ignore them until you have been able to modify the more serious ones. Again, the quickest way to ensure failure of your plan is to try to change too many behaviors at once.

3. Be very clear in your own mind what it is you want to change. This usually means describing in observable, measurable terms the behavior you will concentrate on. Thus, "helping Johnny learn to *finish what he starts—on time*" is a concrete, measurable behavior, while "helping Johnny *be a better student*" is too vague. Note that you target not only the behavior you want to change (never finishes assignments), but also the behavior you want to develop (finishes assignments on time).

4. Inform the student of your

"Disciplinary Strategies," Barbara K. Talent and Suzanne G. Busch, *Today's Education*, February/March 1982. Reprinted by permission.

intention to help him or her behave differently. Pick a time when things have been going fairly well, when the student is fairly calm—*not* a time right after misbehavior. Your explanation should be short, simple, and direct—something like:

> "Janice, you know we've had some trouble getting along in class this school year. I understand that sometimes you feel very angry and that it is hard to control your temper. I have some ideas about what we can do to help you develop more self-control. By self-control, I mean not yelling or hitting or pinching when you are angry and not giving up when you feel the work is hard.
>
> "I know there are times when you are not very pleased with your actions and you would like to make things go more smoothly. I appreciate that, and I know we can make things better. It won't be easy, and it won't happen overnight, but with both of us working together, we can do it."

Make sure that your students understand that you are firmly committed to helping them develop more appropriate behaviors and that you sincerely believe that working together, you will be successful.

5. As far as the rest of your class goes, you will need to be prepared to answer their questions about any special arrangements you make with a particular child (earning special privileges, filling in progress charts, keeping track of certain behaviors). Answer the other students' questions briefly and matter-of-factly: "Janice and I are working together to help her strengthen a weak area. We all have our strengths and weaknesses, and at various times I will most likely have special arrangements with different students in our classroom."

General Techniques

Thoughtfully applied, but liberally meted out, positive reinforcement is one of the most powerful tools you have available for strengthening the behaviors you want children to develop. It is important to be alert for instances of appropriate behavior. Recognize and praise even approximations of the desired behaviors; praise progress and improvement—don't wait until a student has a perfect day.

Shape the target behavior by going over to the student, possibly touching her or him, and honestly praising the behavior: "Janice, I noticed that Steve accidentally bumped your desk, and you looked up, but then kept working. That was really good self-control!" or "Johnny, you are doing a good job of trying hard to solve these math problems, and I know they aren't easy." Praising appropriate behavior shows children when they are acting properly and gives them frequent chances to experience success in their lives.

Positive reinforcement is a tool that is easy to apply to the class as a whole. Let all your students know that you appreciate appropriate behavior. The other behavior management techniques will not be effective unless you regularly use positive reinforcement.

How you praise is an important aspect of shaping behavior. Make sure to praise the behavior you like, not the child. Try to keep praise specific and informative. Thus, "Good job of staying in your seat during math, Johnny," rather than just "Good boy, Johnny," tells Johnny exactly what you liked about what he did and makes very clear what you expect from him in the future.

Again, when trying to help children develop the ability to "keep working even when the work is hard," be sure to reinforce effort rather than just the final product. To feel less frustrated, these children need to learn that trying, even when it's hard, is just as important as "getting it all right."

A second powerful tool for changing behavior is ignoring behavior you want to discourage. Learning to ignore annoying but less severe problem behaviors is quite a challenge. But remember that all attention (both positive and negative) is reinforcing. Stopping a class to correct one student gives that student a powerful dose of attention and actually reinforces the behavior you want to eliminate. A much more effective strategy is to ignore that behavior and attempt to make a model of a child who is behaving in an appropriate manner.

By doing this, you tell students, "Behave appropriately and you will get recognition," not vice versa. If Janice is not working on her assignment, you might walk over to a child near her who is on task and say, "I see you are working hard on your spelling words, Doug. Good job!"

You cannot, of course, ignore all misbehavior. If Johnny gets up and starts to walk around the room, simply say, "During class time, we need to stay in our seats." Then, quickly escort him to his seat with the minimum amount of discussion (attention). Briefly remind him of what he should be doing and then busy yourself with another child who is working. As soon as Johnny picks up his pencil or looks as though he is turning to the assigned page, promptly reinforce this with a remark like, "I like the way you are ready to work. Do you have any questions?"

Developing Better Work Habits

The techniques we have discussed so far should prove helpful regardless of the type of behavior problem you are dealing with. The following suggestions are aimed more specifically at those children who have trouble sticking with tasks they consider difficult or uninteresting.

1. Make sure the child understands the assignment. When you have finished giving the class directions, you might go over and ask the child to explain to you just what he or she is to do.

2. If necessary, break the assignment down into smaller, less overwhelming units. For example, ask the student to start with only one row of math problems or answer only the first three social studies questions, then to raise his or her hand to let you know the work is done. This will allow you to check the student's work and praise effort.

After this bit of encouragement, give the student another short section to do, again briefly checking it when the work is completed. Your goal here is to ensure success, praise effort, and build some independence in work habits. After this student has consistently met with success, you can begin to gradually lengthen the amount of independent work you require.

3. Help the student set realistic short-term goals. Encourage him or her to construct and keep simple progress charts.

For instance, you might make a chart dividing the day into short units (15 to 20 minutes). You and your pupil put checks on the chart for each time period without a temper outburst or without wandering around the room.

When various milestones are reached, a brief note or phone call to the student's home will give parents a chance to congratulate the child for trying hard.

4. Use attainable, enforceable contingencies ("first . . ., then . . ." situations). Make participation in favored activities (e.g., drawing, playing games, time at interest centers) contingent upon "getting your work done first." No exceptions. Verbalize this often.

Phrase the contingencies positively, focusing on the behavior you want, rather than on the undesirable behavior—e.g., "As soon as you finish this assignment, you can draw," not "If you don't finish your work, you can't draw."

If the child you are working with has been particularly good, you might surprise her or him by providing a reward unexpectedly: "You did such a good job of sticking with that assignment that I'd like you to help me put up the bulletin board this afternoon."

5. When a student gets discouraged, provide reminders of other well-handled difficulties: "Remember the division work on Monday? You stuck with it, tried, and did fine."

Disruptive Behavior

What about the child who is behaving in a way that disrupts the whole class? We suggest the use of a time-out place.

The choice of an appropriate time-out place requires careful consideration. A time-out place should be as quiet and unstimulating as possible—a place where the student receives no attention and where there is virtually nothing to do. If you are lucky, a room supervised by an adult might be available. A coatroom is another possibility. If no other room is available, you can set up a corner of your own room as devoid of distracting sights and sounds as possible.

Time out should last for only five to 10 minutes. Time out that lasts longer becomes banishment and is less effective.

Students should know ahead of time that the purpose is to allow them to regain self-control. When you send children to time out, it is very important that (1) you tell them briefly why they are going—e.g., "Janice, you are yelling and disturbing others—time out!" and (2) you do not lecture or scold them. Calmly escort the child to the designated spot, without any arguing or justifying. When the time is up, simply direct the child to rejoin the class.

When disruptive behavior includes angry outbursts of yelling or hitting, the following strategies should be useful:

1. Discuss with the child alternative methods of dealing with anger. Have this discussion when the child is calm, not when he or she is frustrated and angry. The phrase "count to 10" is trite, but still can be an effective reminder to pause for a few seconds instead of giving in to angry feelings.

Let the child know that telling someone how you feel is also a good outlet. Making a real attempt to "ignore little things" is another way the child can try to deal with frustration.

When discussing these strategies, be concrete and specific, and try to give some true-to-life examples: "Suppose Joey walked by and knocked your book off your desk: What could you do?" "What if Ann poked you? What would you do?"

2. Intervene early. If you see a potentially explosive situation, get to the youngster quickly to help him or her regain control. Try using a firm arm around the shoulder and a quiet reminder that there are alternative ways of handling anger.

3. Deal with the child as calmly and matter-of-factly as possible. Help the student gain control through your own relaxed, in-control manner. Try to use your physical presence, too; standing next to the child is far more effective than talking across a room.

A Final Reminder

As we stated earlier, learning to react to children's problem behaviors in a calm, thoughtful, and above all consistent manner is hard work. It is important to remember that you are modifying not only the child's behavior pattern but also your own. This takes time. Behavior change occurs slowly, and progress is marked by many starts and stops.

After a definite improvement has occurred in a child's behavior, some regression is not unusual. If you anticipate this, you won't become disheartened when it occurs. Rather, review the rules with the child and continue your efforts, always remembering to enforce consequences, positive as well as negative. The consistent application of these techniques, coupled with your own knowledge and enthusiasm, will produce improved classroom behavior.

Defusing Discipline Problems

Edward A. Wynne

Edward A. Wynne is associate professor of education at the College of Education, University of Illinois, and editor of Character II.

A FRONT-page article in an issue of *The New York Times* some months ago announced the development of a new student discipline code for the city public schools. Pupil discipline has been the primary parent complaint against public schools in thirteen of the fourteen national Gallup Polls on educational issues. Thus, this New York development has implications for citizens in all communities.

The code is to go into effect this fall. Thomas K. Minter, the associate chancellor of the system, was interviewed about elements of the code, which is designed to provide lesser penalties than expulsion for moderate offenses. As examples of moderate offenses, he mentioned "verbally attacking a teacher or the use of foul language in class." Students engaging in such conduct, he said, would be subject to "reasonable sanctions."

He was asked, "What might 'reasonable sanctions' be?"

He replied, "The student could be required to go to a special counseling program."

This was the only sanction specified in the article. As a professor in a college of education, I thought it would be desirable to know the meaning of the phrase special counseling program.

"And so I asked several of my colleagues for interpretations. One defined the phrase quite literally: "A plan for students to meet frequently and regularly with a trained counselor, to participate in individual and group counseling sessions. Meanwhile, the students would continue in ordinary classes." Another said, "It's my suspicion that the term is just a euphemism. It really means that special classes and schools for undesirables will be set up and that disorderly students will be sent to these places and be subject to tight and unpleasant restrictions." Two other colleagues said they couldn't make an informed guess as to what was meant.

From my research, I concluded that no one could have a good idea of what was meant by "special counseling sessions" in the context of tightening up discipline. The one thing I am sure of is that such ambiguous language—or concepts—bodes ill for the success of any discipline code. A number of studies have demonstrated that firm, consistent, and clear rules and penalties are a common feature of schools that have good student discipline. But how can such policies be developed if obscure language is applied?

Of course, I may be too Machiavellian. Perhaps "special counseling" should be interpreted in its literal sense. Maybe all it means is that students in the New York City schools who engage in moderate acts of "indiscipline" will be sent to regular and frequent counseling sessions, conducted by trained professionals. Why don't I just believe that proposition? First of all, I doubt that there is enough money in the city to pay for such a program. Secondly, even if there was, I believe such counseling, applied without concurrent sanctions, would be a trivial response.

THE INTELLECTUALLY significant part of this matter is that reliance on ambiguous euphemisms is a common pattern in school discipline situations. And my own research has convinced me that such obscurity seriously undermines the process of rule enforcement: students and teachers often feel that the rules lack teeth. And they are right.

The causes for the ambiguity around the *punishment* element—to use an unambiguous word—of student discipline codes are complex, but important. First, we should recognize that student suspension or expulsion is a drastic remedy that properly should only be used in drastic instances; a good discipline

This article appeared first in the Summer issue of AMERICAN EDUCATOR, the quarterly journal of the American Federation of Teachers.

code must include effective lesser penalties. The application of such lesser penalties is often administratively quite difficult. It's not so easy nowadays to apply the old-fashioned device of keeping kids after school. If they are kept, someone must watch them. And many school systems have signed union contracts that permit teachers to leave promptly after the dismissal bell. So it can be hard to find someone to monitor the students being kept. Further, if they are monitored, they should be kept from reading comic books or shooting the breeze so that punishment is really unpleasant. Indeed, detainees might even be restrained from doing their homework so that detention isn't just a place to catch up on studying. This means the adults monitoring the students must treat the assignment seriously, instead of just a chance to catch up on their own paperwork.

Then, if kids are kept, they must get home after the regular school is out. If they travel to and from school by bus, the bus may have made its only run. Or, if the school is in a difficult neighborhood and if the miscreants leave individually, instead of being part of a group of students, who is responsible for seeing them safely home? The students who choose to break the rules? The school? The parents?

Of course, detentions sometimes occur during the school day, when students are kept from regular classes,. or during free periods. There is still the problem of adult supervision. And sometimes it is hard to find available classroom space, so students can be isolated from distractions and amusements.

GIVEN SOME determination, none of the preceding problems is unsolveable. Job descriptions can be amended. Parents can be informed of their ultimate responsibility for bringing their (younger) children home. Older pupils can be reminded that one of the consequences of rule breaking can be an awkward or dangerous trip. Everyone can realize that the economic costs of appropriately monitoring detentions may ultimately result in general savings—resulting from improved discipline.

I believe the administrative problems I have described are only secondary causes for our evident weakness in dealing with discipline problems. The root of our problem is more philosophic that organizational. Many people really do not believe that pupils should be punished—made to feel unhappy, restrained, scorned—for wrongdoing. As a result, we end up with proposals for "special counseling programs." Through many dialogues with anti-punishers, I have come to recognize their rationale. They first contend that punishment doesn't work. But I point out that numerous studies show that punishment actually changes conduct: people who are effectively punished for doing things tend to stop doing them, and others who see such punishments applied tend to avoid acts that stimulate punishment. But the anti-punishers then go on to talk about the secondary effects of punishment. What do students learn from seeing order maintained partly by coercion? What happens to students when they leave school and go to other environments where the punishment structure is not maintained? How will they learn self-discipline? In other words, the anti-punishers redefine and broaden the meaning of punishment "working."

This is a legitimate intellectual tactic. The only problem is that the broader meaning is so broad that it is incapable of being tested via pragmatic research. We cannot know the ultimate effects of punishment unless we follow people for years and study not only those punished, but also those who observe the punishment. Furthermore, to be fair, we would have to compare persons from a punishing environment with persons in an environment where some alternative to punishment—intensive counseling—was applied. I can guarantee that such a project would take a great deal of money and take ten to fifteen years. I doubt that it would supply enough clear answers to satisfy serious partisans of any position.

THE AWKWARD, or interesting, fact is that the way we handle pupil discipline in schools is more related to our views of the nature of man than to any research. The anti-punishers have an essentially Rousseauan view of man. As a result, they believe that social constraints finally inhibit healthy human development. The pro-punishers believe that without such basic social constraints as punishment, many bad and evil things will happen. These dichotomous positions have affected many elements of our educational policy beyond discipline codes. They have shaped grading standards, the homework load we assign students, college admission practices, and pupil promotion policies.

As we have recognized, our society and educational institutions are beginning to shift from Rousseauan views, under the weight of their accumulated—and painful—experience. Perhaps Dr. Minter really intends that a "special counseling program" is something that pupils will really dislike. If so, he may eventually get around to saying that in plain language. And thus the process of incremental improvement will go forward. The first beneficiaries of this improvement will be the myriad rule-abiding pupils who are now forced to attend disorderly schools: schools where the adults are unwilling to take serious steps to restrain the rule-breaking minority.

The Discipline Problem in Our Schools: What's Happening?

Dan Kaercher

During the turbulent Vietnam War era, "down with the establishment" and "up with student rights" were rallying cries in the schools. Now things are quieter.

"You just don't get as many students who are rebellious or hypercritical of adults or institutions now as you did then," says Scott Thomson, executive director of the National Association of Secondary School Principals.

"There seems to be a 'get-tough-on-kids' attitude nationally," adds John Kackley, psychologist for Project PASS in St. Petersburg, Florida. PASS stands for Positive Alternatives to Student Suspension, a model discipline program developed in St. Petersburg area schools over the past decade.

However, Kackley says, adults tend to forget that most students *want* discipline—a term he associates with personal responsibility for behavior, not simply punishment for misbehavior. "Kids want a well-run classroom. They don't want a sloppy, chaotic environment," Kackley says.

What Discipline Approaches Are Being Used These Days?

In-school suspension centers, alternative schools, behavior contracting, and peer counseling are a few of the new programs that are catching on across the country.

The new approaches to school discipline are succeeding best in quelling commonplace disruptions such as rowdiness, insolence, tardiness, and truancy. Infractions like assault and drug abuse still are considered matters for juvenile authorities.

These days school officials aim to keep the majority of disruptive pupils in school, rather than suspend them. Since many children today live in one-parent homes or ones where both parents work, sending a youngster home may backfire.

Some new discipline approaches also stress self-awareness—helping a student realize what he or she has done wrong, and the effects of the misbehavior.

Here's a closer look at some of the innovative new discipline techniques being used today.

In-School Suspension Centers: Keeping Troublemakers off the Streets

In-school suspension centers—also known as crisis classrooms, time-out rooms, and behavior modification centers—are the fastest growing new approach to handling problem students.

In recent years, the centers have appeared in hundreds of school districts—including St. Petersburg, Florida; Houston, Texas; Indianapolis, Indiana; Richmond, Virginia; Columbus, Ohio; Kansas City, Missouri.

Students are sent to the suspension centers for just one period, for a whole day, or for several days as an alternative to being suspended from school entirely.

The advantages: Others in the class aren't distracted from their work, and the troublemakers gets special counseling while keeping up with his or her studies.

In the Houston Independent School District, each of six school "regions" has from one to three single-classroom suspension centers, known locally as "student referral centers."

Houston teachers and administrators credit the referral centers with significantly reducing traditional out-of-school suspensions.

"The kids who were sent home usually just wandered around all day without supervision," says Ginger Harper, supervisor of a community services agency that manages the program with the school district.

Truancy and fighting are the most common offenses that bring students to the centers, which can accommodate up to 20 students each. Typically, a student is required to stay at a center three days.

While at the suspension centers, students must maintain silence and eat lunch alone. Pupils also are required to keep up with regular class assignments. Counseling services are available for youngsters with serious behavior problems.

Like other model programs, the Houston centers emphasize keeping parents informed and involved.

Rather than simply getting a note from the school, parents of youngsters who are referred to the centers are required to attend conferences with their children and school officials.

The Houston centers also offer voluntary counseling services to any student—suspended or not—who is having discipline problems and needs to talk to someone who can help.

In-school suspension centers also have had a dramatic impact on discipline procedures in High Point, North Carolina.

Two years ago, there were 300 traditional suspensions at High Point's Ferndale Junior High. Last year, after the introduction of an "ISS" (in-school suspension center), there were only 85, reports Ferndale principal Betty Thomas.

Alternative Schools: Intensive Care for Problem Students

An even more intensive focus on the needs of problem students is provided at alternative schools that have appeared in communities like St. Petersburg and Daytona Beach, Florida; St. Paul, Minnesota; Wilmington, Delaware; Oxford, Massachusetts; and in Anne Arundel County, Maryland.

The special schools are admittedly costlier than in-school suspension centers, but the results have been judged worth the expense in many school districts.

Alternative schools offer extensive counseling services and remedial academic programs for problem kids, who are often far behind in their classroom studies.

Huntley Cross, principal of the Anne Arundel County Learning Center, says he and his staff make a conscious effort to become involved with students.

"Kids take failure very personally. As a consequence, they don't feel very good about themselves when they come here. We try to change that.

"For at least one period in their lives, we want our kids to realize someone cares."

Enrollment at the Learning Center ranges from 60 to 100 junior-high-aged youths, mostly 14- and 15-year-old males. All of the students have been suspended from other schools in the district, and their attendance at the Learning Center is mandatory, not optional.

The typical student attends school at the center for six to nine months before returning to his or her regular classroom.

Classes at the center are small, averaging ten students each. The academic focus is on basic reading and math skills; the behavior emphasis is on self-discipline. Teachers go over each student's work every 15 minutes and initial daily report cards after each class period.

"Every staff member tries to develop a special relationship with the students," Cross says.

Unruly students at the center must fill out forms listing what they've done wrong and how they plan to improve their behavior. If a student refuses, he or she is sent to the school's "back room," a type of in-school suspension center. Corporal punishment is never used at the Learning Center.

Of the students who have "graduated" from the Learning Center and returned to regular classrooms during the past five years, two-thirds have not been suspended again—an admirable record to students with serious behavior problems.

Behavior Contracting: Drawing the Line on Discipline Problems

In many communities, one solution to the discipline problem has been to spell out exactly what type of behavior is expected of students—and what will happen if expectations are not met.

Behavior codes and contracts cover such matters as getting to class on time, completing homework, and abiding by conduct rules. The written contracts usually are signed by students, parents, and teachers.

Officials at El Camino High School in Sacramento, California, credit a strict new behavior code for a dramatic turnabout in student discipline problems—and the reversal of a serious decline in enrollment.

Before the introduction of the new behavior code, El Camino was losing many of its middle-class students to private schools. Then the school was designated as a fundamental (basics) attendance center within the Sacramento district. Now enrollment is increasing steadily.

"We were at the point where we wanted to see our students educated properly or not at all," principal Joseph Petterle says.

Now El Camino parents and students are asked to sign a contract stating that they understand and will follow school rules "to the letter."

According to Petterle, the emphasis at El Camino is not on catering to troublemakers but on maintaining an orderly environment for the majority of students who are not disruptive.

"There are certain things we won't tolerate here, and

we don't spend a lot of time talking about what's unacceptable," Petterle says.

Petterle explains, "We're trying to focus in a positive way on the majority of the students."

Under the El Camino code, in-school alcohol and drug use are designated as "one strike and you're out" offenses; suspension is mandatory. The behavior code also stresses regular attendance and notification of parents if problems arise, academic as well as disciplinary.

"It's amazing how kids adapt," Petterle says. "It all depends on where you draw the line."

Peer Counseling: Kids Helping Kids

Peer counseling programs are an integral part of discipline programs in Seattle, Washington; Cincinnati, Ohio; Salt Lake City, Utah; and other communities.

According to Larry Neufpickle, chairperson of the counseling department at Taft High School in Cincinnati, peer counseling has helped stretch services that have been limited by budget cuts.

Taft's peer counseling program has been in operation for three years. Student volunteers, who are trained in human relations workshops, make themselves available to other students during lunchtime. The most common problems the peer counselors help fellow students deal with are conflicts with other students and teachers.

"Student counselors get some credit for their work, but it's mostly a volunteer effort," Neufpickle reports.

In three of four Salt Lake City public high schools, student counselors are trained in special social studies courses that often attract students who have discipline problems themselves.

"Students see peer counseling as a way they can plug into the school more productively," says Betsy Thompson, a high school counselor in Salt Lake City. "After the course, the kids acquire the basic skills they need to counsel their friends informally," Thompson says.

The Salt Lake City peer counseling program has been operating for three years. In some instances, potential behavior problems are averted by assigning peer counselors to work with students who have had discipline problems in the past or are new to the school.

Another innovative Salt Lake City program is the Truancy School, which aims to help chronic truants by providing counseling services to both the students and their families.

In the Truancy School, parents who find themselves in juvenile court because they youngster is a chronic truant are required by the court to attend a three-week evening course with the child.

The course includes group counseling and discussion of how to set and achieve behavior goals. School officials report that about 80 percent of students who attend Truancy School with their parents significantly improve their attendance records.

Assertive Discipline: Confidence Is the Key

In many schools, the heart of the discipline problem is a buffaloed classroom teacher.

School administrators say many teachers do not have adequate training in classroom management techniques. As a result, the teachers are insecure and uninformed about how to exercise their authority.

For teachers who need confidence, California education consultant Lee Canter developed his "assertive discipline" program. Canter formulated his approach after observing the best teachers he could find during a six-year period.

Canter's research underscored some commonsense wisdom about classroom discipline: Teachers need to clearly and firmly assert their authority without becoming hostile or indifferent to students.

"Assertive teachers do not tolerate any student who is stopping them from teaching, or preventing other students from learning," Canter says. "And, most important, they recognize and reinforce the behavior of students who behave appropriately."

Since Canter started to spread the assertive discipline gospel in 1976, over 300,000 teachers have studied his methods, primarily at workshops in their schools.

However, Canter's approach has been criticized on the grounds that some "assertive" teachers have tended

Corporal Punishment: Does It Work?

It's an age-old question, but most experts today answer it with a resounding "No!"

Most teachers who have specialized in working with disruptive students say spanking or hitting is ineffective. Further, the teachers say corporal punishment can backfire and compound a student's behavior problems.

Nevertheless, the Supreme Court ruled in 1977 that states can permit corporal punishment in the schools. Since then, the practice has become more widespread and is illegal only in Massachusetts, New Jersey, Maine, Hawaii, and in some local school districts including New York City, Atlanta, Baltimore, and St. Louis.

Irwin Hyman, director of the Center for the Study of Corporal Punishment and Alternatives in the Schools at Temple University, says states where corporal punishment is commonly practiced in schools have higher per-pupil school vandalism costs.

"Kids want justice," says Hyman, who has studied corporal punishment and school discipline for ten years. "When the rules are firm and fair and are seen as reasonable, there are fewer discipline problems. Then the issue of corporal punishment becomes irrelevant."

to neglect the positive reinforcement aspect of his approach.

Canter concedes that there is some truth in the charges about excessive punishments. He warns parents to be aware of inappropriate punishments committed in the name of assertive discipline and discipline in general, such as using unventilated closets for in-school suspension centers.

How Parents Can Help

If you suspect that discipline is a problem in your youngster's school—either too much or too little—discuss the matter with the principal.

Find out how many students are suspended each year or semester and how this compares with other schools in the district. Ask for an explanation of the school's discipline policies, and find out whether any of the innovative approaches discussed in this article are being used. If not, volunteer to help in developing a solution.

In some school districts, budget cuts threaten the survival of alternative schools and in-school suspension centers, which require smaller classes and special counseling services.

Make sure your school board and community leaders are aware of the full benefits of effective student discipline programs. For example, Houston officials credit the student referral centers discussed earlier with lowering the number of youths who are involved in crimes, such as breaking and entering, during the daytime.

Remind officials that such programs make good economic sense, too, since school districts lose state revenue each day a student is suspended from the classroom. Students who are attending classes at alternative schools and in-school suspension centers are still counted in attendance figures.

Finally, make sure you personally set high standards of behavior for your children, and that you enforce discipline appropriately and consistently in your home.

"Parental support is absolutely essential to any effort to improve discipline in the schools," Lee Canter says.

For More Information

• *Student Discipline Problems and Solutions,* published by the American Association of School Administrators, is available for $10.95 per copy. To obtain the report, write to the AASA, 1801 North Moore Street, Arlington, VA 22209.

• *Student Discipline: Practical Approaches,* published by the National School Boards Association, is available for $7.50 per copy. To obtain a copy, write, NSBA Information Services Department, 1055 Thomas Jefferson Street, NW., Washington, DC 20007

• Further information about corporal punishment issues is available from the National Center for the Study of Corporal Punishment and Alternatives in the Schools, 822 Ritter Hall South, Temple University, Philadelphia, PA 19122 (phone 215/787-6091).

—*Written with Jeanne E. Saddler*

There's Only One True Technique for Good Discipline

Susan Ohanian

Susan Ohanian, a contributing editor for Learning, *is a language arts teacher at W.K. Doyle Middle School in Troy, N.Y.*

Four years after our middle school opened, teachers were still grumbling about the absence of an official discipline policy. Then, in the fifth year of our discontent, the school board adopted the Discipline Code—a holy writ of conduct distributed to teachers, parents and children. Teachers, of course, quickly discovered that official rules didn't help them achieve Authority in the Classroom, and the code was filed with other bureaucratic memorabilia.

Our discipline code did not leap full-blown out of the head of an administrator. It was developed by a committee of caring, concerned people—members of the school board, administrators, teachers, parents, students. They meant well; they tried hard. Authority, however, cannot come from a committee. A teacher's authority comes from her own savvy; it is a part of her style and cannot be distributed by fiat or handed out like chalk and rubber bands.

Borrowing from sociologist Max Weber's model, I see three kinds of authority operating in schools: traditional, legal and charismatic. Traditional authority relies on sacred custom. The teacher is always right: respect the office, if not the person. I was raised in that mode: "If you get hit at school, you'll get hit twice at home." The crumbling bulwark of most principals, traditional authority is already dead for most educators outside of military academies and some parochial schools. Nowadays parents are more likely to say, "Stop harassing my child!" And if a student is supended, she comes to the hearing with a lawyer.

With the second kind of authority, legal, committees at the local and state levels hold meetings, set policies, write guidelines. They issue documents to establish law and order in the schools. Principals rely heavily on the edicts spewn forth: "It is state mandated" is a response designed to end all discussion.

Loopholes in the blanket of legal authority have attracted some who aren't schoolteachers, but ed-biz whizzes. Flitting around the country offering teachers the holy grail of classroom management, these trend followers provide a psy-fi fix in the form of barter systems, contracts and the M & M exchange. Too often their programs lead to a student extortion racket: give me a verbal massage (or some candy or gold stars), and I won't drive you nuts.

The third kind of classroom authority, charismatic, is more elusive. This personal authority emanates not from a tradition or a legal document or a manipulative barter system, but from individual personality. It can survive change in reading programs, change in dress code standards, change in ethnic makeup of the student body; it can survive amidst chaos.

One does not find charisma in its pure form very often, nor are descriptions of charismatic authority usually very helpful to educational acolytes. The charismatic teacher holds her kids—in the style of the Ancient Mariner—by her glittering eye, not her handfuls of M & M's. The charismatic teacher knows in her bones when she is right. She doesn't have checklists to prove it. She expresses herself in the work she does, not in pretty slogans and colorful charts.

Several years ago, in *Schools Where Children Learn,* Joseph Featherstone told us that "there are no educational 'models' that can be mass produced." He pointed out that the systems approach is generally inappropriate to education, where most of the problems are human, not technical. "Learning is far more complex in its sequences and motives than the simple models constructed by behaviorists, which are drawn from observations of pigeons eating corn friskies . . ." How naive, then, to suppose that a teacher can take a course, learn a set of dialogues, and parrot a sequence of 63 positive statements to get children behaving correctly.

School administrators intone that "in order for learning to take place, there must be order in the classroom." That may be true, but I feel the emphasis is in the wrong place. In order that learning may take place, there should be something worth learning. Sad to say, an orderly classroom is too often considered accomplishment enough for teachers. One need not take home a book, prepare a lesson, or do anything beyond assign daily reading in class; teachers who never file disciplinary referrals make the administrative honor role.

The behaviorist ed-biz whiz gang has moved in and capitalized on this administrative yearning for order. Once the behaviorists had curriculum whipped into shape with their lists of objectives and criterion-referenced tests and brightly colored skill packets, discipline

Reprinted by special permission of LEARNING, The Magazine for Creative Teaching, August 1982.

became the obvious target. Now they offer their programs as a contract: You do this and the child will do that. Their classroom management schemes—the frozen waffles of junk pedagogy—are packaged in promises and contain few redeeming qualities. I know because I have recently read 15 books on discipline. They have chapter titles like The Ecology of Classroom Discipline, Contingency Contracting, Congruent Communication, Assertive Discipline, Operationally Defined Misbehavior and Minimal Intervention. The self-proclaimed educational experts who write them make a good buck dispensing wisdom and conducting training sessions to show teachers how to organize their classrooms. Training and control are neatly packaged and marketed under the name of "learning." Classroom management and teaching become the same thing in the eyes of the trainers, and, I fear, too often in the eyes of the teachers.

The pseudo-specialized vocabulary of child control adds to the confusion. I am uneasy when I read that a "response cost is defined as the removal of specified amounts of positive reinforcement after (contingent on) a behavior." I read that "punishment is the presentation of an environmental event, contingent on a behavior, which decreases the strength of that behavior," and my brain buzzes. I read of "compliance devices," "token economics," "deceleration targets," "alternate responses," "environmental alterations" and "terminal behavior," and I break out in a rash. I read about the teacher as "operant conditioner," "reinforcer," "facilitator" or "psychodynamicist," and I shout, "NO!" (I must confess, however, to a certain fascination with the expression "terminal behavior." If these guys could guarantee that the next time Selina snaps her gum at me it would be her terminal act, I might sign up for their course.)

The bold assertions amaze me! Without equivocation or hesitation, the behavior mod folks state that the child's "behavior extinguishes since it is no longer successful in obtaining the reinforcement (attention of the teacher) the child desires." Personally, I don't think I've ever extinguished a child's behavior. Furthermore, I agree with James Herndon that all the operant conditioning in the world won't change "simply a mean son-of-a-bitch, no matter how he got that way." Of course, the positive self-image people usually don't talk about the crazies or the 6-foot hoodlum with his fist in your face. Most of their classroom dramatizations deal with children passing notes and speaking without raising their hands.

None of the books I read on classroom management addressed the issue of teacher physical prowess. For inner-city kids at least, body language is more important than sweet words. I am not talking about physical strength or abuse; I have never used physical force on any of my students. I do know, however, that Jack respects me and accepts my authority because one day I put my 103-pound body on the line against him. Jack is a big, angry seventh grader who can't read. He has average intelligence, good auditory memory, and I don't know why he can't associate squiggles on paper with words. I know only that he is in a rage most of the time.

I discovered that mine was one of the few classes in which Jack was disruptive. He was allowed to be absolutely passive in other classes. As long as he didn't cause trouble, no one bothered him. In one class he was given an 80 for "good attitude." He got a 55 in my class because he would not try language experience stories and refused all tests I gave him. One day Jack was leaning back in his chair, needling another boy who was trying to work. The second boy pushed Jack on the chest, causing him to fall over backward onto the rug.

The probability of a blow being struck was about 99 percent. No way could Jack be put down like that in front of his peers without retaliating. I dashed over and shouted, "Jack, you had it coming! You were bothering him!" Jack quickly turned his anger on me. Towering over me, he actually began to huff himself up bigger. I leaned in very close and said, "He was wrong to touch you, but don't make it worse by touching him. You were wrong, too. Calm down."

Jack huffed a couple more times and tried to stare me down. I leaned even closer and stared back. Then he walked out of the room. I followed in a couple of minutes, and he was able to talk to me and eventually to the other boy. They shook hands. I consider this incident one of the most positive things that happened between us in the first five months of school. Jack found out that I wouldn't let him get out of control, that he didn't have to hit me, and that I wouldn't let him hit anyone else. I didn't stop Jack by saying, "You are angry." I stopped him with my voice and my body.

Not long after that confrontation, Jack and I began a different kind of interaction. One day he waited for all the other kids to take their spelling tests, then said, "I'm ready for mine." Five rhyming words. He got 100. He asked me to sign the paper and carried it off. We were in the process of doing winter stories. A bank of marvelous words and phrases—like *icy misery, frozen Arctic regions, shattered water pipes, windy walloper*—stretched the length of the hallway. I told Jack to choose five words, which I'd help him turn into a story. A couple of days later he heard me tell another student to go out in the hallway and find ten good winter words. "You only gave me five," Jack frowned. "I guess I better go get another five."

Jack wrote his stories, read them, typed them, read them again, and hung them in the hallway. To me, this was worth 100,000 gold stars or "I like the way Jack is sitting down" statements. I venture to guess that Jack would rather have those stories than a whole packet of M & M's.

I once heard Jack tell someone, "Ohanian's mean. She don't let you do nothin'." Sometimes in our daily notes he writes to me, "Get off my bak," signs his name and, in tiny letters, adds, "I am jus kidn." Jack's words are high praise. Jack is getting discipline; he is getting a bit of control over his own education; he is learning to do things because he has to.

I tell this long story because I think the teacher who gave Jack an 80 is wrong. He has given up on the kid, but for the sake of peace passes him on.

Only when teachers begin to hate themselves for their toughness are they beginning to grow and to make it as teachers, says Herbert Foster, author of *Ribbin', Jivin', and Playin' the Dozens: The Unrecognized Dilemma of Inner-City Schools*. Foster says that 2 or 3 percent move beyond the "discipline" phase to what he calls humanization. I suspect this latter phase is very similar to what I'm calling charismatic. Students can relax because they know the teacher is in charge physically, spiritually and intellectually. I don't think it is an overdramatization to refer to this physical-spiritual-intellectual power as grace, in Weber's sense of the word. The person who possesses it must constantly revalidate it in action. It is nontransferable: one doesn't get grace in an in-service course.

Most discipline schemes, euphemistically known as classroom management techniques, reek of manipulation. Honest emotion is forsaken in the name of control and quietude. Lee and Marlene Canter, authors of *Assertive Discipline*, would even have teachers plan ahead how they will praise their students; they recommend practicing with a colleague the phrase, "I like the way you did your work." Where is conscience, responsibility, passion?

I see no need to become a different person eight hours a day because I am a teacher. I answer students with myself—with my concern, joy, pleasure, anger—not with the gimmickry of 63 positive responses learned from a manual. Because I regard my style as my essence, I resent it when I tell a positive reinforcer about a good classroom experience only to have her smile tolerantly and tell me, "That's one of our techniques," as if what the children and I do so well together were invented by a behavior mod guru and could best be learned through a copyrighted publication.

These social hustlers are promoting a dangerous panacea. They say, Do it because it works. But if the positive stroking is an end in itself, students may never understand the joy that can come from a job well done. In the words of educator and author Edgar Friedenberg, "Behavior modification is planned to mold desirable behavior directly, without rooting it in ethical purposes. It seeks to operate at Kohlberg's lowest level of moral judgment: behavior is good because it is rewarded. This is a serious denial of the humanity of the person subjected to it." Allegedly humanitarian people who are aghast at the suggestion that electric cattle prods would very quickly bring order to chaotic hallways might ask themselves how they can blithely administer their knee-jerk jolts of positive reinforcement.

The positive approach folks—so glib in their upbeatness—are wrong too when they insist that a teacher's vulnerability (what educator George Dennison calls the "teacher's moment of doubt and defeat") can be manipulated or bargained away. My students know that they can make me cry. The greatest defense against vulnerability is not a prepackaged, fast-fix management system; it is competence. Teachers must be intellectually, spiritually and physically competent—basically able to deal with kids. If they aren't, then all the behavior charts and checklists and magpie jingles in the world will do little good.

My teaching career began in a Queens high school in the middle of a term. To say that my classes were undisciplined is to put it mildly. LeRoy serenaded the class with a trumpet mouthpiece every day. I could never quite catch him with it, and when accused of making disturbing noises, he put on his dramatic "Who, me?" act to further entertain the class. Two of my students were blind. They didn't like each other and did their best to punch each other out. I tried to keep them apart, but if one sensed the other was near, there would be a pitiful flailing of arms and cursing. I dragged myself home every night in utter defeat and tears.

On a most memorable occasion, three quarters of the class got into an ice-cream fight. Kids who couldn't remember to bring a pencil organized themselves to come to class with piles of ice-cream sandwiches, which they promptly spread over one another and the room. Although I knew a teacher was supposed to handle her own dirty linen, I made a desperate call to the department chairman. He gave me some valuable advice. He didn't tell me to punish the kids or to barter with them or to offer them contingency contracts. He told me to become a better teacher. He gave me specific suggestions on how to improve my curriculum. I have never forgotten that discipline "technique." It worked from the very start, and I use the suggestion to this day. When a kid is in trouble in my class, I don't change the way I smile—I alter his curriculum.

That department chairman invested a lot of time in me. He came to my class every Monday and watched how I applied a suggestion for getting across curriculum from the previous Monday's conference. Then he added an item to the list. Slowly, layer upon layer, he helped me to build mastery of the material I was teaching. He borrowed veteran teachers' notes for me, he taught demonstration lessons, he arranged for me to observe other teachers. He was certainly the administrative exception; too often, administrators tell us they have no time to teach demonstration lessons—that it is their job to administer, not to teach. They demand that teacher competence arrive on the first day of school, along with the room keys.

I suspect it is their unwillingness to get involved in teaching that leads administrators to support cosmetic behavior mod schemes so wholeheartedly. Such schemes keep kids out of the office, and that is all that matters. For in their offices, many administrators are busy writing perfect and impossible statements that they expect teachers to enforce. I discovered the truth of that observation —along with other, more heartening, revelations—during my first year of teaching. From on high came a fiat forbidding students to wear denim pants. Right outside the school, kids were fighting a racial gang war. In my classroom, they were threatening to throw one another out the third-story window. And I was supposed to worry about the cotton content of their trousers? You bet I was. From time to time the assistant principal in charge of discipline would stop me and remark that he'd noticed Jerome Wright wearing denim pants and that I hadn't reported it.

The enforcement of strict dress codes has lost some importance in recent years, but every once in a while a principal will come barreling into my room and insist that a kid remove his hat. It seems a terrible waste of administrative energy to me. I'd be more impressed if an administrator came in and asked what I am doing to teach Johnny to read.

I used to think a kid couldn't learn if he was feeling lousy about himself, but now I'm convinced he'll never feel better unless he develops some skills. Control and quiet may be the administrative way of judging teachers, but that does not mean we teachers should settle for such a paltry goal. We are not plumbers; we need to know more than how to locate the on and off spigots of a child's behavior. We need to be more than mere mechanics in the classroom—keepers of compliance devices and counters of environmental events. Educational bureaucrats and their fellow travelers insist that education must be objective and quantifiable. Maybe someday soon, when parents show up at open house, the teacher—or classroom-facilitator—will not need to be present at all. Parents will be able to get all they need to know from a file: Johnny's grade on the CAT, the Stanford, the whatever. They will also see a carefully kept record of how many times Johnny called out without raising his hand and how long it took to "extinguish" this behavior. Let us hope that when this day arrives, someone will have kept in the archives a videotape showing what Maria Montessori called "the first dawning of real discipline." She described this dawning as the moment "a child becomes keenly interested in a piece of work, showing it by the expression in his face, by his intense attention, by his perseverance in the same exercise. The child has set foot upon the road leading to discipline." The teacher doesn't need to say "I like the way Bill has settled down" on such an occasion.

The Myths of Discipline

Richard Kindsvatter and Mary Ann Levine

RICHARD KINDSVATTER is associate professor of education, Kent State University. MARY ANN LEVINE is assistant professor of education at the same institution. Both are members of the Kent State University Chapter of Phi Delta Kappa.

An examination of 12 widely held and attractive but insidious beliefs about the art of managing classroom behavior.

Discipline. The very word has a sobering effect on teachers. They realize that there has been a swing in the balance of power in the schools and classrooms. While the teacher's authority was once taken virtually for granted, now teachers must establish their credibility and authority every day. While simply being confronted by a teacher was once enough to produce compliance, students are now likely to insist on discussing "reasons" and "rights." This assumption of greater power by students has focused greater emphasis on teachers' control behavior. The shift is disconcerting to many teachers, but they have no choice but to cope with it.

Over the years, as teachers have confronted distressing circumstances in their classrooms, their intuitive reaction has been to apply an immediate remedy. Explanations and rationalizations could come later. Efficacious remedies and their rationales protected teacher egos and were gradually embodied in the conventional wisdom. Thus we have a body of current, widely accepted disciplinary practices and notions. Because they have been intuitively derived and remain essentially unscrutinized, they may be termed myths.

Examination of these myths shows many of them to be arbitrary and self-serving, designed to protect the traditional authority of the teacher and the school. But exercising the authority of position has not been an effective solution to a highly complex problem, of which student misbehavior is but a symptom. Meanwhile, the indignity, humiliation, and pain inflicted on students when primitive control methods are used is producing alienation and outrage.

Although we question certain teacher practices in this article, we sympathize with the frustration of many teachers. They have had to face increasingly trying conditions, for it is generally conceded that present-day students are more "difficult" than those of any other recent period. Inability to cope with discipline-related problems is one of the most significant factors in decisions to leave the profession, and it has forced increasing numbers to end what started as a lifetime commitment. The purpose of this article, then, is to examine certain widely held assumptions, hoping that we can help teachers transcend attractive but insidious myths.

Twelve beliefs are examined here. Some deal directly with discipline, and others have important implications for disciplinary practice.

Myth 1 — *Good control depends on finding the right gimmick.* Rudolf Dreikurs reports a study showing that teachers want immediate solutions to discipline problems in their classrooms.[1] Their requests for help often take the form, "What can I do to make the kids pay attention (or quit fooling around, or get to class on time, or be quiet enough that I can teach)?"

However, teachers do not consider that relatively little student misbehavior is spontaneous, the product wholly of the moment. The quality of teacher/student relationships, the clarity and reasonableness of the teacher's expectations, the consistency of the teacher's behavior, and the general level of motivation are among factors that condition student behavior — including misbehavior. These factors become established in the students' minds over time, and changing student perceptions of them in significant ways can also be expected to take time.

Teachers who wish to improve the quality of discipline in their classrooms should first analyze in a dispassionate way the causes of troublesome behavior. We have identified four possible sources of misbehavior: 1) casual or capricious actions by students, 2) chronic emotional or adjustment problems, 3) students' negative attitudes toward the teacher, and 4) volatile intragroup conditions or interpersonal relations. When the source or sources have been identified, strategies that address a particular sort of misbehavior must be devised and used. The process is relatively slow and involved, of course. It requires patience, fortitude, and faith on the part of the teacher. A discipline problem is for the teacher a personal problem that requires a personal solution, because a teacher's discipline-related practices, as an aspect of his or her teaching, are a personal invention closely related to personality and teaching style.

Fritz Redl, an authority on discipline, comments thus on the use of gimmicks:

> Administering discipline is a more laborious task than is taking refuge in a few simple punitive tricks. It is just as much more laborious and challenging as is modern medical thinking compared to

"The Myths of Discipline," by Richard Kindsvatter and Mary Ann Levine, *Phi Delta Kappan*, June 1980. Reprinted by permission.

the proud hocus-pocus of the primitive medicine man. The task of the teacher on his job is to translate the principles of democratic discipline into daily action in the classroom.[2]

Although teachers must take immediate action when misbehavior occurs, preventive measures have greater potential for developing the conditions of good discipline in classrooms. They involve establishing a climate of mutual respect, being firm and consistent, and maintaining a dignified but friendly posture even in trying circumstances.

Myth 2 — *Every teacher can become highly competent in creating the conditions of good discipline.*

One might assume that if teachers were all sufficiently well trained in effective techniques, they could acquire a high level of competence in managing classroom discipline. The effective techniques, however, exist for all teachers at the level of principles, not practices. It is possible to inform teachers of the pertinent principles that relate to discipline, but it is not possible to teach them an infallible process for translating principles into practice.

The preparation of artists provides an apt analogy. It is surely possible to teach an interested person the principles of balance, composition, and color, as well as certain specific skills such as mixing paints and applying them to the canvas. However, no teacher of art would guarantee to produce an artist capable of rendering masterpieces; in fact, guarantees could not be given beyond the technical aspects of art. So it is with preparing teachers to be particularly competent in any but the technical aspects of instruction, for teaching is, in important respects, an art.

Perhaps the most crucial factor determining the teacher's potential for the successful management of discipline is personality. Redl contends that "for the job of establishing good discipline and maintaining it, . . . the personality of the teacher is the most essential factor. Under ordinary circumstances the teacher can get along well with a few technical considerations if this one factor of personality is strongly represented."[3] And Dreikurs maintains that "it is obvious that certain personality types have greater difficulty with power-seeking and defiant children."[4]

Effective classroom discipline grows out of the teacher's leadership qualities, group process skills, and the mutual respect that exists in the classroom. However, the extent to which a teacher can be an effective leader, can acquire and employ principles of group process, and can promote a condition of mutual respect depends upon the existence of that potential within the teacher's personality.

Myth 3 — *The best teachers are those in whose classes students don't dare misbehave.*

An autocratic approach to discipline assumes an adversarial teacher/student relationship; i.e., students won't learn unless they are coerced and won't behave unless they are controlled. If achieving order and unquestioning compliance is a high priority of an institution, then an autocratic, highly controlling approach to discipline can be justified. In a military or prison setting, it may be the only feasible approach. Schools should be different. Schools should develop self-control and personal initiative. Autocratic teachers tend to induce feelings of repression and impotence. A martinet may produce compliant students, but will inhibit initiative and creative thinking. Further, there is no opportunity for an autocratic classroom to model participatory democracy, or for students to learn the habit and satisfaction of self-discipline. This puts an extremely high price on compliance. No good educator takes the position that schools are operated for the convenience of teachers rather than the fullest development of the students, but the classroom martinet has tacitly accepted that position.

In a summary of the research on teacher effectiveness, J. T. Sandefur concluded that "good teachers tend to exhibit identifiable personal traits broadly characterized by warmth, a democratic attitude, affective awareness, and a personal concern for students."[5] This finding tends to confirm what most teachers already believe. If so, why don't all teachers immediately adopt the traits Sandefur identifies? One might as well ask why a swimmer who wishes to break a record doesn't just stroke faster. One doesn't change his personality simply by an act of will, any more than he overcomes physical limitations thereby. The personalities and need patterns of some teachers preclude employing a warm, personal teaching style. This is not to say that teachers cannot have high standards or be demanding and firm when these stances are appropriate; it is only to say that there is no place in the classroom for teachers who are constitutionally unable or unwilling to establish relationships based on kindness, sensitivity, and caring with their vulnerable, impressionable wards. An Indian proverb poetically expresses our belief: "Nothing is so strong as gentleness, nothing so gentle as real strength."

Myth 4 — *The behavior of teachers can be understood only in terms of their instructional role.*

The teacher's task, institutionally considered, is to promote student learning. It is often useful to employ the institutional frame of reference. But from a very personal, human needs view, teaching is the means a person has selected to satisfy certain basic psychological needs, e.g., for power, security, and self-esteem. Students' unwillingness to comply with teacher directions or expectations may undermine the satisfactory fulfillment of those needs. When this happens, the teacher's reaction is to alleviate the resulting discomfiture and reaffirm his or her power, security, and self-esteem. Since this experience has an emotional dimension, it is very likely to stimulate primitive survival instincts, i.e., anger, frustration, extreme self-consciousness, defensiveness, or heightened aggressiveness. When acted out, these instincts take the form of attack, retaliation, or self-justification.

Dreikurs, commenting on teachers' discipline-related behavior, says:

> Many teachers find it extremely distasteful not to respond to the defiance of a power-drunk child. . . . The teacher is afraid for her prestige if she does not try to put the child into his place — regardless of how unsuccessful she may be in the effort.[6]
>
> The first obstacle [to] the solution of the conflict is the widespread assumption that one has to subdue the defiant child and make him respect adult demands. The second stumbling block is the teacher's personal involvement in a power conflict. If one can free himself from such considerations, one can see how amazingly simple it is to resist the power of a child who wants to force us into a struggle.[7]

Much of what we consider to be teaching behavior is learned rather than instinctive. Carl Rinne thoughtfully observed that "the natural behavior for many of us is to maintain the kind of control over other people that we feel most comfortable with. . . ."[8] Our normal human reactions to threat situations (i.e., achieving the kind of control we feel most comfortable with) are often not appropriate as a classroom technique. The fully functioning teacher is one who not only handles the academic aspects of teaching well but uses his or her emotional energy constructively. Firm self-control and the use of appropriate group process techniques must take precedence over self-preservation tendencies.

Myth 5 — *The behavior of students can be understood only in terms of their role as learners.*

This myth is the student counterpart of Myth 4. The institution does predicate the student-as-learner and makes this the basis of curriculum design and of learning activities. We assume that what we teach is good for students, that they should be interested and appreciative. In other words, the school program is designed for students as we would like them to be.

But how are they, really? Their preeminent concerns are not for studying and learning but for socializing, security, attention, and obtaining evidence of self-worth. In varying degrees, classrooms seem almost purposely established to prevent students from achieving these basic needs; socializing is discouraged, anxiety often runs high, individual attention is minimal in a group of 20 to 30, and the accumulating effect of all of these facts precludes obtaining much evidence of self-worth, especially for students who are neither academically inclined nor natural peer leaders.

Students are sometimes confronted with a dilemma, an academic Catch-22. We insist that they be quiet, attentive, polite, cooperative, and generally well-behaved; however, they must, as a psychological imperative, pursue the needs they feel. Many students simply cannot simultaneously accomplish both, within the constraints of the classroom; misbehavior ensues. The fact is that the school sets up unrealistic expectations, then punishes students for not meeting them. Eventually and inevitably, students develop negative attitudes. The process feeds upon itself until by the period of adolescence school becomes virtually intolerable for many students. Daniel Weiner has commented that

> . . . during the peak period of rebelliousness and struggle for maturity (i.e., adolescence), students are being forced into a mold that is scarcely changed from the relatively placid one of preadolescence. This is perhaps the source of the most intense current challenge to classroom discipline, and the educational system has barely begun to consider how to accommodate this stress.[9]

Robert Ardrey has posed the plausible theory that every thinking creature — including, yes, students — has basic drives for identity, stimulation, and security. Failure to satisfy these drives results in anonymity, boredom, and anxiety, respectively.[10] As educators we must realize that our classrooms are likely to become places where anonymity, boredom, and anxiety are highly probable conditions unless we make deliberate efforts to provide for identity, stimulation, and security. And that, as much as anything, may be what good teaching is all about.

Myth 6 — *Punishment is educational.*

Students must be made to understand that they cannot misbehave with impunity, or so the conventional wisdom goes. They should expect and accept the logical consequences of their misbehavior, e.g., being moved if they talk excessively to neighbors, being sent to a time-out site if they persist in disrupting the class. However, in spite of common acceptance, there is virtually no support in the professional literature for harsh punitive practices such as humiliation, abusive language and threats, extra homework, writing a phrase repeatedly, impersonal detention, or striking a student. Although these techniques are doubtless effective in the immediate suppression of misbehavior and sometimes give the teacher a sense of relief, they nonetheless violate the principles of democracy, they have negative long-range effects, and they have no intrinsic educational value. They indicate clearly enough to the student that he or she is out of favor with the teacher, but they do not help the student understand his or her behavior, the standards on which behavior is judged, or what alternatives are acceptable. Finally, teachers who use these tactics model aggressive behavior for students; the message students receive is: "Might is right."

It is very difficult for teachers who encounter unruly, vulgar, inconsiderate, "unmotivated" students on a regular basis not to believe they deserve harsh punishment, even when in dispassionate moments these teachers realize that such students need greater understanding and a compelling reason to change their values. Harsh punishment is so much a part of the tradition of education that it is difficult to conceive of education without it. It is a carry-over from an age when schooling was conducted in a far more simplistic and naive fashion. But to continue to use harsh punishment is to take an anti-intellectual and inhumane approach to managing student behavior. We consider it unconscionable. As professional teachers, we should believe in the science of our profession and order our behavior accordingly.

Myth 7 — *A teacher's response to misbehavior should always be directly related to the misbehavior.*

Misbehavior takes myriad forms in the classroom and throughout the school. The advice that one should make "the punishment fit the crime" sounds quite logical and acceptable on the surface. Implementing that advice for all the many kinds of misbehavior, however, would sorely tax the most imaginative teacher. What should the teacher do, for example, when a student cheats on a test? Tear up the test paper? But that is retaliation; it has nothing to do with why the student felt he or she had to resort to cheating. Lower the student's grade? That defeats the purpose of the test, which is meant to measure a student's level of achievement. Further, it employs grades as a punishment, which is an indefensible use of grades. The teacher might also eliminate that particular test from consideration in determining that student's grade, or give the student another test. These are more appropriate measures, but they may present some difficulties to the teacher.

Some kinds of misbehavior have logical and fairly obvious consequences, as we have noted, but many do not. Many of the punishments teachers regularly use are suppressive but not corrective, and thus they have no educational value. The answer lies, we believe, in adopting a behavior adjustment program that employs a systematic approach to helping students understand their behavior and its consequences.

Myth 8 — *The teacher shouldn't smile until Thanksgiving.*

Well-meaning veteran teachers often give this advice to new colleagues, to help them survive those first difficult weeks. But the advice assumes an adversarial relationship; it emphasizes teacher power; it assigns low priority to respect for student dignity and concern for developing self-discipline. The basis for teacher/student relationships becomes mutual fearing rather than mutual caring.

Smiling, kind, and supportive behavior is by no means an admission of weakness or a request for a truce. Surely a teacher can engage in these behaviors while remaining firm. And if establishing a warm, comfortable climate is to be managed, then smiling and humor will count for far more than sternness. Fritz Redl speaks eloquently in favor of a sense of humor:

> [I]t is so obviously the most vital characteristic of a skillful handler of discipline problems or tough group situations that its possession must be among the prime requisites for the job. If we had to list with it the one personality trait most injurious to successful discipline, we would pick false dignity (i.e., assumed sternness) as our first choice. We know of no other personality trait that causes so much confusion, uproar, and mismanagement as this one.[11]

Myth 9 — *Students do not know how to behave.*

Some teachers take responsibility for directing students' behavior on the assumption that students aren't able to do it themselves. Yet, given certain situations, youngsters of school age conduct themselves quite admirably, e.g., in church, at a friend's home, in a funeral home, or at a formal dance. Young people have sufficient reason to behave with discretion in these settings. Students, therefore, seem not to need to be taught how to behave nearly so much as they need to be convinced that it really is in their best interests to conform to the teacher's and school's expectations.

Teachers have at least five kinds of "power" available to them in effecting student compliance: 1) legitimate power — the power inherent in the position; 2) reward power — the power to award praise or privilege; 3) coercive power — the power to apply sanctions, restrictions, and punishments; 4) referent (personality) power — the attractiveness of the teacher; and 5) expert power — the competence of the teacher.[12] Very often we find teachers relying too heavily on the first three of these to induce compliance. Research has shown that the long-range effects in these cases are negative. But when teachers are able to use referent and expert power, producing a charismatic aura, students find it a sufficient reason to be compliant and cooperative.

Students should, ideally, perceive their classes as places where they and the teacher are partners in achieving worthwhile personal, social, and academic outcomes. If students have this attitude, the likelihood that they will appear not to know how to behave is minimal. In classrooms where students are kept busy, interested, and psychologically comfortable, there is little propensity for misbehavior.

Myth 10 — *Students deliberately test the teacher to find out what they can get away with.*

Students do in fact "test" the teacher, but not, in most cases, deliberately. There is no conspiracy to gauge the teacher's tolerance.

Students are not psychologically comfortable until they know the limits of their freedom in the classroom. For example, students have a strong social drive and will talk to their neighbors if they feel they can do this with impunity. But the teacher expects students to refrain from unsanctioned conversations. The student must determine which of the two forces is the stronger — the internal one for socializing or the external one imposed by the teacher or the classroom conditions.

To the extent that the teacher is inconsistent or the limits of tolerance remain unclear, students will try for clarification. This sort of testing occurs not because of any inherent mean-spiritedness in students but because, psychologically speaking, they have to know. The more clearly the teacher sets the limits and consequences, and the greater the credibility of the teacher in establishing them, the less need the students have to test.

Myth 11 — *Teachers should not look at students' records, so as not to obtain prejudicial information.*

The purpose of inspecting students' records is to obtain information that will be helpful in guiding a student's learning. The more a teacher knows about a student, the more likely it is that he or she can provide for effective learning. It is possible to conceive of a teacher's becoming prejudiced toward a student from reading certain records, but that teacher is hardly a professional practitioner.

If a student has been a behavior problem in the past, the teacher is better off knowing the fact. It should warn the teacher to provide those conditions within which the student is least likely to misbehave. Ignorance is unpreparedness. It can lead to needless confrontations.

The notion that "every student should start off in my class with a clean slate" has a superficial democratic appeal. But it reflects a certain distasteful anti-intellectualism.

Myth 12 — *Being consistent should take precedence over all other considerations.*

Consistency in disciplinary practices is held in high regard among teachers, and rightly so. We have referred four times to consistency as a desirable characteristic of discipline-related behavior among teachers. Nevertheless, the context within which the teacher employs consistency must be considered. The unexamined application of this guideline is not virtue. Sound judgment comes first.

The response a teacher makes to a particular sort of misbehavior should not necessarily be identical from instance to instance. To assume that all students should be treated similarly upon the commission of similar offenses is to overlook the unique circumstances — psychological and social — that impel each student. The child who has a pathological needs pattern and a chronic adjustment problem must surely be treated differently from the student who is merely bored or has a temporary personal problem. Also, a reserved, dependent, usually compliant child will be affected differently by a particular control technique than an aggressive, independent, frequently boisterous child will be.

Carl Rogers, the humanist psychologist, emphasizes the importance of the interpersonal relationship between teachers and children. He has made a convincing argument for a person-centered rather than a rules-centered approach to classroom interaction. If teachers accept Rogers's viewpoint they will give higher priority to the quality of the interaction that occurs than to controlling students as an end in itself.

Ralph Waldo Emerson, as an astute observer of the human condition, noted that "a foolish consistency is the hobgoblin of little minds." He was not telling us to be inconsistent, only that consistency needs a reason.

The insidious aspect of myths is that the person who subscribes to them does not recognize them for what they are. They are accepted as conventional wisdom and are applied without examination. The cost in mismanagement is imponderable. But it is largely avoidable.

To summarize, educators must realize that the problems of teaching, including those related to discipline, will not be resolved through the unquestioning acceptance of conventional wisdom or the pat solutions of so-called experts. We believe that the best hope for the growth and progress of the individual teacher is a three-part approach that involves 1) keeping an open mind and an inquiring posture, 2) taking positions thoughtfully and enthusiastically, but tentatively, on educational issues and practices, and 3) examining one's classroom practices regularly to assure that they are consistent with the best educational thinking one can identify.

---

1. Rudolf Dreikurs, Bernice B. Grunwald, and Floy C. Pepper, *Maintaining Sanity in the Classroom: Illustrated Teaching Techniques* (New York: Harper and Row, 1971), p. 187.
2. Fritz Redl, *When We Deal with Children* (New York: Free Press, 1966), p. 254.
3. Ibid., p. 303.
4. Dreikurs, op. cit., p. 197.
5. J. T. Sandefur, *The Evaluation of Teacher Education Graduates* (Washington, D.C.: American Association of Colleges for Teacher Education, 1970), p. 8.
6. Dreikurs, op. cit., p. 40.
7. Ibid., p. 197.
8. Carl Rinne, "Teaching: The Unnatural Act," *Thresholds in Education*, August 1978, p. 3.
9. Daniel Weiner, *Classroom Management and Discipline* (Itasca, Ill.: F. E. Peacock, 1972), p. 29.
10. Robert Ardrey, *The Social Contract* (New York: Dell, 1970), p. 91.
11. Redl, op. cit., p. 303.
12. John R. P. French and Bertram Raven, "The Bases of Social Power," in Dorwin Cartwright and Alvin F. Zander, eds., *Group Dynamics: Research and Theory*, 2nd ed. (Evanston, Ill.: Row Peterson, 1960), p. 612.

Equal Opportunity and American Education

The people of this nation have a strong commitment to the cause of human rights. The schools of this society are called upon to foster and develop democratic attitudes and improved intercultural relations. They are also called upon to provide equal opportunity in the field of education for all students. This is clearly an enormous task. Yet it is a necessary task if we are to help students become thoughtful and responsible citizens of a democratic social order. The effort to achieve equality of opportunity in the field of education has been a great dream of those who aspire to see the actualization of American Constitutional principles in daily life. It is still a dream, a hope that not all share, but one that inspires those who truly believe that the American Constitutional promise can be fulfilled. Achievement of equal opportunity, or achievement of the optimum attainable level of equal opportunity in the field of education, is a national hope and a national Constitutional responsibility. Few topics either in the field of education or in the political arena have been the subject of such heated national debate. Issues such as desegregation, integration, resegregation, and affirmative action, as well as the equalization of financial bases for education in this nation, are interrelated with this American Constitutional challenge. With increased opposition to busing to achieve racial integration in schools, and trends toward resegregation of many urban and suburban neighborhoods in our major metropolitan regions, the need to consider seriously the topic of equal opportunity in the field of education is as relevant a problem today as it ever has been.

There is now a large body of legal research, as well as historical research, on trends and remedies in dealing with human rights issues in the field of education. The cultural minorities of this nation have engaged in a great social struggle for equality of educational opportunity. School desegregation cases have affected the conduct of education in one way or another in every major American public school system. Questions regarding the provision of equal educational opportunity to all students have been given a high priority as a result of many major federal court decisions in recent years. The nation's schools play a major role in fulfilling the promise of equality for all citizens of the United States.

Looking Ahead: Challenge Questions

What are the Constitutional principles that form the basis for federal and state court cases regarding equality of opportunity in the field of education?

What are a few of the leading principles established by American courts in hearing and adjudicating school desegregation cases?

Can school financing affect the balance of equality of opportunity in the field of education?

What do you believe to be the major merits or faults with proposals to integrate local public school systems in the United States?

Why do great differences still remain for many minority individuals in the opportunities made available for achieving equal education?

What are fair criteria for protecting the rights of all persons involved in educational programming either as students or as teachers?

Why is it necessary to maintain high levels of funding for schools in order to guarantee equality of opportunity in the field of public education? What are the social costs of failing to provide equality?

Which groups suffer most in this society in periods of economic recession? How does this affect the schools? What are some of the consequences on schools when there are high levels of unemployment and underemployment in society at large? How might schools deal with such consequences?

Human Rights: A National Perspective

"IF NOT NOW, WHEN?"

JAMES FARMER

Executive Director, Coalition of American Public Employees; Founder and Former National Director, Congress of Racial Equality, Washington, DC.

At the turn of the century, in 1903, the great Black scholar W. E. B. Du Bois predicted, "The problem of the twentieth century will be the problem of the color line: of the relations between the lighter and darker peoples of the earth in Asia and Africa, in America and the Islands of the sea."

Writing today, I must add the historic problem of anti-Semitism, a virus which has poisoned the atmosphere of so many countries that hardly any are entirely free of it. I must add the problem of women, who face discrimination which is also a violation of human rights. I must specify, as perhaps Dr. Du Bois intended, the problems of other minorities of color, such as the Hispanic Americans and the American Indians.

My perspective is that of one who has been an activist in the struggle within our country. In the 1960's, I headed CORE (the Congress of Racial Equality) and worked with Martin Luther King, Jr.

By that time racism was old in America; it had begun virtually with the founding of our country, as the first slaves were brought over. U.S. racism against Blacks had its roots in the justification of slavery.

Slavery was a profitable economic institution, but somehow it didn't seem moral. Many people, therefore, sought to justify it through religious doctrine. Some theologians of the early slave period used the story of God's curse on Ham and the children of Ham, supposedly the ancestors of the Africans. The early New England Calvinists distorted Calvin's theory of predestination, saying that Blacks were the unelect of God, predestined to be slaves.

Long before the slave period ended at the close of the Civil War, racism had taken on a life of its own. Its supporters used violence to maintain an *apartheid* system in the Southern states, and that was what Dr. King and the other activists of the fifties and sixties were fighting against.

I consider that period to have been one of our nation's finest hours. White and Black, North and South, people of goodwill rallied to a cause that was greater than themselves and fought against the *apartheid* system.

They did not hide behind a preachment of love. As the modern philosopher Gregory Vlastos put it, "He who preaches love in a society based upon injustice can purchase immunity from conflict only at the price of hypocrisy."

They did not fear struggle, because to accept the status quo was to deny their common humanity. As the great old runaway slave Frederick Douglass had said, "Those who profess to favor freedom and yet deprecate agitation are men who want crops without plowing up the ground; they want rain without thunder and lightning. They want the ocean without the awful roar of its many waters."

So after decades of struggle following slavery, the Black movement turned to nonviolent direct action. It was stimulated by the 1954 decision of the U.S. Supreme Court, in the case of *Brown* vs. *Topeka Board of Education*. There, for the first time, the Supreme Court declared segregation according to race in public schools—and, by implication, other forms of *apartheid* practiced in the Southern states—to be unconstitutional.

That declaration stimulated many people to take action. In 1961, for example, we called for volunteers for the Freedom Rides. We got many, White and Black.

The pattern of *apartheid* was that Whites would sit in the front of the bus; Blacks, in the back. At every rest stop there was a White waiting room and, for Blacks, a Colored waiting room. Each waiting room had its own drinking fountain. The Blacks were expected to go into the Colored waiting room and drink Colored water, while the Whites in their waiting room drank White water.

The Freedom Riders reversed the pattern. The Whites sat in the back, and the Blacks sat in the front. They refused to move when ordered. At the rest stops, the Whites would go into the waiting room for Blacks and drink Colored water; Blacks would go into the White waiting room and drink White water.

They were prepared to accept the

 "Human Rights: A National Perspective," James Farmer, *Today's Education*, April/May 1981. Reprinted by permission.

consequences of their actions, and the consequences were often arrest or violence. In one town, a bus was burned to the ground. One White Freedom Rider, a professor of sociology at a state university in the Midwest, was so badly beaten about the head that he suffered a stroke. Nearly 20 years later, he remains paralyzed, confined to a wheelchair. Another White Freedom Rider—and the Whites were more brutalized than the Blacks because the racist Whites considered them treacherous—had 57 stitches taken in his head after he had been left for dead in a pool of blood.

In spite of the racist brutality, we won a victory. Later, we called for volunteers to go to Mississippi to teach Southern Blacks voter education and voter registration. At that time the very act of voting was for a Black an act of courage that risked life and limb. Thousands of college students, White and Black, said, Send me—I'll go.

Working for this cause made people somewhat larger than life. Those who answered our call knew that they were volunteering perhaps to live without a tomorrow. Some, such as Mickey Schwerner, Andrew Goodman, and James Chaney (the first two were Jewish, the third Black) were in fact killed in Mississippi during that campaign.

Anyone who goes South now sees a different country. The *apartheid* system has gone. We have not solved all our problems, but we did stop the denial of shared humanity that forced some people into undesirable places to eat, to ride, to study.

Most of the people of this country were thrilled at the victories of the Civil Rights Movement. We were able to win those victories because we had gotten the majority of the people of the country on our side. Public opinion polls in 1963 (after the great March on Washington where Dr. King made his "I Have a Dream" speech) indicated that more than 75 percent of the American people wanted strong civil rights legislation and wanted that legislation enforced.

That was a change. It came about partly because of the nonviolent tactics the activists used. It came about to a great extent because of Dr. King's magnificent leadership and because television was covering the Movement. The American people sat in their living rooms and watched everything. They were decent people observing indecent activities on the part of some of their compatriots. They said, We cannot tolerate the brutality, the injustice these marchers are meeting—something has to be done.

The effects of the Civil Rights Movement reached farther than we had dreamed. In my opinion, the Civil Rights Movement revitalized the women's movement and influenced the peace movement by saying that the old limitations which exclude people from the mainstream of the nation's life must come to an end, that we must revitalize our nation and make it more perfect.

Now we have moved into a more difficult period. We are dealing with nationwide problems rather than largely Southern problems, more complex issues than the front seat of a bus. We are dealing with how to close gaps between the haves and the have-nots when the have-nots have been deprived through the interaction of poverty and racism.

We are dealing with the question of how to close the income gap between the minorities—the Hispanics, American Indians, Blacks—on the one hand and White Americans on the other. How do we close the income gap, when the median average income of Blacks is about 59 percent of that of Whites? Indians and Hispanics have a smaller percentage than that.

How can we close the educational gap? Because of congested schools, overcrowded classrooms, a lack of teachers, minority children have to be pushed on to make room for their juniors. Many of our youngsters are graduating from high school functionally illiterate, unable to read up to a fourth or fifth grade level.

How can we close the health gap? The gap between the life expectancies of Black males and of White males has widened considerably in the past 15 years. Indeed, the life expectancy of the Black male has actually declined, from 64 to 61, while the life expectancy of the White male is almost 72.

In addition to closing these gaps, we must change the images that many people have of the ethnic, the cultural, the racial minorities. A total culture has produced those images. Until the 1960's the stereotype of Blacks was clear. Many schools used a textbook that spoke of Blacks something like this:

> Negroes made ideal slaves. They fitted admirably into the slave system. They loved and thrived upon the paternalistic love and care of their owners. They enjoyed nothing better than sitting under the magnolia tree and strumming their guitars and singing sweetly of the hereafter.

Thanks to the teacher unions, to the civil rights organizations, to the labor movement, to the progressive movement throughout the country, that image has been eliminated. There has been a demand for Black studies and the inclusion of Blacks in American history courses.

This has not yet happened for American Indians, however. They are virtually ignored in the study of American history. They are demanding more visibility—in some cases, going to jail for it—and they are getting it.

The Hispanics, similarly, are demanding more visibility for their contributions to our history. They are demanding bilingual education, too, because many of their youngsters grow up speaking Spanish at home and then go to a school where the classes and the tests are given in English. They are thus at a disadvantage, so with the support of teacher organizations, they are getting bilingual education.

People's images of themselves do not change easily, however. My father, for example, was a Biblical scholar. He was a Ph.D. in Old Testament and Hebrew from Boston University, the first Black with a Ph.D. in the state of Texas. He could speak, read, write, and think in many languages, including Hebrew, Greek, Aramaic, Latin, French, German, Spanish. Despite all his accomplishments, in his heart of hearts my father believed that Whites were superior, Blacks were inferior. He had been that conditioned by everything he had read growing up as a child in South Carolina and Georgia and by all of the instruments for the dissemination of culture that determined what he thought.

In the Civil Rights Movement, we began to say, Black is beautiful. We did not mean that what is not Black is therefore ugly (although some individuals overstepped that line). We would have liked to believe that Blacks were automatically good, but we soon relieved ourselves of that illusion, too. The point is, Black is not automatically ugly—it's beautiful; and Chicanos and Puerto Ricans, for example, have found the same sense of pride.

Now teachers have responsibility for image building, too. Children who are victimized by poverty and racism may have teachers who in their attitudes or their teachings let slip some feeling that they do not believe that those children can learn as well as the others. Those children will then be handicapped in learning.

Several years ago I was sitting in a school cafeteria in New York City. I heard one Black teacher say to another, "Why do you sweat? You're not training kids to go to Harvard."

That teacher should either be retrained or stop teaching. Her attitude is bound to spread to the kids. They'll say, She's the teacher, and she's telling me just what the society tells me: I'm no good.

Even if the Harvards of this world are now open to those students, such a teacher will make sure those students still have no chance to go there.

Many people have said that teachers are the gatekeepers of our society. As such, they have a duty to help youngsters build good images of themselves and to make them aware that differences can be great—that we don't all have to be the same.

We in this country have learned that it does not damage the fabric of the culture to stress and celebrate the threads that make it up; it strengthens the fabric. We have many races, many cultures, many ethnic groups, and a pluralistic outlook. The minorities now are not trying to forget themselves and become White but are determined to fit as proud and equal partners into that cultural pluralism.

In the words of Hillel, a great rabbi, long ago: "If I am not for myself, who will be for me? If I am for myself alone, what am I? And if not now, when?"

This article was adapted from Mr. Farmer's address to the International Teachers' Conference To Combat Racism, Anti-Semitism, and Violations of Human Rights in Tel Aviv, Israel, in November 1980.

BEYOND RACIAL BALANCE REMEDIES: SCHOOL DESEGREGATION FOR THE 1980s

Almost three decades have passed since "Brown v. the Board of Education." Now, greater attention is needed to improve the quality of schooling wherever black students attend. This can be accomplished through more equitable and effective desegregation strategies.

HUGH J. SCOTT

Hugh J. Scott is Dean of the Division of Programs in Education, Hunter College, City University of New York.

School Desegregation in Retrospect

Nearly three decades of school desegregation have produced neither genuine racial desegregation of public education nor the extension of equal educational opportunity to the majority of black students in America. School desegregation has not been characterized by educational changes that truly make it possible for both black and white students to express the similarity and uniqueness of their personal and group life in an institution that belongs to all Americans. For some black students, school desegregation has resulted in the imposition of an educational environment in which the "cure" is almost as destructive as the "disease." More often than not, school desegregation represents a process that adds token bits of color to institutions controlled entirely by whites.

There remains considerable disagreement between white and black Americans and even among black Americans as to what are the permissible and effective policies and practices in the desegregation of public education. Most white and black proponents of school desegregation accepted the premise that school desegregation was best pursued through the establishment of racial ratios in student assignment that placed black students in a perpetual minority racial relationship with white students. The pursuit of racial balance has been the dominant feature of school desegregation strategies since the *Brown* decision in 1954.

Black Americans did not challenge the constitutionality of *de jure* racially segregated public schools because they believed that black schools by the very nature of their "blackness" were inferior and incapable of teaching black students how to read and write. Segregated public education produced educational systems "that were morally evil, educationally dysfunctional, and constitutionally perverse," but in spite of the numerous evils and inequities of the "separate but equal" era, collaborative ventures between black communities and black schools were formed in the pre-*Brown* era that developed schools that were educationally effective. (1) Black Americans challenged the constitutionality of *de jure* racial segregation in public education because racial segregation was founded on the premise of white superiority and black inferiority and because the "separate but unequal" schools denied black Americans the fundamental right of equal protection under the law.

More black students now attend schools that are identified as racially isolated under *de facto* segregated practices than attended segregated schools under *de jure* segregated practice. (2) The majority of black (and Hispanic) children now live in the large urban centers and attend schools that are predominantly minority. (3) Racial balance remedies concentrated primarily or exclusively on the reassignment of students. They ignored or gave scant attention to the inclusion of intervention components to foster improvements in the educational lot of black students. School boards often challenged efforts of plaintiffs to include compensatory educational programs, in-service training programs for teachers, and guidance and counseling programs as part of the desegregation plan on the grounds that such remedies exceeded the scope of the constitutional violation. It was not until 1977 in *Milliken II* that the U.S. Supreme Court declared that a desegregation plan might have to include programs to undo the inequalities caused by a dual system. (4) The promises of *Brown* for equality in participation and outcome will never be realized for the majority of black students if the "bottom line" in school desegregation strategies is racial balance or cultural assimilation. For the 1980s much greater attention needs to be directed to making *Brown* an instrument for providing effective schooling in mainly black schools.

"Beyond Racial Balance Remedies: School Desegregation for the 1980s," Hugh J. Scott, *New York University Education Quarterly,* Winter 1983. Reprinted by permission.

6. EQUALITY OF OPPORTUNITY

If the "separate but equal" doctrine had produced schools for blacks that were as equal as they were separate, the *Brown* decision probably would have had a much less significant impact on the status quo in American education. Thomas Atkins, Chief Counsel for the NAACP, notes *Brown* stood for the proposition that racial segregation that flowed from public action prevented equal educational opportunity. (5) Atkins acknowledges that desegregation offers no guarantee of a quality education for black students. Equal access alone is not the "necessary and sufficient condition of equal opportunity." (6) Brookover and Lezotte note that those who place the emphasis in school desegregation on racial mixing "are reluctant to look inside institutions and question whether or not students, especially minority students, are receiving equal treatment." (7)

Although a chief proponent of racial balance remedies, Atkins is well aware that racial mixing alone will not safeguard black students from discriminatory treatment. He states that "incompetent local and state educational systems and educators were capable of depriving children of quality education regardless of the racial composition of buildings and classrooms." (8) The commitment to racial balance remedies is socially and educationally unjustified and has not improved the self-concept or academic performance of black students. On the contrary, the massive movement of black students from majority-black to majority-white schools without appropriate intervention components may often hinder their psychological and academic development. (9)

Research findings on the very sensitive and highly important topic of the effects of school desegregation on the academic achievement of white and black students tend to have something to support almost every point of view. The racial composition of a school, when considered alone, does not have a substantial effect on academic performance. Statistically, significant evidence does not exist to support any claim that racial mixing itself contributed to the academic growth of black students. (10) The gap between the achievement of white and black students is present in 1982 just as it was in 1954. Ronald Edmonds has been engaged in the search for and development of effective schools for students from low-income families for a decade. Edmonds believes effective schools for black students are in short supply and effective school systems for large numbers of black students are nonexistent. (11)

A white school superintendent, who heads a major urban school system in the South that has extensively bused black students for more than a decade, testified as an expert witness in a desegregation case involving another large urban school system also in the South. He proclaimed the alleged social and educational merits of racial balance remedies and declared school desegregation had worked in his school system. With no small amount of pride, he informed the court that students in his system performed above the national norms in reading at every grade level. With regard to school desegregation, he stated that black students ought to be in majority-white schools as a means of promoting their integration into the entire society.

At that time, I served as the chief expert witness and educational consultant for counsel for the plaintiffs. In my comments on the testimony of the superintendent, I informed the judge that I did not believe significant gains in academic performance by black students could be attributed solely or primarily to the factor of racial balance. Also, I reiterated my rejection of the universal placement of black students in a minority relationship with white students. I did point out to the judge that the expert witness for the school board had not highlighted how black students in particular had performed in his reporting of system-wide achievement results. The judge agreed and ordered that the figures for black students be obtained. The figures indicated that black students performed well below the national norms at every grade level. The superintendent's school system, like so many others, had for years placed the emphasis on getting black children in white schools with little or no attention given to educational inequalities.

Racial balance desegregation remedies that promote majority white classrooms, schools, and school systems are not in concert with the essential promises of *Brown*: parental choice for black parents and the potential for educationally effective schools for black students. (12) Inherent in racial balance remedies that give priority to the placement of black students in a perpetual minority relationship with white students are the false assumptions that black children inevitably suffer intellectually when their education occurs in all or mainly black schools and that the motivation and achievement of black children necessarily improves when they are enrolled in majority-white schools. Those who subscribe to such assumptions—either in defense of segregation or as an argument in support of integration—deny black children their very humanity as individuals. It is not the addition of black children to a previously all-white school that makes the difference; it is the elimination of many of the negative factors that impede growth and development.

Robert Green, a widely respected desegregation expert, is concerned about the continued and increasing achievement disparities between white and black students in desegregated schools. (13) John Porter, the only black person ever to serve as Superintendent of Public Instruction in Michigan, notes: "many minority students have not yet reached the level of education attainment that was expected. . . ." (14) Green observes that equity in participation and outcome do not often flow from the attainment of equal access. He cites the following as some of the most common discriminatory abuses in desegregated schools (15):

1. Placement of minority students in disproportionately high rates in special education classes and in low ability groups.

2. Excessively harsh disciplinary practices applied to minority students.

3. Various types of discrimination against minority teachers and administrators.

Charles Moody, Sr., Director of the Race Desegregation Center at the University of Michigan, is a dejected desegregationist who is alarmed by the frequent failure of school officials to desegregate with equity. Moody shares Green's concern about discriminatory desegregation (16):

People are still trying to operate school systems under the same kind of policies that they operated under previous to desegregation. This has led to disproportionate minority suspensions and involvement in disciplinary procedures, bias counseling, tracking, inability to participate in extracurricular activities, and black communities not being involved in critical decisions regarding curriculum and governance.

The courts recognize that there is no universal (fail safe) answer to the complexities of school desegregation. The data bank on school desegregation is extensive, complex, and often contradictory. The reassignment of black students from all or mainly black schools, whether or not the reassignment required busing, has been and still is an effective desegregation strategy in some school districts. But sufficient school desegregation history exists to indicate that the path to equal educational opportunity and a quality education for most black students is not via the outworn and inefficacious overreliance on racial balance remedies. The rigid adherence to racial balance remedies—which ignore the diversity among cities, deprecate "blackness," impose inequitable burdens on black students and their parents, give scant attention to the educational essentials of equal educational opportunity, ignore the importance of black history and culture, and/or deny black parents some choice—is not only nonproductive but a denial of equal educational opportunity.

David Kirp asserts that there are no agnostics in school desegregation. (17) School desegregation strategies are derived from the pervasive social beliefs and principal educational assumptions and priorities of those who exercise power in the determination of the permissible policies and practices. The elements of a desegregation strategy are related to the predetermined purposes of desegregation. Racism was a major factor in segregation and is a major factor in school desegregation. For discriminatory and nondiscriminatory reasons most white parents do not want their children in majority-black schools. The fervor and scope of white resistance to school desegregation in the '50s and '60s influenced many black leaders to support racial balance remedies. Some black leaders considered it essential to label all black schools in majority-white school systems as segregated and per se educationally inferior.

White opposition to desegregation and white flight from desegregated schools made it politically more expedient for policymakers to lend their support to racial balance desegregation remedies, particularly those that defined a "viable" racial mixture as no more than 20 to 40 percent black students assigned to any one school. Black leadership, for the most part, supported the premise of *green follows white*: "money in the public schools follows white students, and . . . blacks must enroll their children with white students in order to get the quality of education the school system will provide for whites." (18) The surest antidote for ineffective black schools was considered the creation of more predominantly white schools and the elimination of black schools.

The belief that a racially integrated, effective school for all students in a pluralistic society is the best model for a public school should not be misconstrued to mean that this model is the only acceptable model or that the presence of predominantly or all black schools necessarily represents an infringement of a constitutional right of black students. This challenge to the unrealistic and nonproductive preoccupation with numerically determined educational equity is part of the inevitable debate in the school desegregation arena as to the appropriateness of various ways and means of achieving compliance with the mandates of *Brown*. The fault lies not with *Brown* but with implementing *Brown* in a manner that virtually guarantees that any attention given to educational quality for black students comes not as a consequence of the desegregation strategy.

Cultural Implications

The "melting pot" theory has not worked in America and is a myth. There is no consensus culture in America. The culture of "mainstream" America is a conglomerate of the life styles of all who have participated in the building of America. (19) Culture is the unique achievement of a group that distinguishes it from other people. It includes the basic conditions of the existence of a people, their behaviors, style of life, values, preferences, and creative expressions that emanate from work and play. (20) Andrew Billingsley in *Black Families and the Struggle for Survival* emphasizes that there is no doubt that the ways of life for blacks in America are different in major respects from the ways of whites. (21) It is not the role of the school to function as a "melting pot" for the purpose of seeking cultural sameness. Black Americans have a right to their cultural past and to the freedom and privileges that are enjoyed by those in the more dominant streams of our society.

Of the pioneer immigrants to this nation, the treatment accorded to black Americans has been shamefully unique. No other group of comparable population and longevity in America has been received so poorly by the dominant groups of this democracy. Black people have been engaged in an ongoing and seemingly never ending struggle to prevent their subjugation as a race. The use of race theory to give legitimacy to the establishment of a socioeconomic pattern of segregation of and discrimination against black Americans continues as a factor in shaping the life chances of black people. The black experience in America has conditioned black Americans to approach with considerable apprehension proposals championed by white Americans that purport to bear benefits for black Americans.

In the struggle to become a more viable, functioning group in a society in which power and influence are the guardians of life, liberty, and happiness, black Americans must be keenly aware of their common history and their common predicament as black people. Schools do far more than teach children how to read and write. Society through education attempts to pass on the standards and ideals that society believes are good and necessary for present and future generations. Schools perform a major role in the forming of the American character. The educational system is the single institution that has the major responsibility for dispensing or promulgating those values that identify a group's consciousness of itself. (22) The schools are often called upon to negotiate for the society itself some of the nation's deepest and most severe problems: racism, prejudice, intolerance, and inequity.

Integration is pluralism—rather than assimilation—with respect for differences and is not a desire for amalgamation. The right of black children to attend integrated public schools whether or not blacks elect to exercise this right is fundamental and nonnegotiable. But the Constitution does not state or imply that the right of black Americans to equal treatment under the law can be secured only by blacks integrating with whites. Being a "good" American does not require that black Americans forfeit their cultural heritage or become facsimiles of white Americans.

A black school superintendent in his comments on desegregation noted: "The black culture in America is protected when blacks develop ethnicity. We do not want to exclude those who are different than ourselves, but the black experience has to be recognized within the context of the American society." (23) In 1903 W. E. B. DuBois reminded black Americans about the need for blacks to develop pride and the ability to control the social forces that shape one's environment. (24) DuBois states:

> There must exist a special brand of power which comes from pride in the accomplishments of black people and the powerful thrust toward development of competence in all facets of black public life in America. (25)

The history of black Americans prior to their being heaped upon these shores and the black experience in America have produced a black culture. Black Americans share values, behavioral patterns, and other cultural elements that spring from the black experience and that distinguish blacks from others in the larger population. John Clarke notes that history tells a people where they have been and what they have been, and, most importantly, an understanding of history tells a people where they still must go and what they still must be. (26) As Stokely Carmichael and Charles Hamilton noted in *Black Power*: "Before a group can enter the open society, it must first close ranks." (27) Black consciousness, as it is projected in concert with the basic tenets of the American democracy, is a logical and legitimate form of social behavior. In the pursuit of the kind of life and treatment that establishes, perpetuates, and protects dignity and freedom, black Americans must seek to alter elements of the social structure in order to produce equality of opportunity for all members of the society.

The term "racial balance" is racist and paternalistic. Genuine integration exists when blacks and whites gravitate toward each other as status equals who share decision-making control over institutions and communities. Racial balance implies that a preferred or required distribution formula should govern how whites and blacks are grouped for the receipt of basic institutional services. The Congress of Racial Equality (CORE) in 1970 with its submission of an *amicus curiae* brief in *Swann* declared that any argument that integration is a constitutional requirement suggests the legitimization of inferior status for blacks. (28) The U.S. Supreme Court has neither declared that racial balance is required under the Constitution nor decreed that all black schools in a desegregation case must bus children out or be in violation of the Constitution. But the Court has given its approval to racial balance remedies when prescribed or sanctioned by lower courts. I agree with Derrick Bell's premise: when courts assign black students to racially balance schools, whether or not their parents approve of the reassignment, they "exert under rubric of remedy that character of racial dominance that was the essential evil of the separate but equal era." (29)

Black Communities and the Schools

Education is the chief means through which individuals may improve themselves and their socioeconomic status. The level of entrance into the occupational world is sharply determined by the level that is attained in the educational world. Black Americans should expect that schools will expand the scope of knowledge for, and develop the rational capacities of, their children. They have every right to expect that upon completion of certain courses of study, their children will be capable of entering the world of work as fully functional members of the society. But in terms of service to black students, the public schools have not moved from good to bad or even from average to poor. They have never been adequate.

Public education has been used as an instrument to disfranchise, discredit, and demean millions of black Americans solely on the bases of race and socioeconomic condition. Race and socioeconomic status continue to serve as the chief determinants of success or failure in the schools. The services rendered by teachers are in response to needs that are so fundamental that the failure to meet them seriously interferes with the quality of life and with life itself. While many white teachers have responded to the demands of school desegregation with commendable professionalism, some white teachers cannot or will not change their ways and do not respond to black students and their parents as human beings deserving of respect, goodwill, and equality. White America has exercised an almost absolute control over the quality and intent of public education for black Americans. This monopoly has resulted in black Americans being the most poorly educated, the most severely impaired, and the most deliberately misinterpreted of all the major ethnic groups received in the public schools.

The achievement gap between white and black students ought not be an unexpected byproduct of the socioeconomic discrimination and deprivation imposed on black Americans. The causes of the disproportionately higher dropout rate and distribution of lower achievement test scores among blacks and the poor extend well beyond those effects produced by the consequences of inept and insensitive teachers and administrators. The black indictment of the public schools should be predicated, in large measure, on the culpability of the schools in allowing the achievement gap in academic performance between white and black students to be as extensive as it is. Teachers and administrators cannot justifiably cite socioeconomic factors as the reasons that the public schools across this nation graduate many black students whose cumulative deficiencies in reading, writing, and computational skills classify them as functional illiterates.

The push by black Americans for control over schools that serve large numbers of black students is a criticism of public education for blacks and a recognition of the need to restructure the role that public schools perform in the lives of black Americans. Preston Wilcox notes that white America is learning that it can no longer deceive blacks into believing that white-controlled education means quality education. (30) In the 1960s a group of black educators and parents meeting at Harvard University posed the question: "How do we gain control of our schools; thus the destiny of our children?" (31) Blacks who may be moderates, militants, or extremists in their civil rights activities all hold in common the belief that blacks must take steps to assure that those who created and supported segregated public schools are prohibited from allowing the same educational neglect to occur in desegregated schools.

Education is much too critical to the host of efforts of black Americans to secure the rights of first-class citizenship to be left unchecked in the present condition and structure of control. Many black Americans are demanding and seeking more than just a reexamination of the educational process and reorientation of the social values that undergird that process. They are seeking to restructure the racial composition of the base of power that dictates the educational policies and programs affecting black students. A paramount commitment in black communities is to free black children from the restrictive experiences and massive failures of public education. For an ever increasing number of black parents, this requires control over the schools that their children attend.

Improvements in the education of black students are much more likely to occur when black parents work intimately with, and are not isolated from, the schools that serve their children. There is a significant relationship between the degree of community involvement in the educational process and the quality of education that is offered in the schools. The active participation of parents in school affairs has become an imperative in contemporary school-community relations. In *Milliken v. Bradley*, Judge Robert E. DeMascio declared: "An effective community-relations program must develop a partnership between the community and the schools. . . ." (32) A viable representative structure for community participation in the process of policymaking and program planning and implementation must provide clear and direct access to the decision-making process.

Doctrine of Debt

Black parents do not share the eagerness of policymakers to have their children bused from familiar, friendly, supportive environments into what can often be an unfriendly and hostile environment. They are as concerned as white parents about matters pertaining to what their children are taught, how well they are taught, where they go to school, and how they get to school. In *Kelley* black parents opposed the unnecessary closing of predominantly black schools located in black neighborhoods in the inner city in order to bus black students to predominantly white schools located in almost exclusively white neighborhoods on the periphery of the Nashville-Davidson County school district. (33)

Plaintiffs in *Kelley* did not challenge the belief that there are potential social and educational benefits to be gained by white and black students from the equitable desegregation of the school system. However, black parents did assert that school desegregation in Nashville had not been implemented in a manner that demonstrated respect for the dignity of black people, provided equal educational opportunity for black students, and responded to the importance of black history and culture. Judge Wiseman in *Kelley* agreed that the burdens of busing had not been equitably distributed between white and black students and that the busing out of black students had not been undergirded with adequate program supports to address the distinct educational needs of many of the black students. (34)

The Task Force on Desegregation Strategies has declared: "Improvement in academic performance is not the sole, nor perhaps, even the most important reason for desegregation." (35) The Task Force views the elimination of racial isolation in the large urban school systems as the major challenge confronting school desegregation. Good intentions and past contributions notwithstanding, the Task Force is misguided, and its highest priority is not in the best interests of black students. Of course there are reasons along with the improvement of academic performance for supporting school desegregation, but school desegregation should not only eliminate barriers to blacks gaining equal access to public education, but also it should promote the establishment of educational programs and practices that will ensure equity in participation flows from equal access. The concept of racial balance with its social and educational defects ought not be carried to its illogical conclusion by dissolving mainly black urban school systems.

Mainly black urban school systems are not likely to become fully desegregated in the near future. In many of the mainly black large urban school systems, blacks have secured an unprecedented degree of participation in decision-making as it pertains to policy and administrative matters. Many blacks do not want to see such systems dissolved and are working for their improvement. Equal educational opportunity and quality education for most black students will either be received in mainly black schools or not at all. The preeminent challenge confronting school desegregation in the 1980s is that of using *Brown* as an instrument for making mainly minority schools more effective rather than less nonwhite.

Ben Williams, who heads the Office of Equal Educational Opportunity for the Chicago public schools, notes: "Until we provide good education in minority schools in urban areas, we are not going to have the public's confidence in urban education." (36) Ruth Love, a black educator who heads the nation's second largest school system, remains supportive of school desegregation, but she believes that in Chicago the school system must "focus on the improvement of the quality of education regardless of where black students go to school." (37)

6. EQUALITY OF OPPORTUNITY

The promises of *Brown* will never be realized by the majority of black students if the "bottom line" in school desegregation is racial balance or cultural assimilation. Black Americans need to be more resolute in their insistence upon equitable treatment and viable options in school desegregation. Desegregation strategies that are primarily student reassignment plans predicated on the concept of racial balance "skirt the real issue of desegregation by concentrating on movement of bodies as opposed to planning for improved education for all students." (38) Thirty-five black school superintendents—they represented over one million black students—in responding to my questionnaire soliciting their responses to statements pertinent to school desegregation gave their overwhelming endorsement to the view: "The educational merits of school desegregation strategies noted primarily for the imposition of racial balance remedies are overstated, misconceived, or simply nonexistent." (39)

One black superintendent noted: "Blacks are more interested in good sound basic education than in the need to balance themselves racially with others." (40) Black parents are more interested in the academic consequences of school desegregation than they are in racial balance or racial mixing. Many black Americans would concur with Ulysses Byas's declaration: "If you can have quality and desegregation, good, but if you cannot have both, I will take quality." (41)

As the arbiter of school desegregation compliance litigation, the U.S. Supreme Court has expanded the requirements for compliance with *Brown* from mere destruction of barriers to student assignment to ancillary relief that is "usually ordered when equity in outcome is judged absent and only possible if education components are made part of the overall remedy." (42) *Brown I* broke down the barriers excluding black children from attending schools with white children. (43) *Brown II* required school systems to desegregate with all due speed. (44) *Green* defined the ultimate goal to be a unitary, nonracial system of public education and directed the school board to present desegregation plans that can work and work now. (45) *Swann* utilized transportation of students to achieve racial mix and gerrymandered zone lines and/or noncontiguous zones as permissible remedial devices to achieve a unitary system. (46) *Milliken I* emphasized the remedial nature of the Court's responsibility and expanded the charge to include such action as would nearly as possible restore the victims of discriminatory conduct to the position they would have enjoyed in the absence of such conduct. (47) *Milliken II* approved remediation in the form of educational components designed to restore the victims of discriminatory conduct to the position they would have enjoyed in terms of education. (48) Educational components not only are essential ingredients of a strategy, but also they enhance parental perception of, and support for, the strategy.

For centuries the Constitution's references to justice, welfare, and liberty were mocked by the treatment meted out daily to black Americans by all three branches of our government. (49) For most of the period from 1619 to the present, the courts joined the executive and legislative branches of the government at local, state, and national levels in the denial of basic rights to black Americans. More and more black Americans are now prepared to seek the "doctrine of debt" principle in school desegregation just as vociferously as it is being sought in other institutional settings. The "doctrine of debt" principles hold that society owes something of value to black Americans for 250 years of slavery and for more than 100 years of discrimination after slavery. The scope and severity of the educational needs of black students have for years indicated that some specialized positive treatment should be accorded to black students after centuries of being recipients of demeaning and delimiting treatment. Such a recompense is required if past and present inequities and injustices are to be rectified rather than compounded and perpetuated.

Constitutionally, education is principally the responsibility of each individual state. But in the *Brown* decision of 1954, the U. S. Supreme Court asserted that education where the state has undertaken to provide it is a right that must be available to all on equal terms. (50) While a state can limit the amount of money it will spend on education, a state cannot accomplish such a purpose by invidious distinctions between classes of its citizens. (51)

In *Milliken II* the U.S. Supreme Court decided that it was within the scope of the remedial powers of district courts to require compensatory education programs, in-service training, and guidance and counseling programs as part of the desegregation plan. (52) Intervention components designed to make the desegregation plan successful in terms of educational outcomes were resisted by many school boards. School officials often took the view that since the constitutional violation was racial discrimination in student assignment, the desegregation plan should be limited to the reassignment of students. In his Memorandum Order and Judgment in *Milliken v. Bradley in 1977*, District Judge Robert E. DeMascio ordered the State Board of Education of Michigan and the Detroit Board of Education to implement eleven educational components as a means of eradicating the effects of past segregation. (53) The state of Michigan was required by Judge DeMascio to fund 50 percent of all additional costs, since in the opinion of the court, the local board and the state board participated in practices that created a racially segregated school system. A school official estimates that about 100 million dollars in additional funding has been directed to the implementation of the mandated educational components and support services.

Some black Americans became so enraptured with racial balance or racial mixing that they failed to give the highest priority in school desegregation to the eradication of the educational inequalities produced by constitutional violation in segregated schools and that remained long after the peak period of white flight from previously majority-white school systems. I share Atkins' commitment to resist any effort to relegate black (and other minority) children to second-class education fare as was meted out to black students in the pre-*Brown* era in segregated school systems. (54) Substandard education for black (and other minority) students is discriminatory and injurious regardless of whether the violation occurs in segregated or desegregated school systems. The business of education is education, and the "bottom line" in school desegregation ought to be the pursuit of equity and quality. The desegregation plan should seek to bring minority schools up to the standards of mainly white schools. Derrick Bell notes that black and white students both may deserve more, but it is doubtful that the equal educational opportunity standards in *Brown* permit a court to require more. (55)

Effective schooling does not evolve from osmosis. Robert Ebel is on target when he notes that when the learning of an individual student falters, it may very well be the fault of the student. But when the learning of an entire class or entire school falters, more than likely it is the fault of the teachers and the principal. (56) Effective schools are effective because educators function in an educational climate in which it is incumbent on them to be instructionally effective for all students. (57) The challenge in public education is not to figure out the ideal program of instruction and then impose it on all students. The challenge is to create an educational environment in which educators respect the dignity and importance of those whom they teach and in which educators are "as anxious to avoid things that do not work as they are commited to implement things that do." (58)

For those whose decisions shape the permissible policies and practices in school desegregation, I urge consideration of the following elements in the formulation of a desegregation plan:

1. The preeminent emphasis should be directed to the improvement of teaching and learning in the schools.
2. Resources should be allocated in direct proportion to the degree of the severity of needs of students, with the highest priority being the establishment of programs and services aimed at the alleviation of situations where socioeconomic factors and academic deficiencies combine to present the most demanding challenges to the skills of educators.
3. System-wide intervention programs and services should be aimed at the prevention and remediation of cumulative deficiencies in the acquisition of the basic skills in the areas of reading and math.
4. The concept of multicultural education should be promoted, with emphasis given to the fact that the culture of America is a conglomeration of the life styles of all the groups who have entered into the building of America.
5. The study of black and Hispanic history and culture should be incorporated into the regular curricula of all schools.
6. Any honors program or programs for gifted and talented students should be constituted with a representative number of minority students; and the admissions criteria and procedures for the recruitment and selection of students should be consistent with the principle of equal educational opportunity.
7. Continuous programs of professional development for school personnel for the purpose of enabling them to cope more effectively with the sociological and educational challenges inherent in school desegregation should be established.
8. Policies determining how federal and special state funds are applied to reinforce a commitment to equal educational opportunity and a quality education for all students should be publicly stated.
9. The policy that either black or white students can serve as the minority student population for the purposes of desegregation should be clearly established.
10. Equal educational opportunity and equal employment opportunity must be treated as companion components of school desegregation.
11. The burdens of required disruptions and dislocations should be equitably distributed among white, brown, and black students.
12. The right of choice when busing is proposed must be accorded to minority parents.
13. A testing program that eliminates all vestiges of discrimination should be initiated.
14. A system-wide evaluation program directed toward the determination of the effectiveness of instructional programs should be established and the results of evaluation for planning and policy determinations applied.
15. Structures for community relations at the local, regional, and central levels should be provided, reflecting the racial composition of the school system and offering parents direct access to the decision-making process as it pertains to policy planning and program development and implementation.
16. A comprehensive program of counseling and career guidance for repairing the effects of past discrimination and for responding to the pressures and needs of a pluralistic and highly technological society should be established.

Conclusion

Racial balance remedies in response to *Brown* were never intended to make improvement in the academic performance of black children a major goal. It is time to stop maximizing the minimum in school desegregation. The juxtaposition of numbers as opposed to focus on the improvement of the quality of education regardless of where black children go to school must be ended as a desegregation strategy acceptable to the courts, attorneys for the plaintiffs, civil rights organizations, and parents. White flight created the large, predominantly black urban school systems. Today, blacks would prefer not to be redesegregated, especially if it means more disruptions and dislocations with little or no attention to efforts to improve the educational lot of black children.

Barring major changes in state laws that govern the prerogatives of state boards of education and a significant reduction in housing discrimination that is coupled with impressive improvements in the economic well-being of most black Americans, school desegregation will not erase the reality that quality education for the vast number of black students will be achieved only when there is effective schooling in mainly black schools and school systems. There is no equitable and efficacious means of countering the reality that most mainly black school systems are not likely to become fully desegregated in the near future. The continued adherence to racial balance remedies that required majority-white schools is ludicrous and not conducive to effective desegregation strategies in mainly black school systems that will work now and in the future.

Intelligently conceived and equitably implemented school desegregation strategies remain an imperative in American education. The charge of social inequity and educational inconsequentiality against racial balance remedies is not a preamble for a rejection of *Brown* to a return to the doctrine of "separate but equal" but with full funding support. Racial balance remedies offer no realistic promise of improved academic performance, impose a disproportionately high burden on black students and their parents, divert critically needed dollars to transportation rather than education, and perpetuate the myth of the "rightness of whiteness." Desegregation efforts that allegedly seek to contribute to the process of black Americans securing the blessings and privileges of first-class citizenship cannot succeed if they impose, even temporarily, second-class status on blacks as a means to this end.

In his first inaugural address Thomas Jefferson proclaimed "that though the will of the majority in all cases is to prevail, that will to be rightful must be reasonable; that the minority possess their equal rights, which equal law must protect, and to violate would be oppression." The U.S. Senate's vote in 1982 to curb the power of the courts to require busing for school desegregation is on questionable constitutional grounds, but the vote was not a reflection of the Senate's compassion for the plight of black students. The assault on civil rights from any direction ought not deter black Americans from the pursuit of more equitable and effective school desegregation strategies. Black Americans ought not tolerate ineffective, inequitable, and obsolete desegregation strategies out of fear that to challenge them would give aid and comfort to those who believe in the separation of the races or who would turn back decades of progress in civil rights.

Blackness is neither greater nor less than whiteness. What black Americans are prepared to accept and reject in terms of the permissible policies and practices in school desegregation will provide key indicators of just how deeply rooted in black America are the roots of black pride and consciousness. There is an urgent need for a *Brown III*. *Brown III* would proclaim that school desegregation strategies must respect cultural identity, provide for equitable implementation, and address educational inequalities.

Notes

1. Derrick A. Bell, Jr., *Legal Analysis: Trends in School Desegregation Law*, National Project and Task Force on Desegregation Strategies of the Education Commission of the State, the National Association of State School Boards of Education, and the Council of Chief State School Officers, Denver, Colo. (December 1972), no. 2.

2. Leon Jones, *From Brown to Boston: The Desegregation Struggle* (New Jersey: The Scarecrow Press, Inc., 1979).

3. U.S. Commission on Civil Rights, *Statement on Metropolitan School Desegregation* (February 1977).

4. *Milliken v. Bradley*, 433 U.S. 267 (1977).

5. Thomas I. Atkins, "School Desegregation in the North and West," a paper presented at the Rockefeller Foundation's National Conference on Education Issues convened in New York City on March 13, 1981.

6. W. B. Brookover and Lawrence Lezotte, "Educational Equity: A Democratic Principle," *The Urban Review* (Summer 1981).

7. Ibid.

8. Atkins, "School Desegregation in the North and West."

9. Jeffrey J. Leach, "Busing as a Judicial Remedy: A Social Legal Reappraisal," *Indiana Law Review* (May 1973).

10. Victor Miller, "The Emergent Pattern of Integration," *Educational Leadership* (February 1979).

11. Ronald R. Edmonds and J. R. Frederiksen, *Search for Effective Schools: The Identification and Analysis of City Schools That Are Instructionally Effective for Poor Children* (Cambridge, Mass.; Center for Urban Studies, Harvard University, 1978).

12. Derrick A. Bell, Jr., "A Model Alternative Desegregation Plan," in *Shades of Brown* (New York: Columbia University Press, 1981).

13. Robert L. Green, "School Desegregation and Its Effects: An Introduction," *The Urban Review* (Summer 1981).

14. John Porter, "Desegregation and Improving Student Performance," *Progress*, a publication of the National Project and Task Force on Desegregation Strategies, (Denver, Colo.: Summer 1980).

15. Green, *Urban Review*.

16. From an interview with Charles Moody, Sr., on July 17, 1981.

17. David L. Kirp. "Race, Politics, and the Courts: School Desegregation in San Francisco," *Harvard Educational Review* (November 1976).

18. Bell, "A Model Alternative."

19. Roger D. Abrahams, "Cultural Differences and the Melting Pot Ideology," *Educational Leadership* (November 1971).

20. Andrew Billingsley, *Black Families and the Struggle for Survival* (New York: Friendship Press, 1974).

21. Ibid.

22. Statement extracted from a position paper prepared by the Black Caucus at the Harvard University Conference on Educational Subsystems, January 25, 1968.

23. From an interview with Charles Thomas, Superintendent of Schools in North Chicago, Illinois, on July 17, 1981.

24. W. E. B. DuBois, *The Souls of Black Folk*, (1903; reprint in *Three Negro Classics*, New York: Avon Books, 1965).

25. Ibid.

26. From a speech by John H. Clarke entitled "Struggle Is the Highest Form of Education," presented at the Martin Luther King, Jr., Memorial Forum at Bank Street College in 1972.

27. Stokely Carmichael and Charles V. Hamilton, *Black Power: The Politics of Liberation in America* (New York: Vintage Press, 1967).

28. Motion for leave to file Brief Amicus Curiae on the Merit and Brief Amicus Curiae for the Congress of Racial Equality in the Supreme Court of the United States, October Term, 1970, no. 281, *James E. Swann et al. petitioners v. Charlotte-Mecklenburg Board of Education et al.*, respondents.

29. Bell, "A Model Alternative."

30. Statement by Preston Wilcox, extracted from *The Urban Scene in the Seventies*, James F. Blumstein and Eddie J. Martin, eds. (Nashville: Vanderbilt University Press, 1974) p. 140.

31. Black Caucus Statement at Harvard University Conference.

32. *Milliken v. Bradley*, Memorandum, Order and Judgment issued by Judge Robert E. DeMascio, United States District Court, Eastern District of Michigan, Southern Division, on May 11, 1976.

33. From a Court Memorandum issued by Judge Thomas A. Wiseman, Jr., of the U.S. District Court for the Middle District of Tennessee in *Kelley v. Metropolitan County Board of Education* on August 24, 1979.

34. From Memorandum Opinion issued by Judge Thomas A. Wiseman, Jr., of the U.S. District Court for the Middle District of Tennessee in *Kelley* on May 20, 1980.

35. A Report of the National Project and Task Force on Desegregation Strategies (Denver, Colo.: November 1980).

36. From an interview with Ben Williams on April 23, 1982.

37. From an interview with Ruth B. Love on July 16, 1981.

38. Extracted from the written responses in 1981 by Arthur Jefferson to the author's survey of the responses of black school superintendents to statements pertinent to school desegregation.

39. Survey of black school superintendents conducted by the author in

1981 in conjunction with the presentation of a paper at the Conference on Education Issues convened in New York City in October under the sponsorship of the Rockefeller Foundation.

40. Statement by Carl Sewell, superintendent for Community School District Number 17 in New York City, extracted from an interview on July 16, 1981.

41. Statement extracted from a telephone interview with Ulysses Byas, superintendent of schools in Roosevelt, New York, in June 1981.

42. Green, *Urban Review*.

43. *Brown v. Board of Education*, 347 U.S. 483 (1954).

44. *Brown v. Board of Education,* 349 U.S. 294 (1955).

45. *Green v. County School Board of Kent County, Virginia*, U.S. S. Ct. No. 695, May 27, 1968 88 Ct. 1689.

46. *Swann v. Charlotte-Mecklenburg Board of Education*, 402 U.S. 1. 28 L Ed. 2d 554, 91 S. Ct. 1267 (1971).

47. *Milliken v. Bradley* (Milliken I) 418 U.S. 717. 41 L. Ed. 2d, 1069, 94 S. Ct. 3112 (1974).

48. *Milliken v. Bradley* (Milliken II) 433 U.S. 267. L.Ed. 2d. 745, 97 S. Ct. 2749 (1977).

49. This sentence and most of the material in this paragraph are based on statements made in A. Leon Higginbotham's *In the Matter of Color: Race and the American Legal Process* (New York: Oxford University Press, 1978).

50. *Brown v. Board of Education.*

51. Thomas K. Gilhool, "The Right to Community Services," in *The Mentally Retarded Citizen and the Law* ed. Michael Kindred, Julius Cohen, David Penrod, and Thomas Shaffer (New York: The Free Press, 1976).

52. *Milliken v. Bradley*, 1977.

53. *Milliken v. Bradley*, 1976.

54. Atkins, "School Desegregation."

55. Bell, "A Model Alternative."

56. Robert L. Ebel, "Three Radical Proposals for Strengthening Education," *Phi Delta Kappan* (February 1982).

57. Ronald R. Edmonds, "Some Schools Work and More Can," *Social Policy* (March/April 1979).

58. Ibid.

Achieving Quality Integrated Education — With or Without Federal Help

Willis D. Hawley

WILLIS D. HAWLEY is dean of the George Peabody College for Teachers and a professor of education and political science, Vanderbilt University, Nashville, Tenn. This article is a revised and abridged version of "Effective Educational Strategies for Desegregated Schools," which appeared in the Peabody Journal of Education, *July 1982. An earlier version was presented at the annual meeting of the American Educational Research Association, New York City, March 1982.*

Is school desegregation a policy whose time has come and gone? Probably not. Hundreds of school systems, including some of the largest in the U.S., are involved in the desegregation of racial and ethnic groups. This does not seem likely to change dramatically. Although the flow of new cases into the courts has slowed substantially, courts continue to find that districts must desegregate, and most efforts to achieve relief from the jurisdiction of the courts are unsuccessful.

But two important developments in the last two years suggest that desegregation will not be the same issue in the years to come. First, many education policy makers seem to have decided that high-quality education rather than equal educational opportunity should be the primary goal of public education. (I will resist the temptation to argue that other concerns have *always* been more important than equal educational opportunity.) Clearly, the future acceptance of desegregation by both whites and minorities will depend, much more than it has in the past, on the belief that excellence and equity are mutually reinforcing, rather than competing, goals. Second, the Reagan Administration has reduced both the federal pressure to desegregate and the federal support for desegregation efforts. The Administration opposes mandatory desegregation (i.e., busing) and has essentially repealed the Emergency School Aid Act (ESAA), the primary mechanism through which the federal government encouraged voluntary desegregation. ESAA funds also increased the probabilities that academic achievement would be enhanced when schools desegregated.[1]

Given these changes in attitudes and in federal policies, how can desegregation result in quality integrated education and what can the federal government do to promote this outcome? In trying to answer these questions, I will identify several strategies that school systems can use to increase the benefits of desegregation for students. These strategies do not depend on federal support fôr their efficacy. Then I will explore some low-cost, non-intrusive actions that the federal government can take to improve the quality of education in districts in the process of desegregation.

Overview

Students in desegregated school systems usually exhibit the full range of learning capabilities. Thus effective educational strategies for students in desegregated schools should be a combination of the strategies that are most effective for children who are handicapped, have limited or no English-speaking ability, require compensatory education, are academically gifted, and have no special needs. In other words, most strategies work for different types of children whether their schools are desegregated or not.

In some ways, of course, desegregation makes it more difficult to provide effective education. But before I discuss these problems and their possible solutions, let me call attention to the opportunities that desegregation can create to enhance the education of students. Desegregation can create possibilities for (and sometimes enforce) changes in curricula, classroom structures, instructional practices, and the behavior of teachers and administrators. Moreover, racially integrated schools have one certain advantage over racially isolated schools: They offer opportunities to learn from and about people of different races. In most cases, students in desegregated schools will also have more interaction with persons of different social backgrounds than will students in school systems that have not been desegregated.

The evidence on the overall effects of desegregation shows that in desegregated schools the educational achievement of minorities improves and the achievement of whites is not undermined.[2] Moreover, race relations usually improve where schools take appropriate action to achieve this end.[3] There is also evidence that desegregation in schools improves students' prospects for future employment and increases their chances of attending a desegregated college.[4] These contributions of desegregation to the education of young people are surprising, not only because they fly in the face of popular notions but also because they have been achieved amid considerable opposition, half-hearted implementation, and a lack of shared knowledge about the process. What follows is *not* a full prescription for effective education. I intend to suggest some practices that appear to be important in desegregated schools *in addition* to those that should provide all children with a high-quality education.

People differ on their definition of "quality education." For purposes here, I define quality or effectiveness in terms of 1) academic achievement in mathematics and language arts and 2) tolerance and understanding of people of different races and social backgrounds.

My conclusions are based primarily on the findings of a recent study that reviewed and synthesized 1) the conclusions of about 1,200 books, articles, papers, reports, and commentaries on the effects of desegregation;[5] 2) surveys of educators;[6] and 3) the results of interviews with 135 local and national desegregation experts.[7] Evidence from more recent research is also discussed.

Changes After Desegregation

When school systems desegregate, the relationship of the community to its schools changes. Changes also occur in the context and circumstances in which instruction takes place and educational programs are presented. These alterations in the "conditions of schooling" require special attention if schools are to reap the benefits of otherwise productive educational practices and if the advantages of desegregation are to outweigh its costs. Most of the specific changes in the conditions of schooling that result from desegregation can be grouped into four general categories.

- *Diversity.* Because race is associated with socioeconomic status, interracial schools and classrooms tend to be more heterogeneous academically than their racially segregated counterparts. Traditional instructional strategies are poorly suited to settings in which students have so broad a range of educational needs.[8]
- *Potential conflict.* The possibility of interracial conflict in desegregated schools worries many parents.[9] Moreover, the key challenge of desegregation is to increase student interaction across racial lines so as to enhance race relations in schools and in the larger society.[10]
- *Discontinuity.* Both students and parents feel this change. Parents may feel that desegregated schools are not accessible, because they are far away and unfamiliar. Students may find themselves in environments in which the expectations they experience at home and in their neighborhoods are very different from those they experience in school.[11]
- *Change.* In desegregated schools, teachers, administrators, and students experience substantial change that simultaneously affects the social environment, the nature of instruction and curricula, and personal beliefs. For example, desegregation often requires teachers to take part in a broader range of educational programs, some of which may involve externally imposed requirements and paperwork. Such multidimensional change can greatly increase the workload and sometimes lead to a loss of self-confidence.

Diversity, conflict, discontinuity, and change characterize many schools. But schools that are desegregated by explicit social policy are more likely than others to face these problems and to be forced to resolve them all at once.

These challenges are also opportunities through which more effective education can be achieved. Some school systems have seized these opportunities; others have not. Those that have not seized these opportunities have had their effectiveness reduced and their progress impeded; those that have seized them have often become more effective than they were before desegregation.

Strategies of Response

The challenges posed by the diversity, conflict, discontinuity, and change that often characterize a desegregated school can be met by one or more of a dozen practices.

1. *Desegregate children as early as possible.* Differences in the achievement of students of different races are narrower in early grades, and racial prejudices are not yet ingrained. Thus possibilities for positive, equal interaction among races are greatest at early ages. Such interaction is critical to the mitigation of racial prejudice.[12] In addition, it appears that the positive effects of desegregation on the academic achievement of minorities are greatest in the early grades.[13]

2. *Employ instructional strategies that retain heterogeneous classes and work groups.* Such practices avoid resegregation and encourage teachers to retain high expectations for students of all groups. They also deemphasize competition and encourage student interaction. Examples of such practices are cooperative team learning,[14] the multi-ability classroom,[15] and peer tutoring.[16] Evidence of the effectiveness of such strategies on enhancing achievement and improving race relations is strong.[17] Similarly, there is growing evidence that pull-out strategies are ineffective.[18]

3. *Avoid tracking and other rigid forms of ability grouping.* Tracking usually leads to resegregation within schools and the denial of educational opportunity to low achievers. The increased diversity of students and programs in desegregated schools often leads to a proliferation of pull-out programs and special education assignments. Such assignments may have the effect of tracking and resegregation.[19] Without expertise in classroom management and knowledge of instructional strategies most appropriate for heterogeneous classes, most teachers will be frustrated by extreme student diversity, and the learning needs of students will not be met.[20] Clearly, some students will require special classes if their needs are to be met. But the possible misuse of special programs should be monitored closely.

4. *Retain a critical mass of the minority students in each school and classroom.* When students are in too small a minority, they may be excluded by the majority or withdraw of their own accord. A critical mass of 15% to 20% of students of a given race may help to avoid this problem in desegregated schools.[21] However, in multiracial or multiethnic situations, intergroup conflict tends to be highest when the two groups are about equal in size. Some evidence also suggests that this potential for conflict may be greatest when the students involved are of low socioeconomic status.[22]

5. *Employ minority teachers and counselors.* Minority teachers may act as models for minority children. Some weak but positive evidence exists that minority students do better when they have minority teachers.[23] There is also evidence that minority teachers are less likely to misassign and stereotype students and that they are more likely to relate effectively to minority parents.[24]

6. *Develop a comprehensive approach to human relations that involves substantial interracial contact.* Human relations should be an integral part of the curriculum both in its substance and in the way material is taught. Human relations programs that involve parents are more effective than those that do not,[25] and the most effective human relations programs are those that embody substantial interracial contact.[26] A multiethnic curriculum provides substantive material that may be more meaningful to minority students, and it can provide opportunities for discussing issues that are important to the students' relations with one another. But curricular change alone is not likely to be enough to improve human relations; what teachers do with that curriculum makes all the difference.[27]

7. *Develop interracial extracurricular activities.* Extracurricular activities can offer a chance for success to students whose academic achievement affords them little status within the school. Moreover, extracurricular activities can provide opportunities for interracial contact in cooperative, nonthreatening situations that often require teamwork.[28]

8. *Develop a rigorous but fair disciplinary program.* Developing a well-defined and widely understood code of student conduct and enforcing that code in consistent, firm, and equitable ways are essential elements of an effectively desegregated school. Such a program can help dispel parental anxiety,[29] minimize conflict,[30] and maximize learning.[31]

9. *Create smaller and more supportive learning environments.* Fostering continuity of instruction that avoids anonymity among students and creating a feeling of community that derives from shared values are effective ways to increase order and improve teachers' responses to student needs. Smaller schools and classrooms are not essential to this strategy, but they make it easier to employ flexible instructional strategies and to create manageable environments.[32]

10. *Involve parents directly in the education of their children.* In order to reduce the discontinuity between home and school environments, schools should engage parents directly in the education of their children. Studies on the importance of parental involvement in desegregated schools generally support this conclusion.[33]

11. *Once the desegregation plan is in effect, make an effort to maintain some stability in the educational experiences of*

the child. Such stability helps teachers focus on the educational needs of students, reduces parental anxiety, and gives students a greater sense of security.[34]

12. *Develop a comprehensive program for inservice training.* Staff training is always important, but it becomes even more important when large changes have taken place.[35]

Each of these several strategies responds to at least one of the four conditions of desegregated schooling. Some are positive responses to one or more of the conditions, but they tend to exacerbate one of the others. For example, avoiding tracking and rigid approaches to ability grouping is an appropriate way to respond to student diversity, but it makes it harder for teachers to manage their classrooms.

Implications for Federal Policy

With the demise of the Emergency School Aid Act, the federal government cannot exert the influence it once could on the educational effectiveness of desegregated schools. Through its enforcement powers, the Office for Civil Rights can insist that racial isolation in school systems that have engaged in *intentional* segregation be reduced. Thus it can affect the conditions under which desegregated schools operate. Moreover, housing and employment policies and actions of the Justice Department can affect desegregated schools, but these federal actions do not usually affect the learning process. Assuming that the federal role will no longer involve substantial expenditures or assertive action to require desegregation, let me suggest some general ways that the federal government could enhance the potential educational and social benefits of desegregation for elementary and secondary school students.

Collection and dissemination of information. A fair amount is known about how desegregated schools can become more effective, and many school systems have already implemented successful practices. This information needs to be collected, synthesized, and disseminated. Some steps in systematically collecting information have been taken, but much more needs to be done. The dissemination of research findings has not even reached the federally funded Desegregation Assistance Centers.[36] Among the more than 240 "Ideas That Work" that are publicized by the National Diffusion Network, only *one* deals directly with school desegregation. The National Institute of Education and various federal programs that provide technical assistance and that support professional development could become major vehicles for disseminating information about school desegregation.

Technical assistance and professional development. The largest single federal resource that could influence the instruction students receive in desegregated schools is the set of technical assistance and professional development programs authorized by Title IV of the Civil Rights Act. We now know a good deal more about what works in desegregated schools than we did just a few years ago. But the current "system" that provides assistance is decentralized and uneven in quality. Refocusing these programs — the Desegregation Assistance Centers, the training institutes, state education agencies, and direct discretionary grants to school systems — on improving the education children receive in desegregated schools could make a substantial difference.

Research and development. The federal effort in research and development (especially in the area of desegregation) has been less effective than it might be. Two of the most significant reasons for this failure are the shotgun approach to research funding and the absence of a research and development *system.*

For organizational and political reasons, federal research efforts have distributed available funds widely to address a host of topics. This has meant an inadequate effort in some specific areas, including research on effective desegregated schooling. The justifications for such a shotgun approach to research funding have nothing to do with the development of "usable knowledge." Given limited resources, the federal government should consider focusing attention on a limited number of questions. A good start would be to synthesize what is known and derive from this synthesis a research agenda. Some consensus is required about which issues of high-quality desegregated schooling can be most fruitfully resolved in the near future. Even an imperfect consensus about the issues to be studied would prove more profitable than the scatter-gun approach now in use.

The usual way in which individuals learn can be seen as a cycle that begins in the concrete experiences, dilemmas, or problems that an individual is motivated to consider. These experiential data become the object of reflection and analysis; then concepts and generalizations are derived from them. Next, the implications of these concepts and generalizations are tested in new situations, and the concrete outcomes of these tests provide new data with which to begin the cycle again.[37]

This everyday process is similar to the scientific method used in laboratory research. But the learning cycle for social science inquiry is usually truncated, and responsibility for performing various roles in the development of knowledge is diffused throughout institutions and groups within institutions, often with no explicit connections among them. For example, universities are often organized so that those who perform "basic research" are housed in different places, have different reward systems, and are given higher status than are those who conduct applied research or assist in policy development. The lower rewards for policy-related research and for program evaluation have meant that these functions have been increasingly assumed by contract research firms. These firms, though often technically sophisticated, have no incentives to pursue theory development. Moreover, the cost of field-based research is often so high that resources are unavailable either to test newly developed hypotheses or to replicate studies. Thus, as a society, we learn very slowly and largely without the benefit of well-developed and well-tested theories.

Within its various agencies and programs, the federal government has the elements of a learning cycle. We can think of basic or applied research leading to the development of products or programs that are demonstrated (tested) and then evaluated. The results of the evaluation are then reconsidered in the light of the theory explicit or implicit in the research stage of the process. Unfortunately for the development of knowledge, various stages in the process are the responsibility of agencies whose work is seldom coordinated.

The new Office of Educational Research and Improvement (OERI) in the Education Department (ED) — even after the Education Consolidation and Improvement Act of 1981 — encompasses all the components of the learning cycle (though the evaluation of federal programs rests elsewhere in ED). OERI could structure a research and development process, or, by funding external research consortia, it could link the different stages of the process. Such a strategy, however, would require extraordinary interorganizational cooperation, and the autonomy of some organizations would be reduced. Moreover, both universities and the contract research industry seem likely to resist such efforts.

Parental involvement. Direct involvement of parents in the education of their children seems to be of significant educational benefit. Moreover, parents may increase the sensitivity of educators to discriminatory practices.[38] Most school systems, however, have been ambivalent or even hostile to meaningful parental involvement, though some of the reluctance of educators may be due to a lack of knowledge about ways that parents can be constructively involved.

Federal policies should encourage or require, depending on the program, that districts receiving federal funds actively involve parents. There is no one best way to involve parents, but parent advisory councils at the district level are *not* one of the effective alternatives. Districts should be allowed to construct their own plans to involve parents, and they should be required to make their plans public before they implement them. But parents need to be involved more directly than district-level councils permit. Various technical assistance agencies should know the full range of alternative strategies for involving parents, and the National Institute of Education could publish a handbook on the subject.

Gertrude Stein might have said that a good school is a good school is a good school. But desegregated schools face special challenges in their quest for excellence. With or without federal assistance, desegregated schools can do a great deal to meet those challenges. However, the ability of local school systems to provide high-quality integrated education would surely be enhanced by the relatively inexpensive and non-intrusive federal actions suggested above.

There is no necessary trade-off between equity and high quality. Desegregation creates conditions that require changes in schools, in instruction, and in professional behavior. But the major problems posed by desegregation are not educational; they are political. Most objections that focus on the negative effects of desegregation on students do not hold water. Evidence from research and experience indicates that the difficulties can be overcome and that education in many desegregated districts has improved — especially for minority students.

But the public does not believe the best evidence we have. The reasons for this disbelief raise serious doubt about the possibility of providing high-quality education for all children. Desegregation is more than a challenge to the capacity of schools to provide high-quality education. It is a test of our national commitment to social mobility and to racial equality. So far, we have been doing less well on this test than our schoolchildren have a right to expect. The federal government could help us pass the test by accurately representing the story of the nation's progress to its people.

---

1. John E. Coulson and Anne H. MacQueen, *Emergency School Aid Act (ESAA) Evaluation: Overview of Findings from Supplemental Analyses* (Santa Monica, Calif.: System Development Corp., 1978).
2. Robert L. Crain and Rita E. Mahard, "Some Policy Implications of the Desegregation/Minority Achievement Literature," in Willis D. Hawley, ed., *Assessment of Current Knowledge About the Effectiveness of School Desegregation Strategies, Vol. V* (Nashville, Tenn.: Vanderbilt University, Institute for Public Policy Studies, Center for Education and Human Development Policy, April 1981).
3. Janet W. Schofield, "Desegregation School Practices and Student Race Relations Outcomes," in Hawley, ed., *Assessment of Current Knowledge . . . Vol. V;* and John B. McConahay, "Reducing Racial Prejudice in Desegregated Schools," in Willis D. Hawley, ed., *Effective School Desegregation: Equity, Quality, and Feasibility* (Beverly Hills, Calif.: Sage, 1981).
4. James M. McPartland and Jomills H. Braddock, "Going to College and Getting a Good Job," in Hawley, ed., *Effective School Desegregation. . . .*
5. Willis D. Hawley et al., *Strategies for Effective Desegregation: Lessons from Research* (Lexington, Mass.: Lexington Books, D.C. Heath, 1982).
6. William T. Trent, "Expert Opinion on School Desegregation: Findings from the Interviews," in Hawley, ed., *Assessment of Current Knowledge . . . Vol. V.*
7. Ibid.
8. Valerie Cook, Janet Eyler, and Leslie Ward, *Effective Strategies for Avoiding Within-School Resegregation* (Nashville, Tenn.: Vanderbilt University, Institute for Public Policy Studies, Education Policy Development Center for Desegregation, December 1981).
9. John B. McConahay and Willis D. Hawley, *Reactions to Busing in Louisville: Summary of Adult Opinions in 1976 and 1977* (Durham, N.C.: Duke University, Institute of Policy Sciences and Public Affairs, 1978).
10. McConahay, "Reducing Racial Prejudice. . . ."
11. William J. Tikunoff and José A. Vasquez-Faria, *Effective Instruction for Bilingual Schooling* (San Francisco: Far West Regional Laboratory for Educational Research and Development, 1982), pp. 22-24.
12. Schofield, "Desegregation School Practices. . . ."
13. Crain and Mahard, "Some Policy Implications. . . ."
14. Robert E. Slavin, "Cooperative Learning and Desegregation," in Hawley, ed., *Effective School Desegregation. . . .*
15. Elizabeth G. Cohen, "A Multi-Ability Approach to the Integrated Classroom," paper presented at the annual meeting of the American Psychological Association, Montreal, 1980.
16. Hawley et al., *Strategies for Effective Desegregation. . . .*
17. Robert E. Slavin, "Cooperative Learning in Teams: State of the Art," *Educational Psychologist*, vol. 15, 1980, pp. 93-111; and Shlomo Sharan, "Cooperative Learning in Small Groups: Research Methods and Effects on Achievement, Attitudes, and Ethnic Relations," *Review of Educational Research*, vol. 50, 1980, pp. 241-72.
18. H. Carl Haywood, "Compensatory Education," paper prepared for the National Institute of Education, Vanderbilt University, Peabody College for Teachers, January 1982; and Cook, Eyler, and Ward, *Effective Strategies for Avoiding. . . .*
19. Cook, Eyler, and Ward, *Effective Strategies for Avoiding. . .* ; Roger Mills and Miriam M. Bryan, *Testing . . . Grouping: The New Segregation in Southern Schools* (Atlanta: Southern Regional Council, 1976); and Joyce Epstein, "After the Bus Arrives: Resegregation in Desegregated Schools," paper presented at the annual meeting of the American Educational Research Association, Boston, 1980.
20. Carolyn M. Evertson, Julie P. Sanford, and Edmund T. Emmer, "Effects of Class Heterogeneity in Junior High School," *American Educational Research Journal*, vol. 18, 1981, pp. 219-32.
21. Hawley et al., *Strategies for Effective Desegregation. . . .*
22. Willis D. Hawley, "Effective Educational Strategies for Desegregated Schools," *Peabody Journal of Education*, July 1982, pp. 209-33.
23. Gary Bridge, Charles Judd, and Peter Moock, *The Determinants of Educational Outcomes: The Effects of Families, Peers, Teachers, and Schools* (New York: Teachers College Press, 1979).
24. Epstein, "After the Bus Arrives. . . ."
25. System Development Corporation, *Human Relations Study: Investigations of Effective Human Relations Strategies, Vol. 2* (Santa Monica, Calif.: System Development Corp., June 1980).
26. Schofield, "Desegregation School Practices. . . ."
27. Robert E. Slavin and Nancy Madden, "School Practices That Improve Race Relations," *American Educational Research Journal*, vol. 16, 1979, pp. 169-80.
28. Cook, Eyler, and Ward, *Effective Strategies for Avoiding. . . .*
29. Peter O. Peretti, "Effects of Teachers' Attitudes on Discipline Problems in Schools Recently Desegregated," *Education*, vol. 97, 1976, pp. 136-40.
30. Gary D. Gottfredson and Denise C. Daiger, *Disruption in 600 Schools* (Baltimore: Johns Hopkins University, Center for the Social Organization of Schools, Technical Report No. 289, 1979).
31. Stewart C. Purkey and Marshall S. Smith, "Effective Schools — A Review," *Elementary School Journal*, in press.
32. Hawley, "Effective Educational Strategies. . . ."
33. Coulson and MacQueen, *Emergency School Aid Act (ESAA) Evaluation. . .* ; and Jean B. Wellisch et al., *An In-Depth Study of Emergency School Aid Act (ESAA) Schools: 1974-1975* (Santa Monica, Calif.: System Development Corp., July 1976).
34. Purkey and Smith, "Effective Schools — A Review. . . ."
35. William J. Genova and Herbert J. Walberg, *A Practitioner's Guide for Achieving Student Integration in City High Schools* (Washington, D.C.: National Institute of Education, November 1980); and Mark A. Smylie and Willis D. Hawley, *Increasing the Effectiveness of Inservice Training for Desegregation: A Synthesis of Current Research* (Washington, D.C.: National Education Association, 1982).
36. Willis D. Hawley and Barry Schapira, *The Title IV Race Desegregation Technical Assistance Centers: Some Directions for Change* (Nashville, Tenn.: Vanderbilt University, Institute for Public Policy Studies, Center for Education and Human Development Policy, December 1981).
37. David A. Kolb, Irwin M. Ruben, and James M. McIntyre, *Organizational Psychology: An Experimental Approach* (Englewood Cliffs, N.J.: Prentice-Hall, 1971).
38. Jennifer Hochschild and Valerie Hadrick, *The Character and Effectiveness of Citizen Monitoring Groups in Implementing Civil Rights in Public Schools* (Washington, D.C.: National Institute of Education and the Office for Civil Rights, 1980).

The State of Education for BLACK AMERICANS

Beverly P. Cole

Dr. Cole is Director of Education Programs, National Association for the Advancement of Colored People, New York City.

THE struggle to obtain equal access to quality education for black Americans has been long and arduous. Before the Civil War, every slave state had laws against blacks being educated. When the education of blacks was finally permitted, it was established on a separate and decidedly unequal basis. Not until 1954 (*Brown v. Board of Education*) did the Supreme Court hand down its historic decision that, in the field of education, the doctrine of separate but equal had no place. The court further declared that "It is doubtful that any child may reasonably be expected to succeed in life if he is denied the opportunity of education. Such an opportunity is a right which must be made available to all on equal turns."

In the 1980's, this right is being greatly undermined at the Federal level by anti-busing legislation, severe budget cuts in education and student assistance, proposals for tuition tax credit, the granting of tax-exempt status to schools that blatantly discriminate, the exemption of certain schools from civil rights regulations, the revision of affirmative action requirements, and the abdication to the states of the Federal government's role of monitoring and enforcing equal access to quality education.

On the local level, the right to a quality education is being denied by indifferent and insensitive teachers and administrators, by the lack of school accountability, low expectations of students' potential, pushing-out due to discriminatory disciplinary practices, inadequate equipment, poor curricular and career counseling, racially isolated schools, labeling, tracking, and discriminatory school financing policies.

In spite of these obstacles, blacks have made some progress educationally. There has been a significant increase in school enrollment, with 51% of blacks aged 25 or older graduating from high school. Today, more blacks stay in school longer and go on to college than they did a quarter of a century ago.

On the other hand, this progress has been inadequate to close the gap between black and white educational attainments and, indeed, is miniscule when compared to the overwhelming educational needs of blacks. In many ways, the progress can be described as one step forward and two steps backwards.

In evaluating the educational attainments of blacks, one must not only look at enrollment rates, but also at completion rates, as well as the quality of the educational experience.

- The dropout rate for blacks in high school is 28%, as compared to 17% for whites. Although blacks comprise 10% of the college population, whites are still twice as likely as blacks to be college graduates. Many attribute these statistics to an unresponsive school system.
- In most inner-city schools, where approximately 75% of black students are in attendance, achievement levels are usually two or more years behind the national norm.
- Studies have shown that black children tend to drop below grade level in elementary school and fall further behind as they get older, until, at age 16, at least 35% are below their modal grade.

Many theories have been offered to explain this disgrace; most built upon the notion of "blaming the victim." "Cultural deprivation," "the culture of poverty," the deficit model, "the disadvantaged"—all explained why the low socioeconomic student could not overcome the problems of poverty and social pathology and be expected to learn.

Nevertheless, the results of the "effective schools" research clearly demonstrate that children can be educated successfully, regardless of their family background. However, one of the main prerequisites is a belief and expectation on the part of the teacher and principal that this feat can be accomplished. Schools must demonstrate respect for the dignity of all students and be committed to the principle that all students are educable, regardless of their race or economic background.

Educators know what practices make schools effective, but in many cases are unwilling to implement them. We must hold schools accountable and stop entertaining excuses. As parents and interested citizens, we must also accept our fair share of the responsibility for motivating students, supporting them, and serving as advocates to insure that they receive a quality education.

Improving the quality of education

NAACP branches across the nation are attempting to improve the deteriorating quality of education received by blacks by insisting upon:

- Equal access to quality integrated education at all levels from pre-school to professional schools.
- High expectations on the part of teachers in terms of achievement and behavior.
- Basis academic skills being taught and mastered at an early age (reading, mathematics, written and oral communications).
- A curriculum that develops skills of logic, analysis, problem-solving, and test-taking.
- Multi-cultural textbooks and materials.
- Teachers trained in multi-ethnic education/relations with more inner-city student teaching experiences.
- The utilization of a multi-method approach to evaluation and assessment.
- The elimination of tracking or homogeneous grouping.
- More teacher accountability.
- Counseling programs that encourage and advise students concerning varied career opportunities, the required courses, financial assistance, and other resources needed to pursue post-secondary education or other experiences consistent with their career goals and potential.
- Policies and procedures which insure racial fairness in classrooms and schools such as fair grading and evaluations, fair involvement in student activities, and fair discipline.
- Participation of parents and community leaders in the school process.
- Affirmative action in the hiring and promotion of black teachers and administrators to ensure that black students have appropriate role models.

These goals and objectives were chosen because of various reasons. Black children continue to be confined to separate and unequal schools; over 70% of black students are in predominantly minority schools. When desegregation occurs, research such as the seven-year study on The Effectiveness of School Desegregation produced by Vanderbilt University has shown that the achievement scores of minority students increase significantly and the achievement gains are likely to be maximized when desegregation is begun in the early grades. These findings notwithstanding, "neighborhood school proponents or anti-busing foes are accusing mandatory pupil assignments—for purposes of desegregation—of destroying public education and blighting entire communities across the country with its divisive impact." This is a myth and a gross exaggeration. Approximately 50% of schoolchildren are bused to school and, of this number, only three per cent are bused for purposes of desegregation. It is obvious that busing is not the real issue. The real issue is avoidance of quality integrated education.

Busing is not the goal, but only a means or technique for accomplishing the goal. If the purpose of education were only to teach selected academic subjects, then perhaps there would be no need for the desegregation of schools. All that would be needed is the enhancement of the present racially isolated schools. However, since the education institution is one of society's primary means of socialization, then it needs to teach our children to associate with different races and economic groups in order to exist compatably in this pluralistic country and the world. Integration is an essential component of a quality education for everyone—black, white, brown, yellow, and red. The anti-busing amendment recently passed by the Senate as well as local initiatives are threatening to prevent this ideal from ever becoming a reality.

As was alluded to earlier, teacher expectation is one of the most crucial determinants of student effort, motivation, and achievement. Rosenthal's famous Pygmalion experiment demonstrated how teacher expectation creates the self-fulfilling prophecy. If teachers expect that some children will fail, more than likely the children will fail. This occurs because the varied expectations, based often on race and income, are translated into different behavior. This treatment communicates to the students what behavior and achievement the teacher expects from them and affects their self-concepts, achievement motivation, and levels of aspiration.

The curriculum is another major source of concern. Students must be offered competent instruction in reading, writing, mathematics, and the process of logical thought. Beyond the minimum basic skills, the curriculum should be challenging in order to stimulate students to develop skills of logic, analysis, problem-solving, and test-taking—all of which they will need in this highly technological society. Stressing minimum basic skills is good only if the minimum does not become the maximum offered.

Secondly, our society is a pluralistic one, and the textbooks and materials must reflect this. Black children need to know about the contributions that their race has made to America. They can not learn to be proud of their heritage if all they encounter in school are the achievements of whites. In an effort to enhance the self-image and sense of worth of minority students, as well as to inform white youth, school officials should replace all biased and stereotyped schoolbooks and curriculum aids with materials which accurately reflect in text and illustrations the history and participation of blacks and other minorities.

In order for teachers to be responsive to the needs of minority children, they need more training in multi-cultural/multi-ethnic education and they need more inner-city student teaching experiences. Most teachers have very little knowledge of the poor's urban experiences. For this reason, teachers and administrators should be required to attend in-service training programs geared toward helping them come to terms with their own behavior and attitudes toward students from different cultural, ethnic, racial, and social backgrounds.

In addition, we must press for affirmative action in the hiring of black teachers and administrators to insure that black students have appropriate role models. In order to achieve this, educational systems must set goals and timetables in order to measure the effectiveness of recruitment, retention, and promotion efforts.

In terms of teacher accountability, administrators should expect more and demand more. New procedures need to be instituted for relieving the school system of those teachers who are indifferent, ineffective, and unwilling or unable to improve.

The I.Q. tests, the standardized aptitude tests, and the recent competency tests have been greatly misused in relation to black students and have caused great harm in terms of damaging self-images and life chances. Tests have been used for channeling black students into "slow tracks" and mentally retarded classes and for screening them out of higher education and jobs. For blacks, tests have meant exclusion, rather than inclusion into America's mainstream, and thus have been used to further stratify the society.

It is obvious that some type of assessment is needed, and testing for purposes of evaluation or diagnosis, when used in order to improve skills of the student, is both meaningful and desirable. A good assessment program utilizes a multi-method approach for evaluation. No one sole criterion should be used for such critical determinations as graduation, promotion, certification, college entrance, and hiring. Yet, the reality is that it is much easier to accept a standardized test score than to analyze systematically the strengths and weaknesses of students by multiple means. Therefore, accuracy has been sacrificed for expediency.

Culturally biased I.Q. tests are infamous for causing a disproportionate number of blacks to be placed into "special education" and mentally retarded classes. It would amaze you to know the number of outstanding black professionals who at one time in their early life were labeled in this manner.

Competency testing, which is being used by some 38 states, tends to place the burden of accountability solely on the students. This form of testing should be done at a stage where remedial action can be taken, and teachers as well as students should be held accountable in terms of which skills have been introduced and which skills have been mastered. In those school systems which use competency tests for purposes of promotion, students should be assigned to non-graded classes where they can advance according to their individual achievement and where the stigma of repeating a grade would be avoided.

"Tracking" or homogeneous grouping is synonymous with "trapping" at a very early age. This procedure can cause a child to view himself as being incompetent and consequently establish the self-fulfilling prophecy. Based on test scores, students are often placed into a "slow group" and kept there in the less rigorous dead-end curricula all the way through school, which often creates segregation within a desegregated school. No child is slow in everything. In a heterogeneous environment, there is opportunity for the strong to help and inspire the weak.

Another area that requires careful monitoring is guidance and counseling. The counseling is very limited in inner-city schools; often, a student will not see a counselor unless he is in trouble. It is important that when advice is given it is not based on false assumptions about presumed abilities and aspirations because of the student's racial or class identification. Counseling programs must be provided that will encourage and advise students concerning the required courses and available financial aid to attend college, post-secondary education, or other experiences consistent with their career goals and potential.

In terms of administrative practices, there is a need for the elimination of dehumanizing and exploitative practices for all students. Policies and procedures must be designed to insure racial fairness in classrooms and schools such as fair grading and evaluations, fair involvement in student activities, and fair discipline and suspension. It has been shown that, at the high school level, blacks are suspended three times as often as whites. While minority students are about 25% of the school population, they constitute about 40% of all suspended and expelled students. Furthermore, black students are suspended for longer periods of time. All schools need to examine carefully those conditions at the school which precipitate pushouts and dropouts.

Parental and community involvement are essential ingredients for quality education. Confidence in the school and support for its endeavors occur when parents believe that they have access to school personnel and have some influence over what happens to their children. The family and community must support school efforts and the school must serve the community. Lack of parental involvement in the educational system to a large extent has been primarily because parents feel intimidated and unwelcomed, and lack the skills and information to impact upon the school system. Therefore, many black parents become disenchanted and withdrawn from the educational process. Yet, they still hold high hopes for their children's education, for they know that education is the means to employment, upward social mobility, recognition, and esteem.

Another factor that explains the difference in the scope, content, and quality of the education that blacks receive is the inequitable distribution of revenues and resources to inner-city schools. Despite the overwhelming need, our society spends less money educating inner-city children than children of the suburbs. This is due largely to the declining city tax base and increasing competition from municipal needs (*e.g.*, police, welfare, fire) for the tax dollar. The suburbs, where these demands are less, allocate twice the proportion of their total budgets to education as do the cities. Several judicial decisions have attempted to make school spending independent of property values in order to reduce the gap in per-pupil expenditures between wealthy and low-income school districts.

Researchers have also studied the relationship between students' socioeconomic status and the amount of school resources made available to them and have found that school districts allocate substantially fewer dollars to schools in poor and black neighborhoods. The intra-district disparities are often just as great as the inter-district ones. Other formulas and methods for financing need to be devised.

The budget squeeze

The Reagan Administration has taken steps that will widen the gap between black and white educational attainment. The budget requested for education for 1983 is $10,300,000,000, as compared to $13,000,000,000 proposed to be spent on education in the fiscal year 1982. These proposed budget cuts adversely affect minority education programs the most and represent a big step backward in educational opportunities for the disadvantaged.

The Council of Great City Schools is an organization that represents the nation's 28 largest urban school districts, serving 5,000,000 students, of which 75% are minorities. This council stated that the proposed cuts in education would be especially severe in their areas where 16% of big-city school revenues come from Washington, as compared to the national average of eight per cent.

These school systems estimate a loss of $300,000,000, which will have the cumulative effect of jeopardizing 12,000 jobs and curtailing or eliminating services to about 235,000 inner-city youngsters. The bulk of the cuts would occur in Title I funding, a program designed for low-achieving students in low-income areas. Some 78% of U.S. school districts receive Title I aid and approximately 50% of the children served are from minority groups—29% being black.

Several research studies have shown that the Title I program has been very successful in improving achievement, especially for minority students. The National Assessment of Educational Progress indicated improvement in the relative performance of black youth at ages nine and 13 in five learning areas. It is believed that this may be attributed to Federal programs designed to foster equal educational opportunity, especially Title I.

In spite of Title I's success, the President is proposing to cut its funds by 40% from the 1981-82 funding level. If Congress approves the proposed budget cuts, it would eliminate nearly 2,500,000 children from the program, leaving only 27% of the nation's children who need the services actually receiving them.

Another move which would restrict access to higher education—and consequently to the mainstream of society—is the drastic reduction in student financial assistance. Proposed for 1983 is a 44% reduction in the over-all student assistance program, which will impact approximately 2,000,000 needy students. Since over 80% of all black students enrolled in post-secondary institutions receive some form of Federal assistance either through a loan or a grant or both, black progress in higher education stands to be severely impeded.

The Pell Grant program, the largest of the Education Department's major aid programs for needy students, has been cut by 36% for 1983, requiring parents to contribute more for their children's education. Changes in the eligibility criteria for Pell Grants would eliminate about 1,000,000 students by 1983. Three programs—Supplemental Grants, State Incentive Grants, and National Direct Student Loans—would not receive any funds for 1983. The proposed reduction of college workstudy funding would eliminate 250,000 needy students from the program. The trio program specifically designed for the disadvantaged would be reduced by 47%. The budget would kill three of the five trio programs. The pre-college counseling programs—Talent Search and Equal Opportunity Centers—would vanish under the proposal. Graduate and professional opportunity fellowships as well as assistance to needy students in the law school Cleo program would be eliminated.

Graduate students would be eliminated from the Guaranteed Student Loan program under the new proposal. Six hundred thousand students, more than half the current graduate school enrollment, depend on guaranteed student loans, and the majority of them probably will not be able to stay in school if the Administration's proposal to withdraw graduate aid entirely is approved by Congress. In addition, the Social Security Administration is planning to phase out payments to children of deceased, retired, or disabled parents at the rate of 25% each year until the program ends in 1985—with no checks being issued for the summer months. Any student not enrolled in college full-time by May, 1982, would not be eligible for Social Security aid. It is estimated that over 150,000 high school seniors will become ineligible for Social Security assistance for college.

The cumulative effect of such cuts, at a time of rising college costs (15% to 20%) and reductions in other programs, can tip the balance between the student's looking to education to better his employment possibilities or giving up. For blacks, attrition in higher education to a great extent is affected by financial aid policies. The dropout rate for blacks who do not receive any aid is 46%, as compared to 29% for whites.

Costs to society

The costs to our society of not educating one person in terms of crime, welfare expenditures, and foregone productivity are far higher than the expense of a quality education from birth. When considering the cost effectiveness of programs like Title I, we should remember that it costs $26,000 a year to keep a man in prison.

The black community is quite concerned about Congress placing educational categorical programs such as the Teacher Corps and the Emergency School Aid Act—a program designed to assist school districts struggling with problems of racial isolation and desegregation—into block grants. It is feared that the objectives of these programs will be lost, and that the special needs of the poor and minorities will be left to the discretion of thousands of state and local officials, whose decisions about the allocation of funds will be based upon the political pressure in their jurisdictions. Past experiences have shown that states have not provided sufficient funds for the disadvantaged and minorities, and their funding formulas have been discriminatory.

Increased Federal legislation had to be developed in order to address the needs of the poor and minorities. If more control is relinquished to the local school systems, then the Federal government in turn must ensure that minority and disadvantaged students will receive adequate and appropriate resources.

With the proposed dismantling of the Department of Education and replacing it with the Foundation for Education Assistance, the Administration has decided to redefine the Federal role from one of promoting and ensuring equal access to quality integrated education to one of data collection and analysis, administration of block grants, and student financial assistance. The Foundation's civil rights role is limited to providing counsel, advice, and technical assistance concerning civil rights compliance upon request to recipients of Federal aid. Civil rights enforcement, however, would be turned over to the Justice Department.

Regardless of what happens to the Office of Civil Rights in the Department of Education, the Administration has made it clear that the role of the Federal government is one of advancing civil rights, not enforcing it, using cooperation rather than threatened sanctions to achieve its objectives.

The laws and regulations that took decades to achieve are being dismantled in a matter of months. The new affirmative action regulations would require fewer employees to file affirmative action plans and subject them to fewer reviews. Approximately 80% of the colleges and universities which previously were investigated and ordered to draw up detailed affirmative action plans to hire and promote women and minorities will be exempt. This poses a serious problem not only in terms of employment for minority professionals, but decreases appropriate role models for minority youth as well.

In addition, the Reagan Administration has decided to exempt from anti-discrimination laws those colleges at which guaranteed student loans are the only form of Federal aid. The new rules would significantly limit the number of colleges and universities that must comply with civil rights laws. This shift in policy and reinterpretation of what constitutes Federal assistance is designed to have the same effect as the decision to grant tax-exempt status to schools which racially discriminate.

Finally, the President has introduced tuition tax credit legislation. When you begin to analyze the implications of these actions, you can not help but conclude that access to the mainstream is being deliberately restricted by those who have a stake in their privileged position. When you see being proposed at both the local and national levels legislation that would provide tuition tax credits for parents of children enrolled in private schools, you realize that these tax credits are not designed to provide all parents with a choice concerning the education of their children, for it would not help the 8,600,000 blacks below the poverty level. It was designed to provide relief for the tax-burdened middle class and to encourage escape from the urban public schools with their growing enrollment of poor and minority youngsters. If enacted, these measures would increase social class and racial isolation by establishing a two-tiered educational system in this country—the private schools for the white and middle class and the public schools for the poor and minority. Private education should not be enhanced at the expense of public education, which is the cornerstone of our democracy.

Much remains to be done to finish the uncompleted task of guaranteeing all children in this nation an equal chance at a quality education. The issues of the 1980's are difficult, but not impossible. More concerted effort is needed on the part of all to ensure that black children will receive the kind of training that will equip them to thrive in the pluralistic technological society of which they are a part. We can no longer afford to point the finger and pass the blame. We should all heed the words of Thomas Carlyle: "That there should be one man [to] die ignorant who had the capacity for knowledge, this I call a tragedy."

The Education of Black America: Betrayal of a Dream?

PEARL LUCAS

PEARL LUCAS has taught at many different levels ranging from the elementary school through college. She served as assistant dean of the College of Arts and Sciences at Cornell University for two years and has been on the staff of the New York City Board of Education.

The American dream of work and perserverance toward worthy aims, in recent years, has been all but shattered for many Americans, but for those relatively few black Americans who have followed the demanding and at times all-consuming course of study through higher education, in traditional courses at distinguished institutions, an element of betrayal can be added to the shattered dream.

When the "radical chic" attitude of condescension and patronization towards black Americans was incorporated into public policy, those black Americans who exhibited effort and excellence were castigated for being "white," or mistreated in more subtle ways, while those who practiced indolence and mediocrity were rewarded for being "black." Perhaps the most revealing example of such condescension to have reached public awareness is the reinforcement of the quota system, begun in 1968, that culminated in the federal civil service examination being adjudged differently for minorities. Under such circumstances we see black people being treated as a monolothic group, incapable of competing.

This policy of lowered standards and expectations for minorities is reflected in the evolution of government-sponsored programs, introduced in the mid sixties, intended to change the pattern of poverty by helping the disadvantaged towards a better future through educational opportunity. These programs eventually focused their attention on racial minorities, particularly black Americans. With enthusiastic beginnings, they are today the subject of much controversy.

The fact is that such programs have failed to achieve their original aims, and what is worse, have institutionalized their failure. The very programs that were established to compensate for the inferior education of most minority children in the public schools soon became as obscure in their aims, as poor in quality, and as violent in their administration as is generally characteristic of the educational system from which the children had been drawn. The results are a consequence of years of perverse social theorizing that have obscured the facts or deliberately discounted them, so that despite the many millions of dollars spent by the federal government, little of real value can be demonstrated.

One example of a program that has fallen short of its goals, and that ought to be objectively examined, is Head Start, the federally funded preschool program. From a good beginning, more than a decade ago, that held out high hopes for the social and educational advancement of the children enrolled, the program has changed. Today, encouraged by loose federal guidelines, minor subsidiary objectives and personal and political ambitions have escalated and supplanted the original aim of an educational head start for culturally deprived children—making the pursuit of excellence a lost cause.

The new, though unacknowledged emphasis of the program is on giving employment to neighborhood people, regardless of their qualifications. In contrast to its early years when the quality and dedication of Head Start teachers was often impressive, today's classroom teachers are frequently individuals with little or no training and a minimum of education. Many lack high school degrees and are themselves from culturally deprived backgrounds.

On becoming the director of Head Start for Dutchess County, New York, ten years after I had been a teacher in one of the early Head Start programs, I soon discovered the reason for the teachers' deficiencies. Much to my chagrin, I learned that a committee of uninformed local people, and not I, were to be responsible for reading resumes, holding interviews, and making final decisions as to who would be hired to teach. The result was that individuals with shortcomings similar to their own, who could return political favors, were hired, while well-prepared early childhood teachers, including minorities, were overlooked.

Surprisingly, there are significant parallels between the development of Head Start and the development of programs for minority students at institutions of higher learning, including our most prestigious colleges and universities. Cornell University is one such institution that in the mid sixties, as it approached its 100th anniversary, began a Special Education Program (COSEP) to seek out and enroll disad-

From *Change Magazine,* March 1982, a publication of the Helen Dwight Reid Educational Foundation. Reprinted by permission.

vantaged students from throughout the United States in programs leading to the baccalaureate degree.

COSEP's aims also changed without the consent of those who had voted it into being, in this case, the faculty. A handful of individuals changed the program from admitting disadvantaged students, in general, to admitting primarily black students. And of those students, the academically unprepared were given a preference over the academically prepared, even when their social and economic backgrounds appeared almost identical. As the program evolved and as the participants grew more uniform in color and outlook, the COSEP students came to be viewed as a separate entity by many of the white faculty and students, rather than as a collection of individual young men and women. This perception was encouraged by the self-imposed segregation of the minority students. Their separateness, however, was not simply a natural outgrowth of a homogeneous background and philosophy as might be supposed, and as some theorists would have us believe. On the Cornell campus, it was first encouraged by a black assistant dean of students who speculated that if black students associated with white students it would damage their psyches.

Once the programs for the disadvantaged focused on black minorities, the rhetoric became more extreme and the social theorizing more perverse. And later, when the campus was at the height of its politicization, black minority students who fraternized with white students were threatened with physical harm by self-styled black militants.

As the relatively small group of minority students grew more alienated from their environment and personally insecure, they became, as a group, important to some others who readily manipulated them. They were given roles to play that, with few exceptions, in their fear and anxiety, they willingly acted out, including choosing segregated dormitories over integrated ones; creating thousands of dollars worth of damage to university property; and in the spring of 1969, walking out of a takeover of a student union building armed with guns.

Finally, as with the Head Start program, unqualified people were chosen, not only to counsel the minority students on academic matters, but to instruct them as well. At Cornell this took place largely at the Afro-American Studies Center, a euphemism for a segregated center that was hastily established in response to the crisis of 1969.

What is strangely ironic about both of the programs described here, and typical of other similar programs, is that in each case the educational opportunity that was promised has not been forthcoming; and the pattern of segregation was reinforced rather than modified. The sound education that should have been a genuinely liberating force for these students was impeded at every step.

Why this situation should exist becomes clear when one takes a look at the leadership of these programs and considers how that leadership was chosen. In the middle and late 1960s, individuals and institutions that wished to do things on a mass scale were often moved to action more by slogans and jargon than by reason and sound argument. The result was that it soon became a popular notion where minorities were concerned, that the disadvantaged should lead and teach the disadvantaged. Many black individuals who embody the negative characteristics of the disadvantaged were and are given leadership positions within minority-legislated programs, whereas others who have had the fortitude to overcome their disadvantages and to excel, often with singular perserverance and at personal sacrifice, have been rejected as not being a part of "the black experience."

Many examples of this development could be given, but just a few will serve to illustrate the point. During the strikes, riots, and takeovers at Cornell University, a black professor of economics, Dr. Thomas Sowell, who was graduated *magna cum laude* from Harvard before any special programs were established there, was never consulted by the administration concerning the racial problems at Cornell; nor were the views of nonpolitical black students solicited or welcome.

When the College of Arts and Sciences sought to employ a black student to help in the evaluation of courses, a serious student from a disadvantaged southern background was turned down by a white associate dean in favor of a black woman who had recently returned to her studies after having been suspended for poor grades and for physically attacking another black student. All of the people who had been rejected had in common self-discipline and self-respect and were seen as a threat by those who were riding the bandwagon of "liberalism."

Perhaps worst of all is the inherent violence in the attitude that has allowed these conditions to prevail and persist. It is one that ostensibly accepts a minority group while denying its members the right to develop their individuality and will—something essential to a free person and to the development of his potential. This way of thinking was demonstrated in a ruling passed at Cornell University a few years ago requiring all individuals to pay a minimum fee on campus buses *except* anyone black. This singling out of a group for differential treatment is as bad, or worse, than the most obvious racism.

Similarly, at Harvard University, a black undergraduate student was dissuaded from pursuing her interest in modern European history by a white tutor who suggested that she instead major in Afro-American studies.

This is an attitude that encourages shallowness and an irresponsibility that often breaks forth in criminal acts. At Antioch, when black students were not given the remedial help they needed to enable them to participate with confidence in their course work, they drew together in what was then the self-segregated Unity House dormitory. When three white students, attempting to maintain the Antioch spirit of openness, tried to enter the building, one of them was wounded by a gunshot.

6. EQUALITY OF OPPORTUNITY

The nightmare quality of events that took place during more radical times has disappeared, but there remain inferior educational programs for minorities, supported by government funding, that encourage a subculture of failure and threaten to create a permanent group of second-class citizens.

The most tragic outcome of the perversion of the civil rights movement, however, has been the stultification of the efforts of those who have made real achievements by any system of measurement, and who have been prevented from advancing in accordance with those achievements. One wonders if a separate system of reality has been designed for minorities to flounder around in—one that operates like Lewis Carroll's looking-glass house in which the reverse of what is expected happens, so that if you move forward you end up going backwards. It is a context wherein even if one runs to the point of utter exhaustion, one remains in the same place.

When these things happen in a world where others are not undergoing the same insane experiences, the results are traumatizing. This is seen in the case of a young woman who graduates from the pre-medical curriculum at Mt. Holyoke College and ends up packing crackers in a factory. Another instance is an honor student at Phillips Exeter Academy, a Merit Scholar, who is wait-listed at Cornell University, his first choice, and loses his scholarship money when, bitterly disappointed, he accepts admittance at another university. Ironically, every young white male of his class who applied was accepted at Cornell. The point here is that while this young man's dream was dashed, Cornell continued, under the quota system, to accept only those black students who were perceived to be "authentic" and who fit the "liberal" stereotype.

This is unquestionably a new system of subjugation that debases excellence and humiliates achievers and is a more blazing unjustice to me than a system of enslavement that happened hundreds of years ago to ancestors I never knew.

WE WANT YOUR ADVICE

Any anthology can be improved. This one will be—annually. But we need your help.

Annual Editions revisions depend on two major opinion sources: one is the academic advisers who work with us in scanning the thousands of articles published in the public press each year; the other is you—the person actually using the book.

Please help us and the users of the next edition by completing the prepaid article rating form on the last page of this book and returning it to us. Thank you.

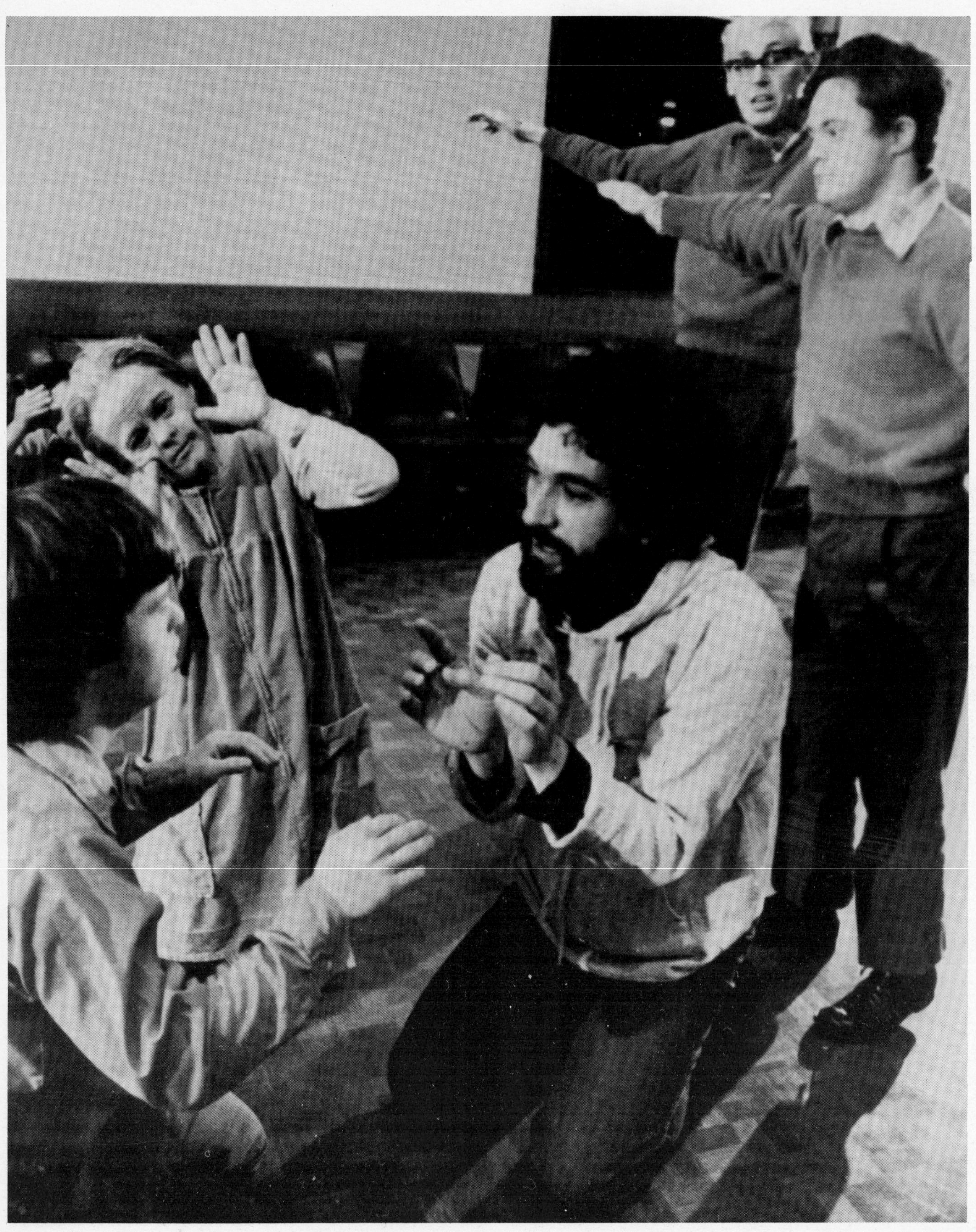

Serving Special Needs and Individualizing Instruction

Young people entering school may have special needs, special abilities, and special disabilities. These children are often called "exceptional." Cognitive, emotional, and social factors all can affect the life of a child in school, so it is imperative that teachers realize the importance of individualized approaches to special learning needs. Helping children adjust to the day to day life of school settings often involves helping them cope with interpersonal problems. Educators and the social systems in which they work are expected to provide many special educational services for students. The range of exceptionality includes the physically handicapped, the learning disabled, the perceptually and neurologically handicapped, and the gifted. Public and professional concern that exceptional students be granted equal and individualized opportunities to pursue their educational goals "in the least restrictive environment possible" has led to government action in recent years. The Education for All Handicapped Children Act of 1975 (PL94-142) requires that as many handicapped learners as possible be integrated into regular classroom settings. The three lead articles for this section address the problems encountered in implementing this law. This policy is known as mainstreaming. The impact of mainstreaming on American schools requires serious professional attention because it raises several educational issues that must be dealt with in fairness regarding the rights and interests of all students.

All nations have to develop policies for serving the educational needs of persons who, for whatever reasons, require some special treatment in gaining an education. The articles in this section focus on issues that are of concern to most teachers. For example, it is interesting to compare differing national practices in the treatment of exceptional learners. The article by Gibson compares some of the major differences between Soviet and American treatment programs for students with special learning problems. Other articles deal with young people who require special, individualized attention because of their placement in school or the effects of traumatic life crises.

Looking Ahead: Challenge Questions

What is mainstreaming? What are some important professional problems to be considered in the implementation of mainstreaming?

In your opinion, what are effective alternative policies to the placement of special students in the classroom?

What are the differences between American and Soviet policies for the education of handicapped or learning disabled students? What are your opinions of these differences?

What can a teacher do to individualize his or her instructional methods? What specific types of classroom planning issues need to be dealt with when individualizing instruction?

Are the professional situations of elementary and secondary teachers different when it comes to individualizing instruction? If so, in what specific ways? If not, why not?

What specific procedures can teachers use to document teaching efforts and learning outcomes from their instructional efforts?

Mainstreaming: Expectations and Realities

Patricia Reed

Guest Editor

Prior to the passage of the 1975 Education for All Handicapped Children Act, teaching of the handicapped was generally considered to be the responsibility of special educators. Current regulations accompanying P.L. 94-142 place expectations relative to educating the handicapped upon all professional educators. All teachers are now expected to demonstrate competencies essential to assure that handicapped students' educational placements constitute the least restrictive environment. These regulations further require that attention be given at both the preservice and inservice levels to the training of general as well as special educators and support personnel.

Translation of these expectations into realities has engendered controversy among professional educators in all fields and at all levels, including colleges and universities. Some of this controversy is attributable to fundamental opposition to the intent of the legislation. Much is related to varying interpretations of the letter of the law. Even more is reflective of the complexities involved in arriving at consensus as to how educational practices can and should be modified to meet the educational needs of all students.

Nowhere are the expectations or their translations into realities more controversial and more difficult than where they relate to educational programming for secondary students. Traditional concepts of roles and responsibilities, organizational patterns, instructional modes, and even the purposes of secondary schools seem to pose almost insurmountable obstacles to "mainstreaming" being accepted and implemented as an educationally sound process.

Two years ago a group of Bowling Green State University faculty who teach professional education coursework required of prospective secondary teachers began to grapple with the controversies and difficulties of placing handicapped students in regular secondary classrooms. Their major goal was twofold: (1) to determine the knowledge, skills, attitudes and values regular teachers need to make mainstreaming "work," and (2) to design and implement a revised curriculum which would assure that beginning teachers have initial competencies in these areas.

Clearly the preparation of teachers is but one aspect of the complex problem of providing appropriate education for the handicapped. That fact itself made the task faculty had before them potentially impossible to achieve—at least on the basis of factors over which they might exercise direct control. Nonetheless they began.

As work progressed, they found their expanding knowledge only generated more questions, thus making it even more difficult to formulate conclusions which could be acted upon with a reasonable amount of assurance. However, after two years of work they arrived at what they believe to be warranted assumptions about what regular secondary teachers can be prepared to do to promote the educational progress of students who need specialized services but need not be restricted to specialized environments. As might have been anticipated, they also arrived at certain assumptions about what other members of the profession can do to make this possible.

The articles which comprise this special issue have been selected to be representative of predominant concerns which surfaced during the two years of work. They are presented as a stimulus for considered thought and action by teachers, administrators, and teacher educators.

More importantly, these articles are evidence that the expectations of P.L. 94-142 are being translated into realities which recognize that the preparation of all teachers affects the teaching of all students.

Presently there is a major movement to "deregulate" P.L. 94-142. If successful, this action will eliminate many expectations now associated with this legislation, including a number pertaining to the preparation of teachers. Perhaps certain expectations of P.L. 94-142 have created realities which are not acceptable or educationally sound. But is the recognition that the preparation of all teachers affects the teaching of all students an unacceptable or educationally unsound reality? Let us think carefully, lest we permit the proverbial baby to be tossed out with the bath water.

Reprinted from *American Secondary Education,* Special Issue, Vol. 12, 1982.

A Holistic View of Mainstreaming

Conrad Pritscher

Conrad Pritscher is a Professor in the department of Educational Foundations and Inquiry at Bowling Green State University in Bowling Green, Ohio.

Teachers who hold a holistic view of education have been doing voluntarily what is now required by Public Law 94-142. Holistic teachers turn the idea of "least restrictive" into the idea of "most enabling" environments for both students and teachers.

A holistic view of education holds that enhancement of students' learning how to learn is a major reason for acquiring various skills and knowledge. According to this view, there is an underlying process that seems to be more fundamental than what is frequently termed the "basics" (i.e., skills and knowledge of reading, writing, arithmetic, and fundamental skills, and knowledge within various disciplines).

Holistic teachers do not view handicapped students in their classes as a burden, since mainstreaming emphasizes the idea of "most enabling environment." Holistic educators have had this emphasis for centuries. However, it is an emphasis that has existed for all students, not only for those who fall into the group called handicapped.

Creating Most Enabling Environments Through Holistic Teaching

When defined as "most enabling environment," the mainstreaming notion of "least restrictive environment" is welcomed by holistic educators as a major step toward the fuller development of each student's free, responsible choice. Holistic educators believe that one cannot make free, responsible choices without basic skills and knowledge, yet they do not usually teach these skills and knowledge apart from active, open-ended student inquiry. Holistic educators further maintain that through this process of open-ended inquiry, basic skills and knowledge are developed.

However, many teachers believe that these basic skills and knowledge ought to be taught in isolation (partly because the curriculum "says" these basic skills and knowledge "must be taught"). Often without wondering or questioning the wisdom of teaching basic skills and knowledge in isolation, these teachers prevent open student inquiry because "the material must be covered" or because "that's the way things are."

The holistic educator has long held that "things are that way" largely because man has made them that way. Furthermore, the holistic educator believes that what man has made, man can change; therefore, more things, processes, and events can be what man wants them to be.

Another characteristic of the holistic notion of "most enabling environment" is that of personal responsibility for what one is and for what one becomes. The holistic educator holds that the teaching-learning relationship with regular and "special" students is partially paradoxical in that the primary emphasis is on the teacher's intervening (directing, guiding, coaxing) so that the students will need less outside intervention, or so that the students will have these interventions primarily when they choose them. The holistic teacher directs in order to enable the student to become more self-directing. Built into this holistic view of teaching is the notion that the teacher helps provide conditions whereby the student relies less and less on outside authority and, instead, more and more on his authority.

Some people say "I do not want to be my own authority." This is acceptable if they are aware of what they are doing, if they choose to do it, and if they are responsible for the consequences. They are then choosing consciously to have somebody else choose for them. This aware, free, responsible choice makes them their own authority regardless of what they say.

Assumptions Underlying Holistic Teaching

Holistic teachers base their decisions and actions upon the following assumptions:

1. Above all else, a holistic classroom is a learning environment where education is viewed as a life-long process in which the learner is guided to his outer limits. In this way, creative, free, responsible choice is maximized to enhance the learner's ability and desire to invent his present and future.
2. Learning is viewed as a process in which the primary emphasis is on learning how to learn, and the secondary emphasis is on acquiring a body of "correct" information.
3. The priority in this learning environment is on the learner's self-image, which is enhanced through fusing intellect and feeling. One's self-image generates most of the achievement.
4. Because the learning process has not yet been fully conceptualized (and may, indeed, be incapable of total conceptualization), this learning environment is a relatively flexible structure. Inherent in this belief is the notion that there are many ways to teach.
5. The learner's inner experience is viewed as a context for learning that is coordinated with the external world as a context for learning.
6. This learning environment promotes whole-brain education in which right-brain nonlinear, intuitive, holistic strategies augment left-brain linear, anlaytical rationality. The learner is viewed as transrational.
7. This learning environment stresses that the human relationships between teachers and learners are of primary importance and technology is seen as a tool to be used by man for the humanization man.
8. This learning environment views the learner as an open system who continuously reconstructs his experience so that he can better invent his present and his future. Inherent in this is the belief that prior to a major reconstructing of experience, a feeling of discontinuity emerges. This discontinuity may be viewed as a productive stress whose intensity ranges from wonder, puzzlement, uneasiness, excitement, creative tension, and confusion, to, at times, anxiety. This learning environment is safe enough to explore, and it encourages exploratory (experimental) effort within the framework of safe emergencies that teachers can help provide. It is assumed that dealing with disequilibrium can foster greater equilibrium.
9. Teaching in this responsive learning environment is primarily an activity that fosters openness to strange new possibilities in which the teacher is a midwife of ideas and a facilitator of learner left-brain/right-brain integration. The teacher believes not only that the learner "causes" the learning, but also that learning can be assisted by providing appropriate conditions.
10. A part of this responsive learning environment is a desire to increase degrees of trust in teacher/learner relations.
11. This responsive learning environment encourages each learner's uniqueness to be developed and cherished.
12. Teachers as well as learners need to deal with ambiguity, puzzlement, conflict, and paradox if noticeable reconstructing (transformation) of experience is to occur. Awareness is a major key in this transforming process. Awareness allows greater access to unconscious anxieties that may stand in the way of this process of reconstructing experience.

As they see more and broad patterns, teachers develop a commo (whole) sense which they can also hel develop within their students (if such i their primary goal). This sense relate to knowledge and skills that they nee to accommodate various handicappe students. Common sense, as the term is being used here, is that which help teachers generate "on the spot" th various skills and knowledge that the need when faced with uniqu situations. Common sense generate inventive resourcefulness. The holisti educator has always believed that no only is each student unique, but so i each day, hour, or minute. Th individualizing of instruction consequently, has been, and continue to be, prized by holistic educators.

Conclusions

Holistic teachers have long been voluntarily doing what is now legally required in the relatively new mainstreaming law (P. L. 94-142) which aims at providing the least restrictive environment for handicapped students. Holistic teachers view their primary function as that of making the classroom the most enabling environment for all students.

Mainstreaming: Is It Secondary At the Secondary Level?

Ellen Williams
Isabel Hansen
Barbara Jackson

Ellen Williams is Assistant Professor in the Department of Special Education at Bowling Green State University.

Isabel Hansen is Assistant to the Director of the Dean's Grant Project at Bowling Green.

Barbara Jackson is a Graduate Assistant assigned to the Dean's Project at Bowling Green.

Preparing secondary teachers to work effectively with handicapped students requires that regular teacher education faculty make a behavioral commitment to incorporating mainstreaming instruction within the pre-service curriculum. Such commitment can be brought about through involvement of faculty in in-service programs which combine knowledge expansion, direct contact with handicapped students, and self-assessment.

It has been postulated that teacher attitude is the critical variable in the successful integration of handicapped students into the regular classroom.[1] If we are intent on providing successful mainstreaming programs for handicapped students, we must address both at the pre-service and in-service levels the issue of teacher attitude toward the handicapped student. Effective mainstreaming competencies cannot be developed at the pre-service level merely through lip service concerning the acceptance of the handicapped. If educators want to promote a positive attitude toward the handicapped among the pre-service population, they must first embrace and demonstrate an attitude of acceptance toward the handicapped.

Avenues have been provided to help faculty examine their own attitudes and promote instructional and curricular change related to mainstreaming through Dean's Grant Projects. Bowling Green State University was awarded a Dean's Grant in 1980 and again in 1981. Its major thrust has been to effect curricular change within the secondary education program by providing in-service education on mainstreaming for those faculty responsible for teaching secondary methods and foundations classes. During its first year of implementation, some of the strategies the Dean's Grant employed for changing attitudes were: 1) knowledge-based experiences, 2) simulation activities, 3) enforced contact, and 4) self-evaluation assessments.

Expanding Faculty Knowledge

As part of the knowledge-based experiences, consultants, resource people, resource information, and bibliographic references were provided throughout the year. The in-service format included lecture, informal discussion and suggested readings of bibliographic material. The education program utilized these sources to explore various aspects of the following: 1) P.L. 94-142, 2) individualized education plans, 3) types of handicapping conditions, 4) mainstreaming the special needs student, 5) accommodating exceptional students in the regular classroom, and 6) support services available to the regular educator.

In addition, faculty were required to participate in such tasks as simulations, panel discussions, examination of course objectives, and field visitations. Following one meeting, for instance, which focused on individual differences and similarities between non-handicapped and handicapped populations, written reactions of the participants were reviewed. Participants' comments reflected uncertainty and frustration:

> My reaction to this session is mixed. I feel that we rehashed philosophical problems that have emerged each time we've met. For that reason, we strayed from the topic at hand. If someone were to ask about characteristics, needs, and behaviors of a mainstreamed student, I'd be hard-pressed to speak in anything but generalities and platitudes. 'Meeting needs' appears to be a dead horse. Let's stop beating it and wrestle with some specifics.

Although the intent of the guest speaker at this meeting was to promote the idea that all too often we look at the handicapped populations in terms of differences, and fail to see the similarities of the handicapped population with the normal population, a number of the participants left the in-service feeling as if there were *no* differences between the handicapped and non-handicapped populations. This reaction and similar comments may reflect the uncertainty and lack of understanding that often precede positive attitudinal change.[2]

When these reactions surface, Hiltenbrand suggests employing a different paradigm for attitudinal change: simulation. Simulation requires the target group members to act out the roles and real-life situations of a dissimilar population. Thus, the target group is applying a practical application of knowledge and developing empathy toward the attitudinal object. Dean's Grant members participated in two types of in-house simulations. In the first simulation professors assumed the role of the regular classroom teacher as they read a case study describing their newly mainstreamed student. The information given to the participants included a brief case study, the student's individualized education plan, and his class schedule. Participants divided into small groups to discuss possible strategies for 1) gaining an understanding of the I.E.P. and its application to the classroom, 2) dealing with the students' behavioral problems (i.e., talking out, tardiness, authority problems), and 3) accommodating for his learning disability (i.e., visual memory problems affecting his reading level).

Participants' reactions to this session were consistently positive, although various viewpoints emerged. One participant noted:

> The session today was stimulating. I enjoyed the interaction with my small group and having to focus on a real problem that could confront any of our students when they get their first teaching job. This was the first time I have ever seen an I.E.P., and found that in itself invaluable. My reaction to the mainstreamed student was that he appeared on paper to be very similar to the average ninth grade student I encounter in urban schools. The session was well designed.

Whereas another member stated:

> Although it was a great experience and some reality contact, teachers are not prepared to deal with a behavioral problem because they are not trained in therapy techniques and group dynamics. I have long advocated an experiential growth-group type experience be required for all teachers. This would pay off for their work with the average student *and* the special student.

The second simulation activity occurred at an established field base site, a local area high school. This simulation differed from the first in that the Dean's Grant faculty participants did not simulate the actual roles, but were asked instead to observe the case staffing as it was role-played by the actual faculty in the secondary school field site. The purpose of the simulation was to provide university faculty with insight into mainstreaming case staffings. The university faculty were given the opportunity to ask questions, comment on decisions, and provide additional comments which they felt were relevant to the mainstreaming case staffing. Most of the participants described the experience as a new, exciting presentation; however, a few had been actual participants in previous staffings and felt that they had gained little additional information on specific strategies for mainstreaming a learning-disabled student. One member exhibited skepticism as a result of this simulation, and commented:

> I found the conference interesting but wondered how often this actually occurs. The regular teacher appeared to be involved only when discussing the student's placement in his class. Shouldn't there be communication among the total professional staff prior to the I.E.P. conference? How is the determination made concerning the child's probability of success in the regular classroom?

Thus it would appear that the simulation activities acted as a catalyst in the attitudinal change process. Although the uneasiness and uncertainty which occurred were not totally removed through the use of simulation, participants did become more cognizant of the "realities" involved in the mainstreaming process. In spite of this, it is unwise to conclude that simulation activities in and of themselves were responsible for helping participants make a more positive transition in the attitude change process, for while they were involved in simulation activities, they were also involved with enforced contact experiences.

Direct Contact Experiences

Enforced contact unites the target person with outgroup members under conditions thought to be conducive to attitude change. Two activities involving enforced contact were provided for the Dean's Grant participants. The first activity was a panel discussion comprised of junior high and secondary educators from a nearby school district. In this experience, the panel members were asked to share with the university faculty their roles and perceptions of the mainstreaming program in their school. During the presentation, the panel pointed out that one of the major criteria for a successful mainstreaming program was the importance of open and consistent communication between special education faculty and regular education faculty. The practical suggestions from these teachers were supported by research studies that view support systems as essential to successful mainstreaming:

> The role of the special teacher should be expanded to become one of resource person: one who is capable of working with other teachers, making recommendations, prescribing materials to be used, and serving as a specialist in the content areas as well as dealing with the general problems of the special student. There is a corollary to this recommendation: that it is necessary that the regular teacher be trained to accept advice and assistance from another person who may be of similar rank in the organization.[3]

This recommendation was supported by the faculty participants following the enforced contact experience between themselves and the secondary panel.

Although the faculty participants felt that they had benefited from contact with secondary school personnel involved in mainstreaming, members expressed a need for direct experiences with the mainstreamed pupil.

Structured field experiences were designed to provide contact between the faculty participants and the mainstreamed students. Each university faculty member was assigned a specific mainstreamed student at the field-based site. The students' handicapping conditions included hearing-impaired, learning-disabled, physically-handicapped, educable-mentally retarded, and behavior-disordered. Prior to meeting with the assigned student, each participant reviewed his student's I.E.P. and interviewed the special and regular teachers involved in educating the student. After establishing a rapport with the mainstreamed pupil through a personal interview, the faculty member arranged to observe the student in his regular and special classes. Each university participant was asked to maintain a log which included a record of actual experiences and evaluative comments related to this field-based observation.

Insights gained as a result of this experience were shared among grant participants at a subsequent in-service. Following the in-service, one participant commented:

> This session was valuable in that each participant had the opportunity to meet a special student firsthand, and to hear what effects the mainstreaming situation had on the student. It was interesting to note that some students were not accommodated or particularly welcomed in some of their mainstreamed classes due to the negative attitude of the teacher...All my colleagues appeared to be enthusiastic about their field visits, indicating that their understanding of special kids in a regular setting had increased considerably.

A second participant reported:

> It is apparent that there is severe human cost when students are misplaced, when teachers who mainstream are indifferent to their students, or when needed resources for support are absent, unknown, or neglected. It's also important to note that there are inspired and dedicated teachers who are doing all they can for their students.

These evaluation comments reinforce the concept that the teacher's attitude toward the handicapped student is critical to the success of a mainstreaming program.[4] The majority of participants indicated that the enforced contact experience promoted a greater understanding of problems facing mainstreamed students.

Assessing Attitudes

Even though the participants' evaluative comments given at the end of each seminar or activity do not provide empirical evidence to show a change in the attitude toward the handicapped, they do, however, tend to support the literature which suggests that effective attitudinal change programs should include direct contact experiences, cognitive information, and experiential activities.[5] Attempts were made, nonetheless, to gather empirical data for determining attitude change among the participants. The Mandell Opinionaire (1976), which measures attitudes toward mainstreaming the mildly handicapped, was administered on a pre-level at the first in-service session, and the post-level at the last in-service session. Using a five-point Likert scale ranging from "strongly agree to strongly disagree," participants were asked to respond to twenty items related to their attitudes towards mainstreaming of the mildly handicapped. Results of the survey were inconclusive, as only 85% of the participants were involved in both pre- and post-tests.

Pre-test results reflected a realistic and positive attitude toward mainstreaming the handicapped student into the regular classroom. The results of the post-test showed no significant change in attitude, but rather a maintenance of that previously held positive attitude. While positive attitudes are critical to effective mainstreaming, it is even more essential that they be translated into behavioral commitment. As noted in a study by Noar and Milgrim on pre-service strategies for regular class teachers for mainstreaming, "Willingness to work with exceptional children is probably a more valid indication of positive attitude change than mere verbal endorsements of positive statements about them."[6] On a comparative note, teacher educators who verbally adopt a receptive attitude toward mainstreaming must also make a commitment to a behavioral intention.

Translating Attitudes in Action

The faculty participants in the Dean's Grant were asked to make such a commitment by selecting and incorporating mainstreaming competencies in their courses for pre-service secondary teachers. Each participant then developed a list of mainstreaming competencies and activities to be implemented in their pre-service teacher training course for the fall of 1981. Thus, faculty participants are attempting to move beyond a positive attitude and into the realm of commitment to behavioral intention. The purpose of the Dean's Grant during its second year of implementation is to provide continued support to the faculty participants as they integrate the mainstreaming competencies into their secondary education teacher program. If the Dean's Grant has been effective, then perhaps the title of the next article will not be entitled "Mainstreaming: Is It Secondary at the Secondary Level?" but rather "Mainstreaming: It Isn't Secondary at the Secondary Level."

Notes

1. D. Mitchel, "Teacher Attitudes Toward Handicapped Children and Regular Class Integration," *Journal of Special Education,* X (1976), 393-400.
2. D. Hiltenbrand, "Detours Towards Dead Ends," *Vocational Education,* LVI (1981), 41-43.
3. V. DuBasik and F.C. Fietler, "Attitudes of Regular Classroom Teachers Toward EMR Students," U.S., Educational Resources Information Center, ERIC Document ED 155 857, 1978.
4. A. Hiroshoren and T. Burton, "Willingness of Regular Teachers to Participate in Mainstreaming Handicapped Children," *Journal of Research and Development in Education,* XII (1979), 93-100.
5. H. Lombana, "Fostering Positive Attitudes Toward Handicapped Students: A Guidance Challenge," *School Counselor,* XXVII (1980), 176-182.
6. M. Noar and R.M. Milgram, "Two Preservice Strategies for Preparing Regular Class Teachers to Mainstream," *Exceptional Children,* XLVII (1980), 126-128.

A Comparison of Soviet and American Approaches to Special Education

Janice T. Gibson

JANICE T. GIBSON is a professor of educational psychology at the University of Pittsburgh. Over the past decade she has spent 12 months in the USSR studying day care and education. In 1977 she was appointed National Academy of Sciences Research Exchange Scholar at the Institute of General and Pedagogical Psychology in Moscow. In 1978, as a member of a delegation from the Council for International Exchange of Scholars to the Soviet Ministry of Education, she interviewed directors responsible for research on education of the handicapped.

Soviet and American views of education and special education differ considerably. The following conversation, recorded in a Moscow school by a member of a visiting delegation of American teachers, points clearly to differences of opinion:

American teacher (politely): The program you just showed us is very impressive. But the work looks so hard! It must be impossible for *all* the students to do it. What do you do with your "slow learners"?

Soviet teacher (puzzled): What is a "slow learner"?

American teacher: There are always a few children who can't keep up with the rest. We call them slow learners.

Soviet teacher: Oh? (Pause) In the Soviet Union, you see, we have no slow learners. Our programs are designed for *all* children to learn.

The American teacher stopped at this point, assuming that the Soviet teacher was spouting "party rhetoric." In fact, there are studies showing that the Soviet Union has approximately the same percentage of mentally handicapped and slow learners as America.[1] The Soviet teacher was not simply reporting the party line, however. Like the foreign tourists, business executives, and scholars who visit the USSR and even live there for extended periods of time, she probably never saw a handicapped child of any kind — on the streets or in school. The reason lies in the Soviet educational system and in the methods by which special children are screened and educated.

In regular Soviet schools it has always been the responsibility of the teacher to assist *all* children to learn. If some children are not learning, it is considered the teacher's, not the student's, problem. The Soviet teacher who was interviewed might not have been telling the entire truth — because admitting that some children don't learn some of the material might reveal a bad job of teaching.

Soviet teachers do, in fact, give very special care to children who have trouble with their lessons. Although schools operate officially six days per week from 8:30 a.m. till 12:30 or 2:30 p.m. (depending on the age of the children), teachers are expected to remain after school for the next several hours to give assistance where needed. They are aided at this task by other children — those who have no trouble with their lessons. It is considered the duty of Soviet children to help their peers. The task of helping society in general as well as other students in the group is one prerequisite for entrance later into Komsomol, the youth Communist league, and, finally, the Communist Party.

The identification of special children in the Soviet Union usually takes place well before it does for their American counterparts. The extensive *yasli* (nursery) and *detskii sad* (kindergarten) programs accept children on an all-day basis as young as three months of age and keep them through age 6. This long preschool period provides the opportunity for caretakers and specialists to screen these children long before first grade at age 7. Pediatricians in the programs identify physically handicapped children. In many cases such children are placed immediately in special preschools for the physically handicapped. Other specialists identify mentally retarded, emotionally disturbed, or learning disabled children, often before they enter first grade.

Children who have trouble learning the fundamentals of reading and writing are usually identified in the USSR before age 7; *detskii sad* programs begin these subjects at ages 5 and 6. This makes it possible for specialists to detect learning difficulties before regular school. Once special children have been identified during the preschool years, the Soviet government provides what it calls "differentiated care," so that these children almost never attend regular primary grades. They attend special schools. It is possible that the Soviet teacher who didn't know what a slow learner is had never had a mentally handicapped child in her classroom. Furthermore, she may not even have had any idea of what kind of education special children receive in their special schools. Even teacher training and program development for these schools are done under separate auspices.

The Soviet Union has been committed since 1919 to a direction quite opposite from that of the U.S. with respect to special children, especially since 1975, when Public Law 94-142 was passed. Rather than mainstream handicapped children together with their normal counterparts, the Soviets have developed an elaborate and specialized system of schools. In most cases, with the exception of some few schools in very large cities, they have used boarding schools for this purpose.

The Soviet System

In order to compare the Soviet system of educating special children with our own in any useful way, we must understand the political-ideological system that gave rise to Soviet beliefs about how all children, including the handicapped, learn. We must also examine ways that Soviets identify children who have special needs. Finally, we need to examine the effects of the programs on the children themselves.

Marxism and its effects on special education. Marxist dialectical philosophy suggests that higher-order mental processes develop through direct interaction with the environment. Soviet researchers, unlike their American counterparts, are not interested in *proving* the role that the social environment plays in learning. Instead, they begin with unquestioned acceptance of this role. Soviet research therefore involves demonstration of *how* the social environment affects learning and what manipulation of the environment produces maximal desired learning.

The work of two famous Soviet psy-

"A Comparison of Soviet and American Approaches to Special Education," Janice T. Gibson, *Phi Delta Kappan*, December 1980. Reprinted by permission.

chologists, A. S. Luria and L. S. Vygotsky, demonstrates this point. Luria's studies are designed to show how schooling affects the abilities to think and solve problems.[2] Vygotsky's research concludes that both language and thinking are social in origin, and, further, that complex thought processes develop early in childhood through manipulation of real objects and through direct interaction with adults.[3] These basic points are used today by Soviet educators. Schooling for all students, including special students, is much more important in Soviet society than in our own. According to the Marxist approach, children who seem to learn more slowly in regular settings require different manipulation of the environment and different interaction with adults. In 1919, in a decree signed by Lenin, the Council of People's Commissars first recognized officially the need for these very specialized environments for handicapped children. The council decided then to care for and educate the blind, deaf, and physically handicapped, and the children with nervous and mental disorders, differently and separately. In recent years research on programs for these children has been consolidated under the auspices of the Institute of Defectology of the Academy of Pedagogical Science. The direction of the schools has been consolidated under one ministry.

Identifying "special needs." Physically handicapped children in the Soviet Union are usually screened first by caretakers at the state-run *yaslis* and *detskii sads*, who send them to pediatricians for examination. When pediatricians think that special help is necessary, they send the children to *yaslis* or *detskii sads* with specialized programs. In the USSR, children whose handicaps are not so severe as to be noticeably crippling usually are picked up earlier for special help than they are in the U.S. (This is because our special screening is normally done privately with preschoolers, and therefore is more frequent among the middle and upper classes.) All Soviet children, by the time they reach age 6, are required to have complete physical examinations. Physically handicapped children who have not been previously screened out by *yaslis* or *detskii sads* are referred to special schools at this time.

Children with mental handicaps that result in learning difficulty are often screened out during the preschool years also. Children at *detskii sad* levels begin to learn the rudiments of reading and writing. By the last year of *detskii sad* (designated the year of preparation for the first grade), caretakers often request that children who exhibit learning problems be given special evaluation.

Methods used to select children with mental handicaps in the USSR differ considerably from those in the U.S. V. I. Lubovskii, head of the Laboratory of Higher Nervous Activity and Psychology of Abnormal Children at Moscow's Institute of Defectology, points out that intelligence, or the ability to think logically and to solve problems, is not a single entity. Thus it cannot be measured quantitatively by a single score such as an IQ.[4] Testing, according to Lubovskii, should not consist of one single administration. It should take place in real-life situations where children are likely to be learning rather than in the artificial, laboratory-like situations in which, Lubovskii points out, American IQ tests are usually administered. Tests designed in Lubovskii's laboratories do not measure the level of functioning until a child makes a mistake. Instead, they measure how much additional information needs to be provided before the child can solve a problem.

Lubovskii and his colleagues are currently comparing their clinical diagnostic procedures with scores obtained on measures similar, they say, to the Wechsler Scales of Intelligence. They report that their multiple diagnostic procedures provide much more useful information, particularly in predicting children's abilities to respond in day-to-day, real-life interactions.

In America we have heard many of the same complaints that Lubovskii and other Soviet researchers are voicing about IQ testing as a method of screening children according to ability. One of the primary reasons that P.L. 94-142 was passed in the U.S. was that parents complained that their children were being classified as handicapped on the basis of "grossly inadequate methods of testing."[5] Parents of minority children, in particular, filed legal suit against the schools because of their belief that their children were being labeled unfairly by culturally biased tests.

The Soviet system of employing "multifaceted clinical assessments" allows many personnel, including teachers, physicians, neuropsychologists, and whatever other experts might be needed, to pool their efforts and to arrive at a consensual diagnosis. Interestingly, the assessment requires much the same information that many American educators feel should be required to develop the individualized educational plans (IEPs) mandated by P.L. 94-142.

Once the recommendation has been made that a child be considered for evaluation, the Soviets collect very specific data. First, they obtain medical and psychological histories from the *yasli* records. They also require complete physical examinations. If specialists believe that a child has a mental or physical handicap, they may give neurological examinations; tests of sensory acuity; electrophysiological evaluations (these include electroencephalographic and rheoencephalographic tests); tests of what the Soviets term "higher nervous activity" (ability to respond in different ways to Pavlovian conditioning); psychological tests involving memory, perception, and cognitive skills; and, finally, extended observation of classroom learning.

What Soviet researchers term "temporarily retarded in psychological development" (TRPD) is a classification very similar to that of "learning disabled" in America. Soviet differential diagnosis of TRPD children frequently shows them to have prenatal medical histories that include mothers who were toxemic during pregnancy; there are no particular measurable neurological symptoms present. Electroencephalographic and rheoencephalographic recordings show electrical recordings from the brain and blood circulation to the brain that differ somewhat from normal children. Tests of higher nervous activity and tests of memory, perception, and cognitive skills show that TRPD children tend to be impulsive and make mistakes but, and this is important, they can profit by instruction. Psycho-educational assessment is used to determine to what extent these children can profit by instruction and what types of instruction are most helpful. A number of tasks are given to determine how effective specialized instruction is and to determine what Soviet researchers call the "zone of potential development." Soviet psychologists suggest that, for TRPD children, unlike mentally retarded children, further cognitive development is possible. The main problem is learning how to organize materials in meaningful ways. The best way for the teacher to help TRPD children, therefore, is to help them internalize appropriate organizational cues, and teach them gradually to do this by themselves.

Programming for "special needs." The goals of the special Soviet schools match those of their regular schools in many respects. The methods of instruction, however, differ considerably, as does the time it takes to meet these goals. As just one example, the program of instruction for the blind or visually handicapped is designed to take 12 years rather than the usual 10.

Using TRPD children as an example of cases in which differentiated care and programming are provided, the following basic components have been designed at the Institute of Defectology:[6]

1. *Integration of instruction with systematic observation.* Teachers have extensive and current daily information describing each child. Their observations include both general debilities and task-specific problems encountered in completing mastery of each skill.

2. *Design of materials and methods based on task analysis.* Soviets agree with American instructional psychologists that the best instruction is composed of tasks divided into logical and small steps, keeping in mind the total task at all times. They believe this to be especially important for TRPD students. Children also need to be taught self-control and specific methods to organize subject matter.

3. *Individualization of instruction.* This is particularly important to the Soviets, because TRPD children's levels of ability are likely to vary more than normal children's.

4. *General transition to independent performance.* TRPD children differ from retarded in that they can learn if the teacher provides the methods. TRPD children then need to be weaned from this type of learning situation to another in which they eventually learn to think independently.

5. *Coordination of theory and practice.* Interestingly, these components all are part of American special education and are today considered useful components of IEPs for many learning-disabled children here. No discussion of special education in the Soviet Union is complete, however, without a description of one last aspect of its special schools. Special education in the USSR is segregated education. It is segregated by design, beginning with the initial 1919 decree establishing special programs and schools. Today, some of the special programs meet goals similar to those of the regular schools, using different methods and different time periods. Children in the special schools for visually or hearing-impaired children, for example, may complete the regular 10-year program in 12 years. Other special schools have different goals. Children in some of the special schools for the retarded, for example, complete elementary and vocational training in eight years. Emphasis here is on development of working skills.

Comparing Methods

Researchers at the Institute of Defectology point out a number of advantages that their special system of schools has for the handicapped student and for the development of truly differentiated learning. First, they say, special schools have lower pupil/teacher ratios than regular schools. They have larger staffs, with counselors and physicians on the premises. They have close physician/teacher relationships. The fact that most of these schools are boarding schools provides an additional benefit: Student learning can be monitored for many more hours per day. Teachers on special school staffs may be better; Soviet publications report that they receive 25% higher pay.[7]

American educators tend to react negatively to the concept of special segregated schools, regardless of the similarity or quality of programming. To Americans committed to mainstreaming, Soviet segregation of handicapped children is of the worst sort: Handicapped children are segregated not only from children with no handicaps but from their families and also from children with handicaps different from their own. How can these children learn how to live in the normal world with other people if they are not exposed to it?

The Soviets respond to this question with some of their own: How can American teachers provide adequate differentiated care for children with different handicaps unless they *all* receive special training and learn to use the special teaching techniques that work most effectively with these children? How is there time for the regular teacher in the regular American classroom to do all of that and still keep up with new research and new methods? These are the same questions that American teachers are asking.

Soviet and American special educators and education programs differ in another significant respect. That is in the ease with which people can answer the very important question, Do the programs work? With some children? With most children? With all children? The Soviet special schools are sufficiently out of sight that it is difficult to measure just what is going on within their walls. The Soviet teacher who asked what a "slow learner" is probably doesn't know how much the TRPD child is learning in the special school nor even, probably, where the special school is. Theory and research, as outlined by the researchers of the Institute of Defectology, do not necessarily dictate the behavior of teachers in special schools, any more than research in graduate schools of education in the U.S. dictates policy within our public schools.

If the Soviet schools are effective in helping handicapped children, they must help these students return to the regular classroom. Lubovskii was somewhat vague in his answer to the question of how this is accomplished. He suggested that additional extensive screening takes place on the advice of teachers. With so little seen of handicapped children, it is unclear just what this means. One possibility is that they are "stuck" in the system.

In the U.S., unlike the USSR, special children are being placed in the forefront of the news and are being taken "out of the closet." Newspapers, magazines, and television make daily issue of our problems, both for our regular and special students. We have few, if any, hidden schools; our dirty linen (if it *is* dirty) hangs in full view for everyone to see. In our new mainstreamed classes, if teachers are not being provided sufficient assistance to deal adequately with their new jobs; if the pains we now are feeling are not, as some suggest, just growing pains; if students are not learning; we shall all soon know. There is no way now to hide mistakes. They will appear in nationally circulated journals. They will be aired on "60 Minutes." They will come in the reports of schoolchildren to their parents. From our mistakes we can develop better programs. This may be, after all, the primary advantage and result of Public Law 94-142.

---

1. Robert Wozniak reports, in "Psychology and Education of the Learning-Disabled Child in the USSR" [in William M. Cruikshank and Donald P. Hallihan, eds., *Research and Theory in Minimal Cerebral Dysfunction and Learning Disability* (Syracuse, N.Y.: Syracuse University Press, 1975), p. 22], that 10% to 11% of school-age children experience difficulties in academic activities. Of these, the mentally retarded account for 3.5%, while the remaining 7% can be grouped as TRPD (temporarily retarded in psychological development), a category closely resembling that of "learning disabled" in the U.S. In contrast, Bill R. Gearhart and Harold Weishahn, in *The Handicapped Child in the Regular Classroom* (St. Louis: Mosby, 1976), report that approximately 5% to 7% of American children fall into these categories, with between 2.5% and 3% mentally retarded (excluding a tiny percentage of severely mentally retarded), and with between 2% and 4% having learning disabilities.

2. A good example of Luria's thoughts on this issue appears in his article, "A Child's Speech Responses and the Social Environment," published in English in *Soviet Psychology*, Fall 1974, pp. 7-39.

3. See Lev S. Vygotsky, *Thought and Language*, trans. by Eugenia Hanfmann and George Vaker (Cambridge, Mass.: MIT Press, 1962).

4. Information obtained from Lubovskii came from a personal interview conducted at the Institute of Defectology in Moscow in September 1978.

5. See, for example, Bill R. Gearhart and Harold Weishahn's descriptions of *Diana* v. *State of California*, pp. 13 and 14 of their book, *The Handicapped Child in the Regular Classroom*, op. cit.

6. Wozniak, op. cit., pp. 106-12.

7. This statistic is reported in the pamphlet, "Education in the USSR" (Moscow: Progress Publishers, 1972), p. 68.

Our Investment in Public Education

CHRISTOPHER JOHNSON

Mr. Johnson is a free-lance writer and former high school English teacher.

The spectacular launch of *Sputnik* in 1957 brought U.S. public education to its greatest crisis since World War II. From the public came a great outcry: How could we have let the Soviets beat the United States into space? What is wrong? In what ways have we failed?

Within two years, the U. S. Congress had responded, with the National Defense Education Act. For the public schools, the result was beefed up curriculums, expanded facilities, more rigorous teacher training, new science equipment. For the nation, the result was the incredible surge of scientific and technological progress in the 1960's that culminated with the 1969 moon-landing.

In many ways, schools today are facing a crisis as great as that of the 1950's. The mass media claim that kids aren't achieving, that fewer and fewer graduates can spell correctly or write intelligibly, that educators aren't holding students to high enough standards. Again, the public is clamoring for better education.

This time around, however, nobody is pouring the resources for effective response into the public schools. Instead of "Let's make the public education system better," many are saying, "Let's abandon the system altogether."

Under attack is not only the job the public schools are doing, but the very idea that they can do the job. Behind this erosion of confidence is the feeling, which many people share, that schools are not cost-effective—that they do not bring a return comparable to the amount of money society spends to support them.

Beyond a doubt, the expenditures on public schools in this country are enormous. The cost of elementary and secondary public education has risen from $15.9 billion in 1960 to $100.2 billion in 1980, and the average expenditure per pupil is $2,400. Each year, we pay about $450 per person (or $749 per taxpayer) to support schools. All told, education consumes 7 percent of our Gross National Product.

Does society reap benefits that justify the expenditure of so many billions of dollars? The question is a difficult one because the service that public education provides is abstract. The "products" are people, and economists from the time of Adam Smith have debated the market value of people. Another problem in determining cost-effectiveness is that the investment we make in the schooling of a child does not start returning benefits to society for 10 or even 20 years after we begin investing.

Figuring cost-effectiveness becomes easier, however, if we break the problem into two questions:

- What economic and social benefits can be traced to public education?
- What are the economic and social costs of *not* providing quality public education?

Few would deny that education provides individuals with substantial economic benefits. It was not until the 1960's, however, that economists started looking at the economic benefits that entire societies derive from education. Since then, researchers have found a correlation between the percentage of a country's young people who are enrolled in school and the rate of that country's economic growth.

How does education translate into economic growth for a society? One way is by creating a literate citizenry. A researcher who has measured the economic value of literacy is John R. Bormuth, an associate professor of education at the University of Chicago. Bormuth found that in 1972, a year in which the national income reached $941.8 billion, employees devoted almost one-third of every workday to reading and writing. Bormuth made the common-sense assumption that these activities must be productive; otherwise, cost-conscious employers would not demand that employees engage in them. He then concluded, after a study involving nine variables, that reading and writing accounted for 23.5 percent of our Gross National Product and for roughly 29 percent of our national income ($273 billion or—using Bormuth's 1976-adjusted figures—$347 billion). Literacy pays. And to the nation belongs the payoff.

Bormuth also calculated what it cost in 1972 to create and maintain literacy. To do so, he looked at two figures: the cost of producing and distributing literacy materials and the cost of teaching people how to read and write.

Bormuth calculated the first cost (again in 1976 dollars) at $31.4 billion. After figuring the percentage of instructional time spent on teaching reading and writing, he

"Our Investment in Public Education," Christopher R. Johnson, *Today's Education*, February/March 1982. Reprinted by permission.

concluded that instruction in these areas cost $28.2 billion, or $135 per person. Together, the costs of literacy instruction and materials—$59.6 billion ($285 per person)—was the total cost of making Americans literate.

The ratio of the benefit ($347 billion) to the cost ($59.6 billion) is 5.8 to 1. Every dollar invested in literacy produces about $6 in national income.

In addition to economic outcomes, however, education has positive social outcomes. For instance, there is growing evidence that the schools have helped change attitudes of ethnic and racial prejudice. In a study completed in conjunction with B'nai B'rith (*The Tenacity of Prejudice*, 1969), Gertrude Selznick and Stephen Steinberg found that the more years of school respondents had completed, the fewer attitudes of prejudice against Jews and Blacks they had.

The researchers distributed a questionnaire measuring anti-Semitic attitudes to respondents with a wide range of educational levels. More than half (52 percent) of the respondents with less than a grade school education gave responses that categorized them as anti-Semitic. The proportion of respondents who were anti-Semitic fell to 36 percent of high school graduates, 24 percent of those with some college, and 15 percent of college graduates.

Surveys weighing anti-Black attitudes yielded the same pattern of results. Among residents of the North, 58 percent of those with only grade school educations were judged anti-Black. The percentage fell to 41 percent of high school graduates, 25 percent of those with some college, and 16 percent of college graduates.

Perhaps the most dramatic results of the study, though, concerned knowledge and acceptance of democratic principles. Selznick and Steinberg reported that respondents were asked whether the U.S. government is permitted to outlaw disagreement with its policies. Forty-eight percent of those with only grade school educations recognized that the Constitution does not sanction federal suppression of such disagreement. Respondents with more education clearly had a greater grasp of the fundamentals of the Constitution: 67 percent of high school graduates and 87 percent of college graduates knew that the government could not legally engage in such acts of suppression.

Backed by their data, Selznick and Steinberg concluded that "the educational institutions are the primary means whereby the individual is integrated into the ideal norms and values that constitute and sustain a democratic and humane society."

This brings us to the second question: What are the social costs of *not* providing quality public education? We can readily examine these costs by studying the effects of dropping out of school, often a result of economic policies that burden schools in their attempts to meet student needs.

First of all, the correlation between dropping out and unemployment is clear. Figures from the Bureau of Labor Statistics show, for instance, that in 1979 unemployment among male dropouts was 8.3 percent, but it was only 5.5 percent among high school graduates and 1.8 percent among college graduates. Among women, the unemployment rate was 4.4 percent higher for dropouts than it was for high school graduates. William Jones, director of the Dropout Prevention Center of the Chicago public schools, notes, "In my experience, dropouts are two or three times overrepresented among the unemployed. It is from this group that we reap many of our social and economic ills."

Dropouts are frozen out of jobs leading up the social and economic ladder. By not spending the money necessary to keep them in school and provide them with marketable skills, society ironically ends up paying more—in both the short run and the long run.

In the short term, we support the unemployable—many of whom are dropouts—with a wide range of social welfare programs. In 1979, 11 million people received direct cash assistance, primarily from the Aid to Families with Dependent Children (AFDC) program. The majority of the recipients are women with young children. As a result of inadequate education, these people have difficulty finding work, and even if they can find work, they cannot make salaries sufficient to allow them to pay the cost of quality day care. Thus, they have little choice but to accept AFDC assistance, which cost federal and state governments $11 billion in 1979. Another $27 billion was spent for in-kind assistance programs such as food stamps, Medicaid, and public housing.

Taken together, the cash assistance and in-kind programs provided an average poor family of four people with as much as $7,300 in assistance a year—more than $1,800 a person, but still very little to live on. Unlike educational costs, though, welfare expenditures do not develop human resources that contribute to the wealth and quality of our society. The expenses are necessary, but they do not develop skills.

Welfare costs are not the only ones incurred as a result of providing too few educational resources. John Gibson, principal of the Cook County Jail School in Chicago, says, "There is a direct correlation between the inability to read and trouble with the law. Ninety-five percent of the school population of this jail consists of dropouts. A sizable percentage are very low achievers, reading at the fifth grade level or below."

Statistics show that, nationwide, more than 60 percent of all jail inmates have fewer than 12 years of schooling and that prisoners have attended school for only a median of 10.2 years. A study of juvenile offenders by the Illinois Department of Corrections found that only 14 percent were reading at the high school level when they entered a correctional facility.

Incarceration costs money—much more money than school does. Valley View, a juvenile facility in Kane County, Illinois, spends $16,425 a year to house each offender. At Illinois' maximum security prison in Joliet, incarceration costs $28,835 a year for each inmate. This is more than 10 times what it costs to educate a child in public school for a year.

Unemployment compensation, welfare, and incarceration all are short-term costs that society incurs by not providing the resources adequate for educating *all* our young people. In the long run, the costs may be even greater. Bearing in mind that each dollar invested in literacy brings a return of $6 in national income, consider the impact of each dollar that is needed but not provided.

Can special programs give potential dropouts a better chance to become productive members of society? To that question Dr. Jones responds with an emphatic *yes*: "In Chicago's Dropout Prevention Center, most of our programs are work-study experiences. In studies we have found that the dropout rate of students in these programs is 2.5 times less than it is among Chicago's school population of the same characteristics. The students' attendance rates are twice as good, and they have one-third the behavior problems." Graduates from the programs have marketable skills and so find it easier to find long-term jobs than if they had dropped out.

We cannot expect any program to bring the dropout rate to zero. We cannot expect the school or any other institution by itself to cure all our social ills. Instead, we should measure the cost-effectiveness of our investment in public education by rephrasing our two basic questions:

- Have the schools played a role in creating the conditions of social and economic progress?
- When we do *not* invest adequately in education, do we pay greater social costs later on?

The answer to both is *yes*. In responding to what it considers a deterioration in the school system, however, the society has turned its back on the facts. As William Jones says, "The problem with our dropout prevention program in Chicago is that we are not able to make the kind of impact we'd like because the programs are not pervasive enough. We just can't reach all the students we need to with the funds that are available to us."

Thousands of educators around the country echo this plaint. As public schools face growing cuts in funding, American society may be on the verge of sacrificing the future because of its refusal to make the necessary investment now—an investment that pays.

Overplacement: RUSHING CHILDREN TO FAILURE

Barbara Johnson and Christopher Johnson

The authors are, respectively, a reading specialist and a former high school English teacher, Framingham, Mass.

JOHN is a first-grader with an IQ of 130 who reads everything he can get his hands on and has been doing so since before he started kindergarten. He knows all there is to know about super heroes like Superman and Spiderman, and he can tell you the batting average of every player in the starting lineup of the Chicago Cubs.

However, John's mother has to drag him kicking and screaming to school every morning. He plays by himself during recess, and during group activities he goes off to a corner of the room. Finally, a month after school has started, John's mother and teacher succeed in settling him into the pattern of school, but, even then, he is not interacting well with the other children.

Not coincidentally, John happens to have a November birthday, so that, while most of his classmates were six when they began first grade, he is only five. Potentially, he is a victim of an educational practice that produces innumerable failures in our schools every year—overplacement. When children are overplaced, they are confronted with work for which they are not yet ready or presented with social/emotional requirements that are beyond their maturity level. All too often, children who are overplaced fall behind academically, are unhappy with school, and never make up the lost ground.

Indications are that overplacement is a more widespread problem than most teachers or parents are aware of. According to Bruce Johnson, former principal of an elementary school in suburban Chicago, "Twenty-five per cent of the children in this school will fail to work up to their potential because of overplacement. And the mean IQ here is 10 points higher than the national mean." Earnest Imbach, a California educator, found that half to two-thirds of the children he studied were overplaced, and the Educational Testing Service surveyed first-grade teachers who reported that 60% of their children were not ready for the academic work of first grade. This sample included 7,000 children from across the country.

These findings are supported by studies concluding that children who are older when they start school demonstrate higher levels of academic achievement than do their younger classmates. These differences in achievement continue throughout elementary school. In a 1977 study of public school children conducted by B. Glen Davis, C. Scott Trimble, and Denny R. Vincent in Kentucky, children who started first grade at the age of six consistently scored higher on reading achievement tests than did those who started at the age of five. Achievement levels of older to younger classmates were compared in first grade, fourth grade, and eighth grade; at each level, the older students registered significantly higher scores. It is little wonder the authors concluded that "Educational leaders should question policies that allow five-year-olds to enter first grade with no specific indication of readiness." Their conclusion is supported by similar research studies conducted in Oak Ridge, Tenn.; Kansas City, Mo.; Austin, Tex; Bloomington, Ind; and other elementary school districts.

The problems caused by overplacement are reflected not only in academic achievement. Fatigue, the inability to complete assignments, daydreaming in class, babyish behavior, aggressiveness toward or withdrawal from peers, complaints about physical ailments, protests about the difficulty of school assignments—all may indicate that a child is in over his head. More than likely, many students whom teachers term "lazy" have often just given up in the face of demands that are too great for their maturity levels.

Teachers are all too familiar with these signs of overplacement, and anyone who has spent time in a classroom is guilty of saying, "Kids always try to get away with doing the least amount of work possible. They've been acting that way for years." If, indeed, children have been acting this way for years, then perhaps the problem of overplacement has been with us for longer than anyone cares to admit. In fact, a survey of schools in 1933 revealed that non-promotion from first to second grade ran as high as 30% or 40% in many communities. Back then, teachers may have been dealing with numerous children who were not dumb or lazy, but who were physically and emotionally unready for the requirements of an academic environment. Since then, schools have eliminated retention except in the most extreme cases, but schools have not eliminated failure.

Compounding the problem

In fact, the educational system has compounded the problem of overplacement by treating all children of the same age as if they have the same maturity level and the same academic readiness skills. Assigning one chronological age for school entrance is the easiest way to get students started in school, but it is also the least accurate way of assuring their successful progress through school. As one first-grade teacher in Glenview, Ill., stated, using chronological age to determine school entrance "is about as fair as a lottery."

Furthermore, a study of kindergarteners in Connecticut found that only one-third of the students were judged to be completely prepared to do the work required, and one-fifth were totally unprepared. Yet, in spite of such studies, we continue to allow children to enter school with no serious consideration of their ability to cope with the structure of the classroom.

Even worse, we continue to assume that children who fall behind in first and second grade will catch up later on in school. However, as Bruce Johnson notes, "The myth of catching up is just that—a myth." Once children are in over their heads, they usually will continue foundering throughout school. They may be promoted for social reasons, but, unfortunately, their peers will keep on growing and developing, and the child who is a little behind in second grade may well be far behind in eighth.

If chronological age is a poor predictor of school success and if it is so hard for many children to catch up once they fall behind, on what other basis can we decide when children are prepared for school? Some school districts have attempted to individualize the school entrance process by giving IQ tests to determine whether particular children have the intellectual potential to benefit from early schooling. The mistake in doing this, however, is to confuse level of intelligence with level of maturity. In interviews, first-grade teachers repeatedly pointed out that IQ is no guarantee of school success. As one Illinois teacher warns, "Parents especially don't understand that intelligence and ability to read are not all that it takes to be successful in school. Social and physical needs must also be met." IQ is certainly a factor in readiness for school, but, taken by itself, it is not much more useful or reliable than chronological age for predicting school success.

To accurately determine whether a youngster is mature enough for school, several other factors must be considered. Is the child physically mature? Children can be bright, yet lack the fine muscle control needed to pick up pencils, use scissors, color, paste, and do the many other tasks that school demands. Eye-hand coordination plays an important role in a child's success with desk work. From 1910 to 1962, a father-son team of opthalmologists in Texas recorded trends in their patients' eyesight and found that the ratio of nearsighted to farsighted children nearly reversed itself over the 50-year period, with nearsightedness far outnumbering farsightedness in the early 1960's. During the same 50-year period, the age at which children started first grade had dropped by two years. Is this a coincidence? Maybe—and maybe not, but there are many who believe that young eyes are simply not ready for the close work that school demands, forcing the eye muscles to adapt in abnormal ways.

Children also need to discriminate between different sounds. In the manual for his widely used auditory discrimination test, Joseph Wepman stresses that some perfectly normal children can not discriminate between sounds like "b" and "d" until they are seven or eight years old. Even tooth development can indicate a youngster's physical maturity—there is evidence that children who are somewhat late in losing their baby teeth also lag developmentally in other areas.

Evidence abounds that the coordination of the eyes, ears, and sensory system into an efficient working system does not occur until well into the primary grades for many children. It is time to ask whether children whose visual maturity has not developed or whose auditory powers are behind schedule have any chance when they are brought into school based on no other information than chronological age.

Social and emotional maturity

Even if children are physically mature and have at least average IQ's, they may still be overplaced if they are not mature in social and emotional ways. One first-grade teacher referred to this area of a child's development as the youngster's "emotional capability to accept the day. A child who is ready for first grade has a sense of knowing who he or she is and what tasks must be performed." School success is directly related to a child's ability to function in and structure the environment. Children who *do* have this ability display a higher degree of self-control and cooperation in both the classroom and on the playground. They have outgrown the emotional volatility, the tantrums, and the aggressiveness toward peers that mark nursery school-age children. What motivates them is the desire for self-reliance. They are responsible for taking their outer clothes off, carrying their lunch money, moving from one classroom to another, and performing other activities that require independence and self-confidence. They are able to work in a group without becoming distraught whenever the chips do not fall their way.

The child who is highly intelligent but emotionally immature may have a particularly difficult time if he or she is accelerated through school. Ames quotes one such adult who writes about her years in school: "How lonely I was. I was always too immature, both physically and psychically, for the group I was with. Many of my social and personal, and even professional, failures in adult life I lay to the fact that I went too fast, much too fast, all the way through school."[1]

Finally, even if a child seems to be physically, emotionally, and socially mature, the question remains whether six-year-olds are ready cognitively for the complex decoding and abstracting processes required in learning how to read. Many researchers agree that not until the ages of seven or eight do children develop logical thinking ability, surely an important capability in being able to make sense out of words. It seems impossible to hurry this development up, and any attempt to do so might only doom a youngster to frustration and feelings of failure. In most cases, overplacement is a result of the youngster's cognitive inability to handle the academic demands; if the child is a slow developer, he or she may fall behind early and never catch up.

The issue of overplacement raises a larger question—whether it is possible to alter or speed up any child's cognitive, physical, or emotional development. The way in which one answers that question depends on how one views human development and education. Arnold Gesell, Louise Bates Ames, and other researchers from disparate fields hold that, although development may be somewhat alterable, it generally obeys biological schedules that must be respected. One child may not be able to master the skill of holding a pencil until he is six years old, no matter how hard his parents try to teach him. His eventual mastery is not due to his parents' efforts, but to the natural development of his fine motor skills at the age of six. Meanwhile, his sister, who obeys a different biological timetable, can hold a pencil as well at three as most second-graders do. The difference is simply one of maturity.

Opposed to this point of view are the environmentalists—those who believe that nurture predominates over nature and that we can speed up the development of each individual's potential. These educators and psychologists have dominated the early childhood education movement and provided the theoretical underpinnings of programs like Project Head Start, which *has* been successful with children from disadvantaged backgrounds. They have given rise to a wide body of popular literature that purports to tell parents how they can speed up their children's learning process—get them to play the violin at three and read *War and Peace* at five.

What these books usually fail to explain is the benefit of all this acceleration. If children read before they enter kindergarten, do their gains last? According to research, the answer is no. Ames reports a study conducted in New York that shows that children who were reading before they entered kindergarten did not register permanent reading gains over other children.[2] Other researchers have questioned the value of early academic training because it appears to give no permanent advantage to children who receive it. Can development be speeded up? Perhaps it can, but to do so requires superb materials, low teacher/pupil ratios, teachers who are particularly dedicated to the goals of the program, and every other advantage of an outstanding education environment. Unfortunately, such a happy convergence of coincidences occurs but rarely in the real world.

Preventing failure

Instead of looking for ways of speeding up the development of some children, we ought to be looking for ways to prevent the failure and disillusionment of a good 20% to 30% of our children. The way to do that is to recognize the problem of overplacement and take the steps necessary to eliminate it. To move in this direction, schools have three options:

Raise the age at which all children start first grade. In their book, *School Can Wait,*[3] Raymond and Dorothy Moore suggest that children not be given formal academic instruction until the age of eight or nine. Louise Bates Ames would like to see formal reading instruction delayed until approximately the same age.

However, less extreme measures than these are certainly possible. In Iowa, for example, a child must be six before June 1 in order to start first grade; there are no late fall cut-offs. Some research indicates that boys should be at least six and one-half years old when they start first grade.

Individualize screening procedures. In Wisconsin, all incoming kindergarteners are routinely screened, no matter what their age. This practice should be extended to all 50 states. Furthermore, the screening should consist of more than IQ tests; it should include evaluations of physical, emotional, and social readiness.

Change the curriculum of early grades. Schools should evaluate the amount and nature of the material that they expect students to master in the lower grades. At a time when the entire nation is alarmed over declining reading scores, it may seem odd to suggest that we not accelerate reading instruction—and perhaps should even delay it, but our emphasis must be on maximizing the effects of early instruction in the early grades, not on hurrying it up. As Bruce Johnson notes, "By holding kids back, we can actually give them a head start." In *School Can Wait*, Raymond and Dorothy Moore report on 300 children who were held out of school for periods of from two to five years. Yet, when those 300 were placed with their peers in the appropriate grades, they caught up and often surpassed the youngsters who had started school at normal ages. It may be more productive to hold off on academic training until children are truly ready for it and then improve the quality of the instruction.

Educators need to shift their focus away from the management of student problems to the prevention of those problems, and an important step could be a radical cut in the number of overplaced children who now populate our schools. Overplacement has been linked to a large number of learning disabilities; it condemns an appalling number of students to the cycle of failure and apathy, and it causes reading problems that must be remediated all the way through elementary and high school.

Yet, overplacement could be prevented, if only we would question some dearly held assumptions; that all children reach school readiness at the same age, that intelligence is the only factor in school success, and that earlier reading means better reading. All too often, schools seem to be run for the convenience of parents, teachers, and administrators. Let us start running them for children and giving a chance to the 20% or 30% of those children who are simply overmatched.

Notes

[1]Louise Bates Ames, *Is Your Child in the Wrong Grade?* (New York: Harper & Row, 1967), p. 138.

[2]*Ibid.*, p. 106

[3]Raymond S. Moore and Dorothy Moore, *School Can Wait* (Provo, Utah: Brigham Young University Press, 1979), p. 100.

The Teacher's Role in Facilitating a Child's Adjustment to Divorce

Patsy Skeen
and Patrick C. McKenry

Patsy Skeen, Ed.D., is Assistant Professor, Child and Family Development, University of Georgia, Athens, Georgia.

Patrick C. McKenry, Ph.D., is Assistant Professor, Family Relations and Human Development, School of Home Economics, Ohio State University, Columbus, Ohio.

"At first it's so terrible you could really die, but then it gets better." (Andy—age 9)

"If I'd only kept my room clean [like Daddy asked], he wouldn't have left me." (Alice—age 4)

"Silence." (Becky—age 5)

These actual responses of children involved in divorce are typical of those observed by teachers. Such observations are increasing as the lives of an alarming number of children are being disrupted—at least temporarily—by divorce. The divorce rate has more than doubled in the past ten years. Currently almost four out of ten marriages end in divorce (United States Bureau of the Census 1976). More than 60 percent of these divorcing couples have children at home. Because almost 50 percent of all divorces occur in the first seven years of marriage, the children involved in divorce are usually quite young (Norton and Glick 1976). It is estimated that 20 percent of the children enrolled in elementary school have divorced parents. In some of the kindergarten and first grade classes, this figure is closer to the 40 to 50 percent level (Wilkinson and Beck 1977).

The period of disorganization following divorce is usually extended. The family living standard is likely to change and a nonworking mother often goes to work. One parent generally leaves the home and siblings can be lost as well (Derdeyn 1977). Because divorce is a crisis involving disruption of the family structure, the role of the school and the teacher are of particular importance. A child's sense of continuity and stability is likely to be dependent upon the availability of extra-familial supports such as the school, as well as upon what protection and concern can be mobilized in the parent-child relationship during this time (Kelly and Wallerstein 1977).

The purpose of this article is to provide information that will enable the teacher to be a positive support to children and families during divorce. Research and theory concerning the effects of divorce on children, parenting through divorce, and the role of the school is summarized. Practical suggestions for the classroom teacher are presented.

Revision of a paper presented at the 1978 National Association for the Education of Young Children Annual Conference.

Children and Divorce

Without exception divorce is a significant event in the life of any child. For the child, divorce may represent a sense of loss, a sense of failure in interpersonal relationships, and the beginning of a difficult transition to new life patterns (Magrab 1978). It cannot be assumed, however, that children will all react to divorce in the same way. For the most part, they are healthy, normal children who are confronted with an extremely stressful situation (Wilkinson and Beck 1977). Research findings indicate that the experience of divorce itself is less harmful than the nature of the parents' personalities and relationships with their children (Despert 1962; McDermott 1968; Westman and Cline 1970). The child's reactions also depend upon such factors as the extent and nature of family disharmony prior to divorce, emotional availability of important people to the child during the divorce period, and the child's age, sex, and personality strengths (Anthony 1974; McDermott 1968).

Some evidence indicates that children of divorce may be better adjusted than children remaining in two-parent homes where there is ongoing tension, conflict, and stress (Nye 1957; Landis 1960; Hetherington, Cox, and Cox 1978). Hetherington et. al. (1978) suggest that divorce is often the most positive solution to destructive family functioning. Divorce can have a positive influence. For example, some children of divorce exhibit more empathy than others, increased helping behavior, and greater independence than children from intact families. However, the ease and rapidity with which divorce may be obtained and the recent emphasis on "creative" and "positive" divorce may mask the pain, stress, and adjustment problems inherent in divorce.

Available research findings on children of divorce tend to agree that divorce is to an extent a developmental crisis for children (Jones 1977; Magrab 1978; Wilkinson and Beck 1977). Wallerstein and Kelly (1977) comment that they drew heavily from crisis intervention theory in their research, and Hetherington, Cox, and Cox (1976) use the term *critical event* to describe divorce as it affects families. Cantor's (1977) review of the literature revealed that in a period of parental divorce, children often show marked changes in behavior, particularly in school, and the changes are likely to be in the direction of acting-out behaviors.

Kelly and Wallerstein (1976) and Wallerstein and Kelly (1975, 1976) have researched the impact of the divorce process on children. In their preschool sample, they found that the children's self-concept was particularly affected. The children's views of the dependability and predictability of relationships were threatened, and their sense of order regarding the world was disrupted. Some suffered feelings of responsibility for driving the father away. Older preschoolers were better able to experience family turbulence and divorce without breaking developmental stride. The older preschoolers were also better able to find gratification outside the home and to place some psychological and social distance between themselves and their parents. However, heightened anxiety and aggression were noted in this group. Almost half of the children in this preschool group were found to be in a significantly deteriorated psychological condition at the followup study one year later.

Kelly and Wallerstein (1976) reported that young schoolage children respond to divorce with pervasive sadness, fear, feelings of deprivation, and some anger. At the end of one year, many still struggled with the task of integrating divorce-related changes in their lives. For older schoolage children, Wallerstein and Kelly (1976) found that divorce affected the freedom of children to keep major attention focused outside the family, particularly on school-related tasks. These children displayed conscious and intense anger, fears and phobias, and a shaken sense of identity and loneliness. At the end of one year, the anger and hostility lingered, and half the children evidenced troubled, conflictual, and depressed behavior patterns.

Hetherington et al. (1976) characterized behaviors of children of divorce as more dependent, aggressive, whiny, demanding, unaffectionate, and disobedient than behavior of children from intact families. Hetherington et al. (1976) noted three areas of anxiety: fear of abandonment, loss of love, and bodily harm. Anthony (1974) noted other behaviors of low vitality, restlessness, guilt, shame, anxiety, depression, low self-esteem, failure to develop as a separate person, a preoccupation with death and disease, inability to be alone, regression to immature behavior, separation and phobia anxiety, and an intense attachment to one parent. With certain groups of children—i.e., handicapped, adopted, and chronic illness cases such as asthmatics, epileptics, and diabetics—the divorce process might precipitate a psychosomatic crisis requiring hospitalization. Jacobson (1978) found the more the amount of time spent with the father was reduced during a 12-month period following divorce, the more a child was likely to show signs of maladjustment. Anthony (1974) concluded that the major reaction *during* divorce is grief associated with guilt, while the major reaction *after* divorce is shame coupled with strong resentment.

Hozman and Froiland (1977) suggested that the experience of losing a parent through divorce is similar to that of losing a parent through death. They adopted the Kubler-Ross model for dealing with loss. In this model, children go through five stages as they learn to accept loss of a parent. Initially, children deny the reality of the divorce. Denial is followed by anger and then bargaining in which children try to get parents back together. When they realize that their efforts cannot persuade parents to live together again, they become depressed. The final stage is acceptance of the divorce situation.

Anthony (1974) and Hetherington et al. (1978) cautioned against expecting all children and parents to react the same way in divorce. Each individual's behavior depends upon his or her unique personality, experiences, and the support system available.

Parenting During Divorce

For parents, divorce is a time of marked stress in everyday living and emotional as well as interpersonal adjustment. Feelings of loneliness, lowered self-esteem, depression, and helplessness interfere with parenting abilities (Hetherington et al. 1978). Several studies have noted a serious deterioration in the quality of the mother-child relationship in divorced families because of the mother's emotional neediness and her ambivalence about her new role as single parent (McDermott 1968; Hetherington et al. 1976; Wallerstein and Kelly 1976). After divorce, some fathers may become freer and less authoritarian. However, other fathers who are absent from the household may become less nurturant and more detached from their children with time (Hetherington et al. 1976; Weiss 1975).

During divorce, specific developmental needs of children are often unmet because of parental preoccupation with their own needs and parental role conflicts. When compared to parents in intact families,

Hetherington et al. (1976) found that divorced parents of preschoolers were less consistent and effective in discipline, less nurturant, and generally less appropriately behaved with their children because of the preoccupation with the divorce process. When compared to parents in intact families, divorced parents communicated less well and made fewer demands for mature behavior of their children (Hetherington et al. 1976).

In summary, parent-child relationships are altered as a result of divorce. Parenting becomes difficult as the structure of the family breaks down and parents must make interpersonal adjustments such as dealing with stress, loneliness, and lowered self-esteem. However, there are many unanswered questions concerning parenting capabilities and behaviors during divorce. A great deal more research needs to be done before we can draw definitive conclusions in this area.

Schools and Divorce

The important role that schools can play in facilitating children's adjustment has not been clearly addressed in the divorce literature. Because children spend a great number of hours in school, as compared to time with parents, it is reasonable to assume that schools may be providing emotional support and continuity to a large number of children from divorcing parents. In other words, schools as a major socializing institution for children may play a more vital role in offsetting some of the negative impact of family disruption that accompanies divorce than previously thought (Jones 1977).

Key relationships in the family are often disrupted in part because of the geographic inaccessibility of the noncustodial parent. In addition, the custodial parent may be emotionally unavailable in the usual role to the child. Therefore, it has been argued that the school has an obligation to intervene with children of divorce to prevent reactions from being repressed and thus to prevent future disorders. Because parents are often involved in conflicts over financial support, visitation rights, and a battle for the children's loyalties, the teacher may be forcibly thrust into the role of an interim parent substitute (McDermott 1968).

Many children find some support within the school setting because their attitudes and performance in school provide gratification which is sustaining to them in the face of divorce stress. Kelly and Wallerstein (1977) found that the attention, sympathy, and tolerance demonstrated by teachers who had been informed about the divorce were supportive to a number of children who were feeling emotionally undernourished at home. In their study, teachers became a central stable figure in the lives of several children in the months following the separation, in some cases the only stable figure in these children's lives.

School personnel should be interested and involved in providing developmental assistance to individuals faced with critical life situations such as divorce. To date, few strategies have been published concerning ways that teachers can provide specific assistance to the child involved in divorce (Wilkinson and Beck 1977). Existing strategies that have been developed have been directed primarily to the school psychologist and guidance counselor. The following specific techniques are suggested for the classroom teacher who perhaps first notices behavioral changes and is in a position to help the child on a long-term basis. The teacher's role is discussed in three sections: working in the classroom, working with parents, and working with counselors.

What Can the Teacher Do?

In the Classroom

Team teachers, Harriet Sykes and George Brown, have just discovered that over one-half of the families of their kindergarten children have been involved in divorce. They decide that they want to help the children in their classroom grow through the divorce experience. What can they do?

Be a Careful Observer

1. Look for behavioral cues that help you understand how a child is feeling and what problems and strengths the child might have. Free play, art activities, puppet shows, and individual talks with the child are particularly good opportunities for observation.
2. Observe the child frequently, over a period of time, and in several types of situations such as at quiet time, in group work, alone, in active play, in free play, and at home. Such varied observations allow the teacher to construct a more complete picture of the total child and reduce the likelihood that judgments will be made on the basis of a "bad day."
3. Be a good listener to both verbalization and body language.

Make a Plan

1. When teachers are attempting to understand, predict, and intervene with behavior, it is important to first determine the child's physical, social, emotional, and cognitive developmental levels. A plan can then be developed to meet the child's individual needs. Direct observation, parents, counselors, and relevant literature are good sources of information to use when planning.

Provide Opportunities for Working Through Feelings

1. Help the child recognize the acceptably express feelings and resolve conflict through the use of curriculum activities such as painting, flannel board, clay, drawing pictures, writing experience stories about the child's family, dramatic play, doll play, books about

alternate family styles, free play, woodworking, music, and movement.

2. If the child appears to be going through the Kubler-Ross stages, prepare to help the child deal with the feelings in each stage. Give the child time for a resolution in each stage.

3. Allow children the solitude and privacy they sometimes need.

4. Support the establishment of divorce discussion and/or therapy groups for children led by trained leaders or counselors.

Help the Child Understand Cognitively

1. Help the child understand cognitively what his or her situation is, how and why he or she feels, how feelings can be expressed, and the consequences of such expression. Many discussions over an extended period of time will be necessary before such cognitive understanding is established.

2. Provide opportunities for the child to be successful in controlling his or her life. For example, make sure equipment and learning materials are matched to the child's abilities. Tell the child about the sequence of the day's events, and notify the child about changes in schedule well ahead of time. Give the child opportunities to make as many choices as he or she can handle.

3. Books and discussions can be used to give information about divorce in general and promote peer acceptance and support for a child from a divorced family. (See Relevant Books.)

Maintain a Stable Environment

1. Remain consistent in expectations for the child. This may be the only area of consistency in a rapidly changing and difficult period in the child's life.

2. Although children must be dealt with patiently and might regress to immature forms of behavior at times, avoid overprotecting the child.

3. Even though the child might have problems, he or she should not be allowed to "run wild." Because parents may be having difficulty setting limits for the child, it is extremely important for the classroom teacher to lovingly, but firmly, set reasonable limits for the child's behavior.

4. Make a special effort to love the child. Let the child know that he or she is important and worthwhile through smiles, hugs, praise, and attention to appropriate behaviors. However, avoid "being a mother or father" or allowing the child to become overly dependent upon you since you and the child will separate at the end of the year.

5. Prepare the child for separation from you at the end of the year (or an extended absence from you during the year) by telling the child ahead of time about the separation, why it will occur, and what will happen to the child. A visit to the new teacher and room can be very helpful. The child must be reassured that you are not leaving because he or she is "bad" or because you have stopped loving the child.

6. Encourage the child to work through stressful situations (e.g., a move to a new house) by talking about and role playing the situation in advance.

Examine Your Attitude

1. Avoid expecting a child to manifest certain kinds of problems simply because parents are divorcing. Children are skillful in "reading" adult expectations and often will behave accordingly. Adults might also assume that divorce is the reason for a behavior problem when in actuality other factors are the causes. Children have different reactions to divorce just as they do to all other aspects of life.

2. Examine personal feelings and values about divorce. Feelings and values consciously and unconsciously affect the way teachers interact with children and parents.

3. Try to help each child grow through divorce. Remember that divorce can have the positive effects of ending a highly dysfunctional family and providing growth opportunities for family members.

Working with Parents

Andy Robinson's mother has just told Andy's teacher, Mr. Wang, that she and her husband are going to get a divorce. She is worried about how this will affect Andy and wants to do whatever she can to assist her son. How can Mr. Wang help?

1. Realize that since divorce is a stressful time, teacher-parent communication should be especially supportive and positive.

2. Understand that parents are in a crisis situation and may not be able to attend to parenting as well as you or they would like.

3. Support the parent as an important person about whom you are concerned.

4. Provide books written for both children and adults for the parent to read concerning divorce. (See Relevant Books.)

5. Encourage parents to be as open and honest as possible with the child about the divorce and their related feelings.

6. Urge parents to assure their children that divorce occurs because of problems the parents have. The children did not cause the divorce and cannot bring the parents back together.

7. Encourage parents to elicit their children's feelings.

8. Assure parents that children will need time to adjust to divorce and that difficulties in the child's behavior do not mean that the child has become permanently psychologically disturbed.

9. Encourage parents to work together as much as possible in their parenting roles even though they are

dissolving their couple role. The attitudes that parents display toward each other and their divorce are vital factors in the child's adjustment. The use of the child as a messenger or a "pawn" in the couple relationship is particularly harmful to the child.

10. Help alleviate parental guilt by telling parents that their child is not alone. Indicate to parents that there is also evidence that children from stable one-parent families are better off emotionally than children in unstable, conflictual two-parent families.

11. Encourage parents to take time to establish a meaningful personal life both as a parent and as an important person apart from the child. This can be their best gift to their children.

12. Provide an informal atmosphere in which parents can share their problems and solutions.

13. Correctly address notes to parents. "Dear Parent" can be used when you are not sure if the child's parents are divorced or if the mother might have remarried and have a different name from the child.

Working with Counselors

Becky's teacher, Ms. Jones, has been patiently listening for two hours to Becky's father talk about the pain he feels and how hard it is to cope with life as a single man after 15 years of marriage. Ms. Jones wants to help but is at her wits end. What can she do?

1. Refer children and parents to competent counselors in the community instead of trying to assume the role of counselor. A great deal of harm can be done by well-meaning listeners who "get in over their heads" and do not know how to handle a situation.

2. The American Association of Marriage and Family Therapists (225 Yale Ave., Claremont, CA 91711) and the American Psychological Association (1200 17th St., N.W., Washington, DC 20036) maintain lists of qualified counselors. Counselors belonging to these organizations also generally indicate such membership in yellow page phonebook listings. However, the teacher should find out firsthand about the effectiveness of a counselor before referrals are made. Former clients, other teachers, and a personal visit to the counselor are good sources of information.

3. Work with the counselor when appropriate. The teacher can provide a great deal of information as a result of daily observation and interaction with the child. The teacher might also help carry out treatment strategies in the classroom.

In summary, divorce is a time of crisis for parents and children. The role of the school becomes particularly important during divorce since the family support system is under stress. Teachers are especially significant to the family since they probably spend as much or more time with the child than any other adult outside the family. When teachers are skilled and concerned, they can help parents and children grow through divorce.

References

Anthony, E.J. "Children at Risk from Divorce: A Review." In *The Child in His Family,* ed. E.T. Anthony and C. Koupernils. New York: Wiley, 1974.

Cantor, D.W. "School-Based Groups for Children of Divorce." *Journal of Divorce* 1 (1977): 183-187.

Derdeyn, A.P. "Children in Divorce: Intervention in the Phase of Separation." *Pediatrics* 60 (1977): 20-27

Despert, L. *Children of Divorce.* Garden City, N.J.: Dolphin Books, 1962.

Hetherington, E.M.; Cox, M.; and Cox, R. "The Aftermath of Divorce." In *Mother/Child, Father/Child Relationships,* ed. J.H. Stevens and M. Mathews. Washington, D.C.: National Association for the Education of Young Children, 1978.

Hetherington, E.M.; Cox, M; and Cox, R. "Divorced Fathers." *The Family Coordinator* (1976): 417-429.

Hozman, T.L., and Froiland, D.J. "Children: Forgotten in Divorce." *Personnel and Guidance Journal* 5 (1977): 530-533.

Jacobson, D.S. "The Impact of Marital Separation/Divorce on Children: Parent-Child Separation and Child Adjustment." *Journal of Divorce* 1 (1978): 341-360.

Jones, F.N. "The Impact of Divorce on Children." *Conciliation Courts Review* 15 (1977): 25-29.

Kelly, J.B., and Wallerstein, J.S. "Brief Interventions with Children in Divorcing Families." *American Journal of Orthopsychiatry* 47 (1977): 23-39.

Kelly, J.B., and Wallerstein, J.S. "The Effects of Parental Divorce: Experiences of the Child in Early Latency." *American Journal of Orthopsychiatry* 46 (1976): 20-32.

Landis, J. "The Trauma of Children when Parents Divorce." *Marriage and Family Living* 22 (1960): 7-13.

Magrab, P.R. "For the Sake of the Children: A Review of the Psychological Effects of Divorce." *Journal of Divorce* 1 (1978): 233-245.

McDermott, J.F. "Parental Divorce in Early Childhood." *American Journal of Psychiatry* 124 (1968): 1424-1432.

Norton, A.J., and Glick, P.C. "Marital Instability: Past, Present and Future." *Journal of Social Issues* 32 (1976): 5-20.

Nye, F.I. "Child Adjustment in Broken and in Unhappy Unbroken Homes." *Marriage and Family Living* 19 (1957): 356-361.

United States Bureau of the Census. *Current Population Reports,* Series P-20, No. 297. Washington, D.C.: U.S. Government Printing Office, 1976.

Wallerstein, J.S., and Kelly, J.B. "Divorce Counseling: A Community Service for Families in the Midst of Divorce." *American Journal of Orthopsychiatry* 47 (1977): 4-22.

Wallerstein, J.S., and Kelly, J.B. "The Effects of Parental Divorce: Experience of the Child in Later Latency." *American Journal of Orthopsychiatry* 46 (1976): 256-269.

Wallerstein, J.S., and Kelly, J.B. "The Effects of Parental Divorce: Experience of the Preschool Child." *Journal of Child Psychiatry* 14 (1975): 600-616.

Weiss, R. *Marital Separation.* New York: Basic Books, 1975.

Westman, J.C., and Cline, D.W. "Role of Child Psychiatry in Divorce." *Archives of General Psychiatry,* 23 (1970): 416-420.

Wilkinson, G.S., and Beck, R.T. "Children's Divorce Groups." *Elementary School Guidance and Counseling* 26 (1977): 204-213.

Relevant Books

Books for Children

Picture Books

Adams, F. *Mushy Eggs.* New York: C.P. Putnam's Sons, 1973.

Caines, J. *Daddy.* New York: Harper & Row, 1977.

Kindred, W. *Lucky Wilma.* New York: Dial Press, 1973.

Lexau, J., *Emily and the Klunky Baby and the Next-Door Dog.* New York: Dial Press, 1972.
Lexau, J. *Me Day.* New York: Dial Press, 1971.
Perry, P., and Lynch, M. *Mommy and Daddy Are Divorced.* New York: Dial Press, 1978.
Stein, S.B. *On Divorce.* New York: Walker & Co., 1979.

Elementary and Middle School

Alexander, A. *To Live a Lie.* West Hanover, Mass.: McClelland & Stewart, 1975.
Bach, A. *A Father Every Few Years.* New York: Harper & Row, 1977.
Blue, R. *A Month of Sundays.* New York: Franklin Watts, 1972.
Blume, J. *It's Not the End of the World.* New York: Bradbury Press, 1972.
Corcoran, B. *Hey, That's My Soul You're Stomping On.* New York: Atheneum, 1978.
Donovan, J. *I'll Get There. It Better Be Worth the Trip.* New York: Harper & Row, 1969.
Duncan, L. *A Gift of Magic.* Boston: Little, Brown & Co., 1971.
Fox, P. *Blowfish Live in the Sea.* Scarsdale, N.Y.: Bradbury Press, 1970.
Gardner, R. *The Boys and Girls Book about Divorce.* New York: Bantam Books, 1977.
Goff, B. *Where Is Daddy?* Boston: Beacon Press, 1969.
Greene, C. *A Girl Called Al.* New York: Viking Press, 1969.
Hoban, L. *I Met a Traveller.* New York: Harper & Row, 1977.
Johnson, A., and Johnson, E. *The Grizzly.* New York: Harper & Row, 1964.
Klein, N. *Taking Sides.* New York: Pantheon Books, 1974.
LeShan, E. *What's Going to Happen to Me? When Parents Separate or Divorce.* New York: Four Winds Press, 1978.
Nahn, P. *My Dad Lives in a Downtown Motel.* Garden City, N.J.: Doubleday, 1973.
Mazer, H. *Guy Lenny.* New York: Delacorte Press, 1971.
Mazer, N. *I, Trissy.* New York: Dell Publishing Co., 1971.
Newfield, M. *A Book for Jodan.* New York: Atheneum, 1975.
Rogers, H. *Morris and His Brave Lion.* New York: McGraw-Hill, 1975.
Simon, N. *All Kinds of Families.* Chicago: Whitman, 1976.
Steptoe, J. *My Special Best Words.* New York: Viking Press, 1974.
Stolz, M. *Leap Before You Look.* New York: Harper & Row, 1972.
Talbot, C. *The Great Rat Island Adventure.* New York: Atheneum, 1977.
Walker, M. *A Piece of the World.* New York: Atheneum, 1972.

Books for Teachers and Parents

Gardner, R. *The Parents Book about Divorce.* Garden City, N.J.: Doubleday, 1977.
Grollman, E. *Explaining Divorce to Children.* Boston: Beacon Press, 1969.
Hunt, M., and Hunt, B. *The Divorce Experience.* New York: McGraw-Hill, 1977.
Kessler, S. *The American Way of Divorce: Prescriptions for Change.* Chicago: Nelson-Hall, 1975.
Krantzler, M. *Creative Divorce.* New York: M. Evans & Co., 1974.
Salk, L. *What Every Child Would Like Parents to Know About Divorce.* New York: Harper & Row, 1978.
Sinberg, J. *Divorce Is a Grown Up Problem: A Book about Divorce for Young Children and Their Parents.* New York: Avon, 1978.
Stein, S.B. *On Divorce.* New York: Walker & Co., 1979.
Stevens, J., and Mathews, M., eds. *Mother/Child, Father/Child Relationships.* Washington, D.C.: National Association for the Education of Young Children, 1978.
Turow, R. *Daddy Doesn't Live Here Anymore.* Garden City, N.J.: Anchor Books, 1978.
Weiss, R. *Marital Separation.* New York: Basic Books, 1975.

Journals

Journal of Divorce. Editor: Esther O. Fisher. Haworth Press, 174 Fifth Ave., New York, NY 10010.
The Single Parent: The Journal of Parents Without Partners, Inc. Editor: Barbara Chase. Parents Without Partners, Inc., International Headquarters, 7910 Woodmont Ave., Bethesda, MD 20014.

HELPING CHILDREN COPE WITH DEATH

Christine L. Roberts

Christine L. Roberts is Professor of Elementary Education at the University of Connecticut in Storrs, Connecticut.

The rationale for teaching about death and dying is simple: death is a part of life. The person who cannot grieve is crippled emotionally, unable to experience and benefit from the full range of human emotions. Sylvia Plath (1972), visiting her father's grave years after his death, couldn't understand why she was crying so hard.

> Then I remembered that I had never cried for my father's death. My mother hadn't cried either. She had just smiled and said what a merciful thing it was for him he had died, because if he had lived, he would have been crippled and an invalid for life, and he couldn't have stood that, he would rather have died than had that happen (p. 137).

Grief is an essential reaction to loss; to repress grief is to repress emotional growth. If children are to grow up to be whole, integrated adults, they need to learn how to cope with catastrophe and crisis (Gorer, 1965)—with *any* loss in their lives.

It is normal for children to show curiosity about death; it also seems natural for parents to ignore their questions to spare them from pain. As children internalize their parents' avoidance behaviors, they learn to "field questions," "be strong," and deny their anguish. Unfortunately, these culturally acceptable responses are not healthy.

Children and youth need solid information in order to neutralize "the pornography of death" they see in movies and on television: the highly stylized and ritualized brutality, sadism, and murder that render life and death trivial or meaningless. Susceptible children who see such impersonal violence may believe that their own lives are irrelevant, precisely at an age when they are searching for meaning and intimacy (Jackson, 1972). They need to learn about death in order to explore the ramifications of such taboo topics as abortion, suicide, euthanasia, cryogenics, and triage. They need to learn how to cope with catastrophe and crisis whenever they meet it. Expressing their emotions is a necessary first step in this coping process.

We know much about children's fears and needs (Nagy, 1948). Understanding the stages of child development can make it easier to know when and how to go about teaching children the meaning of death.

- Children *under six months* of age are too young to understand death. However, bonding—an early, warm, loving relationship with a parent or surrogate—is critical to babies (Brown, 1978).
- Toddlers from *one to two years* still have a need for bonding: They sense and reflect their parents' anxieties and recognize separation, which they react to by crying. Toddlers love to play "peek-a-boo," which literally means "alive or dead" in old English (Kastenbaum, 1969), but they still cannot grasp the concept of death.
- For *three- to five-year-olds,* death is temporary and reversible; dead persons or animals will return someday just as the characters who die on TV return later in another show. They believe that the dead can read, eat, write, and sleep in the grave (Nagy, 1948), and that death happens to others, not to themselves. They have no fear of death, injury, or mutilation. Tots also like to hear nursery rhymes, even though they contain many morbid actions. In fact, in all 200 nursery rhymes, there are eight allusions to murder, at least one case of death by choking, devouring, decapitation, dismemberment, squeezing, shrivelling, starving, boiling, hanging, and drowning; 21 other unclassified deaths; five death threats; and several references to undertakers, graves, and body snatching (Baring-Gould, 1962).

• From *five to nine years,* children fear personification of death—skeletons, werewolves, and ghosts. Seven-year-olds may pick flowers in a cemetery, but in a year or two they will be afraid of graveyards. They also fear haunted houses, fire, loud storms, "bad" people such as robbers, darkness, strange sights, and being alone (Foster and Headly, 1966). While they know that the body decays in death, they believe the spirit still lives. This is the time to talk openly about death to clear up misconceptions and lessen fears. Children should come to understand that everything that lives must die, that dead plants cannot grow, and dead flies won't fly away anymore. They should be able to cope with accompanying an adult on a visit to a relative's grave or bury a dead pet with dignity. They should also be taught to respect varied religious definitions of death (an end, a mystery, a stepping stone to an afterlife).

• From *ten years of age and up,* children can understand and accept a mature, realistic explanation of death as final and inevitable. They may want to refuse to believe that they themselves are mortal, and they may cover up any feelings of incompetence (Jackson, 1972). Around the age of 14, many children abandon their belief in spiritual immortality, and they are more apt to be aware of death around them. Children over ten should be taught that (1) it is normal to feel sad, angry, and lonely when a favorite pet, relative, or friend dies; (2) it is all right to talk and cry openly over a death; (3) both the dying person and the living need to say goodbye to each other; and (4) life is precious and should be preserved. It's also not too early to teach children that alcohol and drug abuse, pollution, starvation, and disease are all forms of slow death to be avoided.

• By the time children reach their *mid and upper teens,* they are able to understand the issues of death, such as war, abortion, suicide, murder, slavery, child abuse, and rape. They can deal emotionally with hospitals and nursing homes, battlefields, or war museums. Most important, they can evaluate on their own the language and subliminal messages of advertising, which persuade them to think young, look young, and stay young. Guntzelman (1975) calls America "the most death-denying culture of all time."

Kubler-Ross (1969) describes five stages through which people must pass when confronted with death, either their own or another's. These stages were recently dramatized in the movie *All That Jazz.* They may differ in length and intensity, and a person may regress to an earlier stage before progressing to the next or appear to be in two stages simultaneously. To block or repress emotions felt in any of the stages is unhealthy.

• Stage 1—denial and isolation. "Oh no, not me! This can't be true!" The person who is dying or the person who faces the death of a loved one temporarily permits the psyche to collect itself and mobilize defenses.

• Stage 2—anger. "Why me? Why not somebody else?" Denial hasn't worked, so the person feels angry and displaces and projects the anger to others.

• Stage 3—bargaining. "Just let me live until the baby comes." Denial and anger have both been ineffective, so the next step is to bargain with the purveyor of misfortune for a little more time—usually in exchange for good behavior.

• Stage 4—depression. This comes as a reaction to the realistic sense of loss, including feelings of guilt and shame for failing to function adequately. It is painful for mourners, but it is worse for the dying person who now realizes everything will be lost.

• Stage 5—acceptance. As long as the earlier feelings have been sufficiently expressed, the individual will be able to feel peace, acceptance, and resignation. Eventually the person who is to die loses interest in everything, grows weak and tired, and desires only to remain undisturbed or with one or two loved ones.

These stages are recognizable in anyone who has faced a traumatic disappointment—from death to loss of a job, divorce, or failure to get a promotion. Learning to face loss and disappointment is an important developmental task in the wholesome integration of personality. Older children, as well as adults, can recognize them and should feel free to pass through them unselfconsciously.

There are several ways in which parents and teachers can make death seem less unnatural and horrible and more acceptable to children. In order to do so, they should first confront their own anxieties about death and stop using such euphemisms as "passed away" for the word "died."

When a hospitalized parent is obviously dying, family members should talk freely to the patient and permit themselves to express grief. Terminally ill patients can recognize a conspiracy of silence among family members who would prefer to avoid the subject of death—ironically, at a time when the dying individual really wants to discuss it. Once it becomes known that the patient is dying, doctors visit less often, nurses take longer to answer calls, and even hospital volunteers avoid the patient, who by this time has been moved to a private room. Often, the hospital's cleaning staff are the only ones left to linger, talk, and listen. Yet this is the time when family members and other adults need to visit often, listen to the patient, and talk candidly (Glaser and Strauss, 1965).

Parents should never send their children away to avoid a mourning period; they should permit the children to hear everything. While they need to answer all questions honestly, they should avoid overanswering, as this betrays anxiety. The child should understand the cause of death and, if he or she wishes, participate in the funeral.

After the funeral parents should continue to discuss the dead person, but they should not glamorize death. One mother whose husband died in an auto accident told her young son that "Daddy is up in Heaven now, and he is very happy there doing everything he always wanted to do." Her young son went outdoors and deliberately hit his head on a rock so that he could join his father in that wonderful place (Doyle, 1972).

There is some advice, too, for parents and families of dying children. If the child is very young, the family will need to reassure him or her that everything possible will be done to help and that death is not a punishment for being naughty. They will need to answer all questions as they arise. Children as young as 15 months old can sense parents' anxiety, especially when it causes the parents' behavior to fluctuate between frantic closeness and cool emotional distance. At first, the child can sense danger in the frantic closeness; however, perceiving the emotional distance, the child usually reacts with protest, then despair, and finally total detachment (Bowlby, 1961). Siblings of the dying child may suffer hysterical symptoms—enuresis, headache, school phobia, depression, abdominal pains (Binger and others, 1969)—perhaps because they feel guilty or rejected by the parents, who now spend much time and energy on the dying child.

If that child is a teenager, parents and family need to understand the psychology of the adolescent: teenagers prize their physical powers and attractiveness and feel guilt and shame at finding themselves sick and weak. They may believe their growing up years were all for nothing, an idea vividly illustrated by an infant epitaph found in a British churchyard, "It is so soon that I am done for; I wonder what I was begun for." Dying teenagers may bitterly resent the fun-filled lives of their peers. They need to continue to develop their own special talents and hobbies right up to the day of their death. In one hospital where personnel were trained for grief counseling, a counselor worked with a despondent teenager named Michael, who had given up on everything, including playing his beloved guitar. The counselor found a soundproof room where Michael taught guitar classes to other patients and wrote a rock mass for four guitars. The mass, which Michael completed just a few weeks before his death, was played at his memorial service (Doyle, 1972).

Like sex education, death education takes a long time: it cannot be taught or learned in a three-day or three-month unit of study. Death education begins naturally the first time the young child sees a dead bird or plant; it continues when the child grieves for the death of loved ones, and it ends with his or her own death.

References

Baring-Gould, William, and Baring-Gould, Ceil. *The Annotated Mother Goose.* New York: Bramhall House, 1962.

Binger, C. M., and others. "Childhood Leukemia." *New England Journal of Medicine* 10 (February 1969): 414-416.

Bowlby, J. "Childhood Mourning." *International Journal of Psychoanalysis of the Child* (December 1961).

Brown, Nancie Mae. *Bonding: The First Basic in Education.* Bloomington, Ind.: Phi Delta Kappa, 1978.

Doyle, Nancy. *The Dying Person and the Family.* Public Affairs Pamphlet No. 485. New York: Public Affairs Committee, 1972.

Foster, R., and Headly, N. *Education in the Kindergarten.* 4th ed. New York: American Book Co., 1966.

Glaser, B., and Strauss, A. *Awareness of Dying.* Chicago: Aldine, 1965.

Gorer, Geoffrey. *Death, Grief and Mourning.* New York: Doubleday, 1965.

Guntzelman, Joan. *Reconciliation and Children: Suffering, Death and Dying.* Kansas City, Mo.: National Catholic Reporter, 1975. (cassette.)

Jackson, Edgar N. "Understanding the Teenager's Response to Death." In Sarah S. Cook, *Children's Perceptions of Death.* New York: Department of Psychiatry, Columbia University, and Foundation of Thanatology Cooperative Symposium and Workshop on Anticipatory Grief, 14 April 1972.

Kastenbaum, Robert. *Explaining Death to Children.* Edited by Earl Grollman. Boston: Beacon Press, 1969.

Kubler-Ross, Elisabeth. *On Death and Dying.* New York: Macmillan, 1969.

Nagy, Maria. "The Child's Theories Concerning Death." *Journal of Genetic Psychology* 73 (1948): 3-27.

Plath, Sylvia. *The Bell Jar.* New York: Bantam Books, 1972.

The Profession of Teaching Today

The profession of teaching has undergone great change and experienced much upheaval in recent years. This section addresses major issues affecting the present status of the teaching profession in the United States. American teachers are confronting serious challenges relating to the conditions of their work and the socio-economic pressures upon them. They must deal with the same pedagogical and curricular issues that teachers all over the world face; yet they also have to deal with some social pressures that are unique to the American system of school governance. American teachers are affected by economic frustrations caused by the fact that their wages have lost ground to inflation in the twenty years between 1964 and 1984, and, in many areas of the nation, their wages continue to decline in value. But this is only one of their problems. All of the financial gains won by American teachers in the first half of the 1960s have been lost. It is becoming very difficult once again to attract talented people into the profession. This has happened in spite of the development of collective bargaining for teachers in many states between 1967 and the present. Now collective bargaining for teachers is being attacked at a time when the earning potential for teachers is extremely limited because of recessionary economic conditions and high rates of unemployment in the country. Local public school districts are less able to pay their teachers well, while many school administrators take an adversarial view of teachers' bargaining rights. One question that teacher leaders raise is: What would teachers' wages be like today if both the National Education Association (NEA) and the American Federation of Teachers (AFT) had not demanded collective bargaining for teachers?

Severe emotional strain has also become a factor in the day to day working lives of many teachers as a result of increases in school discipline problems, low professional morale in some communities, and the economic and status problems cited above. The economic and the emotional stresses on many teachers have influenced the development of what is called "teacher burnout." Teacher burnout is an emotional downturn in a teacher's professional motivation and morale that leads to a crisis in the teacher's perception of happiness in the profession. When a teacher experiences burnout his or her effectiveness as a teacher declines. The major teacher organizations in the United States are deeply concerned about the sharp downturn in the morale of many teachers. Many are leaving the profession after only five to ten years; others are expressing their professional frustrations in other ways. Even though the teaching profession in the United States has had a relatively high rate of entrance into and exodus from the profession, the conditions (professional, economic, and social) under which teachers work today are somehow aggravating this historical phenomenon. Teachers never have been one of the more protected or privileged working groups in this nation. However, social pressures are affecting them the same way that these pressures affect other members of the nation's labor force.

In the past there were more incidences of teachers leaving the profession to advance themselves economically. Now, however, emotional pressures caused by demands for formalized measures of evaluation of teacher performance and competency are forcing many capable teachers out of the profession. Contrary to popular belief, teachers often find careers in business and in the corporate world to be less, not more, stressful than teaching. This is a fact the American public needs to understand before it loses more of the best of its professional corps of teachers.

Looking Ahead: Challenge Questions

Is teaching an art? What dimensions of teaching make it an art? Why is teaching more of an art than a science?

What seem to be the most pressing social pressures on American teachers?

What are the best reasons for a person to choose a career in teaching?

Why are so many talented undergraduate students refusing to consider teaching as a viable career opportunity?

What are the special professional and social circumstances of American teachers as opposed to teachers in other countries?

What ought to be the minimal literacy and computational competencies of anyone entering the teaching profession?

Why do teachers experience burnout? What should be done to help teachers who experience this problem?

What are the reasons for teacher tenure laws? What would you state as the best criteria for deciding whether or not to grant tenure or merit pay to a teacher?

What are some of the pros and cons of collective bargaining for teachers? What are your reasons for your position?

Scapegoating The Teachers

DIANE RAVITCH

Diane Ravitch's latest book is *The Troubled Crusade* (Basic).

THE MOST common response to the current crisis in education has been to assail public school teachers. Not only are they incompetent, goes the charge, but good people have abandoned or are shunning the teaching profession. Teacher competency tests, which have spread during the past five years to some three dozen states, have produced embarrassing results in many districts; for example, when a third of Houston's teachers took a competency test, 62 percent failed the reading section and 46 percent failed the mathematics section (and the scores of hundreds of other teachers were ruled invalid because of teacher cheating). Those who major in education in college tend to have below-average grades in high school and lower scores on their SATs than the already depressed national average (in 1982, the national average on the SAT-verbal was 426, while the average for those planning to major in education was only 394).

This state of affairs has prompted a plethora of proposals. Some call for merit pay. Others call for increased salaries across the board. To some reformers, the answer lies with the designation of master teachers or with the promotion of more doctorate degrees in educational practice. Still others argue that the teacher problem would be ameliorated by abolishing schools of education.

THE PROBLEM of teacher competence is serious, since there is no chance that the schools will improve unless the teachers know more than the students do. Yet the rush to attack teachers and teacher education programs smacks more than a little of scapegoating. Teachers did not single-handedly cause the debasement of educational standards, and their preparation is better today than it was twenty years ago, when test scores began to fall. Though we now look back to 1962-63 as the golden age of student achievement, these years coincided with the publication of two major critiques of teacher education, James Koerner's *The Miseducation of American Teachers* and James B. Conant's *The Education of American Teachers*. Teachers, it seems, can't win: when scores go down, they are to blame; when scores are high, they get no credit.

It is comforting to blame teachers for the low state of education, because it relieves so many others of their own responsibility for many years of educational neglect.

—Why not blame the colleges and universities for lowering entrance requirements, thus undermining high school graduation requirements? Why not blame them for accepting hordes of semiliterate students and establishing massive remedial programs, instead of complaining to the high schools that gave diplomas to the uneducated?

—Why not blame businesses and employers, who set

up multimillion-dollar programs to teach basic skills to their work force instead of telling the public, the school boards, and the legislatures that the schools were sending them uneducated people? Why didn't representatives of major employers—like the telephone company and the banks—join forces to demand improved education?

—Why not blame state legislatures, which quietly diluted or abolished high school graduation requirements? Why were they willing to pile on new requirements for nonacademic courses (drug education, family life education, consumer education, etc.) while cutting the ground away from science, math, history, and foreign languages?

—Why not blame the press, which has been indifferent to educational issues, interested only in fads, and unaware of the steady deterioration of academic standards until a national commission captured its attention?

—Why not blame the federal government, which has toyed with the curriculum and introduced programs, regulations, and practices that narrowed the teacher's professional autonomy in the classroom?

—Why not blame the courts, which have whittled away the schools' ability to maintain safety and order? (Several weeks ago, the New Jersey Supreme Court invalidated evidence that students were selling drugs in junior high, because the drugs had been illegally seized in one student's purse and in another student's locker—the court's decision that the students' right to privacy outweighed the school's obligation to maintain order nullified the school's obligation to act in loco parentis.)

With so many guilty parties still at large, it should be clear why almost everyone seems eager to pin responsibility on the teachers for the bad news about the schools. The reality is that teachers should be seen not as perpetrators of the deleterious trends in the schools, but as victims of them. As teaching conditions worsen, it is teachers who suffer the consequences. When judges rule that disruptive youths cannot be suspended, it is teachers who must lock their classroom door and worry about being assaulted.

JUST AS SERIOUS as the problem of teacher competence is the state of the teaching profession. Some teachers insist bitterly that teaching is no longer a profession, but has been reduced to a civil service job. Other professionals are subject to entry tests and to supervision by senior professionals, but they usually retain a large measure of control over where they work and how they perform their duties; in teaching, governmental agencies and policymakers have bureaucratized hiring practices, curriculum development, student placement, and other areas that once engaged the experience and participation of teachers. The effort to make schools "teacher-proof" ends by making the teachers technical functionaries, implementing remotely designed policies. With so many laws and regulations and interest groups on the scene, wise teachers look for protection to the rulebook, their union, their lawyer, or to some job with more dignity. For the person who simply wants to teach history or literature, the school has not been a receptive workplace.

In response to declining enrollments and worsening working conditions, the number of people who want to be teachers has dropped sharply over the past decade. The number of undergraduate degrees awarded in education reached a peak of two hundred thousand in 1973, when they were 21 percent of all bachelor's degrees awarded in the nation, but have dropped to only one hundred and eight thousand in 1981, fewer than 12 percent of all bachelor's degrees awarded. The tight job market has meant not only a decline in the number preparing to teach, but a decline in the ability of those who want to teach. Apparently the brighter students were smart enough to pick another field, and the flight of academically talented women to other fields has particularly depressed the quality of the pool of would-be teachers. The low starting salary for teachers is undoubtedly a factor in shrinking the pool: a college graduate with a bachelor's degree in mathematics would get a starting salary in teaching of about $13,000, while the same person would receive about $17,000 as an accountant in private industry.

The outlook for a better pool in the future is not very promising. In the fall of 1970, 19 percent of college freshmen said that they wanted to teach in elementary or secondary school. A year ago, less than 5 percent of college freshmen expressed the same ambition. Less than 2 percent wanted to teach in high school, a choice that was doubtless informed by their own recent observation of the life of high school teachers.

Would reforms in teacher education help the situation? For years, critics of education have heaped scorn on schools of education and on the required education courses that prospective teachers must take. Thirty years ago, critics like Arthur Bestor and Mortimer Smith charged that entry to the teaching profession was controlled by an "interlocking directorate" made up of schools of education, bureaucrats in state education departments, and teacher associations, and that the hurdles these groups erected (such as "Mickey Mouse" courses in educational theory and methods) excluded talented people from the public schools. Since the early 1950s was a time of baby boom and teacher shortage, nothing much came of the grumbling, and the agencies of certification and accreditation are, if anything, even more powerful today.

YET SCHOOLS of education are not solely responsible for the intellectual inadequacies of those entering teaching. The important fact to bear in mind about students preparing to teach is that they take most of their courses outside of the undergraduate education department. Would-be high school teachers take only about 20 percent of their courses in education, and would-be elementary teachers take about 40 percent of their courses in education. If their academic preparation is deficient, the fault lies with the arts and sciences faculties.

Even though education majors take most of their courses outside the education department, it would be preferable if there were no education majors at the undergraduate level, if every would-be teacher majored in some subject or combination of subjects. As matters now stand, the one hundred and eight thousand bachelor's degrees in education awarded in 1981 were divided up among students preparing to be elementary teachers (35 percent), physical education teachers (17 percent), special education teachers (13 percent), and teachers of such specialized areas as home economics, vocational education, prekindergarten instruction, and health education. Less than 3 percent of the education degrees went to secondary teachers, which suggests (happily) that those who want to teach in high school take their Bachelor of Arts degrees in the subjects they want to teach and get their education credits on the side or in graduate school.

Elementary teachers need a wide preparation, since they will be teaching reading, writing, mathematics, science, social studies, art, and music. But they can take the courses in how to teach these subjects to young children while majoring in a discipline or combination of disciplines. The case for requiring physical education instructors to major in a subject area is even stronger, because a large number of them teach their minor subject (usually social studies) and end up as high school principals.

Since prospective secondary teachers rarely major in education in college, they do not get counted or measured by the researchers who examine the quality of the teaching pool. In most studies and government reports, statistics are gathered only for those who major in education in college. Thus the numbers that are tossed about refer *only* to those who are academically weakest. In fact, when we are warned about the onrushing tide of incompetent teachers, we are hearing only about the coaches, the school nurses, the elementary school teachers, and the shop teachers, but not the would-be teachers of history, the sciences, English, and mathematics. We should still be concerned, particularly about the low academic ability of those who are supposed to teach young children the basic skills and impart to them their attitudes toward learning, but we should recognize that the data are biased.

GRADUATE SCHOOLS of education have shown little interest in training teachers. Some professors and programs involve themselves with the public schools, but most of these institutions emphasize research and the training of educational administrators. Because they are parts of universities, their concept of status derives from the traditional academic model. They have low status within the university, which considers the graduate school of education little better than a vocational school.

Yet the graduate school has a useful role to play. In particular, it cares about education, which is one of the major social and economic activities in the nation. This sets it apart from the rest of the university, which tends to look down upon any interest in or involvement with the public schools. Just last summer, however, the presidents of Harvard and Stanford met with leading university presidents and their education deans to discuss how to help the schools and how to overcome the traditional snobbery that has kept the "ed" schools out of the academic mainstream. Whether this resolve is translated from rhetoric into programmatic commitments remains to be seen.

Perhaps a personal note at this point will explain my own bias. In 1972, when I had been out of college for a dozen years, I decided to get a Ph.D. in history while writing a political history of the New York City public schools. I approached a young history professor at Columbia, who told me that I was a bad bet for his department: "You have three strikes against you," he said. "First, you are a woman; second, you are more than ten years away from your B.A.; and third, you are interested in education." At Teachers College, the graduate school of education at Columbia, none of those characteristics was considered a handicap, and I pursued my studies there. This lack of interest in elementary and secondary schooling and in education as a profession and as a research field is typical of major research universities.

The present crisis in education and the depressed condition of the teaching profession offer an unusual opportunity to reassess our present arrangements for preparing teachers. As Gary Sykes, until recently the National Institute of Education's specialist on the teaching profession, has observed, the profession needs both "screens and magnets," ways to keep out incompetent teachers and ways to lure in the highly talented. The traditional screen—state certification—is almost entirely ineffective, since it guarantees only that a prospective teacher has taken required courses and received a degree. Recognizing that a college degree today certifies very little, a number of states have begun to adopt teacher examinations and to reassess their requirements for entry into the profession. If school boards and state legislatures were to raise their hiring standards—to insist that new teachers have an undergraduate major other than education, for instance, and to determine whether the education courses they require are valuable—the message of the marketplace would be heeded by institutions that prepare teachers.

Developing magnets to attract good people to teaching will be far more difficult. It must involve better pay, so that a life of teaching is not equivalent to an oath of penury. It may or may not involve some form of salary differentiation for teachers who win the respect and admiration of their peers, but some salary incentives should be available to keep gifted teachers in the classroom. It should involve generous public fellowships to underwrite the education of those willing to commit themselves to the classroom for several years. It should mean a readiness by school boards to provide teachers with opportunities for continuing intellectual and professional growth. It should mean a flexibility by teachers' unions to permit the employment of graduate students in science and mathematics, college-educated housewives, and professional writers to meet critical shortages on a temporary or part-time basis. It requires a willingness by education officials to defend the teacher's professional autonomy and to preserve a climate in the schools that honors teaching and learning.

Like every other educational problem, the difficulty of attracting top-flight people to teaching will not yield to simple solutions. Demography contributed to the problem; smart people looked for other jobs as enrollments declined. But demography may help ease the problem, as enrollments begin to grow again, increasing the demand for new teachers. The opening of other career opportunities has shrunk the talent pool, but teaching will continue to be an attractive occupation for those who wish to combine a career with family responsibilities.

As a mass, public profession, teaching will never offer salaries that compare favorably with law or medicine, but it does offer satisfactions that are unique to the job. In every generation, there are people born with a love of teaching. They want to open the minds of young people to literature, history, art, science, or something else that has seized their imagination. To recruit and hold onto such people, the nation's schools must not only reward them adequately but must provide the conditions in which good teaching can flourish. That will not come about through public incantations; it will demand realistic programs and imaginative solutions. But a nation that has led the world in popular education for more than a century owes it to itself to meet the challenge.

THE ART OF TEACHING

STEVEN M. CAHN

Steven M. Cahn is director of the Division of General Programs at the National Endowment for the Humanities in Washington, D.C., and adjunct professor of philosophy at the University of Vermont.

Teaching is an art, and, as in the case of all arts, even its most gifted practitioners can improve their skills through review of fundamentals. But is it possible to explicate the essentials of good teaching? To meet that challenge I begin with the basic principle that a teacher is responsible to both students and subject matter. Sacrificing either one for the other amounts to failure.

Consider the simple case of teaching a friend how to play chess. You start by explaining the different possible moves of the various pieces, and soon your friend assures you that he has grasped these basic maneuvers. Suppose, then, after stressing the importance of strong openings, you proceed to demonstrate your favorite, the slashing King's Gambit. Knights, bishops, and pawns whiz back and forth over the board, accompanied by your running commentary on the strengths and weaknesses of the complicated variations. At last, you complete this detailed analysis and look up proudly, awaiting your friend's approval. He stares at the board, shakes his head, and finally remarks, "I guess I'll stick to checkers. I like it better when all the pieces move the same way."

King's Gambit may have been flawless, but while concentrating on the details of the subvariations, you have overlooked your friend's confusion as he tried to keep in mind such fundamentals as how pawns can move and where knights can jump. A good instructor anticipates such difficulties, realizing how tenuous a beginning student's claim to understanding may be. Lacking this insight, you might succeed as a chess analyst but not as a chess teacher.

Assume, however, that in an effort to sustain your friend's involvement, you do not warn him about the complexities of opening theory but merely advise that he attack quickly with his queen. You regale him with anecdotes of your triumphs over weak players who fell into such elementary traps as the Fool's Mate. Your friend supposes he has mastered a surefire strategy and, full of confidence and enthusiasm, marches to the nearest chess club. There he soon encounters some intermediate players who deftly parry his premature assaults and defeat him with ease.

What went wrong this time? Unless your friend eventually realizes the inadequacy of the preparation you provided and possesses the dedication to study the technical materials you suggested he bypass, he will again and again be beaten badly, quickly grow discouraged, and perhaps give up the game altogether. He may, nevertheless, have thoroughly enjoyed his lessons with you. If so, you succeeded as an entertainer but, again, not as a teacher.

Anyone who thinks teaching is easy has never stood in front of a class of thirty restless teenagers and tried to arouse and maintain their interest while simultaneously attempting to communicate a subject's complexities. In such circumstances, individuals quickly become aware that not everyone cares who they are or what they have to say.

Of course, the mechanics of sheer drill backed by the pressures of reward and punishment will normally result in some learning. But if the attention of students is engaged only by gold stars or raps on the knuckles, the removals of these reinforcements may well be accompanied by loss of interest. Students will thus have failed to acquire that most important of qualities, the desire to continue learning. Persons whose educations end when they leave school are doomed to spend much of their lives in ignorance. Good teaching, therefore, is not merely the transmission of information and skills, but the encouragement of zest for further study.

Sheer gusto, however, is not sufficient. If it were, teachers could succeed merely by going along with the whims of their students. If the students wanted to learn history but not economics, instructors could teach history and not economics. If students found most history boring but were fascinated by the history of the American cowboy, instructors could teach that

This article first appeared in the Fall 1982 issue of AMERICAN EDUCATOR, the quarterly professional journal of the American Federation of Teachers.

history and nothing else. If students wanted to see cowboy movies but not read any books about the West, instructors could turn their classrooms into movie houses. And if students wanted just to picnic in the park, instructors could make themselves useful cooking the hamburgers.

THE INTERESTS of students, however, may not match either their own needs or the needs of a democratic society whose welfare depends in great part on the understanding and capability of its citizens. Teachers, therefore, have the responsibility to lead their students to master appropriate subject matter without misrepresenting or diluting it yet at the same time arousing appreciation for it. How can they achieve this result?

Since teaching is a creative endeavor, there are no infallible guides to success. Good instruction, however, typically involves four elements: motivation, organization, clarification, and generalization.

As to motivation, I have found it useful to distinguish two types of teachers: those who pull the subject matter behind them and those who push the subject matter in front of them. The former use their own personalities to attract students and then try to transfer the students' interest from the instructor to the subject. The latter minimize their own personalities and seek to interest students directly in the material itself.

Those who pull the subject behind them usually have little difficulty in arousing enthusiasm, but their characteristic pitfall is the failure to redirect student interest away from themselves and toward the subject matter.

As Sidney Hook in *Education for Modern Man: A New Perspective* (Knopf) has noted, a teacher "...must be friendly without becoming a friend, although he may pave the way for later friendship, for friendship is a mark of preference and expresses itself in indulgence, favor, and distinctions that unconsciously find an invidious form....A teacher who becomes 'just one of the boys,' who courts popularity, who builds up personal loyalty in exchange for indulgent treatment, has missed his vocation. He should leave the classroom for professional politics."

But this is not to say that teachers who pull the subject behind them cannot be superb instructors. Indeed, if they succeed in involving students as much in the material as in the instructors' own manners, they can exert an enormously beneficial influence on an extraordinary number, for such teachers invariably attract many devoted admirers who will follow wherever such instructors lead.

On the other hand, those who push the subject in front of them need have no worry about misdirecting a student's interest. Their worry, rather, is whether such interest will be aroused at all. In many cases they must overcome the necessarily abstract quality of their subjects and make apparent the connections between the seemingly esoteric material and their students' own sphere of experience. Perhaps the most reliable tool for doing so, and one instructors need to master, is the use of well-chosen examples that relate to the purposes or passions of the students. The subject itself thus becomes their personal concern.

But whatever the particular approach of their instructors, students should be led to appreciate the subject not merely as a means but as an end, something of intrinsic worth to be enjoyed on its own account. Their lives will thereby be enriched and the material rendered more vivid and even more useful when serving some purpose beyond itself.

Teachers who fail to convey the significance of what they are discussing can see their own inadequacy reflected in the eyes of their apathetic students. Obtaining a sound education is difficult enough for a person interested in the work; for one who is bored, the process is intolerable.

A MOTIVATED student is ready to learn, but a teacher must be organized enough to take advantage of this situation. Admittedly, inflexibility can hinder an instructor from making the most of opportunities that arise spontaneously in the course of discussion, but a rambling presentation may well dissipate initial enthusiasm. What is too often forgotten is that lack of planning usually leads to stream-of-consciousness instruction, resulting in the sort of class that meanders idly from one topc to another, amounting to nothing more than an hour of aimless talk.

Each day before setting foot in the classroom, teachers should decide exactly what they intend to accomplish during a particular session and precisely what they expect their students to know by the time the period ends. In the words of Alfred North Whitehead in *The Aims of Education and Other Essays*, "a certain ruthless definiteness is essential in education." A teacher's obligation is to guide students, and to guide requires a sense of where one is headed. If the teacher does not know, then everyone is lost.

Careful organization, however, must be complemented by an equal concern for clarification. Otherwise, even the most highly structured course of study may prove incomprehensible to the uninitiated.

Since academic subjects tend toward complexity, classrooms are often rife with confusion. But good teachers foresee this problem and substantially reduce it by making every effort to be as clear as possible. They use concrete cases to exemplify abstract concepts, and, realizing that individuals differ in how they arrive at an understanding of particular ideas, good instructors take pains to explain fundamental principles in a variety of ways.

Of course, not every train of thought can be rendered in very simple terms. A book entitled *Kant Made Easy* is surely the work of a charlatan or a fool. Effective teachers, therefore, must be shrewd judges of both the difficulty of their materials and the ability of their students.

Why do some instructors seem to make so little effort to express themselves clearly? Many do not realize that good teachers direct their remarks not only at the best student, or at the top 10 percent of the class, or even at the majority; instead, good teachers speak so that virtually all their listeners can follow. These teachers realize that when more than one or two students complain they are lost, many others, whether they themselves realize it or not also need help.

Having now discussed motivation, organization, and clarification, I turn to the fourth element of good instruction: generalization. Because a thorough knowledge of any subject matter depends upon a firm grasp of its details, the tendency of many instructors is to emphasize analysis at the expense of synthesis. But to master a subject requires awareness of its connections to related areas of inquiry. Details are necessary to understanding, but they are not sufficient. Also required is perspective, and that can be achieved only by viewing specific information within a broad framework.

I still vividly recall my high school history teacher who insisted that we memorize the dates, locations, and names of the commanding generals for every major battle of the Civil War. Only in my college years when I heard a series of enthralling lectures on the causes, strategies, and results of that war did I come to understand and share my earlier teacher's fascination with the events of that period.

A student should not be allowed to become lost in minutiae. For although generalizations without details are hollow, details without generalizations are barren.

I HAVE thus far been considering the components of good teaching, but great teaching involves yet another element. Great teachers not only motivate their students, organize the class, clarify their material, and provide illuminating generalizations, they also project a vision of excellence.

Even after considerable study, it is not easy to distinguish what is adequate from what is excellent. How many of us, observing two physicians, would know which was merely competent and which superb? How many of us, reading a history of Europe, would realize whether the account was exceptional or just satisfactory? Recognizing such distinctions depends upon an awareness of critical subtleties, and each great teacher in inimitable ways leads students to acquire and prize such insight.

Excellence is not only of value to those who possess it. Equally important is its significance for those who have been taught to appreciate it, for by developing the acuity and sensitivity needed to comprehend the magnificent achievements of which human effort is capable, one's perceptions are rendered more vivid and one's experience enormously enriched.

The hallmark of superb instruction is not the applause of students but rather their informed and abiding commitment to recognize and respect quality. Achieving that goal is the ultimate challenge inherent in the noble profession of teaching.

Tenure: Do We Need It?

Patricia Palker

Patricia Palker is a writer who specializes in education.

Patricia Makris is a second-grade teacher who has tenure. She has a master's degree and nine years teaching experience in District 123 of the Oaklawn-Hometown (Illinois) school system. Patricia Makris also has a letter of dismissal. Her position has been eliminated because declining enrollment is forcing the closing of four of the district's 10 schools.

Tenure didn't save Makris' job. Yet teacher tenure is often equated with job security, a subject of much concern as declining enrollments and budget cuts cause layoffs throughout the country. Tenure has also been associated—by those who are against it—with protecting incompetent teachers.

Such concerns and varied opinions about tenure raise a number of questions: What actually is this thing called tenure? Just how much security does tenure provide? What are key points in the debate about the value of tenure? Where do union controls fit in? Do teachers need tenure?

For answers to these questions, I talked with national and local teachers' union representatives, teachers, school board officials and school administrators.

What Is Tenure?

Webster's defines tenure as "a status granted after a trial period to a teacher protecting him from summary dismissal." Tenure laws are those state laws that outline the conditions for reaching that status and the conditions and procedures for holding onto it. Forty-six states plus the District of Columbia have tenure laws and 39 of these laws apply statewide. They were designed to raise the teaching profession above the political "spoils system" of staffing, to give teachers the freedom to teach without fear of coercion or reprisals and to improve education by encouraging a more permanent, more experienced staff.

Generally, tenure laws accomplish three goals. First, they specify that a teacher is entitled to permanent employment status after the successful completion of a probationary period (two to five years, depending on the state). Second, tenure laws list specific reasons for which a tenured teacher can be dismissed. In Connecticut, which is typical, those reasons are (1) inefficiency or incompetence; (2) insubordination; (3) moral misconduct; (4) disability, as shown by competent medical evidence; (5) elimination of the position to which the teacher was appointed, if no other position exists to which he or she may be appointed if qualified (the circumstances of Patricia Makris' dismissal); (6) "other due and sufficient" cause.

Third, tenure laws outline procedures that are designed to protect the tenured teacher's rights—such procedures as requiring that the teacher be given written notice of termination and of the charges against him or her, and be allowed a fair hearing to present witnesses in his or her own defense.

For example, Massachusetts' tenure laws require the school committee [board] to set a date for a meeting at which the vote on the dismissal is to be taken and must notify the teacher at least 30 days prior to that date. The law also requires that, upon request, the teacher be allowed a hearing before the school committee and be given a written statement of the charges. The teacher has the right to be represented at the hearing by an attorney and to present evidence and call witnesses. The superintendent must make a recommendation regarding the dismissal, and the school committee must be able to substantiate its charges. Finally, two-thirds of the entire membership of the school committee must vote for dismissing the teacher. If the teacher is not satisfied, he or she can appeal the decision in a court within 30 days after the vote.

In the four states—Mississippi, South Carolina, Utah and Vermont—and the parts of others without tenure laws, most teachers have one of two types of contracts. The "continuing contract" promises the teacher that he or she will be notified by a certain date if the contract is not to be continued; it does not promise that the teacher will be given the reason for dismissal or has due process rights. The "annual," or "long-term," contract does not even promise advance notification of dismissal.

How Much Security?

The kind of protection that tenure laws provide for teachers who have been accused of incompetence, insubordination or misconduct varies widely throughout the country. In most states, as in Massachusetts, the school committee is both prosecutor and judge at the teacher's dismissal hearing. In some states, such as Nevada and North Carolina, teachers can choose to have their cases heard by a five-member panel drawn from a Professional Review Committee. The panel then makes a recommendation to the school board, which makes the decision on the teacher's dismissal.

In still other cases, as in Washington State, teachers can, instead of requesting a hearing before the school board, opt to take their case directly to court. In those states and areas where school committees are both prosecutor and judge, some laws, like those in Arizona and Delaware, allow teachers to appeal decisions to the courts.

In other states, like Indiana and Iowa, the decision of the school board is final.

However, in no state does tenure prevent a teacher from being laid off as a result of declining enrollment. Most tenure laws, such as those in Illinois (where Patricia Makris teaches) and in Connecticut, say that a teacher can be dismissed if the position he or she holds is eliminated and no other position for which he or she is qualified exists.

Such laws have usually been interpreted to protect the tenured teacher as much as possible. Nontenured teachers have been bumped from their jobs if a tenured teacher's job is eliminated and that teacher can possibly qualify for the nontenured teacher's position. In some cases the system has resulted in unlikely and maybe unsuitable job assignments. For example, a career junior high social studies teacher might wind up teaching first grade. Most districts begin to lay off the tenured teachers only after the nontenured are all gone.

Many teachers' unions have negotiated clauses into their contracts that specify procedures to follow in deciding who will be laid off. The procedure is usually based on seniority and certification. That was the case this past February in Chicago when the board of education, because of financial difficulties, announced it would lay off 1,375 teachers. Because the contract included a seniority clause, no tenured teacher was dismissed.

If, however, a situation arises in a district where all of the nontenured teachers for a particular level or subject area have already been let go, and if the tenured teacher isn't certified to teach in any other area, he or she can be dismissed.

In Patricia Makris' case, many of the teachers still teaching in her district have more seniority than her nine years. The ones who had less seniority had received dismissal letters in previous years—60 last year; 40 the year before; 51 the year before that. Over the past six years the student population of this suburban Chicago elementary school district has declined from roughly 6,000 to about 2,000. In previous years, most of those who received letters (which were sent out in March) were reinstated by September when other teachers retired or moved. But this year, because of the four schools closing, Makris thinks rehiring is less likely. She says she plans to just wait and see . . . and hope.

The Debate

Though tenure has been a subject of debate since the first tenure law was passed, the debate intensifies whenever there is a surplus of teachers. (See "A Brief History of Tenure," next page.) Many administrators and school board members argue that tenure procedures are so cumbersome, time-consuming and expensive that it is difficult, if not impossible, to dismiss incompetent teachers.

Says Ronald Gister, executive director of the Connecticut Association of Boards of Education, "Tenure procedures are so legalistic that there is virtually nothing that can be done [with an incompetent teacher] except when there is an overt act. So administrators get locked into personnel who are mediocre—not really horrible, but not really good. It is so legalistic that everyone is afraid to touch it . . . things are resolved by judges on points of procedure rather than on the issue at hand."

Paul Salmon, executive director of the American Association of School Administrators (AASA) says that most school districts do not have the number of administrators they need in order to evaluate teachers properly and to gather and document enough information so that dismissals will be upheld under tenure laws. In fact, a 1978-79 survey of AASA members ranked "dismissal of incompetent staff" as the third most serious problem of administrators (surpassed only by "cost reduction" and "adequate school financing").

"I know that when I was superintendent in Sacramento," Salmon said, "I was totally incapable of separating an incompetent teacher in any of my high schools because I didn't have enough staff to do the job and to adhere to the due process requirements of tenure."

Salmon says that because dismissing tenured teachers is "sometimes an unwieldy and awkward process requiring a tremendous amount of time, what often happens instead in many of the big city districts is that they have what they call the 'pass around the turkey day.' That is, that if you've had a certain teacher for this year, now where can we send him or her so that the community can tolerate this teacher for whatever length of time? It's 'Don't fire them; ship them off.' But don't require one administrator to have the teacher any great length of time."

The arguments against tenure go on outside the education community, too. Parents and taxpayers, disappointed in the education system, are seeking greater accountability for teachers. Despite all the arguments, they see tenure as an obstacle to achieving that accountability. The complaint heard most often: "People in other professions don't have tenure; why should teachers? The security makes them so comfortable that they become lazy."

Some teachers agree, but others say that teachers have special reasons for needing tenure. They say that teachers work for a virtually monopolistic employer. A shoe salesman who has a falling out with his employer can often find another shoe store in town to work in. A doctor who loses patients can find others. But a teacher who loses his or her job with a school district must often pick up and move to another area.

Richard Leonard, president of the Westport, CT, Education Association, compares teachers' protection with that of other unionized employees. "In no other union category that I can think of does it take management three years to make up its mind and then give the job security, seniority rights and fair dismissal procedures . . . Whether you speak of carpenters or truck drivers or chemical workers, a worker taking a new job or moving into a new job category establishes seniority, job security, fair dismissal procedures—that is, he becomes nonprobationary—within 30 to 90 days."

Others argue that many public jobs covered by statute, as well as private jobs covered by collective bargaining agreements, have job security provisions similar to tenure. They require just cause for dismissal and the burden of proof of incompetence is on the employer.

Not surprisingly, national representation of the American Federation of Teachers (AFT) and the National Education Association (NEA) argue in favor of tenure, too. "Tenure does work," says John Dunlop, manager of negotiations for the NEA. "They (people who criticize tenure) tend to forget their history. It protects teachers from political pressures that exist in the community and it makes for better education by having secure employees . . . To say tenure protects incompetent teachers is like claiming the Bill of Rights protects criminals.

"When you've got a surplus of labor," Dunlop continues, "then people have all sorts of reasons for getting rid of experienced teachers; for one thing, they cost more. I realize it's probably a relatively jaundiced view of the motivations of the other side, but I just don't see tenure being the difficult mechanism that some administrators make it out to be."

Despite all the debate, no states have adopted or repealed tenure laws in recent years. But what has happened recently is that teachers' unions have been negotiating provisions into their contracts that clarify and expand their statutory tenure protections—a move that the AFT and NEA say has left teachers with more job security than they ever had before. In fact, provisions now being written into teacher contracts as a result of negotiations may be making the debate about tenure irrelevant. What's happening in Miami could be the beginning of a trend in which union contracts take over tenure's role.

The Emergence of Contract Tenure

Last year Pat Tornillo, executive vice president of the United Teachers of Dade (Dade County, FL, which includes Miami) spearheaded ratification of a contract that will eliminate the possibility of tenure for new teachers. But that stand doesn't mean Tornillo is against tenure. He says he views the basic provisions of tenure—that a teacher can only be dismissed for "just cause" and that he or she has the right to due process—as absolutely essential.

What Tornillo doesn't like about tenure is that "the total misunderstanding of what it is or isn't on the part of the public, the media and the teachers themselves" hurts the teaching profession. "The myth that surrounds tenure is an albatross around the necks of teachers" he says. "Tenure doesn't protect incompetent teachers. Incompetent administrators protect incompetent teachers." Still, he said, the misunderstanding hurts us.

When the United Teachers of Dade took steps to reject the Florida tenure statute they set a national precedent; but at the same time they wrote "just cause" dismissal provisions into their contract—provisions that Tornillo says afford more protection than the statute.

Such clauses are not new; they were among the first types of clauses to be negotiated once states began enacting laws giving teachers collective bargaining rights in the 1960s, according to Dunlop of the NEA. Unions in Michigan were among the first, in 1965, to bargain these kinds of clauses into their contracts. The clauses typically clarified or expanded upon rights provided by statute. Presently in Michigan and Wisconsin, which Dunlop says are fairly representative states, about 65 percent of all contracts have just cause dismissal provisions.

James Ward, director of economic research for the AFT, calls the unions negotiating to gain just cause clauses "the largest single trend (in negotiations) in the past three years." However, Dade County teachers are the first to use the clauses instead of, rather than in addition to, their state tenure statute. Under the new Dade contract (its tenure-related aspects have not been implemented this year because the Florida legislature has not yet made the necessary state changes) teachers who already have tenure will be able to choose to keep it. On the other hand, no teacher in the first or second year of probation will be awarded tenure. The proposed changes would allow teachers' unions in each district of Florida to choose either to negotiate for just cause dismissal clauses in their contracts or to be covered by the state law.

Do Teachers Still Need Tenure Laws?

Opponents of statutory tenure say that with the increase of contract tenure, the statutory variety is no longer needed. They also point to protections for teachers that the courts have drawn from constitutional amendments. The courts have, as far back as 1923, interpreted the Fifth and Fourteenth Amendments (which say that a person cannot be deprived of life, liberty or property without due process of law) as providing due process for teachers' right to work. In 1923, the Supreme Court ruled that the concept of liberty included freedom to engage in one's chosen profession. Some courts have also, since then, ruled that when a person enters an occupation he or she acquires a "property" right that cannot be arbitrarily taken away.

The opponents of tenure also like to point to school districts that appear to be running quite well without the statutes. One is the Salt Lake City School District. There, teachers and administrators work under a novel shared governance contract that includes peer evaluation. Any teacher (or administrator) whose supervisor judges his or her performance to be inferior is placed on a five-month remediation program designed and run by a four-member team. In the case of teachers, the team consists of the principal, a learning

A Brief History of Tenure

• The first teacher tenure law was enacted in 1906 at a time when teachers were being fired for just about any reason at all. It is on record that some teachers were fired for attending the theater, which was forbidden them in some communities. Others lost their jobs if they dared to smoke cigarettes or get married. Almost any kind of nonconformity could be cause for dismissal.

That first tenure law was born 23 years after the Pendleton Act set up the Civil Service Commission, doing away with the corrupt "spoils system" in federal government employment. And it came about 20 years after the National Education Association (NEA) had first begun to fight for tenure.

• By 1918, seven states plus the District of Columbia had tenure laws. Gradually, up until the depression, other states passed laws. But during the early thirties, the movement ground to a halt and then slid backwards.

On July 6, 1934, the tenure committee of the NEA reported:

"During the past three years the seriousness of the financial problems of our public schools has tended to hide the invasion of politics into the schools of certain communities; the increase in the discharge of competent, experienced teachers to make room for cheaper, inexperienced teachers or for personal friends or relatives of board members; the elimination of important school subjects and activities; the overloading of classes; and the injection of fear of unjust discharge into the consciousness of teachers. In many communities teaching morale is being destroyed; the building of a teaching profession has been halted."

• In the mid 30s the tenure movement began to recover and make up for lost time. National studies were written on the topic of academic freedom. In 1934 the NEA voted $10,000 for the work of its tenure committee and also passed strongly worded resolutions demanding academic freedom for teachers. In 1944, 44 states had tenure laws. By 1960, only four states—Mississippi, South Carolina, Utah and Vermont—were without them.

• During the 1960s, as states began adopting collective bargaining laws, teachers' unions rushed to negotiate contract clauses that would strengthen the rights they had gained through tenure laws.

• In the 1970s, tenure came under heavy attack. During 1971 and 1972, its opponents tried in about half the states to repeal or weaken the laws. None of the laws were rescinded, however, and very little change has occurred in state tenure laws in the past decade.—*P.P.*

specialist and two other teachers who are chosen from a list supplied by the teachers' union. At the end of the five-month remediation period, each member of the team must vote on whether to retain or fire the teacher.

Since 1974, when the program began, about 60 of Salt Lake City's 11,000 teachers and administrators have been placed on remediation. Of those, 30 left the district, most of them by resigning. Only two had to be terminated. And neither of those cases resulted in court battles, according to Donald Thomas, superintendent of schools. During the year before the program started, he says, there were three court cases that were related to terminations.

Proponents of state tenure statutes say that it is not realistic to believe that the Salt Lake City system could be widely duplicated. It requires teachers to take an active part in their own evaluation—a task that they feel is the job of administrators. They also say that the constitutional interpretations are still not in actuality as strong a protection as tenure statutes.

Finally the NEA and the AFT feel very strongly that, despite the rise of contract tenure, state tenure statutes are extremely important. Their leaders point out that not every local union in the country is large enough or powerful enough to win such clauses. Though teachers may be NEA members, there are no bargaining rights in many areas of the country. Thus—since not every teacher is necessarily covered by just cause dismissal clauses—if state laws were repealed, many teachers would be left totally unprotected.

"There are gaps in the coverage through collective bargaining," Dunlop of the NEA says, "and those gaps are very significant because we're out to protect all teachers, not just those who happen to have a powerful bargaining agent."

Despite all of the debate surrounding tenure, or perhaps because of it, many that I spoke with agreed that teachers have more job security now than they ever have had. In the 1980s, most observers predict that protection will increase, but so will administrators' success in using the laws to weed out incompetent teachers. More and more contracts will include just cause dismissal provisions, and as that happens, the word "tenure," which is associated with protection by state statute, may well fade from use.

To Improve Schools, Teachers Must Lead Children in a New Direction

"We must get the government off our backs" is a catch phrase that captures the social philosophy currently dominant in the United States. There is less wrong with what this view encompasses than with what it leaves uncovered. Merely cutting back government will not set America on a course of recovery unless these efforts are coupled with a period of reconstruction—of family, schools, neighborhoods and nation, and above all, of individual renewal.

Amitai Etzioni

Amitai Etzioni is a professor at George Washington University in Washington, D.C. This article is excerpted from An Immodest Agenda: Rebuilding America Before the Twenty-first Century *by Amitai Etzioni.*

With the words above, Amitai Etzioni, a former White House adviser for the Carter administration and currently a professor at George Washington University, introduces his recently published book, An Immodest Agenda: Rebuilding America Before the Twenty-first Century *(McGraw-Hill), in which he warns that if we hope to restore America's economic, social, political and ethical vigor, and if we expect to achieve this through decreased government intervention in our lives, we are going to have to take more responsibility for ourselves and for one another, "to be less preoccupied with self and more with 'us.' "*

What does this "period of reconstruction" entail? Etzioni calls for an end to the kind of excessive individualism and "ego-centered mentality" (characterized by the "do-your-own-thing" proponents of popular psychology) that sets self-fulfillment above all else, including family, other people and community. What's needed, he says, is a better balance between ego and other, between individualism and community-mindedness—what Etzioni refers to as mutuality*—as well as a resurgence of* civility*—a willingness to play by the rules and to become involved in commonweal concerns. "All said and done," Etzioni exhorts, "citizens will have to become less private, more public, more actively committed and involved in the shared concerns of the community."*

The family, being the first educational institution—and the place where mutuality is first experienced and civility is first taught—is the key to reconstruction, says Etzioni. Its ability to educate, particularly to develop personality and character, affects all the institutions that follow (schools, community, the workplace). But right after the family come the schools, "the second educational institution," and they, too, says Etzioni, are in need of reconstruction, *"although hardly for the reasons usually given."*

What follows is the first article of a two-part series in which Etzioni suggests the real reasons many (though far from all) American schools have failed in their first duty: to educate.*

It is a commonplace to suggest that American schools are a diminished, hollowed institution. Reports abound of rampant violence, drug abuse and alcoholism; of teacher "burnout"; of disappointed parents and resentful taxpayers; of declining test scores; of both long delays in adopting new teaching materials and methods (said to require a generation) and a rudderless pursuit of unproven fashions in the teaching of subjects from math to reading.

My readings of the data on school performance suggest that the criticisms of schools are, on the one hand, too sweeping, and on the other hand, misfocused. A nationwide study of the scope of violence in schools, for instance, conducted for Congress by the National Institute of Education, indicates that violence and highly disruptive behavior are concentrated in only about 15 to 20 percent of the schools, mainly inner-city public schools.

The lament of declining reading, writing and other school achievements, as well as declining SAT scores, has reached the level of cliché. However, the low point may well already have been passed, with both local and national scores slowly starting to mend. This is not to deny that scores are low nationwide compared to other advanced countries, and that whatever improvements are discernible began at rather low levels. Still, these data do not show that young Americans are functionally illiterate, or that "Johnny can't read" or "can't count," or that, as John R. Silber, the president of Boston University, put it, "Today's high school diploma is a

*For second part of series, see article 9, pg. 42.

fraudulent credential." Such statements and many similar ones about schools in general are much too sweeping. It is bad enough that maybe as many as half of the nation's schools do not function effectively; we need not go beyond that and declare that the schools *in toto* are failing.

Aside from being too broad, the criticisms commonly focus on the wrong issue. Cognitive learning is the preoccupation of most school critics. The continuing exposé of why Johnny can't read, for example, not only overstates the cognitive deficiency of young Americans but rests on the assumption that the schools stand or fall on their ability to teach cognitive skills.

This cognitive preoccupation is revealed both by those who urge that kids not be graduated, nor promoted from class to class, unless they demonstrate "minimum competence" in certain skills, and by those who oppose such educational policy on the ground that it is biased against minorities or enforces an all-too-low standard. It is the focus of those who favor a "core" curriculum as it is of those who favor plenty of electives; of those who see salvation of reading in the use of phonics as of those who advocate "sight reading." It sustains the proponents of "mastery learning" and modular, of new math and old, and so on through all the various teaching panaceas.

Character Formation, Mutuality and Civility

In evaluating the status of American schools and contemplating reconstruction, the first criterion I suggest we ought to use is contribution to personality development, to character formation. This requires special attention to school-generated experiences, which educate young Americans in the broadest sense.

To put it briefly first, a significant proportion of the children who enter American schools each year seem to be psychically underdeveloped. Their families have not helped them mature to the point that they can function effectively in a school, relate constructively to its rules, authorities and "work" discipline. It might be said that to relate well to many of the nation's schools—to their burned-out teachers, uninspiring principals, arbitrary rules and tedious assignments —would itself be a mark of maldevelopment on the side of the young generation. However, I refer here to a *general* incapacity to deal with authority, rules and "work," a deficient capacity to mobilize self and to commit it, whatever the setting.

Many schools—I estimate roughly a third—seem to add psychic damage to the psychic deficiencies new pupils import from their homes. These schools do little to develop underdeveloped personalities and quite often provide opportunities for further maladjustment. As a result, many young people are unable, for psychic reasons, first to learn effectively in the schools and then to function effectively in the adult world of work, community and citizenship. Thus, the root problem is not that millions of high school graduates have great difficulties in reading, writing and 'rithmetic; these all-too-common deficiencies are *consequences* of insufficient self-organization, of inadequate ability to mobilize and to commit. These graduates enter the adult world *twice* handicapped. They suffer both from continued psychic underdevelopment *and* from the inadequate cognitive preparation this underdevelopment helped to cause.

Let us look for a moment at a simple incident. A young secretary, recently hired, was asked to use the Yellow Pages of the telephone directory. When she was unable to do so, it became evident that she did not command the alphabet nor understand the principles of categorization and subcategorization involved.

Such inability would usually be counted an example of a cognitive deficiency, of poor teaching if not low IQ. However, if one asks why it is difficult to teach someone a list of 26 items and the principles of a very simple classification, one soon realizes that something more is amiss than that no one ever provided the needed time and effort. Nor could it be a question of IQ for most pupils, because so little comprehension or intelligence is involved.

Think what it would take you to memorize, say, a telephone number of 26 digits—a considerable amount of effort, but *not* cognitive; instead, concentration, control of impulse, self-motivation, ability to face and overcome stress (in order to resist distractions and accept the "routine" work involved in memorizing). This element of psychic organization, or capacity to mobilize and commit psychic energy to a task, is what those who are not learning well seem to me to be most lacking. It is what seems to account for their "inability" to do elementary computation (i.e., to memorize a few rules and discipline oneself to adhere to them), or to write a coherent paragraph (i.e., to remember the rules of punctuation, grammar, and so on—we are not dealing with effective writing, but straight English exposition).

The significance of psychic deficiencies for cognitive learning, for the acquisition of skills, can hardly be overstated. The relevance of personality development to the ability to work is elementary; young persons who cannot cope effectively with authority figures, rules and routines in schools cannot be expected to do so on most jobs.

At the foundation of civility and mutuality is a capacity to control impulse and mobilize ego's energies *in part* for acts other than the satisfaction of biological needs. The newborn infant has next to no such capacity; it is preoccupied with its immediate biological needs. The process of education, starting with the family, channels some of these drives to "energize" a regulator, to modify behavior by introducing a "personality" or character. This is achieved by tying biological satisfaction to socially acceptable gratifications (sublimation, if you wish); by relating satisfaction to sensitivity to others and deriving satisfaction from the affection and respect of others, the psychic basis of mutuality; and by building ego-restraints, the basis of playing by the rules, and ego-involvement in the transcending (public) realm and issues, the basis of civility.

It is possible to overeducate and draw too much of ego's energies into these spheres, a process that has concerned social scientists in the past and that has led to a call for less education and more freedom for ego. However, the historical context of present-day America seems to require the opposite: schools that, making up for undereducation in the family, lay the psychic foundation for mutuality, civility and work in the adult world —and in the schools themselves.

Structure and Self-Discipline Vs. Ego Psychology

While the common preoccupation with the cognitive agenda thus focuses on consequences rather than on the prime cause, a parallel concern with discipline is much closer to the mark. In one public opinion survey after another, teachers and parents rank discipline as the number one problem of the schools. This attention to discipline is highly relevant: It focuses on the school as a structure in which learning is to take place, and suggests that in a classroom where the proper relationships between pupils and teachers, and between students and rules and routines, cannot be developed and maintained, learning is not possible. Violent schools, the public correctly perceives, are not only unsafe but also provide institutional conditions under which schools cannot discharge their teaching duties.

So far, so good. Unfortunately, the focus on discipline itself is partially misdirected, although at least it calls attention to the right issue, the psychic one. Discipline, as most people understand it, is highly external: Teachers and principals "lay down the law"; students "show respect" (rise when the teacher enters the room, do not speak unless spoken to and so forth). What the pupil—and the future adult—really needs is *self*-discipline, *self*-organization, the ability to mobilize and commit self. This in turn is developed in structured conditions, but not in authoritarian ones.

The line between structure and authoritarianism is easy to illustrate but not to define. Basically, what is needed is not close, continuous external supervision, but a school structure—authority figures, rules and organization of tasks—that will build up the capacity of the student to regulate self. This is achieved best, it seems, when what is required of the student is clearly stated, and the link between requirements and educational goals is clearly and fully explained, rather than arbitrarily announced, changed at will and whim, and aimed as much at teachers' egos as at educational enhancement. Advancing self-organization requires that assignments be "do-able," appropriately checked and rewarded. When they are excessive and mechanical (such as excessive memorizing) or when rewards are allocated by irrelevant criteria (such as being teacher's favorite or having influential parents or minority status), requirements become dictates, not sources of involvement and ways to build commitments.

Of course, deficient self-organization—and school structure that neglects its development—is by no means limited to inner-city schools where violence and disruptive behavior are prevalent. Indeed, many suburban schools, schools in upper-middle-class parts of cities, and private schools suffer from a lack of structure and concern for self-discipline.

Structural weakness in these schools is often promoted by an educational version of the ego-centered mentality. One version is a bastardization of Freud that calls for "working out," "letting go," "expressing primordial urges" and "listening to one's inner feelings" as needed for ego growth. In schools these notions provide the ideology for an understructured social environment, and the withdrawal of authority both in practice and principle.

Two minor incidents provide quick, vivid illustrations. In a kindergarten on New York City's West Side, Freddy, age 4, bullies and brutalizes other kids for better than a week. The teacher does nothing to restrain or dissuade him; she firmly believes Freddy is "going through a stage" and must "work out" his hostilities. After that, she says, there will be an opportunity for some other kid to "find his victim." Lesson imparted: Yield to your impulses; society is a sequential jungle in which victimizers and victims take turns, as opportunity arises.

In a primary school in Montgomery County, Md., Jim sticks a pencil through the lip of David in the course of a fight, requiring David to have stitches. The following day the teacher explains to David's parents: "First of all, it was a very hot day, and Jim's parents are just in the middle of the worst divorce fight ever." Implication: What can be *explained* from the viewpoint of ego psychology is taken care of. Attention is focused on ego rather than on the needs of mutuality and civility. Lesson imparted: Do not rely on shared rules; take "the law" into your own hands.

Current Remedies Are As Bad as Current Abuses

The enthusiastic following won by popularized developmental psychology does not help. Particularly relevant in education have been the theories that portray children's learning as a natural unfolding from within, a process initiated and basically carried out by the child herself or himself.

Educational pop psychology's focus on ego and immediate satisfactions rather than on self-organization has been most evident in the open classroom movement, with its planned lack of structure. Students initiate their own "learning experiences" according to their interests and capabilities; the role of the teacher is to facilitate and encourage rather than to guide. For the pupil, enjoyment and spontaneity are said to be as important as growth and achievement. The open classroom movement explicitly repudiates deferment of gratification and ability to play by the rules, and advocates instead the educational equivalent of "do your own thing."

As I see it, this approach imposes too much on the child and too little on the educators and the schools. Moreover, this sunny view ignores the elementary fact that what children are when they begin school is not what children are by nature. At birth, when their "nature" is most evident, children are unformed creatures who, left to their own devices, will learn little. And what schools and teachers face is not children's unadulterated nature, but what families—and neighborhoods—have made of it. Schools cannot ignore the fact that many of the children who reach them are neither eager to learn nor good at it; they must first be won over to learning, in effect rehabilitated, and helped to develop learning habits.

I say "habits" deliberately. Not all learning can be made fun and games, and it should not be even if it could, because it would then provide a poor preparation for the post-school world. There the ability to defer gratification is required; not all work, not even all thinking, can be made intrinsically rewarding.

Critics of existing schools and advocates of alternative approaches often zero in on valid problems exhibited by traditional and bureaucratic schools, but then go overboard in their criticisms and, above all, in the reforms they suggest. Thus, critics correctly see many schools as too large, insensitive to children, and teacher oriented. But their more extreme corrections—such as making schools and teachers heed kids' cues almost exclusively, or closing the schools and letting kids learn by following adults around ("the way they did in primitive tribes")—take reform too far, both practically and conceptually.

That structure in schools is often excessive—that teachers with rigid, preset agendas, indifferent to children's interests and pace, will not be effective—cannot be argued. Yet learning needs structure, so the solution is not to eliminate structure, but to make it more effective for education. And recognition that teachers command superior knowledge and represent the adult world, that children are immature and often must be prodded to grow, and that not all growth is enjoyable and self-propelled, must balance the proper rejection of teacher authoritarianism.

MERIT PAY the great debate

Marge Scherer

Marge Scherer is managing editor/editorial of INSTRUCTOR.

"If we're going to give schools only one improvement, let it not be merit pay."

"I do not know how anyone, especially a teacher, can be against the idea of merit pay."

"Merit pay could restructure the entire teaching profession by providing the career ladder we've been needing."

"Merit pay! In an underpaid profession, it's like putting icing on a cake that doesn't exist."

The voices in the debate on merit pay are discordant even when they are all addressing the same proposal, which isn't often the case. For, as newscasters, presidential candidates, and the general public join in the discussion raised by the National Commission on Excellence in Education, the deceptively simple issue of merit pay threatens to disrupt the education profession to the same degree as the allegation of mediocrity has. Complicating matters is the fact that the merit pay plans are as various as they are numerous.

The recent furor over an issue that is at least 75 years old has prompted the NEA to decide to monitor all merit pay and master teacher plans. At the same time, it is on record as opposing any compensation system based on "favoritism, subjective evaluation," or arbitrary standards, including those based on student achievement or grade and subject taught. The AFT, on the other hand, passed a resolution that said, "While merit pay is not AFT policy, under certain circumstances state federations may feel the need to negotiate" plans that would promote significant numbers of teachers to more highly paid master teacher positions.

Meanwhile, in circles in and outside of education, people on opposite political and ideological sides continue to endorse and attack concepts rather than specific plans. Some proponents who want schools to improve but who are convinced that the vast majority of teachers are mediocre, feel merit pay is the way to reward good teachers and avoid paying the rest. Other merit pay advocates feel some of the plans could provide teachers more recognition, more career latitude, more money, as well as attract and keep better teachers and help to increase student achievement.

Many educators who have not been enthusiastic about merit pay in the past now feel that taking advantage of the current national interest in education is the astute thing to do. If merit pay is the way to get higher salaries for teachers, they say "so be it," but they want teachers to speak out about what kinds of merit pay are adopted in their districts. Both critics and proponents of merit pay warn that the wrong merit plan, the wrong procedures, could increase competition among teachers, lower student and teacher morale, and, worst of all, by inaccurately defining what it means to be a good teacher, effectively cut off true educational reform.

What kinds of plans are being discussed?

Bonus pay based on student performance What some people are talking about when they say "merit pay" is a bonus given to teachers for what is considered to be superior teaching and not given to those who don't meet the criteria. For instance, in Seiling, Oklahoma, merit pay is a $500 bonus given to every teacher in the elementary school if all children in school average above the targeted increase in reading scores. In addition, each teacher may receive another $250 for each of his or her classes whose reading scores reach the target and another $250 if math scores meet the goal. The maximum merit pay an elementary teacher can earn is $1,000.

A committee of teachers headed by the superintendent sets the target, each year trying to increase the standard over the previous year. Scores from standardized, criterion-referenced, and teacher-made pre- and post-tests are keyed into a computer that is programmed to convert the scores to Normal Curve Equivalency points, and to figure the class average, school average, and amount of bonus each teacher will receive. So far, all participating teachers (38 out of 42 this year) have earned the $500 because the school each year has exceeded the target. About 85 percent of these teachers have earned additional bonus money above and beyond their salaries, which range from $15,000 to $21,000.

Gerald Daugherty, Seiling superintendent, says the system "rewards extraordinary teachers and encourages those who are teetering on the brink of mediocrity." The four-year-old plan, which is not used as a substitute for annual salary raises, has resulted in "a definite trend toward higher scores and greater teacher concentration on goals."

Teachers in Seiling mention drawbacks in the plan—a major one being that students are aware their scores control merit pay for teachers and that some deliberately score low on the tests of teachers they don't like. (The tests do not necessarily affect students' grades.) To protect against this problem, the top and bottom 10 scores are disregarded in figuring class averages. Other criticisms by teachers are that the tests don't accurately measure the full scope of what is being taught; that tests take valuable time; and that teachers must teach to the tests, although not exclusively.

Educators outside the system direct their criticism not at the Seiling plan but at the general principle of using student achievement as the basis of merit pay. Their major criticism is that reliance on such tests indicates a narrow notion of what teaching is. "Teachers are seen as review books, not educators," says Samuel Bacharach of Cornell University, who is currently reviewing all arguments for and against merit pay for the National Education Association. He says that any system based on student tests reflects a belief in the scientific objectivity of tests to a degree of predictability and accuracy we just don't have.

Thomas Good of the University of Missouri, author of *Looking in Classrooms* and *Teachers Make a Difference,* comes to the same conclusion: "If good teaching means high test scores, then teachers will mobilize all teaching to that purpose." Because it is easier to come up with valid measures in math and reading as opposed to social studies, art, or music, the latter subjects may be neglected. "Not only is the content of what is being taught narrowed, but teaching students abstract processes like problem-solving and self-evaluation are dropped in favor of teaching them what is measured on tests. . . .I would be very much interested in the attitudes of the students in such a system. Do they see classrooms as more answer oriented than learning oriented?"

Richard Murnane, an associate professor of economics at the Harvard Graduate School of Education, voices another concern about using student achievement tests for the purpose of merit pay. "It could put a premium on having the brightest students in the classroom and result in teachers lobbying for students who would respond well to instruction," he says. In other systems that are weighted in favor of average achievers, "teachers would allocate less time to both the gifted and low ability children, figuring the gifted would make a year's gain with very little teaching, and the lowest students, even with great effort, might not achieve the target." Despite the fact that seniority-based contracts may unfairly pay both the poor and the good teacher the same amount, Murnane thinks that the system is truer to the concept of equal opportunity for students than are many merit pay plans.

Increments based on teacher performance A completely different approach, an incentive increment plan, is taken in Ladue, Missouri, where teachers are observed and evaluated by principals three times a year. Teachers are awarded points in such categories as classroom performance, interaction with colleagues, effective communication with the community, contributions to the school district, and professional self-improvement. Each year the school board determines how much the points are worth. In the 1982-83 year a teacher could earn $300 per point, and teachers could earn up to $4,500 in merit pay. About 10 to 15 percent of teachers get the maximum amount, giving some teachers salaries in the $38,000 range. (The beginning salary is $14,500, and the average salary about $30,000.)

Carol Hampton, a Ladue teacher, says the system works because "when it started, the teachers and administrators had a family feeling that has filtered down through the years." The system has an appeal procedure that teachers can use, as well.

Charles McKenna, Ladue superintendent, says that when he came to Ladue 20 years ago, 10 years after the program started, he took a "look-and-see attitude." Now he's convinced: "There's no way to defend using college credits and years of experience as the only criteria for paying teachers. Everyone's willing to admit there is such a thing as a good teacher, yet few are willing to say how outstanding performance can be determined. Any kind of evaluation program requires time and effort and training for those who will conduct it. There's a margin of error in our system but less than if we had a strictly automatic seniority-based system."

Those who question the plan say that while it might work in Ladue, they have their doubts that such a system would work in a less wealthy or less closely knit group, mostly because the merit increments would not be enough to matter or because charges of favoritism would be overwhelming.

Glen Robinson of the Educational Research Service, a nonprofit corporation sponsored by eight national associations, found in a 1978 national study that many districts that had abandoned merit plans did so because evaluation procedures were unsatisfactory. Among problems reported were difficulties in determining who deserved extra pay, inconsistency among evaluations, poor evaluative instruments, too much record-keeping, and a belief of teachers that impartial ratings were impossible.

A major decision to make in such plans is which person or group will be responsible for the evaluation. Principals who do not often visit classrooms or know curricula are not the best evaluators, and problems may result with peer review as well. "I had a wonderful review one year," says New York teacher Valerie Bang-Jensen, who recently studied merit pay proposals for a graduate course. "But I felt my evaluators did not really understand what I was trying to do in the classroom. Some evaluators have philosophical blinders and may like what they see only if it coalesces with their own educational theories." Others may be impressed with the obvious—straightened blinds or a creative desk arrangement.

If evaluators come from outside the district, they may not understand the specific school situation. If they come from inside, the politics of the district may override their objectivity. Even if an evaluation is done with care and integrity, whether it really measures the quality of superior teaching or is at all related to student achievement are two more questions worth debating.

"It's so much easier to describe what is not working in a classroom than it is to describe the difference between an average classroom and a good one," Thomas Good says. "Too often we evaluate teachers as if they were actors on the stage," noting their movement, appearance, voice quality, and enthusiasm, but "part of the quality of teaching is continuity—building meaning over time. . . . Our rating systems usually are based on three or four observations; it all boils down to the question 'How spellbinding was she?' "

Evaluators also tend to assume that if something is good, more will be better, Good says. Thus if evaluators consider that homework leads to student achievement, the teacher who assigns a good deal of homework may be rated superior. Research doesn't bear that out though, he says. "A teacher can assign too much homework, ask too many questions, even allow too much time for response. What we should really consider is the effect on the student."

Educators also criticize using evaluations of teacher performance as a basis of merit pay because administrators often have to impose a quota system on the number of teachers eligible for merit pay. If a superintendent does not impose some limits, everyone will receive excellent ratings, and the merit pay will be spread too thin, says Joe Shedd, a doctoral candidate in industrial relations at Cornell University. "And if grade creep does occur, the school board will request extra documentation. . . . It will be such a headache to document a high or low rating, they might find it easier to give average ratings." And if quotas are imposed, the collegiality of the staff will suffer. "Effective school research shows that education is a group effort," Shedd says. "The very worst thing to do is to set up a compensation system that rewards only individual effort and discourages teachers from sharing ideas and advice with one another."

Another question often raised in the debate on merit pay is who is most motivated by it—the average teacher, the new teacher, the extremely good teacher, or the poor teacher? The average teacher who could be good but needs more money might well decide to moonlight at another job rather than put extra effort into teaching, Bang-Jensen says. And if money is the object for bright new teacher candidates, there are many other career options open.

Gerald Daugherty says in his experience, the average teachers benefit most. "Good teachers whose egos are wrapped up in their students and teaching will do yeoman's work no matter what you pay. And no amount will make a sorry teacher into a great one." But for the majority, "a little incentive causes them to be more concerned with the outcome of their work." Samuel Bacharach says the person who is *hurt* the most by a merit pay system is the one who aims for merit pay and doesn't get it. "The average worker thinks he is better than 80 percent of his coworkers. No person will be as frustrated as the one who is *almost* a good teacher."

Individualized Productivity Plan A third type of merit pay proposal attempts to combine the best features of other merit plans and to avoid their problems. Developed by the Educational Research Service, the plan is based on student achievement and on teacher performance, and if adequately financed, theoretically would be available to all who qualify. It has not yet been put into practice, according to Glen Robinson, ERS president, but a number of school districts are studying it.

Under this plan, a teacher could be awarded merit pay when he or she had met his or her own individual productivity goals and submitted an individualized performance plan for verification to an approved committee. In this plan a seventh-grade math teacher might suggest she could teach the same content in less time than she did previously while maintaining or improving test scores, and then would use the remaining time to teach a computer literacy course. If that teacher could satisfactorily prove she had met her own goal, she would receive the agreed upon bonus. Other personal productivity proposals might include ways of increasing student learning (including that of a special group of students with learning or behavior problems); improving student attitudes; teaching more students while maintaining achievement; and so on. The key to this plan is that the teacher is responsible for designing the proposal and objectively measuring whether it's been successful, says Robinson. It ideally would be used in conjunction with a conventional evaluation plan based on staff relations, classroom management, and techniques of instruction to help teachers improve performance. The productivity plan would not take teachers out of the classroom or establish a hierarchy of teachers, but would raise the morale of all, Robinson says.

Whether or not such a plan is practical depends greatly on what types of proposals are made and on the committee who accepts or rejects them. "I'd want to know who's on the committee, what role parents have, and how varied the plans could be," Richard Murnane says. "I'd also want to know who determines which students teachers get because many times the more difficult and harder to handle students would not be those who teachers feel increase their personal productivity." Yet the plan has potential, he says, and although he can't see it working in urban Philadelphia with 30,000 teachers negotiating proposals, he believes the program might work in smaller districts.

Thomas Good concurs with the idea of rewarding careful teaching and encouraging teachers to think instead of "trying to standardize what it means to be a good teacher." The quality of the proposals would have to be good, however. Individualized criteria could not be gratuitous or silly. "Any goal can be reached if set low enough." Another consideration is whether such a proposal could expect too much of teachers. "If teachers are expected to broaden their capabilities they would have to be very skillful indeed to do it without changing their classroom situations in any material way. They should have the option of requesting additional equipment, additional help, someone to help them grade papers, a team of teachers to work with. . . .We should think of adding more resources as well as altering compensatory systems if we are going to achieve excellence."

Differentiated staffing The differentiated staffing approach differs significantly from bonus or incentive plans to the extent that some persons who advocate them disavow the use of the term *merit pay*. Instead of giving extra pay for superior teaching, these plans assign higher salaries to positions considered to be more important, have more responsibility, or be in more demand.

David Rhone, president of National Management Associates in Shippensburg, Pennsylvania, proposes a plan that would pay teachers of "more difficult" subjects more; for instance, first-grade and math teachers would receive higher salaries, with middle school teachers' salaries falling in the middle range, and possibly driver education teachers' in the lowest. The idea behind the plan is to relate compensation to job and "to stop paying everyone the same rate based on years of time in the system. . . .Each district would have to determine which jobs to reward more, making it necessary for the community to think hard about what it values the most," Rhone says.

The Houston Second Mile Plan incorporates differentiated staffing as well as other ways teachers can earn stipends. Teachers in a school with many disadvantaged students; those who teach subjects where there are staff shortages (bilingual education and secondary mathematics, for instance); and those whose schools exceed predicted achievement on standardized tests all can apply for stipends ranging from $400 to $2,000. Teachers who miss five or fewer days in attendance are also eligible for stipends ranging from $50 to $500. The multiple provisions in the plan reflect specific needs of the district and are ways to respond to teacher shortages, staff absenteeism, and the need for improved standardized test scores. Criticism of the arbitrariness of some of the provisions aside, educators say the problem with differentiated staffing is in establishing the relative importance of different teaching jobs. NEA and AFT affiliates have both opposed the plan, and many teachers question the judgment of those who say math is more important than social studies.

The career ladder approach This approach differs from differentiated staffing in that it creates new career steps and promotes teachers to more highly paid teaching levels. Under such a plan, teachers at higher levels may be responsible for teaching and evaluating other teachers or developing the curriculum. Some may teach more hours and months, as well. Tennessee Governor Lamar Alexander's career path approach establishes four career levels: apprentice, professional, senior, and master teachers. Teachers advance to the next highest level based on the number of years at the previous level (at least three); performance evaluations by supervisors; competency or subject-area tests; and student performance. In addition, those who are advanced to the master teacher level would have to demonstrate the ability to work with and evaluate other teachers. State and local committees of evaluators would be formed to continuously reevaluate and recertify teachers.

Under the plan, professional teachers would receive $1,000 in incentive pay in addition to across-the-board raises; senior teachers (25 percent of Tennessee teachers would be eligible) would get $2,000 or $4,000 more, depending on whether they had a 10- or 12-month contract; and master teachers (another 15 percent) could earn from $3,000 to $5,000 more. Senior and master teachers would work in the summer with gifted or remedial students, or they would conduct inservice for teachers or develop curricula.

The advantage of the plan, says Chester Finn, professor of education and public policy at Vanderbilt University, is that it fulfills teachers' needs. "A good teacher is motivated by intrinsic rewards, a decent salary, and by being recognized by others in society," he says. "In the last few years the intrinsic rewards have been harder to achieve and material rewards have been less. This plan will keep good people in the system."

One major problem may be that apprentice teachers will want to achieve promotions at a faster rate. "For new teachers it will take 11 years before they become master teachers. If they're real hotshots, other careers could pay off sooner," Finn says.

Other unknowns about career ladder systems are how teachers who remain in the lower categories throughout their careers might be affected and how their students and students' parents will react to not having the "best teachers." (In the Tennessee plan, apprentice teachers must advance at least to the professional level in a certain period of time or lose their position.)

Most career path systems also establish an additional bureaucracy of evaluators, and require a great deal of record-keeping, and much time given to evaluating teachers. Most master teacher plans also take those judged to be the best teachers out of the classroom or require them to take on an additional work load. "The good teacher

Questions to ask

Eric Rhodes, the president of the consulting firm Educational Futures Research, suggests the following questions to ask before considering a merit pay plan.

1. What's your purpose? Is it to improve instruction, reward outstanding teachers, attract better teaching candidates, motivate teachers?
2. Will you evaluate teachers on the basis of their assignment and degree of responsibility? on students' standardized test results? on peer or administration observation of performance? or a combination of the above?
3. How will teachers' associations and unions participate in decisions about implementing merit pay? What will your appeal process be?
4. What is your time line? (A year of planning is realistic.)
5. What costs are you willing to bear? Rewards must be sufficiently attractive, at least 10 percent of average salary. A merit pay plan in a district of 500 teachers with an average salary of $20,000 could cost a minimum of one-third of a million dollars.

might want to spend the energy and effort in the classroom," Valerie Bang-Jensen suggests.

What else is there?

Many merit pay plans have a primary objective to attract or to keep good teachers and thereby to improve the quality of education for students. According to a great many educators, merit pay is surely not the only way of doing that. Almost all mention that a reasonable salary to begin with is most important. "If we want to attract excellent teachers, we won't do it just by dabbling with merit pay or master teachers programs," says Louis Fischer, a professor of education at the University of Massachusetts, Amherst. "One of my key concerns is that through endorsing merit pay for a few people, we provide a rationalization for not looking at greater salaries for all concerned."

Beyond that, educators offer their own ideas for what else besides money motivates good teachers. Harvard's Richard Murnane suggests that "trying to make the job of teaching more pleasant will go a longer way in improving education than merit pay will." To do this he suggests decreasing bureaucracy so that teachers with good ideas can put them into effect, and dividing large-school faculties into teams of teachers working with smaller groups of students. To attract new candidates to teaching, he thinks a dramatic salary boost in the second year ("if you're going to get good, you get good fast") coupled with on-the-job help from older teachers would improve the performance of young teachers more-so than would the possibility of having a career ladder in later years.

When Karen Zumwalt, associate professor, Teachers College, Columbia University, conducted a survey to determine why veteran teachers had positive feelings about their teaching jobs, she found that the teachers identified respect, recognition, and reinforcement as those things that had improved their teaching. Participating in research studies; being a member of a teaching team; earning grants for curriculum development; as well as being encouraged by principals, parents, colleagues, and students all motivated these teachers to keep striving for excellence. She believes, "It's a leap of faith to think merit pay will solve our problems. We'll need merit pay, plus a lot of other things."

Teacher Burnout: A Psychoeducational Perspective

Barry A. Farber
Teachers College, Columbia University
Julie Miller
New York University

In the last decade, probably no professional group has been criticized as frequently or as intensely as teachers. Teachers have been accused of failing to adequately teach students, of failing to control student violence, of failing to be sensitive to racial differences among their students, and even of failing to be professionally "responsible" in their salary demands. When schools become battlegrounds teachers are accused not only of instigating the war but of profiting from the spoils.

It has become apparent, however, that teachers, as well as students, are victimized by problem-laden schools. Indeed, *teacher burnout* has become a problem of increasing public and professional concern. Major newspapers, magazines, and television news shows have recently carried stories about teacher burnout,[1] and the National Education Association (NEA) made teacher burnout the central theme of their 1979 convention. According to NEA, as a result of burnout, "thousands of sensitive, thoughtful and dedicated teachers have already left teaching and thousands more may well be contemplating such a move."[2] In this regard, too, a recent NEA poll noted that one-third of the teachers surveyed stated that if they were starting their careers over again they would choose not to become teachers; in addition, only 60 percent reported that they planned to remain in teaching until retirement.[3] Further evidence of disillusionment is supplied by the fact that whereas in 1962, 28 percent of all teachers had twenty years experience, by 1976 that number had been reduced by half.[4]

Teacher burnout has already reached serious, if not crisis, proportions. The societal implications of this problem are great. As Sarason noted:

> If it becomes increasingly the case that professionals experience a widening discrepancy in work between expectations and satisfactions, the negative consequences for their lives will have ramifications far beyond the spheres of their individual existence.[5]

Among teachers themselves, burnout will continue to potentiate "radical career changes" as well as increased demands for alternative sources of satisfaction. However, the most critical impact of teacher burnout will surely be on the delivery of educational services, particularly to that growing segment of the population that can ill afford a further deterioration of an already lacking educational system and is most certainly unable to gain access to private schooling.

These trends portend ominously for the future state of public education. Yet despite increasing awareness of the deleterious effects of teacher burnout on individuals as well as on communities, there remains a notable paucity of adequate empirical research on this topic. Moreover, it is our contention that even recent attempts to develop a conceptual framework for understanding teacher burnout have been incomplete or inadequate. These efforts have too often viewed teacher burnout as a problem of individual "overload" or psychopathology and have failed to adequately acknowledge the salience of historical or even environmental factors in the burnout process.

Burnout

Freudenberger[6] originally coined the term "burnout" to describe the emotional and physical exhaustion of staff members of alternative health care institutions. In recent years a small but growing number of studies have investigated the burnout phenomenon.[7] Maslach, for example, in studying a broad range of health and social service professionals, found that burned-out professionals "lose all concern, all emotional feelings for the persons they work with and come to treat them in detached or even dehumanized ways."[8] Burned-out professionals may become cynical toward their clients, blaming them for creating their own difficulties or labeling them in derogatory terms. Furthermore, the

We would like to express our appreciation to Maxine Greene and Seymour Sarason for their helpful ideas and encouragement.

"Teacher Burnout: A Psychoeducational Perspective," Barry A. Farber and Julie Miller, *Teachers College Record,* Winter 1981.

emotional frustrations attendant on this phenomenon may lead to psychosomatic symptoms (e.g., exhaustion, insomnia, ulcers, headaches) as well as increased family conflict.

Although burnout is a topic of growing interest to researchers, no study to date has systematically investigated the process of dimensions of teacher burnout. The literature bearing on the topic consists primarily of (1) research on the general dimensions of professional burnout as noted above; (2) impressionistic or autobiographical accounts of the difficulties of teaching;[9] (3) clinical descriptions of "battered teachers" or of teachers suffering from "combat neurosis";[10] and (4) empirical research on teacher stress[11]—a concept that is related but not identical to that of burnout. While this literature fails to provide an entirely adequate data base for clarifying the nature of teacher burnout, it does provide some useful hypotheses regarding the etiological, symptomatic, and treatment components of the phenomenon.

Etiology

The proposed causes of teacher burnout include discipline problems (student violence and abusiveness), student apathy, overcrowded classrooms, involuntary transfers, excessive paperwork, excessive testing, inadequate salaries, demanding or unsupportive parents, lack of administrative support, and public criticism of teachers. The most salient factors appear to be those related to issues of school discipline. In the recent NEA poll, nearly three-fourths of all respondents (74 percent) felt that discipline problems impaired their teaching effectiveness, at least to some extent; moreover, 45 percent of teachers polled believed that the school had not done enough to help them with their discipline problems.[12] Predispositional factors may also contribute to teacher burnout. Bloch, for example, reports that teachers who are obsessional, passionate, idealistic, and dedicated (as measured by the Minnesota Multiphasic Personality Inventory—a well-established and often-used psychological test) are more prone to the "battered teacher syndrome."[13]

Symptoms

The symptomatic manifestations of teacher burnout are anger, anxiety, irritability, depression, fatigue, boredom, cynicism, guilt, substance abuse (alcohol or drugs), psychosomatic symptomatology, and, in extreme cases, paranoid ideation. Marital and family crises are also likely to arise among teachers who are burned out. On a professional level, the consequences of these symptoms may include diminished professional performance, excessive sick leave, and premature retirement. Stated more descriptively, teachers who become burned out may plan classes less often or less carefully, may be less sympathetic toward students, may expect less effort from their students and less reward from their jobs, may have a lower tolerance for frustration in the classroom, may frequently feel emotionally or physically exhausted, may develop a numbed or "depersonalized" state as a way of distancing themselves from perceived threats, may fantasize or actually plan on leaving the profession, and, in general, may feel less committed and dedicated to their work.

Treatment Approaches

No standardized treatment plans have been established. Proposals for either preventing teacher burnout or reducing its severity include additional teacher training that would more adequately prepare teachers to cope with violence and stress; firmer and more consistent administrative responses to student violence; increased sensitivity of administrative staff to teacher problems; grants to afford instructors respite from their teaching duties and an opportunity to participate in educational research; physical exercise and participation in fulfilling outside activities; periodic shifting of grade or even school assignments; education of the public to increase the status of teachers in society; school-based crisis intervention teams; community-based hot lines; teacher drop-in centers; and the establishment of coalitions among teachers, administrative staff, parents, and community leaders. It should be noted that these proposals are primarily based on a crisis-intervention model. That is to say, the implicit task revolves around "treating" teachers after they are already burned out.

Stress, Teacher Burnout, and School Structure

As noted above, the traditional view of teacher burnout is that it is a phenomenon attributable exclusively to pressures caused by student violence and apathy, overcrowded classrooms, inadequate salaries, public criticism, and so forth. These conditions undoubtedly do lead to stress and even trauma. However, it is our hypothesis that teacher burnout is attributable not only to overt sources of stress but often to unexamined factors within school structures that lead to a lack of a *psychological sense of community*[14]—a lack that produces feelings on the part of teachers of both isolation and inconsequentiality.

Let us offer an example to illustrate this point. Teacher A and Teacher B are both sixth-grade teachers in inner-city schools. Both have experienced discipline problems in their classrooms, both have had only limited success in improving their students' reading scores, and both have had a history of frustrating, unproductive meetings with parents. In short, both teachers appear to be equally stressed and equally prone to burnout. However, Teacher A works in a school where she feels herself to be an integral part of a common group tradition and mission, and is identified with a network of relationships reciprocal in nature and mutually enhancing. When stresses arise for Teacher A, she enjoys a psychological sense of community that validates her worth and supports her needs. Teacher B, on the other hand, perceives that she has no such opportunities for collaboration and support. When stresses arise for Teacher B they are magnified by her sense of isolation and, in turn, invariably make her feel as if her professional efforts are in vain. What we are contending, therefore, is that a psychological sense of community may mitigate the impact of stress and prevent or reduce the intensity of teacher burnout.

Empirical support for this position is suggested by a study investigating correlations between absenteeism, personal characteristics of teachers, and structural aspects of schools. Bridges and Hallinan[15] found no significant relationship between teacher absenteeism (which may be viewed as a consequence of stress) and such factors as sex, age, or marital status. Significant correlations were, however, found between subunit size (number of persons a teacher was involved with on a daily basis) and work system interdependence (how many people made up the teacher's actual work team). Absenteeism rates were lowest in small schools where a great deal of contact was usual among small numbers of people. Additional evidence of the importance of affiliation to teachers comes from studies by Super and Holland.[16] Their findings indicate that in comparison with other occupational groups, teachers are highly "social" and greatly value opportunities to interact with co-workers.

Social and political factors in the last two decades have contributed considerably to teachers' growing sense of isolation. The middle 1960s marked the end of an era of widespread public reverence for teachers.[17] Teachers then were grossly underpaid but enjoyed the admiration and respect of a public that regarded them as highly competent professionals. If a child was not doing well in school it was the child's "fault" and the parents' shame; the teacher was considered sacrosanct. But in the early and mid 1960s—an era that saw thousands of idealistic young people become teachers, an era of social awareness and protest, an era when "the system" became the focus of abuse—a transformation occurred. Violence in schoolchildren was now seen as the inevitable product of an unresponsive, morally bankrupt nation; the onus of educational failure began to shift from the child to the teacher. Teachers no longer received the same kind of respect and admiration, and, now, if a child was not doing well in school it could be regarded as the fault of an uncaring, incompetent, and possibly even racist teacher. The child was now the highly respected and often sacrosanct institution; a child's failure was now considered the school's fault and the teacher's shame. This trend might appear to be progressive, but it is ironic and unfortunate that many of the same educators, critics, and concerned citizens who applauded the demise of the "deficit model" of the inner-city child—a model ascribing the failures of urban education to cultural, emotional, and intellectual deficiencies in the child—are now subscribing to a deficit model of the teacher, believing that school failures are primarily the result of teacher deficiencies. The wholesale adoption of this model by a public eager to scapegoat some group, any group, for educational failures has certainly driven many teachers into a stance of embittered isolation.

As it stands, teachers' needs for affiliation and support are often unfulfilled. For the most part, teachers are terribly alone in their helping roles. They not only function independently, but, within the confines of their classrooms, they become the sole repository for skills, stamina, and enrichment—a role that cannot long be endured by any single individual. As a further contributory factor to teachers' lack of a psychological sense of community, it should be noted that schools are settings where learning and change are viewed as goals for someone other than the helping professional.[18] Thus, in spite of the obvious impact of teacher satisfaction on pupil performance, schools are inadequately designed to meet the needs of teachers. In short, Levine's notion of "teaching as a lonely profession"[19] clarifies an essential aspect of the etiological basis of teacher burnout—an aspect too long ignored by those preferring to view the problem within the paradigm of individual, rather than environmental, pathology. While the symptoms of teacher burnout form an observable clinical profile, their origins must be properly located in a social-environmental context.

Strategies for Intervention

The prevention of teacher burnout requires that the overarching goal of all intervention efforts be the development of a structurally enduring psychological sense of community. We propose that in order for this to occur, the environment of the school must be altered in such a way that it becomes a growth-producing, motivating one for teachers and other educational personnel. Reppucci[20] has offered several guidelines for the creation of settings conducive to the needs of helping professionals, among them "a guiding idea or philosophy which is understandable to, and provides hope for, all members of the institution"; an organizational structure encouraging consistent collaboration among all levels of staff personnel; and the necessity of active community involvement. Based on these principles, schools in which teachers experience a psychological sense of community might feature, for example, ongoing case conferences geared not only to acute student crises but to the long-term expression of teachers' needs, concerns, and interests; a team-teaching concept of education; variation in teachers' scheduled routines; consistent program- and problem-oriented contact with administrative as well as paraprofessional personnel (apart from the usual adversary meetings); an active in-school teachers center; use of school facilities for teachers after hours; recruitment and utilization of community volunteers; and effective coalitions among teachers, administrators, parents, and community leaders. In regard to this last point, we have found that active collaboration among all segments of the educational community reduces the institutionalization of teaching as a lonely profession; reinforces the teacher's esteem for peers, community members, and self; and may rejuvenate a teacher's commitment to and investment in the children in the classroom. To be sure, these are but a few examples of the kinds of situations that may lead teachers to experience themselves as part of a schoolwide, and indeed communitywide, effort to educate children. What is important to recognize is that all such innovations should grow out of a sensitivity to the fact that the experience of work is intimately related to a psychological sense of community.[21] It is worth noting, too, that while the creation of social-professional support networks to combat professional burnout has been encouraged by researchers in the field,[22] with few exceptions (e.g., the formation of a Teachers Center in the Bayshore, Long Island, public school system[23]), this general concept has not been widely or successfully adopted on a grass-roots level.

A teacher burnout becomes an issue of increasingly greater public concern—and it surely will as its impact on children becomes more apparent—pressure to arrive at "immediate" solutions will intensify. It is likely that these solutions will consist of treatment plans whereby teachers will be brought together to compile a list of stresses or "horror" stories with the hope that these efforts will offer cathartic relief. Undoubtedly, some teachers will be temporarily gratified by the opportunity to share their experiences in an atmosphere of acknowledgment and support. It is our contention, however, that the majority of such treatment efforts lend themselves, at best, to the illusion of short-term benefits. These efforts fall within the category of "first order change,"[24] that is, they do not alter the nature of the malfunctioning system (the school in this case) and, in fact, serve to perpetuate present misconceptions regarding the nature and treatment of the problem. First-order strategies are of the type that bring to mind the classic French proverb, "the more things change, the more they stay the same." Even, however, when first-order change fails, that is, when teachers begin to perceive "gripe sessions" as unproductive and outside consultants as essentially unhelpful, first-order strategies are likely to be continued. In fact, the nature of social science problem solving is such that failure most often leads to *increased* use of the same or similar strategies. The usual administrative prescription is for more of the same.

Effective remediation of teacher burnout requires second-order change strategies, that is, a reconceptualization of the problem in a different manner and subsequent modification of the system's functioning. In this case, the reconceptualization involves understanding that burnout is not an inevitable result of the inevitable stress a teacher faces; the modification of the system involves utilizing principles underlying a psychological sense of community.

It is, of course, clear that social problems do not have "solutions" in the same sense as do mathematical or biochemical problems. And though the establishment of social-professional support networks within a general psychological sense of community cannot guarantee the prevention or abolition of teacher burnout within a school it can, and does, offer a more comprehensive and potentially enduring solution to this problem.

Notes

1 See "The ABC's of School Violence," *Time,* January 23, 1978, pp. 73-74; "What about Teachers?" *Sixty Minutes* (CBS Television), March 1979; Fred Hechinger, "About Education," *New York Times,* 15 July 1980, pp. C1, C4; Sally Reed, "Teacher Burnout, A Growing Hazard," *New York Times,* 7 January 1979, section 13, 1; and "Teacher Burnout," *Wall Street Journal,* 25 July 1979, p. 20.

2 William H. McGuire, statement on teacher burnout distributed at the meeting of the National Education Association, Detroit, June-July 1979.

3 William H. McGuire, "Teacher Burnout," *Today's Education* 68, no. 4 (1979): 5-7.

4 These figures cited in "Teacher Burnout: How to Cope When Your World Goes Blank," *Instructor* 6 (1979): 57. Note too, however, that even those teachers who stay in the field may be performing at less than optimal efficiency—a recent Rand Corporation study showed that teachers tend to "peak out" after five or seven years on the job.

5 Seymour B. Sarason, *Working, Aging, and Social Change: Professionals and the One Life-One Career Imperative* (New York: Free Press, 1977), p. 232.

6 Herbert J. Freudenberger, "Staff Burnout," *Journal of Social Issues* 1 (1974): 159-64.

7 See Cary Cherniss, Edward S. Egnatios, and Sally S. Wacker, "Job Stress and Career Development in New Public Professionals," *Professional Psychology* 7 (1976): 428-36; Herbert J. Freudenberger, "Burnout: Occupational Hazard of the Child Care Worker," *Child Care Quarterly* 6, no. 2 (1977): 90-99; Robert Kahn, "Job Burnout: Prevention and Remedies," *Public Welfare,* Spring 1978, pp. 61-63; Christina Maslach, "Burned Out," *Human Behavior* 5 (1976): 16-22; and Ayala Pines and Ditta Kafry, "Occupational Tedium in the Social Services," *Social Work* 23 (1978): 499-507.

8 Maslach, "Burned Out," p. 16.

9 In the last two to three years there have been many descriptive accounts of teacher burnout written by teachers and administrators that have been published in popular teacher magazines. See, for example: Jan Adams, "Send Me No Apples," *Instructor* 88, no. 2 (1978): 118-26; Madeline Hunter, "Getting Ready—Counter-Irritants to Teaching," *Instructor* 87, no. 1 (1977): 122-24; Robert Scrivens, "The Big Click," *Today's Education* 68, no. 4 (1979): 34-35; and Bettie B. Youngs, "Anxiety and Stress—How They Affect Teaching," *NAASP Bulletin* 62, no. 421 (1978): 78-83.

10 Alfred M. Bloch, "The Battered Teacher," *Today's Education* 66, no. 2 (1977): 58-62; and idem, "Combat Neurosis in Inner-City Schools," *American Journal of Psychiatry* 135, no. 10 (1978).

11 See Glenese Keavney and Kenneth E. Sinclair, "Teacher Concerns and Teacher Anxiety: A Neglected Topic of Classroom Research," *Review of Educational Research* 48, no. (1978): 273-90; and Chris Kyriacou and John Sutcliffe, "Teacher Stress: Prevalence, Sources, and Symptoms," *British Journal of Educational Psychology* 48 (1978): 159-67.

12 In New York City, crime against teachers in the public schools declined during the last academic year for the first time in sex years. However, despite this improvement, the United Federation of Teachers stated that teachers still faced an "intolerable situation."

13 Bloch, "The Battered Teacher."

14 Seymour B. Sarason, *The Psychological Sense of Community: Prospects for a Community Psychology* (San Francisco: Jossey-Bass, 1974).

15 Edwin M. Bridges and Maureen T. Hallinan, "Subunit Size, Work System Interdependence, and Employee Absenteeism," *Educational Administration Quarterly* 14, no. 2 (1978): 24-42.

16 Donald E. Super, *Work Values Inventory* (Boston: Houghton Mifflin, 1970); and John Holland, *Making Vocational Choices: A Theory of Careers* (Englewood Cliffs, N.J.: Prentice-Hall, 1973).

17 According to the annual Gallup Poll of public attitudes toward education, the percentage of parents who would like their children to become public school teachers has dropped from 75 percent in 1969 to 48 percent in 1980.

18 In this regard see Seymour B. Sarason, *The Culture of the School and the Problem of Change* (Boston: Allyn and Bacon, 1971).

19 Murray Levine, "Teaching Is a Lonely Profession," in *Psychology in Community Settings: Clinical, Educational, Vocational, Social Aspects,* ed. S. Sarason et al. (New York: John Wiley, 1966).

20 N. Dickon Reppucci, "Social Psychology of Institutional Change: General Principles for Intervention," *American Journal of Community Psychology* 1, no. 4 (1973): 330-41.

21 Still another concept of Seymour Sarason's. See, for example, Sarason, *Work, Aging, and Social Change.*

22 See, for example, Maslach, "Burned Out"; and Kahn, "Job Burnout."

23 Bill Fibkins (in Bayshore, Long Island, New York) has written a fascinating, though still unpublished, account of his work in creating this teacher center ("Teacher Centers and Professional Burnout").

24 The concepts of first- and second-order change have been proposed by Paul Watzlawick et al., *Change: Principles of Problem Formation and Problem Resolution* (New York: Norton, 1974).

Reflections on the Profession

BY REBECCA R. TURNER

Colorful high-interest posters written and designed specifically for kids are a special feature in every issue of Learning. *These posters are accompanied by teaching notes, which appear on this page and provide additional background information, teaching suggestions and recommended children's books.*

This month, however, since most kids are still enjoying their summer vacation, we've created two Learning Posters especially for you. Each celebrates teachers and teaching, and invites posting in your home or in your school's teachers lounge.

The content of this poster guide *(continued on page 65)* *also differs from the usual in that its focus is not on students but, rather, on you and your profession.*

Here's Looking at You

At any given moment—during nine months of the year—you might be guiding your class in the use of math manipulatives, decorating a bulletin board, helping a student write a story or trying to eat your lunch while maintaining order on the playground. It's all in a day's work, and it's part of a day in the life of a teacher. But there's another side to being a teacher, the one that links you with colleagues throughout the country by common concerns and personal characteristics.

It's difficult, however, to get a handle on these collective concerns and characteristics that on some level, at least, describe the 2,138,572 elementary and secondary teachers in this country: who they are, what they're thinking, how much money they make and where they're headed professionally. In search of such a statistical portrait of today's teachers, *Learning* combed the yearly reports of organizations such as the Bureau of the Census, the National Education Association (NEA) and the National Center for Education Statistics (NCES) to find information that would enable you to step back from your routine and see teaching from a different perspective.

A Profile of Today's Teachers

According to the number keepers, the person at the front of the classroom is likely to be a white, married mother of two. Twenty-three students fill the desks before her, and even though she spends 7.3 hours a day with her class, her job requires still more time. Like the others on the predominantly female staff of her school (only 33.1 percent of all teachers are male), she works an average of 46 hours each week.

The median age of all teachers is on the rise again after falling steadily from 41 in 1961 to 33 in 1976. At age 36 (37 for both sexes), today's typical teacher is twice as likely as her 1961 counterpart to have a master's degree. Her years of education and the 12 years she's spent teaching in the classroom aren't reflected in her salary, however. Her paychecks haven't made the satisfying leaps seen by veteran members of other professions.

Granted, you may not be white, female and 36 years old, but statistics also reveal a bit about the not-so-typical individuals who are teaching in today's schools. For instance, black teachers make up only 7.8 percent of the teaching force. The geographic distribution of minority teachers varies considerably and tends to correlate with the number of minority residents in any given area.

Your age, if it's much above or below 37, makes you part of a minority—and a shrinking one at that. In 1980, about 65 percent of all teachers fell in the 25- to 44-year-old age range. People under 25 made up 16.6 percent of the teaching force in 1970, but they constitute approximately 8 percent of all teachers today. And although women tend to stay in education longer than men, only about 10 percent of today's teachers are over 55.

Selected Characteristics of U.S. Public School Teachers†

	1961	1966	1971	1976	1981
Median age:					
All teachers	41	36	35	33	37
Men	34	33	33	33	38
Women	46	40	37	33	36
Race (percent):					
Black	ND	ND	8.1	8.0	7.8
White	ND	ND	88.3	90.8	91.6
Other	ND	ND	3.6	1.2	0.7
Sex (percent):					
Men	31.1	31.1	34.3	32.9	33.1
Women	68.7	69.0	65.7	67.0	66.9
Married status (percent):					
Single	22.3	22.0	19.5	20.1	18.5
Married	68.0	69.1	71.9	71.3	73.0
Widowed, divorced or separated	9.7	9.0	8.6	8.6	8.5
Highest degree held (percent):					
Less than bachelor's	14.6	7.0	2.9	0.9	0.4
Bachelor's	61.9	69.6	69.6	61.6	50.1
Master's or six years	23.1	23.2	27.1	37.1	49.3
Doctor's	0.4	0.1	0.4	0.4	0.3
Median years of teaching experience	11	8	8	8	12
Average number of pupils per nondepartmentalized elementary class	29	28	27	25	25
Average annual salary	$5,264*	$6,253	$9,261	$12,005	$17,209

†From *Status of the American Public School Teacher.* Nation Education Association, 1980–81. ND: No data

*Includes extra pay for extra duties

Data are based upon sample surveys of public school teachers. Because of rounding, percents may not add to 100.

Another group of teachers found beyond the perimeters of what's typical in education today is the 11 percent who teach in inner-city schools. The percentage is even smaller on the outskirts of urban areas, where only 9 percent of the teaching force works. Rural areas employ 16 percent of today's teacher corps, leaving the great majority in suburban (31 percent) or small-town (33 percent) schools.

A statistic of interest to all teachers—regardless of background, age or location—is salary. A bachelor's degree, it seems, goes much further in private industry than in teaching. The average starting salary for teachers in

1982–83 was $13,500, a wage surpassed even by those who entered the private sector with an amorphous "liberal arts" major to their credit.

In 1983, the average teacher salary was between $20,500 and $21,000—well below the income level designated that year by the U.S. Labor Department Bureau of Statistics as providing an "intermediate" standard of living for a family of four. This figure continues the trend in which teacher salaries have fallen further below the "intermediate" cost-of-living standard every year since 1971.

Teachers fare better, however, when their salaries are compared with those of other municipal employees. One recent study reports that teachers could expect to earn between $500 and $2,500 more than health, welfare and hospital workers.

Percentage of Women Awarded Degrees in Selected Professions: 1950 to 1980†

	1950	1955	1960	1965	1970	1975	1980
Doctors	1.0	4.7	5.5	6.5	8.4	13.1	23.4
Dentists	.7	.9	.8	.7	.9	3.1	13.3
Lawyers	ND	3.5	2.5	3.2	5.4	15.1	30.2
Engineers	.3	ND	.4	ND	.8	2.2	8.8
Education	46.0	64.0	64.0	67.0	67.0	68.0	71.0

†From *The American Teacher*, Feistritzer Publications, 1983. ND: No data

A Profession in Flux

Discontent lurks within many teachers, according to a 1981 survey of teacher opinion. When asked if they would become teachers if they could start all over again, only 21.8 percent stated that they "certainly would." In 1961, 49.9 percent answered this question in the affirmative.

An adamant 12 percent reported that they "certainly would not" return to teaching; only 2 percent of those questioned gave this response in 1966. In 1981, the situation was a draw between those who "probably would" and those who "probably would not" choose teaching again.

Teachers ranked the public's attitude toward schools as foremost among the reasons for their discontent. Also frequently named as having a negative effect on morale were: ill treatment of education by the media, student attitude toward learning, low salaries and the status of teachers in the community. Student behavior and class size were at the bottom of the list, with under 50 percent of the respondents listing these factors as having a negative impact on their job satisfaction.

The typical and not-so-typical teachers of tomorrow may bear little resemblance to those of today. The education picture is rapidly changing as fewer people enter the profession each year. In 1972, colleges and universities awarded 194,210 bachelor's degrees in education; by 1980, the number had fallen to 118,102, a decline of 40 percent.

But even the decline in the total number of graduates does not tell the whole story. Of the 177,200 people newly qualified to teach in the spring of 1977, only 49 percent were teaching full-time by February 1978. Among the influences deterring those graduates from teaching, one might list budget cuts, teacher layoffs and competency-based certification requirements—the last being an increasingly common factor in teacher employment: By 1981, 17 states had adopted provisions for such requirements.

The composition of the teaching population also changes as fewer women go into education every year. In fact, the proportion of female graduates decreased more sharply over the last decade than did the proportion of males. Increasing opportunities for women in other fields —30.2 percent of graduating law students in 1980 were women, as compared to 5.4 percent in 1970 —contributed to the overall decline, as did the salaries and prestige associated with other professions.

Teacher shortages are appearing in pockets all over the country, and developing technology demands that more and better-trained teachers both enter and stay in the profession. As a result, quality has come to the forefront as a personal and collective goal for teaching professionals. Innovative strategies for accomplishing this end —strategies such as free tuition for graduate study and in-service programs—are becoming increasingly available to teachers. Out of all the changes rocking education today will arise a new statistically typical teacher. But in the end, the basic issue remains the same: no matter the setting, the wage or the age, it's the teacher who makes the difference. Always has, always will. ■

Rebecca R. Turner is an editor for Learning.

Opinions of Public School Teachers Toward Their Profession*

"Suppose you could go back to your college days and start over again; in view of your present knowledge, would you become a teacher?"

	1961	1966	1971	1976	1981
	Percentage Distribution of Responses				
Certainly would	49.9	52.6	44.9	37.5	21.8
Male	35.2	38.0	33.0	27.3	16.0
Female	56.6	59.2	51.1	42.5	24.8
Elementary	57.3	59.6	50.1	43.5	26.4
Secondary	40.0	44.9	39.1	31.7	18.1
Under age 30	ND	49.2	41.4	35.6	28.5
Age 30 to 39	ND	50.9	40.1	34.5	16.2
Age 40 to 49	ND	48.9	47.1	41.6	21.3
Age 50 and over	ND	60.2	53.0	41.3	27.3
Probably would	26.9	25.4	29.5	26.1	24.6
Chances are about even	12.5	12.9	13.0	17.5	17.6
Probably would not	7.9	7.1	8.9	13.4	24.0
Certainly would not	2.8	2.0	3.7	5.6	12.0

*From *Status of the American Public School Teacher*, National Education Association, various years. ND: No data

A Look to the Future

Reliable thinking about the future of American education should be based on analysis of trends in the past and present. Scenarios of possible futures must be based on accurate data regarding economic, ideological, demographic, and other relevant social forces of the past and present. Whatever happens in a nation's educational institutions is always the outgrowth of cultural, ideological, economic, and political forces. Visions of the future should be humanistically conceived and well documented portraits of possible developments. Accurate anticipation of attainable probabilities can only come from an accurate understanding of the past and present.

Thoughtful persons in and out of the academic life are currently studying methods to develop more accurate projections of possible future courses of action in educational planning and development. This inquiry is proceeding in order to ascertain and meet anticipated future educational requirements of our nation and the world. It is interesting to wonder how educators at the turn of the twenty-first century will deal with those issues reflected in the professional literature of 1984 and 1985. What will be the educational clichés of the future? The current revolution in microcomputers will transform some, if not most, dimensions of the educational process in the elementary and secondary schools, as well as in the university. What can be learned from all of this? For instance, will efforts to help gifted learners in the 1980s and 1990s be as half-hearted as they were in the 1970s? Will adequate programs for the physically and learning disabled in the 1980s be successfully implemented? Which philosophical positions and which learning theories will dominate educational development in the years to come? Or will the present confusion of philosophical eclecticism continue to predominate in the United States?

What trends may shape the future of American education? The essays in this unit contain valuable insights into demographic and empirical data which could affect future educational development.

Looking Ahead: Challenge Questions

People in every era seem to believe that the period in which they live is a time of monumental crises and turbulent transition. Is there anything about the contemporary view of life that seems different or unique in this regard?

What can one do to teach students to map out alternative future plans or actions for themselves?

What are some concerns a teacher might have about his or her ability to cope with future educational problems?

How will the revolution in microcomputers benefit students and teachers at all levels in the national educational system?

What knowledge or skills would be most helpful to prepare students for adjustment to continuing change? What do you believe will be the great curriculum issues of the 1990s?

Are any of the biases of the authors in this book built into their views of our possible educational futures? What does your answer to this question tell you about the process involved in developing projections concerning the future?

CURRICULUM IN THE YEAR 2000: TENSIONS AND POSSIBILITIES

Michael W. Apple

MICHAEL W. APPLE is professor of curriculum and instruction and educational policy studies at the University of Wisconsin, Madison. He has written extensively on the relationship between curriculum and society. Among his books are Ideology and Curriculum *(1979) and* Education and Power *(1982). He thanks Shigeru Asanuma, Esteban De La Torre, David Hursh, Ki Seok Kim, Dan Liston, Yolanda Rojas, and Leslie Rothaus for their important contributions to this article.*

Predictions of the future, even in the best of times, are hazardous. So many unforeseen variables and unexpected circumstances can influence outcomes. If this is so in the best of times, it will be even more the case in the next few decades, for these are certainly not the best of times. Thus all of my claims in this article should be preceded by a single word: *if.*

Much of what I am predicting about U.S. education in general and the curriculum in particular depends on political and economic factors. For example, I am not very optimistic about the future for urban school districts. I see the curriculum in urban schools becoming more dated and less flexible in the next 10 to 20 years. I arrive at this prediction from a sense — backed by a decent amount of evidence — that our economy will continue to sputter, if not to stall, in the foreseeable future, thereby creating a serious dilemma for the hard-working teachers and administrators in numerous school districts across the U.S.[1] However, there are also hopeful signs, especially in attempts — even in the face of serious financial difficulties — to keep necessary programs alive and to make curricular content more representative and honestly reflective of a significant portion of the U.S. population.

Basically, though, I see the next two decades as a time of increasing conflict in curriculum. School programs will reflect the splintering of common interests and the polarization of the larger society, trends largely caused by pressures and conflicts over which the schools have little control. A significant amount of the blame will also lie in curricular decisions made as long ago as the early Sixties or as recently as today.

Before going further, I must review some important social and economic facts. It is unfortunate but true that 80% of the benefits of current social policies go to the top 20% of the population. Moreover, the gap between the haves and the have-nots is widening, due in part to the severe economic problems that the U.S. is now experiencing.[2] To their credit, most Americans feel uncomfortable about this situation. But this general discomfort will not prevent many interest groups from arguing that it is not "our" responsibility to alter economic disparities. Nor will it prevent economic inequities from creating serious tensions in U.S. education. If anything, the state of the economy and contradictory attitudes toward it will exacerbate the problems that educators now face. In the next two decades, the curriculum will reflect many of these tensions in the larger society. This should not surprise us. Only rarely has curricular content *not* reflected what is happening outside the school.[3]

I will focus here on three interrelated areas: the content of the curriculum, its form (or how it is organized), and the process of decision making that shapes it. Only by considering all three factors can we understand the forces, building today, that will set limits on and create possibilities for the curriculum in the year 2000.

One major issue that is brewing now and will continue to grow is the debate about "basics." This is not a simple problem. There are many competing conceptions of what everyone should be taught, of what knowledge will be the most valuable to students and to the society. The current controversy over bilingual programs in elementary schools and contemporary proposals to "upgrade" content and to reduce electives in the secondary schools are cases in point. Defining the basics will prove to be one of the most difficult issues that the schools will face, because schools will serve as arenas in which various groups will do battle for their differing conceptions of what the society should value.

It is clear, for instance, that the content of the curriculum has become a major political issue. The activism of conservative and extremist groups has increased measurably. This activism will continue to grow, feeding on past successes that result in increased funding. Mel and Norma Gabler of Longview, Texas, are prime examples; they speak for a larger movement that spends considerable time denouncing textbooks that are "unpatriotic," that reject "absolute values" and "free enterprise," that emphasize too strongly the contributions of minority groups, and so on. Armed with the notion that God is on their side, they are likely to scrutinize an ever-broader swath of curricular content, intent on purging it of any taint of "un-Americanism" and "secular humanism." The increase in book banning and the evolution/creation controversy document the growing willingness of such groups to enter into debates over what should be taught in the schools. Thus educators will have to give more attention to justifying *why* they teach what they do. And this task will be increasingly difficult, because teacher-training institutions are moving toward greater stress on *how* to teach, not on providing justifications for and skills in arguing about *why* educators teach particular information, skills, and attitudes. Unless this trend is reversed, teachers and administrators will be hard pressed to defend curricular decisions against well-organized and well-funded attacks.

Tension between business and organized labor will also manifest itself in conflict over curricular content. On the one hand, we are currently witnessing the emergence of industry as a powerful pressure group that seeks to influence education. Businesses across the U.S. have established departments whose goals are to distribute curricular materials to schools, to convince textbook publishers to tout the benefits of free enterprise, to lobby state legislators, and to provide summer internships for teachers that will help them develop a more positive perspective on business. I see no sign that this type of pressure will abate.[4] On the other hand, labor unions have begun to stress the importance of labor education. A movement is growing to teach labor history and to encourage students to examine critically the problems of the U.S. economy and the imbalance in economic planning. These conflicting goals — to teach content that will produce citizens who will meet the needs of industry and simultaneously to examine critically industrial models and power and the putative lack of concern of big business with the needs of workers — will create a good deal of friction over what should be taught.

This friction will be heightened by the growing cooperation between state departments of education and the business community. In times of economic difficulty, when tax revenues are lower and jobs are hard to find, it is not unusual for school programs to become more closely aligned to the needs of business. We can expect to see more emphasis on teaching job-related skills and on disciplining students according to the norms that guide the workplace. This shift will be difficult to accomplish, because the U.S. job market is clearly changing. New skills rapidly become obsolete, and new jobs are not being created quickly enough.[5] Furthermore, many individuals will object to this closer relationship between the schools and industry, arguing that business generally has its own profits, not the common good, at heart. Thus one more conflict over curriculum will arise.

These two "political" issues — defining the basics and determining the proper relationship of the school to business and to labor — will not be the only ones to surface. The basics will also be expanded to include academic areas that now seem to receive less attention than they deserve. Clearly, there will be attempts, largely positive, to strengthen the teaching of mathematics and science. Several states are already preparing to mandate more science and mathematics courses for high school graduation and the retraining of teachers at state expense, in an effort to reverse the current shortage of qualified math and science teachers. This increased emphasis on mathematics and science will be accompanied by a greater focus on computers in all areas of the curriculum, but especially in math and science. We must be exceptionally cautious and avoid jumping on yet another technological bandwagon. There is no quick fix for the difficult problems we face. Without higher salaries and greater prestige to attract and keep well-trained teachers in these curricular areas, the prospects for success are mixed.

An unfortunate trend will accompany this increased emphasis on mathematics, science, and technology: increased differentiation of the curriculum. Schools will try to identify "gifted" students much earlier. We will see a return to tracking systems and more ability grouping than is currently in evidence. When large amounts of financial, material, and human resources are available, such differentiation may make it easier for teachers and support personnel to meet individual needs by working intensively with students, taking each to the limit of his or her capabilities. But in a time of fiscal crisis, such resources will not be readily available; in such a time, the reinstitution of differentiated curricula and tracking systems will often have the opposite effect: to ratify the low socioeconomic position of many children.[6]

The fiscal crisis will have other profound effects. Since less money will mean fewer teachers and support services, we will see an accompanying steady decline in curricular alternatives as well. There will simply be fewer programs and options.

Moreover, fiscal constraints will hinder the replacement of existing instructional materials (which provide the foundation for nearly all curricula); the average age of textbooks used in the schools will increase and perhaps even double. This trend will be most evident in large urban areas, because they will suffer disproportionate declines in tax revenues and in state and federal support. As a result, the gap in the quality of curricular offerings and instructional materials will broaden between cities and their more affluent suburbs. Thus curricular content will differ by race and social class.

As I have already noted, we must consider curricular content, form, and the process of decision making simultaneously. There is no guarantee that President Reagan's New Federalism will go beyond rhetoric, but evidence suggests that decision making will shift to the state level. Oddly, this shift — though aimed at increasing the responsiveness of state authorities to local districts — will actually decrease curricular diversity. As decision-making power coalesces at the state level, publishers will tailor their textbooks increasingly to the values of those states that encourage statewide textbook adoptions — generally through reimbursements to local school districts for some portion of the cost if they select their instructional materials from an approved list. For publishers, getting materials placed on such lists is quite important, since it nearly guarantees high sales and profits. Given this economic fact, states such as Texas and California, which have state textbook adoption policies, will have disproportionate power to determine which textbooks and resources will be available throughout the U.S. Hence we will see even greater standardization of the curriculum. The curriculum will become "safer," less controversial, less likely to alienate any powerful interest group.

I have argued that curricular content will become both a political football and more homogenized (due to economic pressures on publishers and political and economic pressures on local and state education authorities). A third trend will also become apparent: The form or organization of the curriculum will become increasingly technical and management-oriented. And this will have a serious impact on teachers.

A fundamental change in the curriculum of the American school began in the early 1960s, especially at the elementary level. Sputnik inspired fear that the teaching of mathematics and science lacked sufficient rigor and that the academic disciplines were not central enough in the curriculum; in response, the U.S. government funded a large number of projects that focused on producing new curricular materials. A significant proportion of these materials turned out to be "teacher-proof." They specified everything that a teacher had to know, say, and do. Often, they even specified acceptable student responses. This approach — to specify *everything* and leave nothing to chance — was tacitly sexist, since it seemed to assume that elementary school teachers (most of whom were women) could not cope on their own with sophisticated mathematics and science.[7] To insure that these materials would be purchased and used, the government reimbursed school systems for the bulk of their costs.

Although many of these new materials were not used in the ways that their developers had envisioned,[8] they did signal an important modification in the curriculum — one that we will be living with for years to come. The curriculum became less a locally planned program and more a series of commercial "systems" (in reading, mathematics, and so on). These systems integrated diagnostic and achievement tests, teacher and student activities, and teaching materials. Such integration has its strengths, of course. It does make possible more efficient planning, for example. But its weaknesses may prove to outweigh its strengths.

What we have actually seen is the *deskilling* of our teaching force. Since so much of the curriculum is now conceived outside the schools, teachers often are asked to do little more than to execute someone else's goals and plans and to carry out someone else's suggested activities. A trend that has had a long history in industry — the separation of conception from execution — is now apparent as well in U.S. classrooms.[9]

This trend will have important consequences. When individuals cease to plan and control their own work, the skills essential to these tasks atrophy and are forgotten. Skills that teachers have built up over decades of hard work — setting curricular goals, establishing content, designing lessons and instructional strategies, individualizing instruction from an intimate knowledge of each student's desires and needs, and so on — are lost. In the process, the very things that make teaching a professional activity — the control of one's expertise and time — are also dissipated. There is no better formula for alienation and burnout than the loss of control of the job. Hence, the tendency of the curriculum to become totally standardized and systematized, totally focused on competencies measured by tests, and largely dependent on predesigned commercial materials may have consequences that are exactly the opposite of what we intend. Instead of professional teachers who care about what they do and why they do it, we may have only alienated executors of someone else's plans. Given the kinds of materials that now dominate many classrooms in such curricular areas as mathematics and reading, this danger seems likely to increase over time.

The economics of this process of deskilling is worth noting. In essence, we have established a capital-intensive curriculum in our classrooms. Simply to keep the program going, a large amount of money must be set aside for the ongoing purchase of consumable materials. School districts may soon find themselves burdened with expensive "white elephants," as school budgets are reduced and money is no longer available to purchase the requisite workbooks, tests, worksheets, revised editions of "modules," and so forth. School districts will then have to turn to their own staffs to create materials that are less expensive and more responsive to their students' needs — only to find that the necessary skills for doing this have been lost. This will be a very real predicament.

At the same time that teachers are being de-skilled, however, they are gaining greater control over which curricular materials and textbooks will be purchased for use in their classrooms. Curricular decision making is becoming more formally democratic; less power now resides in central curriculum offices or with select groups of administrators. Both teachers and parents are becoming more involved. Meanwhile, an increasing concern for accountability and for measurable achievement outcomes in a few "basic" areas will also bring a movement toward more standardized testing, more objectives, more focus on competencies, more centralized curricular control, and more teaching to the tests.

As this movement gains momentum, a vicious circle will develop. Publishers will further standardize content, basing it on competency tests and routinizing it as much as possible, so that their materials will produce measurable outcomes with little variability that will fit cost/control models.

Thus far, I have not been very optimistic about what will happen in the areas of curricular content, form, and decision making. I do not intend simply to be a nay-sayer. It is critically important to be realistic about the very difficult times that we educators will confront in the not-too-distant future. Only then can we begin to plan how to cope with what may happen. I would be remiss, however, if I did not point out some of the very beneficial tendencies that will become more visible by the year 2000.

Certain content areas — quite positive ones, in my opinion — will receive more emphasis than they do at present. Just as greater attention will be focused on mathematics and science (which, I hope, will be taught *not* as mere technical skills, but as creative and powerful ways of constructing meaning[10]), so, too, will teachers devote more time to the topics of ecology and peace. People from all walks of life, representing a variety of political persuasions, will coalesce around the topic of peace and urge that it be given more attention in the curriculum.

However, positive outcomes from additions to the curriculum will not be the dominant trend in a period of fiscal constraints. In fact, many school districts will be forced to save money by eliminating necessary programs. But this may prove beneficial, as well — especially in generating closer and more cooperative bonds between school personnel and the communities they serve. Teachers and parents will form coalitions to save programs that they see as essential. Difficult decisions will cause closer relationships to develop between community groups and the educators who must make those decisions. In a period of declining revenues and with the projected rise in enrollments, few outcomes will be more important. Funds will be needed to hire new teachers, to maintain and expand curricular offerings, to deal with students with special needs, and to carry on other essential tasks. Such funds can be generated only through greater cooperation with and increased support from the public. Even the scrutiny of the curriculum by conservative groups, to which I alluded earlier, should not be seen as merely a threat. The fact that parents — of whatever political persuasion — take a serious interest in their children's education suggests possible avenues for cooperation and fruitful discussion.

If we were freed from some of the tensions, conflicts, and pressures that will probably affect us as we strive to build or preserve a high-quality educational program for the children entrusted to us, what might we do about content, form, and decision making? Here I must be honest. A portion of what I will say has been recognized for years by knowledgeable educators. But such educators have seldom had the time, the resources, the support, or the freedom from contradictory pressures to act on this knowledge.

Let us look first at content. As attempts accelerate to redefine and to drastically limit what is taught to children, we should *broaden* our definitions of literacy and of the basics to include not only reading and writing — which are very important and must not be neglected — but also social, political, aesthetic, and technological literacy. Community action projects that provide curricular links between students and their local communities can help youngsters develop social and political responsibility and learn the necessary skills for active participation in the society.[11] At the same time, we should expose all students to beauty and form, aesthetics, and various ways of creating personal meanings — including research, poetry, dance, the visual arts, and film making. In other words, we should give equal weight to both "discursive" and "nondiscursive" subjects, so that each student has an opportunity to discover his or her talents and to develop the wide range of tools with which individuals control their own lives and their futures.[12] Thus we must define the "basics" very broadly.

Given the important role of technology in the future, *all* students — not just a select few who are "gifted and talented" — should be literate both in using computers and microcomputers *and* in analyzing their social implications. For example, computers and video-display equipment increase efficiency, but they may also cause untold thousands of workers (primarily women) to lose their jobs, become de-skilled, or work under stressful conditions. "Literacy" means the ability to analyze and deal with the social as well as the technical implications of this new technology.

In a recent column in the *New York Times*, Fred Hechinger noted that, if we approach computer literacy as a narrow vocational issue, we are bound merely to add one more relatively ineffective career education program to the many that already exist. As he put it:

> The visions of brave new electronic worlds of microchips and robots raise simultaneous demands for a schooling that looks to the future by learning from the past. Yes, the computer must be mastered by all, regardless of race, sex, or economic condition. But at the same time . . . the computer must be mastered by young people who are secure in a broad understanding of what used to be called general education — including language, history, economics, mathematics, science, the arts; in short, the human condition.[13]

To focus on a broad and general education requires that we be sensitive to the fact that the curriculum must represent us all. A "selective tradition" has operated in curriculum to date. This tradition may be more visible in some subjects than in others, but it is quite clear that the knowledge of some groups is not represented adequately in the curriculum.[14] For instance, we tend to teach military history or the history of U.S. Presidents; we teach less rigorously the history of the U.S. working class. Obviously, we have made advances here, just as we have made advances in teaching the real histories, contributions, and cultures of ethnic minorities and of women. Our progress in eliminating sexism and racism and in recapturing the lost past of U.S. labor is too important to allow these advances to slip away in the next decade or two. We must continue to pursue curricular balance. The content that we teach cannot be determined solely by the needs of any one group, even in times of severe economic difficulty. That would be short-sighted.

The curriculum must simultaneously be both conservative and critical. It must preserve the ideals that have guided discourse in the U.S. for centuries: a faith in the American people, a commitment to expanding equality, and a commitment to diversity and liberty. Yet it must also empower individuals to question the ethics of their institutions and to criticize them when they fail to meet these ideals. Curricular content should give people the ability to interpret social change and to reflect critically on what is happening in their daily lives. This is not a formula for an "easy" curriculum. It requires hard work and discipline on the part of both teachers and students.

Moreover, participation in such a curriculum is not merely an individual act; it is a profoundly social act as well. In an interdependent society, the curriculum should encourage cooperation and the testing of each individual's ideas against those of others. This requires countering — at least to some degree — the individualized instructional models now widely practiced in schools. All too many children sit isolated from one another in the elementary grades, completing worksheet after worksheet with little or no opportunity for serious discussion, deliberation, debate, or cooperation. Individualization is important; however, to be truly meaningful, it must be balanced by a sense of social responsibility.

The issue of time looms large here. Educators must have time to consider the curriculum carefully. Too many curricular decisions today focus on *how* to teach, not on *what* to teach. Teachers and other educators must have opportunities to discuss in detail what they want to do and why they want to do it. Creative scheduling is essential, in order to make time available for frequent, in-depth discussions of curricular content among local educators.

Obviously, teachers are not the only ones who are affected by what is taught. As much as possible, all individuals who are affected by a curricular decision should be involved in making it.[15] This includes parents, concerned citizens, organized labor and other interest groups, and, when possible, the students themselves. I recognize that such broad participation can lead to political conflict and to interminable meetings, but it can also lead to a greater sense of trust and cooperation on the part of all those involved. Indeed, broad participation may be one way to bolster flagging community (and financial) support of public education.

Educators who act on this suggestion must be willing to take risks and to work hard. School officials must aggressively present their curricular proposals and programs to the community — especially to the most disenfranchised groups. They must show their publics what they offer and communicate the justifications for these offerings. They must take criticisms seriously and respond to them honestly.

I have good reasons for making these suggestions. Available evidence suggests that, unless participation in curricular planning is widely shared among teachers, principals, central office staff members, students, and parents, the amount of support for any program is significantly reduced.[16]

In addition, direct parental involvement in the classroom tends to foster both more and longer-lasting changes in the daily activities of teachers. And evidence suggests that *how* a program is carried out is just as important as the specific content of a program.[17] The prospect of a continued decline in educational funding will give impetus to broad participation in the classroom. Parents will have to become more deeply involved, since schools will be hard pressed to afford many of the programs essential to high-quality education. As parents (and the elderly, I hope) volunteer to serve as tutors, as resource people, as counselors, and in other capacities, they will become more knowledgeable and more skillful at dealing with curricular issues. This is an important step toward a genuinely cooperative effort to guarantee high-quality programs for children.

If parental participation in decision making is important, teacher participation is even more important. There tends to be a very high correlation between the involvement of teachers in decisions related to changes in the curriculum and "effective implementation and continuation" of such changes.[18] When we consider going from what *is* to what *should be*, there are few things we know for certain. However, we do have some guidelines for strategies that seem to foster more effective and lasting changes in the curriculum, in what teachers do, and in what students learn. The findings of several studies have suggested that "what should be" will be enhanced to the extent that there is: 1) concrete, extended, and teacher-specific training related to the curricular change; 2) continuing classroom assistance from the district; 3) opportunities for teachers to observe similar projects in other classrooms, schools, or districts; 4) frequent meetings among the people involved that focus on practical problems; 5) local development of materials, insofar as this is possible; and 6) emphasis on teacher participation in curricular decision making.[19] As the financial crunch worsens, these guidelines will become even more important, especially in larger school districts.

So far, I have suggested certain attitudes and activities that should guide our policies on curriculum content, form, and decision making. However, this article would be both incomplete and deceptively simplistic if I did not add that, just as many of the tensions and conflicts over the curriculum arise outside the school, so too do many solutions to these problems require changes in the larger society. The issues of raising students' achievement levels and preventing dropouts are cases in point; solving these problems will require coordinated efforts by the larger society.

Educators have given a good deal of attention to reforming the secondary school curriculum to prevent dropouts. These reforms have had mixed results, in part because focusing solely on internal curricular changes is too limited a strategy. As Christopher Jencks has recently shown, the economic benefits for students who complete secondary school are still *twice* as great for whites as for blacks.[20] Moreover, completing secondary school provides relatively few benefits to students from economically disadvantaged backgrounds. Jencks and his colleagues have summarized their findings thus: "Apparently, high school graduation pays off primarily for men from advantaged backgrounds. Men from disadvantaged backgrounds must attend college to reap large occupational benefits from their education."[21] Clearly, those minority and economically disadvantaged students who stay in secondary school longer receive few economic rewards for their efforts — regardless of what common sense tells us about the benefits of increased schooling.

I am *not* arguing against making the curriculum more responsive to the needs of such youngsters. Rather, I am saying that, without a societal commitment to altering the structure of the economic marketplace so that these more responsive programs pay off for participants, such efforts may be doomed to failure. Why should such students wish to take part even in well-designed programs, if the statistical probability that these programs will improve their lives is very low? We *do* need better secondary programs, but these programs will be successful only to the extent that students feel that the school has something to offer — both now and for the future.

Improving the achievement of students poses similar problems. We have spent many years and huge sums of money attempting to raise achievement — especially scores on reading tests — through better instructional materials and curricula, more intensive teaching strategies, and so on. Yet these efforts, too, have had mixed results. We may have to take seriously the evidence that suggests a marked relationship between socioeconomic status and achievement in schools. The answers to many of the curriculum questions we face now and will certainly face in the next two decades — such as how best to increase the achievement of minority and poor students — may be found as much in social policies as in better teaching and curricula. As I mentioned earlier, doing well in elementary and secondary school does not guarantee economic success in later life.

The implications of this fact are striking. If we are really serious about increasing student mastery of content, especially among economically disadvantaged groups, then we might consider embarking on a serious analysis of the prevailing patterns of educational financing, of the possibility of redistributing income, and of ways to create jobs that would make possible a decent standard of living for the many families who will suffer the most if the economy continues its downturn. However, such analysis must not serve as an excuse for failing to do the important work of revising the curriculum and teaching practices. My point is that we must take seriously the complications that hinder the schools from reaching their goals. If we are to reach these goals by the year 2000, we will have to consider how our ability to do so is linked to the existing distribution of resources in our society.

If our aim is a society in which all people are more equal in their opportunities to experience success and to exercise control over their own destinies, not a society in which the chasms between groups grow larger every day, then we must deal now with these larger social issues. Otherwise, the public will continue to blame the school and its curriculum, its teachers, and its administrators for something over which they have much less control than do other social agencies.

If I am correct that the success of the schools is very much tied to conditions in the larger society, then the training of curriculum specialists, teachers, and administrators for the year 2000 cannot be limited to such things as techniques of teaching, management approaches, and methods of financial planning. We must focus more rigorously — starting now — on the skills of democratic deliberation about such questions as social goals, the proper direction for schools to take, and what we should teach and why.[22] We will never have a curriculum free of tensions and conflicts. And it would probably not be good if we did, since such conflicts demonstrate the vitality of democracy. We must learn to work creatively with conflicts, seeing them not as hindrances but as possibilities for cooperative improvement of education.

The results of the decisions we make today about curriculum policies and classroom practices will be with us in the year 2000, which is just around the corner. It is crucial that we debate now the questions of what we should teach, how it should be organized, who should make the decisions, and what we as educators should and can do about (and in) a society marked by large and growing disparities in wealth and power. I hope that I have stimulated such debate, because that is the necessary first step to taking seriously the question of what the curriculum should be in the year 2000.

---

1. I have discussed this in much greater detail in Michael W. Apple, *Education and Power* (Boston: Routledge and Kegan Paul, 1982). See also Manuel Castells, *The Economic Crisis and American Society* (Princeton, N.J.: Princeton University Press, 1980); and Lester Thurow, *The Zero-Sum Society* (New York: Basic Books, 1980).
2. For a detailed analysis, see Martin Carnoy and Derek Shearer, *Economic Democracy* (White Plains, N.Y.: M.E. Sharpe, 1980).
3. See Michael W. Apple, *Ideology and Curriculum* (Boston: Routledge and Kegan Paul, 1979).
4. See, for example, Sheila Harty, *Hucksters in the Classroom* (Washington, D.C.: Center for Responsive Law, 1979); and Apple, *Education and Power*, esp. Ch. 5.
5. Castells, pp. 161-85.
6. For a review of the literature on tracking and differentiation, see Caroline H. Persell, *Education and Inequality* (New York: Free Press, 1977); and Thomas Good and Jere Brophy, *Looking in Classrooms* (New York: Harper and Row, 1978).
7. Michael W. Apple, "Work, Gender, and Teaching," *Teachers College Record*, in press.
8. See, for example, Seymour Sarason, *The Culture of the School and the Problem of Change* (Boston: Allyn & Bacon, 1971).
9. For an empirical analysis of what is happening to some teachers in elementary schools because of this separation, see Andrew Gitlin, "School Structure and Teachers' Work," in Michael W. Apple and Lois Weis, eds., *Ideology and Practice in Schooling* (Philadelphia: Temple University Press, forthcoming). See also Apple, *Education and Power*.
10. For an interesting discussion of various forms of meaning and "representation," see Elliot Eisner, *Cognition and Curriculum: A Basis for Deciding What to Teach* (New York: Longman, 1982).
11. Fred Newmann, Thomas Bertocci, and Ruthanne Landsness, *Skills in Citizen Action* (Skokie, Ill.: National Textbook Co., 1977). See also Fred Newmann, "Reducing Student Alienation in High Schools," *Harvard Educational Review*, Winter 1981, pp. 546-64.
12. Elliot Eisner, *The Educational Imagination* (New York: Macmillan, 1979).
13. 10 August 1982, Sec. 3, p. 7.
14. Apple, *Ideology and Curriculum*, pp. 6-7.
15. Joseph Schwab, "The Practical: A Language for Curriculum," in Arno Bellack and Herbert Kliebard, eds., *Curriculum and Evaluation* (Berkeley, Calif.: McCutchan, 1977), pp. 26-44.
16. Paul Berman and Milbrey W. McLaughlin, *Federal Programs Supporting Educational Change, Vol. VIII: Implementing and Sustaining Innovations* (Santa Monica, Calif.: Rand Corporation, May 1978), p. 14.
17. Ibid., p. 24.
18. Ibid., p. 29.
19. Ibid., p. 34.
20. Christopher Jencks et al., *Who Gets Ahead?* (New York: Basic Books, 1979), pp. 174-75.
21. Ibid., p. 175. It is unfortunate that most of this research has dealt only with men.
22. Kenneth Zeichner is doing some of the best work on helping teachers to develop the skills of deliberation and reflection. See his "Reflective Teaching and Field-Based Experience in Teacher Education," *Interchange*, vol. 12, no. 4, 1981, pp. 1-22.

Instructional Computing In 2001: A Scenario

William H. Pritchard, Jr.

WILLIAM H. PRITCHARD, JR. (North Central Florida Chapter) is coordinator of the computer literacy program at Vassar College, Poughkeepsie, N.Y.

Jim yawned and stretched as he pushed himself away from the comsole.* He glanced at the clock and exclaimed, "Good grief, it's already seven!" He was always amazed at how quickly time flew when he worked with his computer system. He was aware, too, of the quick passage of time since his graduate student days in 1981. That was 20 years ago. "So much has happened since," he thought.

Working at the comsole, Jim often felt as though the world were at his fingertips — and, of course, it really was. Simple instructions made any piece of information instantly his. It was addictive; the greater his capacity to receive information, the greater his potential for discovering new relationships, new concepts, and new frontiers of information. Jim was oblivious of time when he was working at the comsole. "It's lucky," he thought, "that I have a model that's programmed for automatic rest periods!" The comsole didn't need the rest, but he did. Thus his comsole featured factory-installed automatic shut-off points. These intervals virtually forced the purchaser to eat, to exercise, to interact with others, and to take care of those functions essential to human life.

Jim often cursed his comsole when it imposed a rest period; privately, however, he blessed the interruption. Rest periods gave him time to think independently, without the pressure of constant pushing by the machine. He did not care what others believed; he *knew* there was qualitative difference between human thought and machine thought.

It was during rest periods that Jim pondered the relativity of time and its relationship to information flow. He thought it puzzling that, the more time he spent at the comsole, the less aware he was of the passage of time. It was as if time stopped when he sat down at the comsole; only the flow of information was important. He was amused by the deception that time and his brain tried to play on him. After almost 50 years, his body knew — and frequently reminded him — that he was not young anymore.

"Ah, to be young again," he sighed, thinking back to graduate school in 1981. That was about the time he first became aware of the revolution already under way in information processing. In retrospect, it seemed a simple, naive time.

Few people had sensed in 1981 the changes that were taking place. Jim had suspected that change was coming, but he could not predict its direction or magnitude. What prescience he had in those days came from a course in curriculum and instruction that had introduced him to microcomputers and their capabilities. Jim recognized that these machines and their progeny were going to change the world, the ways people thought about the world, and even the ways that people related to one another. He sensed, too, that education would be radically altered.

Jim's premonitions had proved accurate. Education *had* changed since those days, and he had been caught up in the process. That was how time and his brain became partners in deception. The time was intense and heady, both for Jim and for education. Events occurred so rapidly and were so strongly influenced by the interactions of social change and technological advance that, in retrospect, it was hard for him to keep it all straight. He remembered that the first hand calculator had appeared in the Seventies. Shortly thereafter, slide rules disappeared. By 1981 education was beginning to feel the impact of the microcomputer.

In a survey Jim conducted while in graduate school, he had found that 60% of the school districts in his state used microcomputers in some way for instruction. He recognized even then that this did *not* mean that 60% of all schools used computers — or even that 60% of all students worked directly with computers. He had been impressed, nonetheless, by the substantial inroad the new technology had made in the schools.

During the past 20 years microcomputers had so saturated the culture that guidelines for federal education programs now mandated the ownership of some type of computer. A home without a computer immediately classified its occupants as living below the poverty level. The government now considered home computers as essential as indoor plumbing.

Overcome by nostalgia, Jim glanced at the comsole and noted, to his delight, that the "on" light was glowing again. His next idea came with a rush. He recalled writing a paper — such an obsolete process — predicting the changes that microtechnology would force on education. Now he hoped to locate those predictions, and he knew that the comsole would help. The only problem might be his own failure to store that paper during the national electronic storage operations in 1989. He had discarded many of his old files, but he vaguely remembered saving that particular paper to serve as a sort of personal time capsule in the future.

"Search through the graduate school records of Jim Arnold, 328-44-8688," he said to the comsole. "I'd like to have a copy of a paper; the subject was future problems for educators as computer technology gained wider use in education."

"I think I've found what you want," replied the comsole. Jim winced at the word *think*. In spite of all the time he spent working with the comsole, he still was not accustomed to the fact that it could think — or that it thought it could.

"If you will look at the videoscreen," the comsole continued matter-of-factly, "you will find a listing of papers written by Jim Arnold, 328-44-8688, and stored in the central data bank. This list reflects graduate work only."

Jim read the list and soon located the paper. He was tempted to scan the others, especially his dissertation, but he decided to do that another time.

"Please give me a facsimile of number 17," he told the comsole. Producing such a copy was many times more expensive than using the video screen, primarily because the world's forests — the source of all paper — had been so drastically reduced by population growth. For this reason, the government had mandated electronic information storage in 1989. Jim preferred to read old works in their original form, however. The feeling of

*A comsole is a communications console.

"Instructional Computing in 2001," William H. Pritchard, Jr., *Phi Delta Kappan,* January 1982. Reprinted by permission.

paper in his hands evoked special memories.

As the facsimile appeared from a slot in the comsole, Jim retrieved it gently but eagerly. He read the title: "Future Problems and Issues for Educators in the Use of Computer-Based Instruction: A Paper to Fulfill the Requirements of EDG 6905 — The Future and Education." The paper contained a list of problems that Jim had foreseen in 1981 as those that educators would face in the future. He wanted to compare the list with what had actually happened in the past 20 years.

Jim's eyes raced down the page until he found the first problem he had prophesied: teacher computer literacy. He had felt in 1981 that this problem was the most pressing. "In an increasingly computerized world," he had written, "we cannot expect our students to emerge from school computer literate unless our teachers are first computer literate. . . . At present, students bring computer literacy into schools. The schools do not bring computer literacy to the students." From his own research in his state, Jim had predicted a crisis in public school systems precipitated by the rapid growth of the microcomputer industry. He knew from his survey that school systems already owned computers that were gathering dust because teachers did not know how to use them. The technology was more available than were educators prepared to use it.

Jim recognized the accuracy of his first prediction. Microcomputers had proven much easier to mass produce than computer-literate teachers. As computers swept through society, however, educational institutions were forced to change. By 1985 most teacher training institutions required of their graduates some knowledge of computers, and many had established separate departments for the scientific study of computerized instruction.

By 1990 technologists had developed programming languages that used human voice commands for input, and these advances created new pressures for change in education. Not many years later, technologists developed computers so sophisticated that they could accept commands in conversational English. As technology bounded ahead, the role of teachers also changed dramatically. No longer were they the primary disseminators of knowledge. The comsoles in each home assumed that role. Teachers were trained instead in interpersonal skills, and children attended school to learn social graces. "The first problem that I foresaw is no longer relevant," Jim decided, "but it sure was, back in 1981."

Jim had listed the short-term lack of high-quality courseware as the second major problem to be faced by educators. Now he had trouble remembering instructional computing as it had been in 1981. It had been a very crude art form at best. The PLATO system had boasted the most sophisticated courseware, but even PLATO had had its limitations. It was relatively expensive, tied to a somewhat temperamental central mainframe, and lacking stand-alone sound or color capability.

"The growing popularity of microcomputers," he had written, "will bring a parallel increase in the dangers awaiting ill-prepared educators. Some commercial producers may respond to the need for instructional courseware by marketing faulty or substandard products." Jim had gone on to note that "courseware developed by teachers to meet their own instructional purposes would be the ideal, but most teachers are currently illiterate when it comes to computers. This phenomenon is the 'Catch-22' of educational computing," he added. "Until teachers are literate, low-quality courseware will be the albatross that we educators must endure."

In retrospect, Jim felt that he had been accurate about this issue. Initially, computer experts — not educators — had dominated the instructional computing scene and had directed the production of educational courseware. By the mid-Eighties, however, the quality of the courseware had improved markedly, thanks primarily to pressures from teachers who demanded instruction in educational computing and who used computers in their homes. By 1989, when the Library of Congress collection was stored electronically, courseware quality was no longer an issue. Five years later, virtually every U.S. home contained a computer that was connected to other home computers by cable and satellite communications technology. Shortly thereafter, public schools ceased functioning as institutions for academic learning and became social-skills centers, instead.

"Two for two — *not bad*!" Jim thought as he turned the page. "Uh-oh, this one's a little different," he observed, when he saw the third problem that he had foreseen in 1981: the toy/game mentality.

As a graduate student, Jim had been concerned about the use of microtechnology in toys and games, for fear that the toys-and-games mentality would spill over into the classroom. He worried that electronic games would convince children that computers are toys, suitable only for recreation. He worried, too, that children would come to believe that excessive competitiveness — a characteristic of nearly all the electronic games — was acceptable behavior in the real world.

The advantages of hindsight told Jim that he had been overanxious about children seeing computers as merely toys. Fun had proved to be a major attraction of computerized instruction — for him and for everyone else. Moreover, the intervening years had seen the advent of sophisticated computer games that accurately simulated life. Such games had useful applications as learning tools in every field from astronomy to zoology.

Jim had been even more concerned that electronic games would cause youngsters to value competition too highly. Wide reading had convinced him that the world was becoming increasingly interdependent and that only international cooperation would enable humankind to solve the problems occasioned by overpopulation and depletion of resources.

Sadly, Jim saw that he had been correct in his concern about competition. The 1980s and 1990s had been rough for everyone — economically, environmentally, and socially. Widespread starvation became common in Africa, South America, and Asia. The continued reliance on petroleum resources maintained high standards of living for the industrialized nations but created serious long- and short-term problems. In the mid-Eighties the Reagan Administration reacted to resource depletion by placing severe restrictions on immigration. The U.S. Congress also appropriated funds to construct barbed-wire and laser-light fences along the Mexican border, precluding the entry of illegal aliens. According to the Reagan Administration, illegal immigrants from Central and South America — hoping to escape the poverty of their homelands and "to take advantage of the federal largesse" — were pouring into the U.S. After the mid-Eighties no one was able to immigrate, and the U.S. refugee program was abolished. President Reagan and the U.S. drew strong criticism from Third World nations for "elitist and exclusionist" policies, but these policies were continued nonetheless.

Jim sighed. He knew that immigration was an old problem, not easily or quickly resolved. Realizing that he could spend a great deal of time on this issue alone, he decided to push on to the fourth problem he had anticipated back in 1981: the narcissistic self-reinforcement of computerized instruction.

As Jim thought seriously about this issue, memories of his idealistic youth depressed him. He recalled the discouragement that the self-centered "Me Generation" of the Seventies had inspired in him. He remembered the concern he had felt about self-aggrandizement after reading *The Culture of Narcissism* by Christopher Lasch. He had feared that computerized instruction, an individualized and intrinsically rewarding activity, would only aggravate the widespread alienation and self-centeredness. He had argued that the problem went beyond courseware design; it had to do with the intrinsic power of computers. Having that much intellectual power under one's control — and, more especially, having that power wait for one's input or response — struck him as inherently rewarding to the ego. "The American dream of a chicken in every pot and a computer for every kid," he had written, "may have dangerous consequences as well as benefits. Our children need to learn to communicate with *each other*, as well as with a computer."

Jim realized that he had been a voice crying in the wilderness. The American infatuation with new gadgets and technology, combined with public demands for a return to the basics and a new emphasis on accountability, created a wave of enthusiasm for the new technology. Calls for restraint and a study of negative side effects — especially such subtle effects as increased narcissism — went unheard in the headlong rush for equipment and courseware. It was not until the mid-Nineties that rest times became a federal requirement for comsoles. Even then, the public opposed this restriction on much the same ground as it had opposed automobile seat belts and airbags in the Seventies.

Jim sighed again. He knew he had been right; computerized instruction increased narcissism. He also knew that he was hopelessly addicted to his own comsole, primarily because of the ego rewards it afforded him. It was time to change the subject.

He turned to the fifth problem he had predicted in 1981: the speed of computers and appropriate "wait time" in instruction. The early computers had emphasized the speed of performing given functions. This emphasis became more important when large systems, supporting many terminals, were on time sharing. Back in those days, one operator or function could control an entire system, but only at great expense. As a result, instructional programs, housed with systems that had also been designed for other uses, were assigned low priority and could provide only erratic responses for the learner. On systems dedicated solely to instruction, by contrast, the response was virtually immediate. Jim had cited the research of Mary Budd Rowe, which indicated that delayed responses from the instructor (in this case, the computer) often facilitated learning. He had emphasized this point by quoting Ivan Illich: Tools should be "convivial." That is, they should be used with control instead of letting their design dictate inherent standards of control. "A computer that gives an instantaneous response to a student is not necessarily an educationally convivial tool," Jim had written. "It is speeding up the learner to meet the demands of the technology instead of adjusting itself to the needs of the student."

From informal observations of himself and others, Jim had noted signs of hyperactivity and feelings of increased tension after several hours of using a computer. He had attributed these symptoms to the subtle demands for rapid responses that a computer places on its user. He laughed out loud now, remembering that the hyperactivity and increased tension had come instead from his own excitement and the uncomfortable position he had assumed while working with the machines. Those feelings had not been the result of speed factors or of any "deadly emissions from the cathode ray tube," as he had suspected in 1981.

On the problem of wait time and on the need for convivial computers, he had been accurate, however. Once colleges of education began to set up separate departments for instruction and research in instructional computing, his fears had been alleviated. By the late 1980s all high-quality courseware allowed the student to determine individual wait time, either directly or indirectly.

Jim moved on to the sixth problem he had anticipated two decades earlier: the computer and its compatibility with learning styles. In 1981 Jim had been concerned about the prevalent notion that the computer was equally attractive to and effective with all learners. He had disagreed. Research on personality characteristics and cognitive styles clearly indicated that individuals learn in different ways. But the use of computers for instruction in those days called for a specific learning style. Computers required a certain degree of manual dexterity at the keyboard (for input), attention to detail and accuracy, and an aptitude for learning visually. "No longer relevant," Jim thought, "now that we have synthesized speech and verbal input." Computers in 1981 also demanded a degree of physical passivity and a willingness to sit still. "These attributes are still somewhat relevant," Jim thought, "although miniaturization and remote units now allow for increased mobility." The 1981 computers required, in addition, a preference for working alone and strong intuitive and diagnostic ability. "Both are still very relevant," Jim mused.

All in all, Jim felt the greatest satisfaction about this part of his paper. By pointing out the need for learning-style compatibility in 1981, he had gained the attention of other instructional computing specialists. This had become a popular

But he was saddened by the evolution of the schools into centers for teaching only social skills. Implicitly, these centers suggested that humans do not think well in groups — that their highest intellectual achievements come only with the support of machines. He believed the human mind to be far more capable and versatile than that. In fact, Jim had recently organized a group of people who met regularly for intellectual discussions without the aid of machines. He was confident that there existed a qualitative difference between machine intelligence and human intelligence. And he preferred the latter, particularly in light of recent advancements in the chemical and genetic enhancement of human intelligence.

"And now, my final prophecy," Jim thought. He scanned the page until he found it: language and equipment compatibility. During the late Seventies and early Eighties the computer industry had expanded rapidly, experiencing greater growth and innovation than any other industry in world history. That period had been characterized by extraordinary creativity in the industry. New designs and innovations in hardware and software occurred almost daily. It had been impossible for an individual, let alone a school system, to keep up. Jim recognized the need for such creativity, but he felt that there was also a need for uniformity of standards in educational computing.

Back in 1981 there had been a few computer languages specifically designed for computerized instruction, but individuals had been working to develop courseware in many other languages. The problem, as Jim had seen it, was to find a way of sharing courseware when language capabilities differed. Simply put, there had been no standardized language or hardware for educators to use back in those days. Fortunately, one of the first concerns of programmers of computerized academic instruction had been to develop just such standards. The irony was that, just about the time educators had settled on standards for language and hardware, the computer industry had developed machines capable of handling conversational English. Once again, education was behind the times.

"Speaking of time," Jim thought aloud, "what time is it?"

"Eleven-thirty," responded the comsole. "You missed your human discussion group."

Jim sensed a pompous note in the comsole's voice — but that was not possible. Or was it? "Why didn't you remind me of the meeting?" he asked querulously.

"You did not instruct me to do so," replied the comsole.

Jim sighed. The comsole was right. Perhaps he should add the problem of haughty computers to his list.

The Coming Enrollment Crisis

Focusing on the Figures

David W. Breneman

David W. Breneman is a senior fellow at the Brookings Institution in Washington, D.C. He serves as executive editor of Change *and president of Kalamazoo College. This article is excerpted with permission from the monograph "The Coming Enrollment Crisis: What Every Trustee Must Know" published by the Association of Governing Boards, Washington, D.C. Copyright 1982, Association of Governing Boards.*

Those concerned with the well-being of higher education may have noted a curious—and troublesome—paradox. On the one hand, most people are aware that the "baby-boom" generation has passed through the nation's colleges, and that for the next fifteen years colleges and universities in most states will face the much smaller "birth-dearth" generation.

Many people also know that the traditional college-age population will decline in number between now and the mid-1990s by roughly 25 percent. On the other hand, a recent national survey of college and university presidents reported that only 16 percent of the presidents expected their institutions to lose enrollments, while 42 percent expect their enrollments to increase! The remainder see their enrollments as holding steady. This paradox suggests that most presidents are either incurable optimists or they know something that the rest of us do not. A more troubling possibility is that most presidents are unwilling to admit—or do not believe—that enrollment decline will hit their colleges, although they fully expect other institutions to have trouble.

The purpose of this report is to provide college and university trustees with information about enrollment prospects, and to suggest questions that trustees might ask in order to probe the adequacy, comprehensiveness, and realism of the institution's long-range planning. Although the report does not advance its own enrollment projection, it does accept the rather widespread view that between now and the mid-1990s, enrollments will decline nationally by about 15 percent.

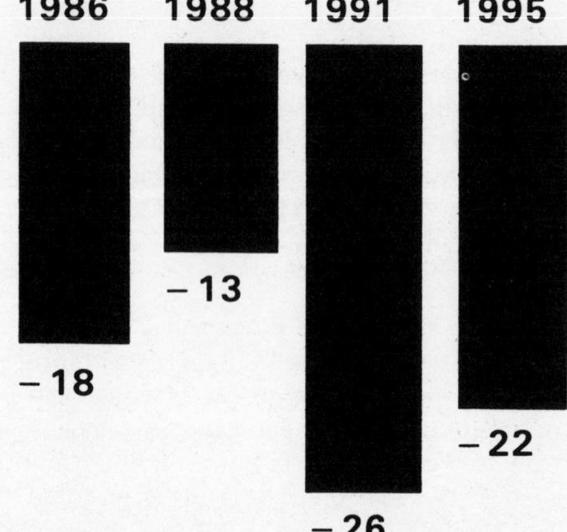

Percentage of change in the number of 18-year-olds calculated on the base year of 1979. Projections by the Western Interstate Commission for Higher Education.

One of the main reasons that the Association of Governing Boards commissioned this report was the concern that far too many colleges and universities were entering this difficult period without sound long-range plans or management techniques suited to an era of retrenchment. There was particular concern that many trustees are not fully aware of the challenges ahead, and could benefit from a brief discussion of what is known—and not known—about enrollment projections and the economic environment in which higher education will be functioning.

Enrollment Projections

In looking ahead, the one solid piece of information that we have is the future age distribution of the popula-

From *Change,* March 1983. Reprinted with the permission of the Association of Governing Boards of Universities and Colleges in Washington, D.C. The full publication on which this article is based is available from AGB.

tion, including the number of 18-year-olds for each of the next eighteen years. These are counts of people already born, and thus are hard data, not forecasts. The size of this age group from 1950 through 2000 reveals three important points.

First, the number of 18-year-olds roughly doubled between 1950 and 1980, with the most rapid growth occurring in the 1960s (45 percent increase) and a considerably slower rate of growth in the 1970s (13 percent increase). These data help to explain why the 1960s witnessed such explosive growth in higher education enrollment, while the 1970s witnessed continued growth, but at a slower rate.

Second, the figure shows the sharp drop in this age group that will occur between 1979 (the peak year) and 1994 (the trough). The population drops from 4.3 million to 3.2 million, a 26 percent decline, which helps to explain why the years between now and the mid-to-late 1990s are of great concern to higher education.

Finally, the population of 18-year-olds begins to climb again in the last years of the 1990s, reflecting an "echo" baby boom—the children of the earlier baby-boom generation. This final point is important because it shows that enrollment decline is not forever. The nation's colleges and universities must weather a difficult fifteen years, but they can expect enrollments to climb again in the late 1990s. The fact that the downturn is not permament must be factored into each college's long-range plan, and state officials must weigh the financial benefits of closing programs or campuses now against the costs of rebuilding them when once again enrollments surge.

While research findings on college enrollments are useful both to institutional and governmental planners and policymakers, many imponderables influence the college-going decision, complicating efforts to forecast future student behavior. Furthermore, the next ten to fifteen years will be very different from the last two decades, making extrapolation of past patterns of behavior a dubious activity. The biggest change will be the shift from a seller's to a buyer's market, and no one understands fully the implications of that change. One can say with certainty, however, that the competition among colleges will get much stiffer, and that a poorly prepared and poorly directed institution will be highly vulnerable to institutional decline, even closure.

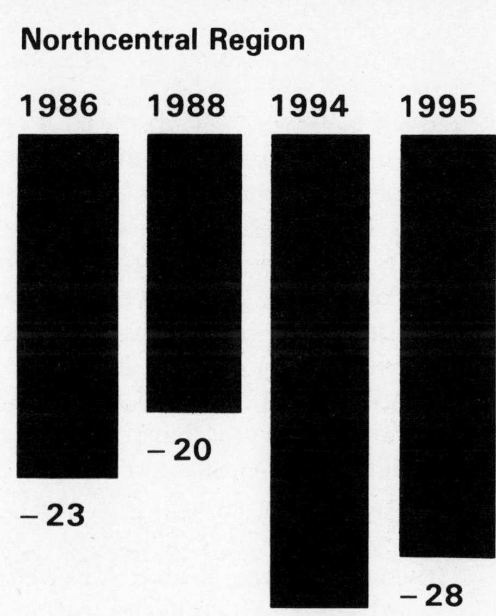

When we move beyond birth statistics to enrollment projections, considerable uncertainty is introduced. Consider the factors that have to be included in making an enrollment projection:

- High school graduation rates;
- College entry rates;
- College retention rates;
- Enrollment rates for older age groups;
- Enrollments of foreign students;
- Enrollments of graduate and professional students;
- Full-time vs. part-time attendance (in order to measure full-time equivalence).

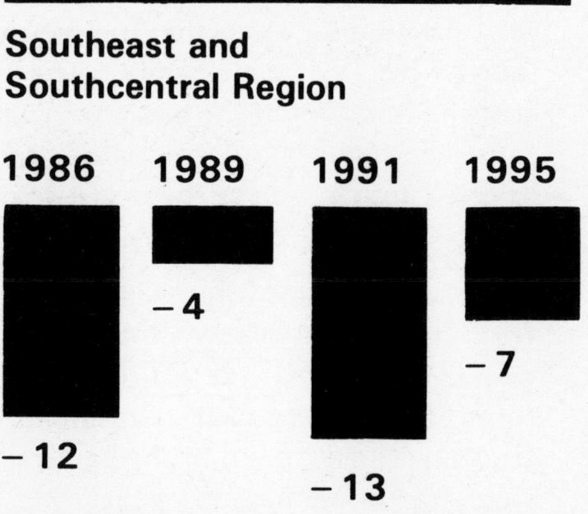

Projections of high school graduates are of particular importance because recent graduates still comprise the bulk of full-time enrollments. William R. McConnell of the Western Interstate Commission for Higher Education (WICHE) recently made such projections for each of the fifty states by year to 1995. McConnell's projections take into account differences in birth rates by state as well as migration patterns among the states. The Northeast and Northcentral regions will be the hardest hit, with projected declines from the 1979 level of 40 and 32 percent, respectively. By contrast, the Western and Southeast-Southcentral regions are projected to decline by only 16 and 13 percent. Because many colleges and universities draw their enrollments from the state or region in which they are located, it is clear that the pattern of enrollment decline will not be distributed evenly among institutions.

The projections for individual states are even more sobering. Several states, such as New York, Massachusetts, Connecticut, Rhode Island, and Delaware, are projected to have declines in excess of 40 percent, while others, such as Pennsylvania, New Jersey, Maryland, Michigan, Illinois, Minnesota, Ohio, Wisconsin, and Iowa, have projected declines of between 34 and 40 percent. Most of these states have large numbers of public and private colleges and universities, making the adjustment to greater-than-average enrollment decline particularly severe.

Possible Offsets

Faced with falling numbers of traditional college-age students, many colleges and universities have sought increased enrollments elsewhere. A report written by Carol Frances and published by the American Council on Education in 1980 received widespread attention. (See *Change*, July–August 1980.) Titled *College Enrollment Trends: Testing the Conventional Wisdom Against the Facts*, it discussed several strategies for increasing enrollments in the years ahead. These were:

- Increased high school graduation rates of students who would otherwise drop out;
- Increased credentialing by testing of high school dropouts;
- Increased enrollment of low- and middle-income students;
- Increased enrollment of minority youths;
- Increased enrollment of traditional college-age students;
- Increased retention of current students;
- Increased enrollment of adults;
- Increased enrollment of women aged 20 to 34;
- Increased enrollment of men aged 35 to 64;
- Increased enrollment of graduate students;
- Increased enrollment of persons currently being served by industry;
- Increased enrollment of foreign students.

The report presented estimates of the potential enrollment gains nationally that could be made between 1980 and 1990 with each of these strategies. It also provided an illustrative example in which the combined effect of three strategies—enrolling more lower- and middle-income young people, more adults over age 25, and more foreign students—could by 1990 result in a 3.5 percent increase over 1980 enrollments.

Leaders in higher education are concerned that institutions are not preparing adequately for enrollment decline, and view the optimistic interpretations of the Frances report as both unrealistic and counterproductive—the future seen through rose-colored glasses. They worry that the report might mislead presidents and trustees, or be used by some presidents as a justification for putting off difficult decisions that would have to be made if a substantial drop in enrollments were the accepted forecast.

In retrospect, it seems clear that the controversy surrounding the report need not have occurred. At the level of the individual institution, there is no inherent conflict between a careful effort to assess possible sources of new students, and an equally careful effort to make realistic enrollment projections for the institution. A residential liberal arts college of 1,200 students in a rural town of 8,000 people, for example, simply does not have the same possibilities for enrolling older part-time students that an urban university has.

It would be irresponsible, however, to approach those strategies for increased enrollments on the assumption that each college will find some combination of nontraditional students to offset the loss of the traditional college-age population. Several of the strategies outlined are not within the power of colleges and universities to determine. Actions of others will be required if high school graduation rates for majority and minority youths are to increase, or if greater numbers of dropouts are to earn high school certificates through equivalency tests.

The fact that black and Hispanic youngsters will make up a growing percentage of the 18-year-old population between now and the late 1990s must also be considered, for these minority students have substantially lower rates of high school completion than majority youngsters. In 1977, the high school graduation rate for whites 18 to 24 years old was 83.9 percent, for blacks 69.8 percent, and for Hispanics 55.5 percent. In the absence of concerted action to raise the completion rates of blacks and Hispanics, their increasing numbers in the age group will cause the high school graduation rate to fall—not rise—over the next fifteen years.

Perhaps the most promising strategy for boosting enrollment of younger people is to increase retention rates of those already enrolled. Presumably, students who drop out of the university were fit for admission, suggesting a need to look within the institution for possible reforms. While attrition can never be eliminated, most colleges can probably do a better job of keeping more of their current students enrolled. This strategy is hardly new, however, and many colleges may have reduced attrition about as far as possible.

Older students constitute the group most commonly looked to as an offset to the declining population 18 to 24 years old. Indeed, between 1970 and 1978, the number of students 25 to 34 years of age did increase significantly, with enrollment of women experiencing a particularly sharp 187 percent increase.

Community colleges accounted for much of this enrollment growth, with over 27 percent of their students in the 25 to 34 age group in 1978, compared to 14 percent in the four-year colleges. Projecting enrollments for the population over age 25 is subject to great uncertainty, but those who have examined the matter closely do not expect enrollment rates to continue rising as rapidly as they did in the 1970s. One reason is an assumption that the sharp increase of female enrollments is a one-time "catching-up" phenomenon that will not repeat itself. In recent years, younger women have enrolled in college in roughly the same proportion as men, whereas those in the generation preceding them did not. Women from this older generation enrolled in large numbers during the 1970s, making up for educational opportunities missed earlier. A second reason that adult enrollments may grow less rapidly in the 1980s is the expiration of GI Bill benefits for Vietnam veterans. Older students drawing these benefits contributed substantially to enrollment growth during the 1970s.

The vast majority of students over age 25 enroll part time, usually in evening courses offered at a convenient location near the student's home. It must be remembered that several part-time students are required to generate the equivalent workload and revenues of one full-time student, so head-count projections must be discounted to full-time equivalence.

A similar caution concerns increased enrollment of foreign students. In

1980–81, some 312,000 non-immigrant foreign students were enrolled at 2,734 U.S. colleges and universities, making up a little more than 2.5 percent of total enrollments. This figure represents more than a doubling of such enrollments since 1970–71, when 1,748 institutions enrolled 145,000 foreign students. Over 43 percent of the foreign students in 1980–81 were enrolled in engineering or business management programs, areas currently crowded with U.S. students.

Few foreign students enroll in humanities or education programs, where excess capacity currently exists on many campuses. Given this pattern of foreign student enrollments, it is far from certain that the nation's colleges could absorb a further doubling in the number of such students during this decade.

How best to evaluate the potential net effect of these several strategies for combating enrollment decline? Each suggests a wide range of possible forecasts that could be made, depending upon the assumption adopted. Several analysts have independently arrived at an estimated enrollment decline of about 15 percent. This figure incorporates a view that various recruitment strategies will offset about 40 percent of the 25 percent decline that would follow from demographic factors alone. As mentioned earlier, even if this rough national estimate turns out to be accurate, considerable variation will occur among regions and institutions.

Other Factors that Influence Enrollments

In addition to the demographic considerations discussed above, a number of other factors will affect enrollment patterns during the 1980s and beyond. Among these are the state of the economy, both nationally and locally; trends in federal and state student aid; the rate of increase in college prices relative to the general rate of inflation and to the growth in family incomes; employment prospects for new graduates; and the relative attractiveness of alternatives to college, such as military service or the labor market.

Factors such as quality and diversity of programs, location, prestige, price relative to competitors, and recruitment policies will largely determine how students distribute themselves among the various campuses.

For the foreseeable future, it would be prudent to assume that federal student aid will be less plentiful and a less reliable source of support. Although additional student and family resources may be forthcoming, it also seems likely that a bumping process will occur, in which some students shift from high- to low-priced institutions, some from full- to part-time status, and some from resident to commuter status, while others withdraw from college altogether. Clearly, the overall effect will be both to reduce and redistribute enrollments.

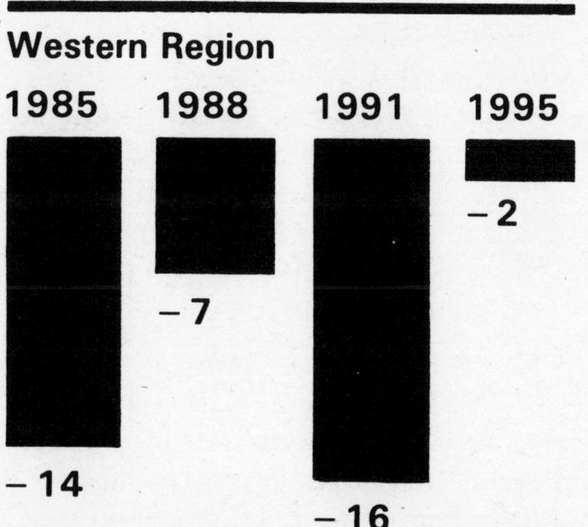

One bright spot that may help to shore up enrollments later in this decade is a likely upturn in the labor market for college graduates. The flip side of declining enrollments is a reduced labor supply of new graduates. All else being equal, a reduced supply of college graduates should lead to a stronger market for their services, an effect that should be visible by the mid-1980s. An improved market, in turn, may help to restore student interest in those liberal arts fields that have suffered in recent years from the emphasis on vocationally focused majors.

In general, one can expect the relative scarcity of young people over the next fifteen years to enhance the opportunities available to them, not just in college but in the labor market and in the military as well. Competition for their services will increase, and colleges will find themselves competing not only with each other but also with the all-volunteer military and with employers.

Prospects for the Sectors of Higher Education

How will the different types of institutions be affected by the prospect of enrollment decline? Are there any generalizations that might be helpful to trustees?

A fairly broad consensus exists that two groups of colleges and universities are particularly at risk—nonselective private liberal arts colleges and public state colleges and universities, many of them former state teachers colleges. Private junior colleges are also highly vulnerable to enrollment decline.

By contrast, state university systems, and particularly the flagship campuses, should experience limited loss of enrollments because in most states these institutions have an excess of applicants and can largely determine the size of entering classes. Similarly, the high-prestige private colleges and universities will fare well in the competition for enrollments because they draw on national pools of applicants. Public community colleges are also favorably positioned by their relatively low prices, their ability to serve the adult part-time population, and their flexibility in shifting program offerings rapidly in response to changing demands. In general, institutions located in urban settings will have more opportunities to offset enrollment decline than will those located in rural areas.

But even the more favored institutions will face dilemmas that require hard thinking, sound planning, and dedicated effort. Research universities, public and private, can expect difficulties in financing graduate programs and maintaining their strength as research institutions. Prestigious private colleges will have to struggle to maintain diverse student bodies rather than becoming enclaves for the very rich and a limited number of the very poor. Community colleges will face stiff competition from four-year institutions and universities for the traditional college-age students who enroll in transfer programs, and will have difficulty financing the large number of part-time students who enroll in noncredit courses.

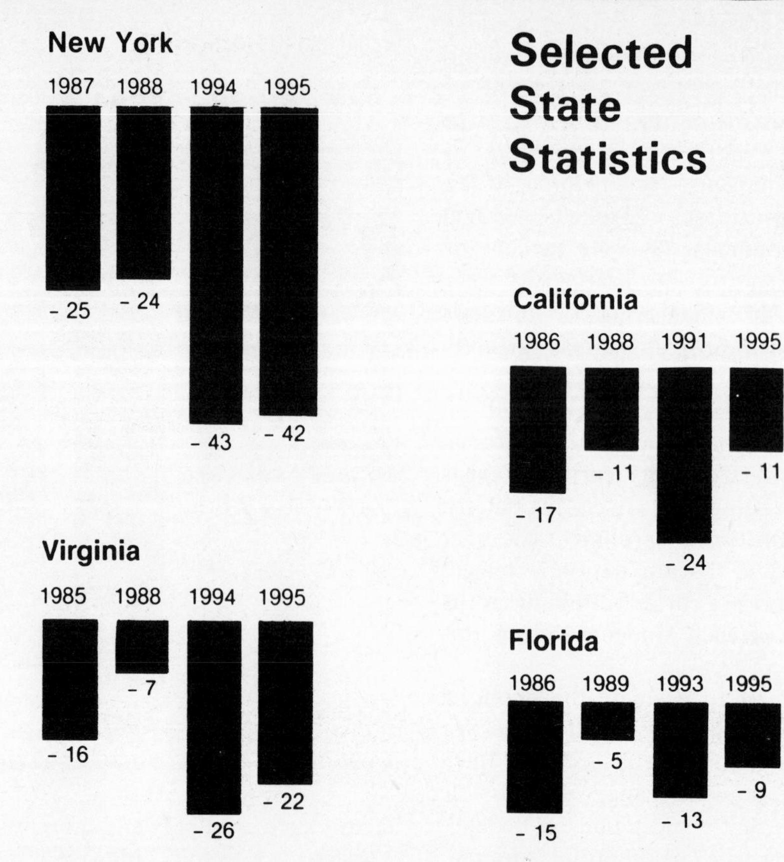

No group of institutions, in short, will escape the need to plan for—and adapt to—the difficult circumstances in which higher education will find itself over the next fifteen years. Well-informed trustees who raise thoughtful and timely questions for college administrators and for themselves will be of extraordinary value to their institutions.

The following questions are illustrative of those that should be raised. A caution is in order, however: Some of these questions are more easily answered than others, and some must be addressed first by the board as matters of policy.

General Questions

- Is the college's present planning process adequate for the years ahead? How realistic are institutional enrollment projections? How accurate have past projections been, and are current projections congruent with state and regional figures? If not, why not?
- What have been the relationships between enrollment levels, costs, and revenues in recent years? What approximate effect would a 10 or 15 percent decline in enrollments over the next five years have on costs and revenues?
- What is the student attrition rate from the various degree programs, and how has it changed over time? Has the institution taken any steps to try to reduce it?
- Average costs per student are not useful for the type of analysis that focuses on changes in costs as enrollments rise or fall. Instead, colleges should have estimates of marginal (incremental) costs or estimates of fixed and variable costs. Can such data be estimated for the college for use in planning and financial analysis?
- In light of possible enrollment decline and the accompanying loss of revenues, should the college take a fresh look at its pricing policies? Is there a case for charging different tuition rates by program or level of study to reflect cost differences more accurately? Should the college match, exceed, or lag behind price increases of its competitors? Have fee structures been examined recently to align them more closely with current costs?
- Should the college seek to attract new clientele groups to maintain enrollments? If so, what will be the impact on the institution's tradition mission? Will a change in educational emphasis help or harm the college's attractiveness to its traditional clientele groups?
- Given current staffing patterns, how flexible is the college in shifting program direction? Would new programs require a net increase in faculty, or will retirements and normal attrition offset the addition of new faculty? Is faculty development and redirection a realistic possibility? At what point, under what circumstances, and with what procedures might it be necessary to dismiss tenured faculty?
- Are there alternative uses for campus buildings (including dormitories) that are rendered superfluous for a

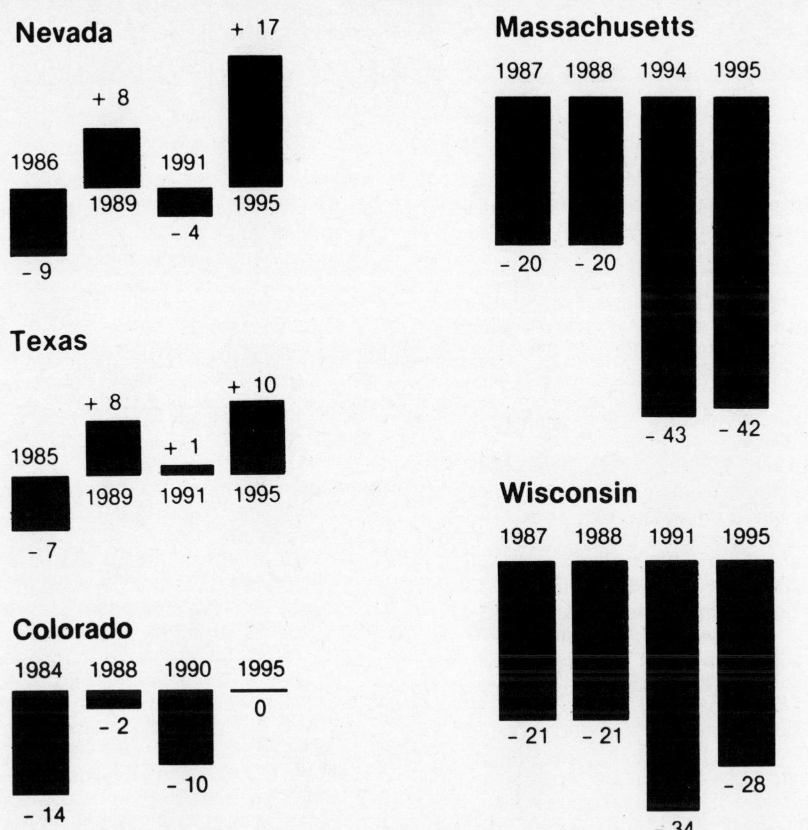

decade or more by enrollment declines? Can these surplus physical assets be converted into revenue producers? What can be done to avoid defaulting on long-term loans covering such properties?

- At what point will continued deferred maintenance and aging equipment adversely affect enrollments?
- How dependent has the college become on federal and state student aid? Is it possible to estimate the proportion of the student body that would withdraw if significant cuts were made in grant and loan programs? Can the college realistically plan to replace government aid by support or credit commitments from new sources?
- How much of the institution's own money is being spent on student aid? What percentage of the educational and general operating budget is being used for such aid, and how has that percentage changed over time? How much is drawn from restricted and unrestricted funds?
- How have the college's annual costs of attendance changed relative to the consumer price index and family income over the last decade? Has the college's competitive pricing position changed relative to the institutions with which it competes for enrollments?

Next Steps

After reading this candid report on enrollment prospects and problems facing the nation's colleges and universities, there is a danger that trustees may be overwhelmed by the difficulties ahead, and not know how to proceed. Stunning trustees into inaction, however, is not the purpose of the Association of Governing Boards in publishing this paper. Instead, the intent is to disabuse trustees of the notion—should some still hold it—that the position they occupy is not demanding and is largely ceremonial.

As the report makes clear, the next ten to fifteen years will be utterly unlike those of recent decades, when the challenge facing colleges and universities was to meet the demands of growth. The challenge now is not just to survive, but to do so while enhancing the quality of instruction, research, and public service rendered by the institution during a time of general retrenchment.

Those who serve and those who attend the nation's colleges and universities must rely on the support and informed guidance of trustees to a degree not required before. This report will have served its purpose if the discussion that it generates on campus leads to improved decision making and stronger institutions for the years ahead.

INDEX

Credits/Acknowledgments

Cover design by Charles Vitelli

1. Perceptions
Facing overview—United Nations photo/Y. Nagata. 18—Photograph courtesy of The National Catholic Education Association.
2. Continuity and Change
Facing overview—International Business Machines Corporation
3. The Struggle for Excellence
Facing overview—United Nations photo/O. Monsen.
4. Morality and Values
Facing overview—United Nations photo/Y. Nagata.
5. Discipline Problems
Facing overview—United Nations photo.
6. Equality of Opportunity
Facing overview—United Nations photo/S. Dimartini.
7. Serving Special Needs
Facing overview—United Nations photo/Jane Hanckel.
8. The Profession
Facing overview—United Nations photo/Marta Pinter.
9. A Look to the Future
Facing overview—United Nations photo.

WE WANT YOUR ADVICE

ANNUAL EDITIONS: EDUCATION 84/85

Article Rating Form

Here is an opportunity for you to have direct input into the next revision of this reader. We would like you to rate each of the 56 articles listed below, using the following scale:

1. **Excellent: should definitely be retained**
2. **Above average: should probably be retained**
3. **Below average: should probably be deleted**
4. **Poor: should definitely be deleted**

Your ratings will play a vital part in the next revision. So please mail this prepaid form to us just as soon as you complete it.
Thanks for your help!

Rating	Article
	1. Hard Times, Hard Choices: The Case for Coherence in Public School Leadership
	2. When Rituals Are Not Empty
	3. The Educational Pendulum
	4. The Twentieth Century Fund Task Force Report on Elementary and Secondary Education Policy
	5. How to Save the Public Schools
	6. End of the Permissive Society?
	7. The Fifteenth Annual Gallup Poll of the Public's Attitudes Toward the Public Schools
	8. What's Still Right with Education
	9. Restructuring the Schools: A Set of Solutions
	10. Keys to Computer Literacy
	11. Video Games Go to School
	12. Computers and a New World Order
	13. Bilingual/Bicultural Education: Its Legacy and Its Future
	14. Multiethnic Education: Historical Developments and Future Prospects
	15. The New Pioneers of the Home Schooling Movement
	16. The Debate About Standards
	17. A Nation at Risk: The Report of the National Commission on Excellence in Education
	18. A Nation at Risk: How's That Again?
	19. The Bold Quest for Quality
	20. A Time for Re-Examination and Renewal Commitment
	21. The Decline of American Education in the '60s and '70s
	22. Are Soviet Schools as Good as They Look?
	23. The Conflict in Moral Education: An Informal Case Study
	24. Schools and Democratic Values
	25. The Role of Self-Discipline
	26. Values and Morality in Early Twentieth Century Elementary Schools
	27. No Empty Heads, No Hollow Chests
	28. How to Encourage Moral Development
	29. Disciplinary Strategies
	30. Defusing Discipline Problems
	31. The Discipline Problem in Our Schools
	32. There's Only One True Technique for Good Discipline
	33. The Myths of Discipline
	34. Human Rights: "If Not Now, When?"
	35. Beyond Racial Balance Remedies: School Desegregation for the 1980s
	36. Achieving Quality Integrated Education—With or Without Federal Help
	37. The State of Education for Black Americans
	38. The Education of Black America: Betrayal of a Dream?
	39. Mainstreaming: Expectations and Realities
	40. A Holistic View of Mainstreaming
	41. Mainstreaming: Is It Secondary at the Secondary Level?
	42. A Comparison of Soviet and American Approaches to Special Education
	43. Our Investment in Public Education
	44. Overplacement: Rushing Children to Failure
	45. The Teacher's Role in Facilitating a Child's Adjustment to Divorce
	46. Helping Children Cope with Death
	47. Scapegoating the Teachers
	48. The Art of Teaching
	49. Tenure: Do We Need It?
	50. To Improve Our Schools Teachers Must Lead Children in a New Direction
	51. Merit Pay: The Great Debate
	52. Teacher Burnout: A Psychoeducational Perspective
	53. Reflections on the Profession
	54. Curriculum in the Year 2000: Tensions and Possibilities
	55. Instructional Computing in 2001: A Scenario
	56. The Coming Enrollment Crisis

(continued on back)

ABOUT YOU

Name ______________________ Date __________
Are you a teacher? ☐ Or student? ☐
Your School Name ______________________
Department ______________________
Address ______________________
City ______________________ State ________ Zip ________
School Telephone # ______________

YOUR COMMENTS ARE IMPORTANT TO US!

Please fill in the following information:

For which course did you use this book? ______________________
Did you use a text with this Annual Edition? ☐ yes ☐ no
The title of the text: ______________________
What are your general reactions to the Annual Editions concept?

Have you read any particular articles recently that you think should be included in the next edition?

Are there any articles you feel should be replaced in the next edition? Why?

Are there other areas that you feel would utilize an Annual Edition?

May we contact you for editorial input?

May we quote you from above?

EDUCATION 84/85

BUSINESS REPLY MAIL

First Class Permit No. 84 Guilford, CT

Postage will be paid by addressee

The Dushkin Publishing Group, Inc.
Sluice Dock
Guilford, Connecticut 06437